Zoning and the American Dream

Promises Still to Keep

Zoning and the American Dream

Promises Still to Keep

Edited by

CHARLES M. HAAR *and* JEROLD S. KAYDEN

PLANNERS PRESS
AMERICAN PLANNING ASSOCIATION
Chicago, Illinois   Washington, D. C.

In Association with
The Lincoln Institute of Land Policy

Copyright 1989 by the American Planning Association
1313 E. 60th St., Chicago, IL 60637
ISBN 0–918286–57–3
Library of Congress Catalog Card Number 88–71466

Contents

Preface **vii**

Foreword: Zoning at Sixty—
A Time for Anniversary Reckonings **ix**
Charles M. Haar and Jerold S. Kayden

Part I. The Historical Setting   1
 1. **The Office File Box—Emanations from the Battlefield**   3
    Arthur V. N. Brooks
 2. **Professors, Reformers, Bureaucrats, and Cronies: The Players in**
    Euclid* v. *Ambler   31
    William M. Randle

Part II. Zoning Applied (Misapplied): An Experiment in Social and
    Physical Order   71
 3. **Arenas of Conflict: Zoning and Land Use Reform in Critical**
    Political-Economic Perspective   73
    Joe R. Feagin
 4. **Expulsive Zoning: The Inequitable Legacy of *Euclid***   101
    Yale Rabin
 5. **Planning and Zoning**   122
    Peter L. Abeles
 6. ***Euclid* and the Environment**   154
    Earl Finbar Murphy
 7. **Legislating Aesthetics: The Role of Zoning in Designing Cities** 187
    Michael Kwartler

Part III. Zoning and the Courts: A Steady Legal Legacy?   221
 8. **Judges as Planners: Limited or General Partners?**   223
    Jerold S. Kayden
 9. **The Prescience and Centrality of *Euclid* v. *Ambler***   252
    Michael Allan Wolf
10. ***Euclid's* Lochnerian Legacy**   278
    Robert A. Williams, Jr.

v

Part IV. Zoning and Economics: Are They Compatible?   297

11. **Zoning Myth and Practice—From *Euclid* into the Future**   299
     Robert H. Nelson

12. **Zoning and Land Use Planning: An Economic Perspective**   319
     William C. Wheaton

Part V. Anticipating the Future   331

13. **Reflections on *Euclid:* Social Contract and Private Purpose**   333
     Charles M. Haar

Appendix: *Village of Euclid* v. *Ambler Realty Company*   355

Index   373

Contributors   385

Preface

This book had its genesis in a Fall, 1986 meeting of the Lincoln Institute's Land Policy Roundtable in Cambridge, Massachusetts. There, planners, lawyers, historians, sociologists, economists, developers, bankers, judges, and other practitioners and scholars met to discuss, evaluate, and occasionally argue about the central land-use planning mechanism of the twentieth century: zoning. The occasion celebrated the sixtieth anniversary of the 1926 U.S. Supreme Court decision, *Village of Euclid* v. *Ambler Realty Co.* Many of the papers collected in this volume were initially presented at that 1986 meeting. Other papers were outgrowths of discussions at the meeting.

The book does not purport to contain an exhaustive review of zoning's every aspect, even though it touches on many of the central features. Part I, The Historical Setting, animates zoning's most famous courtroom encounter, the *Euclid* case, by delving into the personalities, legal strategies, and social context behind the opinion's written words. Part II, Zoning Applied (Misapplied): An Experiment in Social and Physical Order, traces the impact of zoning's near-universal adoption and application, with criticism and praise for its social, economic, environmental, and physical ramifications. Part III, Zoning and the Courts: A Steady Legal Legacy?, examines the active participation of judges in the planning and zoning of American communities, a participation that sometimes shook and other times maintained the status quo. Part IV, Zoning and Economics: Are They Compatible?, offers economic critiques and suggestions about a technique that, by its very nature, interferes with private property markets. Part V, Anticipating the Future, looks at the past, present, and future realities and prospects of zoning, uncovering commonalities and conflicts that simultaneously energize and ennervate its ultimate utility.

The editors wish to thank the Lincoln Institute of Land Policy for its generous support as well as present and former Institute officials Ben Chinitz, Ron Smith, and Arlo Woolery for their personal encouragement. Sylvia Lewis of the American Planning Association shepherded us through the publication process with a needed mixture of humor and deadlines.

Charles M. Haar
Jerold S. Kayden
Cambridge, Massachusetts
January, 1989

Foreword: Zoning at Sixty— A Time for Anniversary Reckonings

Charles M. Haar and Jerold S. Kayden

The year 1986 marked the sixtieth anniversary of the landmark United States Supreme Court decision, *Village of Euclid* v. *Ambler Realty Co.,* upholding the basic constitutionality of local zoning. The year also marked 70 years since New York City enacted the country's first zoning ordinance, and 25 years since that original ordinance was replaced by a nationally influential successor. Like some astrological alignment of Jupiter, Mars, and Earth, the coincidence of anniversaries called for recognition and evaluation of this central land use control technique.

When first introduced, zoning promised to fulfill goals at once simple and majestic. Through its *height and setback* controls, zoning would ensure sufficient light and air at street level so cities would not be labyrinths of dark and dreary canyons. Through its *use* controls, zoning would prevent incompatible uses from locating cheek by jowl so residential neighborhoods would be protected from factories. Through its *density* controls, zoning would guarantee congestion-free central business districts and the ability of municipal infra-

structure to keep pace with growth. In short, zoning would help create the City Beautiful.

Although it may be hard to understand through today's lenses, zoning's original boosters were almost messianic in their support. Social progressives and conservatives rode the same bandwagon, bolstered by beliefs in the power of planning to better order people's lives. In the 1920s, Herbert Hoover, then secretary of commerce, would chair the national commission to draft a model state enabling act to authorize zoning. More than half a century later, almost every large city and small town in America has a zoning code that guides development.

How has the 70-year record of zoning measured up to these original hopes? What are its overall successes and failures? The following list provides some answers.

1. *Zoning helped establish the principle that the interests of private property owners must yield to the interests of the public.* It is easy to forget how completely zoning and its near universal adoption have recast the terms of the debate. Today's arguments are about how far, not whether, private property must yield to the public weal. Short

of depriving landowners of reasonable use of their property, the public sector may regulate to serve legitimate government interests.

2. *Zoning has delivered on its simpler promises such as keeping incompatible uses separated.* In situations where there is little controversy about the goal, zoning has been able to produce a better built environment. By institutionalizing the common law of nuisance, zoning has kept *Euclid* author Justice Sutherland's pig in the barnyard and out of the living room.

3. *Zoning has failed to deliver on its loftier promises of producing high-quality working and living environments.* Many of our major cities have overbuilt downtowns that are straining with cars and people. Many of our suburbs are little more than sterile bedroom communities. Extant zoning ordinances—although relied on heavily—have done little to prevent these occurrences. But perhaps the true failure rests with elected and appointed government officials charged with drafting and administering our zoning codes. Like many political issues, zoning is subject to the push and pull of many groups, including developers, environmentalists, low-income housing advocates, big business, neighborhoods, and others. If people do not have the environments they want, then perhaps our representative democracy is to blame. After all, zoning is merely a tool: With the appropriate political will, it can mandate that no building in San Francisco be taller than 15 stories and can encourage diversity of uses in suburban neighborhoods to mitigate boredom engendered by rows of single-family houses.

4. *Innovative techniques such as incentive zoning have provided small-scale public amenities.* Zoning's Model T ordinance has new fins: Under incentive zoning, floor area bonuses are granted to developers who agree to provide plazas, parks, theatres, low-income housing, and other public amenities. Although some of the amenities have been poorly designed, and some developers have received more bonus floor area than necessary, the overall record is not as bad as some would maintain. For example, New York City has obtained around 270 public spaces—and many of them are heavily used—through its incentive zoning program.

There are those who argue that trading floor area for amenities distorts the fundamental purpose of zoning. But is it wrong for a community to decide it will tolerate greater density and congestion from larger bonused buildings if more low-income housing for needy people is produced?

5. *Zoning has been misused by suburban communities to exclude low-income and minority families.* Suburban communities have employed zoning requirements to lock the doors on city residents. Too often, local ordinances still employ large lot and minimum floor space requirements as mechanisms for exclusion of low-income and minority families striving to leave the city, locate near job opportunities, and enjoy the good life. It does not take a real estate expert to understand that, when a town is zoned only for single-family housing on minimum one-acre lots, low-income families are not going to have the chance to live in that community. And while such zoning may help preserve small town character, which in and of itself is an acceptable objective, the question remains whether local interests should yield to solve broader problems.

6. *Zoning engenders corruption, but so does all government exercise of power.* Although much of the evidence is anecdotal, it seems clear that the administration of zoning has been accompanied by corruption. Zoning's basic concept of uniform treatment within and among districts, designed to guarantee against arbitrary and capricious action, has been frequently undercut by issuance of variances, exceptions, and special permits. Such discretionary action, conferring or taking away value, invites pay-offs. But zoning's history is probably no more or less rife with corruption than the experience of all government programs invested with a healthy dose of discretionary power.

7. *Zoning has not dealt adequately with regional problems.* This is not an inherent aspect of zoning, but a political reality. Although states legally authorize local communities to zone, it is the communities—and their residents—that view zoning as a strictly local power. Because of such parochialism, opportunities for intelligent regional solutions to planning problems have been missed.

8. *Zoning can mandate only so much, and only in times of economic well-being.* Some cities are beginning to use their zoning codes to *require* office and residential developers to contribute funds for low-income housing. This trend—for zoning to become a Christmas Tree on which public officials hang an increasing number of ornaments—can be justified only so long as taxed developers truly are responsible for creating low-income housing needs. When zoning loses a planning rationale for its application, it becomes more susceptible to an attack on its validity.

An anniversary also invites speculation about the future. What, then, are the challenges that will face zoning during its next 70 years? Zoning must continue its attempt to strike that elusive balance between preservation and growth. While protecting our quality of life, it must not become a regulatory strait-jacket making economic revitalization impossible. It should tie itself ever more closely to comprehensive planning and capital budgeting, if it is to continue providing meaningful guidance to growth and change. It must avoid being abused to serve the interests of the few and the powerful. Zoning is here to stay, as firmly entrenched a part of the landscape as the buildings it regulates. In the final analysis, its future success or failure will depend not so much on modifications to the technique itself, but upon its application by those who write and administer its provisions, and the willingness of the public to oversee those officials.

The chapters in this book represent an evaluation of the promise and record of zoning, from its early days in the 1920s to the present. There is a story here, of historical figures and movements, of community and individual aspirations, of the shaping of a technique to guarantee or frustrate the needs of different groups. Zoning affects the basic organization of our human environment. As the chapters themselves reveal, there is little agreement but much fascination with history and ideas, enough to assure a stimulating rethinking of this central public policy.

I

The Historical Setting

The world of law revolves around the interpretation of words penned in judicial opinions. The social context leading to the need for judicial resolution is all too frequently a casualty of a linguistic preoccupation—we forget that real human beings and events are the basis of, not the background for, legal disputes. The written words of the Supreme Court decision *Village of Euclid* v. *Ambler Realty Company,* stored in Volume 272 of the United States Reports, tell only the conclusion of a story involving strong-willed individuals, controversial strategy decisions, surprising coalitions, major political movements, and debates about the nature of private property. It is this story that holds the key to understanding the birth and enduring health of traditional zoning.

Ten years before the *Euclid* case, New York City had enacted the country's first zoning ordinance, regulating land and buildings according to their use, shape, and bulk. And in 1924, Secretary of Commerce Herbert Hoover's committee issued the standard state zoning enabling act. With sales of 50,000 copies, zoning was a best-seller. Euclid's ordinance was neither the first nor the most innovative—indeed histories of the *Euclid* case pay the least attention to who drafted the ordinance, who prepared the planning reports, and who was zoning director of the village.

Nonetheless, it is the year 1926 that traditionally marks the birth of zoning, and it is the name Euclid (and Euclidean) that attaches most readily to the technique of zoning. The Supreme Court's validation of Euclid's ordinance not only brought fame to the village, but also tended to place in cement the form of zoning espoused by the village, a form similar in large measure to New York City's ordinance. The dramatis personae in the famous legal battle included George Baker, the lawyer for Ambler Realty Company; James Metzenbaum, the lawyer for the village of Euclid; Alfred Bettman, the lawyer writing the "friend of the court" brief in support of zoning; and Justice George Sutherland, the author of the *Euclid* opinion.

This was great drama, and it is recounted with flair and detail in the following two chapters. In "The Office File Box—Emanations from the Battlefield," Arthur V. N. Brooks exhumes the dusty files of the case to reveal the thinking behind the thinking. It is rare that such files ever see the light of day, and their revelations of unfolding trial strategy and high principle are fascinating. William Randle's "Professors, Reformers, Bureaucrats, and Cronies: The Players in *Euclid* v. *Ambler*" delves into the personal backgrounds of the actors, connecting events and influences to their roles and acts in the zoning saga. He paints a disconcerting picture of crude racism and unholy academic-professional-business alliances surrounding the birth of this ubiquitous technique.

1

The Office File Box— Emanations from the Battlefield

Arthur V. N. Brooks

This was clearly no ordinary office file box. On one of the three jackets, dusty and dog-eared, was handwritten: "Papers Mr. Baker took to Washington" and (in red) "Save Forever."

Here was the Pandora's Box of zoning law in the United States: The notes, briefs, and correspondence of one of the foremost advocates of his day in a case which has both profoundly affected the physical development of the United States and cast a lengthy shadow of controversy which continues to this day. Not only was Newton D. Baker a towering figure in Cleveland's history, he was a statesman of national stature who very nearly was nominated for the presidency on the fifth ballot at the 1932 Democratic National Convention.[1] Not incidentally, Mr. Baker was the founding partner of our Cleveland, Ohio, law firm. One approaches the exhumation of such a file with the same sense of trepidation associated with the cinematic "Lost Ark."

This chapter will review the contents of "The Box" to discover what it may tell us about the theory, objectives, tactics, and result of the case, as Mr. Baker saw them, and will close with one lawyer's observations on the conduct of the case—gingerly offered—from the standpoint of the perfect hindsight of 60 years.

CONTENTS OF THE BOX

What remains in the box, 60 years later, is an edited closed file of papers, perhaps representing the collective judgment of Mr. Baker, his secretary, Dorothy Cook, and his associate, Henry S. Brainard, Esq., as to those documents which might have some value to lawyers dealing with the subject in later years. As with other cases significant to our law firm, the briefs were once bound in a volume for future reference. The bound volume contained interleaved typed notes, apparently reflecting Mr. Baker's dictated views concerning the opponents' briefs. Regrettably, this volume has been misplaced.

Correspondence. The correspondence in the file covers the period from January 2, 1923, to January 22, 1934. Of central interest is Mr. Baker's extensive correspondence with lawyers and judges in other parts of the country concerning the timing, theory, progress, and result of the case. The correspondence consistently reveals the grace, charm, courtesy, and

3

wit with which the lawyers of that day corresponded.

Pleadings, Briefs, and Court Papers. Among the numerous court papers in the file are the complaint and answer in the district court, miscellaneous motions in both courts, and the extensive briefs of the parties in the district court. They are not chronologically arranged and stand more or less as the unassembled pieces of a complex legal jigsaw puzzle.

Miscellaneous. Among the notes, memoranda, notices, and clips in this folder are, most importantly, what appear to be Mr. Baker's handwritten notes for the Supreme Court argument on rehearing. The folder also contains the original Euclid Zoning Ordinance, copies of cases from state court jurisdictions, and notes and memoranda of legal research. Much of the writing is unattributed but can be presumed to be the work of Mr. Baker; Henry S. Brainard, his associate; or Judge Robert Morgan, his co-counsel.

"Papers Mr. Baker Took to Washington." In addition to the principal briefs, this full file jacket contains what appear to be parts of draft briefs directed largely toward answering Alfred Bettman's[2] famous "Brandeis brief" in favor of comprehensive zoning. The jacket also includes a hand-annotated printed brief in the Ohio Supreme Court case of *Pritz* v. *Messer*, 12 Ohio St. 628 (1925), a case in which both Mr. Baker and Mr. Bettman appeared, *amici curiae*, to contest the constitutionality of zoning in Ohio. There is also an enigmatic handwritten folio, marked to the case in the United States Supreme Court, containing a few case summaries in which the anonymous writer notes the author of the opinions and, usually, the "strength" of his opinion.

WHAT'S NOT IN THE BOX

Since nondiscovery of the expected may have some significance, it is noted that the file does

not contain the record of testimony in the district court, any notes concerning the testimony of witnesses therein, or the typed transcripts of oral argument in either court.

A BRIEF CHRONOLOGY

The Euclid Zoning Ordinance was adopted on November 13, 1922. Mr. Baker was retained in April 1923 by the Ambler Realty Company and 14 other owners of substantial properties in Euclid Village, who each executed an "expense underwriting agreement" by which the sum of $14,650 was subscribed to cover legal fees and expenses.[3] The bill of complaint was filed in the United States District Court in Cleveland on May 5, 1923, and assigned to Judge David Westenhaver.[4] The ordinance was amended on June 11, 1923. The Village's motion to dismiss the complaint was argued on November 8, 1923, with the constitutional questions reserved until the motion was disposed of. Before deposition testimony in the case had been fully concluded, the final oral arguments were made by the parties on December 21, 1923, and the court's decision against the village was entered on January 14, 1924. The appeal of the case was allowed by the United States Supreme Court on April 1, 1924, and the principal briefs were filed by James Metzenbaum (for the village) in late 1925, and by Mr. Baker in January of 1926. The case initially was argued on January 26, 1926. Both sides presented reply briefs following oral argument, the last of which was filed in February 1926. The parties were formally notified of the rehearing of the case in March 1926. Mr. Bettman (who had not appeared at the initial hearing) obtained leave to file his brief, *amicus curiae*, in August 1926. Mr. Metzenbaum alone submitted a supplemental brief on rehearing in the fall of 1926. The case was reargued in the Supreme Court on October 12, 1926, and the Court's decision was rendered on November 22, 1926.

During the period from October 1921 to the date of the decision in November 1926, four justices of the Supreme Court were appointed by President Warren Harding, including Justice George Sutherland,[5] who wrote the decision. During the pendency of the case in the Supreme Court, Justice Harlan F. Stone was appointed by President Calvin Coolidge to replace Justice Joseph McKenna.

ORIGINS

Ambler—A Question of Property Rights vs. Communal Control

It is not difficult to imagine the seriousness of the threat which the village of Euclid's comprehensive zoning posed to the Ambler Realty Company and the other property owners who retained Mr. Baker to challenge the ordinance.

Since about 1912, the Ambler Realty Company had owned, among other substantial properties, a 68-acre tract in a level area near the eastern boundary of the city of Cleveland. The tract was located between Euclid Avenue, a major east-west thoroughfare extending through Cleveland into Euclid and beyond, on the south, and the Nickel Plate Railroad on the north. Ambler held the property in anticipation of the industrial development that surely and naturally would occur as Cleveland developed along the railroad lines and major thoroughfares to and beyond its eastern boundary. In 1912, less than 2,000 people resided in Euclid in an area of some 16 square miles. It was still largely a rural community of 5,000 to 10,000 people when, in 1922, it became the third municipality in Ohio to adopt a comprehensive zoning ordinance separating all of the land uses in the village into six districts. All of the land in the village was divided into height, lot area, and use districts or zones in the conventional pyramid fashion.[6]

To the chagrin of Ambler and the other property owners, industrial zoning was limited largely to the area between the two major railroads that bisected the community. Nearly half of Euclid's 68-acre tract was zoned residential, including more than 1,800 feet of frontage along Euclid Avenue.[7] As Ambler and the others saw it, a great part of the use value of undeveloped land in the village had been "taken" by public action for some imaginary—or at least elusive—public purpose or benefit, without compensation. Looked at as a cloud on Ambler's title, zoning impaired the salability and severely depressed the value of the tract to the extent of "several hundred thousand dollars."[8]

The property owners' choice of Mr. Baker to serve as their counsel was shrewd. Apart from his national reputation as a courtroom advocate, Mr. Baker, a progressive Democrat, had served both as law director and mayor of Cleveland. He had been a champion of the 1912 amendment to Ohio's constitution, which granted home rule authority to each of Ohio's municipalities. At one time he had been a strong proponent of the public ownership of utilities and other public service facilities. Mr. Baker's appearance on behalf of the property owners would itself provide eloquent support for rational limitations on public control of the use of private property. Somewhat surprisingly, the file does not suggest that the choice for Mr. Baker was particularly difficult or that his own views on the subject varied substantially from the strong position that he took on behalf of his clients.

Perhaps the best expression of his view of the zoning issue is contained in a July 1926 letter to Mr. Frank Hunter, a lawyer in Chester, Pennsylvania, who was then handling a major zoning case in the Supreme Court of Pennsylvania:[9]

It plainly is not possible to draw hard and fast

lines and to say that "zoning" either is or is not constitutional. That a city may be zoned for fire protection has long been thoroughly established. That it may not be zoned on purely aesthetic grounds has been often held and is generally conceded. Between these two extremes, each case has to stand on its own facts and it is difficult to state a principle by which the facts can be discriminated. In the conflict between the police power on the one side and the integrity of the right of private property on the other, there are two embarrassing circumstances: first, that with the progress of science, the police power necessarily reaches new conditions which are brought within the scope by knowledge of their effect which was not previously suspected; second, by the presumption in favor of the acts of the legislature which the courts always indulge.

Mr. Baker saw the nexus of these two "embarrassing circumstances" as providing potentially unlimited legislative power over private property:

> On the other hand if the right of private property is subject to the unrestrained caprice of village councils and the courts can do nothing more helpful than retire behind a conclusive presumption of soundness in legislative action, no matter how capricious or burdensome it appears on its face, then obviously we have outgrown the civilization established by the Constitution and have surrendered into a sort of communistic ownership and control. . . .

So, in support of private property and against the "collectivism" of the "zoners," Mr. Baker marshalled a test case of the constitutionality of the Euclid zoning ordinance.

Euclid: In Defense of the American Home

Needless to say, Euclid saw the matter quite differently and with great conviction. Zoning

was sweeping the country with the support of the U.S. Department of Commerce and the U.S. Chamber of Commerce, among others. All but a handful of states had adopted zoning enabling legislation. Planners and visionaries saw it as the key to the prevention of urban blight and decay. More than 20 million people lived in the urban and urbanizing communities that had then adopted zoning. Zoning had more than broken even in the lower courts as a justifiable exercise of local police power to protect public health, safety, and welfare.

Most importantly, zoning afforded Euclid an opportunity to "preserve the present character of the Village"[10] in the face of the incipient pressures of growth and industrialization inherent in its location. The Euclid ordinance, therefore, severely confined industrial and business development in order to protect and encourage the development of single-family residences on the lakeshore and on the hill to the south of Euclid Avenue. Zoning, in effect, guarded against the encroachment of industry on existing and future single-family residences. Single-family—not industrial—development was the "natural and normal" pattern of suburban development; the Ambler Realty Company itself had recognized this by developing acreage immediately *adjacent* to its 68-acre tract for single-family residential purposes.[11] Ample territory in Euclid remained for the development of industry. Any loss in value was pure speculation since no present demand existed for Ambler's property.[12] Zoning was rational and scientific, not arbitrary and capricious. Hardship, mistakes, or changed conditions could be handled by administrative appeal or by amendment.

James Metzenbaum, a prominent Cleveland lawyer, served as chairman of the Euclid Planning and Zoning Commission and undertook representation of the village on his own time, as a hobby, and for what the *Plain Dealer* characterized as a "small fee from the Village Council." Mr. Metzenbaum's style fairly can be characterized as contentious and full of the zeal and hyperbole of the reformer.[13] He conceded nothing; not even the size or location of the village itself. In Mr. Metzenbaum's hands, Euclid became something of a battlefield in a larger class struggle, ironically with the industrials cast in the role of the proletariat:

[W]e wish to avert to the question of that so-called "greater public welfare" about which the Supreme Court of the United States itself has spoken.

We refer to the question of the American Home.

The New York Commission . . . found . . . that the modern tendency is rapidly destroying and undermining the continuance of separate . . . homes and residences.

The best minds of America are exhorting Congress and the states to do all that is possible to stem and prevent this tendency. . . .

The bulwark and the stamina of this country has [sic] always been credited and conceded to the home owning tendencies of the American People.

It is generally conceded that the home owner who has the opportunity to have his little garden and to rear his family in a house and to raise his children with a greater freedom of fresh air and abundance of light, is one of the most important factors in the sustaining of the American People.

It means not merely comfort and wealth but it means greater safety for the children, a more vigorous generation due to plentifulness of fresh air and sunlight . . .; it means less accidents for the young ones because they have a yard in which to play. . .; it means a greater interest in public welfare and in civic affairs. . .; it means a greater relationship to the schools, a more restful condition for the head of the family and a place where the yard affords recreation and the opportunity for flowers and plants which are the highest accompaniment of a growing generation, and which means better children and men and women and health.

. . .

Is it not doubly to the general welfare of all suburban municipalities to look after the safety and the health, the general welfare of those who have, and the many who want to come just because they found a haven and a promised land in the suburbs in their effort to escape from the congested, accident producing and smoke-filled condition of the city and where, in the suburbs, they hope to find fresh air and sunlight and a yard for children? [Affirmative brief of defendant, *Ambler* v. *Euclid,* Equity #898 at 16.]

Thus were the battle lines drawn by two forceful advocates: Zoning seen either as a protection of the suburban American home against the encroachment of urban blight and danger, or as the unrestrained caprice of village councils claiming unlimited control over private property in derogation of the Constitution. At the time, of course, neither the Ohio Supreme Court nor the United States Supreme Court had determined finally the constitutionality of zoning and the *Euclid* case from the start assumed the larger proportions of a test of the constitutional limits on the exercise of the police power over the use of private property.

In the district court, Mr. Metzenbaum was joined by W.C. Boyle, of Squire, Sanders and Dempsey, on behalf of the Cleveland Chamber of Commerce, and Alfred Bettman, on behalf of The Ohio State Conference on City Planning, as *amici curiae.*

THE BATTLEFIELD—U.S. DISTRICT COURT

Mr. Baker's task was the more formidable. Apart from the generous private and public support for zoning and the emerging trend of the case law, Ambler had no current proposal for the sale of its property for industrial purposes and had made no application either for a permit or for a variance to use it. Its complaint, as the Supreme Court later observed, was against the "mere existence" and "threatened enforcement" of the Euclid ordinance.[14] Moreover, a result favorable to Ambler with respect to the zoning of its property would not necessarily result in the desired test of the constitutionality of the zoning principle. Euclid could rest on home rule and the presumption of validity of its action, leaving to Mr. Baker the task of proving that the ordinance had no rational basis.[15] Mr. Baker also was faced with the threshold questions of whether the remedy of injunction was available and whether the village action was tantamount to the state action required to obtain federal court jurisdiction. The interplay between jurisdictional and substantive issues and between the broader and narrower grounds of attack plagued his case from the start. Mr. Baker chose the broader ground.

Baker: The Broad Attack

Mr. Baker's complaint on behalf of Ambler was a model of subtlety and lofty expression. Euclid was but an undeveloped portion of the Cleveland metropolitan area—"a highly organized industrial community of more than one million people." Industrial development contributed to the rapid growth and prosperity of Cleveland and to the growth and prosperity of the United States. Industrial development "naturally follow[ed] the established railroad and other transportation lines" so that only about 15 percent of the entire metropolitan district, including Ambler's 68 acres, was available for industrial purposes. By reason of its location, therefore, the Ambler tract was "peculiarly adapted to industrial development" and for such uses had a present market value of "about $10,000 per acre"; but if limited to residence uses, "for which it had no special availability", its market value would not exceed $2,500 per acre. Moreover, the Euclid Avenue frontage (restricted by the ordinance to two-family residential development) drew its major "usefulness" from the character of the street as a principal business street "for the whole space of 13 miles from Public Square" in Cleveland. Its value for "mercantile and business uses" was at least "twice" its value as so restricted. Not only was all of this true with respect to Ambler's property, it was also true with respect to the entire area of undeveloped land in the village situated in the level area adjacent to the railroads and along the major thoroughfares.

In the face of these and other economic and geographic imperatives, Euclid had interposed its zoning ordinance, destroying these intrinsic property values, and imposing a cloud upon title—a cloud made all the more severe by criminal sanctions and by provisions severely limiting its amendment or variance.

Plaintiff was not complaining, however, about the provisions of the ordinance which restricted against nuisance uses or which were necessary for the prevention of fire or which adopted maximum density requirements for living units:

> but the plaintiff says that the ordinance, to the extent that it (otherwise) restrains or prohibits the use of building upon its . . . lands, is arbitrary, unreasonable and burdensome in its operation and effect; that it was enacted for the purpose of preserving the ideas of beauty officially entertained by the members of the council . . . and excluding uses of private property

...offensive to the eccentric and supersensitive tastes of said members of council and arresting and diverting the normal and lawful development of the lands of the plaintiff and other similarly situated lands . . . from those industrial, commercial and residence uses for which it is best suited and most available, all of which this plaintiff avers is done by lines arbitrarily and irrationally drawn and by restrictions which invade alike the rights of private property and personal liberty guaranteed by the Constitution of the United States. . . .

In his "Brief for Plaintiff on Motion to Dismiss" (at 7–9), Mr. Baker maintained the broad attack on the Euclid ordinance:

The contention of the complainant . . . is that the Ordinance . . . is void, as being in excess of the power conferred on the Village by the Constitution of Ohio, as being in excess of any power which the legislature of Ohio can confer upon the Village and being in excess of any power which even the Constitution of Ohio could confer upon the Village to invade, impair and deny rights . . . [of] citizens to hold their property in the full vigor of private ownership, subject only to the rights of eminent domain and regulations enacted under the police power as the latter term is lawfully defined. . . .

Our contention is that the whole body of legislation is unreasonable and void in that it constitutes a taking of the property of the complainant without compensation, and that the regulations sought to be imposed are not justified by any rational or legal definition of the police power.

Thus, despite the "severance" clause included in the ordinance:

[T]he Ordinance is so interwoven as to its illegal, its doubtful and its valid provisions that the Court would find it difficult, if not impossible, to separate them, and when the valid provisions are separated they constitute so great a departure from the professed purpose of the council in enacting the legislation that it would be quite impossible for the court to say that the Village would have adopted the Ordinance at all if it had been conscious at the time of its action of the real limitations upon its power.

Mr. Baker then called the court's attention to the numerous weaknesses and inconsistencies in the entire ordinance, not just those which affected the Ambler tract, suggesting both unreasonableness and an aesthetic or exclusionary purpose not connected to the public health and safety.[16]

Metzenbaum: In Defense of All Zoning

Mr. Baker's broad attack on the Euclid ordinance drew Mr. Metzenbaum into a curious point-by-point rebuttal of each allegation and a lengthy affirmative argument citing every conceivable "fact" and authority in support of zoning generally and of the Euclid ordinance in particular.

This omnibus approach clearly worked to Mr. Baker's advantage. In effect, the burden shifted to Mr. Metzenbaum to *sustain* the ordinance in all its particulars when all that was required, perhaps, was a narrow argument addressing itself to the procedural and jurisdictional issues, the presumption of validity, and the rational basis for the classification of Ambler's property.

Bettman and Boyle: "With Friends Like These . . . ."

Mr. Bettman, of course, appeared solely for the purpose of addressing the general question of the constitutionality of comprehensive zoning, "as illustrated by the Euclid ordinance." This perhaps further encouraged the court to view the case as a test of the constitutionality of zoning itself.[17]

Mr. Boyle, on the other hand, urged the court to limit its consideration to the effect of zoning on the Ambler tract. He even suggested in his brief as filed (and later withdrawn at Mr. Metzenbaum's urging) that the zoning be modified with respect to the residentially zoned portion of the Ambler tract along the Euclid Avenue frontage:[18]

> All unite in saying that the restriction of the first 150 feet for single- or two-family residences on Euclid Avenue is not the best or most profitable use to which it could and should be put.

In substance, therefore, as submitted to Judge Westenhaver, Mr. Baker's general thesis remained more or less undisturbed: The ordinance as a whole created a cloud on Ambler's title imposed for largely aesthetic or class reasons ("to erect a dam to hold back the flood of industrial development") in derogation of the property rights protected by the United States and Ohio Constitutions:

> Our cities ought to be increasingly beautiful and comfortable in order that life in them may be happier and more complete, but this public good cannot be sought by imposing the cost of it vicariously upon the owners of certain property and by arbitrarily transferring value from one owner to another in defiance of the natural law by which the value in money of property follows its increasing value in use.

Thus put, the case fell more closely within the rationale of Justice Oliver W. Holmes's decision in *Pennsylvania Coal Co.* v. *Mahon*[19] as a case of police power regulation which had gone too far, and the court so held, limiting its decision, perhaps inevitably, to the ordinance as applied to the Ambler property.[20]

Judge Westenhaver's opinion paralleled Mr. Baker's argument and his private views in almost all respects. Since the ordinance prevented Ambler from realizing the "normal and reasonably to be expected increased value" of its land for "trade, industrial, and commercial purposes," Euclid had taken Ambler's property without compensation.[21] The police power must be delimited by something more substantial than a declaration that the public welfare is served; to be valid, regulations must "bear a real and substantial relation to the maintenance and preservation of the public peace, public order, public morals, or public safety"; for example, where they bear an "intimate relation to the prevention of nuisances."[22] Here, by contrast, the "true object" was the exclusionary purpose of regulating "the mode of living of persons who may thereafter live in Euclid," and the "aesthetic" purpose of making "the Village develop into a city along lines now conceived by the Village Council to be attractive and beautiful."[23]

THE BATTLEFIELD—WHETHER TO LEAVE WELL ENOUGH ALONE

The district court's decision left Euclid in a difficult, but not completely untenable, position. The court, in its final decree, found, in sum:

> That the facts alleged by the plaintiff in its bill are true and that the plaintiff is entitled to the relief prayed for.

With this sweeping result, an appeal became a highly doubtful proposition. Of course, Euclid was left with the simple expedient of amending the ordinance, as it affected Ambler's property, to conform to the court's order. However, apparently because of the broader issues involved, this was a case that neither party wanted to win—but that neither could afford to lose.

To the Members of the Ohio Conference on City Planning:

Enclosed are copies of the briefs of Messrs. Alfred Bettman and W.C. Boyle in the Euclid Village zoning case.

Mr. Bettman and Mr. Boyle agree that Judge Westenhaver's opinion is a barrier but not entirely an insurmountable obstacle to zoning progress in Ohio. Both of them hope that the Euclid Village zoning authorities will amend their Ordinance in accordance with this opinion, and not appeal the case. If, however, the case is appealed, we shall very much need Mr. Bettman's help in the next court.

Charlotte Rumbold,
Secretary-Treasurer[24]

In the face of such views, it is not known what, other than the zeal of the advocate, prompted the Euclid appeal to the United States Supreme Court. Mr. Bettman, for his part, did not again engage his talents in the case until *after* the first hearing on appeal. Indeed, it is one of the great ironies of the *Euclid* case that Mr. Bettman entertained the private view that the Euclid case was a poor one with which to test the constitutionality of zoning:

The City made no scientific survey, and in an effort to keep the village entirely residential, the local authorities zoned all as residential and business, except a very narrow piece along the railroads, too narrow for a practical industrial development. It was a piece of arbitrary zoning and on the facts not justifiable. . . . Everybody advised against an appeal, because on appeal the decision is sure to be affirmed, even though the upper court disagrees with the opinion.[25]

All along, however, Mr. Bettman suspected that Mr. Baker and his "special interest" clients were part of "a larger group seeking to destroy the zoning movement" and that they singled Euclid out because of the weaknesses in its ordinance.[26] His return to the battlefield, for whatever reason, later assumed great—even decisive—importance.

AN UNEASY CALM

Considerable delay attended Mr. Metzenbaum's effort to perfect an appeal to the Supreme Court, and time did not work to Mr. Baker's advantage.

A new front was opened on March 11, 1925, in the Ohio Supreme Court. Messrs. Baker, Morgan, and Bettman appeared, on reargument, in two zoning cases that later would be cited as sustaining the constitutionality of comprehensive zoning in Ohio.[27]

Meanwhile, Euclid opened another front by its public actions following Judge Westenhaver's decision and Mr. Baker returned to court to prevent Euclid from doing piecemeal what Judge Westenhaver's decision had prevented it from doing all at once.[28]

Other cases, too, were making their way onto the Supreme Court's docket from around the country, leading to the growing certainty that an historic decision was in prospect.

THE BATTLE—SHIPS PASSING IN THE NIGHT

Whether by a perversity of court rule, devious strategems, or ubiquitous fate, the arguments of the two parties in their principal briefs in the Supreme Court proceeded without reference to the other.

The Appellant: An Embarrassment of Riches

Mr. Metzenbaum was a tireless and persistent advocate. In the face of a district court opinion that found all of the facts against him, he undertook to retry the case on the facts in the Supreme Court. For 45 pages under 27 separate "billboard" headings,[29] Mr. Metzenbaum belabored the facts. For the next 29 pages he expounded upon "the philosophy of zoning," interposing various references to the case among a host of favorable references to zoning generally. At page 56, he paused briefly to state "The Basic Question" of the case as he saw it, that is, the abstract validity of zoning:

> Otherwise worded, the issue is really freed from the question of the reasonableness or unreasonableness of the particular restriction and the subject really narrows down to the sole and completely *legal* and *fundamental* question as to whether there is a *constitutional power* to enact such ordinances as the one in question.

He then proceeded to offer "factual" support for the principle of zoning ("zoning increases values, and tends to great safety," "one intrusion without ordinance steals neighbors' values," "zoning prevents huddling and indiscriminate throwing together of homes and factories and stores," etc.). Not until page 76 was the opinion of the court below discussed at any length. Similarly, not until page 82 did Mr. Metzenbaum call the court's attention in any effective way to the presumption of validity and the severe burden placed on the appellee to demonstrate the unconstitutionality of the Euclid ordinance.[30] If, by the time the steadfast reader reached page 131, any doubt remained about Mr. Metzenbaum's essential agreement with Mr. Baker on the breadth of the issue or that Euclid had undertaken, on the proof, to *sustain* the entire ordinance (despite the presumption of validity), it was there put to rest:

> In the earlier part of this brief we endeavored to indicate that the limitation in question was not confiscatory, that it was reasonable, that it was closely related to public health, safety and welfare and that it not only did not lessen but that it really enhanced the value of the Complainant's land and that its use for indus-

trial or commercial purposes would be distinctly inimical to the public welfare.

The brief then concluded with Mr. Metzenbaum's history of the regulation of growth and development in the United States (in which support for zoning was found even among "street car officials" and "street cleaning departments"), at the end of which the finishing touch (at 139) was put on what can only be seen as a major concession to Baker that the principle of zoning was the real issue in the case:

> Many states, hundreds of municipalities and several millions of the people are eagerly looking forward with the hope and trust that this Court may find that there is such a relationship between these ordinances on the one hand and the public health, safety and welfare on the other hand, as to warrant this exercise of the Police Power in order to bring about a Greater Public Welfare.

The Appellee: A Delicate Question

Apparently unaware of Mr. Metzenbaum's eagerness to join the larger issue (or if not, at least apprehensive about the Supreme Court's willingness to reach the issue), Mr. Baker drew a delicate balance[31] between the narrower (and more certain) and the broader (and more difficult) objectives of his case:

> Primarily the Court's attention must be directed to the restrictions sought to be imposed by the ordinance on the land of the Appellee. Since, however, it is claimed by the Appellant that Ordinance 2812 is a comprehensive piece of legislation and that the damage suffered by the Appellee is merely the incidental result of a large scheme enacted in the general public welfare, it is necessary for the Court to consider No. 2812 generally. . . .
>
> [W]hile it will be necessary for us to discuss

"zoning" and point out what we believe to be the point of collision between the so-called zoning power and the Constitution of the United States, the Appellee's primary interest is to protect its property against the damage wrought by this particular ordinance.

In two introductory paragraphs Mr. Baker then reiterated his principal thesis: While municipalities have the power to regulate the height of buildings, area of occupation, strengths of building materials, modes of construction and density of use and may divide the community into zones for such purposes

> a municipality may not, under the guise of the police power, arbitrarily divert property from its appropriate and most economical uses or diminish its value by imposing restrictions which have no other basis than the momentary taste of the public authorities. Nor can police regulations be used to effect the arbitrary desire to have a municipality resist the operation of economic laws and remain rural, exclusive and aesthetic, when its land is needed to be otherwise developed by that larger public good and public welfare, which takes into consideration the extent to which the prosperity of the country depends upon the economic development of its business and industrial enterprises.
>
> The municipal limits of the Village of Euclid are, after all, arbitrary and accidental political lines.

In the main argument (at 46–47), Mr. Baker elaborated on the important distinction drawn in the district court between the police power and eminent domain:

> The limitations imposed by the police power do not have to be compensated for, for the reason that they are inherent in the ownership. If I buy a piece of land I have no means of knowing whether or not it will be needed for the

public use, and if any need develops, I must be compensated when the public takes it. But I always know when I buy land, that I may not devote it to uses which endanger the safety, health or morals of others or make its use a common nuisance to the prejudice of the public welfare. Because of its nature, the exercise of the police power has always been restrained to those uses of property which invade the *rights* of others, and courts consistently decline to permit an extension of the police power to uses of property involving mere questions of taste or preference or financial advantage to others.

Even where the objects to be achieved are genuinely benevolent and praiseworthy, Mr. Baker argued, the courts nevertheless guard against the tendency gradually to "relax . . . guardianship over the constitution."[32]

These general observations set the framework for Mr. Baker's discussion of the state court decisions on zoning, which Mr. Baker believed were impossible to "reconcile" and did not present an "authentic definition and application of the constitutional restraints upon unlimited extensions of the police power." The Ohio cases were cited as generally conforming to the reasoning of Judge Westenhaver as to limitations upon the police power, despite apparently contrary *dicta* in *Pritz v. Messer*.[33]

Having stated his thesis and reviewed the cases, Mr. Baker then attempted to apply the law to the facts by reviewing specific provisions of the ordinance, addressing the delicate balance between the ordinance viewed as a whole and the provisions that related specifically to Ambler's tract:

> The appellee's rights depend upon the operation of this ordinance upon its property. If an inspection of this ordinance shows that it is not addressed in general to the proper objects of

the police power but is drawn on the erroneous assumption that the village has the power to regulate the use of private property in the interest of entirely fanciful or fantastic social or aesthetic grounds, then the particular restrictions applying to the appellee's property get their color and purpose from the general purpose of the enactment, and since the main purpose thus established for the ordinance as a whole is inadmissible, the appellee cannot be required to make the enormous contribution out of its property to its accomplishment which these restrictions entail.

Mr. Baker then concluded (at 82–84) with an eloquent summary statement, noting the effects, *in terrorem,* of the philosophy of zoning. It is a statement that appears calculated to speak directly to the philosophical leanings of the majority of the Supreme Court:

> Many of the benefits claimed by counsel for the Village of Euclid to flow from "zoning" are, in fact, the familiar consequences of processes of recognized validity. Building regulation, city planning and the concerted voluntary action of proprietors have accomplished and can accomplish all the protection which the safety, health and morals of a community require and many objects of an aesthetic kind as mere incidents. But the zoning power for which counsel contends is a power different in kind and is in effect a political and communal control of the uses to which an owner may devote his property. It is not the power merely to negative dangerous or anti-social uses, but the power affirmatively to select among admittedly harmless uses those which the political power deems the most popular and to prohibit all others. We do not believe this power exists. Nor are we at all sure that if there were such communal control recognized by the Constitution, its fruits would justify it. The theory of our liberty has always been to maintain the right of the individual to his liberty and to his property and to allow free play to economic laws, private contract and personal choice. . . .

> To assume that the Council of the Village of Euclid, or any other village is able to measure, prophetically, the surging and receding tides by which business evolves and grows, to foresee and map exactly the appropriate uses to which land shall be developed and the amount necessary for each separate use, in a complicated classification, is to assume a degree of wisdom which not only does not exist in municipal councils but does not exist anywhere.

> Yet the theory of zoning, in its ampler definitions, assumes that the municipal councils will be able to do, comprehensively, what private owners, most interested, have found it difficult to do, even on a small scale. Thus to subdivide a municipality, to classify it and crystallize restrictions into laws, is to embed a fly in amber. The forces of movement are stayed and growth is arrested. Around such an ordinance there come to be interests which feel themselves vested and changes in the ordinance, to respond to new needs, have to be made against the protest of those who have come to rely upon arbitrary artificial restrictions rather than to feel themselves subject to the operation of general economic and social laws, which they can measurably foresee and discount.

> That our cities should be made beautiful and orderly is, of course, in the highest degree desirable, but it is even more important that our people should remain free. Their freedom depends upon the preservation of their constitutional immunities and privileges against the desire of others to control them, no matter how generous the motive or well intended the control which it is sought to impose.

With the briefs in this posture, the oral arguments were made to the United States Supreme Court on January 26, 1926. Of what then transpired, the only clues provided by the file are those contained in the reply briefs of the parties filed shortly after the hearing; we do know, however, that for $60 a transcript was available and neither side obtained one.[34]

The Reply Briefs: Ships Distantly Acknowledge One Another

To this point the arguments of Messrs. Baker and Metzenbaum proceeded along almost completely separate lines: Mr. Metzenbaum attempting to contradict the factual and legal bases for the plaintiff's whole case as stated in the complaint and Mr. Baker effecting a "delicate balance" between his overall and specific constitutional attacks. Mr. Metzenbaum now had a clearer and narrower target.

First, he complained about the apparent reversal of Mr. Baker's position from the broader to the narrower ground, asserting that this reversal made it important for the Court more closely to consider the proof of damages. In Mr. Metzenbaum's view, the record actually showed that the ordinance had enhanced the value of Ambler's property. This was a difficult and unnecessary burden but, for the first 19 pages, he assumed it, point by point and witness by witness.

Had he stopped there, the issues in the case may have been somewhat more sharply drawn for the Supreme Court. However, with boundless conviction and energy, Mr. Metzenbaum then undertook to rebut all points, large and small, made or inferred by Mr. Baker, drawing his case into what appeared to be a complex morass of petty disagreements. In the process, important concessions inadvertently were made.

To almost all of this Mr. Baker made only brief general reply, calling the Court's attention to the thoroughness of the proceedings below and noting:

> Counsel for the Appellants plainly did not feel that the trial court had failed to consider any part of the evidence, as no motion for a new trial was urged and no attempt made to call attention to matters now suggested to have been overlooked.

Mr. Baker then proceeded to reframe his overall argument in its narrower and broader aspects into three simple propositions: (1) the State cannot "restrict the uses of private property by selecting among admittedly innocent uses . . . those which it prefers . . . and prohibiting others equally inoffensive," (2) the ordinance itself demonstrates the unlimited extent of the power claimed by Euclid over the uses of land and shows that it is, on its face, "arbitrary, irrational, and confiscatory and that the damage done to the lands of the plaintiff cannot be justified" as incidental to a valid exercise of the police power, and (3) the ordinance has destroyed the salability of the lands of the plaintiff by restricting its appropriate and legitimate uses and by "notifying prospective purchasers . . . that the Village . . . claims to exercise large but undefined, if not undefinable, powers of regulation and control."

In this way (at 10), the broader and narrower issues were harmonized:

> Counsel for appellee, of course understands that this Court cannot properly be asked to accept anything so vague as the "validity of zoning" as an issue of law to be decided. But it is manifest that the Village of Euclid would have no purpose in imposing the restrictions . . . upon plaintiff's land unless it could lawfully impose many, if not all, of the restrictions . . . upon the rest of the land in the village.
>
> If, therefore, the village has wholly misconceived its power and is pursuing a purpose

which it may not lawfully pursue, that fact will appear from an examination of this entire ordinance. One of the virtues claimed for the ordinance is that it is comprehensive and hangs together in all its parts. . . .

According to Mr. Baker, Mr. Metzenbaum had inadvertently provided in his reply brief a perfect opening illustration of the "unreasonable and arbitrary" nature of the ordinance in its other aspects (*ibid.*):

> That the ordinance is thus unreasonable and arbitrary is conceded by counsel for the appellant in his reply brief. On page 22 he discusses the provisions of the ordinance which exclude churches, schools, orphan asylums and other like desirable structures from U1 and U2 territory, and makes the remarkable defense that these objectionable provisions of the ordinance were not put in in good faith to be taken at face value, but are rather a device, cunningly conceived, for the purpose of requiring persons, who plan to build such structures, to consult with the City Planning Commission in order that they may be advised and guided by the wisdom of that body. It is easy to see what sort of advice would be given to the trustees of an unpopular religious denomination who sought to build a church in the village or to the trustees of an orphan asylum or school whose wards were of a particular race or religion, and so suggested those distinctions upon which our most hateful and virulent prejudices are aroused.

Mr. Metzenbaum also had provided Mr. Baker with an illustration of the proper versus the improper use of the police power as it applied to the Ambler tract (at 13):

> It is suggested in oral argument and said in the reply brief of the appellant that the purpose of these prohibitions is to prevent the building of railroad switch tracks up to Euclid Avenue, but the obvious way to prevent that is to prohibit it in plain terms, and in any case railroad switch tracks are not necessary for apartment houses, churches, banks and many other uses which are preemptorily prohibited in U2 and U3 territory.

After reviewing the evidence on the question of damage, Mr. Baker addressed a question evidently put to counsel in oral argument as to whether other zoning ordinances resembled "in a general way" the Euclid ordinance. Mr. Baker first suggested that, in general, use restrictions (as distinct from height and area restrictions) had drawn such justification as they then had from the presence of nuisance features. He then quoted the residential use district regulations of several large city zoning ordinances to support his overall response (at 22) that:

> Most of these cities have undertaken in a large way to separate residence uses, business uses and industrial uses, but the Village of Euclid imposes far more burdensome restrictions and devotes more than half of its area to single-family residences, while it thrusts apartment houses, hotels, clubs, churches and banks, to say nothing of retail dry goods and grocery and drug stores, down either into or immediately adjacent to the district declared by it to be appropriate for heavy industrial uses.

Finally, Mr. Baker returned to the Ohio cases, arguing that from them "the most that can be claimed . . . is a declaration that [the Ohio Supreme Court] will sustain use regulations which are necessary for the preservation of the public health, welfare and safety . . . against [which] position we have nothing to urge."

With the filing of the last reply brief in February 1926, the case was submitted to the decision of the Supreme Court essentially as two distinct cases: Mr. Baker's legal and philosophical attack on use district zoning in general, in which Euclid provided the context, and Mr. Metzenbaum's detailed "factual" and legal justification of the Euclid ordinance as proof of the validity of zoning generally.

THE BATTLEFIELD—REINFORCEMENTS

This case is restored to the docket for a reargument and assigned for Monday, October 4 next . . . .

What prompted the above announcement has been one of the more intriguing and enduring mysteries of the *Euclid* case. Justice Stone's law clerk saw it this way:

Justice Sutherland . . . was writing an opinion for the majority in *Village of Euclid* v. *Ambler Realty Co.*, holding the zoning ordinance unconstitutional, when talks with the dissenting brethren (principally Stone I believe) shook his convictions and led him to request a reargument, after which he changed his mind and the ordinance was upheld.

Another observer[35] has it that:

Baker's arguments carried the day; after the first oral argument, the Justices split 5–4 in favor of Ambler Realty. It was then that . . . Alfred Bettman . . . took the unorthodox step of urging his friend, Chief Justice Taft, to set the case for reargument and to allow an *amicus* brief to be submitted.

Mr. Baker's correspondence reveals yet another interpretation:[36]

In connection with that matter, and this morning, I had a talk with a man that had been the private secretary to Mr. Justice Brandeis, [and]

who had just come from Washington. He is now practicing law here in Minneapolis and told me that he had had a conversation with Brandeis's secretary, who told him that the order for the reargument in the Village of Euclid case came about by reason of the fact that the court was so closely divided that neither side dared to risk a vote.

Brandeis and Holmes certainly are in favor of this zoning business, McReynolds, Van Devanter and Butler opposed to it, with Taft an uncertain quantity, Stone a new member who was not fully conversant with the situation, and who desired more time that he may acquaint himself.

I got the impression from what he said that the reargument was made at Stone's suggestion.

In any event, the file shows that, at this point, the interest and attention of lawyers from all parts of the country were drawn even more widely to the case and, in correspondence, Mr. Baker urged as many as possible to file briefs with the Supreme Court:[37]

I hope a substantial number of briefs will be filed from various parts of the country because it seems quite certain that the "zoners" will file poetic and romantic disquisitions on behalf of the principle by which they think they are going to solve all the problems of society and ultimately produce a better and handsomer human race.

In June, the Supreme Court fixed the date of reargument at October 11 and Mr. Baker pondered the filing of a supplemental brief.

George T. Simpson of Minneapolis was a regular correspondent whom Mr. Baker had suggested file an *amicus* brief in the *Euclid* case. In July, Mr. Baker indicated that he would "probably . . . determine after seeing [Mr.

Simpson's brief] whether I shall try my hand with a supplement to the brief . . . already filed."[38] Mr. Simpson's brief was received in early August:[39]

> In the preparation of the brief, I have had in mind, not only my idea of the invasion of property rights by these zoning ordinances, but the fact that the brief will be scanned by Pierce Butler, who is personally familiar with the entire situation here in the Twin Cities.

Mr. Baker was pleased with the brief pointing out that there were points that "had not occurred to [him] . . . particularly the illustrations . . . dealing with the economic situation in the Northwest as affected by restrictions imposed in the Twin Cities," continuing:[40]

> No doubt Mr. Justice Butler's long residence in Minneapolis would make this brief particularly helpful to him.
>
> As I have had Mr. Justice Butler's opinions and appeared before him as a judge, I have come to have a very deep respect for his learning and earnestness and feel sure that if we can get the principles involved in our case fairly stated to him, he will give the matter a scholarly and high-minded study.

Judge Charles D. Elliot, also of Minneapolis, had another zoning case in the Supreme Court which he desired to advance and consolidate with the Ambler case for argument. Mr. Baker agreed to divide his time with Mr. Elliot,[41]

> but if there are other cases or other counsel appearing *amicus curiae,* it may be necessary for us to discuss the situation after we get to Washington. . . . I, for instance, have already argued my case once and did not say enough to satisfy the Court, so while I am eager for a fresh chance, it may be that I do not deserve it.

In July, Mr. Bettman prepared his brief and in August requested formal consent from Mr. Baker to allow the brief to be filed.

Robert Morgan prepared a memorandum for argument in August and the file clearly shows that Mr. Baker, at that time, was preparing to write a supplemental brief. Mr. Morgan proposed "doing three things to help in this matter":[42]

> First, see if I cannot find some authorities to back up our claim that in cases of this sort the rule of decision requires the court to find the *fact* of public benefit to accrue, or public damage to be avoided; second, point out from the cases favorable to zoning how the courts have based their decisions entirely on the assumption of validity or on a statement of inability to see that the public interest would not be advanced. Then I thought I could run the late zoning cases so that we might check them over for points in our favor.

In September, Mr. A. J. Hill, counsel opposing the Los Angeles Zoning Ordinance, corresponded with Mr. Baker concerning the advancement of his case for argument with the *Euclid* case, to which Mr. Baker replied:[43]

> I have no doubt the court will advance your case for hearing with ours. I would be glad to consent to the motion so far as any action on my part is either necessary or helpful.
>
> It will be better for the court to have as many phases of this omnibus power before it as possible.

Later in the month, Mr. Metzenbaum telegraphed Mr. Hill to obtain from a transcript in his possession a passage from Mr. Baker's first argument and Mr. Hill wrote to inform Mr. Baker:[44]

I am in receipt of another telegraph from Mr. Metzenbaum, which is as follows:

> *"Several places but particularly near opening Baker stated principal objection was unconstitutionality because of unreasonableness as applied to Ambler parcel and not because of unconstitutionality of all zoning ordinances."*

and in reply thereto am mailing to him the following excerpt:

> *"(A map was placed upon the frame in front of the bench). Mr. Baker (continuing). I want to say, in the first place, that I do not assume the burden of demonstrating the general and comprehensive invalidity of all zoning ordinances; and I have no special argument to make against an abstract philosophy on that subject."*

This is for your information.

Mr. Baker responded:[45]

> the extract which you supplied him seems to me to be innocuous and I shall not be terrified at meeting it again.

On October 5, Mr. Baker advised Messrs. Hill and Elliott that the court was going to deny all motions to advance but would welcome briefs, *amici curiae.* As the date for argument approached, only Messrs. Simpson, Bettman, and Metzenbaum had provided briefs supplemental to those previously filed.

THE BATTLEFIELD—LAST SHOTS AND A RESULT

Between the filing of his reply brief earlier in the year and the time of preparation of his supplemental brief, Mr. Metzenbaum's thinking had further evolved. He now believed that the *only* issue properly raised before the Supreme Court was the "Basic Unconstitutionality" of the Euclid ordinance (at 3):

> [B]ecause of the facts and conditions admitted by the Ambler Company, it does not have the right . . . to bring into issue any questions of reasonableness or unreasonableness of the ordinance as it applies to its land, even though the Village concedes that the Ambler Company may in the pending case have the right to bring into issue the question of the basic and per se unconstitutionality of the ordinance.

Mr. Metzenbaum then cleverly used Mr. Baker's statement from the previous hearing (obtained from Mr. Hill) to urge that Mr. Baker had placed principal, if not exclusive, reliance on the unreasonableness of the ordinance *as applied,* and therefore (at 17):

> the complainant stand(s) before this court without any strong or real ground of asking for court intervention.

In his fashion, however, this *tour de force* was weakened somewhat by the presentation of 26 "unanswerable facts" and not a few digressions, such as this feisty quibble with Mr. Bettman (at 42–43):

Brief of *Amici Curiae*

We wish here to advert to the brief filed by the National Conference on City Planning, as *Amici Curiae.* With no intention of criticism and with a fitting respect for this brief, the Village nevertheless feels that in defense of its own position it does not wish this brief, like its predecessor in the Trial Court below, to prejudice any of the rights of the Village, for (a) the Village earnestly finds itself unable to subscribe to several of the doctrines urged in this brief just as they were urged in the Trial Court, and (b) in addition thereto the Village—having studiously refrained from resting upon citations of so-called "nuisance" and "semi-nuisance" cases as supporting zoning ordinances—the Village cannot conscientiously subscribe to the citation of such cases in the brief of the *Amici Curiae.* (Kindly note disclaimer at middle paragraph of page 76 of Village Original brief.) (c) Some of the other citations are not fully accurate, among these particularly being the North Dakota decision, which has long since been favorably ruled upon by the Supreme Court of that State and is no longer confined to the favorable opinion of its lower court.

Much has been said and written about Mr. Bettman's "Brandeis brief" in the *Euclid* case and no further comment need be made here except to suggest that, in context, it stood between the more extreme arguments of Messrs. Baker and Metzenbaum. It both engaged Mr. Baker on the loftier philosophical and legal grounds and lent dignity and reasoned and focused authority to Mr. Metzenbaum's omnibus defense of zoning; for the Court, it gave reassurance that the application of analogous authority—not any radical departure from precedent—was all that was required.[46]

The oral arguments were made on October 12, 1926.[47] As far as can be told from scant clues in the file, Mr. Baker attempted both to rebut certain of Mr. Bettman's main points (such as the legitimacy of the use of the police power to *prevent* rather than *suppress* nuisances) and to develop a clearer rationale for the Court to distinguish between legitimate police power regulation and taking. His thinking, too, had evolved and he presented this concise distinction to the Court:[48]

> When the public power is used negatively, that is to say, merely to restrain people from making use of their property or of their personal rights in such fashion as to deny others equal freedom, the public power used is the police power. When the public power is used affirmatively, that is to say, to construct a public benefit at the expense of the private property and personal rights of citizens, the power used is eminent domain and can proceed only upon compensation.

However, the opinion of Justice Sutherland, when it was announced on November 22, 1926, contained no reference to this interesting distinction and, in tribute to Mr. Bettman, followed his major theses in almost all respects.[49] To Mr. Metzenbaum, the opinion gave not only the satisfaction of victory but credit, perhaps, for his late season emphasis on the "ripeness" of the case for adjudication on the grounds of unreasonableness of the ordinance as it applied to Ambler's property.[50]

THE RESULT INTERPRETED

Mr. Baker, for his part, expressed only mild disappointment and "hurt pride" that the Court "did not think it wise to go more fully into the philosophy of the decision" and had not defined any outer limit on the police power such as the one he had suggested in oral argument:[51]

> I spent the whole summer trying to work out some distinction that would be philosophically sound, but since Mr. Justice Sutherland in his opinion did not even refer to my discovery, I am forced to assume that it was not as impressive to them as it seemed sound to me.
>
> . . .
>
> Of all the people I know, Mr. Justice Sutherland seemed to me the unlikeliest to write such an opinion as the one handed down. When he was president of the American Bar Association in 1917, he made a presidential address at the annual meeting in Saratoga Springs in which he said, "It is not enough, however, that we should continue free from the despotism of a supreme autocrat. We must keep ourselves free from the petty despotism which may come from the vesting of final discretion to regulate individual conduct in the hands of lesser officials." If he has not subjected us to the petty despotism of lesser officials in this opinion, I confess I do not see how it could be done.

Mr. Simpson saw the matter somewhat more darkly:[52]

> Frankly few of us here can understand the attitude of the court, for I am convinced that if this opinion stands in its present nakedness, the property interests of this nation, on which, I think, perhaps, the whole court would agree the future welfare of the nation depends, are in danger.
>
> George Sutherland is generally understood to be a property man. I know all about his appointment, and, to have George Sutherland write an opinion of this kind makes a fellow stop and think.

Looking to future cases, Mr. Baker expressed the view that:[53]

> What the court has actually decided is that the general principle of zoning to an extent necessary to separate residence from industry and commercial uses is within the police power but that the reasonableness of any particular exercise of that power must be determined in each instance on its own facts and my own judgment is that the Supreme Court, having stated this much, intends to leave to the Circuit Courts of Appeal the work of the details and the imposing of rational restraints upon municipal activities. . . .
>
> I have felt it would be entirely useless for me to ask for another reargument before the Supreme Court of the United States in the Ambler case but I do not think it useless to urge specific instances of unreasonableness in the case as they arise and I have no doubt that by the time we get done pointing out the detailed evils, the police power will be gradually reduced to much less menacing proportions than it seems to have in the Ambler opinion.

Mr. Bettman gave Mr. Baker credit for introducing the "metropolitan factor" in the case:[54]

> but . . . this factor [was pushed] beyond its just desserts, and the opinion of the Supreme Court that the suburban community is not required to merge its welfare completely in that of the metropolitan region is salutary and refreshing.

Mr. Bettman also observed, somewhat patronizingly:[55]

> So able a lawyer as Newton D. Baker . . . felt it necessary to rely upon an extreme statement of early nineteenth century laissez-faire political philosophy, which seemed to be about as appropriate to twentieth century cities as electric traffic control would have been to wilderness cross-roads at the time of President Washington.

Mr. Metzenbaum, graceful in victory, wrote to Mr. Baker on February 8, 1927, charmingly rejecting the idea of his drafting any final decree in the case:[56]

> I have not forgotten your telephone call of last week, but I simply cannot bring myself to dictating or drafting any journal entry against you.
>
> If you wish, you may even place it on the basis that I do not know how to do this, for I simply will not do it. . . .
>
> I do not take this position out of any spirit of stubbornness or the like, but solely because of my sincere and affectionate regard for you.
>
> If there is anything to be written which will be adverse to you, you will be obliged to do the writing, for I will not do it. I will take your instructions in reference to subjects which will aid you, but I will not do so regarding situations which are unfavorable to you.

OBSERVATIONS—GINGERLY OFFERED

What, then, may be said of the conduct of the case from the perfect hindsight of 60 years? Surely *Euclid* provided a landmark departure from the jealous guardianship by the Court of common-law property rights, foreshadowing the great enlargement of governmental authority sanctioned by the more liberal courts of later years.

What stands out, in retrospect, is the absence in the opinion of any cogent rationale, other than the elusive test of reasonableness, for delimiting the scope of the police power. The *Euclid* case, in consequence, has accorded to local zoning officials—just as Mr. Baker envisioned—a power unlimited in theory, impenetrably defended by a near conclusive presumption of validity.

It is unfortunate that Mr. Baker did not avail himself of the opportunity to respond to Mr. Bettman's analysis more directly in the United States Supreme Court. He had done so with great force in the Ohio Supreme Court:[57]

> Without further quotation, we submit that the court will find on every page of his brief an admission that the advocates of zoning seek to substitute the opinion and desire of the municipal legislature for the operation of the natural laws of competition and self-interest in the building and regulation of cities. . . .
>
> Thus . . . the court will find a description of the way zone plans are made. But it is exactly because the founders of our government were unable to persuade themselves that legislatures would always be wise, and always benevolent and always just that the great constitutional guaranties were enacted. . . .
>
> The society organized by our constitution is one in which the individual is guaranteed his liberty of person and his right to possess and use, as he will, property, real and personal, subject . . . only to those restraints which are necessary to prevent his use of his personal freedom or of his property from impairing the like rights in others. If it be said that zoning still leaves a substantial part of these constitutional liberties, it must be conceded that it leaves them impaired and less extensive than they were in the minds of the framers of the Constitution, and that they have been impaired by a process which, if extended, will substitute community control for personal control, alike of personal conduct and privately owned property.

It is likewise unfortunate that Mr. Baker's late developing rationale[58] to distinguish between valid police power regulation and a taking could not have been presented more completely to the Court. The adoption of this thesis would have served both to delimit the exercise of police power and (by incorporating eminent domain principles) to reserve the presumption of validity in zoning cases. Similar views have found quite recent expression,[59] encouraged, somewhat, by recent decisions of the Supreme Court:

> If the state does not desire (or require) the acquisition of a fee simple ownership of particular property, but wants merely to appropriate an easement right or to prevent certain nonnuisance land uses, a dilemma is presented. Regulation of private land use, other than to prevent common law nuisances, should not normally be permitted without compensation (purchase of interest appropriated). This was the clear intent of the framers of the fifth and fourteenth amendments. The state obtains an interest in the burdened property whenever it denies the owner the full, nonnuisance use and enjoyment of his property. Hence, zoning restrictions, land use controls and other forms of property regulation should, absent compensation, be presumptively invalid.

It seems likely that the Court discounted both the unyielding absoluteness of Mr. Metzenbaum's claims on behalf of zoning and, as Mr. Bettman has suggested,[60] Mr. Baker's lofty dependence on the principles of nineteenth century laissez-faire political philosophy. At bottom, Mr. Metzenbaum was defending the American home and, at bottom, Mr. Baker flatly rejected the whole concept of zoning:[61]

> The more experience I have had with zoning ordinances, and I have now examined a very great many of them, the more satisfied I am that the whole theory is wrong. Nobody knows enough or can know enough to zone a city. As a matter of fact, cities do not grow and will not grow according to any plan, no matter how wise. Their growth is a necessary resultant of economic forces and economic accidents which nobody can foresee.
>
> In conspicuous cases, the truth of this observation, of course, is clear. In Detroit, for instance, any plan for the growth of Detroit before the advent of the motor car industry there would have been entirely useless and probably worse. Here in Cleveland the opening up of a suburban real estate development has changed the whole character of the city within the past dozen years. Within the last two years the location of a railroad terminal has started a new redistribution of the city's activities and growth. In every instance with which I am acquainted a zoning ordinance has become out of date within two or three years after its passage, sometimes generally out of date and sometimes sporadically out of date, with the result that the normal development of the territory has been artificially interfered with. People who rely upon the apparent stability of conditions established by zoning ordinances find themselves defeated in their expectations and in some of the cases of which I have knowledge the results are cruel.

Finally, one might ponder the role of "facts" in determining the outcome of the case. For Mr. Baker, the only relevant facts were those that tended to show damage to his client and, from the map and ordinance itself, their exclusionary, aesthetic, or irrational purposes. Generally, the facts were discounted by the district court and were, in effect, assumed by the Supreme Court. In retrospect, one wonders whether more could have been made of the lack of any comprehensive plan, the paucity of preparatory studies and "scientific" analyses mentioned by Mr. Bettman,[62] and perhaps, most importantly, the *bête noir* of all land use measures: the underlying rationale for the drawing of particular district boundaries.[63] With such an emphasis it is possible that the Court might have been drawn into an analysis which better defined the proper antecedents of valid zoning.

The *Euclid* case is full of delicious irony: Mr. Baker's conversion from "progressive" to "mossback" theology while, at the same time, advocating metropolitan dominance over home rule; Mr. Metzenbaum's elaborate justification of the "NIMBY" ("not-in-my-backyard") principle on the grounds that it actually enhanced the value of the Ambler tract; and Mr. Bettman's stirring defense of a zoning ordinance he privately believed to be a "piece of arbitrary zoning."[64] Perhaps the ultimate irony of the case, however, lies in the physical fact that on Ambler's famous 68 acres today, there stands—adjacent to Euclid Avenue and extending to the tracks of the Nickel Plate Railroad—The Inland Plant of the General Motors Corporation.[65]

NOTES

1. Elliot A. Rosen, "Baker on the Fifth Ballot? The Democratic Alternative: 1932," *Ohio History*, Autumn 1966.

2. Alfred Bettman was a prominent Cincinnati lawyer

active in reform city politics. His lifelong interest in city planning may have stemmed from his appreciation of the work of Rabbi Isaac Meyer Wise "who fused reform Judaism into a gospel of urban reform." Mr. Bettman is credited with securing passage of the first municipal planning enabling act in Ohio. As a member of the Advisory Committee on Housing and Zoning of the U.S. Department of Commerce, Mr. Bettman worked on the Standard State Zoning Enabling Act. (The foregoing is based on Timothy Alan Fluck, *"Euclid* v. *Ambler:* A Retrospective," 52 *Journal of the American Planning Association* (1986): 23, note 4 and accompanying text.) While Messrs. Baker and Bettman addressed each other by their first names, the file hints at a certain coolness in their relationship. For example, Mr. Baker's office apparently sidestepped Mr. Bettman's repeated requests for copies of the Ambler briefs until Mr. Baker himself forwarded a copy of his February 1926 reply brief to Mr. Bettman on October 20, 1926, eight days *after* the arguments in the U.S. Supreme Court. Mr. Baker disappointed Mr. Bettman in other respects as well. See notes 54 and 55 and accompanying text.

3. Among the larger contributions were those from the New York Central and Nickel Plate Railroads at $2,000 each. Except for the wider interests of the railroads, the subscribers did not appear to represent any larger regional or national interests:

> The undersigned are owners of lands in the Village of Euclid, Ohio, and believe their rights as such owners are seriously prejudiced by the provisions of Zoning Ordinance #2812 of said Village, adopted November 13, 1922.
>
> WHEREAS, the undersigned believe that most of the provisions of said Ordinance having the effect of restricting the use of said lands are unconstitutional, and therefore the undersigned are desirous of having an appropriate action or actions brought in the joint or several names of one or more of said undersigned to test the validity of said Ordinance in such court or courts as counsel selected may in his or their discretion think best.
>
> WHEREAS, the undersigned having retained NEWTON D. BAKER of the Cleveland Bar to act for them as attorney and counsel in such matters, he to have the right in his discretion to select other attorneys as he wishes to aid him in the matter, at his own expense.

4. As an equity case, of course, there was no jury trial.

According to one source, the assignment of Judge Westenhaver was a felicitous one for Mr. Baker.

> David Westenhaver had been persuaded to move to Cleveland in 1903 by his close friend, Newton Baker. Thanks to the sponsorship of Secretary of War Baker, President Wilson had nominated Westenhaver to a federal judgeship in 1917. [Timothy Alan Fluck, *"Euclid* v. *Ambler:* A Retrospective," 52 *Journal of the American Planning Association* (1986): pp. 326, 329.]

5. Justice Sutherland, a Republican from Utah, was appointed to the Court in 1922. As senator from Utah, Justice Sutherland had opposed the Federal Reserve Act, the Federal Trade Commission and Clayton Antitrust Acts, and the imposition of the Federal Income Tax. Clearly conservative in outlook, he quickly joined the majority in outlawing the minimum wage for women. He later became a leading spokesman for the Court's conservative majority in rulings unfavorable to New Deal legislation.

6. In the pyramid scheme only single-family districts are exclusive of other uses, i.e., at the "top" of the pyramid. In each other category, uses are cumulative with the higher uses; that is, for example, single-family residences could be built anywhere. While typical of other zoning ordinances in this respect, the pyramid scheme was vulnerable to attack as evidencing an aesthetic or exclusionary purpose:

> If there were any genuine purpose in this ordinance to segregate family life from an industrial and commercial environment, no such situation would be tolerated. [Brief and argument for appellee *Euclid* v. *Ambler Realty,* Case No. 665, U.S. Supreme Court, October Term, 1925 at 78.]

7. The original Euclid ordinance classified only the 500 feet nearest to the Nickel Plate Railroad (approximately one-quarter of the tract) for industrial purposes, and the entire remainder was zoned for two-family residential purposes. By amendment, the industrial area was roughly doubled and a narrow strip, 130 feet wide, was added for apartment uses.

8. Despite much argument by the parties, neither court determined the amount of Ambler's zoning-related loss. From the facts shown in the opinion, however, both were apparently willing to assume that its loss in value was as alleged in the bill of complaint [See *Euclid* v. *Ambler Realty,* 272 U.S. 365, 384 (1926).]

9. Mr. Baker was fascinated by Mr. Hunter's case on

behalf of the Bell Telephone Company of Pennsylvania relative to the location of telephone exchanges:

> This is an excellent illustration of a thesis I have been trying to demonstrate in *Ambler* v. *Village of Euclid* to the effect that nobody knows enough to draw up a zoning ordinance. To demonstrate for instance, the location of a new central exchange requires a highly specialized scientific study to determine the true efficient and economical wire center. I have not the least doubt the same would be true of the location of a police station, fire station, and, in a diminishing degree, of everything else from public libraries down to corner grocery and drug stores. In the normal process of social development, locations for things like this are determined one at a time, either by study or experience, and when thus determined the experience is not so extensive that an error is incorrigible. If a man puts his drug store in the wrong place, he soon learns it by finding that he has no patronage and moves to a new location with relatively little economic loss to the community. When the thing is attempted comprehensively, however, by one of these zoning ordinances, mistakes are far more burdensome and their correction more costly and difficult. [Letter from Newton D. Baker to Frank M. Hunter dated July 10, 1926]

10. This phrase was contained in the "Preamble" to the Euclid zoning ordinance, preceded by recitals that described the community as a "residential suburb," the street, sewer, and water systems of which were designed and constructed to take care of such restricted uses and were inadequate for more congested uses. The preamble contained a "finding" that the territory made available for manufacturing, industrial, and commercial uses was sufficient for such purposes. To Mr. Baker, this seemed to be a clear expression of an intention to "forcibly change the character of the Village," in restraint of the "obvious prospect" of industrial development along the railroads in the major part of its whole area, in effect, to "erect a dam to hold back the flood of industrial development." *Brief for Plaintiff on Motion to Dismiss, Ambler* v. *Euclid,* Equity No. 898, at 9.

11. This fact was alleged in the answer of the village to the initial complaint:

> That . . . the said Complainant, itself, laid out and dedicated another street (Cushman Road) running from Euclid Avenue . . . to the Nickel Plate tracks. . . .

> That said Complainant . . . sold off all of its [lots] on [Cushman Road], with restrictions . . . restricting and limiting each and all of the lots . . . for single residences alone. [*Answer, Ambler* v. *Euclid,* Equity No. 898, at 4–5.]

12. Euclid's answer alleged that there were but 16 factories in Euclid, only two of which were located along Euclid Avenue (at 2). Moreover, "not a single factory has been built or constructed anywhere at all in Euclid Village, for more than four years prior to the enactment of [the] Ordinance."

13. As the *Plain Dealer* observed in reporting on Mr. Metzenbaum's victory in *Euclid* on November 22, 1926:

> Metzenbaum, the hero of the *Euclid* case, has not the physique usually associated with trial lawyers. He is a bantamweight, hardly more than five feet tall, and the Supreme Court Justices had to crane their necks to see him over the edge of the bench.
>
> They had no trouble hearing him however, for he has a reputation of being one of the most persistent men in town. He is an experienced debater and conversational grappler, and excels in discourse and argument.

14. 272 U.S. 365, 395 (1926).

15. That is, that the ordinance was "arbitrary and unreasonable having no substantial relationship to the public health, safety, morals, or general welfare." See *Cusack* v. *Chicago,* 242 U.S. 530, 531 (1918).

16. In addition to his prescient claim that the "general welfare" was not limited to the 4,500 residents of Euclid, Mr. Baker made a number of arguments from the face of the ordinance itself, noting, for example, that (a) bathrooms were required in single- and two-family dwellings but not in apartments (at 12); (b) churches or schools were not permitted at all in single- or double-family districts and fire and police stations were excluded from all residence districts (at 13); (c) since "accessory uses" had to be on the same lot with the primary use, "if a man owned two lots of fifty feet each he could not have his house on one and his garage on the other" (at 14); (d) because of the "pyramid" scheme, the ordinance did not "attempt to protect residences from the proximity of industrial undertakings, but only to protect certain sections of land from being occupied by both uses" (at 16); (e) (with respect to lot areas) "if the health, safety and comfort of a family are adequately provided for by a minimum of 700 square feet in any part of the Village, the same minimum will serve the same purpose in every

part of the Village" (at 17); and (f) (with respect to amendments) besides the requirement that changes contrary to the recommendation of the City Planning and Zoning Commission be adopted by a three-fourths vote, if the change was to a *less* restricted use, the objecting petition of the owners of 20 percent of the land within 200 feet of such area would also require such a vote ("considerations of public safety, health, and comfort do not depend upon preferences of property owners" (at 19–20)). These and other provisions:

> show that [the objectives of the ordinance] cannot be the public health, safety or welfare, but . . . the "preservation of the present character of the Village."

17. Mr. Bettman did argue that the case might not be "ripe" for adjudication and that, in consequence, the broader question of constitutionality need not be reached (Brief on Behalf of the Ohio State Conference on City Planning, Amicus Curiae, *Ambler* v. *Euclid,* Equity No. 898 at 18); Mr. Metzenbaum was unhappy with Mr. Bettman's brief, as he later noted in his supplemental brief in the U.S. Supreme Court on rehearing, perhaps in part because of the brief's sober, detached perspective. It is possible that there was tension concerning Mr. Bettman's private views on the Euclid ordinance (*see* note 25 and accompanying text). Although Mr. Bettman dutifully noted in his brief that the Euclid ordinance was a "conscientious, careful piece of work" and that there was no evidence that it was "arbitrary in the sense of absence of care or genuine application of thought," he also noted that even a comprehensive ordinance might be unreasonable if it were a piece of "slap-bang guess work" (at 2).

18. When this argument reached Mr. Metzenbaum's full attention, Mr. Boyle was forced by him to withdraw this portion of the brief, prompting a delightful exchange of correspondence between Messrs. Baker and Boyle. Mr. Baker responded to this turn of events in his letter of January 10, 1924:

> I have your letter of January 9th enclosing the substituted sheets for your brief. I perfectly understand the situation there and will, of course, seek no advantage from the frankness of your original brief, although with a judge like Westenhaver I fancy it makes very little difference whether we let him draw the inferences or aid him in drawing them.

And, Mr. Boyle responded on January 11, 1924:

> I thank you sincerely for your very frank and manly letter of December (sic) 10th, as it greatly tends to relieve me from the embarrassment that has oppressed me throughout this trial.

19. 260 U.S. 393 (1922).

20. *Ambler Realty Co.* v. *Village of Euclid,* 297 F. 307 (N.D. Ohio 1924).

21. Judge Westenhaver relied principally on a takings analysis. He was persuaded that the "high water" mark of the Supreme Court's willingness to tolerate invasions of property rights under the police power had been reached in the rent law cases arising from World War I. In his view, in order to justify intrusion on the use rights of private property (which were inseparable from property itself), there had to be a clearer connection to the prevention of some public harm. Even then, the police power was not without limit, as demonstrated in the *Mahon* case. Given the composition of the Supreme Court and the state of the authorities, he was clearly justified in holding to this view.

22. The modern reader is somewhat staggered by Judge Westenhaver's comparison of *Ambler* to *Buchanan* v. *Warley,* 245 U.S. 60 (1918), a case in which the Supreme Court invalidated an ordinance "districting and restricting residential blocks so that white and colored races should be segregated":

> It seems to me no candid mind can deny that more and stronger reasons exist, having a real and substantial relation to the public peace, supporting such an ordinance than can be urged under any aspect of the police power to support the present ordinance as applied to plaintiff's property.
>
> . . .
>
> The blighting of property values and the congesting of population, whenever the colored or certain foreign races invade a residential section are so well known as to be within judicial cognizance.
>
> [297 F. 307, 312–13.]

23. 297 F. 307, 316.

24. Bulletin sent under date of February 15, 1924, on the letterhead of the organization.

25. Mandelker, Daniel R., and Robert A. Cunningham, *Planning and Control of Land Development,* 2d ed., 1985, at 71, quoting from a 1924 letter of Alfred Bettman.

26. Fluck, *supra* note 4, at n.35.

27. *Pritz* v. *Messer,* 112 Ohio St. 628 (1925); *City of Youngstown* v. *Kahn Brothers Building Co.,* 112 Ohio St. 654 (1925).

28. Letter from Mr. Baker to Mr. Malcolm B. Sterrett dated December 26, 1924.

29. For example: "Euclid is 9 to 14 miles from Cleveland," "The bill of complaint does not square up with the facts," "Though Railroads have been there for all these years, there are only 16 industrials in total and not one has built along or near the street line."

30. There then followed an argument on the police power in general (three pages); the presumption of validity (five pages); a (highly curious) section denying that taking under the police power was prohibited; some miscellany ("Classification is permitted and even necessary," "Not invalid if there could have been a valid basis," "Court will not substitute its judgment for legislative division," "The GENERAL application and not one single instance must be the guide," "Constitutionality of board of appeals," and "Appeal board is legal"); and a long recital of state court cases favoring comprehensive zoning.

31. At this juncture, Mr. Baker faced the prospect of a kind of draw: The Court could dispose of the case on the issue of timeliness or on the issue of the effect of zoning on Ambler's property, separately considered, upholding or reversing the district court on a narrow application of police power principles and the presumption of validity. These were the narrow and safer grounds for the Court. Nevertheless, both Mr. Baker and Mr. Metzenbaum pressed their larger and bolder theses.

32. Mr. Baker did not hold to the view that the objects of zoning were "benevolent and praiseworthy" (at 48):

Even if the world could agree by unanimous consent upon what is beautiful and desirable, it could not, under our constitutional theory, enforce its decision by prohibiting a land owner, who refuses to accept the world's view of beauty, from making otherwise safe and innocent uses of his land. The case against many of these zoning laws, however, is much stronger than this. The world has not reached a unanimous judgment about beauty, and there are few unlikelier places to look for stable judgments on such subjects than in the changing discretion of legislative bodies, moved this way and that by the conflict of commercial interests on the one hand, and the assorted opinions of individuals, moved by purely private concerns, on the other. We respectfully submit that counsel for appellant, in his fervor for an extension of the police power which will permit municipalities to accomplish all the great goods at which zoning aims, overlooks the fact that, after all, this is merely a desire of some people to tell other people how to use their property.

33. This case unfairly plagued Mr. Baker, because the Ohio Supreme Court had reached out, in *dicta,* to uphold Cincinnati's comprehensive zoning ordinance. Its views, *ex cathedra,* were incorporated into the syllabus of the opinion—thus making them an official statement of the Court.

34. Fluck, "*Euclid* v. *Ambler:* A Retrospective, p. 31, relates that Justice Sutherland was not present at the argument and that Chief Justice Taft interrupted Mr. Metzenbaum to request clarification of the "fundamentals of zoning." He also notes that (since Mr. Baker went last for his one-hour argument) the last 15 minutes of Mr. Baker's argument substantially agitated Mr. Metzenbaum. He believed both that Mr. Baker had improperly shifted his position from the broader to the narrower grounds and that he had distorted the facts. This led Mr. Metzenbaum to go to extraordinary lengths to obtain leave to file a reply brief:

Metzenbaum was convinced that these final 15 minutes of Baker's presentation meant victory for the opponents of zoning. He could not sleep that night on the train from Washington to Cleveland. He resolved to telephone a Washington lawyer to appear in person before the Court the next day—the last day before a one-month adjournment to decide cases—to move for permission to file a reply brief.

But because of a snowstorm, in the morning the train was still in Pennsylvania, not Cleveland. Unable to telephone from the train, Metzenbaum drafted a telegram to Taft:

. . . Because of the importance of the cause and not for any mere purpose of winning, am compelled by conscientious duty to request permission to file short Reply Brief. . . .

As the train slowed along a siding where freight cars were being shoveled out of the snow, Metzenbaum shouted to a workman, tossed the telegram form wrapped with money, and saw it land in a bank of snow. Only after reaching Cleveland did he learn that the telegram had been sent. It would not be until February 2, 1926, that Metzenbaum would receive the Court's permission to file a reply brief within one week.

35. A. Dan Tarlock, "*Euclid* Revisited," *Land Use Law and Zoning Digest* 34 (1982): 4, 5.

36. Letter from George T. Simpson to Newton D.

Baker dated May 22, 1926. Mr. Baker replied on May 25, 1926:

> I have your very interesting letter of May 22. I had heard none of the probable line-up with regard to the zoning question but it seems a more or less natural division.

37. Letter from Newton D. Baker to George Simpson dated May 25, 1926. Mr. Baker had his own additional example of unreasonable zoning:

> I have in another case here in Ohio an instance in which a Jewish Orphanage Asylum, which is one of the best managed institutions of its kind in America, has been excluded from a village in which it owns a twenty-acre tract and in which it proposed to build a modern cottage-system orphanage. The question of permitting this building was referred to a so-called zoning committee and by them reported adversely because they did not think it would be good for the village to have a large number of Jewish children in it. If I were to tell that story to the court it would be regarded as an improper effort to arouse religious prejudice and yet, of course, that is exactly the kind of misconduct we can expect from municipal authorities if they are given a free hand to indulge all their prejudices and preferences.

This case was later carried to the Circuit Court of Appeals with a decision favorable to Mr. Baker's client on the grounds of "reasonableness." *Village of University Heights* v. *Cleveland Jewish Orphans' Home,* 20 F.2d 743 (6th Cir. 1927).

38. Letter to George T. Simpson dated July 10, 1926.

39. Letter from George T. Simpson to Newton D. Baker dated August 5, 1926.

40. Letter to George T. Simpson dated August 11, 1926.

41. Letter to Hon. Charles B. Elliott dated August 12, 1926. Mr. Elliott's case was *Beery* v. *Houghton,* decided by the Supreme Court after *Euclid* and reported at 273 U.S. 671 (1927).

42. Letter to Newton D. Baker dated August 17, 1926.

43. Letter to Mr. Hill dated September 11, 1926. The case was *Zahn* v. *Board of Public Works,* decided by the Supreme Court after *Euclid* and reported at 274 U.S. 325 (1927).

44. Letter to Mr. Baker dated September 25, 1926.

45. Letter to Mr. Hill dated September 30, 1926.

46. In effect, Mr. Bettman argued that the Supreme Court had already sustained the validity of zoning regulations in *Welch* v. *Swasey,* 241 U.S. 91 (1909) (height regulation), and *Hadacheck* v. *Sebastian,* 239 U.S. 394 (1915) (use regulation). Quite clearly, Mr. Bettman's abstract vision of a valid comprehensive zoning ordinance differed markedly from the actual facts found by the district court to pertain with respect to the Euclid ordinance. As even he conceded (at 10–11),

> Property derives its value from its appropriateness, by reason of location, for certain uses, and the fact that a zoning ordinance causes a substantial impairment of value may be evidence, not conclusive or presumptive, but an item of evidence of arbitrary, unreasonable zoning; that is of zoning which, in fixing the boundaries between the various zones, has been careless of or has ignored this factor of appropriateness of location. The reasonableness of the plan . . . is, of course, in issue in any case in which the validity of the plan is attacked. . . .

47. The *Plain Dealer* reported the arguments this way:

> Mr. Baker reiterated today that his intention is not to demonstrate the general and comprehensive invalidity of all zoning ordinances, but that he holds a particular ordinance unconstitutional.
>
> Mr. Metzenbaum insists that basic constitutionality is the only question open to the realty company, and that sixteen states have "through their highest tribunals so firmly stamped their approval and validation, that the question of fundamental unconstitutionality has successfully been denied, literally, from coast to coast."

48. Letter from Mr. Baker to George T. Simpson dated December 13, 1926. Mr. Baker's handwritten notes for oral argument suggest that he planned to (1) begin with a description of the "physical situation" and the showing of damage (from "2nd Brief p. 15"), (2) describe the new features of the case, i.e., Mr. Simpson's brief, the *Beery* and *Zahn* cases, and Mr. Bettman's brief, (3) discuss the police power vs. the 14th Amendment (a) distinguishing between the "suppression" and "prevention" of nuisances ("Police power a shield not a sword," "Prevent injury not construct benefits," *"sic utero,* etc.—limit on right of private property also basis of doctrine of nuisances" [believed to be *sic utero tuo ut alienum non laedes:* Use your own property in such manner as not to injure that of another], (b) develop tests: "reality of public danger versus damage or inconvenience and relative injury to

individual," (c) discuss "illustrative cases": Pennsylvania case (?), *Terrace Park* case, orphan asylum case, Simpson (Wood Products), *Beery, Zahn, Buchanan, Truax, (v. Corrigan), Meyer, Wolf Packing,* and *Mahon;* and (4) apply (the foregoing?) to "our case"; Ordinance—"Public good is served?" "Health, Safety Morals." "Comparison of Ordinances 2nd Brief 23," Enactment of Experiments and Theories" (unintelligible) "prejudices and neighborhood passions."

49. Mr. Bettman's argument, of course, was directed only to the constitutionality of comprehensive zoning in principle and not to the "reasonableness or arbitrariness" of the Euclid village ordinance itself or as it applied to the Ambler property. It seems likely that this general argument not only lent great force to Mr. Metzenbaum's substantive arguments but also served to direct the Court's attention away from Mr. Baker's specific arguments against the Euclid ordinance. The resulting opinion validated an ordinance that Mr. Bettman privately believed to be "a piece of arbitrary zoning." An excellent analysis of Mr. Bettman's brief is found in *Tarlock, supra* note 35 at 6–8.

50. The Court, of course, sustained the ordinance in general terms, leaving to another day cases in which "the provisions of the ordinance . . . come to be concretely applied to particular premises . . . or to particular conditions, or to be considered in connection with specific complaints." *Euclid* v. *Ambler Realty,* 272 U.S. 365, 395 (1926).

51. Letter to Charles J. Eisler dated December 6, 1926.

52. Letter from George T. Simpson dated December 11, 1926.

53. Letter to George T. Simpson dated December 13, 1926 referred to in n.48 *supra.*

54. Alfred Bettman, *The Decision of the Supreme Court of The United States in the Euclid Village Zoning Case,* 1 U. Cin. L. Rev. 184 (1927).

55. *Id.* at 187.

56. The final decree was prepared by Mr. Baker, but not without a final quibble from Mr. Metzenbaum in a letter dated June 7, 1927, and sent to Judge Westenhaver:

> Not for any purpose of being technical nor with any idea of suggesting any mere capitous [sic] objections, I really believe that a weighing of the third and fourth lines of the second page of the decree as submitted by Mr. Baker, will indicate that it may not be inadvisable to eliminate the word "as" which appears in the third line on page 3 between the word "Euclid" and the word "described."
>
> It is my further judgment that a period added

after the word "complaint" at the end of the third line of page 2 and then the elimination of all of the words in the fourth line of page 2, would be somewhat more in keeping with the final decision.

57. Brief of Newton D. Baker and Robert M. Morgan *Amici Curiae, Pritz* v. *Messer,* No. 18, 750 at 15–16.

58. The distinction between the "affirmative" and "negative" use of the police power may have been drawn from Freund, *Police Power,* Section 511, which Mr. Baker quoted in his principal brief in the Supreme Court (at 50):

> Under the police power, rights of property are impaired not because they become useful or necessary to the public, or because some public advantage can be gained by disregarding them, but because their free exercise is believed to be detrimental to public interests; it may be said that the State takes property by eminent domain because it is useful to the public and under the police power because it is harmful, or as Justice Bradley put it, because "the property itself is the cause of the public detriment."
>
> From this results the difference between the power of eminent domain and the police power, that the former recognizes a right to compensation, while the latter on principle does not.

Regrettably, Mr. Bettman enlisted Freund (at Section 26) to greater effect:

> The Police Power endeavors to prevent evil by checking the tendency toward it and it seeks to place a margin of safety between that which is permitted and that which is sure to lend to injury or loss. [Brief on Behalf of The National Conference on City Planning, etc. *amici curiae, Euclid* v. *Ambler,* #665, at 27.]

59. Mark S. Pulliam, *Brandeis Brief For Decontrol Of Land Use: A Plea For Constitutional Reform,* Sw. L. Rev. 13 (1983): 435, 461.

60. Letter from George T. Simpson dated December 6, 1926.

61. Letter to W. Calvin Chestnut dated December 15, 1925.

62. Mandelker and Cunningham, *Planning and Control,* p. 71, quoting from a 1924 letter of Alfred Bettman.

63. *See Nectow* v. *City of Cambridge,* 277 U.S. 183 (1928), one of the few land use cases to be dealt with by the Supreme Court between 1925 and *Village of Belle Terre* v. *Boraas,* 416 U.S. 1 (1974). Mr. Baker furnished copies of

the *Euclid* briefs to John E. Hannigan, Esq., of Boston, who represented *Nectow,* in October 1926. When the decision was announced, Mr. Baker noted (in a letter dated October 1, 1928, to Mr. Valjean Biddison in Oklahoma) that *Nectow* "was so much like the Ambler case that we were unable to discover the difference, although a different result was reached in the Supreme Court."

64. Sadly, the file reveals another irony: of the $14,650 subscribed by the property owners in April, 1923, only $8,881.08 apparently was actually paid. Expenses totaled $1,571.27, leaving about $7,000 in fees, ostensibly to be split between Messrs. Baker and Morgan.

65. The author is indebted to Ms. Diane Hinderliter, a second-year law student at The University of Michigan Law School, for her thoughtful assistance and to Mr. Dayne R. Myers, a first-year law student at The Harvard Law School, who, among his many contributions, jogged by the site and reported not only on the existence of the General Motors plant but on the presence of gas stations, a restaurant, a beverage store, and a medical building along the north side of Euclid Avenue, to the west (all with homes just behind), and a gas station (also with homes behind) immediately adjacent to the west of the plant.

2

Professors, Reformers, Bureaucrats, and Cronies: The Players in *Euclid* v. *Ambler*

William M. Randle

Propinquity breeds special relationships. The urban influence and territorial aggrandizement accompanying the growth of Cleveland, Ohio, had significant impact on the adjacent village of Euclid.[1] Euclid, located along the eastern shores of Lake Erie, was separated from the Cleveland–Collinwood section (annexed in 1910) by East 185th Street.

Lakewood, the "City of Homes" next to the city on the western Lake Erie shore, resisted annexation as did Cleveland Heights, East Cleveland, and Euclid.[2] All became single-family, middle-class residential suburbs. In the early 1920s, aided by zoning experts (led by Robert H. Whitten), each of the suburbs developed a comprehensive zoning ordinance.

Cleveland lawyer James Metzenbaum lived in Euclid and was appointed chairman of its board of zoning appeals. There was an immediate challenge to the zoning law and Metzenbaum successfully defended the first case against the city. Additional attacks led the city council to amend the original ordinance to meet the demands of the Ambler Realty Company and other firms with extensive property holdings near the New York Central and Nickel Plate railroad rights-of-way.[3] However, according to Metzenbaum, "property owners demanded the right to go entirely unregulated and completely unrestricted and so they banded together, employed some of the country's outstanding legal talent and proceeded to assail both the original and the amended ordinances."[4]

Ambler Realty Co. v. *Village of Euclid*[5] was brought before District Judge Dale C. Westenhaver. Westenhaver was the federal judge who had tried the *Debs* case in 1917. He was a former political associate and law partner of Harry and James R. Garfield (sons of assassinated President James A. Garfield), Frederic C. Howe (the publicist-reformer), and Newton D. Baker (ex-mayor of Cleveland and Woodrow Wilson's secretary of war). Baker was the attorney for the Ambler interests. He charged the Euclid zoning law was a direct violation of the Ohio and United States Constitutions.

Metzenbaum had been Baker's protégé during the Tom L. Johnson reform era, selected because he was "brilliant." He was "a loner who is no one's confidant," according to a contemporary source.[6] Metzenbaum's briefs were presented to Judge Westenhaver who made his decision after more than a year of reading extensive depositions and volumes of zoning facts and cases.

Written in his office in the massive Federal Building on Cleveland's Public Square, Westenhaver's prescient opinion stated: "In the last analysis, the result to be accomplished is to classify the population and segregate them according to their income or situation in life."[7] Based on Metzenbaum's "mistaken" view of property and overextended view of the proper use of the police power, Judge Westenhaver supported Newton D. Baker's arguments and declared the ordinance unconstitutional.

Metzenbaum described the decision as "the undoing of all the efforts of the men and women who had preached and sincerely believed in the very necessity of zoning in order to safeguard the public welfare."[8] Alfred Bettman, a leading constitutional scholar who had aided Metzenbaum on the case, reacted quite differently. Bettman wrote: "Regarding the Euclid Village zoning decision, the case was unfortunate . . . . It was a piece of arbitrary zoning and on the facts not justifiable . . . . Everybody advised against an appeal, because on appeal the decision is sure to be affirmed, even though the upper court disagrees with the opinion."[9]

"Everybody" failed to recognize the Euclid attorney's monomaniacal identification with the "cause" of zoning. The case became a crusade for the diminutive lawyer and he appealed directly to the United States Supreme Court. The case was first heard in January 1926. Baker's final argument caused Metzenbaum to file a reply brief. The Court ordered the case to be reargued, an unusual occurrence.[10]

In the interim, Alfred Bettman had given the case considerable thought. Since Metzenbaum had appealed and the "future of zoning" was now at stake, it was imperative that a more sophisticated brief be presented. Bettman wrote, "There is ample ground for the suspicion that the Ambler Realty Company, while genuinely the party plaintiff, still represented a larger group seeking to destroy the zoning movement, and that the Euclid ordinance was chosen for this purpose because of certain weaknesses which were felt to inhere in its provisions." He also worried that Westenhaver's opinion, if affirmed, "would invalidate all zoning."[11]

Bettman, as a result, submitted an *amicus curiae* brief that *City Planning* called "remarkable" and "so overwhelming an array of arguments for zoning that it will be generally useful beyond its undoubted effect on the attitude of the Supreme Court."[12] Commentators have described Bettman's brief as the primary source of Justice George Sutherland's opinion in *Village of Euclid* v. *Ambler Realty Co.* (1926), the decision that constitutionally validated height, area, and use of property regulations based on a comprehensive zoning plan as a reasonable use of the state's police power.[13]

Authorities have reached near consensus that *Euclid* is the most significant case in zoning and land use history. It is the "foundations under" the development of the law of zoning in America.[14] The importance of the case lies not only in its seminal role in the development of land use law in America. The roots and effects of *Euclid*, still relatively obscure, run deep in our society. These include the professors, bureaucrats, reformers, and cronies who formed the corps of secondary players in the case; the philosophical warfare between the forces of laissez-faire and collectivism; the revolution in transportation systems; and the growth and diffusion of cities and their suburban satellites.

THE REFORM/SINGLE TAX BACKGROUND

James Metzenbaum credited his personal zoning expertise to the efforts of Secretary of Commerce Herbert Hoover and the work of Dr. John M. Gries's housing staff. Newton D. Baker, during the war, had been the prime mover in the development of housing to serve the expanding industrial effort. Demobilization brought an end to this large-scale program. There was an immediate congressional reaction to the cancelling of these innovative housing efforts and the new Division of Building and Housing was created as a bureaucratic answer to the critics. After July 1, 1921, Gries's section was staffed with "experts" such as John Ihlder and used outside zoning authorities Edward M. Bassett, Lawrence Veiller, and Alfred Bettman.[15]

Metzenbaum characterized New York lawyer Edward M. Bassett as the "dean of zoning" and the man primarily responsible for the adoption of the first New York zoning ordinance in 1916.[16] Attorney Frank B. Williams's 1922 book on zoning law and the monthly zoning decisions published in *The American City* also were important.[17] He named as influential in the development of zoning practices Lawson Purdy, Bruno Lasker, Harland Bartholomew, John Nolen, and Robert Whitten. All were significant contemporaries, major theorists and practitioners in city planning. They were the cutting edge of the rapidly expanding philanthropic and governmental bureaucracies that were the legacies of progressivism and Woodrow Wilson.[18]

In the early days of the century, successful movements for reform laid the groundwork for the growth and development of new ideas for social change and redistribution of political and economic power. "Efficiency in the . . . tasks of city administration (became) the goal of idealists."[19] The initial defeat of the bosses by urban reformers led to a transfer of power that, in the Michigan and Ohio areas, gave control of the political process to dedicated followers of Henry George, the single tax ideologist.[20] Among those followers were Tom L. Johnson, Newton D. Baker, and Frederic C. Howe, all of Cleveland. Associated with these political leaders were Edward W. Bemis, Delos F. Wilcox, and Robert H. Whitten.[21]

NEWTON D. BAKER

Newton D. Baker, lead counsel for the Ambler Realty Company in the *Euclid* case, was born in 1871 in Martinsburg, West Virginia. He grew up in the Reconstruction and "Bloody Shirt" era of West Virginia politics under the early influence of his youthful friend Dale C. Westenhaver. Baker graduated from the prestigious Johns Hopkins University during the era of Woodrow Wilson, Richard T. Bly, Edward W. Bemis, and other academic giants.[22] Frederic C. Howe, Baker's fraternity brother and roommate, wrote of these college years: "I came alive. I felt a sense of responsibility to the world. I wanted to change things."[23]

After graduating from Johns Hopkins, Baker took his law degree at Washington and Lee University (1894). He was a lawyer in Martinsburg, worked in Washington, D.C., as a political appointee, and traveled and studied in Europe. Returning to Martinsburg in 1879, he became the junior partner of Flick, Westenhaver & Baker.

Two years later, Frederic Howe (by then a partner in the Garfield family law firm in Cleveland and a successful politician) was asked by former Congressman, later Judge, Martin Foran to recommend a new attorney for his firm; Baker got the position.[24] Twenty years later Foran wrote the precedential opinion in *State ex rel. Morris* v. *East Cleveland* [25] that is significant for his extended discussion of the "apartment problem" and the use of the police power to control such building through zoning ordinances, one of the basic *Euclid* concepts.[26]

Baker came to Cleveland (1899) when the city was undergoing a tremendous surge of reform. The Garfields were powerful political figures along with the legendary Mark Hanna. It was their split with Hanna interests that permitted Tom L. Johnson's Single-Taxers to take over the city. Johnson fought Hanna for control of the street railway in Cleveland and made a fortune in iron and steel ventures before his conversion to Henry George's theories.[27]

Frederic C. Howe and Newton D. Baker were stalwart Johnson followers and active politicians. When Baker came to Cleveland to practice law, "He was a splendid speaker, fluent, resourceful, and adaptable." "He did his work easily, mastered intricate legal subjects quickly, and had time for wide and carefully selected reading."[28] Baker was made Johnson's law director in 1902; his major efforts for the city included more than 50 lawsuits related to street railway franchises and the controversial "three-cent fare." In 1903, Baker persuaded Dale C. Westenhaver, his West Virginia mentor, to join him in Cleveland in the franchising battles. Johnson later wrote "The interests of the city and of the low-fare line were in the hands of . . . Baker and D.C. Westenhaver . . . . He did most of the fighting for the low-fare companies."[29]

Baker, credited by Johnson as the brains behind his numerous reforms, was given extraordinary support in his efforts by Professor Edward W. Bemis. Bemis had been fired by the University of Chicago and became one of the first municipal experts, working closely with other developing specialists in taxation and franchising; among them, Delos F. Wilcox and Robert H. Whitten. Bemis, ostensibly the Cleveland superintendent of waterworks from 1901–1909, was actually Johnson's draftsman and manager of legislation.[30]

Frederic C. Howe, a Johns Hopkins Ph.D. and corporation lawyer-reformer, split his energies and became a millionaire while he maintained his Progressive political role.

The Baker-Howe-Garfield network expanded with the addition of D.C. Westenhaver. He joined Howe when Baker brought him to Cleveland; the firm became Garfield, Howe & Westenhaver. After the Garfields retired, Howe, active in state politics, left the firm. A Democrat during the Tom Johnson years, Westenhaver later became an independent. He was proud of his West Virginia heritage when "he had to struggle with poverty and adverse conditions . . . in order to secure an education" and "paid his way for his university training by teaching district school, by farm work, and by loans from his friends."[31]

Another important Johnson-Baker associate was John H. Clarke, an outstanding Ohio corporation lawyer and newspaper publisher. Although he was a conservative (who supported the use of troops against Eugene V. Debs's union in the Pullman strike; he was counsel for the firm), he was also an anti-imperialist and entered politics to "curb trusts and regulate industry."[32] Clarke ran for the U.S. Senate against Mark Hanna after nominating Tom Johnson for governor against Myron T. Herrick; Hanna and Herrick were elected. Johnson died in 1911 and was replaced as mayor of Cleveland by Newton D. Baker.

Clarke was appointed a federal district judge by President Woodrow Wilson in 1914 and with Baker's support advanced to justice of the Supreme Court in 1916. He was opposed by Ohio Senators Attlee Pomerene and Warren G. Harding, staunch supporters of Utah Senator George Sutherland. Sutherland had been defeated for reelection because of his rejection of Wilson's New Freedoms. He was an outstanding conservative legal theorist. Clarke's replacement in the Ohio federal district judgeship was D. C. Westenhaver in 1917. Pomerene and Harding again opposed the Baker-influenced appointment but after an eight-month delay a Cleveland newspaper headlined: "Westenhaver, Baker's Choice, Named U.S. District Judge."[33]

Clarke was a member of the Supreme Court from 1916 to 1922. He was considered a liberal and maintained his long-standing friendship with Newton D. Baker (in 1932 Clarke led the drive to nominate Baker for the U.S. presidency against Franklin D. Roosevelt). His interest in the League of Nations led him to resign from the Court in 1922. President Warren G. Harding nominated George Sutherland and he easily was confirmed. If Clarke had not retired in 1922, he would have been on the Court at the time of *Euclid* and Sutherland's opinion probably would never have been written.[34]

Just prior to Clarke's retirement, Newton D. Baker (after serving as secretary of war under Wilson) returned to Cleveland to revitalize his law partnership with Joseph Hostetler and Thomas Sidlo.[35] He soon accepted a case brought to him by the venerable Ambler realty family, one of several firms with speculative property interests in the village of Euclid negatively affected by a new zoning ordinance.[36]

FREDERIC C. HOWE

The zoning ordinance involved in *Ambler Realty Co.* v. *Village of Euclid* [37] was the result of a long and tortured history of attempts to solve the problems of American cities. While zoning was not constitutionally challenged in the Su-

preme Court until *Euclid,* reformers had been trying for decades to alleviate congestion and eliminate the slums that plagued urban America. The brilliant reformer Frederic C. Howe, the Cleveland associate of Johnson, Clarke, Baker, Bemis, and Westenhaver, was one of the first to write a major study of the problems. His successful book, *The City: The Hope of Democracy* (1905), was one of a series of reform analyses of urban conditions (Delos F. Wilcox, the Michigan tax and franchise expert, and Benjamin Marsh, a New York reformer-publicist, also published contemporary "city" books).[38]

Howe was a dedicated follower of Henry George and devoted his life to promoting and publicizing the concept of the single tax as a panacea to solve contemporary land use questions. He was a scholarly tax specialist for Cleveland during Johnson's administration and brought New York tax expert (and single tax enthusiast) Lawson Purdy to Cleveland to develop a new valuation of property taxes based on George's ideas.[39] Howe believed completely in the use of property tax valuations and political power to achieve desired social goals, even if they had to be disguised or reached by devious methods. He confessed later in his career that the tax system he and Purdy imposed on Cleveland was "the first step toward the single tax by increasing the valuation of the land and reducing the valuation placed on improvements."[40]

Howe later, in conjunction with other Henry George disciples (Kiefer and Bigelow of Cincinnati), worked for direct elections and the initiative and referendum in Ohio. Their "primary interest was in using the device of the initiative to speed the introduction of the single tax. For fear of frightening farmers and others, however, they kept this motive in the background. . . ."[41] The same group fought for home rule and a new constitution for Ohio; they were successful in 1912.

Howe was politically active outside of Ohio and was an early associate (with Louis Brandeis) of Wisconsin's Robert M. LaFollette. Howe came into conflict with his former law partner James R. Garfield, the major strategist for Theodore Roosevelt, over Progressive policies and, after the collapse of LaFollette's campaign, Howe joined Newton D. Baker in support of Woodrow Wilson.[42] Wilson, after his election in 1912, appointed Howe U.S. commissioner on immigration for the Port of New York.[43]

Baker was offered a cabinet post in 1912. He rejected Wilson's position because of his determination to continue Johnson's policies as mayor of Cleveland. After Wilson's reelection in 1916, Baker was appointed secretary of war.[44]

When Howe went to New York in 1910 he immediately joined forces with Lawson Purdy, Delos F. Wilcox, Benjamin Marsh, Robert H. Whitten, Dr. Frank Goodnow, and the settlement house principals (Mary K. Simkhovitch of Greenwich House and Florence Kelley of the National Consumers' League). They were in the forefront of the New York housing reform movement (initiated at the turn of the century by Lawrence Veiller).[45]

Kelley had been the catalyst for the New York Committee on Congestion of Population that had produced a successful "Congestion Show" and focused national attention on urban problems. This led to the First National Conference on City Planning in Washington, D.C., in 1909 (promoted by Benjamin Marsh and other Single-Taxers) and was the beginning of the enormously important series of annual meetings that set the standards for zoning and housing programs in the country. Howe and Purdy lobbied for the "unearned increment" ideas of Henry George as well as related

European developments; for example, the zoning of German cities.[46]

The emphasis on single tax doctrines, led in New York by Howe and Purdy, was stimulated after 1905 by the interest of Joseph Fels, the soap maker.[47] Tom Johnson had worked closely with Fels and, at his death, was an executive of the Fels Fund, as was Howe. The original aim of the Fels' campaign was "to put the single tax into effect somewhere in the United States within five years."[48]

In New York, the Georgites organized to attack land use problems on several fronts. They were well represented in the original congestion group and were appointed by Governor Hughes and later New York Mayor Gaynor to "prepare a comprehensive plan for the present relief and future prevention of congestion of population. . . ."[49] This committee also included Allan Robinson, president of the Allied Real Estate Interests in New York.

The original emphasis of the several committees was to tax buildings at lower rates than unimproved land, a direct attack on land speculators and major real estate interests. This had been the battle cry of Henry George's followers for decades. Mayor John P. Mitchell continued studies of reforms and held public hearings in 1915.[50] Progressives like Lawson Purdy, Frederic C. Howe, and Delos F. Wilcox were also responsible for major state legislation (including the Herrick-Schaap Bill). Organized resistance by the real estate industry killed such legislation.[51] "Very much of the opposition was based on the ground that having the tax rate on buildings was merely an entering wedge for the single tax."[52]

The final effort by Howe and the reformers was their participation in Mayor Mitchell's Committee on Taxation of the City of New York, created in 1914. Howe was the secretary; his constant academic opponent to single tax ideas, Professor E.R.A. Seligman of Columbia

University, was chairman of the executive committee. After exhaustive studies and volumes of reports, the committee presented its final comments in 1916 recommending "against the adoption of the principle of untaxing buildings . . . ."[53] The report emphasized that the scheme would need "laws to regulate the height of buildings and to provide for a proper zoning system."[54] The dream of Frederic C. Howe and Lawson Purdy to institute a form of the single tax at this time was ended; "unearned increment" was a dead social and political issue.

SCIENTIFIC MANAGEMENT, BUREAUCRACY, AND ZONING

Lubove credits "the combined pressure of housing, taxation, and other social reformers in alliance with conservative business interests" for the final enactment of the 1916 New York comprehensive zoning code.[55] He logically assumed that "American zoning reformers . . . believed they had found in zoning a tool with which to control land speculation, the fluctuation of property values and, above all, congestion."[56] The reform spirit and a contemporary need for controls of Fifth Avenue real estate values coincided to produce legislation.

It was not so simple. Major real estate interests, after soundly defeating the reform single tax lobby, immediately adopted the "laws to regulate the height of buildings and . . . a proper zoning system" that had previously been anathema to their interests. Zoning, without the tax valuation emphasis promoted by Howe and Purdy, became New York law and the prototype for most municipalities.[57]

Purdy, unlike Howe, was a realistic and flexible example of the new "experts" and sophisticated urban professionals (many powerfully dedicated to long-range reform ideologies) who proliferated as urban areas developed. The product of scientific management, rapidly emerging managerial cohorts dominated growing municipal bureaucracies.[58]

There had always been such an infrastructure of engineers, lawyers, accountants, tax officials, and staff that kept cities running even under the "boss" system.[59] Purdy, for example, was a tax expert for Tammany Hall. He was also a dynamic reformer and tax authority who modernized municipal tax law through his work as a practitioner and writer. As the president of the National Municipal League (1916–1919) he played an important role in the expansion of zoning law throughout the United States.

Lawrence Veiller, an early tenement and slum control pragmatist, became a "political strategist, propagandist, and lobbyist, technical advisor, legislative draftsman, and administrator."[60] He was active in the 1913 New York Commission that researched and developed the basic sources for the 1916 Commission which drafted the first comprehensive zoning laws.[61] The 1916 group included Lawson Purdy and was dominated by the ideas of Robert H. Whitten and Edward M. Bassett.

EDWARD M. BASSETT

Toll says: "(I)f American zoning has a father, he is Bassett."[62] Bassett, however, credits Whitten who "contributed far more to the upbuilding of zoning in this country than I did."[63] Both men were archetypical municipal "consultant-experts" operating as conduits between the political process and city managements.

Bassett was a lawyer-politician-crony of New York Democrats. Often described as a reformer, he was a Columbia University-trained lawyer (1886), businessman, and one-time Congressman (1902), who specialized in bankruptcy and real estate law. Brought into New

York politics by his law school classmate Charles Evans Hughes, Bassett became a rapid transit specialist and, under the aegis of Lawson Purdy and George McAneny (an important liaison figure in zoning history), a city planning "expert."[64]

Bassett was a peripatetic booster of zoning law, traveled extensively (on political and zoning matters), wrote a number of influential books and articles, and actively aided in the drafting of national zoning enabling acts.[65] Bassett's victory of accommodation (aided and abetted by Purdy) over Howe and the other reformers in 1916 was continued by the institutionalization of these acts.[66]

The narrow conceptual and legalistic framework validating the use of the police power as the basis for zoning law was followed by an overwhelming majority of municipalities. Tarlock writes, "Zoning was taken up by its most likely client groups—the real estate industry and then-Secretary of Commerce Herbert Hoover—precisely because it has been stripped of any potential for harm."[67] Bassett and Purdy (with the technical support of Robert H. Whitten) were responsible for the emasculated compromise zoning system that was designed to convince builders and real estate operators of the "enhancement" and "stabilizing" effects of zoning laws.[68]

Purdy in 1918 advocated the takeover of the Newton D. Baker war time government housing developments, again using a Henry George tactic (an "increment" value formula). His friend Veiller commented on the proposal as "sort of camouflage for the single tax idea . . . . It is also a form of communism." But "(I)t may be a very wise thing to do." Purdy responded that his "Own Your Own Town" concept was "not the single tax. That is too beautiful to be talked about just at this time."[69]

Frederic C. Howe wrote a major book in 1919 that promoted an even more ambitious collaboration of architects, planners, and educators with the underlying implications of the need for taxation and valuation systems that would redistribute the "unearned increment."[70]

ROBERT H. WHITTEN

Robert H. Whitten is one of the city planning experts recognized by James Metzenbaum as a significant influence on his *Euclid* career. Veiller lists Whitten (with Bassett and Ford) as "the three chauffeurs on the job" of the New York Commission.[71] Born in 1873 in Indiana, Whitten graduated from the University of Michigan (1896), where he was strongly influenced by Charles Horton Cooley and John Dewey (as was his classmate Delos F. Wilcox). Whitten followed Dewey to the University of Chicago and studied administrative law (1897), finishing his Ph.D. at Columbia in 1898, just two years after Wilcox.[72]

From 1898 to 1907, Whitten worked in New York libraries as a researcher-writer and librarian-statistician, specializing in legislative references and editing the *Yearbook of Legislation*. From 1907 to 1914, he worked for the New York State Public Service Commission. He joined Edward Bassett as secretary to the city planning commission of the Board of Estimate and Apportionment from 1914 to 1917, during which time he played an increasingly important role as researcher, draftsman, and legislative technician.

By 1917 Whitten was nationally known. He worked closely with Delos F. Wilcox and wrote major treatises on street railways, taxation, and franchising. His two-volume *Valuation of Public Service Corporations* (1912) was the standard legal authority until the late 1930s (in 1928 Delos F. Wilcox revised Whitten's work).[73] Whitten aided Wilcox in producing *Municipal Franchises* (1910), also the standard work in the field.[74] The two men were recognized as the outstanding experts in their several fields.[75]

Whitten's basic zoning philosophy was simple: "The protection of the homes of the people is probably the primary purpose of use districting."[76] He had been working in Cleveland since 1917 as a city planning advisor, writing statutes, and developing a thriving ancillary zoning consultancy business. His expertise as a "planner" and "expert" was nationally marketed by his books, articles, and lectures. His problem-solving skills (traffic congestion surveys, promoting legislation, and drafting comprehensive plans) made him a highly paid and in-demand professional.

During his stay in Cleveland, Whitten developed zoning ordinances for Lakewood, East Cleveland, and Cleveland Heights (as well as Providence, Rhode Island, and Dallas, Texas), created an acquisition program for Cleveland's 200,000-acre "Emerald Necklace," and designed a comprehensive outer parkway system that dramatically enhanced the value of suburban areas.[77]

Whitten was as evangelical as the most dedicated reformers. "On the economic side, zoning means increased industrial efficiency and the prevention of enormous waste. On the human side, zoning means better homes and an increase of health, comfort, and happiness for all the people."[78] Unsuccessfully trying to implement a zoning plan for Cleveland, he wrote that its "haphazard development has resulted in enormous waste and destruction of property values. But this enormous economic waste is not nearly as important as the social and civil loss. . . . Zoning is absolutely essential to preserve the morale of the neighborhood."[79]

The 1919 East Cleveland zoning case that became the local precedent for Metzenbaum's *Euclid* briefs was the product of Robert H. Whitten's expertise, energy, and advocacy. Euclid, Cleveland, Cleveland Heights (Judge

Westenhaver's home), and East Cleveland were subjected to tremendous pressure from apartment house developers after 1918. The high cost of living and rent-gouging by unscrupulous landlords were a national problem. There was a rush to meet the postwar housing shortage by building high-density apartment buildings. Cleveland suburbs resisted with lawsuits, technical delays, and zoning ordinances originating with Whitten.

Lakewood had resisted annexation to Cleveland (a move led by Morris Black).[80] Lakewood had benefited tremendously from the Whitten-inspired parkway design and billed itself as "The City of Homes." Whitten wrote the Lakewood zoning ordinance after the 1918 attempt to annex the area and, as a direct result of his law and covert restriction techniques, Lakewood was able to maintain its segregated suburban residential character.

Euclid's border with Cleveland was a heavily working class neighborhood with major industrial and railroad complexes. The railroad rights-of-way passed through Euclid on their way to Pittsburgh and the East. Ambler Realty properties paralleled the tracks and were the areas in dispute in the litigation.

Euclid, as a result of the Lakewood and East Cleveland apartment house litigation, developed a similar zoning ordinance to keep its population "stable." East Cleveland, as the result of its zoning ordinance, had been sued by a major apartment builder. Judge Martin Foran returned the original *Morris* v. *East Cleveland* case for a rehearing after discussing the "apartment problem" thoroughly and indicating the desirability of maintaining "family" environments.[81]

The subsequent opinion, after a new hearing, was written by Judge Samuel Kramer. Kramer vigorously upheld the right of the suburb to use the police power to establish a systematic and complete zoning plan.[82] The

testimony of Haven Emerson (a New York
health commissioner), Paul Feiss (chairman of
the Cleveland Chamber of Commerce housing
committee), and zoning expert Robert H.
Whitten convinced Judge Kramer that public
residential zoning restrictions, as part of a
comprehensive plan, were legal.[83]

East Cleveland was related directly, in origin and geography, to Euclid. It was the success of Whitten's zoning law that led to the
Euclid ordinance of 1922. The *East Cleveland*
case, although it was decided in a minor court,
was cited extensively and was a nationally famous opinion.[84] James Metzenbaum, fully
aware of the decision, was convinced that it
completely validated Euclid's ordinance. He
believed that Kramer's "comprehensive" language was particularly applicable to the village.

JUDGE D.C. WESTENHAVER

Judge D.C. Westenhaver did not see the case
that way. He was a precise and meticulous
man, an "efficiency expert" with an impecca-
ble reputation, and was considered "unreach-
able." His legal philosophy was rigid and
deterministic. Garland Ashcraft, a Cleveland
newspaperman, wrote that Westenhaver had
a "dispassionate legal mind, austere and inexorable . . . with the cold, impersonal precision
of a calculating machine." He was not a reformer and considered efforts to rehabilitate
people "trivial" and "useless." Westenhaver
said he "sat on the bench and punished people, not to reform them, but to coerce them,
and through their fear, stabilize society, and
render it temporarily endurable."[85]

It is clear from his decisions that Westenhaver was an extremely conservative judge.
Chafee said of the *Debs* trial that Westenhaver's "charge gave the jury such a wide
scope that Debs was probably convicted for an
exposition of socialism. . . ."[86] However,

Chafee also lists Westenhaver's permission for
Debs to speak on his own behalf (a high point
of the trial) as a very important policy decision
giving "great latitude to the defendant's proof
and urging upon the jury the necessity for the
dispassionate consideration of evidence."[87]

The judge's history as an open shop enthusiast and his issuance of antilabor injunctions
sustaining "yellow dog" contracts and lock-
outs during the 1920s West Virginia and Ohio
coal mining wars, including rulings in favor of
the notorious Baldwin-Felts strikebreakers,
made him anathema to liberals. He had himself been involved in the importation of armed
thugs during the Cleveland traction strike of
1908 (aided by Baker, Howe, and Johnson).[88]

Westenhaver was strongly opposed to the
"New Immigration" from Eastern Europe and
was active in immigration restriction movements. He had been influenced by Edward W.
Bemis, who advocated as early as 1888 a literacy test to control immigration. The idea was
picked up by Henry Cabot Lodge and promoted by Boston lawyer-legal historian Charles
Warren through his Immigration Restriction
League (especially by John Fiske) after 1894.
Warren, an associate of Alfred Bettman in the
Department of Justice during the war, was responsible for many cases dealing with radicals
and immigration, often opposed by Frederic C.
Howe.

Westenhaver also was influenced by racist
theories such as Madison Grant's *The Passing of
the Great Race* (1916) and Harvard Ph.D Lothrop
Stoddard's *The Rising Tide of Color* (1920). Along
with Richard T. Ely, Westenhaver thought of
the new immigration population "surviving in
the slums and intensifying all those social evils
which have their origins in urban congestion."[89]

The "unwanted" in the 1920s were primarily immigrants and "Negroes." Millions of the
Eastern European immigrants were Jews. The

real reasons for the newly emergent interest in zoning among New York real estate operators and Fifth Avenue merchants were cultural and class differences, as well as economic: "Fifth Avenue versus the garment industry." It was "racism with a progressive, technocratic veneer."[90] Toll concluded, "The immigrant is in the fiber of zoning . . . ."[91]

Major immigration problems ended with the Johnson-Reed Act (1924) and a system of admission quotas based on national origin.[92] New laws effectively blocked the flow of undesired groups and, coordinated with an intensive Americanization program, neutralized the political and social concerns of the majority.[93]

The migration of millions of blacks from the South to urban areas during and after the war added to the congestion in cities and exacerbated racial tensions. The result was explosive growth of the Ku Klux Klan, lynchings, violent race riots, and the development of restrictive property covenants and zoning laws.[94] Although *Buchanan* v. *Warley*[95] held racial zoning unconstitutional on its face, the decision was vitiated by postwar housing shortages, unchallenged discriminatory ordinances, and spatial (and *de facto*) segregation in a majority of towns and cities. Racist attitudes and legislation clearly defined the place of minorities and, for all practical purposes, enclosed them in semipermanent ghettoes.[96]

The constitutional validation of zoning in *Euclid* in 1926 gave local governments the full use of the police power to determine uses, subject only to a rational basis test, the reasonableness of the ordinances in question, and an understood deference to the legislative body enacting the laws. Zoning, as a result, provided suburbs and other local government entities with a powerful tool to limit and define their areas on economic, social welfare, and (in practice and covertly) class and racial bases.

Like Lakewood and Euclid, such communities were able to maintain pristine middle-class segregated communities while avoiding their "fair share" of the potential social and economic costs of urban sprawl and blight.

One commentator, supported by a number of critics, described America's explosive urban social conditions as "a direct result of the nation's acknowledged failure to insure that all social and racial groups are able to gain access to suburban land."[97] There is evidence that "(E)xclusionary policies have played a major role in shaping the residential patterns of both cities and suburbs."[98] Zoning reflects the insidious and pervasive racism that permeates the fabric of political and social policies and is a constant factor in American history.[99]

If Judge Westenhaver (like many Progressives and reformers) was a racist, why did he decide *against* zoning in 1924? His opinion, founded on the racial and exclusionary aspects of the legislation, anticipated the legal actions of civil rights advocates 40 years later.[100] Westenhaver was either a firm believer in precedants (particularly *Buchanan* v. *Warley*) or he was influenced in his pro-Ambler decision by his lifelong friendship with Newton D. Baker.

There was little question in his mind that Euclid's use of the police power was supported by a far less rational basis than the ordinance in *Buchanan*. Louisville's use of districting as a segregation technique had as its genesis, according to Westenhaver, "a real and substantial relation to the public peace" and "more and stronger reasons exist . . . supporting such an ordinance than can be urged under any aspect of the police power to support the present ordinance (Euclid). . . ." The judge went on with his opinion that, "The blighting of property values and the congesting of population, whenever the colored or certain foreign races invade a residential section, are so well known as to be within the judicial cognizance."[101] In other words, if obvious dangers had not been enough to influence the Court in *Buchanan* (in addition to his other analysis) there was no rational basis for a different decision given the Ambler facts.

WHITTEN AND RACISM

When Metzenbaum's case was rejected by the district court, it was really the legal work and philosophies of Robert H. Whitten that went down to defeat. Where the original concerns of property owners were based on the "stability of property values" and control of "undesirable neighbors," those neighbors were generally apartment buildings, retail stores, and factories that constituted nuisances. Whitten was well aware of the ethnic, racial, and social class effects of zoning legislation and strongly defended them.

In 1920, a Bruno Lasker article in *The Survey* suggested that zoning resulted in the "exclusion of the middle class as a potent influence on policies and services."[102] Charles H. Cheney, the West Coast equivalent of Whitten and the Eastern zoning "experts," responded to Lasker's article and claimed, "(T)o remove the social barriers in cities and to give the poor man, and particularly the foreign-born worker an equal opportunity to live and raise his family . . . is one of the prime objects of the recent city planning and zoning regulations. . . ."[103] However, in his own developments, Cheney built expensive areas like Palos Verdes, "the most carefully planned and highly restricted garden suburb of the 1920s."[104]

Lasker wrote that zoning used class differences as a basis for discrimination and was basically a method for screening out "undesirable neighbors."[105] His perception of the real motive for zoning was confirmed two years later by Whitten's openly racist and segregationist Atlanta (Georgia) zoning law. Whitten, described by Lasker as "perhaps the most influential zoning adviser in the United States . . .,"[106] had written the Lakewood, Cleveland Heights, and other Ohio ordinances at the same time.

Racial tensions were so high that even in Cleveland Heights (where Judge Westenhaver lived) daily incidents took place. In 1924, scurrilous handbills were circulated to all home owners attacking a family trying to move into the area, commenting on "Black-mail," "Black Gold Diggers," and "certain niggers," ending with the statement "(L)et them know we can duplicate riots in Tulsa, St. Louis, Chicago, and Baltimore."[107]

In 1926, contemporary with *Euclid,* restrictive covenants in private land contracts (to prevent the sale or rental to blacks and Jews, among others) were upheld in *Corrigan* v. *Buckley.*[108] This real estate contract device further intensified the plight of racial and religious minorities.

Whitten had described Cleveland Heights, a city of 15,000, as "a high-class residence suburb" with a popular mandate to "preserve it as such." "This public demand, fortified as it is by consideration of the general public interest and welfare, is being carried out in the zoning plan and ordinance. . . ."[109] However, given the opportunity to zone a Southern city, Whitten's Atlanta plan was "the first to embody in an outspoken form segregation along the line of social composition of the population." "It subdivides residential districts into three race districts, white, colored, and undetermined." He continued "No colored family may move into the select areas reserved for whites. . . ."[110]

Whitten's report accompanying the segregated zoning plan states: "It is essential in the interest of the public peace, order and security and will promote the welfare and prosperity of both the white and colored races."[111] Lasker reported Whitten also was opposed to any zoning that mixed families of "different economic status." The result: "As a precedent it opens up the possibility of new zoning ordinances embodying restrictions against immigrants . . . persons of certain occupations, political or religious affiliations, or modes of life."[112]

Whitten responded to Lasker in a letter to *The Survey,* writing that Atlanta was already a segregated city where "A race riot is a terrible possibility . . . . Establishing colored residence districts has removed one of the most potent causes of race conflict." This was "a sufficient justification for race zoning which is simply a common sense method of dealing with facts as they are." He proceeded, "Coming back to the main criticism that zoning tends inevitably toward the segregation of the different economic classes, I admit the fact but do not consider this result either anti-social or undemocratic in its tendency." Further, "A reasonable segregation is normal, inevitable and desirable and cannot be greatly affected, one way or the other, by zoning."[113]

PROFESSOR RICHARD T. ELY AND HIS CRONIES

Whitten was hardly alone in his professional racism. One of his most powerful mentors and associates was University of Wisconsin Professor Richard T. Ely. Ely held firmly in 1924 to his turn-of-the-century beliefs in the "fundamental and inescapable fact that the ideals of political democracy and equality of economic opportunity are empty of meaning except for a fairly homogeneous people . . . . Exclusion must be practiced."[114] His contemporary, the eclectic Edward Allsworth Ross, shared his views and was responsible for the widespread concept of "race suicide" as a result of immigration. Edward W. Bemis originated the concept of the "literacy test" nearly 40 years before it was enacted into law.

Woodrow Wilson's career reflects a continuing pattern of racism in action. And even Henry George, the father of the single tax reformers, considered unrestricted immigration "hordes" to be "human garbage." The Populist and Progressive professoriate and leadership were a major factor in legitimating public hostility to ethnic and racial minorities.[115]

Historians are in complete discord in their approaches to the study of the twentieth century in America. While the major writers fall into relatively distinct categories (progressive, consensus, revisionist), the range of disagreement is extensive and the sharpness of the debate intensifies. The early analyses of Mowry, Hicks, Woodward, DeWitt, and Faulkner contrast with the work of Hays, Schlesinger, Fine, Commager, Hofstadter, and Link, and are diametrically opposed to cliometrician revisionists like Kolko, Wiebe, and Weinstein.[116]

David Donald described R.H. Wiebe's progressive era as a "fundamental shift in American values" from the small-town 1880s to the "new, bureaucratic-minded middle class by 1920."[117] These were "largely urban professional men and women who developed the new values of 'continuity and regularity, functionality and rationality, administration and management' in order to cope with twentieth century problems."[118]

There is growing consensus among historians that the industrial and managerial revolutions required a concomitant government bureaucracy. The structural-functionalist and entrepreneurial historians are not far removed from the Wisconsin theorists led by Richard T. Ely (or the economic determinism of Seligman, Beard, Smith, Commons, or Perlman) in their beliefs that larger economic and historical developments were an inevitable, necessary, and progressive process.[119]

The renewed interest in associated scholars such as Arthur F. Bentley and the potential revival of the thought of Charles Horton Cooley as major theorists indicate the vitality and power of these important voices of the past. There is significant justification for contemporary analysis in the genius of Lester Ward, Thorstein Veblen, John Dewey, Lewis H. Morgan, Roscoe Pound, and Frederick W. Taylor, among others equally dynamic and contemporary.[120]

It was Taylor's concept of scientific management that initiated the cult of efficiency in 1895. His "differential rate system" was expanded by H. L. Gantt's "bonus system" in 1901.[121] Although labor resisted, American industry adopted the ideas to increase efficiency and profits. The American Plan, the anti-union open shop movement of the 1920s, derives directly from Taylorism.[122] The National Grange adopted the plan and the National Association of Manufacturers, Chambers of Commerce, and the American Bankers' Association were major supporters. Newton D. Baker advocated the system as secretary of war but was defeated by Samuel Gompers's American Federation of Labor.[123] After the war, in 1922, Baker headed the open shop movement and lost his liberal credentials.[124]

The new skills of public relations, originated by Ivy Lee for the Rockefellers, were refined during the war by George Creel and Walter Lippmann under Baker's aegis. Eric Bernays and Roger Babson, the leaders of postwar business public relations, admitted, "The war taught us the power of propaganda. . . . . Now when we have anything to sell to the American people, we know how to sell it. We have the school, the pulpit and the press."[125] It was this new expertise that helped Edward Bassett "sell" zoning to the real estate industry and the public.

Commager wrote the new bureaucracies brought "a growing appreciation of the realities behind the formalities of political, civil, and personal rights." But there was a "gap between formal promises and actual fulfillment."[126] While there were conflicts between individualism and collectivism as competing value systems, the real world operated "to accommodate these two and imperfectly to reconcile the indispensable values which are inherent in them both."[127]

Richard T. Ely and his cronies were outstanding examples of this academic-governmental interaction. Reacting to the oppressive complexities of urban congestion, the impact of scientific management concepts, the rise of bureaucracies, the shocks of industrial violence and fears of radicalism, the revolution in transportation, the nationalization of education and culture, and the vagaries of economic "boom" and "bust," the new professionals deplored the evils of the system and trumpeted their newly popular answers to the spectrum of social and economic problems.

Among the new experts and professionals were the social workers, growing out of the original settlement house movement. They were led by Jane Addams, Lillian Wald, Mary Simkhovitch, Florence Kelley, the Goldmark sisters, Alice Hamilton, Edith and Grace Abbott, and Mary Richmond, among others.[128] While some critics were concerned by the bureaucratization and professionalism of the voluntary philanthropies, "The trend toward professional social work was inexorable."[129] Scientific philanthropy and credentialing institutions melded with government bureaucracies to create a massive power base, originally designed as an instrument of social change.[130]

For example, the concept of an efficient social organization based on an ideal of service was the source of the city planning movement. The social reformers, however, were no match for the technicians and businessmen. The original agenda of the planning conferences (to solve the problems of urban congestion and improve living conditions in cities) was ephemeral. "When the conference met the next year . . . it was obvious that the architects and engineers . . . had taken over."[131] The social workers and Single-Taxers were no longer significant players.

The growth and development of large and well-funded government agencies, departments, and commissions was influenced by the new sciences of statistics (General Walker, Richmond Mayo-Smith, and Wesley C. Mitchell) and public administration (W.F. Willoughby). These organizations became models of efficiency that led to the proliferation of specialized groups and programs, supported largely by the new army of academics and "experts."[132]

The cooptation of the universities, as well as the domination of the regulators by regulated industries, was the outcome of such accommodation. The flow of social reformers to Washington and state capitals to staff the bureaucracies was steady and appreciative.[133] What had been a rarity when Judge Thomas Cooley headed the Interstate Commerce Commission became commonplace after the war time growth of the federal bureaucracy under Woodrow Wilson.[134]

One of Ely's closest associates, Edward W. Bemis, was already well established by 1900. He was "then creating for himself his own job as expert adviser to municipalities in their contests with privately owned utilities over questions of regulation and public ownership."[135] After working for Tom L. Johnson and Newton D. Baker in Cleveland, Bemis continued his work and was nationally recognized as a franchise "expert" along with Delos F. Wilcox and Robert H. Whitten.[136] Their joint efforts, books, and public testimony were important factors in rate cases, franchise renewals, and regulation matters. Such testimony by "experts" was challenged by the utility companies in the mid-1920s in the Denver Tramways case and public interest testimony was excluded in future litigation.[137]

Ely had tremendous influence through his students, the expanded political science and economics departments in all major universities, his widely read texts and popular books, a constant stream of articles and lectures, and a sophisticated exploitation of the giant industrial firms that dominated American business.

One part of his multivalent career was dedicated to the development of zoning laws in the United States as an answer to urban problems. He played a most significant role by creating his land use center, developing a curriculum and textbooks for the real estate industry, and publishing the major zoning works at the time the idea required massive academic legitimation.[138]

The genesis of Ely's intensive interest in zoning was the revival of single tax activity after 1914. Defeated in the New York zoning and tax battles, the followers of Henry George received new foundation funding after the death of Joseph Fels. The High-Cost-of-Living panic after the war and the attempt to take over Baker's government housing projects brought forth a new single tax movement; there was immediate reaction from the real estate boards. Since Ely had been a long-standing opponent of Henry George's ideas, he was recruited by the real estate industry to professionalize it and, through publications and curriculum, to counteract the Single-Taxers.[139]

Ely founded his Institute for Research in Land Economics (1920) at the University of Wisconsin. He incorporated it as an independent research and educational institution in 1922.[140] His early interest in the Chautauqua movement had given him "an interest in adult education that I have never lost."[141] The use of the Institute as an adult education system was "directed particularly toward those in the real estate business which we wanted to help put on a professional basis."[142] One of Ely's first publications was the first major study of zoning law, the Frank Backus Williams's treatise. The school's first offering included Ely's own course on land economics, John Burton's appraising class, real estate management, and a comprehensive planning course taught by Robert Whitten.[143]

Ely had large contracts for developing the standard texts for the National Real Estate Boards' real estate courses. These were regularly offered through the YMCA and the American Association of Collegiate Schools of Business beginning in 1923.[144] The real estate boards in all cities were powerful organizations by the 1920s and had tremendous influence on local legislation including sewers and water supply, street lighting and railways, traffic congestion, zoning ordinances, and, particularly, tax valuation systems.[145] The real estate boards vigorously opposed the Single-Taxers, their most radical critics, on local, state, and national levels.

The influence of the real estate boards in developing a professional credentialing system paralleled similar activities in most professions. The boards were successful. By 1925, Northwestern University had full credit courses (derived directly from Ely's text and curriculum) on "real estate principles and practices," "land economics," "valuation," and "real estate financing."

The University of Michigan hired E.M. Fisher, director of education for the board schools (and an Ely Institute executive), as the first full-time professor of real estate in an American University (1926, School of Business Administration). A board-developed and sponsored collegiate major in real estate was available at more than 40 colleges in 1926; the

two-year vocational course of 1923 was revised and in use in more than 200 cities by 1925.

Ely, through his contracts with Macmillan and other publishers, became the major source of books on real estate and related land use studies. In addition to Williams's very influential law of zoning, Ely produced a library of standard references by reputable authorities to serve real estate personnel and management in addition to the municipal market and colleges and universities. He publicized Cleveland real estate experts' books on zoning and valuation problems (widely used in the industry after 1923). Harlean James's comprehensive land planning work was published in 1926.[146]

Ely was an active real estate speculator and developer who sought financial support from major business interests for his institute. "But the money which comes to us must be free from any restriction or limitations of any sort whatsoever. We have been told simply to state the facts. . . ."[147] However, Ely's methods were "highly questionable" and he used scare tactics "exploiting the fears of special interest groups. Large property holders appeared particularly vulnerable to a revived single tax agitation, which arose from the acute housing shortage. . . ."[148] Ely's institute's motto became "Progress without Confiscation."

Ely's reputation suffered with the release of information that he and his institute (and many of his published writers) were in fact heavily subsidized by the real estate boards and utilities companies. The National Electric Light Association (NELA) of Cleveland paid him thousands of dollars a year for his work in their behalf. NELA was headed at the time by Merlin Aylesworth, later president of the National Broadcasting Company. A Federal Trade Commission report was used to show that "Aylesworth ordered payments right and left to college professors and newspapermen who would spread his propaganda, and secretly paid for the writing of textbooks suitable to the public-utilities promoters."[149]

Without such self-aggrandizement, Ely would have been merely one of a number of significant people in zoning history. It is evident, however, that his institute and "experts" cloaked the commercial and business aspects of zoning with academic respectability and provided the network and resources (books, curriculum, schools, professionals) that Edward M. Bassett, Robert H. Whitten, and others used to expand zoning throughout the country.[150]

The question of using tainted money was nothing new. Washington Gladden and the Social Gospel adherents had lamented the Rockefeller grants to churches and the University of Chicago. Stanford, Harkness, and Carnegie flooded universities with hundreds of millions of dollars in endowments. Justice John H. Clarke, Baker's friend, left well over a million dollars to Western Reserve University in Cleveland.[151] Metzger indicated that such philanthropy was "welcomed . . . by its very grateful inhabitants." The reason, "the most compelling of motives—self-interest and the desire for social approval."[152]

The Russell Sage Foundation, which published *The Survey* and backed social surveys and public service legal projects, was established by Margaret Olivia Sage, wife of the notorious financier.[153] The head of the fund for many years was Robert W. DeForest; Lawson Purdy also served in that capacity.[154] Many of the Sage grants were in support of city and regional planning efforts. The foundation was the single most important factor in the growth and development of private American social welfare services.[155]

The Sage Foundation, due to its support of child labor and minimum wage cases, often was opposed by leaders of the American Bar Association, including George Sutherland. The ABA was highly conservative in its membership, publications, philosophy, and influence on the legal system. It consistently opposed "Populist" and "majoritarian" state legislation.[156] Its leadership fought vigorously to turn back Louis Brandeis's nomination to the Supreme Court.

The ABA was particularly active against social legislation proposed by Florence Kelley and Josephine Goldmark, Brandeis's sister-in-law. Kelley, a lifelong friend of Frederic C. Howe and Newton D. Baker, was a former settlement house worker who, losing her belief in the potential of social work, became a political activist. She headed the National Consumers' League for many years.[157] Goldmark was a sophisticated and dynamic social change agent, specializing in research and brief writing for league-backed cases.[158]

It was Josephine Goldmark who first developed the extended sociological legal brief in a New York child labor case.[159] She was later responsible for the brilliant *Muller* v. *Oregon* (1908) research that made Brandeis a national figure when Justice Brewer accepted the innovative brief.[160] Her work on the subsequent *Bunting* v. *Oregon* (1917) brief was given full credit by Felix Frankfurter.[161] Kelley and Goldmark are best known for their 1,100-page "Brandeis brief" for *Adkins* v. *Children's Hospital* (1923).[162] This was the minimum wage case in which Justice Sutherland shocked reform sentiment with his reaffirmation of *Lochner* v. *New York*.[163]

ALFRED BETTMAN

It was a "Brandeis brief" that Alfred Bettman wrote for *Euclid* v. *Ambler.* Metzenbaum, although he sharply rejected early Bettman suggestions, called him one of "the stout champions of zoning . . . whose pen was constantly employed in the advancement of the cause."[164] Bettman was a former city solicitor and municipal reformer in Cincinnati whose interest in city planning led him ultimately to the *Euclid* case. He graduated from Harvard Law School (1898) after receiving an undergraduate degree and a masters degree from the same institution. On his return to Cincinnati he was admitted to the Ohio bar (1898) and immediately became active in the affairs of the city.[165]

Bettman's interest in city planning, an outgrowth of his concern with street congestion, overcrowding, and public health conditions in Cincinnati, brought him national prominence. His early association with the National Conferences on City Planning and his papers written for professionals in the field began in 1913.[166] Bettman's enabling acts were the basis for Ohio cities to create planning boards after 1917. From 1923, cities had the right to regulate ancillary suburbs. Bettman, in coordination with Edward Bassett and others, prepared Standard City and State Zoning Enabling Acts after his return from government service in 1919.[167] From 1921 to 1927 these model statutes guided the majority of cities in the country through their zoning problems.[168]

From 1917 to 1919, Bettman was a special assistant to Woodrow Wilson's Attorney General Thomas Gregory and was associated closely with John Lord O'Brian in the War Emergency Division of the Justice Department.[169] Bettman, like Charles Warren and other lawyers working for the government during that period, drafted a number of war time restraint measures. It is his actions during this period that have earned him an enduring reputation as a principal civil libertarian.[170]

Bettman's government and Cincinnati experience brought him to national attention in 1921 with the release of the massive Cleveland Foundation publication *Criminal Justice in Cleveland,* under the direction of Dean Roscoe Pound and Professor Felix Frankfurter.[171] Frankfurter wrote of Bettman: "(He) proved to an uncommon degree that mere citizenship is the most important office in a democracy. Bettman held strong convictions without intolerance and fought wrong without rancor. He had enthusiasm born of imagination, and ardently pursued the American dream. . . ."[172]

It was this ability to focus on major problems and consistently apply his skills and time to their solution that raises Bettman from the visionary reform category to the pinnacle of measurable and significant achievement in advancing the society in which he lived and worked. He had "no illusions about recreating a world by means of legislation" as did Florence Kelley and the Goldmark sisters, although he knew them and, like Baker, worked on a number of progressive legislative matters.[173] However, he was a positive and dynamic person and the "great problem on which he 'brooded and labored was to make planning not merely fit into, but actually preserve and strengthen democracy.' "[174]

Bettman, convinced that zoning based on a comprehensive plan and involving a reasonable use of the police power was indeed constitutional (and in spite of his early expressed opinion that the *Euclid* appeal would result in a higher court upholding Westenhaver's decision), decided to submit a brief to the Court in support of the village's case. He was influenced greatly by his victory over Newton D. Baker in *Pritz* v. *Messer,* in which Judge Florence Allen's opinion stressed the importance of the comprehensive zone plan and its integral relationship to the city plan as factors supporting the constitutionality of the ordinance in question.[175]

For Bettman, the constitutionality of zoning rested absolutely on the reasonableness of the use of a comprehensive plan to promote the "health, safety, convenience, prosperity and social welfare of the people of the city . . . (and) . . . a genuine taking of the economic and social factors into account. . . ."[176] Bettman had long viewed zoning as a proper use of the police power in the areas of traffic, public health, noise, and safety, and emphasized its role in "the promotion of common prosperity by stabilizing and protecting property values and reducing the difficulties and expense of municipal administration, and the promotion of community welfare . . . ."[177] He believed completely in the flexibility and applicability of the police power to control zoning "regulating private property and . . . conduct in the interest of community welfare . . . (T)he nature of this police power . . . cannot have any definitely stable limits . . . . It necessarily changes. . . ."[178]

Bettman's renewed confidence in the *Euclid* appeal is indicated in his contemporary publications on zoning law. In October 1925, his paper at the Ohio State Conference on City Planning heralded the year as "a triumphant one for the constitutionality of zoning" since it had been upheld by the highest courts of California, New York, Louisiana, Wisconsin, Massachusetts, Ohio, Minnesota, and Kansas.[179] In Ohio, the Cincinnati case indicated a significant shift in judicial attitudes in the state. Only in Missouri, Maryland, and New Jersey had zoning been negated constitutionally and "none of these three states . . . had a general state zoning law of the type of the modern zoning statute and . . . each of them is now engaged in drafting and, no doubt, passing such a statute."[180] Bettman also pointed out that, contrary to his prior interpretation of the Westenhaver opinion, "the decision did not necessarily invalidate all zoning. In fact, the same court (Westenhaver) has since upheld one of the regulations in the same ordinance."[181]

As a result of the events of the past year, Bettman unequivocally stated, "There can be no doubt whatever . . . that the overwhelming weight of authority supports the constitutionality of zoning; and American urban communities may safely proceed upon the assurance that the validity of zoning is established."[182] Bettman was, of course, correct. In 1926, Justice George Sutherland's opinion reversed Judge D.C. Westenhaver's decision and held in *Euclid* v. *Ambler* that zoning was constitutional.[183]

JUSTICE GEORGE SUTHERLAND

Professor Tarlock writes, "A student of constitutional history must ponder how it was that Justice Sutherland, a leading constitutional conservative, agreed to write the majority opinion in *Euclid.*"[184] Sutherland's biographer theoretically answers the question by analyzing the fears of overpopulation (the Malthusian doctrine contemporary with Herbert Spencer and Social Darwinist ideas) and urban congestion (reflected in the popular works of Charles Dickens and Jacob Riis) as facts requiring social and political controls to protect the public welfare. The resulting arguable thesis was that zoning was an answer to such problems and, in addition, enhanced and stabilized the value of property. Sutherland decided that such a reasonable approach permitted the use of the state's police power.[185]

Sutherland focused on the question of whether the *Euclid* ordinance was a valid use of "some aspect of the police power, asserted for the public welfare," admitting that drawing such a line "is not capable of precise delimitation." He had to balance (using Holmes's adapted adjudicative calculus) the vested rights of some property owners with the rights of others. Adjusting those rights through the use of the police power was constitutional: "In a changing world, it is impossible that it should be otherwise."[186]

The police power is defined as "the right of the government to promote order and to protect the public safety, health, morals, and general welfare within constitutional limits."[187] While Professor Haar describes "aesthetics" as a "brooding omnipresence" and "property," "political externalities," and the "comprehensive plan" as controlling the parameters of permissibility in zoning laws,"[188] the general rule is that property can be regulated to a certain extent; past that point, the result is a taking.[189]

Ernst Freund's authoritative treatise[190] clarified the balancing of harms and benefits from the use of the state's power. While the narrowing of the idea of the police power by Bassett and the zoning ordinance drafters was not in line with Freund's approach to his own theory, their concept prevailed in *Euclid.* "Freund believed that zoning must reflect the cultural values of society to be effective."[191] The approach of Bassett and the zoning legal fraternity was more pragmatic.

Justice Holmes had "sweepingly" expanded the concept of the police power in 1911 in *Noble State Bank* v. *Haskell,*[192] the definition Harold Laski called "the modern charter of the federal state."[193] It "extends to all the great public needs" that are "greatly and immediately necessary to the public welfare."[194] The taking question was resolved in *Pennsylvania Coal Co.* v. *Mahon.*[195] The police power and balancing calculus gave Sutherland the analytical tools he needed to validate zoning. His was a logical, if tenuous, extension of the jurisprudence of Justice Holmes.

Felix Frankfurter, later Justice, misunderstood the genesis of Sutherland's thought and relegated him to "the era of great big sterile absolutes—(when) 'liberty of contract' was riding high." He writes Sutherland was "limit-

ed because his basic ideas came from a predominantly different social and economic society than was asserting itself in the twenties. . . ."[196] Sutherland, however, was careful to insist there was no such thing as "absolute freedom of contract." There was only a general rule that required "the existence of exceptional circumstances" for the use of legislative power to abridge it.[197]

We are indebted to Paschal for an intensive study of the career of Justice Sutherland[198] and to Mason for insights into his "world."[199] Sutherland, the son of an English immigrant (a Mormon apostate and quondam lawyer) was a Westerner with educational and political roots in Utah and Michigan. Permanently influenced by the social thought of Herbert Spencer (primarily through his Mormon teacher Karl Maeser), the Social Darwinists, and the "constitutional limitations" theories of Thomas Cooley, he was an aggressively individualistic and anticollectivist "dual federalist."[200]

Sutherland's culture base was the dynamic era of powerful business interests and the industrial revolution, ably defended by a brilliant corps of legal minds. Their major tool against legislation negative to powerful vested interests was the concept of the corporation as a person combined with the expansion of the Fourteenth Amendment in the new doctrines of due process and equal protection.[201] Due process became a positive and judicially enforceable restriction on state legislation and use of the police power. The result: a "perpetual censorship" of social legislation beginning in 1890 with the victory of Justice Field's judicial activist concepts in the *Minnesota Rate Cases*[202] and peaking in *Lochner* v. *New York.*[203] *Lochner* fixed the legal parameters of economic liberty. Among the ideas included was liberty of contract.[204]

Sutherland's views reflected such conservative judicial theories. His controversial opinion in *Adkins* v. *Children's Hospital*[205] was no less doctrinaire than Judge Van Orsdel's "Of the three fundamental principles which underlie government, and for which government exists, the protection of life, liberty, and property, the chief of these is property. . . ."[206] The "Brandeis brief," developed for Felix Frankfurter by the tireless Goldmark sisters and Florence Kelley, was not enough to create a crisis mental set for Sutherland to affirmatively respond.[207] He found it "interesting but only mildly persuasive."[208]

The Brandeis-Frankfurter use of statistical, social, and economic information in persuasive briefs reflected Justice Holmes's early interest in the application of science to the law. The effect of such briefs on the Court in *Muller* and *Bunting* had been significant. But in *Adkins,* Sutherland decided the facts were merely examples of the fine technical lawyering he found attractive in Brandeis and Frankfurter but not persuasive. He remarked such briefs were easy to amass, their effectiveness diluted by countervailing materials. In this assessment of the value of "Brandeis briefs," Sutherland was ahead of his time.[209]

The inconsistency of Sutherland's thought is exemplified in his agreement with Justice Holmes's dissent in *Meyer* v. *Nebraska* (1923).[210] A later Court generation was to use *Meyer* as a major citation in the new civil liberties judicial activism of the 1960s.[211] The very reasoning Sutherland used in *Adkins* to permit Willie Lyons to work for any wage she could "freely exact from her employer" was used by McReynolds in *Meyer* to denote "the right of the individual to contract, to engage in any of the common occupations of life, to acquire useful knowledge, to marry, establish a home and bring up children, to worship God according to the dictates of his own conscience, and generally to enjoy those privileges long recog-

nized at common law as essential to the orderly pursuit of happiness by free men."[212]

Herbert Spencer's ideas are emphasized by Paschal as the primary source of Sutherland's judicial language and thought in action. Spencer was a "celestial guide for Sutherland in his odyssey as lawyer, legislator and judge."[213] For us to accept Sutherland's few quoted letters and depend on "The Spirit of Brigham Young University"[214] with its eulogization of the influence of Karl Maeser is difficult. The "Spirit" comments were made at the end of his life in the context of the receipt of an honorary degree. Sutherland's public speeches are suspect as contrived and rhetorical commentary. They were written for special occasions and audiences using a forensic style and method derived from his experience as orator and Senator.[215]

Paschal's emphasis on the influence of Judge Cooley on Sutherland, while widely cited and accepted, is also a tenuous position. Cooley was, after all, Sutherland's law professor for less than a year.[216] His other professor was the equally important James V. Campbell, like Cooley a major writer and judge on the Michigan Supreme Court.[217] There is, however, no question of the impact on Sutherland (and the legal profession) of Cooley's classic *Constitutional Limitations.*[218]

That early educational experiences are significant in the growth and development of an individual is obvious. Thomas A. Cooley had considerable influence in the early life of his son Charles Horton Cooley, still a major figure in sociological theory.[219] Yet, even under the pervasive influence of his "hard-driving ambitious extrovert" father, he did not become a Social Darwinist.

Cooley was interested in Spencer's ideas but he was far more influenced by the writings of Jane Addams, Lewis Henry Morgan, William James, and the anti-Spencerian Lester

Ward.[220] He became a mild Progressive, a brilliant and innovative social theorist of the changes resulting from urbanization and a modern industrial society.

Certainly Charles H. Cooley, teaching Delos F. Wilcox and Robert H. Whitten in his first classes at Michigan, had as much influence on them (and the history of zoning) as his father had on Justice Sutherland.

While Paschal credits Maeser and Judge Cooley as primary conduits of Spencerian thought in Sutherland's development as a politician-Justice and William Graham Sumner as the basis for his Social Darwinism, it is probable that the conservative American Bar Association hierarchy, of which he was a distinguished member, was a more pervasive and consistent ideological influence.[221]

The 1916 revival of Spencer's social and political theories was a frontal attack (through a revival of laissez-faire doctrines) on Woodrow Wilson's New Freedom policies. These were vigorously rejected by Sutherland, an opposition that lost him his seat in the United States Senate.[222]

The Truxton Beale best-selling edition of Spencer's *The Man Versus the State* (1916) contained the adroit polemics of William Howard Taft, Elihu Root, Charles Eliot, Henry Cabot Lodge, David Jayne Hill, Nicholas Murray Butler, Elbert Gary, and Harlan Fiske Stone (later a Justice of the Supreme Court). It must have been read reflectively by Sutherland.[223]

The interstitial notes of the distinguished commentators adapted Spencer's ideas to the specific conditions of 1916. They emphasized the "growing tyranny of officialism" through the "extension of official control over the private life and activities of the individual" and the "subordination of personal liberty to the dictates of a ruling class acting in the name of the State."[224]

The politician-popularizers of Spencer asserted government was becoming "more coercive, legislation more restrictive, and the State more omnipotent." There was a "gradual imposition of a new bondage in the name of freedom," a specific reference to President Wilson's administration.[225]

After 1915 the massive works of Professor William Graham Sumner were revived and "Sumnerology" became a dynamic and viable academic and political force. This culminated in the postwar reaction against government intervention and "return to normalcy" proclaimed by Warren G. Harding and managed by George Sutherland.[226]

Sumner's thought, distilled through Spencer's ideas and mixed with Republican-party prerogatives and imperatives, played a major role in Sutherland's career after 1916. Spencerian evolutionary and individualistic doctrines coincided with Sumner's concept of the futility of social initiatives. "The greatest folly of which a man can be capable, (is) to sit down (and) plan out a new social world."[227]

Sutherland's interpretation of Sumner, reflected in his opinions as a Justice, was to maintain a self-adjusting society operating with a minimum of state interference and a maximum of voluntary participation. This policy was the best answer to the problems of rapidly changing social and economic realities. It was this thought process, influenced by the revivalism of laissez-faire ideals, that supported Sutherland's *Adkins* decision.[228]

Florence Kelley (and the majority of those in the minimum wage, child labor, and women's movements) attacked Sutherland's ideas. However, a number of leading feminists did not see *Adkins* as a reactionary throwback. They cited the sweeping implications of his opinion on women's rights as a progressive statement of equal rights for women. Alice Paul, a leader of the Women's Party and the writer of the 1923 Equal Rights Amendment, wrote in *The Survey* that Sutherland's opinion treated women as "adult human beings" who were now "standing on an equal plane with men."[229]

Even as harsh a critic as Alexander Bickel admitted "Sutherland had his moments," referring to his support of Andrew Furuseth and the Seamen's Act of 1915 and his position on workmen's compensation bills.[230] However, there was a personal relationship and philosophical affinity involved here. Furuseth was a Jacksonian Democrat (like Judge Thomas Cooley) "fearing the state and opposing government ownership." He was antiradical and anti-Industrial Workers of the World (IWW) and viciously attacked his adversaries.[231] Furuseth was an antibureaucratic, highly conservative individualistic thinker. He and Samuel Gompers of the American Federation of Labor enthusiastically supported Sutherland for the Senate in 1916.[232]

It is in the areas of party politics, protectionism, and Spencer's antibureaucracy that Sutherland was remarkably consistent. As a senator, his domination by Republican party leaders was complete. His early aberration in favor of Bryan in 1896, prior to his Washington years, was clearly based on Western voters' mania for "free silver."[233]

It was Nelson W. Aldrich and William Howard Taft, his political mentors, who determined Sutherland's practical politics. In the Pinchot-Ballinger controversy, his first contact with the genius and skills of Louis Brandeis, Sutherland supported Ballinger and Taft, endearing himself to the president and beginning the split with Theodore Roosevelt and his followers, among them James R. Garfield and the Pinchots.[234]

Unlike Spencer and Cooley, whose individualism derived from the free trade theories of Adam Smith, Sutherland was a staunch believer in protective tariffs as the basis of American prosperity, aiding manufacturing and industry.

With only a few exceptions, Sutherland consistently opposed any expansion of government bureaucracies. His concept of Spencer's "Superfluous Government" was presented in a 1914 Cleveland speech where he denounced the creation of "an army of official agents, government bureaus and all sorts of Commissions to pry into our affairs, smell out our shortcomings and tell us what we may and . . . may not do." He fought against bureaucracy as a basic source of a flood of "unwise or unworkable or unnecessary" laws.[235]

During his career he demonstrated a mild progressive attitude in his thought. He supported the Pure Food and Drug Act, the Hepburn bill, postal savings, and the Children's Bureau, acts which contrasted with his expressed antipathy to the "insurgent soothsayers" and their "cabalistic utterances respecting the initiative, the referendum (and) the recall . . .," which he considered useless devices to achieve the social millennium.[236] He was opposed to the income tax, the Federal Reserve Act, and the Federal Trade Commission.

Sutherland was able to reconcile himself as a Justice to contemporary realities and compromise with his fellows. *Grosjean,* for example, was a reflection of the educating influence of Justice Cardozo's ideas on Sutherland; his writing derives from Cardozo's alternate concurrence.[237] One writer claims Sutherland's apparent change of position in *Euclid* was probably the result of Justice Stone's influence.[238]

Burner writes of him as "the intellectual spokesman" for the "Four Horsemen." He describes Sutherland's opinions as "tightly reasoned and systematic; his thinking . . . subtle and complex."[239] Justice Stone said Sutherland "put a great deal of faith in experience and very little in mere experiment," and added, "He was profoundly convinced that ill-considered experimentation in government in pursuit of passing fashion in legislation . . . would in the end prove to be the real enemies of true democracy, and a grave danger to constitutional government . . . . Few would be so bold as to deny those dangers."[240]

Rodell described Sutherland as "the ablest and hardest working" of the conservative Justices.[241] The collectivist constitutional commentator Louis Boudin reflected on him as a "tricky" realist who represented a negative view of potential social change in America.[242] McCloskey views Sutherland somewhat positively as a "judicial activist."[243] Even Justice Frankfurter was able to point to Sutherland's *Powell* opinion as "a notable chapter in the history of liberty."[244]

Still, Woodrow Wilson wrote to former Justice Clarke in 1922 that he had "no reason to suspect him (Sutherland) of either principles or brains. . . ."[245] And to a leading journalist of the thirties, he was "a lame duck senator," "tall and slender with a neatly trimmed gray beard," "an attractive and scholarly looking person" who was a major reactionary force on the Court.[246]

Why did Sutherland seemingly reverse himself ideologically in *Euclid?* The answer may well be that he did not. He was able to adjust to the realities of a changing world, particularly when major elements (immigration, congestion, the role of the family, new property interests) required a more sophisticated and flexible response.

A RESPONSIVE ERA

While the Progressive era and Harding "Normalcy" certainly maintained a continuing ideological warfare, the 1920s represented a pragmatic political environment responsive to actual and implied power structures.

The background of zoning in America represents the initial efforts of the liberal-reformers, "an extraordinarily compelling lot, vivid and powerful personalities, they demanded to be heard."[247] They were "vigorous, active, creative, dramatic . . . the antithesis that carrie(d) the seeds of the future."[248] But, operating within the middle-class mainstream, they were unable to compete with more powerful social and economic interests. Reformers were unable to withstand the shock of postwar prosperity and were fragmented, ideologically and individually. Zoning, as a result, was not a reform product; it became a fundamental technique in maintaining the power of property.

The flexible and opportunistic pattern of accommodation that is represented in *Euclid* is merely one example of the compromise basis of American politics, based on the written Constitution and carried out in its evolving history. The consequences of the case and its progeny are still developing. The ghost of Robert Whitten walks through the current realities of racism and "exclusionary zoning." And the specter of Henry George's single tax (in subtle and convoluted ideological forms) still haunts the dreams of those who live in the "House of Have." It is also a potentially powerful idea for the varying constituencies in the "House of Want."[249]

AUTHOR'S NOTE

The author was aided in the research and production of this chapter by the staffs of the Cleveland Public Library, the Cleveland State University Library, the several libraries of the Case-Western Reserve University, the Oklahoma City University Law Library, and the Bizzell Library of the University of Oklahoma. Susan MacFarland, Department of Political Science, the University of Oklahoma, aided in the concept and development of the chapter.

NOTES

1. The village of Euclid derived from a secondary distribution of land in the Western Reserve. Harlan H. Hatcher, *The Western Reserve: The Story of New Connecticut in Ohio* (Indianapolis, Ind.: Bobbs-Merrill, 1949).

2. William Ganson Rose, *Cleveland: The Making of a City* (Cleveland, Ohio: World Publishing Company, 1950), pp. 636, 689.

3. Euclid, Ohio, Ordinance 2812 (November 13, 1922), amended by Ordinances 3367 and 3368 (June 11, 1923).

4. James Metzenbaum, *The Law of Zoning* (New York, N.Y.: Baker, Voorhis and Company, 1930), p. 111.

5. 297 F. 307 (N.D. Ohio 1924).

6. N. R. Howard, "Brilliant Metzenbaum Led Melancholy Life," Cleveland *Plain Dealer,* January 7, 1961. File, James Metzenbaum, *Cleveland Press* Collection, Cleveland State University Library.

7. *Ambler Realty Co.* v. *Village of Euclid,* 297 F. 307, 316 (N.D. Ohio 1924).

8. Metzenbaum, *The Law of Zoning,* p. 112.

9. Letter, Alfred Bettman to D.J. Underwood, September 29, 1924, quoted in Daniel R. Mandelker and Roger A. Cunningham, *Planning and Control of Land Development: Cases and Materials* (Indianapolis, Ind.: Bobbs-Merrill, 1979), p. 213, n. 5.

10. Metzenbaum, *The Law of Zoning,* pp. 116–120.

11. Alfred Bettman, "The Decision of the Supreme Court of the United States in the Euclid Village Zoning Case," *U. Cin. L. Rev.,* Vol. 1, no. 2, (March 1927): pp. 184–192; Alfred Bettman, *City and Regional Planning Papers,* Arthur C. Comey, ed. (Cambridge, Mass.: Harvard University Press, 1946), p. 51.

12. *City Planning,* Vol. 3, no. 4 (April, 1927): p. 132.

13. *Village of Euclid* v. *Ambler Realty Co.,* 272 U.S. 365 (1926).

14. Donald G. Hagman, *Public Planning and Control of Urban Land Development: Cases and Materials* (St. Paul, Minn.: West Publishing Company, 1980), pp. 465–466.

15. Metzenbaum, *The Law of Zoning,* pp. 106, 135.

16. Id. at p. 105.

17. Frank Backus Williams, *The Law of City Planning and Zoning* (New York, N.Y.: The Macmillan Company, 1922).

18. Metzenbaum, *The Law of Zoning,* p. 107.

19. Thomas Harrison Reed, *Municipal Government in the United States* (New York, N.Y.: The Century Company, 1926), p. 101.

20. "Henry George," *Dictionary of American Biography* 7 (New York, N.Y.: Charles Scribner's Sons, 1931), pp. 211–215. See Hoyt Landon Warner, *Progressivism in Ohio 1897–1917* (Columbus, Ohio: Ohio State University Press/Ohio Historical Society, 1964); Michael H. Ebner and Eugene M. Tobins, eds., *The Age of Urban Reform: New Perspectives on the Progressive Era* (Port Washington, N.Y.: Kennikat Press, 1977); John D. Buenker, *Urban Liberalism and Progressive Reform* (New York, N.Y.: Scribner's, 1973); David D. VanTassel and John Grabowski, eds., *Cleveland, A Tradition of Reform* (Kent, Ohio: Kent State University Press, 1986); Jack D. Elenbaas, "Detroit and the Progressive Era: A Study of Urban Reform, 1900–1914," (Ph.D. dissertation, Wayne State University, 1968); Melvin G. Holli, *Reform in Detroit: Hazen S. Pingree and Urban Politics* (New York, N.Y.: Oxford University Press, 1969). For a brief survey of the era, *see* Page Smith, *America Enters the World: A People's History of the Progressive Era and World War I* 7 (New York, N.Y.: McGraw-Hill, 1985), pp. 72–98.

21. "Tom Loftin Johnson," *Dictionary of American Biography* 10 (New York, N.Y.: Charles Scribner's Sons, 1933), pp. 122–124; Tom L. Johnson, *My Story,* Elizabeth J. Hauser, ed. (New York, N.Y.: B.W. Huebsch Company, 1911); Carl Lorenz, *Tom L. Johnson, Mayor of Cleveland* (New York, N.Y.: A.S. Barnes, 1911); Robert L. Briggs, "The Progressive Era in Cleveland, Ohio: Tom L. Johnson's Administration, 1901–1909" (Ph.D. dissertation, University of Chicago, 1963). See "Newton Diehl Baker," *Dictionary of American Biography* 22 (New York, N.Y.: Charles Scribner's Sons, 1958), pp. 17–19; Clarence H. Cramer, *Newton D. Baker, A Biography* (Cleveland, Ohio: World Publishing Company, 1961). *See also* "Frederic Clemson Howe," *Dictionary of American Biography* 22 (New York, N.Y.: Charles Scribner's Sons, 1958), pp. 326–328; Robert Arthur Huff, "Frederic C. Howe, Progressive" (Ph.D. dissertation, University of Rochester, 1967). Bemis, Whitten, and Wilcox are extensively profiled *infra.*

22. The influence of German universities and scholars (Heidelberg, Göttingen, Kiel, Berlin, Leipzig, Halle, Jhering, Ranke, Schmoller, Gauss, Helmholtz, Gumplowicz, among others) was enormous; 13 of the 53 professors at The Johns Hopkins University in 1884 had German doctorates. Professors such as G. Stanley Hall and Richard T. Ely taught students such as John Dewey, Edward Webster Bemis, Albert Shaw, and John R. Commons; Woodrow Wilson, Frederick Jackson Turner, and Simon N. Patten influenced brilliant students to pursue academic careers; among those students were Frederic C. Howe and Newton D. Baker. *See* Charles Franklin Thwing, *The American and the German University, One Hundred Years of History* (New York, N.Y.: The Macmillan Company, 1928); Hugh Hawkins, *Pioneer: History of the Johns Hop-*

kins University, 1874–1889 (Ithaca, N.Y.: Cornell University Press, 1960).

23. Frederic Clemson Howe, *The Confessions of a Reformer* (New York, N.Y.: Charles Scribner's Sons, 1925), p. 1.

24. Cramer, *Newton D. Baker, A Biography,* pp. 30–31. The firm was Foran, McTighe & Baker.

25. *State ex. rel. Morris* v. *East Cleveland,* 31 Ohio Dec. 98 (1919).

26. Id. at pp. 106–120.

27. "Harry Augustus Garfield," *Dictionary of American Biography* supp. three (New York, N.Y.: Charles Scribner's Sons, 1973), pp. 292–294; "James Rudolph Garfield," *Dictionary of American Biography* supp. four (New York, N.Y.: Charles Scribner's Sons, 1974), pp. 316–318; "Marcus Alonzo Hanna," *Dictionary of American Biography* 8 (New York, N.Y.: Charles Scribner's Sons, 1932), pp. 225–228; Herbert David Croly, *Marcus Alonzo Hanna, His Life and Work* (New York, N.Y.: The Macmillan Company, 1912).

28. Howe, *The Confessions of a Reformer,* p. 190. See Eugene R. Moulton, "An Evaluation of the Speaking Effectiveness of Newton D. Baker" (Ph.D. dissertation, Western Reserve University, 1954), for an analysis of Baker's legendary skills as a public speaker. Moulton was the first researcher given access to the Baker archives prior to their transfer from Baker, Hostetler control to the collections of the Library of Congress.

29. Johnson, *My Story,* p. 247; Charles E. Kennedy, *Fifty Years of Cleveland, 1875–1925* (Cleveland, Ohio: The Weidenthal Company, 1925), p. 336. The complex history of traction franchise battles in Cleveland (and other cities) is one of suit, countersuit, delay, bribery, and corruption. *See* Johnson, *My Story,* pp. xxi, 221–249, 276–291. A thorough contemporary description of street railway franchises is included in Delos Franklin Wilcox, *Municipal Franchises* vols. 1–2 (Chicago, Ill.: University of Chicago Press, 1910).

30. Daniel M. Holmgrem, "Edward Webster Bemis and Municipal Reform" (Ph.D. dissertation, Western Reserve University, 1964); "Edward W. Bemis" (Obituary, *New York Times,* September 27, 1930).

31. File, "D.C. Westenhaver," Cleveland Public Library Reference Room; Elroy McKendree Avery, *A History of Cleveland and its Environs* vol. 2 (Chicago, Ill.: The Lewis Publishing Company, 1918), pp. 22–24. The firm became Westenhaver, Boyd & Brooks.

32. Hoyt Landon Warner, *The Life of Mr. Justice Clarke* (Cleveland, Ohio: The Western Reserve University Press, 1959); "John Hessin Clarke," *Dictionary of American Biography* supp. three (New York, N.Y.: Charles Scribner's Sons, 1973), pp. 167–168.

33. Warner, *The Life of Mr. Justice Clarke,* pp. 59–60; File, "D.C. Westenhaver," Cleveland Public Library Reference Room.

34. Clarke's resignation was a surprise to Baker. The two men corresponded regularly and met frequently in Washington during the time Baker was secretary of war and Clarke a Justice. Howe, unlike Baker and Clarke, considered the League a reactionary police force for the big powers. *See* Frederic Clemson Howe, "Economic Foundations of the League of Nations," *Annals of the American Academy of Political and Social Science,* vol. 83 (May 1919), pp. 313–316.

35. Joseph C. Hostetler, assistant city solicitor, and Thomas L. Sidlo, public service director, were Johnson-Baker officials. They formed, with Baker, the Baker, Hostetler & Sidlo law firm.

36. Ambler was a veteran real estate operator in Cleveland, responsible for major downtown and suburban developments. An Ambler specialty was assembling large contiguous areas for speculative ventures.

37. 297 F. 307 (N.D. Ohio 1924).

38. Howe, *The Confessions of a Reformer,* pp. 113–140; Frederic Clemson Howe, *The City: The Hope of Democracy* (New York, N.Y.: Charles Scribner's Sons, 1905); Robert H. Bremner, "Honest Man's Story: Frederic C. Howe," in "The Civic Revival in Ohio," *American Journal of Economics and Sociology* vol. 8, no. 4 (July 1949), pp. 413–422. *See also* Benjamin C. Marsh, *An Introduction to City Planning* (New York, N.Y.: 1909); Delos Franklin Wilcox, *The American City: A Problem in Democracy* (New York, N.Y.: The Macmillan Company, 1904).

39. The single tax was Henry George's solution to the economic problems of the capitalist system. He was a theorist on the use of the tax power to redistribute wealth. His primary work is Henry George, *Progress and Poverty* (New York, N.Y.: Doubleday & McClure, 1879). Howe's interpretation of George's ideas is found in Frederic Clemson Howe, *Privilege and Democracy in America* (New York, N.Y.: Charles Scribner's Sons, 1910); Howe, *The City: The Hope of Democracy,* pp. 191–192, 205–207, 225, 237, 249–250, 263, 267. John Dewey ranked George as "one of the great names among the world's social philosophers. . . . No man, no graduate of a higher educational institution has a right to regard himself as an educated man in social thought unless he has some first-hand acquaintance with the theoretical contribution of this great American thinker." John Dewey, "Introduction," *Significant Paragraphs From Henry George's Progress and Poverty* (Garden City, N.Y.: Doubleday, Doran & Company, 1928), pp. 1–2.

40. Howe, *The Confessions of a Reformer,* pp. 95–99, 127,

136, 226. *See also* Warner, *Progressivism in Ohio, 1897–1917*, pp. 87–104; Robert H. Bremner, "The Single Tax Philosophy in Cleveland and Toledo," in "The Civic Revival in Ohio," *American Journal of Economics and Sociology*, vol. 9, no. 3 (April 1950), pp. 369–376; Robert H. Bremner, "Tax Equalization in Cleveland," in "The Civic Revival in Ohio," *American Journal of Economics and Sociology*, vol. 10, no. 3 (April 1951), pp. 301–312.

41. Warner, *Progressivism in Ohio, 1897–1917*, pp. 195, 296. *See also* Lloyd L. Sponholtz, "Progressivism in Microcosm: An Analysis of the Political Forces at work in the Ohio Constitutional Convention of 1912" (Ph.D. dissertation, University of Pittsburgh, 1969).

42. David P. Thelen, *Robert M. La Follette and the Insurgent Spirit* (Boston, Mass.: Little, Brown, 1976), p. 82; George Edwin Mowry, *Theodore Roosevelt and the Progressive Movement* (Madison, Wisc.: The University of Wisconsin Press, 1946), pp. 23, 75–83; Robert M. La Follette, *La Follette's Autobiography* (Madison, Wisc: The Robert M. La Follette Publishing Company, 1913), pp. 532–534, 574–576. *See also* Francis Russell, *The President Makers From Mark Hanna to Joseph P. Kennedy* (Boston, Mass.: Little, Brown, 1976).

43. Howe's integrity as a public man is exemplified in his service as immigration commissioner. He resigned his post after a running battle with Congress and the Department of Justice over deportation policies. Howe analogized federal immigration laws to "fugitive slave laws" and said they were "a disgrace to any country." Frederic Clemson Howe, "The Alien," in Harold Stearns, *Civilization in the United States: An Inquiry by Thirty Americans* (New York, N.Y.: Harcourt, Brace and Company, 1922), pp. 337–350, 348.

44. Baker's reputation as a reformer and liberal was seriously damaged by his activities as secretary of war (Pershing's punitive invasion of Mexico in search of Pancho Villa, the lack of support of prewar pacifist friends such as Herbert S. Bigelow, the harsh treatment of conscientious objectors) and his postwar open shop policies. Baker was termed a Tom Johnson liberal who "turned corporation attorney . . . (and) defended the very forces that he and Johnson had attacked, and died without the regard and often the respect of his closest associates in his reforming days." Oswald Garrison Villard, *Fighting Years: Memoirs of a Liberal Editor* (New York, N.Y.: Harcourt, Brace and Company, 1939), p. 249. Baker and Villard had been outspoken pacifists who worked with Jane Addams and Emily Greene Balch before the war.

45. *See* "Lawrence Turnure Veiller," *Dictionary of American Biography*, supp. six (New York, N.Y.: Charles Scribner's Sons, 1980), pp. 654–655. For a comprehensive treatment of Veiller as a housing reformer, see Roy Lu-bove, *The Progressives and the Slums: Tenement House Reform in New York City, 1890–1917* (Pittsburgh, Pa.: University of Pittsburgh Press, 1962). *See* "Lawson Purdy," *Dictionary of American Biography*, supp. six (New York, N.Y.: Charles Scribner's Sons, 1980), pp. 521–523; "The Reminiscences of Lawson Purdy," Columbia University Oral History Collection. Dr. Frank Goodnow was later president of the Johns Hopkins University. Benjamin Marsh was a vigorous reform publicist throughout his life. *See* Benjamin C. Marsh, *Lobbyist for the People* (Washington, D.C.: Public Affairs Press, 1953). Mary Simkhovitch was an important figure in the development of public housing programs during the New Deal and was a prime mover in the passage of the Wagner-Steagall Act of 1937. Timothy L. McDonnell, *The Wagner Housing Act: A Case Study of the Legislative Process* (Chicago, Ill.: The Loyola University Press, 1957). These and related personalities are profiled extensively in Allen F. Davis, *Spearheads for Reform: The Social Settlements and the Progressive Movement: 1890–1914* (New York, N.Y.: Oxford University Press, 1967).

46. For example, Frederic Clemson Howe, "The Municipal Real Estate Policies of German Cities," *Third National Conference on City Planning* (Boston, Mass.: University Press, 1911), pp. 14–26.

47. *See* "Joseph Fels," *Dictionary of American Biography* 6 (New York, N.Y.: Charles Scribner's Sons, 1930), pp. 314–315; Mary Fels, *Joseph Fels, His Life-Work* (New York, N.Y.: B. W. Huebsch, 1916); Frederic Clemson Howe, "Joseph Fels," *The Survey*, vol. 31, no. 26 (March 28, 1914), pp. 812–813; and Arthur Power Dudden, *Joseph Fels and the Single-Tax Movement* (Philadelphia, Pa.: Temple University Press, 1971). For a comprehensive analysis of the role of the Fels Fund in single tax activities, see the definitive Arthur Nichols Young, *The Single Tax Movement in the United States* (Princeton, N.J.: Princeton University Press, 1916).

48. Fels Fund Commission Circular, "Is It Worth While?" (1908).

49. Young, *The Single Tax Movement in the United States*, p. 218.

50. "Taxation Problems in New York City," *The Survey*, vol. 35, no. 10 (December 4, 1915), p. 231.

51. This group included Richard Hurd, Clarence Kelsey, Louis Bright, and Allan Robinson. National and New York area real estate magazines vigorously opposed these measures, as did the *New York Times*.

52. Young, *The Single Tax Movement in the United States*, p. 222.

53. *Final Report of the Committee on Taxation of the City of New York* (New York, N.Y.: The O'Connell Press, 1916), p. 15.

54. Id. at pp. 32–35.

55. Lubove, *The Progressives and the Slums*, p. 237.

56. Id. at p. 230.

57. The role of Allan Robinson, the major figure in the opposition to Howe, Goodnow, and the tax reformers, requires additional research. In addition to the basic real estate groups, there is considerable activity by city and state politicians (such as Al Smith) and financial institutions involved in land use areas (Metropolitan Life Insurance Company) in these events.

58. Martin J. Schiesl, *The Politics of Efficiency: Municipal Administration and Reform in America, 1800–1920* (Berkeley, Calif.: The University of California Press, 1977), and, particularly, Blake McKelvey, *The Emergence of Metropolitan America, 1915–1966* (New Brunswick, N.J.: Rutgers University Press, 1968).

59. For the functions of city personnel prior to the era of "experts," see Blake McKelvey, *The Urbanization of America: 1860–1915* (New Brunswick, N.J.: Rutgers University Press, 1963) and Mel Scott, *American City Planning Since 1890* (Berkeley, Calif.: University of California Press, 1969).

60. Toll called Veiller a "reformer with an atypical set of views. He was not at first enamored of either zoning or the garden city. . . ." Seymour I. Toll, *Zoned American* (New York, N.Y.: Grossman Publishers, 1969), p. 149.

61. Id. at pp. 140, 149, 172, 187. The documents are *Report of the Heights of Buildings Commission* (1913) and *Report of the Committee on Building Districts and Restrictions* (1916).

62. Toll, *Zoned American*, p. 143.

63. Id. at p. 185, quoting Edward Murray Bassett, *Autobiography* (New York, N.Y.: The Harbor Press, 1939), p. 127.

64. *See* "Edward Murray Bassett," *Dictionary of American Biography*, supp. four (New York, N.Y.: Charles Scribner's Sons, 1974), pp. 55–57, and Bassett, *Autobiography*.

65. Toll, *Zoned American*, pp. 143–146, 167–168, 194–202, 310.

66. Purdy, according to Toll, was smooth enough to reassure real estate interests that zoning would "enhance the value of land and conserve the value of buildings," ensuring the passage of the 1916 zoning law. Toll, *Zoned American*, p. 150. *See also* Stanislaw J. Makielski, *The Politics of Zoning: The New York Experience* (New York, N.Y.: Columbia University Press, 1966), p. 20, and Scott, *American City Planning Since 1890*.

67. A. Dan Tarlock, "Euclid Revisited," *Land Use Law and Zoning Digest*, vol. 34, no. 1 (January, 1982): p. 5.

68. Whitten worked directly with Bassett and Purdy as a highly sophisticated researcher, legislative liaison, and draftsman. His work was comprehensive and significant.

69. Frederick Law Olmsted, Lawson Purdy, and Lawrence Turnure Veiller, "War Housing," *Tenth National Conference on City Planning* (Boston, Mass.: 1918), pp. 88, 107–116, 120, 122–124.

70. Frederic Clemson Howe, *The Land and the Soldier* (New York, N.Y.: Charles Scribner's Sons, 1919); Frederic Clemson Howe, *The High Cost of Living* (New York, N.Y.: Charles Scribner's Sons, 1917).

71. Lawrence Turnure Veiller, "Districting by Municipal Regulation," *Eighth National Conference on City Planning* (New York, N.Y.: 1916), pp. 147–158.

72. Delos Franklin Wilcox, *Municipal Government in Michigan and Ohio* (New York, N.Y.: Columbia University Press, 1896); Robert Harvey Whitten, *Public Administration in Massachusetts: The Relation of Central to Local Activity* (New York, N.Y.: Columbia University Press, 1898). Cooley described Whitten as "an expert in city planning" and commented on Wilcox's "distinguished career as a specialist—always on the side of the public—in franchises and public utilities administration." Charles Horton Cooley, *Sociological Theory and Social Research: Being Selected Papers of Charles Horton Cooley* (New York, N.Y.: H. Holt and Company, 1930), p. 7. Cooley was the son of Judge Thomas McIntyre Cooley, considered by biographers of Justice George Sutherland to be a major influence on his thought.

73. Robert Harvey Whitten, *Valuation of Public Service Corporations*, 2 vols. (New York, N.Y.: The Banks Law Publishing Co., 1912), revised ed. Delos Franklin Wilcox (1928). Whitten earlier had written *Taxation of Corporations in New York, Massachusetts, Pennsylvania, and New Jersey* (Albany, N.Y.: University of the State of New York, 1901); *Supervision of Street Railways in England and Prussia* (Albany, N.Y.: J.B. Lyons Co., 1909); and *Regulation of Public Service Companies in Great Britain* (New York, N.Y.: Public Service Commission for the First District, 1914). Whitten's zoning plans were also published and widely circulated, including *The Atlanta Zone Plan* (Atlanta, Ga.: City Planning Commission, 1922) and *The Columbus Zone Plan* (Columbus, Ohio: City Planning Commission, 1923). He wrote major articles for prestigious law reviews including "Fair Value for Rate Purposes," *Harvard Law Review* vol. 27 no. 5 (March 1914), pp. 419–436. His collaborative works include those with Delos Franklin Wilcox as well as Robert Harvey Whitten and Thomas Adams, *Neighborhoods of Small Homes* (Cambridge, Mass.: Harvard University Press, 1931), volume 3 of the Harvard City Planning Series, and Robert Harvey Whitten, Frank Backus Williams, Alfred Bettman, and Edward Murray Bassett, *Model Laws for Planning Cities, Counties and States* (Cambridge, Mass.: Harvard University Press, 1935), volume 7 of the Harvard City Planning Series. An annotated bibliogra-

phy of Whitten clearly indicates that he was one of the most important theorists and practitioners in planning history.

74. Delos Franklin Wilcox, *Municipal Franchises* 2 vols. (Chicago, Ill.: The University of Chicago Press, 1910).

75. Both men (as well as Edward Webster Bemis) testified regularly before local and national regulatory agencies and in local, state, and federal courts. Rulings such as *The Denver Tramways Case* diminished their importance as "public interest experts" when such testimony was severely restricted in rate cases.

76. Robert Harvey Whitten, "The Zoning of Residence Sections," *Tenth National Conference on City Planning* (Boston, Mass.: 1918), pp. 34–46.

77. *Fourteenth National Conference on City Planning* (Springfield, Mass.: 1922), pp. 200–210. Whitten was also active during the Florida "boom." *See* Scott, *American City Planning Since 1890.* During Whitten's Cleveland period (1917–1921), he produced a major "thorofare" plan (1920) but was hampered in zoning the city by local political opposition. His work for the Boston City Planning Commission (1927–1931) included a major "thorofare" project (1930).

78. Robert Harvey Whitten, "Zoning and Living Conditions," *Thirteenth National Conference on City Planning* (1921), pp. 22–30.

79. Id. at p. 25.

80. He is not to be confused with Morris Black, Frederic C. Howe's political associate and Harvard Law School graduate. Morris A. Black was an active "civitist" (the reformers' term) who led the Civic League after 1905. Black headed the Cleveland City Plan Committee from 1913 and was a "booster" who strongly favored the annexation of Lakewood and Euclid to Cleveland in 1918. He was a fervent proponent of zoning who worked closely with Whitten, although there are elements of anti-Semitism in Whitten's Lakewood zoning efforts at this time. "Jewish elements" are attacked in local publications for advancing apartment projects in the area. The same tactics were used in East Cleveland.

81. *State ex rel. Morris* v. *East Cleveland,* 31 Ohio Dec. 98, 106–120 (1919).

82. *State ex rel. Morris* v. *East Cleveland,* 22 Ohio N.P. (n.s.) 549 (1920).

83. Id. at p. 564.

84. *See* Metzenbaum, *The Law of Zoning,* pp. 105–106, 215; Williams, *The Law of City Planning and Zoning,* pp. 285, 288; Newman F. Baker, *Legal Aspects of Zoning* (Chicago, Ill.: The University of Chicago Press, 1927), pp. 47, 134–135, 157; and Robert Harvey Whitten, "The Zoning of Apart-

ments and Tenement Houses," *American City,* vol. 23, no. 2 (August, 1920): pp. 140–142.

85. File, "D.C. Westenhaver," Cleveland Public Library Reference Room; File, "D.C. Westenhaver," *Cleveland Press* Collection, Cleveland State University Library.

86. Zechariah Chafee, Jr., *Free Speech in the United States* (Cambridge, Mass.: Harvard University Press, 1941), p. 84.

87. Id. at p. 77, citing John Lord O'Brian, "Civil Liberties in War Time," *Rep. N.Y. Bar Association* vol. 42 (1919): pp. 275, 310.

88. Philip Sheldon Foner, *The AFL in the Progressive Era, 1910–1915: History of the Labor Movement in the United States,* vol. 7 (New York, N.Y.: International Publishers, 1980), p. 71. Baldwin-Felts was infamous in labor history due to brutal murders in the West Virginia coal mining strikes and the Colorado "Ludlow Massacre." Martinsburg, West Virginia (Baker's and Westenhaver's birthplace), was the scene of the first major railroad strike in 1877. *See* Robert V. Bruce, *1877: Year of Violence* (Chicago, Ill.: Quadrangle Books, 1970). For contemporary background on labor injunctions, see Felix Frankfurter and Nathan Greene, *The Labor Injunction* (New York, N.Y.: The Macmillan Company, 1930). The Northern District of Ohio was a source of numerous labor injunctions, beginning with Judge Picks in 1893 and continuing throughout Westenhaver's tenure.

89. Richard Theodore Ely, *Outlines of Economics,* fourth ed. (New York, N.Y.: The Macmillan Company, 1924). p. 63.

90. Frank J. Popper, *The Politics of Land-Use Reform* (Madison, Wisc.: The University of Wisconsin Press, 1981), p. 55.

91. Toll, *Zoned American,* p. 29.

92. *See* Carl Frederick Wittke, *We Who Built America* (New York, N.Y.: Prentice-Hall, Inc., 1939); John Higham, *Strangers in the Land: Patterns of American Nativism, 1860–1925* (New Brunswick, N.J.: Rutgers University Press, 1955); Robert D. Parmet, *Labor and Immigration in Industrial America* (Boston, Mass.: Twayne Publishers, 1981); Robert E. Bouwman, "Race Suicide: Some Aspects of Race Paranoia in the Progressive Era" (Ph.D. dissertation, Emory University, 1975). The 1924 law was the result of years of intensive restrictionist lobbying. A 1907 commission appointed by Theodore Roosevelt resulted in the massive 41-volume Dillingham series of immigration studies. For the racist implications of the Dillingham reports, see William Randle, "Racism and Immigration: The Language of Prejudice, 1900–1924" (paper; Carol Wittke and Harvey Wish, eds., Western Reserve University, 1961).

93. *See* William Spencer Bernard, *American Immigration Policy* (New York, N.Y.: Harper, 1950); Maldwyn A. Jones, *American Immigration* (Chicago, Ill.: The University of Chicago Press, 1960); Edward P. Hutchinson, *Legislative History of American Immigration Policy, 1798–1965* (Philadelphia, Pa.: University of Pennsylvania Press, 1981); and Victor Greene, "Immigration Policy," in *Encyclopedia of American Political History,* vol. 2, Jack P. Greene, ed. (New York, N.Y.: Charles Scribner's Sons, 1985), pp. 579–593. Americanization programs originated as public policy during World War I although settlement houses and related philanthropic groups had worked to integrate immigrants into American society from the 1880s. *See* Horace M. Kallen, *Culture and Democracy in the United States* (New York, N.Y.: Boni and Liveright, 1924) and Edward George Hartmann, *The Movement to Americanize the Immigrant* (New York, N.Y.: Columbia University Press, 1948).

94. *See* William M. Tuttle, *Race Riot: Chicago in the Red Summer of 1919* (New York, N.Y.: Atheneum, 1970); John Hope Franklin, *From Slavery to Freedom* (New York, N.Y.: Alfred A. Knopf, 1947); and St. Clair Drake and Horace R. Cayton, *Black Metropolis* (New York, N.Y.: Harcourt, Brace and Company, 1945).

95. *Buchanan* v. *Warley,* 245 U.S. 60 (1917).

96. Jane Jacobs, *The Death and Life of Great American Cities* (New York, N.Y.: Random House, 1961); Derrick A. Bell, *Race, Racism and American Law* (Boston, Mass.: Little, Brown, 1980); Richard Bardolph, *The Civil Rights Record: Black Americans and the Law, 1849–1970* (New York, N.Y.: Crowell, 1970); Kenneth L. Kusmer, *A Ghetto Takes Shape: Black Cleveland, 1870–1930* (Urbana, Ill.: The University of Illinois Press, 1976); and Gilbert Osofsky, *Harlem: The Making of a Ghetto* (New York, N.Y.: Harper & Row, 1966). Exclusionary practices are described in Michael N. Danielson, *The Politics of Exclusion* (New York, N.Y.: Columbia University Press, 1976); Richard F. Babcock, *The Zoning Game, Municipal Practices and Policies* (Madison, Wisc: The University of Wisconsin Press, 1966); Richard F. Babcock, *Exclusionary Zoning: Land Use Regulation and Housing in the 1970s* (New York, N.Y.: Praeger, 1973); and, particularly, Mary Brooks, *Exclusionary Zoning* (Chicago, Ill.: American Society of Planning Officials, 1970).

97. Davidoff and Gold, "Exclusionary Zoning," Yale Rev. L. & Soc. Act. vol. 1 (1970), pp. 57–58.

98. Danielson, *The Politics of Exclusion,* p. 2.

99. Gunnar Myrdal, *An American Dilemma* (New York, N.Y.: Harper & Brothers, 1944); Thomas F. Gossett, *Race, The History of an Idea in America* (New York, N.Y.: Schocken Books, 1963); Thomas G. Dyer, *Theodore Roosevelt and the Idea of Race* (Baton Rouge, La.: Louisiana State University Press, 1980); Ruth Benedict, *Race, Science and Politics* (New York, N.Y.: The Viking Press, 1945).

100. Archibald M. Cox, Mark DeWolfe Howe, and James Russell Wiggins, *Civil Rights, the Constitution and the Courts* (Cambridge, Mass.: Harvard University Press, 1967); Harry Julian Abraham, *Freedom and the Court: Civil Rights and Liberties in the United States* (New York, N.Y.: Oxford University Press, 1972); Jonathan D. Casper, *Lawyers Before the Warren Court: Civil Liberties and Civil Rights 1957–1966* (Urbana, Ill.: University of Illinois Press, 1972); Harrell R. Rodgers, Jr. and Charles S. Bullock, III, *Law and Social Change: Civil Rights Laws and Their Consequences* (New York, N.Y.: McGraw-Hill, 1972).

101. *Ambler Realty Co.* v. *Village of Euclid,* 297 F. 307, 312–313 (N.D. Ohio 1924).

102. Bruno Lasker, "Unwalled Towns," *The Survey,* vol. 43, no. 19 (March 6, 1920): pp. 675–680, 718. Lasker was a European-trained social scientist and publicist who reviewed books and wrote numerous articles and books on public issues. He had worked extensively with Howe, Marsh, and other reformers prior to his social journalism; his progressive analysis continued into the 1940s. *See* Bruno Lasker, *Race Attitudes in Children* (New York, N.Y.: H. Holt and Company, 1929); Bruno Lasker, *Filipino Immigration* (Chicago, Ill.: University of Chicago Press, 1931); Bruno Lasker, *Peoples of Southeast Asia* (New York, N.Y.: Alfred A. Knopf, 1944); "Bruno Lasker," Columbia University Oral History Collection.

103. Charles H. Cheney, "Removing Social Barriers By Zoning," *The Survey,* vol. 44, no. 8 (May 22, 1920): pp. 275–278.

104. Cheney was an architect, engineer, builder, and land developer as well as a prominent city planning and zoning expert. He worked with Harland Bartholomew, Robert H. Whitten, Frederick Law Olmsted, and other planners on large-scale zoning surveys and metropolitan highway planning. *See* Scott, *American City Planning Since 1890,* pp. 209, 228, 233.

105. Bruno Lasker, "The Issue Restated," *The Survey,* vol. 44, no. 8 (May 22, 1920): pp. 278–279.

106. Bruno Lasker, "The Atlanta Zoning Plan," *The Survey,* vol. 48, no. 4 (April 22, 1922): pp. 114–115.

107. *Negro Housing: Report of the Committee on Negro Housing, The President's Conference on Home Building and Home Ownership,* John M. Gries and James Ford, eds. (Washington, D.C.: 1932), p. 46. Gries was the Hoover-appointed expert who headed government agencies responsible for the zoning enabling laws.

108. *Corrigan* v. *Buckley,* 299 F. 899 (1924); 271 U.S. 323 (1926).

109. Robert Harvey Whitten, "Zoning and Living

Conditions," *Thirteenth National Conference on City Planning* (1921), pp. 22–23.

110. Bruno Lasker, "The Atlanta Zoning Plan," *The Survey*, vol. 48, no. 4 (April 22, 1922): p. 114.

111. Id.

112. Id. at pp. 114–115.

113. Robert H. Whitten, "Social Aspect of Zoning," *The Survey*, vol. 48, no. 10 (June 15, 1922): pp. 418–419.

114. Ely, *Outlines of Economics*, p. 67.

115. The Bemis literacy test was first proposed in Edward Webster Bemis, "Restriction of Immigration," *Andover Review*, vol. 9, no. 3 (March, 1888): pp. 251–264; it became law in 1917. Higham, *Strangers in the Land: Patterns of American Nativism, 1860–1925*, p. 42; John Higham, "Origins of Immigration Restriction, 1882–1897: A Social Analysis," *Miss. Vall. Hist. Rev.*, vol. 39, no. 1 (June, 1952): pp. 77–88; Oscar Handlin, *Race and Nationality in American Life* (Boston, Mass.: Little, Brown, 1957).

116. Louis Morton Hacker, *The Triumph of American Capitalism* (New York, N.Y.: Simon and Schuster, 1940); Harold Underwood Faulkner, *The Decline of Laissez-Faire* (New York, N.Y.: Rinehart, 1951); Sidney Fine, *Laissez-Faire and the General-Welfare State* (Ann Arbor, Mich.: University of Michigan Press, 1956); Edward C. Kirkland, *Dream and Thought in the Business Community, 1860–1900* (Ithaca, N.Y.: Cornell University Press, 1956); and Joseph Dorfman, *The Economic Mind in American Civilization*, vols. 1–5 (New York, N.Y.: The Viking Press, 1946–1959) are not far removed from the contemporary critiques of Gabriel Kolko, *The Triumph of Conservatism: A Re-Interpretation of American History, 1900–1916* (New York, N.Y.: Free Press of Glencoe, 1963); Alfred Dupont Chandler, *Strategy and Structure: Chapters in the History of the Industrial Enterprise* (Cambridge, Mass.: M.I.T. Press, 1962); James Weinstein, *The Corporate Ideal in the Liberal State, 1900–1918* (Boston, Mass.: The Beacon Press, 1968) and David W. Noble, *The Progressive Mind, 1890–1917* (Chicago, Ill.: Rand-McNally, 1970).

117. Robert H. Wiebe, *The Search for Order, 1877–1920* (New York, N.Y.: Hill and Wang, 1967), pp. vii–viii. *See also* Robert H. Weibe, *Businessmen and Reform: A Study of the Progressive Movement* (Cambridge, Mass.: Harvard University Press, 1962).

118. Wiebe, *The Search for Order, 1877–1920*, p. viii.

119. Ely's writings (along with those of Selig Perlman and John R. Commons) are regularly cited by revisionist theorists. However, even more powerful thinkers such as J. Allen Smith, Charles Beard, and E.R.A. Seligman are less trendy. Seligman's *The Economic Interpretation of History* (New York, N.Y.: Columbia University Press, 1902) had enormous impact, as did Beard's similar determinist approach. Seligman's later scholarship is exemplified in the huge *Encyclopaedia of the Social Sciences*, vols. 1–15 (New York, N.Y.: The Macmillan Company, 1930–1935). The contemporary emphasis of deconstruction and structuralism in the modern literature community of scholars is typical of the tensional disequilibriums between competing theories in all disciplines. There is a vitality in social thought that often transcends specific eras and dynamically impacts current approaches to problems; the influence of Pigou on Keynes and the derivative legal theories of Ronald Coase are immediate examples. Robert Merton's answer to this dilemma (along with Talcott Parsons) is to develop conceptual frameworks to countervail doctrinal stasis of the more conservative revisionists. *See* Robert King Merton, *Social Theory and Social Structure* (Glencoe, Ill.: Free Press, 1949).

120. Arthur Fisher Bentley, *The Process of Government* (Chicago, Ill.: The University of Chicago Press, 1908). John Dewey wrote with Bentley. See John Dewey and Arthur Fisher Bentley, *Knowing and the Known* (Boston, Mass.: The Beacon Press, 1949); "John Dewey," *Dictionary of American Biography*, supp. five (New York, N.Y.: Charles Scribner's Sons, 1977), pp. 169–173; George Dykhuizen, *The Life and Mind of John Dewey* (Carbondale, Ill.: Southern Illinois University Press, 1973). Dewey's interest in single tax teaching methodologies developed in an experimental community school in Fairhope, Alabama, headed by Marietta Pierce Johnson and is chronicled in Lawrence Arthur Cremin, *The Transformation of the School: Progressivism in American Education, 1876–1957* (New York, N.Y.: Alfred A. Knopf, 1961), pp. 148–152. The most important works of Thorstein Veblen are *Theory of the Leisure Class* (New York, N.Y.: The Macmillan Company, 1899), *The Higher Learning in America* (New York, N.Y.: B.W. Huebsch, 1918), and *The Engineers and the Price System* (New York, N.Y.: B.W. Huebsch, 1921), relevant to this period. For the role of Veblen and the cluster of genius of his era, see Joseph Dorfman, *Thorstein Veblen and His America* (New York, N.Y.: The Viking Press, 1934); "Thorstein Bunde Veblen," *Dictionary of American Biography*, vol. 19 (New York, N.Y.: Charles Scribner's Sons, 1936), pp. 241–244. *See also* "Lewis Henry Morgan," *Dictionary of American Biography*, vol. 13 (New York, N.Y.: Charles Scribner's Sons, 1934), pp. 183–185; Lewis Henry Morgan, *Ancient Society* (New York, N.Y.: H. Holt, 1877). Professor Leslie White was the primary factor in the revival of interest in Morgan's work, particularly his influence on Marxist theory.

121. "Frederick Winslow Taylor," *Dictionary of American Biography*, vol. 18 (New York, N.Y.: Charles Scribner's Sons, 1936), pp. 323–324. *See* Frederick Winslow Taylor,

The Principles of Scientific Management (New York, N.Y.: Harper & Brothers, 1911); Samuel Haber, *Efficiency and Uplift: Scientific Management in the Progressive Era, 1890–1920* (Chicago, Ill.: The University of Chicago Press, 1964). Louis Brandeis, influenced by Josephine C. Goldmark, argued favorably for "efficiency" (a Taylorism) in the *Eastern Rate Cases* (1911). The application of scientific management techniques to public education, a John Dewey idea, is chronicled in the Gary Plan, a major experimental curriculum introduced in 1907. Cremin, *The Transformation of the School,* pp. 153–160.

122. The "American Plan" was headquartered in Cleveland, Ohio, during the 1920s.

123. Daniel R. Beaver, *Newton D. Baker and the American War Effort, 1917–1919* (Lincoln, Neb.: The University of Nebraska Press, 1966), p. 6. *See* Albert K. Steigerwalt, "The National Association of Manufacturers: Organization and Policies, 1895–1914" (Ph.D. dissertation, University of Michigan, 1952). Commons credits scientific management theories for the conflict between the open shop proponents and labor during this period. John Rogers Commons, *Myself* (New York, N.Y.: The Macmillan Company, 1934), p. 178.

124. Baker had long been influenced by Ralph Easley's National Civic Federation, an ostensibly neutral but, in practice, powerful anti-labor group originally funded by Mark Hanna. Wilcox, Bemis, Commons, Ely, and Whitten were among the many academics and experts who worked on NCF projects and were staunch and vocal supporters of Easley's ideas. Commons said he "found in Easley the most illustrious combination that I had known of executive ability, astute insight, and critical acumen. . . ." (Commons, *Myself,* pp. 82–83). Easley attacked Jane Addams, Florence Kelley, Crystal Eastman, Charles Beard, Scott Nearing, and other Progressives as "Reds" after World War I. He was consistently opposed to industrial labor organizations and, after the passage of the Wagner Act, was considered to be one of the most extreme reactionaries fighting the C.I.O. and other new unions. *See* Gordon M. Jensen, "The National Civic Federation: American Business in an Age of Social Change and Social Reform, 1900–1910" (Ph.D. dissertation, Princeton University, 1956) and Marguerite Green, *The National Civic Federation and the American Labor Movement, 1900–1925* (Washington, D.C.: Catholic University of America Press, 1956); *see* Foster Rhea Dulles, *Labor in America: A History* (New York, N.Y.: T.Y. Crowell Co., 1955), p. 94.

Baker was never considered to be a reactionary in spite of his corporation lawyer role in his later career. He was, by any standards, a fine and honest man who never de-

serted his basic ideals. He supported Jane Addams and Florence Kelley when they were named by committees as subversives and publicly repudiated such attacks. He stated that "Miss Jane Addams . . . lends dignity and greatness to any list in which her name appears." *The Survey,* vol. 41, no. 18 (February 1, 1919): p. 649. His statement was an open letter rejecting the printed lists of "Reds" released by the New York State Lusk Committee.

Baker's interest in civil liberties was circumscribed by his role as secretary of war (although he did defend his Ohio single tax friend, Herbert Seeley Bigelow, when he was attacked physically and in print for his pacifist stance; Bigelow was later elected a U.S. Congressman from Cincinnati). Baker, like Alfred Bettman (writing briefs in the *Debs, Schenck,* and *Abrams* cases for the Department of Justice), was still a civil libertarian and continued his activities after the war.

In the late 1920s, convinced of the importance of a complete trial record (for the public as well as the legal profession) of the Sacco-Vanzetti trial, Baker and others financed and published *The Sacco-Vanzetti Case: Transcript of the Record of the Trial of Nicola Sacco and Bartolomeo Vanzetti in the Courts of Massachusetts and the Subsequent Proceedings, 1920–1927,* vols. 1–5 (New York, N.Y.: H. Holt & Company, 1928–1929). Baker was also a "true internationalist and humanitarian" who opposed Adolf Hitler and Nazi theories as early as 1933; he was active in the fight against anti-Semitism and wrote extensively on the subject. Although he was consistently described as an apologist for business interests, he was originally responsible for the selection of the Muscle Shoals power site (a controversial public power project opposed by major utilities companies and Henry Ford): "(S)afety lies alone in the Government's retaining this property . . . rather than passing it . . . to any private corporation whatsoever." Richard Lowitt, *George W. Norris, The Persistence of a Progressive, 1913–1933* (Urbana, Ill.: The University of Illinois Press, 1971), p. 212. Baker's Muscle Shoals decision earned him the bitter hatred of Henry Ford, whose anti-Semitic newspaper, the *Dearborn Independent,* vilified Baker as a "secret Jew." *See* Albert Lee, *Henry Ford and the Jews* (New York, N.Y.: Stein and Day, 1980). Baker, however, was opposed to the TVA and was engaged in a vigorous controversy over that power project with Alfred Bettman, its primary legal supporter and his adversary in *Euclid.*

125. Howard K. Beale, *Are American Teachers Free?* (New York, N.Y.: Charles Scribner's Sons, 1936), p. 546.

126. Henry Steele Commager, *The American Mind* (New Haven, Conn.: Yale University Press, 1950), pp. 340–341.

127. David Morris Potter, *History and American Society,*

ed. D.E. Fehrenbacher (New York, N.Y.: Oxford University Press, 1973), p. 276.

128. Lubove, *The Progressives and the Slums;* Davis, *Spearheads for Reform;* Clarke A. Chambers, *Seedtime of Reform: American Social Service and Social Action, 1918–1933* (Minneapolis, Minn.: University of Minnesota Press, 1963); Paul S. Boyer, *Urban Masses and Moral Order in America 1820–1920* (Cambridge, Mass.: Harvard University Press, 1978).

129. Lubove, *The Progressives and the Slums,* p. 200. *See* Judith Ann Trolander, *Professionalism and Social Change: From the Settlement House Movement to Neighborhood Centers, 1886 to the Present* (New York, N.Y.: Columbia University Press, 1987). While some revisionists have attacked some reformers and settlement house interests as conservatives (as did Frederic C. Howe), others describe them as dedicated social change agents. *See* Staughton Lynd, "Jane Addams and the Radical Impulse," *Commentary,* vol. 32, no. 1 (July, 1961): pp. 54–59; Roy Lubove, *The Professional Altruist: The Emergence of Social Work as a Career, 1880–1930* (Cambridge, Mass.: Harvard University Press, 1965). For the functionalist view of professionalism, see Talcott Parsons, "The Professions and Social Structure," *Social Forces,* vol. 17, no. 4 (May, 1939): pp. 457–467. See also John H. Ehrenreich, *The Altruistic Imagination: A History of Social Work and Social Policy in the United States* (Ithaca, N.Y.: Cornell University Press, 1985), Magali S. Larson, *The Rise of Professionalism* (Berkeley, Calif.: University of California Press, 1977), and Howard M. Vollmer and Donald L. Mills, eds., *Professionalization* (Englewood Cliffs, N.J.: Prentice-Hall, 1966) for overviews ranging from neo-Marxist to conservative.

130. *See* Don S. Kirschner, *The Paradox of Professionalism: Reform and Public Service in Urban America, 1900–1940* (Westport, Conn.: Greenwood Press, 1986); Michael B. Katz, *Poverty and Policy in American History* (New York, N.Y.: Academic Press, 1983); Robert H. Bremner, *From the Depths: The Discovery of Poverty in the United States* (New York, N.Y.: New York University Press, 1956); John F. McClymer, *War and Welfare: Social Engineering in America, 1890–1925* (Westport, Conn.: Greenwood Press, 1980). For the revisionist view of philanthropy as a system of maintaining the power of entrenched interests, see Robert F. Arnove, ed., *Philanthropy and Cultural Imperialism: The Foundations at Home and Abroad* (Boston, Mass.: G.K. Hall, 1980), particularly the chapter "Looking Backwards: How Foundations Formulated Ideology in the Progressive Period," a Gramscian analysis of the Russell Sage and other ameliorative funds.

131. Davis, *Spearheads for Reform,* p. 73. Charles E. Merriam, Jr., the brilliant University of Chicago political scientist-social activist, believed that "grim necessity (drove) city builders of our day to that . . . careful coordination and systematization of diverse factors which we call planning." Charles E. Merriam, "Remarks," *Ninth National Conference on City Planning* (New York, N.Y.: 1917), pp. 280, 284. That he was not naive in his observations and actions is indicated in Charles E. Merriam, *Chicago* (New York, N.Y.: The Macmillan Company, 1929), particularly the chapters "The Big Fix" (pp. 24–69) and "City Builders" (pp. 70–89). Zoning is discussed at pp. 73–80. Merriam was one of the most important political science theorists and a major innovator in policy studies; his students and ideas are pervasive in the field. *See* "Charles E. Merriam, Jr.," *Dictionary of American Biography,* supp. five (New York, N.Y.: Charles Scribner's Sons, 1977), pp. 484–486.

132. Herbert Hoover, as secretary of commerce, created numerous committees and conferences that reflected the new efficiency within the federal government. W.F. Willoughby's Institute for Governmental Research was the prototype for dozens of similar organizations. The Interstate Commerce Commission (first headed by Judge Thomas M. Cooley) and the Department of Agriculture were major sources of the new expertise. General Francis Walker incorporated statistics into the Census Bureau after 1880, a new methodology furthered by Richmond Mayo-Smith, *Science of Statistics,* vols. 1–2 (New York, N.Y.: The Macmillan Company, 1895), expanded by the Bureau of Labor Statistics and, after World I, developed into a specialization by price theorist and business cycle analyst Wesley C. Mitchell.

133. The cooptation of the regulators by the regulated is well demonstrated by the Hoover conferences on radio broadcasting and the housing industries. The Federal Radio Commission of 1927 derived directly from such conferences. *See* Edwin G. Krasnow, Lawrence D. Longley, and Herbert A. Terry, *The Politics of Broadcast Regulation* (New York, N.Y.: St. Martin's Press, 1982). The influence of Dr. John Gries and his zoning group is described in this chapter. While the "capture" theory of regulation is too simplistic to maintain the original concept of Samuel P. Huntington, "The Marasmus of the ICC," *Yale L. Journal,* vol. 61, no. 4 (April, 1952): pp. 467–509, there is little doubt that efficiency is the primary purpose of government regulation. Kenneth J. Meier, *Regulation: Politics, Bureaucracy and Economics* (New York, N.Y.: St. Martin's Press, 1985), pp. 6–7.

134. Of the major players in the *Euclid* case, only James Metzenbaum had not been involved in federal government activities.

135. Commons, *Myself,* p. 65.

136. The networking of Commons, Ely, Bemis, Whitten, and Wilcox during this period is obvious from their writings and professional interactions. An example is John Rogers Commons, "Taxation in Chicago and Philadelphia," *Journal of Political Economy,* vol. 3, no. 4 (September, 1985), pp. 434–460; Robert H. Whitten, "The Assessment of Taxes in Chicago," *Journal of Political Economy,* vol. 5, no. 2 (March, 1897), pp. 175–200; and Edward Webster Bemis, "The Taxation Problem in Chicago," *Bibliotheca Sacra,* vol. 54 (October 1897); p. 746. Bemis worked with Wilcox and Whitten on rate cases when he was a member of the Advisory Board of the Valuation Committee of the Interstate Commerce Commission from 1913–1923.

137. "Delos Franklin Wilcox," *Dictionary of American Biography,* vol. 20 (New York, N.Y.: Charles Scribner's Sons, 1936), pp. 202–203.

138. "Richard Theodore Ely," *Dictionary of American Biography* supp. three (New York, N.Y.: Charles Scribner's Sons, 1973), pp. 248–251; Richard Theodore Ely, *Ground Under Our Feet: An Autobiography* (New York, N.Y.: The Macmillan Company, 1938); Benjamin G. Rader, *The Academic Mind and Reform* (Lexington, Ky.: University of Kentucky Press, 1966). Ely's books were great popular and academic successes. His first major textbook, Richard Theodore Ely, *An Introduction to Political Economy* (Chautauqua, N.Y.: Chautauqua Press, 1889) sold more than 200,000 copies.

139. Ely projected an anti-single tax book (F.B. Garver, *The Single Tax*) as part of his Macmillan series for the National Association of Real Estate Boards' courses. Ely's antipathy to the single tax is reflected in most of his textbooks; *see* Richard Theodore Ely, *Property and Contract in their Relations to the Distribution of Wealth,* vols. 1–2 (New York, N.Y.: The Macmillan Company, 1914).

140. This was known by several names, among them the Institute for Economic Research and the Institute for Research in Land Economics and Public Utilities. Extensive research and publications resulted from Ely's self-aggrandizing but productive entities. *See* Rader, *The Academic Mind and Reform,* pp. 196, 204–215.

141. Ely, *Ground Under Our Feet,* p. 243; Robert L. Utlaut, "The Role of the Chautauqua Movement in the Shaping of Progressive Thought in America at the End of the Nineteenth Century" (Ph.D. dissertation, University of Minnesota, 1972).

142. Ely, *Ground Under Our Feet,* p. 243.

143. Id. at p. 244. The genesis of these and other Ely-developed courses is described in H.U. Nelson, "The Objectives and Content of Real Estate Courses," in *General Real Estate Topics: Proceedings of General Sessions and Special Conferences at Eighteenth Annual Convention,* vol. 1 (1925), pp. 195–211.

144. Williams, *The Law of City Planning and Zoning,* was edited by Ely to be used in conjunction with Frederick M. Babcock, *The Appraisal of Real Estate* (New York, N.Y.: The Macmillan Company, 1924). Nelson was the research director of the YMCA schools and his curriculum concepts derived directly from the Chautauqua movement, agricultural extension courses of the land grant colleges and universities (especially the programs of the University of Wisconsin under President Charles Van Hise), and the evening school courses originated at the Johns Hopkins University in the 1880s. Such courses and programs were, of course, an integral part of the settlement house movement.

145. Pearl Janet Davies, *Real Estate in American History* (Washington, D.C.: Public Affairs Press, 1958); Ernest McKinley Fisher, *Principles of Real Estate* (New York, N.Y.: The Macmillan Company, 1925); Everett C. Hughes, "Study of a Secular Institution: The Chicago Real Estate Board" (Ph.D. dissertation, The University of Chicago, 1928); Marc Allen Weiss, *The Rise of the Community Builders: The American Real Estate Industry and Urban Land Planning* (New York, N.Y.: Columbia University Press, 1987).

146. Stanley L. McMichael and Robert F. Bingham, *City Growth and Values* (Cleveland, Ohio: The Stanley McMichael Publishing Organization, 1923), was by Clevelanders who worked closely with Morris Black, Robert Whitten, and others in the development of zoning ordinances for the city. McMichael's treatises were nationally distributed; he was an important person in the transmission of practical information to the real estate industry. Harlean James, *Land Planning in the United States for the City, State and Nation* (New York, N.Y.: The Macmillan Company, 1926) was the ninth volume in the National Association of Real Estate Boards' series of texts under Richard T. Ely's direction.

147. Ely, *Ground Under Our Feet,* p. 264.

148. Rader, *The Academic Mind and Reform,* p. 204.

149. Ferdinand Lundberg, *America's Sixty Families* (New York, N.Y.: The Vanguard Press, 1937), p. 281. Rader, *The Academic Mind and Reform,* pp. 208–213. Aylesworth was a close Baker associate from the time he was an executive with the Utah Power and Light Company; the friendship continued during the Cleveland NELA years.

150. The historical implications of the networking of zoning experts, the real estate industry, academicians, and bureaucrats are obvious. It may be that the interactions and linkages are integral and necessary for the process to function optimally. Intensive study of these networks can expand understanding of the complexities

of the regulatory systems. *See* Meier, *Regulation: Politics, Bureaucracy, and Economics,* pp. 9–36; Harold D. Lasswell, *Politics: Who Gets What, When, How?* (New York, N.Y.: McGraw-Hill Book Co., Inc., 1936); Bentley, *The Process of Government.*

151. Ernest Victor Hollis, *Philanthropic Foundations and Higher Education* (New York, N.Y.: Columbia University Press, 1938), pp. 303–306.

152. Richard Hofstadter and Walter P. Metzger, *The Development of Academic Freedom in the United States* (New York, N.Y.: Columbia University Press, 1955), p. 419.

153. Mrs. Sage's philanthropies were the most important private funding source for social services during this period. An example of the excellent work done under the aegis of the Russell Sage Foundation was the huge *Pittsburgh Survey* done by Paul Kellogg, Crystal Eastman, and others; the survey derived from a journalistic venture of the *Charities and Commons* (later *The Survey* magazine), and was funded by Mrs. Sage. The Foundation set up the Department of Surveys and Exhibitions in 1912; from 1907–1928 more than 2,700 surveys were taken, based largely on the new methods of applied social science research. Jean M. Converse, "The Reformist Ancestor of Policy: The Social Survey," in *Survey Research in the United States: Roots and Emergence 1890–1960* (Berkeley, Calif.: University of California Press, 1987), pp. 11–53.

154. "Robert Weeks DeForest," *Dictionary of American Biography* supp. one (New York, N.Y.: Charles Scribner's Sons, 1944), pp. 236–237.

155. A countervailing view is Arnove, *Philanthropy and Cultural Imperialism.*

156. Arnold M. Paul, *Conservative Crisis and the Rule of Law: Attitudes of Bar and Bench, 1887–1895* (Ithaca, N.Y.: Cornell University Press, 1960); Barbara C. Steidle, "Conservative Progressives: A Study of the Attitudes and Role of Bar and Bench, 1905–1912" (Ph.D. dissertation, Rutgers University, 1969); Frank J. Goodnow, *Social Reform and the Constitution* (New York, N.Y.: The Macmillan Company, 1911).

157. Kelley, like Crystal Eastman and a number of feminists, was a lawyer. Mrs. Kelley had translated the works of Freidrich Engels and was a tireless, dedicated, dynamic, and "Impatient Crusader." She was a life-long friend of Newton D. Baker but disagreed with him often after World War I; however, he was the speaker at her funeral. His comment "Everyone was brave" when she (Kelley) walked into the room has been permanently recorded in William L. O'Neill, *Everyone Was Brave: The Rise and Fall of Feminism in America* (Chicago, Ill.: Quadrangle Books, 1969). *See* Josephine Clara Goldmark, *Impatient Crusader* (Urbana, Ill.: The University of Illinois Press, 1953).

158. Goldmark was a multi–faceted reformer, a writer, a researcher, activist, leader, and educator. Josephine C. Goldmark, *Fatigue and Efficiency: A Study in Industry* (New York, N.Y.: Charities Publication Committee, 1912) reflects her interest in Frederick W. Taylor's scientific management theories. The book includes a number of important briefs researched by Goldmark.

159. *City of New York* v. *Chelsea Jute Mills,* 43 Misc. 266 (1904); Goldmark, *Fatigue and Efficiency,* p. 250.

160. 208 U.S. 412 (1908).

161. 243 U.S. 426 (1917).

162. 261 U.S. 525 (1923).

163. 198 U.S. 45 (1905); 261 U.S. 525, 548 (1923).

164. Metzenbaum, *The Law of Zoning,* pp. 106–107.

165. *See* Zane L. Miller, *Boss Cox's Cincinnati: Urban Politics in the Progressive Era* (New York, N.Y.: Oxford University Press, 1968); Warner, *Progressivism in Ohio 1897–1917;* Joseph Lincoln Steffens, "Ohio: A Tale of Two Cities," *McClure's Magazine,* vol. 25 (July, 1905), pp. 293–311; Joseph Lincoln Steffens, *The Shame of the Cities* (New York, N.Y.: McClure, Phillips & Co., 1904). Cincinnati housing conditions are described by Veiller and DeForest: "(A)fter New York and Boston, (Cincinnati) has the worst housing conditions of any city in America. . . ." Robert Weeks DeForest and Lawrence Turnure Veiller, eds., *The Tenement House Problem,* vol. 1 (New York, N.Y.: The Macmillan Company, 1903), p. 144.

166. Alfred Bettman's writings have been collected in Bettman, *City and Regional Planning Papers.* There is need for a comprehensive bibliography of his equally important civil liberties materials, including the Department of Justice briefs and his series of assaults on the criminal syndicalism laws in Ohio and Michigan.

167. Scott, *American City Planning Since 1890,* pp. 193–195, 237–240, 242–248.

168. Toll, *Zoned American,* pp. 201–202; Metzenbaum, *The Law of Zoning,* p. 135.

169. "Alfred Bettman," *Dictionary of American Biography* supp. three (New York, N.Y.: Charles Scribner's Sons, 1973), pp. 65–67.

170. Carl Resek, ed., *The Progressives* (Indianapolis, Ind.: Bobbs-Merrill, 1967), p. 361. Roger Baldwin, a pacifist and one of the founders of the American Civil Liberties Union, credits Bettman and John Lord O'Brian as "committed" and "real friend(s)" of civil liberties. For additional comments on Bettman as a civil libertarian, see Stanley Coben, *A. Mitchell Palmer: Politician* (New York, N.Y.: Columbia University Press, 1963), pp. 201–202, 207–208, 242; Chafee, *Free Speech in the United States,* pp. 67,

147, n. 341, 442, 470–471, and n. 472. O'Brian's references in Chafee (including the identification of their joint actions) are at id., pp. 36–37, 64–69, 77, 99, 101–102, n. 198, 283, 292, 443–444, n. 470, 471. The resistance by Bettman and other lawyers to the excesses of the Palmer "Red Scare" was an extraordinary event in American legal history. *See* William Preston, Jr., *Aliens and Dissenters: Federal Suppression of Radicals, 1903–1933* (Cambridge, Mass.: Harvard University Press, 1963); Harry N. Scheiber, *The Wilson Administration and Civil Liberties, 1917–1921* (Ithaca, N.Y.: Cornell University Press, 1960). For a complete report by former government lawyers and academic critics, see National Popular Government League, *Report Upon the Illegal Practices of the United States Department of Justice* (1920).

171. The Cleveland Foundation did landmark studies in education, health, police, public administration, and related areas during this period. Like the Russell Sage Foundation, the Cleveland Foundation spent millions of dollars in annual income to study and combat social problems, especially in the cities.

172. Bettman, *City and Regional Planning Papers*, pp. xviii–xix.

173. Id. at p. xvii.

174. Id. at p. xvii.

175. 112 O.S. 628 (1925). Alfred Bettman, "The Present State of Court Decisions on Zoning," *City Planning*, vol. 2, no. 1 (January, 1926): pp. 24–34. Bettman and Baker had submitted *amicus curiae* briefs in this case; Bettman's prevailed and zoning was decided constitutional by the Ohio Supreme Court. Judge Florence Allen's decision was nationally reported and cited in subsequent cases in other states. Judge Allen was one of the first women to reach high appellate court levels; her early career had been greatly aided by Newton D. Baker.

176. Alfred Bettman, "The Present State of Court Decisions on Zoning," p. 26. *See also* Alfred Bettman, "Constitutionality of Zoning," *Harv. L. Rev.*, vol. 37, no. 7 (May, 1924): pp. 834–859.

177. Edward Murray Bassett, "Constitutional Limitations on City Planning Powers," *Ninth National Conference on City Planning* (New York, N.Y.: 1917), pp. 199–214; Alfred Bettman, "Discussion," id. at pp. 214, 218.

178. Alfred Bettman, "How to Acquire Parks and Other Open Spaces," *Planning Problems of Town, City, and Region: Nineteenth National Conference on City Planning* (Philadelphia, Pa.: Wm. P. Fells Co., 1927), pp. 181–192, 183.

179. *City Planning*, vol. 2, no. 1 (January 1926): p. 24.

180. Id. at p. 24.

181. Id. at p. 24.

182. Id. at p. 25.

183. *Village of Euclid* v. *Ambler Realty Co.*, 272 U.S. 365 (1926).

184. Robert C. Ellickson and A. Dan Tarlock, *Land Use Controls: Cases and Materials* (Boston, Mass.: Little, Brown, 1981), pp. 50–51.

185. Joel Francis Paschal, *Mr. Justice Sutherland: A Man Against the State* (Princeton, N.J.: Princeton University Press, 1951), pp. 126–127, 166, 242–243.

186. *Village of Euclid* v. *Ambler Realty Co.*, 272 U.S. 365, 387 (1926).

187. Patrick J. Rohan, *Zoning and Land Use Controls*, vol. 1 (New York, N.Y.: Matthew Bender, 1965), p. 82.

188. Charles M. Haar, *Land Use Planning: A Casebook on the Use, Misuse, and Re-Use of Urban Land* (Boston, Mass.: Little, Brown, 1977), pp. 392–393. The aesthetics of the Progressive era reflected social and economic as well as artistic ideologies. The development of the Cleveland Group Plan is a classic example of the role of aesthetics in planning, influenced greatly by Daniel Burnham and Frederick Law Olmsted. *See* Holly M. Rarick, *Progressive Vision: The Planning of Downtown Cleveland, 1903–1930* (Cleveland, Ohio: Cleveland Museum of Art, 1986). The early influence of Frederic C. Howe and his friends is described in Howe, *The Confessions of a Reformer*, pp. 80–82 and Howe, *The City: The Hope of Democracy*, pp. 243–245. Abram Garfield, the architect brother of Harry A. and James R. Garfield, was a prime mover in this concept. The Federal Building (where Westenhaver wrote his original *Euclid* opinion) was the first to be completed (1911). The original Gateway design was destroyed by the Van Sweringen brothers' Terminal Tower complex, which moved the railroad hub to the Public Square area to serve as the downtown anchor of their multi-billion-dollar Shaker Heights suburban development and its associated urban rapid transit empire. Newton D. Baker was attacked by reformers for his role in legally defending the site changes.

189. *Pennsylvania Coal Co.* v. *Mahon*, 260 U.S. 393, 415 (1922).

190. Ernst Freund, *The Police Power* (Chicago, Ill.: Callaghan and Company, 1904), pp. 546–547; Ellickson and Tarlock, *Land Use Controls*, p. 136. *See* "Ernst Freund," *Dictionary of American Biography* supp. one (New York, N.Y.: Charles Scribner's Sons, 1944), pp. 323–324.

191. Tarlock, "Euclid Revisited," pp. 5, 7.

192. 219 U.S. 104, 110 (1911).

193. Quoted in Samuel J. Konefsky, *The Legacy of Holmes and Brandeis* (New York, N.Y.: The Macmillan Company, 1956), p. 34.

194. 219 U.S. 104, 111 (1911).

195. 260 U.S. 393, 415 (1922).

196. Harlan B. Phillips, *Felix Frankfurter Reminisces* (New York, N.Y.: Reynal, 1960), pp. 103–104, 293.

197. 261 U.S. 525, 546 (1923).

198. Paschal, *Mr. Justice Sutherland. See* "George Sutherland," *Dictionary of American Biography* supp. three (New York, N.Y.: Charles Scribner's Sons, 1973), pp. 753–756; David Burner, "George Sutherland," in *The Justices of the United States Supreme Court, 1789–1969,* vol. 3, Leon Friedman and Fred L. Israel, eds. (New York, N.Y.: Chelsea House/Bowker, 1969), pp. 2133–2143.

199. Alpheus Thomas Mason, "The Conservative World of Mr. Justice Sutherland," *American Political Science Review,* vol. 32, no. 3 (June 1938): pp. 443–477.

200. Paschal, *Mr. Justice Sutherland,* pp. 3–114.

201. The long and involved legal history of the Fourteenth Amendment, its initial meaning (based on the ideas, philosophies, and political immediacies of Charles Sumner, Thaddeus Stevens, and their followers), the later "conspiracy" theory of Roscoe Conkling, and the numerous interpretations and revisionary analyses (Bickel, Corwin, Cushman, Ely, Mason, Boudin, Tribe, Warren, Twiss, McCloskey, and others) are too complex for this writing. However, it seems clear that, whatever the original meaning of the document, it has served all segments of the ideological spectrum in American legal thought and practice. Edward Samuel Corwin, *The Twilight of the Supreme Court* (New Haven, Conn.: Yale University Press, 1934); Lawrence M. Friedman, *A History of American Law* (New York, N.Y.: Simon & Schuster, 1973), pp. 299–302.

202. 134 U.S. 418 (1890); 134 U.S. 467 (1890).

203. 198 U.S. 45 (1905).

204. "Freedom of contract" doctrine was based solidly on the interpolation of laissez-faire theories into the Fourteenth Amendment's due process and equal protection clauses. The flexibility of such analysis permitted clausal limitations of progressive social legislation. *See* Robert E. Cushman, "The Social and Economic Interpretation of the Fourteenth Amendment," *Mich. L. Rev.,* vol. 20, no. 7 (May 1922): pp. 737–744; Benjamin R. Twiss, *Lawyers and the Constitution: How Laissez-Faire Came to the Supreme Court* (Princeton, N.J.: Princeton University Press, 1942); Charles Warren, *The Supreme Court in United States History,* vols. 1–3 (Boston, Mass.: Little, Brown, 1922).

205. 261 U.S. 525, 548 (1923).

206. *Children's Hospital* v. *Adkins,* 284 F. 613, 622 (1922).

207. *District of Columbia Wage Cases, Brief for Appellants* (1923).

208. 261 U.S. 525, 560 (1923).

209. The quality of the Goldmark-Kelley-National Consumers' League briefs was far superior to most of the later "Brandeis briefs." These became a mechanical technique rather than exemplifying the original sociological jurisprudence of Brandeis, Pound, and Frankfurter. The briefs in *Brown* v. *Board of Education,* 347 U.S. 483 (1954), and *Wisconsin* v. *Yoder,* 406 U.S. 205 (1972), are outstanding exceptions to this trend of hack briefing.

210. 262 U.S. 390, 412 (1923) (Holmes, J. dissenting; Sutherland, J. dissenting).

211. The expansion of Justice McReynolds's language in *Meyer* has been the basis for significant contemporary decisions; for example, *Roe* v. *Wade,* 410 U.S. 113 (1973); *Loving* v. *Virginia,* 388 U.S. 1 (1967); *Griswold* v. *Connecticut,* 381 U.S. 479 (1965); and similar "fundamental rights" cases.

212. 262 U.S. 390, 399 (1923).

213. Paschal, *Mr. Justice Sutherland,* p. 9.

214. "The Spirit of Brigham Young University," reprinted in *The Messenger,* vol. 18, no. 10 and cited in Paschal, *Mr. Justice Sutherland,* pp. 4–6, 235–236.

215. Id. at pp. 49–53, 62–66, 73–81, 93–95, 108–111.

216. "Thomas McIntyre Cooley," *Dictionary of American Biography,* vol. 4 (New York, N.Y.: Charles Scribner's Sons, 1930), pp. 392–393; G. Edward White, *The American Judicial Tradition: Profiles of Leading American Judges* (New York, N.Y.: Oxford University Press, 1976), pp. 113, 115–122; Alan Robert Jones, "The Constitutional Conservatism of Thomas M. Cooley: A Study in the History of Ideas" (Ph.D. dissertation, University of Michigan, 1960).

217. "James Valentine Campbell," *Dictionary of American Biography,* vol. 3 (New York, N.Y.: Charles Scribner's Sons, 1929), pp. 455–456.

218. Thomas McIntyre Cooley, *Constitutional Limitations,* second ed. (Boston, Mass.: Little, Brown, 1871); Clyde Edward Jacobs, *Law Writers and the Courts: The Influence of Thomas M. Cooley, Christopher G. Tiedeman, and John F. Dillon Upon American Constitutional Law* (Berkeley, Calif.: University of California Press, 1954).

219. Charles Horton Cooley, *Human Nature and the Social Order* (New York, N.Y.: Scribner's, 1902); Charles Horton Cooley, *Social Organization* (New York, N.Y.: Scribner's, 1909); Charles Horton Cooley, *Social Process* (New York, N.Y.: Charles Scribner's Sons, 1918).

220. Edward Clarence Jandy, *Charles Horton Cooley: His Life and His Social Theory* (New York, N.Y.: The Dryden Press, 1942).

221. Paschal, *Mr. Justice Sutherland;* Jay Benson Saks, "Mr. Justice Sutherland: A Study in the Nature of the Judicial Process" (Ph.D. dissertation, The Johns Hopkins University, 1940); Alan Jones, "Thomas M. Cooley and 'Laissez-Faire Constitutionalism': A Reconsideration,"

Journal of American History, vol. 53, no. 4 (March 1967): pp. 751–771.

222. This stinging defeat, a personal loss of power and prestige for George Sutherland, was followed by a dramatic series of Wilson legislative victories, emphasizing the values of his "New Freedoms" and exacerbating the political wounds of the defeated conservatives.

223. The Justice was an avid reader of journals and scholary books. His letters reflect an intense interest in current events and political debates. Paschal, *Mr. Justice Sutherland.*

224. Herbert Spencer, *The Man Against the State,* Truxton Beale, ed. (New York, N.Y.: M. Kennerley, 1916), p. ix.

225. Id. at pp. ix-x.

226. "William Graham Sumner," *Dictionary of American Biography,* vol. 18 (New York, N.Y.: Charles Scribner's Sons, 1936), pp. 217–219. Sumnerology caused an academic debate similar to the Darwin-Spencer controversies. Edward Youmans, through his Appleton publishing lists and popular magazines, was again important in spreading Sumner's ideas. Youmans also published Henry George, Edward Bellamy, and other social thinkers whose ideas were controversial. *See* Richard Hofstadter, *Social Darwinism in American Thought, 1860–1915* (Philadelphia, Pa.: University of Pennsylvania Press, 1945) for a thorough discussion of Darwin, Spencer, and Sumner and their impact on American society. *See also* Richard Hofstadter, *The Age of Reform: From Bryan to F.D.R.* (New York, N.Y.: Random House, 1955); Fine, *Laissez-Faire and the General-Welfare State;* Raymond Jackson Wilson, *Darwinism and the American Intellectual* (Homewood, Ill.: The Dorsey Press, 1967); Robert G. McCloskey, *American Conservatism in the Age of Enterprise: A Study of William Graham Sumner, Stephen J. Field and Andrew Carnegie* (Cambridge, Mass.: Harvard University Press, 1951). For a specialized study of Sumner as a "progressive," see Bruce E. Curtis, "The Middle Class Progressivism of William Graham Sumner" (Ph.D. dissertation, University of Iowa, 1964).

227. William Graham Sumner, "The Absurd Attempt to Make the World Over," in *War and Other Essays,* Arthur Keller, ed. (New Haven, Conn.: Yale University Press, 1913), pp. 195–210.

228. The success of his Harding campaign management was a powerful affirmation of Sutherland's conservative ideology, which he had maintained for most of his professional and political life. The Paschal theory of the combined influences of Maeser, Spencer, and Cooley is too simplistic to explain the genesis of Sutherland's thought and answer the questions posed by his more complex behavior as a Justice of the United States Supreme Court.

229. "The Minimum Wage-What Next?," *The Survey,* vol. 50, no. 4 (May 15, 1923): pp. 215–222, 256–263. Kelley, Mary Anderson, the Goldmark sisters, the Abbotts, and others had a vested interest in the legislative process as an instrument of social change; they resisted Alice Paul and the Woman's party protagonists. *See* Lois Scharf and Joan M. Jensen, eds., *Decades of Discontent: The Women's Movement, 1920–1940* (Westport, Conn.: Greenwood Press, 1983); Christine A. Lunardini, *From Equal Suffrage to Equal Rights: Alice Paul and the National Woman's Party, 1912–1928* (New York, N.Y.: New York University Press, 1986).

230. Alexander M. Bickel and Benno C. Schmidt, Jr., *The Judiciary and Responsible Government 1910–1921: History of the Supreme Court of the United States,* vol. 9 (New York, N.Y.: The Macmillan Company, 1984), p. 486. Bickel and Schmidt, referring to the work of Sutherland on employers' liability and workmen's compensation, write, "This was the newer 'progressiveness' to which even as conservative a politician as Senator Sutherland adhered. . . ." Id. at p. 210. Other commentators have been less grudging in their remarks. *See* Jane J.M. De Long, "Brandeis and Sutherland: Apostles of Individualism" (Ph.D. dissertation, Harvard University, 1971).

231. George P. West, "Andrew Furuseth and the Radicals," *The Survey,* vol. 47, no. 6 (November 5, 1921): pp. 207–209.

232. Paschal, *Mr. Justice Sutherland,* pp. 97–98.

233. Id. at p. 36.

234. Id. at pp. 61–62, 96, 116.

235. Id. at p. 90.

236. Id. at p. 76.

237. *Grosjean* v. *American Press Co.,* 297 U.S. 233 (1936); Laurence H. Tribe, *God Save This Honorable Court* (New York, N.Y.: Random House, 1985), pp. 35–36.

238. Alfred McCormack, *Colum. L. Rev.,* vol. 46, no. 5 (September 1946): pp. 710–718.

239. Burner, "George Sutherland," in *The Justices of the Supreme Court,* p. 2133.

240. Justice Stone held similar beliefs; his comments are, as a result, in context favorable to Sutherland. However, Stone was a far more important Justice.

241. Fred Rodell, *Nine Men: A Political History of the Supreme Court from 1790–1955* (New York, N.Y.: Random House, 1955), p. 219.

242. Louis B. Boudin, "Justice Holmes and his World," *Lawyers Guild Rev.,* vol. 3, no. 4 (1943); pp. 26–27. Boudin refers to McReynolds, Sutherland, and Butler as "the true 'realists' on the Supreme Court. . . ." Id. at p. 27. *See* Louis B. Boudin, *Government By Judiciary,* vol. 2 (New York, N.Y.: W. Godwin, Inc., 1932), pp. 480–484, 491–498 for

perceptive comments on Sutherland's opinions of this period.

243. Robert G. McCloskey, *The Modern Supreme Court* (Cambridge, Mass.: Harvard University Press, 1972), pp. 132, 184.

244. *Powell* v. *Alabama,* 287 U.S. 45 (1932). Frankfurter was otherwise almost totally opposed to Sutherland's ideas, which usually contravened his own progressive and sociological jurisprudence concepts. *See* Bickel and Schmidt, *The Judiciary and Responsible Government,* pp. 18, 24, 200–201, 260, 599–601 for comments on Frankfurter's ideas.

245. Quoted in Alpheus Thomas Mason, *William Howard Taft: Chief Justice* (New York, N.Y.: Simon and Schuster, 1965), p. 165.

246. Drew Pearson and Robert S. Allen, *The Nine Old Men* (Garden City, N.Y.: Doubleday, Doran & Company, Inc., 1937), p. 198.

247. Page Smith, *America Enters the World,* p. 1029.

248. Id. at p. 1030.

249. George, *Significant Paragraphs from Henry George's Progress and Poverty,* published through the support of the Robert Schalkenbach Foundation, a fund set up to keep the writings of Henry George perpetually in print. The Foundation was headed in the 1930s by Lawson Purdy, still waiting for that wonderful idea that was "too good to be true at this time."

II

Zoning Applied (Misapplied): An Experiment in Social and Physical Order

For defenders and critics of Euclidean zoning, its 60-year history is grist for their respective mills. Zealous critics must nevertheless agree that its near-universal application indicates a substantial degree of public acceptance. At the same time, ardent supporters must acknowledge that zoning can be and has been misused to achieve ends never envisioned by some of its creators and judicial approvers.

Zoning's traditional separation of uses into distinct districts, its control over building heights and shapes, and its regulation of density all influence the social and physical environments in which we live. Segregating single–family homes from apartment buildings does more than separate different building types—it frequently means government-guaranteed homogeneous income, class, and racial neighborhoods. Requiring a one-acre lot for a home means significant consumption of open space by a relatively small number of people. Allowing substantial building footprints and generous floor area ratios ensures the development of skyscrapers in our downtowns.

The following chapters review the record of zoning since its approval in the *Euclid* decision.

Chapter 3 is Joe R. Feagin's "Arenas of Conflict: Zoning and Land Use Reform in Critical Political-Economic Perspective," in which Feagin rejects a traditional narrow analysis of zoning for a broader indictment reflecting his view of capitalism's shortcomings. For him, zoning's history has been written by divergent class and race interests and by differing conceptions of property values ("exchange" versus "use" value). He urges a redefinition of property rights that would make land widely available to all citizens and distribute such rights through a process of maximum participation (life-space, not commodity-space).

In his loosely empirical Chapter 4, "Expulsive Zoning: The Inequitable Legacy of *Euclid*," Yale Rabin unearths a disturbing zoning strategy, different from exclusionary zoning, but used with equal effectiveness to perpetuate class and racial discrimination. He presents informal case studies describing how certain communities have zoned viable black and poor neighborhoods for disruptive commercial and industrial uses, while existing middle-class white neighborhoods are zoned against such intrusions. As a first step toward explor-

71

ing this misuse, Rabin's chapter makes clear the need for further rigorous research.

In Chapter 5, "Planning and Zoning," Peter Abeles relies on his extensive experience as an urban planner and developer to analyze the technique's strengths and weaknesses. Portraying the changes in the demographic, economic, social, and physical environments of America's cities, suburbs, and rural areas over the past century, Abeles sees zoning principally as a tool for suburban communities. He too cites the misuse of zoning, describing the application of exclusionary zoning practices by some New Jersey communities documented by the now–famous *Mount Laurel* series of cases.

Earl Murphy and Michael Kwartler focus on *Euclid's* legacy for our natural and physical environments. In Chapter 6, "*Euclid* and the Environment," Murphy opines that Justice Sutherland's use of the word "environment" in his *Euclid* opinion surely would encompass today's environmental concerns. The concern expressed in *Euclid* about industrial incursion into residential neighborhoods includes notions of potential environmental degradation caused by industrial activities. Whether properly denominated as zoning or environmental controls, Murphy argues, the scope of the police power adumbrated in *Euclid* is broad enough to cover regulations preserving open space, clean air, and clean water. In Chapter 7, "Legislating Aesthetics: The Role of Zoning in Designing Cities," Kwartler shows how zoning's originally neutral *intent* vis-a-vis building design had anything but a neutral *effect.* The "wedding cake" design of buildings produced under New York City's 1916 ordinance, with its setbacks based upon street widths, would be replaced by the glass and steel towers encouraged by the city's 1961 comprehensive zoning amendment. Kwartler urges a zoning that stresses urban design rather than building design, administered as a matter of right through performance-based criteria. His is a clarion call to architects and urban planners for full involvement in the drafting of ordinance language.

3

Arenas of Conflict: Zoning and Land Use Reform in Critical Political-Economic Perspective

Joe R. Feagin

An adequate understanding of zoning and related land use regulation issues requires an assessment of their historical and political-economic contexts. Many land use controversies can be viewed as part of a century-long struggle in U.S. society over conflicting land use interests: "exchange value" interests versus "use value" interests. Pursuit of divergent land use goals is imbedded in a capitalistic system with distinctive historical features. That political-economic system has unrestrained growth as its internal combustion engine. Individual and corporate investors aggressively pursue their capital investments across rural and urban space, across national and international space, and even into outer space.

Land is a unique type of commodity in this expansive investment process. In terms of the new urban political economy perspective discussed in this chapter, "exchange value" is often the dominant value in land-related decisions under capitalism. This can be seen in the investment actions of developers and speculators seeking to profit from the sale of and construction on land itself. But exchange-value decisions often come into conflict with use value concerns emphasizing the utility rather than profitability of space. Such use-value concerns, for example, motivate the decisions and actions of neighborhood residents seeking to keep large-scale urban development projects from intruding on their "home space." Often reflecting use-value concerns, home owner-supported zoning and similar land use controls throw up barriers to the unrestrained expansion of capitalistic investment across urban space. Historically, much pressure for such land use regulation has come from worker-home owners concerned with protecting family spaces and neighborhoods against economic, social, and racial incursions. Their commitment to the land is primarily to its use value as a place to live and raise a family. Other pressures for land use controls have stemmed from local capitalists, such as New

73

York merchants concerned with protecting certain Manhattan spaces for profitable marketing uses. In this case the commitment to the land is primarily to its use value as a place to make a manufacturing or commercial profit. Thus we have three basic interests in land: (1) in the exchange value of the land itself; (2) in the use value of the land for living, family, and neighborhood; and (3) in the use value of the land for commercial or industrial profit making.

The history of successful and unsuccessful attempts at implementing land use regulations in the United States is one of conflict, which has taken various forms, including racial conflict, interclass conflict, and intraclass conflict. Often the language of struggle is technical and abstract-legal, but the technical terms are sometimes little more than obfuscating euphemisms for the aforementioned land-related interests. Much discussion in the planning, law, and policy literatures on land use emphasizes the need to seek the "public good." Indeed, in the *Euclid* case Ambler Realty viewed the zoning ordinance to be in conflict with the general "public interest," which meant in reality its exchange-value interest. Under capitalism, what is called the public good or the generalized public interest usually is a parochial interest; because of the major and fundamental class (capitalist/worker) and race divisions there can be *no* general consensus on most issues of urban development, environmental degradation, and land use controls. Conflict of interests is the common condition.

This chapter examines the struggle over land use controls, particularly zoning, in the light of a critical political-economic perspective. After reviewing the replacement of the now–in–decline urban ecological paradigm with the new urban political-economy paradigm, the chapter examines the development of zoning laws in the early decades and assess-

es certain conflicts over zoning and land use controls in recent decades with the aid of insights from the new urban paradigm. The next section provides a critical review of land use reform proposals in the 1960s and 1970s; a concluding section discusses an alternative slate of reforms with land use relevance, as seen from a progressive-democratic perspective.

THE NEW URBAN PARADIGM IN THE SOCIAL SCIENCES

Mainstream Urban Ecology

In the last decade, the dominance of an urban sociology rooted in the ideas of Herbert Spencer has been challenged by a more critical power-conflict paradigm substantially influenced by a sophisticated reading of Marx, Weber, and recent European theorists such as Henri Lefebvre, David Harvey, and Manuel Castells. The first major burst of energy in urban sociology in the United States occurred in the 1920s and 1930s at the University of Chicago. There, researchers such as Robert Park and Ernest W. Burgess drew on nineteenth century theorists, especially Herbert Spencer, in crafting an ecological framework for viewing urban life. Park and Burgess derived their concept of competitive relations between human groups from the Spencer tradition; competition "invariably tends to create an impersonal social order in which each individual, being free to pursue his own profit . . . invariably contributes . . . to the common welfare" (Park and Burgess 1924, p. 507). Together with geographers, these urban sociologists viewed this market competition as resulting in unplanned regularities in urban land use patterns and thus as generative of a social map of concentric *zones* moving out in waves from a central business district. These zones were considered to be naturally segregated areas of location for a diverse human population. Segregation of these zones was viewed as ensuring the "common welfare," another term for the generalized "public interest."

In the decades that followed, most mainstream ecologists have been more interested in broad demographic trends (e.g., the statistical analysis of metropolitan deconcentration) than in the zonal mapping of Burgess; yet for mainstream ecologists today competition, conflict, and accommodation still take place within a "framework of rules approximately the same as those advocated by Herbert Spencer—with room for social evolution, enterprise, and the survival of those most fit to survive" (Greer 1962; p. 8). A string of important books and articles from the 1950s to the 1970s (Hawley 1950; Berry and Kasarda 1977) established the dominance of this ecology paradigm in the urban social sciences. The basic assumptions of this framework include an uncritical acceptance of a self-regulating market system (viewed as operating for the public good), a pervasive technological determinism, a downplaying of inequality, and a structuralist approach deemphasizing human actors and classes of actors. While there were some early critics (Form 1954), since the 1950s ecologists have dominated much discussion of U.S. cities. In Hawley's theoretically oriented analysis, as well as that of other less theoretical ecologists, the central problem of inquiry is usually how a population organizes itself in adapting to a changing environment ("sustenance organization"). There is a strong concern with (societal) balance and equilibration. This equilibrium-seeking ecological view is an

> example of what passes for mainstream urban science today, namely, the use of mystifying abstraction and an emphasis on a noncontentious process of adjustment and functional integration to hide the important concrete issues of everyday life arising from the unequal distribution of resources, which

both Weber and Marx recognized as a principal driving force of social history. [Gottdiener 1985; p. 39]

Mainstream ecologists frequently view the functional complexity of cities as determined by transportation and communication technologies. Changes in urban form are explained in terms of some type of technological transformation, particularly in terms of shifts in rail and automotive transport systems. The political-economic history and decision-making context that resulted in the dominance of one type of transport over another is largely ignored. Thus the role of government (e.g., federal highway programs or the FHA) is often left out of mainstream discussions of such topics as metropolitan deconcentration and suburbanization. However, federal intervention in the form of subsidies of home mortgages, highways, oil production, and decentralized airports significantly encouraged urban deconcentration by reducing the cost of decentralized suburban development. Urban processes such as suburbanization are not simply the natural result of market forces, but rather the result of intentional actions by powerful economic and political actors. Mainstream ecologists have little interest in corporate capitalists or urban residents as actors, preferring instead to emphasize self-regulating markets and market-determined equilibria (cf. Logan and Molotch 1986, pp. 8–9).

Mainstream ecological analysis tends to be conservative in social-justice terms; that is, mainstream analysis tends to see city patterns as inevitable, even as efficient and neutral. The actual patterns of city development are not neutral; they reflect social inequality. The work of mainstream ecologists in sociology, as well as in geography and economics, has on occasion been used to buttress the existing urban system with its built-in social injustices. Thus a 1980 report sponsored by the Carter administration suggested that the federal government should look with favor on corporate growth in Sunbelt cities, to the point of letting northern cities die. Prepared by the President's Commission for a National Agenda for the Eighties (1980), the report called on the federal government to refrain from assisting the declining cities of the north. This market-knows-best view of the Frostbelt–Sunbelt shift in capital investment drew on the work of such ecologists as John Kasarda (1980) and Brian Berry (1982). In some of Kasarda's work, profit-seeking by capitalist entrepreneurs appears to be the intelligent directive force in metropolitan expansion and contraction: "An Urban Policy apropos northern cities should be well informed by the favorable business climate that has fostered so much recent economic development in the South" (1980, p. 389). Profit is also described as an innate sense that drives entrepreneurs to avoid the "negative externalities" of innercity locations. The controllers of capital follow the "beneficent" logic of a capitalistic system, which creates good business climates in Sunbelt cities and which dictates that the needs of working people in northern cities for adequate jobs be sidestepped in the quest for profit. Mainstream ecological analysis has not dealt adequately with such critical factors in urban development as inequality, class conflict, vested capitalist interests operating in space, and government subsidy programs that are pro real estate. In an overview book, *Sociological Human Ecology* (Micklin and Choldin 1984), numerous urban ecologists and demographers review the question of how humans survive in a changing environment, including cities, but with no significant discussion of inequality, conflict, or poverty.

In addition, mainstream ecologists generally neglect the role of the state in urban and regional development. Not one of the dozen authors in the aforementioned Micklin and Choldin collection discusses issues of government or politics. Earlier books by Hawley (1950) and Berry and Kasarda (1977) give brief attention to such topics as the effect of population shifts on local governments or government housing policies, but no serious attention to the growing and extensive role of government intervention in shaping urban economies. There is an interesting contrast between contemporary ecologists and earlier ecologists such as Park and Burgess. The latter go beyond a strict laissez-faire view to argue that the growth of people, communication, and organizations in cities has so increased mutual interdependence that some state intervention is necessary. Park and Burgess had a Darwinist view of the urban scene, but a "reform Darwinism" or a "corporate-liberal" view which accepted the necessity of an independent state adjudicating conflict and protecting essential values such as private property (Park and Burgess 1924; pp. 512, 558–559). The reason for this emphasis is that Park and Burgess argued that in periods of rapid population growth competition is converted into conflict; the expansion of judicial and other governmental institutions are necessary to mediate this conflict. Many contemporary ecologists, in contrast, seem to have moved away from this corporate-liberal framework back to the neo-individualist framework of the nineteenth century.

The New Urban Political Economy

By the mid-1970s, a number of European social scientists had published critical assessments of the ecology paradigm (Harvey 1973; Castells 1977). The winds of paradigmatic change had blown across the Atlantic; by the 1980s this European influence was one of several important ingredients in the maturing of the new urban paradigm. Over the past decade much published work in urban social science has directly challenged the fundamental assumptions and explanatory schemes of the mainstream ecological paradigm. To take one important example, Gottdiener (1985) develops a new sociological framework following the lead of Henri Lefebvre, a French urbanist who has accented space as a central feature of modern capitalism and who has portrayed the users of urban space as caught in a web of economic, political, and cultural forces. Gottdiener argues that spatial production is the material manifestation of complex political and economic processes associated with phases of capitalist development. Sociospatial patterns are the outcome of the many complex contradictions in capitalistic development, but not always the direct result of a particular capitalist's actions. What is crucial here is that the "valorization of capital" requires a spatial complex and that class conflict and capital accumulation do not occur in space, but rather they are about space.

The new urban analysts examine the processes and contradictions of capital accumulation in direct relation to urban spatial development. Prototypically, accumulation by a small capitalist elite involves mobilizing and transforming the inputs for production and then selling the output of that production, with the profit from the sale cycled back into production. Investment and concern for exchange value are the guiding forces behind this forever-expansive accumulation process. Since even in this contemporary period of oligopoly capitalism there are usually at least a few corporations in competition in most industrial and other sectors, capitalists are action-oriented and seek investments and profits by transforming labor processes, generating supplies of labor, increasing capital

goods, and transforming rural and urban space. The constant renewal of profits is at the heart of this process; profits are invested and reinvested, thus generating change. Late capitalism is not a post-industrial society, as analysts such as Daniel Bell have suggested. Rather, the modern U.S. economy is one which for the first time in history has a condition of generalized industrialization, an economy characterized by the generalization and expansion of mechanization, standardization, overspecialization of labor, and the concentration of capital in virtually all sectors (Mandel 1978). Indeed, the extension of these industrialization, mechanization, and concentration processes to previously neglected areas such as agriculture and urban real estate development is a major characteristic of the current period.

Central in shaping the sociospatial patterns of cities is the development sector of capital (McAdams 1980; Feagin 1983; Gottdiener 1985). Since the 1940s, the development process has involved at least five major categories of development-related decisions—corporate location, land ownership, land development, building construction, and land and construction financing. Some land-oriented entrepreneurs and companies specialize in one area, such as land ownership, but most such companies are multifaceted. Numerous industrial corporations, such as Exxon, have added real estate development subsidiaries in recent decades. Many land use actors operate in dozens of cities across regional and international boundaries. For example, as of the early 1980s, Canada's Cadillac-Fairview Corporation, one of the ten largest firms operating in the U.S., had eight divisions, including a financing division, a shopping center division, and a construction division. Since the 1940s large firms have increasingly dominated commercial construction in cities (and, to a growing extent, residential development). Some firms started after World War II as local firms tied into a local growth coalition, but they later became complex bureaucracies developing projects in numerous cities and engaging in a variety of financial, landowning, construction, and marketing operations.

The capitalist system of investment, production, and marketing is a powerful engine for the social and physical transformation of cities. Growth in capitalist cities typically hinges on the decisions made by industrialists, bankers, and real estate entrepreneurs calculating profit at the firm level. Social costs have been defined as the negative consequences of for-profit production, as costs that are not paid for by an individual firm but which are shifted onto third parties, onto individuals, and onto communities (Kapp 1950). Urban real estate investment decisions commonly create social costs because the decisions are calculated at the microeconomic level of the individual company in terms of its exchange-value concerns: profits, future net revenues, and share of the market. Many problems in cities are generated because decision making affecting the use-value concerns of neighborhoods and communities is done at the level of the individual firm. As a result, much traditional analysis of urban economies has had trouble dealing with the broader social costs linked to private investments. The economist Kapp (1950) has surveyed the literature and suggested that many traditional accounts emphasize Alfred Marshall's concept of social problems as externalities, of problems as more or less isolated cases of market failure, or they accent outside factors such as rapid technological change or large population shifts stressed by mainstream ecologists. While these latter factors can be important, they themselves are often dependent on more fundamental factors central to the decision-making process of a capitalist system.

Cities are in the first instance physical and geographical environments into which human action has intruded. The physical environment has its own regularities and laws—for example, ground and surface water flows. If these givens are ignored when investment and production decisions are made, then the negative consequences of such decisions may well be substantial. In addition, the high velocity of contemporary investment capital affects social costs. Bluestone and Harrison (1982, p. 106) have noted that the impact of city growth is greatly shaped by capital velocity:

> How much expansion can be absorbed, and how quickly, depends on the dynamics of the people and the environment of the community involved . . . . With suitable planning and reasonable forecasts, new schools can be built, teachers hired, roadways, water, and sewage systems constructed, and job training . . . . But when the capital influx is totally unrestrained, the absorptive capacity of the social system can be quickly overwhelmed.

The absorptive capacity of a particular city varies not only with the dynamics of its environment but also with the role of government in that context. When governments operate to facilitate profit making by pollution-causing firms or when they retreat from the planning and intervention to deal with the problems created by private profit making, they cooperate in inflicting social costs on the citizenry. The new urban political-economists give particular attention to the role of government (the state) in modern capitalism, drawing in part on the work of James O'Connor (1973) and Jurgen Habermas (1973). The state in late capitalism, according to O'Connor, has had to cope directly with the social crises of capitalism. Government under capitalism must try to meet certain obligations: (1) enhancing capital accumulation and (2) maintaining the legitimacy of the system in the eyes of the public. Capital accumulation is fostered by local and federal government action that increases productivity of labor and the rate of profit, such as government-subsidized industrial development parks, urban renewal projects, airports, and large-scale utility projects. Feagin (1985) has added to O'Connor's list a third type of state intervention: regulation. Many types of government regulation, including land use controls, have been implemented under home owners' or capitalists' pressures for government to rationalize a too-irrational capitalism.

While there is still much diversity among the scholars adhering to this new perspective, there is a growing consensus on certain basic concepts and assumptions:

1. Societies are fundamentally shaped by their means of production. Societies are more than demographic assortments of people; rather, they are socially organized along class lines and are fundamentally shaped by the logics of production and reproduction.

2. In this historical period, U.S. and Western European countries are organized around and structured by the capital accumulation process; they are shaped by a class system rooted in that process.

3. This capital accumulation process is centered in firms calculating profit at the firm level and thus results in irresolvable contradictions, such as major social costs not figured into firm accounts, capital flight, and periodic overaccumulation and underaccumulation crises. Capital accumulation involves an ever-expanding exploitation of labor (inequality) on a national and an international scale.

4. This capitalistic class structure and accumulation process articulates with space (place) to generate patterns of urban structure, growth, and decline.

5. The state in modern capitalistic societies, usually under the control of capital, plays a crucial role in fostering capital accumulation, in groping with market contradictions, in mediating struggles between classes and fractions of classes, and in enhancing the legitimacy of the established political-economic system in the eyes of its inhabitants (Gottdiener and Feagin, forthcoming).

The contrast with mainstream Spencerian ecology is clear. From this critical perspective, society is characterized by antagonistic class relations that generate change; change is not simply generated, as the mainstream ecologists would have it, by a biotic integration and equilibrium upset only by outside social influences such as the incursion of new technologies (e.g., the automobile). Much change flows out of the conflict-ridden capitalistic system and its mode of production. U.S. and West European societies have seen the emergence of strong capitalism-conditioned states, which attempt to intervene to solve crises in market functioning and capital accumulation, as well as to mediate intra- and interclass conflict. The inequality of power, of control over economic and political resources, is a central feature of capitalistic societies, and thus of their cities, and *not* an inevitable consequence of societal organization as the mainstream ecologists would have it (Hawley 1981, p. 224). In addition, the new urban approach emphasizes the point that no society is an island in time or space; it must be analyzed in light of its political-economic history and its position in an increasingly globalized capitalistic system.

ZONING IN POLITICAL-ECONOMIC PERSPECTIVE

The new urban paradigm points to the import of broader historical and political-economic frameworks for a deeper understanding of developments in governmental land use policy such as zoning and similar regulations. Let us now turn to the early decades of zoning in the United States.

Investment Expansion and City Growth

Between 1916 and the late 1920s, zoning and related land use laws became dominant governmental policy in U.S. cities. This state intervention in economic matters did not take place within an economic or social vacuum. Indeed, it was the direct result of efforts to alleviate some of the negative effects (so-called externalities) of rapid capitalistic expansion—of the accelerating capital flows moving into industries in numerous U.S. cities between 1870 and 1930. Industrial capitalists usually sought out cities for labor supply reasons. There were already workers in many towns and cities from the commercial capitalist period prior to the 1870s. Labor migration and population growth also followed capital investment. The concentration of the new industries in many cities stemmed from decisions of top corporate executives or free-wheeling entrepreneurs establishing dominant major industries. As plants and factories became situated in certain cities in this national investment process, the new urban workplaces attracted workers from rural areas, from the South, and from Europe. In this 1870–1930 period, cities were booming and industries of a dozen major varieties were locating hundreds of plants in them. Professional, managerial, technical, and skilled blue-collar workers increased to significant numbers, opening up by the 1920s a new market for consumer goods, including mass-produced automobiles and houses in central cities and the suburban rings. By 1922 there were 135,000 homes in the suburbs of 60 cities that were dependent on an auto-centered transport network (Flink 1975, p. 164). Without the significant increase in a relatively affluent group of white-collar and skilled blue-collar workers, there probably would have been no suburban expansion and thus no zoning litigation.

This suburban expansion slowed dramatically in the 1930s because of an overproduction crisis in U.S. capitalism. Overproduction in the automobile industry during the mid-1920s triggered huge layoffs in all auto-related industries, thus precipitating the general economic crisis called the Great Depression (Flink 1975). Sharply expanded state investments during and after World War II bailed the nation out of that major crisis and further accelerated the growth of suburban development and zoning regulations.

The Interventionist State

Ecologists and other urban analysts have often neglected the critical role of the capitalist-conditioned *state* in shaping U.S. cities. The history of cities in the last century is not only a history of boom-bust capitalism, of capital investments and capital strikes, but also a history of gradually increasing *state* intervention, at several levels of government, into the national and urban economies, in large part to deal with market-generated pressures, crises, and contradictions.

This state role in urban structuring and restructuring has taken a number of different forms. There are numerous state subsidies to foster accumulation in favored industries. Both the federal and local governments, for example, have played a central role in subsidizing the growth of the auto-truck industry. By the 1910s and 1920s, state subsidies for transport systems were shifted away from interurban rail systems and intraurban mass transit to highway systems and other infrastructural facilities necessary for the auto-truck industry to expand production and sales. This "socialized" infrastructure facilitated the dominance of and profit making in the auto and truck firms, a situation unique among major capitalistic countries. One result of this state action was the fostering of a distinctive expansion of suburbia in U.S. conurbations. Moreover, after World War II suburban expansion continued to be related to an expansion of an auto-centered highway system. This socialized highway system cost local, state, and federal governments no less than $249 billion between 1947 and 1970. The nationalized, auto-centered system and its accompanying car culture occurred "less because of consumer demand in a competitive market than because of the government's massive indirect subsidization of the automobile and oil industries, especially through the Interstate Highway Act of 1956" (Flink 1975, p. 213). Rail transit, utilized for people transport, was a major casualty of this state bias toward the automobile. O'Connor's theory of the role of the state in modern capitalism, particularly his emphasis on the role of the state in facilitating capital accumulation—and thus in this case facilitating urban deconcentration and zoning segregation—can be seen in these historical events.

Local and federal support of capital accumulation in this period was accompanied by growth in the number and significance of local governmental units. From the 1890s to the 1930s, and again after World War II, there was a major increase in the incorporation of municipalities around cities. By 1920, Cook County (Chicago) had 109 such municipalities walled off from the central city. Pittsburgh had 107 and New York City had 204. During the decade of the 1920s, new suburban areas were created by the dozens around U.S. cities (Judd 1984, p. 173). After World War II, moreover, the numbers of walled-off suburban municipalities continued to increase. This balkanization of cities reflected a growing concern for the externalities of expansionist investment, a concern among those managers,

professionals, and affluent blue-collar workers able to decentralize their residences. These suburban areas (and protosuburban areas, e.g., the village of Euclid) sought to protect their families, homes, and neighborhoods from the noise, pollution, congestion, and other negative consequences of industrial expansion, as well as from white immigrant and nonwhite workers drawn to cities by the new industries. In their origin, zoning and related regulations represent an attempt to use government to solve the negative problems created by the aggressive exchange-value expansionism of industrial and commercial capitalism. The willingness to give up a laissez-faire approach to government for increased intervention appears by the 1920s, not only in regard to zoning but also in regard to the regulation of many aspects of the American economy.

The zoning regulations used in suburban municipalities had first emerged in central cities, with New York City being the most important of these. By 1910, the New York Real Estate Board had advocated limiting the height of buildings. Reportedly, real estate values in the retail section of Manhattan had decreased by half in the decade prior to 1916; in particular, Fifth Avenue retail merchants were worried about the encroachment of the Jewish garment merchants, their new buildings, and their immigrant workers. The 1916 New York zoning law resulted from pressure from these central Manhattan merchants, rather than from home owners. In this case, the concern was primarily with the commercial use value of the land, a concern for retail marketing and profit making by merchant capitalists concerned with maintaining a presence in a particular urban land space. Yet this New York law was influential in broadcasting the concept of zoning to cities across the country. By 1920 there were 904 zoning ordinances, according to a survey of the U.S. Bureau of

Standards. Altogether, 82 of the 93 largest cities, those over 100,000 in population, had zoning laws. By April 1932 there were 766 comprehensive zoning ordinances (Davies 1958, p. 146). Under the zoning acts of the 1920s state governments delegated land use planning and controls to local governments, which in turn provided zoning ordinances.

Central city merchants and suburbanites played an important role in the emergence of zoning and allied planning regulations, but there were other powerful actors as well. There were those actors whose principal concern in real estate transactions was with the exchange value of land, particularly builders, developers, and real estate brokers. Before there were large developers engaged in residential and commercial construction in central cities and suburbs, there were smaller developers often called "builders." Initially, some business leaders representing these builders were opposed to zoning. In 1911, one leader argued at a National Planning Conference that the "German policy" of city zoning may come in the future, but "it is as yet undemocratic" and "savors too much of class-consciousness, to be popular in America" (Davies 1958, p. 78). Soon, however, the views of the leadership of the National Association of Real Estate Boards reflected the fact that local boards were strong supporters of zoning (Davies 1958, p. 78). According to Davies (1958, p. 146), these U.S. real estate boards played an important role in framing the model zoning enabling act in 1925.

Zoning Validated.

In *Village of Euclid* v. *Ambler Realty Co.*[1] the Supreme Court dealt with a zoning statute passed by the village of Euclid, an area adjacent to Cleveland and just beginning to be a suburb. By 1920, the village of Euclid had 3,363 inhabitants and was still mostly farm-

land. Some areas of the village were being developed for residences, but much was still undeveloped. In 1922, the village adopted an ordinance establishing comprehensive zoning of all land. The intent of the ordinance was to reserve much of the village land for residential development and to segregate industrial plants near the major rail lines. When much of the land owned by Ambler Realty was designated for nonindustrial use, Ambler pursued its lawsuit. Ambler Realty argued that zoning regulations will "throttle the great metropolises with a multitude of local regulations, in conflict with the general public interest" (Fluck 1986, p. 326). As with many real estate corporations, special pleading for profit was couched in terms of the general public interest. As the new urban political economy has demonstrated, in a class-stratified capitalistic society there is often no general consensus on land use matters. There is the interest of corporate investors and there is the interest of worker-home owners in suburban areas. Indeed, arguing for Ambler, attorney Newton Baker pointed out that *no* village or suburb could anticipate in its planning the freewheeling expansionism of capitalistic investors: "the surging and receding tides by which business evolves and grows" (Baker, p. 653).

Reportedly, the author of *Euclid*, Mr. Justice George Sutherland, initially viewed the ordinance in a negative light, but he was convinced to alter his view. Influenced by the thought of Herbert Spencer, the prominent nineteenth century sociologist who influenced mainstream urban analysis, Sutherland was a foremost advocate of laissez-faire. Sutherland was similar to many early and contemporary urban ecologists in his respect for Spencer's thought, which apotheosized the public benefits of a market system free from government interference. Like the ecologists, Sutherland was "so immersed in the Spencerian philosophy that he had no power to criticize it judiciously . . . no vantage point from which to see how much of Spencer was merely the expression of an age" (Paschal 1951, p. 242). In Spencer's view, government resulted from such an increase in population that people came into conflict with one another. But government was not neutral and should be limited to settling disputes and preserving order in the face of overcrowding (Paschal 1951, pp. 9–15). Going beyond Spencer a step or two, both ecologists such as Park and Burgess and jurists such as Sutherland accepted *some* governmental intervention into the complex workings of a capitalistic economy. Thus in *Euclid* Sutherland argued that growth in population meant growth in social complexity; and that growth in complexity required the intervention of the state to protect private property. Zoning was not a taking of property, but in fact a protection of property. Common law permitted the abolition of nuisances; the Euclid zoning law protected residential property (residential use values) from the nuisance of the industrial development sought by the Ambler firm. Since in Sutherland's view the problem was created by significant demographic growth and overcrowding, the zoning ordinance was beneficial in that it protected private property from divergent land use incursions (Paschal 1951, pp. 26–27).

CONFLICT OVER ZONING

Early Criticisms

Zoning regulations had become the target of much criticism by the 1930s. In that decade, questions already were being raised about the large number of zoning variances being granted in various cities. City councils and boards of adjustment were accused of destroying zoning maps and thus of breaking down the integrity of the zoning districts (Toll 1969, p. 281). Zoning variances had become "marketable

commodities, with investors subverting the law." This problem has persisted since the 1930s. For one example, in the 1960s the executive director of the American Society of Planning Officials cited with approval the statement of the city planner: "You can buy with money any kind of zoning you want in half the communities of the United States" (quoted in Toll 1969, p. 301). The complaint here seems to be with the way in which local developers and land entrepreneurs gain concessions. Because the governments in cities and municipalities historically have depended on taxes from development to survive, they often have gone out of their way to provide zoning concessions to local developers. Not unexpectedly, bribery scandals have been common in the history of zoning. In recent decades there have been payoff scandals in New Jersey, California, New York, and Chicago (Popper 1981, p. 52).

While residential use-value concerns seem to underlie some of the criticism of zoning variances, there have also been many criticisms from those real estate actors preoccupied with the exchange value of land. By the 1930s, some leaders in the real estate industry were criticizing certain failures of zoning laws. Walter Schmidt, then NAREB president, called for replanning and rezoning because "in the average American city many times as much property as can ever be used has been allocated for apartments, business, manufacturing, and industrial purposes, crowding out and destroying home neighborhoods" (quoted in Davies 1958, pp. 184–185). He acknowledged that real estate people were "the most aggressive group in the organized planning movement" and were partially responsible for "blunders made." An early advocate of zoning reform and streamlining, Schmidt anticipated the reformers of the 1970s when he called for state housing and planning acts to coordinate and simplify local codes.

Challenges to and Conflicts over Land Use Restrictions

There was no real challenge to zoning at the Supreme Court level until the early 1970s. Yet in the decades before and after the early 1970s there has been conflict over land use and land use controls. Much of this has centered on three areas of dispute: (1) low-income and minority apartment buildings; (2) environmental quality and no-growth issues; and (3) community attempts to restrict expansion by big developers. Each of these areas of dispute has involved zoning and related land use ordinances, but each also has encompassed different sets of actors. Thus the issue of low-income apartments has often been a struggle between low-income minority families and civil rights advocates on the one hand and white suburban families on the other. The struggle over the environment has often pitted environmentalists and local residents against developers and their allies. And the third struggle has seen suburbanites and residents in other residential subdivisions struggling to keep out large-scale urban development projects such as the shopping malls, power plants, and highways desired by large development firms.

The Civil Rights Challenge to Exclusionary Zoning

Racial and ethnic separation and exclusion have been at the heart of urban land use regulation since the 1880s. Indeed, the first zoning actions were taken in San Francisco in the 1880s in order to stop the spread of Chinese laundries. The 1916 New York City ordinance originated from Protestant and German Jewish merchants on Fifth Avenue pressing for zoning to protect their marketing area from the garment factories of southern and eastern European Jewish industrialists and workers. Popper (1981, p. 55) calls this "racism with a progressive, technocratic veneer."

This technocratic racism has persisted in suburban zoning laws used to exclude minority families. In this case, the dubious use-value concerns of *affluent* suburban home owners have been enshrined in land law, but the use-value concerns of less well off Americans have not been recognized in this fashion. Many suburban areas ringing U.S. cities are self-governing; most such areas are controlled by whites, with no blacks participating in the establishment of local government regulations. "Exclusionary zoning" in suburbia usually includes such things as prohibition of multi-family units and mobile homes and minimum lot size restrictions. Suburban zoning laws have been successful in excluding not only low-cost housing, but also many minority families.

Moreover, the location of publicly subsidized housing in city and suburban areas has provoked considerable discussion of exclusionary zoning laws. Local governments control the sites for public housing, while the federal government provides most of the money. But federal agencies have provided little protection for minorities against discrimination by local governments. Instead, federal agencies have played an important role in perpetuating the encapsulation of minorities in ghetto areas by allowing federally subsidized housing projects to be concentrated by local governments in segregated areas. Although the federal government has the authority to cut off funding to local agencies that do not comply with fair housing laws, it has shown a preference for local wishes. White fear has prompted suburban governments to turn down federal funds in order to retain local control and exclude public housing, and thereby minority families.

In the mid-1960s, the Chicago Housing Authority (CHA) presented a proposal to the city council to construct low-rent public housing projects throughout the city. At that time virtually all of the public projects already built were located in ghettos. The CHA proposal was rejected by the city council; the CHA then made an unsuccessful appeal to federal officials in Washington, following which the CHA retreated to the segregated policy the city council desired. A group of black tenants and applicants filed suit in 1966 against the CHA, charging it with selecting its public housing sites to keep blacks out of white neighborhoods. The federal government was charged with financially supporting these discriminatory practices. Three years later in *Gautreaux* v. *CHA*,[2] the federal district court found CHA guilty of violating the constitutional rights of black tenants by its discriminatory site selections and tenant assignments and ordered the CHA to disperse future housing in all-white neighborhoods, discontinue its discriminatory assignment procedures, and move rapidly to increase the supply of nonsegregated units. In a subsequent case, the federal housing agency was also found guilty of helping to perpetuate "a racially discriminatory housing system in Chicago." The CHA's refusal to comply with the order prompted a maze of further litigation (Feagin and Feagin 1978, pp. 108–110).

In *Hills* v. *Gautreaux*,[3] the Supreme Court held that the federal housing agency must provide low-income housing in the Chicago suburbs. But the Court allowed local municipalities to retain their zoning powers. The white mayor of a Chicago suburb said, "I really don't think the federal government will go charging out to the suburbs to put in housing where it's not wanted. If you don't have local cooperation,

you'll have a hell of a situation." Alexander Polikoff, an attorney who has been involved with the public housing debate for a long time, argued that the Court's decision to uphold local zoning powers would limit the effectiveness of the low-income housing dispersal order: "Any community that wants to oppose subsidized housing can use its land use powers just as it always has" (Feagin and Feagin 1978, pp. 110–111).

Arlington Heights, an affluent Chicago suburb, resisted the building of low- and moderate-income multifamily housing units by using its zoning regulations. The publicly expressed concern did not explicitly touch on race, but rather on the way in which local property values in this single-family area would be affected by multifamily housing units. However, the real concern was keeping neighborhoods exclusive. After the local zoning board voted nine to two against the necessary rezoning proposition, the case went to the federal courts. Because there was no evidence of racially exclusionary action on intentional grounds, the Supreme Court upheld this zoning decision in an important case, *Village of Arlington Heights* v. *Metropolitan Housing Development Corp.*[4] The Supreme Court had retreated to the position that racial discrimination must be proven by complainants to be intentional in order for it to be ruled illegal (Feagin and Feagin 1978, pp. 111).

With the Supreme Court showing a reluctance to deal with the obvious discrimination institutionalized in zoning in the suburbs, it has been left to the New Jersey Supreme Court to order change in segregated housing patterns. In a celebrated case, *Southern Burlington County NAACP* v. *Mount Laurel*,[5] the New Jersey justices unanimously reaffirmed an earlier *Mount Laurel* decision and ordered Mount Laurel and similar suburban communities to develop inclusionary zoning practices; in effect, "every municipality's land use regulations . . . must provide a realistic opportunity for decent housing for its indigenous poor" (Babcock and Siemon 1985, p. 212). The New Jersey court had in effect suggested that 20 percent of any new housing development be set aside for low- and moderate-income families. The exact figures for particular communities have been the source of much debate, but the radical implications of this New Jersey decision are quite clear: Towns and cities must allow for the housing of people of all income levels. The Republican governor of New Jersey even went so far as to say that the decision was "communistic" (Babcock and Siemon 1985, p. 215). The New Jersey Builders Association, made up primarily of smaller developers, expressed opposition to this government intrusion into the free market economy. As in other cases of state action, some larger developers, in contrast, have seen the new situation as an opportunity, for they have the greater resources to comply with the development regulations. For them, at least, it is helpful that these particular land use regulations are consistent across the state of New Jersey (Babcock and Siemon 1985, p. 220). Nonetheless, New Jersey stands virtually alone as the state which has sought to recognize as legitimate the use-value interests of the bottom third of the U.S. population, the concerns of moderate-income tenants for decent living space.

The No-Growth Restrictions: Zoning for Use Values

Zoning and related land use laws have been used for a variety of purposes. One purpose has been to exclude minorities. Yet another purpose has been to try to maintain a certain quality of life. In the last two decades, numerous cities and towns have become greatly concerned about the social costs of urban growth; some have passed growth-control ordinances.

Many of these costs have stemmed from the decisions of commercial, industrial, and real estate capitalists calculating company profits at a microeconomic level. As the urban political economy perspective would suggest, because corporations do not figure social costs into their balance sheets, the costs are not charged against the profits the firms make from producing and marketing products. As Bluestone and Harrison (1982) noted in the passage above, unrestrained capital influx, whether in the form of large subdivisions or rapid industrial expansion, can overwhelm local government capacity to cope with the capital flow.

It is not surprising then that cities and towns in the growing areas of the U.S., such as the Sunbelt, have been the most likely to regulate growth. The no-growth movements in many towns and cities have increased the number of local laws with which developers must cope. In the last decade the no-growth movement from Florida to California has resulted in laws specifying large-lot zoning, restrictions on the number of sewer and water taps, limits on housing permits, and delayed service provision for large projects. This has sometimes created a war between development interests and local citizen groups and their governments. The expansion of local zoning and planning ordinances to regulate growth runs directly counter to the interests of most development capitalists. Moreover, it is of interest that communities of various income levels, from moderate to very rich, have barricaded themselves against the intrusion of development interests and fought growth with new controls (Babcock and Siemon 1985).

Environmental Restrictions on Land Use

A related land use conflict has grown up around land use restrictions aimed at reducing environmental problems. In the 1960s, a number of activists working in the environmental movement began to target the negative impact of development on the urban and rural landscapes. Since most local zoning and other land use ordinances seemed inadequate to the task of environmental protection, many pressed for regulation at the higher levels of government. By the early 1970s, numerous environmental laws had been passed into law. Indeed, the 1970s have been called a "decade of quiet federalization." Laws coming out of Congress attempted to regulate air pollution, water polution, utility siting, land conservation, strip mining, and wilderness lands (Meyer 1979, p. 55). The new laws have covered large projects such as power plants and strip mines, as well as coastal and mountain areas. State governments have taken back some of the police powers delegated to local governments. Thus the 1972 Coastal Zone Management Act gives 30 seacoast and Great Lakes states federal dollars to regulate coastal developments (Popper 1981, p. 16–17). Toward the end of the decade, Representative Morris Udall estimated that there were about 140 federal programs that shaped local government land use decisions, ranging from direct regulation to federal funding of state regulation, and from broad guidelines to detailed stipulations. In addition to federal laws, state governments have passed hundreds of land use laws since the early 1970s (Meyer 1979, p. 56).

This wave of environmental regulation has been strongly opposed by some powerful real estate actors, particularly developers. Often arrayed against environmentalists have been development corporations and their local government allies, although there have been temporary coalitions between environmentalists and some big development firms. As Popper (1981; p. 6) notes, "this opposition has not succeeded in stopping land use reform legislation, but it has imposed a variety of prode-

veloper concessions and compromises on what began as strictly environmentalist bills." This major struggle has often involved local home owners and environmentalists primarily interested in use values on the one hand and certain factions of capital, such as real estate developers interested in exchange values, on the other. But the picture is often complex; some communities with unemployed residents have preferred the social costs of corporate investment to what they have regarded as the "purism" of environmentalists. The logic of capitalism, as it is currently structured, often forces a Hobson's choice between a clean environment and jobs.

Conflict over Large-Scale Development Projects

In recent decades, localized zoning and other land use regulations have been increasingly attacked by big developers and their allies among land use reformers. Prior to the 1940s, most urban development projects were carried out by small builders and developers. Beginning in the 1940s and 1950s, large developers such as Levitt and Sons began to build very large suburban development projects. By the 1960s there were numerous big developers constructing large shopping malls, office buildings, warehouses, and residential subdivisions. In the late 1960s and early 1970s, many large firms put together or acquired their own development subsidiaries, such as ITT taking over Levitt and Exxon creating the Friendswood Development Corporation. At the peak of corporate involvement in the 1970s, many top executives expected to reap new profits from shifting investments into large-scale urban development projects. With much surplus capital to expend, large industrial firms moved capital into real estate investment circuits, including large planned unit developments (PUDs), such as Kaiser Aluminum in Rancho, California, Gulf Oil in Reston, Virginia, and Exxon in developments in Clear Lake City, Texas. Independent real estate development corporations grew ever larger as capital became more centralized and concentrated in firms like Cadillac-Fairview, Gerald Hines Interests, and Olympia and York, Ltd.

As the scale of urban development projects increased, local regulations became problematical for the big developers: "Traditional zoning and subdivision regulations with their piecemeal approval, density limits, and fixed-use districts were not in accordance with the new scale and design of major projects" (Walker and Heiman 1981, p. 71). The Urban Land Institute (ULI), the research arm of big developers, took an active part in pressing for land use reform. One ULI publication notes that "broadening the concept of zoning to meet the needs of large new communities and redevelopment projects" is a goal of "planning bodies, redevelopment authorities, large corporations and foundations and those qualified to engage in large-scale developments" (ULI 1961, p. 59).

Shopping malls are one major type of large-scale development project. Existing zoning maps map the locations for commercial projects, but in the view of large developers the "prezoned, mapped commercial strips are usually not suitable locations for shopping centers" (McKeever, Griffin, and Spink 1977, p. 51). This quote is from the *Shopping Center Development Handbook* of the Urban Land Institute. The *Handbook* continues by noting that in numerous communities zoning laws have not been "revised to automatically provide for the planned unit concept (and the shopping center *is* a planned unit)." The *Handbook* calls for the updating of ordinances so that existing building height, lot size, and setback regulations will not prevent large shopping mall projects.

The shopping mall project is said to be in the public interest because of the increased taxes accruing to the local community and because the community is relieved of the need to provide parking facilities (McKeever, Griffin, and Spink 1977, p. 53).

In the 1960s and 1970s, large-scale infrastructure projects using public money also ran into local land use barriers. Local communities used land use controls to keep out power plants, highways, and airports. Plotkin (1987) cites cases of successful citizen mobilization: the Tocks Island dam in New Jersey, the Miami-Dade Jetport, and the North Expressway project in San Antonio. Backed by large-scale development interests, these projects were attempts to improve the local transport-energy infrastructure using federal government funds. Such land use conflicts have been viewed as "the result of poor planning" or a "lack of coordination," to quote Senator Henry Jackson (quoted in Plotkin 1987, p. 183). But they represent something far more fundamental, again the use-value concerns of urban and suburban residents versus the exchange-value concerns of, to use the ULI language above, "those qualified to engage in large-scale developments."

Proponents of large-scale development projects have seen themselves as positive forces for social change. Thus Berry (1973, p. 24) notes that the "planning commission in a social sense and the zoning ordinance in a real estate sense . . . are holding operations against the forces of social change." The defenders see local opponents of growth as opposed to progress. It has often been asserted that large-scale development projects can better meet the goals of racial desegregation, can lower housing costs, and can better protect the environment than the disorganized and fragmented projects of smaller developers. However, Walker and Heiman (1981, pp. 79–81) have demonstrated that for the most part such assertions cannot be supported from the existing data on large developments.

THE STRANGE CAREER OF LAND USE REFORM

Regulation versus Profit?

Land use reform has been on the nation's agenda since the late 1960s. Land use reformers have been committed strongly to race and income desegregation of the suburbs, rational planning and control of the environment, and greater efficiency in the location of large-scale development and infrastructure projects. Popper (1981, p. 212) portrays the land use battles as between those who view land as "a resource that was subject to stringent centralized regulation" and those who see land as a "loosely and locally regulated commodity on which its owners could make a profit." But Popper misses the complex reality of the class backgrounds and interests of many of the reformers. Indeed, the struggles over land use have involved a diverse array of competitors and actors, some concerned with the use value of land as living space, some concerned with the use value of land for commercial profit making, others with the exchange value of land. Worker-home owners have often pressed for territorial separation; mall developers, for investment expansion. But the picture can be complex; land-use politics often brings together strange bedfellows.

The 1960s and 1970s were a period of great debate over zoning and other land use ordinances. Because of the problem of land-use localism, big business interests worked through private planning groups such as the Regional Plan Association of New York, the Bay Area Council of San Francisco, and the Committee for Economic Development in order to press for metropolitan reorganization and planning. In the 1960s there were numerous foundation-funded critiques of local political and zoning fragmentation. Particularly important have been the Ford and Rockefeller Brothers foundations. The Ford Foundation funded a study on this subject by the Regional Plan Association of New York. In 1961, the Ford Foundation gave a grant to the American Society of Planning Officials to review zoning laws, with Richard F. Babcock as the key evaluator. Two years later, Ford also gave a half million dollar grant to the American Law Institute to study zoning laws and to propose a model law. Out of this latter project came draft proposals for a Model Land Development Code that would bring up to date the Standard Zoning and Planning Acts of the 1920s. In *The Zoning Game* (1966), Babcock argued that the patchwork quilt of such local laws should be transformed into a set of development controls operated by higher levels of government. He argued that existing zoning practice deifies municipal plans and "enshrines the municipality at a moment in our history when every social and economic consideration demands that past emphasis on the municipality as the repository of 'general welfare' be rejected" (Babcock 1966, p. 123). For Babcock, as for many reformers, the public good (of big developers?) can be better preserved at a level of government beyond the local level.

Major government-funded reports took up the cause of land use reform in the late 1960s. One major reform issue grew out of the civil rights protests. One response to the intense black ghetto riots was the 1968 Kerner Riot Commission's strong critique of exclusionary zoning by suburbs as a cause of the central city racial crisis. The report of the 1968 National Commission on Urban Problems also argued vigorously against the use of land use controls to segregate housing. That report argued that the right of minority individuals to achieve their housing choices must be given priority over the desire of white neighbors to exclude them: "The principle, of course, is well established in such matters as the invalidity of racial zoning . . . there are many gray areas, however, in which a regulation with a purported 'physical' objective (e.g., a minimum house or lot size) may have a dominant motive of exclusion" (National Commission on Urban Problems, 1968, p. 241). The commission recommended that state governments amend zoning acts to include as a legitimate zoning purpose the inclusion of housing sites for persons of all income levels.

The report of the 1973 Rockefeller Brothers Fund Task Force on land use and urban growth, called *The Use of Land,* was a major step in the struggle for national land use reform. It also called for removal of exclusionary zoning laws that keep minorities out of suburban areas. Moreover, this report pressed vigorously for new governmental action to facilitate capital accumulation by big developers frustrated by local zoning and planning regulations. In its attacks on small-scale development, the report reflects the interests of big developers:

> The small scale of most development remains a major obstacle to quality development. Although an increase in scale does not guarantee high quality, it significantly increases the developer's opportunity to achieve quality. [Reilly 1973, p. 28]

The Use of Land is aggressive in proposing large-scale developments as a solution to urban development problems and in arguing for the abolition of local planning and zoning barriers that interfere with large projects. It proposes state government entities, such as New York's pioneering Urban Development Corporation, with the "power of eminent domain, the power to override local land use regulations,

and the power to control the provision of public utilities, when necessary, to overcome the barriers that now prevent most developers from operating at the larger scales that the public interest requires" (Reilly 1973, p. 29). The report further calls for depriving "local governments of the power to establish" various land uses in excess of state government statutes and for a remolding of the regulation process so as to reduce the control of governments over land use regulation "that significantly affects people in more than one locality" (Reilly 1973, pp. 27–28).

Major Federal Legislation

A centerpiece of the reform movement was the National Land Use Policy Act introduced in various incarnations by Arizona Rep. Morris Udall and Washington Senator Henry Jackson between 1968 and 1976. This bill would have given state governments dollars "to devise comprehensive land use programs to regulate large developments and other building in environmentally fragile areas" (Popper 1981, p. 17). It passed the Senate easily in 1974, but was defeated by four votes in the House. While Senator Jackson claimed his land reform was "the best possible protection for basic property rights" and that the $100 million provided under the act would not allow the "federal government to substitute its own policies for those of the states," it was clear that the law would require the states to set up detailed land use planning requirements and agencies as a condition of eligibility. House supporters such as Udall saw the bill as a national land use planning policy, one needed because there was "no real order, no overall policy to cope with future land development and the struggle between speculators and preservationists" (quoted in Meyer 1979, p. 57). The Jackson bill was presented as "policy neutral" and as oriented toward greater efficiency in land use planning. But the bill actually shifted power away from local governments to the federal and state governments.

Classes and Class Factions in the Land Use Reform Struggle

The new urban political economy perspective would suggest an in-depth investigation of the relationship of the land use reform commissions and bills to the larger class and political-economic context, in particular to oligopoly capitalism and attempts to rationalize the chaos of a profit-centered market system. Because of the class-structured character of capitalism and of state intervention, there is typically no consensus on land use goals. Reformers have included not only environmentalists and civil rights advocates, but also those representing the interests of big developers and those planners committed to rationalizing the problems of cities under advanced capitalism. Some large-scale development interests have worked for land use reform, particularly major development and industrial companies that see centralized policy-making as neutralizing local regulations and reducing local no-growth barriers to development.

Environmentalists testified for the Jackson bill, together with big corporations and their real estate and banking allies: the National Wildlife Federation, Exxon, Bank of America, the National Association of Realtors, and the Conservation Foundation. Energy and utility companies have sometimes been supportive of a certain type of national land use policy. The environmentalists wanted a law that would protect the U.S. environment against rape from local interests. But the large corporations "preferred a system that would minimize the risks inherent in an uncoordinated and decentralized approach to land use planning" (Meyer 1979, pp. 57–58). Not surprising, thus, was the testimony by an Exxon executive be-

fore a Senate committee that emphasized that "we believe the time has come for a more orderly, disciplined way of planning for and managing for future growth of the nation" (Meyer 1979, p. 58).

Zoning reformers have noted the problems that local zoning laws create for large firms interested in urban development. Thus Babcock notes that these "sophisticated advocates are chagrined to discover that village codes often are a major barrier to marketing their dwelling-related products . . . . In short, there are powerful and conservative forces that would welcome an erosion of local land use control" (Babcock 1966, pp. 59–64). The point is that localism in land use regulations is a major headache for large development firms. Thus a national land use law is in order to rationalize local "irrationalities" in land use regulations.

The 1920s *Euclid* zoning debate was centered on getting what was seen as a *reform* past the judiciary of that era. In the 1960s and 1970s, reformers such as Babcock wanted to remake that reform. Babcock seems to fear that the "one-man, one-vote" concept increases the power of the suburbs in state legislatures and thus makes zoning reform difficult. In this sense, his corporate-liberal view is basically antidemocratic. He and other reformers prefer state and federal legislatures to reform the laws in spite of what voters might want (Toll 1969, p. 306). Big firms and their advocates seem to prefer centralized planning because they more easily can influence decisions at these state and federal levels of government than smaller developers and the general public can. Large developers need standardized zoning and planning regulations to facilitate huge development projects over large geographical areas. Moreover, the participation of federal and state authorities can help steer development projects away from the most resistant and assertive local communities.

Corporate land use reformers and their professional allies had the value commitments and practical wisdom to try to build a coalition with civil rights advocates who find exclusionary zoning repulsive and environmentalists who find certain traditional state practices as degrading of the environment. In a review of the literature of the late 1960s and early 1970s, Walker and Heiman (1981, p. 73) found numerous calls "for alliance between developers and proponents of environmental quality, social equity, and growth control." The major land use commission studies pressed hard (1) for streamlined regulations for large-scale development and (2) for restrictions on exclusionary zoning, goals supported by divergent factions in the reform coalition. However, from the beginning there were major tensions in any coalition of this type. The benefits of large-scale projects have been exaggerated, and environmentalists often disagreed with big developers on such matters. Many minority activists have also been ambivalent about land use reform. While they recognize its potential for reducing racial zoning, they also fear that new environmental rules will create the possibility of new types of exclusionary zoning. For example, one group of middle-income whites in Newark was able to block a low-income housing project by questioning the environmental impact of the project, using the environmental impact law (Popper 1981, pp. 70, 258).

Another set of allies for the national land use reformers were the environmentalists who had succeeded in getting Congress to pass laws regulating water and air pollution. Many environmentalists supported the use of state police powers to regulate the environment, and they supported the national land use planning legislation in the 1970s. But this love affair did not last long. The environmentalists' concern with pollution controls ultimately "stood in opposition to developer interests . . . The latter disapproved of protecting critical environmental areas without balancing this with the power to override local restraints on development elsewhere" (Walker and Heiman 1981, p. 75).

Localized Opposition to Land Use Reform Bills

The most effective opposition to national land use planning legislation came from local forces. When they lost, some reformers saw their opponents as right-wingers who conducted a "campaign of strident sloganeering" (Meyer 1979, p. 58). But the opposition was more substantial than this implies. Local business and government officials, small farmers, and local developers opposed the National Land Use Policy Act. For example, Chicago Democrats, controlled by Mayor Richard Daley, provided crucial votes to defeat the act. Popper (1981, p. 62) suggests that the reason for this opposition was a concern that higher levels of government would get the power to regulate land use; local government officials wanted that power, as well as the political contributions given by local builders and developers to those politicians in control. But Popper gives too much weight to the political officials. The land use struggle was between a national and rationalized land use system of the corporate-liberal, land use reformers and a localized land use system of suburban home owners and local real estate actors.

Plotkin (1987) notes that the nationally oriented land use elite pressing for the rationalization of development ran into the basic problem that few local people wanted land use law changes. For these local officials land use decision making was a stabilized and routinized activity, with routine access for the powerful actors at the community and city level. In some areas, the application of zoning and other ordinances favored growth, but in other areas decisions favored zoning and no-growth. In any event, most local real estate actors had little reason to support federal government intervention.

The defeat of the comprehensive land use law has led some reformers to target more restricted goals such as expanding regional action. Some large developers and allied reformer-lawyers have tried to participate on regional environmental bodies, in order to influence regional land use policies. Others have tried to piggyback onto the conservative (laissez-faire) deregulation movement of the 1980s, arguing that streamlined land use is necessary in order to deal with the "dramatic increase" in local regulations.

ALTERNATIVE STRATEGIES FOR DEALING WITH URBAN DEVELOPMENT

Large-scale Organizations and Corporate Liberalism

Large-scale industrial, real estate, and development organizations increasingly have come to dominate American urban landscapes. Corporations often have annexed the power of the state to help them in private profit making. At the core of the struggle over a streamlined national land use policy has been a corporate-liberal approach to the problems of modern capitalism. The corporate-liberals long have disagreed with their laissez-faire conservative brethren and have pressed for more government involvement in dealing with the irrationalities of the capitalist system. Urban protest movements, such as that in Santa Monica (see below), have raised fundamental questions about capitalist cities including questions about the quality of life, the pervasive profit criterion of investment, and the dominating influence of capitalist elites. While recognizing the significance of these urban movements, those adhering to the corporate-liberal ideology remain committed to a capitalist system and see the solution to many problems in more centralized regulation and in coopting certain elements of popular protest. But the corporate-liberal solutions are illusions, since the real issue is not the "obsolescence of zoning and small-scale development" but the "obsolescence of organizing social life around class inequality and the accumulation of capital" (Walker and Heiman 1981, p. 83).

Corporate liberalism appears to be a reform effort. Yet in reality corporate-liberalism offers "equality of opportunity" for real equality; bureaucratic regularity and rationalization for expanded citizen participation; and consumer goods for democratic control of workplaces (Lustig 1982, p. 248). The problem with corporate liberalism is that it encompasses a strong faith in a profit-oriented capitalism, albeit a state-administered and rationalized capitalism. But profit-oriented production and development frequently do not respond to basic human needs very well, either in the short run or in the long run. And a concern with making city development more rational and efficient is not the same as ridding cities of deepening injustices. If we are to meet the needs of all city dwellers, we must move beyond the choice of twentieth century corporate liberalism and the choice of a renewed nineteenth century individualism and Social Darwinism.

DEMOCRATIZING LAND USE CONTROLS: ACCENTING HOME USE VALUES

Henry George (1962, p. 264) long ago argued that it is the work and effort of all the people in communities that create land values and bring whatever advances in land prices that do occur. In his view, land dealers and real estate speculators secure, unjustly and without much effort, the increased prices generated by community labor. Extending this insight, George argued that the inequality of property holding and property control was a major source of the extreme imbalances in wealth and poverty in the United States. Real estate capital—and other land-interested capital, one might add—often is concerned only with the exchange value of urban space itself or the use value of space for moneymaking, whereas most ordinary worker-renters and worker-home owners view their residential urban spaces in terms of family use values, as "home." When capital becomes highly expansive and mobile, great tensions can occur. Critical to the health and progress of U.S. society have been certain basic social and cultural arrangements—stable neighborhoods and communities, dependable social relationships, and a sense of the limits to destructive capital investments. Yet these family-home arrangements are being destroyed by the world-oriented operation of modern corporate capitalism. A capitalism that has always operated as though "community, tradition, family, and morality made no difference, now finds them disappearing in fact" (Lustig 1982, p. 256).

A major problem with the national land use reform proposals of the corporate-liberal reformers is that they would reduce citizen input, input that has been expanding at the local level in recent years. Certain land use reforms may be appropriate, but they should be set in a context of human concern with use values and citizen participation.

Major class and income inequalities, major imbalances in political power, racial exclusion in matters of housing, struggles over air and water pollution, conflict over siting of large developments and utility projects—all these reflect the "normal" problems of the elitist system we call capitalism. As long as that elit-ist system is in place, reforms will be biased in favor of the exchange value interests of the powers that be. The existing social relations of capitalistic production set significant limits on reform, so in the end capitalism will have to be replaced. But there is still a need for reforms "in the meantime." Urban land use reforms can be related to more progressive and democratic goals rather than the corporate-liberal or reactionary Social Darwinist goals. What progressive reforms might be, or have been, attempted?

Plotkin's Proposal

In a provocative analysis, Plotkin (1987, p. 241) has suggested the need for a National Community Security Act bringing together five basic goals often considered separately by progressive analysts:

1. To achieve full employment;

2. To control prices in oligopoly sectors;

3. To eliminate speculation and to control housing prices;

4. To restrict corporate flight from communities;

5. To establish integrated planning and investment controls.

The first step here would be to provide the breadwinners in every family with a decent income and a guaranteed job and thereby to reduce the residential isolation of poor minorities now suffering job and racial discrimination. Adequate incomes would be corrosive of exclusionary zoning. Controlling prices for primary commodities (e.g., food and energy) would involve regulation of only a few major firms and would control inflation. Housing could be treated as a basic necessity and valued for its home use value, rather than its speculative exchange value. For example, Congress could pass legislation controlling the prices of all houses built with federal aid or federal tax subsidies. A heavy tax on undeveloped land could be used to reduce speculation, as Henry George proposed. Racial exclusion might be reduced because there would be less of an income and housing cost differential between city neighborhoods. Plant-closing legislation is necessary to reduce the negative impact of capital flight. Without control of job-creating investments, cities are without control of their futures. Plotkin suggests the further step of actual contracts between companies and cities such as those made by professional sports teams. The new law would require that a corporation that violates its written contract by leaving would be liable for the costs of abandonment.

"Contracts" between Communities and Corporations

The idea of a contract between communities and corporations has been broached by other analysts of the urban scene. David Smith (1979), for example, has argued that the "reliance" doctrine can be linked to a conception of "implied contracts." There is in the common law a "reliance" doctrine. If a local government promises to build a sewer and water system for an area and a builder constructs houses on that promise, and if the government fails to deliver, the builder has a legal right to sue for breach of contract. There was no written contract, but there was an implied contract on which the builder took action. Smith (1979, p. 7) has suggested that this principle should be applied to decisions by private companies as well. When a company locates a major plant or office facility in an area, it not only attracts people to work there but also encourages people to settle in for the long term with their families, to build schools and city buildings, and to take out long-term mortgages on their homes. Tax breaks are granted to the company by the local community. Workers and their families develop strong social ties to the community. There is an implied contract between the company and the people; the company implicitly has agreed that it is there for the long term. But, if a company leaves after a short time or with a few weeks' notice, it has clearly violated that implied contract. Yet in such a case there is as yet no way for citizens to sue a company for damages or to force compliance with community needs. Today, a basic community necessity is to build into American law such contracts in order to hold corporations accountable for the broader community costs for investment and disinvestment.

In Europe, pressures from organized workers have resulted in some laws restricting corporate flight. A company in Great Britain desiring to close or relocate must get an industrial development certificate from the government's Department of Trade and Industry. Corporations are thereby discouraged from leaving a troubled area and are encouraged to enter high unemployment cities. In cases where firms must close, workers are required to be given training, relocation, or job severance pay benefits. Similar laws are in operation in France and West Germany.

But what is the relevance of this to urban land use debates? There are two points here that are relevant to an alternative progressive perspective. One central point is that capital flight is indeed a *land use issue.* When companies abruptly leave a community, they destroy the viable context for securing home and neighborhood use values, and they take capital with them that has been created by the collective efforts of the workers in the community. In many apologies for capitalism, capital itself is viewed as a *privately* generated resource, and thus as legitimately beyond the control of citizens and local communities. But companies frequently borrow money from banks and other lenders, or they draw on past profits.

Where does that money come from? Smith (1979, p. 7) has put this well:

> Capital is a social resource. The people created it collectively, by their labor, savings, and their presence in a community which creates markets. It is absurd to say that once this money moves into the hands of some financial intermediary, it ceases to be theirs and is no longer accountable to public concerns.

Capitalists often borrow from the savings of workers in banks, insurance companies, and pension funds. Or they draw on the past profits generated by the labor of their workers. It is ironic that capital created by people's sweat and savings in a particular locality is used to create unemployment there as companies abandon that place for lower-wage labor markets around the globe.

A second point is that Smith's conception of an implied contract and of much capital as a resource created collectively by people's labor and savings can be extended to land-development corporations and their relationships to communities. The latter come into communities seeking profits; they too can be viewed as making an "implied contract" with the community residents whose labor and efforts there give land a price—and a rising price. And they too—for example, in hit-and-run developments or in environmentally disastrous projects—can create major social costs for community residents to pay. Moreover, real estate firms draw on lenders' capital whose source is, partially at least, collective in the sense that Smith eloquently describes above.

Forging Contracts with Developers

Progressive policies regarding land use have been implemented in a number of U.S. cities in the last decade (cf. Clavel 1986); but Santa Monica seems to have moved the most sub-stantial distance in the direction of forging major agreements and contracts with real estate development firms. Santa Monica, a beachfront city of 90,000 surrounded by Los Angeles, has been the site of major conflict over the use value of land. In the 1970s, housing in Santa Monica became a critical issue, particularly for senior citizens. Housing price increases outran incomes by eight to one in the late 1970s (Clavel 1986). Speculative sales of residential units increased tenfold; between 1970 and 1978 landlords increased rents twice as fast as landlords elsewhere in Southern California. While moderate-rent apartments were being razed in large numbers for larger-scale development projects, expensive condominiums and homes accounted for most new units being privately developed (Capek 1985; Feagin and Capek 1986).

The business-dominated city council repeatedly suggested that moderate-income residents were "second-class citizens." In response, a group of senior citizens in 1978 spontaneously organized to put a rent control initiative on the ballot. It lost, but Proposition 13 won. Proposition 13 was a property tax measure publicly linked to promises of rental savings for tenants. When landlords instead increased rents, opposition formed against this "exchange value" solution. This time voters passed a strict rent control law. Two years later, the successful grassroots electoral coalition targeted the destruction of the city by landlords and developers and elected a slate of progressive candidates to the city council.

The new city council took some dramatic steps, including a moratorium on all real estate development. Unlike most cities, which typically vie with each other to capture footloose investments, Santa Monica's democratically elected progressive council forced developers to negotiate givebacks to the community in exchange for the right to make a profit there.

Santa Monica exacted a whole new category of social goods: low- and moderate-income housing, day care centers, public parks, energy-saving features, and affirmative action hiring. The projects themselves were made to conform to a "human scale" construction. For example, one developer came to the Santa Monica council for permission to build a multistory office complex. The council agreed, but only after the developer committed himself to meeting major community needs as part of the project: an affirmative action program of hiring, a public park, 30 units of low- and moderate-income housing, a 1,500-square-foot community room, and a day care center. In addition, an agreement between the city of Santa Monica and another real estate firm specified that a significant portion of a proposed commercial-office project be constructed to house low- and moderate-income citizens, including units for senior citizens and families with children. In another agreement with a real estate developer, Welton Becket Associates, the Santa Monica city council reportedly reshaped a 900,000-square-foot commercial-office-hotel complex to include the following: 100 rental units in new (or existing) buildings for low- and moderate-income renters (including the aged and handicapped); three acres of landscaped park areas with athletic sport facilities; a day care center; promotion of car pool, bicycling, and flex-time arrangements to reduce traffic programs; and an arts and social services fee (Feagin 1983, pp. 203–205).

Reviewing the Santa Monica proceedings, Lindorff (1981, p. 20) noted the extraordinary character of such negotiations between a city council and important developers. These are rare written contracts because in big cities, such as New York, "developers routinely threaten to drop projects if the city doesn't give them something (usually a height exemption and a giant tax abatement)." The usual procedure is for city councils and other government officials to rush to the aid of developers with subsidies and to require no negotiations with developers for contributions to community needs or meeting social costs. The new council, not dependent on development interests for its campaign financing, argued that developers should pay for some social costs they create, including housing destruction and increased city service expenditures. Other city council innovations stressing democracy and local control included city funding of neighborhood organizations, the creation of citizen task forces, development policies encouraging open space and public amenities, a housing policy to preserve the income and racial mix of the city, an innovative anticrime program, toxic disclosure regulations, and farmers' markets (Shearer 1982; Feagin and Capek 1986).

Democratization of decisions about urban land use is a central feature of the reforms in Santa Monica and a number of other towns and cities across the United States. But the expansion of democratic input does not come easily. The progressive politicians in Santa Monica faced a host of problems. While they had laid down some new people's rules governing their city, they could not control the regional economy and investment flows into and out of that region. Landlords besieged the city with expensive lawsuits. Progressive city council members often faced hostile community groups and found that democracy was limited by the existing hierarchical (antidemocratic) structure of city hall and by constant pressures on the city by the larger political-economic system in which it was embedded. Organizing a routinized government and regulating real estate development resulted in the city council members compromising their ideals in order to take effective action in a capitalistic economy. Even the aforementioned developer agreements signal the compromises made by progressive council members who were initially opposed to all private development in the city. At the same time, the Santa Monica people's movement raised democratic participation in the city significantly and rewrote the traditional urban script on land use decision making in a way that favored non-elite actors (Feagin and Capek 1986).

CONCLUSION: LESSONS FOR LAND USE DECISION MAKING

The democratic reform impulse has not been limited to a few city councils. We have noted the progressive elements of the New Jersey (*Mt. Laurel*) court decisions concerning the income and racial desegregation of housing in that state's suburbs and cities. The negative consequences of exclusionary zoning practices there slowly became evident to judges who were in no sense "radicals," although their actions were taken, accurately, by conservatives as fundamentally radicalizing for traditional land use practices. The judges recognized that "freedom and equality for all U.S. citizens," an American ideal since at least 1776, has a force of its own which in the long run is difficult to resist. People of all income levels and racial backgrounds have a right to secure home and neighborhood use values. This principle of the right to a life-space is one that could well become a guide to future planning and court decisions in regard to U.S. cities. The essential ideal has two parts. First, maximize the resources available to all citizens, even if that requires redistribution of income or housing rights down the status ladder (cf. Rawls 1971). Secondly, maximize the participatory rights of the entire citizenry, even if that entails the sacrifice of the tradition of elitist decision making on behalf of that citizenry. This democratization ideal can be seen as encompassing both the political and the economic spheres—and

thus as challenging the maldistributions of rights and of wealth which are grounded fundamentally in a capitalistic political-economy.

It has been pointed out that in order to exist, capitalism must continuously convert life-space into commodity-space in order to sustain profits. Whole communities created by a large developer—or organized around a particular industry—may be defined as commodity-space; particular neighborhoods may be singled out to be converted into investment space, as in gentrified areas from New York to San Francisco. In the process of expansive capital investment, life-space often is rendered abstract economic space and separated from the fact that it is a place where people carry on their lives. It is in this sense that capitalism must swallow "roots" of people to stay alive. Such a process raises basic questions of fairness. It does not take place without a struggle, as Santa Monica illustrates. And by enshrining the private property principle, capitalism creates its own nemesis—people want to defend their life spaces, their use-value concerns, and thus stand in the way of capitalism's restless appropriation of urban space.

NOTES

1. *Village of Euclid* v. *Ambler Realty Co.,* 272 U.S. 365 (1926).
2. *Gautreaux* v. *CHA,* 304 F. Supp. 736 (1969).
3. *Hills* v. *Gautreaux,* 96 S. Ct. 1538, 1549 (1976).
4. *Village of Arlington Heights* v. *Metropolitan Housing Development Corp.,* 429 U.S. 252 (1977).
5. *Southern Burlington County NAACP* v. *Mount Laurel,* 456 A. 2d 390, 410 (1983).

REFERENCES

Babcock, Richard F. 1966. *The Zoning Game.* Madison Wis.: University of Wisconsin Press.

Babcock, Richard F. and Charles L. Siemon. 1985. *The Zoning Game Revisited.* Boston Mass.: Oelgeschlager, Gunn & Hain.

Baker, Newton D. 1975. "Brief and Argument," *Landmark*

Briefs and Arguments of the Supreme Court of the U.S. Vol. 24. Edited by P. Kurland and G. Casper. Arlington, VA.: University Publications of America, Inc.

Berry, Brian J. L. 1982. "Islands of Renewal—Seas of Decay." Paper presented at Urban Policy Conference, University of Chicago, June 18–19, 1982. In *The New Urban Reality,* Edited by P. Peterson. Washington, D.C.: Brookings, 1985, pp. 69–98.

Berry, Brian J. L. 1973. *The Human Consequences of Urbanization.* New York, N.Y.: St. Martin's Press.

Berry, Brian J. L. and John Kasarda. 1977. *Contemporary Human Ecology.* New York, N.Y.: Macmillan.

Bluestone, Barry and Bennett Harrison. 1982. *The Deindustrialization of America.* New York, N.Y.: Basic Books.

Capek, Stella. 1985. "Progressive Urban Movements: The Case of Santa Monica." Ph.D. dissertation, University of Texas.

Castells, Manuel. 1977. *The Urban Question.* Cambridge, Mass.: MIT Press.

Castells, Manuel. 1983. *The City and the Grassroots.* Berkeley, Cal.: University of California Press.

Clavel, Pierre. 1986. *The Progressive City.* New Brunswick: Rutgers University Press.

Davies, Pearl J. 1958. *Real Estate in American History.* New York, N.Y.: Public Affairs Press.

Feagin, Joe R. 1983. *The Urban Real Estate Game.* Englewood Cliffs, N.J.: Prentice-Hall.

Feagin, Joe R. 1985. "The Social Costs of Houston's Growth." *International Journal of Urban and Regional Research.* June, 9:164–185.

Feagin, Joe R. and Clairece Booker Feagin. 1978. *Discrimination American Style.* Englewood Cliffs, N.J.: Prentice-Hall.

Feagin, Joe R. and Stella Capek. 1986. "Grassroots Movements in a Class Perspective." Paper presented at annual meetings of Society for the Study of Social Problems, New York, August 1986.

Flink, James J. 1975. *The Car Culture.* Boston, Mass.: MIT Press.

Form, William H. 1954. "The Place of Social Structure in the Determination of Land Use: Some Implications for a Theory of Urban Ecology." *Social Forces* 32:317–324.

Fluck, Timothy A. 1986. "*Euclid* v. *Ambler:* A Retrospective." *American Planning Association Journal,* Summer.

George, Henry. 1962. *Progress and Poverty.* New York, N.Y.: Robert Schalkenbach.

Gottdiener, Mark. 1985. *The Social Production of Urban Space.* Austin, Tex.: University of Texas Press.

Gottdiener, Mark and Joe R. Feagin. 1986. "The Paradigm Shift in Urban Sociology." Unpublished manuscript.

Greer, Scott. 1962. *The Emerging City.* New York, N.Y.: Free Press.

Habermas, Jurgen. 1973. *The Fiscal Crisis of the State.* New York, N.Y.: St. Martin's Press.

Harvey, David. 1973. *Social Justice and the City.* Baltimore, Md.: Johns Hopkins University Press.

Hawley, Amos. 1950. *Human Ecology.* New York, N.Y.: Ronald Press.

Hawley, Amos. 1981. *Urban Society.* Second edition. New York, N.Y.: Wiley.

Judd, Dennis R. 1984. *The Politics of American Cities.* Second edition. Boston, Mass.: Little, Brown.

Kapp, Karl. 1950. *The Social Costs of Private Enterprise.* New York, N.Y.: Schocken Books.

Kasarda, John. 1980. "The Implications of Contemporary Redistribution Trends for National Urban Policy." *Social Science Quarterly* 61:373–400.

Lindorff, David. 1981. "About-Face in Santa Monica." *Village Voice,* December 2–8.

Logan, John and Harvey Molotch. 1986. *Urban Fortunes.* Berkeley, Cal.: University of California Press.

Lustig, R. Jeffrey. 1982. *Corporate Liberalism.* Berkeley, Cal.: University of California Press.

Mandel, Ernest. 1978. *Late Capitalism.* Trans. J. De Bres. London: NLB-Verso.

McAdams, D. Claire. 1980. "A Power-Conflict Approach to Urban Land Use," *Urban Anthropology* 9:292–318.

McKeever, J. Ross, Nathaniel M. Griffin, and Frank H. Spink. 1977. *Shopping Center Development Handbook.* Washington, D.C.: Urban Land Institute.

Meyer, Peter. 1979. "Land Rush." *Harper's.* January, 258:45–60.

Micklin, Michael and Harvey Choldin, eds. 1984. *Sociological Human Ecology: Contemporary Issues and Applications.* Boulder, Colo.: Westview Press.

National Commission on Urban Problems. 1968. *Building the American City.* Washington, D.C.: U.S. Government Printing Office.

O'Connor, James. 1973. *The Fiscal Crisis of the State.* New York, N.Y.: St. Martin's Press.

Park, Robert E. and Ernest W. Burgess. 1924. *Introduction to the Science of Society.* Chicago, Ill.: University of Chicago Press.

Paschal, Joel F. 1951. *Mr. Justice Sutherland.* Princeton, N. J.: Princeton University Press.

Plotkin, Sidney. 1987. *Keep Out: The Struggle for Land Use Control.* Berkeley, Cal.: University of California Press.

Popper, Frank J. 1981. *The Politics of Land-Use Reform*. Madison, Wisc.: University of Wisconsin Press.

President's Commission for a National Agenda for the Eighties, Panel on Policies and Prospects. 1980. *Urban America in the Eighties: Perspectives and Prospects*. Washington, D.C.: U.S. Government Printing Office.

Rawls, John. 1971. *A Theory of Justice*. Cambridge: Harvard University Press.

Reilly, William K., ed. 1973. *The Use of Land: A Citizen's Guide to Urban Growth*. New York, N.Y.: Crowell.

Smith, David. 1979. *The Public Balance Sheet*. Washington, D.C.: Conference on Alternative State and Local Policies.

Shearer, Derek. 1982. "How the Progressives Won in Santa Monica." *Social Policy*, Winter, pp. 7–14.

Toll, Seymour. 1969. *Zoned American*. New York, N.Y.: Grossman Publishers.

Urban Land Institute. 1961. *New Approaches to Residential Land Development*. Technical Bulletin 10. Washington, D.C.: Urban Land Institute.

Walker, Richard A. and Michael K. Heiman. 1981. "Quiet Revolution for Whom?" Annals of the Association of American Geographers. March, 71:67–83.

4

Expulsive Zoning: The Inequitable Legacy of *Euclid*

Yale Rabin

The values and concerns that motivate reformers often bear little resemblance to the legislative measures that result, or appear to result, from their efforts. In a society in which land is primarily a commodity—highly valued and actively traded—it should come as no surprise that measures intended to influence its development and use, whatever their ostensible purpose, should function, in practice, to protect and promote the interests of those who trade in and develop land. Nor should it seem unusual that such measures are employed to reinforce long-standing patterns and practices of racial discrimination and segregation. Zoning is an acknowledged example of such measures.

What follows sets forth the hypothesis that zoning, in addition to its well-recognized use as an exclusionary mechanism, also has been frequently employed in ways that have undermined the character, quality, and stability of black residential areas; that zoning not only has been used to erect barriers to escape from the concentrated confinement of the inner city, it has been used to permit—even promote—the intrusion into black neighborhoods of disruptive incompatible uses that have di-

minished the quality and undermined the stability of those neighborhoods. For reasons explained later, I refer to this practice as *expulsive zoning*. The hypothesis that expulsive zoning has been widespread is based on anecdotal evidence and on the consistently reinforcing relationship which that evidence bears to the attitudes, values, and motives that influenced the evolution and adoption of zoning.

Zoning, the regulation of land use by districts, was initially advocated by urban planners and social reformers as a means of eliminating urban blight, slums, and congestion—conditions that they saw as a consequence of unconstrained greed and corruption. While characterized as a comprehensive planning tool, what was sanctioned instead by the Supreme Court in *Village of Euclid* v. *Ambler Realty Co.* was a public mechanism for promoting and stabilizing private development, reducing risk in property investment, and protecting the character and quality of single-family residential neighborhoods.

This last objective was a central focus of the decision in *Euclid,* which found that the intrusion of nonresidential uses into residential areas was sufficiently detrimental to the welfare of those areas and their residents to warrant their legal exclusion. It must follow from *Euclid,* then, that zoning that fails to provide this protection—or worse yet, promotes the intrusion of offensive industrial or commercial uses into residential areas—must be judged an impermissible use of the police power, violative of the rights of those who are thus adversely affected.

While neither the literature on zoning nor the courts appear to have addressed this issue directly, there is evidence to suggest that expulsive zoning practices have been relatively commonplace in black residential areas. The record, while admittedly fragmentary, indicates that in the years following the Court's rejection of racial zoning in 1917 and continuing through the thirties, and perhaps much later, a number of cities—mainly, but not exclusively, in the South—zoned some low-income residential areas occupied mainly, but not exclusively, by blacks for industrial or commercial use. These practices were sometimes carried out even in neighborhoods of single-family detached houses, thus undermining the quality of the very types of neighborhood which zoning ostensibly was intended to protect. To the extent that these practices were effective—that is, to the extent that residential uses were replaced by industrial or commercial uses, residents were displaced. Therefore, the term *expulsive zoning.* Because it appears that such areas were mainly black, and because whites who may have been similarly displaced were not subject to racially determined limitations in seeking alternative housing, the adverse impacts of expulsive zoning on blacks were far more severe and included, in addition to accelerated blight, increases in overcrowding and racial segregation.

Evidence of expulsive zoning emerged as a by-product of case studies I have conducted of racially discriminatory government practices. These studies, conducted in many areas of the country between 1966 and 1986, were undertaken mainly to provide the basis for expert testimony in civil rights litigation. Among the principal issues on which this litigation focused were school segregation, voting rights, housing segregation, discrimination in the provision of municipal facilities, and in one case, exclusionary zoning. In no case was the issue of expulsive zoning litigated, although, in two cases, relief from expulsive zoning was ordered.

A common concern in many of these studies (55 in all) was the need to assess the role of government action in creating or perpetuating patterns of residential segregation by race. In the course of those studies, the frequent observation that black residential areas, particularly older ones, were interspersed with industrial and commercial uses led me, in 12 cases, to investigate the zoning of those areas. In all 12 cases expulsive zoning was a significant influence on both public and private actions affecting the conditions of the area. To suggest that such findings result from mere coincidence is to stretch the limits of credibility. On the contrary, these findings strongly suggest that additional studies in similar circumstances would yield similar results leading to the conclusion that expulsive zoning has been widespread.

Moreover, these expulsive zoning practices are entirely consistent with the more general findings of my studies: that the land-use-related policies and practices of government at all levels, but particularly the decisions and initiatives of local government, have been and continue to be instrumental influences on both the creation and perpetuation of racial segregation. Expulsive zoning, as one of these practices, does not occur as an isolated or independent action, but as one element in a web-like pattern of interacting public practices that serve to reproduce and reinforce the disadvantages of blacks. Urban renewal, public housing site selection, school segregation, highway route selection, and code enforcement are a few of the other frequently encountered cords in the web.[1]

In addition, given the low economic status of blacks, the consequent low value of the housing they occupy, and the pervasive disregard for their welfare, expulsive zoning is also consistent with the fundamental nature and actual—as opposed to ostensible—purpose of Euclidean zoning. Separation, or exclusion in order to preserve or enhance value, is zoning's very essence, and racial and ethnic separation have been recurrent themes in its evolution, adoption, and implementation. The acceptance of zoning as a regulatory restriction on the rights of private property became a reality only after its potential for enforcing separation and protecting established privilege was understood and appreciated. My findings strongly suggest what one might reasonably infer from the history of zoning, and indeed expect to find, that resourceful local officials, not to be deterred by the Supreme Court's 1917 rejection of racial zoning in *Buchanan* v. *Warley,* have continued to use zoning adaptively to pursue the same goals by less racially explicit means.

DARWINISM, PROGRESSIVISM, AND PROPERTY VALUES

The process of regulating land use by districts or zones had its origins in the last decades of the nineteenth century in Germany.[2] There, and soon afterwards in England, the decisions to impose such controls were prompted by alarm at the poor physical condition of city workers in general and of urban military conscripts in particular. Under the growing influence of Darwin's ideas, it was believed that better living conditions would improve ". . .

the health and efficiency of its working people," and contribute to the ". . . courage and loyalty of its fighting men,"[3] thereby preventing the deterioration of the race[4] and promoting the general welfare of the state.

On this side of the Atlantic, the early advocates of zoning came from among the ranks of the urban reformers in the Progressive movement. However, there were others who were quick to recognize the potential of regulation for promoting land sales. Most notable among these were the real estate developers who were instrumental, in 1908, in the adoption by the city of Los Angeles of a "Residence District Ordinance" and an "Industrial District Ordinance." These measures, which foreshadowed the later adoption of comprehensive zoning, were supported by developers who shrewdly identified land use regulation ". . . as an important vehicle for strengthening Los Angeles's most appealing selling point."[5] The urban social reformers, on the other hand, were deeply distressed by the growth of disease-ridden, unsanitary, and congested slums, and angered at the uncontrolled greed and corruption that they perceived to be the primary determinants of those deplorable urban living conditions.

Among those reformers, Benjamin Marsh was one of the earliest and most committed advocates of zoning. His 1909 book, *An Introduction to City Planning: Democracy's Challenge to the American City,* was the first American publication setting forth the principles of city planning and zoning. That small book was an enormous influence in its time and is considered widely to have been the catalyst in the series of events that led to the ultimate incorporation of these processes into the machinery of local government. Marsh's introductory reflections unmistakably express his point of view.

To open the door of opportunity for health we must close the door for exploitation of land.

No city can count itself civilized when any of its normal workmen must pay one-third of their income for reasonable housing.

Congestion would lose its charm for the landowner if the city taxed away all his profits instead of rewarding him by relieving him of the costs.[6]

Marsh and his followers believed planning to be the antidote for the spread of urban congestion and blight:

The conservation of the health of the people is one of the most vital purposes of modern, progressive town planning, and in no place can health be better or more easily conserved than in the home.[7]

And they believed zoning to be the process by which plans were to be implemented ". . . even though it may reduce the flow of speculative dollars into the pockets of the landlords."[8] The reforms they proposed were influenced by a growing faith in environmental determinism, and by the conviction that government reform could, and would, bring progressive change. They were struck also by the contrast between the conditions in American cities and what they believed to be the achievements of land use regulation that they had observed in Germany. Their basic concerns were similar to those of their European counterparts.

Marsh considered the congested slum housing conditions of New York, the port of arrival for millions of immigrants, to be a threat to the national welfare because so many of those immigrants, after remaining in New York for a while, moved on to settle in other parts of the country.

While the transition period may not permanently affect the physique of these people, it nevertheless has a most important influence upon them and no degree of subsequent care can compensate for the evil results of their adoption of the standards of housing and living of New York's congested districts or exonerate the country for exposing them to such dangers.[9]

Marsh and his fellow zoning supporters had been to Europe and had returned impressed by what they had seen. Frederic Howe, who wrote frequently in American periodicals of Germany's achievements in urban improvement, declared to the Second National Conference on City Planning in 1910 that, "The Germans have built the most wonderful cities in modern times."[10] Two years later another speaker enthusiastically reported to the Fourth National Conference:

. . . that within the span of about a quarter of a century the industrial classes of Germany have been translated from hovels and dens reeking with disease, degeneracy, and vice, to pleasant homes, surrounded with all the comforts, conveniences, and privileges that make for health, happiness, and good citizenship; and all this has been accomplished mainly by breaching the one-time sacred wall of vested rights and establishing the principle that the economic progress of the nation and the integrity of its social fabric transcend the prerogatives of the individual.[11]

These glowing, and probably exaggerated, reports of dramatic improvements in the lives of Germany's working classes were impressive but did little to convince American lawmakers that this alien system of land use regulation was anything but ". . . an unwarranted invasion of property rights incompatible with the American idea of freedom."[12]

The efforts of Marsh and his colleagues,

while national in scope, were focused on New York where they sought the enactment of what in 1916 would become the first comprehensive zoning ordinance in the United States. The story of those efforts has been vividly reconstructed by Seymour Toll in his 1969 book, *Zoned American.*

What emerges from Toll's narrative is the account of a transformation. What began as a means of improving the blighted physical environment in which people lived and worked, was transformed into a device for protecting property values and excluding the undesirable. And what was conceived as a process for implementing plans for an improved future was transformed into a mechanism for preserving the status quo and committing the future to its reproduction.

It was not the desire to eliminate what Marsh had termed the "evil influence" of slum tenement districts that motivated New York's lawmakers to adopt comprehensive land use regulations. Instead, it was growing demands by the luxury merchants and wealthy residents of Fifth Avenue for protection from the unwelcome incursion of the expanding garment industry, whose thousands of Eastern European immigrant workers crowded the sidewalks in front of their elegant shops and ". . . violated the ambience in which luxury retailing thrives."[13]

Although the Commission on Building Districts and Restrictions, which drafted the New York ordinance, included among its 19 members a few of the early reformers, it was dominated by a combination of Fifth Avenue merchants and real estate interests. A resolution drafted to guide the work of the Commission, and later embodied in the ordinance, enjoined them to ". . . pay reasonable regard to the character of buildings in making zoning regulations in order to enhance the value of land and conserve the value of buildings."[14]

Both the process and its underlying objectives were described frankly and openly by important members of the Commission. Edward Bassett, chairman of the commission who later embarked on a nationwide campaign to promote zoning, told a group that had been created to draft a zoning ordinance for Chicago in 1922 that

> . . . in New York the city did not know how to zone, so it went to the people, the property owners to find out, and it was advised by every section of the city and every kind of property owner, so when the plan was formed, it was purely the "property owners" plan. That was the only thing that prevented . . . beating the life out of it.[15]

Lawson Purdy was the commission's vice chairman. With an eye to the inevitable future legal challenge, Purdy urged his colleagues at the Tenth National Conference on City Planning, eight years before *Euclid,* to:

> . . . think in terms of values a great deal, popularize the idea of preserving the value of a man's house, of a man's lot. Get that talked about. When you meet one of those judges tell him about it, so that when, bye and bye, a case comes before him as a judge, it will be entirely familiar to him.[16]

He later noted in his memoirs that ". . . the principle we followed (was) to raise the value of land."[17] It is hardly surprising that Toll concluded that, "Despite genuine professions about making zoning the major instrument of American urban planning, their pioneering work turned out to be an exercise in drafting the will of a handful of New York's property holders."[18]

Based on the evidence of early zoning ordinances, it must have been believed widely that zoning not only could but would indeed enhance property values. The early ordinances of many cities were expressions of an apparent unquestioning faith in the power of legal designation to bring into being land uses that would increase property values. In Duluth, Minnesota, the residential zoning envelope[19] created a capacity to accommodate a population of 1 million, but provided for office space to serve a population of 20 million; Burbank, California, which in 1919 had an estimated population of 20,000, created a residential capacity of 125,000, but zoned enough land for business to serve a population of 1.5 million; Los Angeles zoned enough land for business to accommodate all the business activity existing in the United States at that time.[20] In the 1916 New York ordinance, a residential capacity of 77 million people was created, and enough commercial space allowed to accommodate a working population of 344 million.[21] One commentator noted in 1934 that, "It is not unusual to find a city with 600 percent more land zoned for business than is being used for business."[22]

SOUTHERN PROGRESSIVES AND SEGREGATION

While northern Progressives were enacting zoning as a mechanism for protecting and enhancing property values, southern Progressives were testing its effectiveness as a means of enforcing racial segregation. During the first two decades of this century, the Progressive era, ". . . racism took deeper roots in American society than at any time since the Civil War."[23] Racism was conceived of by some as the very foundation of Southern Progressivism:[24]

> . . . black disenfranchisement and segregation—was itself the seminal "progressive reform" of the era. So far as most whites were concerned, counting out Negroes politically and socially made possible nearly every other

reform they might undertake—from building better schools to closing the saloons.[25]

Zoning was suited ideally for this purpose. The protection of racial purity and the protection of property values were, after all, mutually reinforcing objectives.[26]

The first racial zoning ordinance was enacted in Baltimore in 1910, and within a few years was followed by ordinances in cities across the south and extending as far west as Texas.[27] These ordinances varied somewhat in form, but in common they established separate residential areas for blacks and whites and prohibited members of either race from occupying residential property in the district set aside for the other. The cities that enacted such ordinances included, among others: Richmond, Norfolk, Roanoke, and Portsmouth in Virginia; Winston-Salem, North Carolina; Greenville, South Carolina; Birmingham, Alabama; Atlanta, Georgia; Louisville, Kentucky; St. Louis, Missouri; Oklahoma City, Oklahoma; New Orleans, Louisiana; Indianapolis, Indiana; and Dallas, Texas.

Racial zoning was struck down by the Supreme Court in 1917 in *Buchanan* v. *Warley*, in which the Court found that the ordinance enacted by Louisville, Kentucky, violated the right of a white property owner to dispose of his property to a buyer of his choice. While this decision marked a favorable change in the Supreme Court's handling of cases dealing with racial segregation, it did not put an end to racial zoning ordinances. In the 1920s New Orleans, Norfolk, Dallas, and Indianapolis all enacted segregation ordinances. Winston-Salem adopted a racial zoning ordinance in 1940[28]; a Dade County, Florida, attempt to establish racial zoning was struck down by the Florida Supreme Court in 1946[29]; and in 1949 the last in a series of post-*Buchanan* racial zoning ordinances enacted by the city of Birmingham was struck down. In defense of that ordinance the city claimed it had been designed to alleviate racial friction and protect property values.[30]

These persistent attempts to legislate housing segregation, despite its rejection by the Supreme Court, reflect the depth of antiblack feeling and the determination that was so widespread during the Progressive Era to achieve and maintain racial separation. When viewed in the context of the wave of Jim Crow legislation sweeping across the South at that time—requiring racial separation in the use of everything from prostitutes to Bibles[31]—racial zoning can be understood as the most fundamental and potentially most powerful of the legal weapons deployed in the cause of racism. It would be naive to imagine that the cause was abandoned in the aftermath of *Buchanan.* What is far more likely, and what my own findings strongly suggest, is that racial separation continued to be pursued by every available means—and that zoning, in the form sanctioned by the Court in *Euclid,* was enlisted expediently in the cause.

The ability, through zoning, to employ economic segregation in the cause of racial exclusion is too well understood to warrant much discussion here. It is sufficient to note that blacks, being of generally lower economic status than whites, could be excluded from white areas by the establishment of differential lot size and housing type restrictions, which rendered areas occupied by—and reserved for—whites as unaffordable to blacks. For those few blacks who could afford the cost and who sought to intrude, intimidation or deception effectively could be brought to bear.

However, in the South the desire to exclude blacks from white areas—and sometimes from entire towns[32]—was not the only motive in the adoption of zoning. Southerners also were influenced by belief in the ability of zoning to enhance land values by stimulating economic development. Had the extravagant development fantasies expressed in the ordinances described earlier, and in others like them, been played out in undeveloped areas, they would—at least in retrospect—seem merely foolish and ill-conceived. But, where those grandiose expectations exceeded the capacity of existing vacant land, they often were superimposed on developed black residential areas. Whether the dominant motive in these instances was economic development or the displacement of blacks is not important. In either case, the pursuit of profit or the expression of prejudice, the interests and welfare of blacks have been equally expendable.

EXPULSIVE ZONING

In reviewing the zoning literature, I have encountered only two references to what I have termed expulsive zoning—instances in which it was clear that an area in residential use had been zoned in order to promote the development of other than residential uses. The first was described by Professor Garrett Power, of the University of Maryland Law School, who has written extensively about the history of Baltimore's development. He writes that after the city's third racial zoning ordinance fell in response to the 1917 *Buchanan* decision, pressure developed to follow in the footsteps of New York and adopt comprehensive zoning. Spurred in part by the national zoning promotion efforts of Edward Bassett and assisted by New York planning consultant Robert Whitten, Baltimore enacted its first comprehensive zoning ordinance in 1923.[33] During this period Whitten was retained by many cities as a consultant in the preparation of zoning ordinances. Only a year earlier, he had advised the city of Atlanta that ". . . home neighborhoods had to be protected from any further damage to values resulting from inappropriate uses, including the encroachment of the colored race."[34] Power is clear about the expulsive intentions of the ordinances, which in this instance were not limited to blacks.

> . . . the south and southeast Baltimore tenement districts which housed first-generation immigrants, and the alley districts which housed poor blacks, were placed in industrial districts so as to encourage their displacement by factories.[35]

Power found that ". . . the strategy worked and American Sugar, Glidden Paint, Standard Oil, Procter and Gamble, and Lever Brothers came to town."[36]

Unfortunately no further detail is provided. There is no account of how many households—immigrant or black—were displaced or of the secondary impacts of the displacement. But two inferences can be readily drawn. First, the zoning-induced displacement increased levels of overcrowding among blacks because access to housing outside ghetto areas was denied them. Second, because whites who were displaced were not similarly restricted in seeking alternative housing, levels of racial segregation were increased.

The other example of expulsive zoning found in the literature is from St. Louis, which like Baltimore had earlier tried to enforce segregation through zoning. In response to a request from the mayor, the St. Louis Plan Commission in 1926 undertook a study of the relationship between zoning and land use patterns. In its report, dated October 22, 1936, it notes that:

> More than one-third of all the residence property in St. Louis is zoned for a lower classification such as commerce or industry. . . . Residential areas are thirty-seven percent (37%) underzoned. By such zoning we are de-liberately planning to reduce our total population from 822,000 to 517,000. . . . Zoning of this sort is totally unsound and accomplishes nothing other than the deliberate creation of slums.[37]

The report makes no mention of race, but the city's history of racial zoning makes it reasonable to assume that the bulk of those intended for displacement by this draconian population reduction measure were black. It is clear from the report that the level of overzoning for commerce and industry was absurdly unrealistic; what was therefore occurring was the blighting intrusion of scattered industrial and commercial uses into the industrially zoned residential areas.[38]

The two examples of Baltimore and St. Louis illustrate the range of impacts of expulsive zoning, from large-scale displacement to scattered intrusion and consequent neighborhood deterioration. My own findings would suggest that because extravagant overzoning for nonresidential uses was so widespread, the effects experienced in St. Louis were more typical. Evidence of this was found in the frequency with which such areas were later designated for clearance as urban renewal projects. It was in this relationship with urban renewal that I first encountered expulsive zoning.

PULASKI, TENNESSEE

This first encounter with expulsive zoning took place in 1966 in Pulaski, a town of approximately 7,500 (in 1966) in south-central Tennessee. Black residents of an area designated for clearance as an urban renewal project had sought assistance and advice in their attempt to delay or modify the project. The focus of their concern was the absence of adequate relocation housing resources, not the feasibility or legality of the project itself, which was intended to provide a site for a shopping center. Even such a modest intervention represented a bold move by blacks at that time. To have raised fundamental questions about the validity of the project would have been unthinkable then, in the light of their painfully conditioned belief in the unlimited authority of government to work its will on them.

The project area consisted of several sparsely developed blocks containing 44 black-occupied single-family houses, 5 vacant houses, a combination tavern and residence, and two small, single-story structures, one occupied as an office and the other vacant. The houses were mainly owner-occupied. The project was bounded on the south by railroad tracks; by a lumber yard and scrap metal yard on the west; by white-occupied housing and a small convenience shopping center on the east; and by a vacant parcel approximately the same size as the project area on the north. The project area itself, the blocks immediately to the west, south, and east, as well as the vacant parcel to the north, were all zoned industrial, a condition of which no one I encountered in the project area was aware. To the west, north, and east of the vacant parcel was a modest white residential area mostly zoned residential. One of the factors cited by the city to HUD in support of its selection of the project area was the nonconforming status of the black-occupied housing in an industrially zoned area.

My survey of the project area revealed that 10 of the houses (5 of these were vacant) were in a dilapidated condition. The remaining houses, while some were in need of repair, were generally well maintained. Streets were paved; the area was well served by utilities; there were many mature shade trees; lots were of adequate size and yards and gardens were attractive. In terms of convenience to residen-

tial amenities and shelter from through traffic, the area compared favorably with any other residential neighborhood in the city. It was, in fact, the best of the predominantly black occupied areas in Pulaski.

By contrast, the houses in the small white residential area (my best recollection is 12 to 15 houses) immediately adjacent on the east were more dilapidated than the houses occupied by blacks in the project area; but although these also were zoned industrial, they had nevertheless been excluded from the project. The selective use of zoning to justify displacing only the blacks clearly was racially motivated. A report of these findings in an administrative complaint to HUD resulted in cancellation of the prior project approval and withdrawal of the funds.

HAMTRAMCK, MICHIGAN

Instances in which intervention came in time to forestall such clearance were infrequent. In Hamtramck, Michigan, a city entirely surrounded by Detroit, the city embarked during the 1960s on a series of urban renewal projects that eliminated about a tenth of the city's housing supply and displaced almost a third of Hamtramck's black households. The purpose of these projects was to provide land for the expansion of several automobile manufacturing plants located within the city. Because no relocation housing was available, displaced black households had been forced to leave the city.

In 1971, black residents of Hamtramck filed suit against the city and HUD seeking to require the provision of relocation housing facilities for those who already had been displaced as well as for those who were about to be displaced by a forthcoming project. That suit, *Garrett* v. *Hamtramck,* resulted in a finding in favor of the plaintiffs and an order by the court on November 22, 1971, that the city return in 90 days with a relocation plan, ". . . designed to remedy the wrongs suffered by virtue of defendant's conduct."[39] When the city failed to come forward with such a plan within the required time, I was appointed by the court to prepare one on the city's behalf.

My study revealed that in addition to the displacement contemplated by the forthcoming renewal project two other black residential areas, both adjacent to automobile plants, were slowly being displaced by acquisitions and demolitions by the automobile firms. By the time of the litigation, one had largely been converted to industrial use. The other, called Grand Haven, remained predominantly residential. Both areas were zoned industrial but, unlike most other examples in which the industrial zoning was an old designation, in Hamtramck the areas had been rezoned from residential to industrial only after the race of the residents had changed from white to black. In accord with the relocation plan I prepared, the court ordered that the Grand Haven area be rezoned residential and that the city be further enjoined from taking any action:

> (a) to rezone any part of Grand Haven to an industrial or commercial category, or (b) to grant a variance for commercial or industrial use in Grand Haven, or (c) to issue any building permits for nonconforming uses, or (d) to grant any demolition permits for Grand Haven (except in the case of unmistakable emergency as discussed above), or (e) to acquire or condemn any property in Grand Haven for nonresidential public use.[40]

CHARLOTTE, NORTH CAROLINA

In Charlotte, North Carolina, the examination of the relationship between zoning and housing patterns was part of my broader study of the impacts of government policies and actions on residential racial segregation. That study, which also included the effects of urban renewal, highway construction, public housing site selection, and tenant assignment, was conducted in 1968 and early 1969 in connection with *Swann* v. *Charlotte-Mecklenberg,* the Charlotte school desegregation case. I found substantial differences in the zoning of black and white residential areas.

Charlotte was bisected by a band of railway lines and adjacent industrial uses that ran roughly from northwest to southeast through the city. With the exception of a small enclave of black-occupied housing in southeast Charlotte, all blacks at that time lived in west Charlotte, which was interspersed with industrial uses. Blighted housing was concentrated mainly in proximity to these industrial uses, and several such areas had been or were in the process of being cleared through urban renewal at the time of my study.

Under the provisions of a major zoning ordinance revision that had been adopted in 1962, between one-quarter and one-half of west Charlotte was zoned for industry, including extensive areas in black residential use. While there were some very small industrially zoned areas in east Charlotte, none of those covered areas in existing residential use. The most significant area of industrial zoning in east Charlotte formed a buffer between the only existing black residential area in east Charlotte and the white residential area to the north of it.

This 1962 ordinance also included some more subtle distinctions in the zoning of black and white residential areas. No black residential area of Charlotte—not even those subdivisions that conformed to lowest density zone requirements—were zoned for either of the two lowest density residential categories. And 12 of the 15 white residential districts in east Charlotte included strategically located areas zoned for small neighborhood convenience commercial uses including such uses as physician's offices; only 4 of the 13 black residential districts in west Charlotte had similar zoning provisions.

The ordinance that had been in effect prior to the 1962 ordinance was one that had been adopted in 1947. A comparison of the map from that ordinance to a map of 1940 population distribution by race in Charlotte revealed that with the exception of two tiny areas—one of them surrounding a small black college—all of black west Charlotte had been zoned industrial; the only industrial zoning in east Charlotte had been the strip that bordered the only black enclave there.

The principal effects of government policies, among which expulsive zoning was a significant element, were the creation and reinforcement of physical barriers of industrial use between black and white residential areas, the introduction of blighting uses into black but not white areas, and the steady extension of the all-black residential area to the west and northwest as a consequence of the combined effects of displacement, public housing policy, and the barriers to the east.

NASHVILLE, TENNESSEE

The north Nashville area of Nashville, Tennessee, designated in 1970 as a Model Cities Area (MCA), was overwhelmingly black and overwhelmingly residential, with some interspersion of mostly small, industrial structures. Extensive areas of north Nashville had always been and continued to be zoned industrial. A study conducted by the Model Cities planning agency found almost 5,100 residential structures, about a third of all the housing units in the MCA, to be blighted. Among the nearly 400 industrial structures, more than three-fourths were found to be blighted, and among those employed in industry in the MCA, more than three-fourths were determined to be

whites who commuted, mainly by automobile, from outside the MCA. Within the industrially zoned portion there also existed a 700-acre undeveloped site.

The plan developed by the city for the MCA concluded that because of their deteriorated condition and the ongoing blighting effect of industry, the 5,100 blighted housing units would require demolition. No proposals were made for eliminating or improving the blighted industrial structures or for abating the pollution, traffic, and noise that the study had identified to be the ongoing blighting effects on the MCA. The Model Cities Plan proposed that the 700-acre vacant site be developed as an industrial park, and that 2,500 replacement housing units be built on various blight-cleared sites in the MCA.

In 1970, black residents of the MCA filed suit in federal court alleging that Nashville's Model Cities proposals failed to comply with the requirements of the Demonstration Cities and Metropolitan Development Act, and violated rights under the Fourteenth Amendment and Title VI of the 1961 Civil Rights Act. I was retained by plaintiffs to assess the city's proposals and their impacts in connection with that litigation.

I found, in addition to the facts noted above, that during the several years in which the city had conducted its study of existing conditions in the MCA, there had been a virtual halt to code enforcement there and that the number of blighted housing units in the MCA had nearly doubled during that period.

All of these facts were brought to light in the hearing of *North Nashville Citizens Coordinating Committee v. Romney*, which took place in June 1971 in Federal District Court in Nashville. After having testified during direct examination to the plan's evident inequity in failing to meet relocation housing needs while committing all of the available vacant land to industrial development, I was asked on cross-examination whether or not I was aware that the vacant land was zoned for industry and therefore could not be used for housing. I recall my response being interrupted by the judge who, with some annoyance, reminded the city's attorney that the city had zoned the land for industrial use, and was perfectly free to rezone it for another use.

Unfortunately, the court, in an opinion handed down on July 28, 1972, found none of the city's actions to be violative of black plaintiffs' rights, thereby leaving the city perfectly free not to rezone the vacant land at all. A subsequent appeal by the MCA residents also failed; the city of Nashville then was permitted to proceed with the implementation of its expulsive Model Cities proposals.

KANSAS CITY, MISSOURI

In Kansas City, Missouri, as in Charlotte, my investigation of zoning was undertaken as part of a broader examination of land-use-related policies in connection with school desegregation litigation. That case was *Craig Jenkins* v. *State of Missouri.* The available zoning information was more limited than in Charlotte, but revealed some interesting differences in the use of expulsive zoning. What was available as base data in Kansas City was a 1933 zoning map and a 1930 map showing distribution of black population. The pattern revealed by the population map consisted of a major black residential area immediately adjacent to the southeast edge of the central business district and containing nearly 70 percent of the city's black population plus 12 small black neighborhoods—each of them several city blocks in size—outside the main black residential area. These housed the remainder of the black population.

Those black enclaves to the north and west of the central business district were zoned in-

dustrial as were portions of the northern edge of the main black residential area. The remainder of the main black residential area and the enclaves to the south and southeast were zoned for residential use.

In 1954, anticipating the effects of pending urban renewal and highway projects, the city commissioned a study to determine the relocation needs of blacks who were likely to be displaced and to explore the extent to which there might be interest in relocating outside the main black residential area. However, the only area about which the survey inquired was southeast Kansas City.

During the next 15 years a series of urban renewal and highway projects eliminated all of the industrially zoned black enclaves north and west of the main black residential area, as well as the northern portion of that area that had been industrially zoned. To no one's surprise, the area immediately to the southeast of the main black residential area underwent rapid transition from white to black, simply extending the ghetto in that direction and absorbing the other black enclaves; by 1970 more than 91 percent of all blacks in Kansas City lived within the single main black residential area.

JACKSON, TENNESSEE

The most extensive and blighting effects of expulsive zoning that I have encountered have been in Jackson, Tennessee. Here expulsive zoning has been and continues to be a fundamental influence on other land-use-related policies and actions of the city which adversely affect the welfare of black residents. My study in Jackson began in 1978 and was undertaken to identify and describe the responsiveness of white elected officials there to the housing and municipal service needs of the city's black residents, in connection with a voting rights suit, *Buchanan* v. *City of Jackson.*

South Jackson, a section of the city which until the mid-1960s housed approximately half of the city's black population, had been zoned industrial since the city first adopted zoning in 1928. The other half of the city's black population lived in northeast Jackson, in an area surrounding all-black Lane College. That area had been and continues to be zoned residential. Housing in the Lane College area, while modest, is, with the exception of a few scattered pockets of slum housing, sound and well maintained.

Although south Jackson is bounded along its southern edge by a number of labor-intensive, forestry- and agriculture-related industries, the area itself always has been overwhelmingly residential. The area's residents have been the city's lowest income blacks; the housing they occupied was of poor quality and what remains has become severely blighted as a direct consequence of city policies and actions.

Since the early 1960s the city has repeatedly and publicly made clear its intentions to redevelop much of south Jackson for industrial and commercial use and since that time has halted all code enforcement and municipal improvement in the area. At the time of my first visit in 1978, two urban renewal projects were underway. One, at the southwestern edge of the city, was to provide land for industrial development, and in the other, in the center of south Jackson and adjacent to the central business district, a civic center was already under construction. By the city's own estimates, these two projects involved the displacement of approximately 940 black families including more than 2,600 people—about one-fifth of the city's black population. Between the two projects there remained an all-black-occupied public housing project and nearly 20 city blocks of black-occupied slum housing and unpaved streets.

One of the consequences of this large-scale displacement has been the racial transition of the low-income white residential area that formerly separated south Jackson from the Lane College area. By the time of the trial in the voting rights case, which took place in October and November 1986, that area had become nearly all black, and what was emerging was a single concentrated black residential area in east Jackson.

Despite subsequent clearance of additional housing in south Jackson and near total neglect of the rest, there remained in the summer of 1986, within a few blocks of the new civic center, 127 black families awaiting escape from the dilapidated housing they still occupied and the littered vacant lots and abandoned shacks that formed the remains of their neighborhood.

By failing to require even minimal maintenance of housing and withholding maintenance of infrastructure, the city accelerated the deterioration of the housing in south Jackson and reduced the costs to the city of subsequent property acquisition. By failing to provide relocation resources they caused an increase in the level of racial segregation and overcrowding in the city, and prolonged the time during which south Jackson residents were subject to that area's deplorable living conditions.

The city's response to these allegations during trial was that south Jackson had been zoned industrial from the outset because its low-lying character and proximity to industry made it unfit for human habitation. They were unable, however, to explain why in the light of their own reasoning they had built the first public housing project for blacks in the midst of this industrially zoned and ostensibly uninhabitable area.

SELMA, ALABAMA

During the 1960s, Selma, Alabama, became a nationally recognized symbol of oppressive racial policies. Its well-deserved reputation was based largely on the brutal treatment of the city's black residents by its law enforcement officers. However, less well recognized, but no less oppressive, was Selma's systematic use of its land-use-related policies and practices to maintain racial segregation, to perpetuate a lower standard of residential quality for blacks than for whites, and to impose on blacks a disproportionately large share of the burden of the city's economic growth and development. These practices and their impacts were described in a report I prepared for the NAACP Legal Defense Fund in February 1970.[41] Among those practices zoning played a prominent role.

Except for a small isolated enclave of black-occupied housing in otherwise all-white west Selma, blacks lived in an L-shaped area north and east of the city's central business district. In Selma's application in 1961 to the federal government for urban renewal eligibility the city made no attempt to conceal its intention to use zoning to reinforce existing patterns of racial segregation. Referring to the enclave described above, Selma's Neighborhood Analysis noted that,

> Area No. 1 is a small Negro area completely surrounded by good standard white houses. The area is definitely substandard and is exerting blighting effect on the good nearby houses. It is proposed to redevelop the area into lots of Zoning District R–1 which will largely insure white residential reuse. Number one priority is indicated for this project.[42]

In black west Selma about one-sixth of the developed residential area was zoned industrial and was interspersed with industrial and commercial uses. Most houses were on tiny lots, and blight and overcrowding were widespread. Zoning was a factor here as well. Within the six residential categories established by Selma's zoning ordinance, virtually all of the city's white residential area was in the two lowest density zones, while virtually all of the city's black residential area was in the two highest density zones. By this means, blacks, who comprised approximately half the city's population in 1970, were relegated to less than one-fifth of the city's residential land.

Zoning appeared to affect even the distribution of street paving. More than half of all black families in Selma lived on unpaved streets, while only 3 percent of white families lived on unpaved streets. Of the approximately 15 miles of unpaved streets in black east Selma, the greatest concentrations were in the residentially developed but industrially zoned areas. Because the platting that resulted in the street pattern predated the adoption of zoning, land was divided into small blocks suitable for high-density housing, but inappropriate for accommodating the extensive site needs of contemporary industrial development. In these circumstances, the lack of paving could reasonably be attributed to the combined effects of public disregard for the welfare of blacks and the unwillingness of the city to commit public resources to street improvements to serve residential uses that the zoning ordinance indicated to be only temporary.

In October 1970, after failing in attempts to negotiate settlement of a wide range of housing and land-use-related grievances with the city and HUD, black residents of Selma filed suit in federal court. *Clarke School Urban Renewal Project Committee* v. *Romney* sought relief from city policies, plans, and practices which:

• Would displace blacks through urban renewal and highway construction without providing adequate relocation housing;

- Maintained racially segregated public housing;
- Zoned black residential areas for either industrial or high-density use;
- Provided inferior municipal facilities to black residential areas;
- Denied blacks a meaningful role in the deliberations that produced these policies, plans, and practices.

Through the patient and persistent efforts of the HUD area office director, Jon Will Pitts, a group representing all the parties to the litigation was convened (in which I served as planning advisor to the plaintiff representatives), and over a 15-month period, reached agreement on the major issues. That agreement, known as the *Selma Accord for Housing and Community Development,* was signed in February 1972 and was incorporated in the court order dismissing the action. Included among its provisions was a commitment by the city of Selma to revise its zoning ordinance in order to:

a. Recognize and protect existing areas in residential use by preventing the encroachment of conflicting land uses and safeguarding neighborhoods, against land speculation which might threaten stability.

b. Provide for the orderly coordination of land development and the provision of municipal facilities and services.

c. Create a choice of residential densities in all sections of the City.[43]

ALEXANDRIA, VIRGINIA

For nearly 20 years, low- and moderate-income black home owners in the downtown area of Alexandria, Virginia, have been subjected to steadily increasing displacement pressures. Urban renewal, highway construction, and code enforcement all have contribut-

ed to a reduction in the number of black home owners in the downtown from 843 in 1970 to 704 in 1980. Since 1984, expulsive pressures have been increased substantially by the city's blatantly unwarranted designation of the overwhelmingly black Parker-Gray neighborhood as an historic district.

Adjacent to Parker-Gray on the south and east is a neighborhood that has for many years attracted affluent Washington-area families to its many blocks of nineteenth century row houses and the nearby Potomac River. In 1946, that southeastern section of Alexandria's downtown formally was designated as an historic district and became known as Old Town. The boundaries of Old Town were extended several times and by 1965 the historic district abutted the Parker-Gray neighborhood.

Formal designation as an historic area is accompanied by the adoption of special design criteria and regulations administered by a board of architectural review. These regulations govern all new construction and exterior renovation, and serve to maintain the character and quality of the district. They also have the effect of significantly increasing the cost of renovation and repair. In addition, under laws in effect at that time, historic area property owners were entitled to deduct the cost of some renovations under federal tax regulations.

While downtown Alexandria has been attractive to affluent whites, it has also long been home to Alexandria's black community, among whom many can trace their roots in the city back to the 1700s.[44] As recently as 1960, 91 percent of Alexandria's black households lived downtown, most of them in Old Town and Parker-Gray. Among the downtown black households in 1960, 34 percent were home owners compared to 21 percent for whites. By 1980, these figures had approximately reversed becoming 23.5 percent and 34.5 percent respectively.

In the late 1960s and early 1970s, an urban renewal project displaced more than 300 black families from Old Town and the area immediately adjacent to it on the west. That project was intended to clear 14 city blocks of deteriorated housing which were to be replaced by federally subsidized housing—230 townhouses and 84 garden apartments—to accommodate the displacees. It became evident after the displacement took place that there was a great demand by affluent whites for the blighted vacant housing. The city then sought and obtained permission from HUD to amend the urban renewal plan to permit the sale and renovation of the housing. These changes substantially reduced the amount of vacant land available in Old Town for the construction of relocation housing, and what was ultimately built were 25 townhouses and 300 garden apartments.

The attractiveness of Old Town's nineteenth century village character increased as the renovations and restorations took place. By 1973, the demand for restorable Old Town housing exceeded the supply.[45] Scattered older houses in areas adjacent to Old Town were purchased and rehabilitated, but purchasers sought assurance that the character and quality of Old Town would be maintained in those areas. In the fall of 1973, pressure from real estate interests led to the introduction in Alexandria's city council of a measure to extend the boundaries of the Old Town district to include almost all of the Parker-Gray neighborhood.

Low- and moderate-income black residents of Parker-Gray, who had been petitioning the city council for some relief from the enormous property assessment increases that were undermining their ability to retain their homes, objected strenuously to the proposed extension, and after much debate the measure was rejected. Pressure by aspiring gentrifiers continued, however, and additional unsuccessful attempts were made to enact scaled-down versions of the proposed historic district extension. In 1977, a survey of the Parker-Gray neighborhood by the director of the Virginia Historic Landmarks Commission resulted in a letter to the city stating his opinion that the area did not qualify for designation as an historic area.

Would-be buyers were not deterred. If historic houses did not exist, they could modify post-World War II row houses or create new facsimiles—as long as their investments could be subsidized by tax benefits and protected by design standards. On June 26, 1984, the Alexandria City Council finally succumbed to the pressure, and over the continuing opposition of black neighborhood residents, formally designated more than 25 blocks as the Parker-Gray Old and Historic District. A report by the Alexandria City Planning Commission recommending approval of the historic area designation identified 53 buildings within the new district that were 100 or more years old, 39 of which were concentrated in a three-block area at its southern edge. The 53 buildings composed less than 5 percent of the housing units in the district.

MOUNT LAUREL, NEW JERSEY

Mount Laurel, New Jersey, is probably best known for the successful challenge to its exclusionary zoning practices in *Burlington County NAACP* v. *Township of Mount Laurel*. Less well known is the fact that Mount Laurel also employed expulsive zoning practices to displace a low-income black and white community that had existed in the township for many years. This community, known as Springville, was not provided with water, sewer, or paved streets as were the other developed areas of the township.

Because the lots in the Springville area did not conform to the requirements of the zoning ordinance, the residential uses there were defined by the township as nonconforming. This designation was used by the township as a rationale for the refusal to issue required permits for the replacement, repair, or renovation of the houses. Inspections, condemnations, and demolitions served to steadily reduce the number of low-income housing units. Even though required under New Jersey law, no relocation assistance was provided, and almost all who were displaced were forced to leave the township. Between my surveys for the first and second trials in 1972 and 1977, the number of low-income families in Springville was reduced by a third, from 120 to 80. These facts were introduced at the second trial, but the court, focused as it was on the issue of exclusion, did not respond and thus failed to provide any relief or protection from Mount Laurel's expulsive practices.

BALTIMORE COUNTY, MARYLAND

In 1970, the U.S. Commission on Civil Rights undertook a nationwide study of minority group access in housing in the suburbs. As an element of that study, I was asked to examine the impacts of development controls in Baltimore County, Maryland, on housing opportunities for blacks. The principal focus of the commission's concern was exclusionary zoning, and Baltimore County provided ample evidence to justify that concern. Approximately 90 percent of the undeveloped residentially zoned land in the county permitted no more than one house per acre.

However, there were 20 black residential areas scattered throughout the county, some of them tracing their origin back to the mid-nineteenth century. These ranged in size from clusters of fewer than 20 houses to one community with nearly 1,500 black households. Most consisted of between 50 and 100 homes.

A demographic report prepared by the staff of the Civil Rights Commission indicated that in 1950 Baltimore County had a total population of 220,273, of which 18,026 or about 6 percent were black. By 1960, the black population had decreased to 17,535 or 3.3 percent of the total county population of 492,418. By 1964, although total county population had increased to approximately 541,600, black population had further declined to 16,580, or 3 percent of the total.[46]

From interviews and examinations of county records, I determined that more than 350 houses that had been occupied by black families had been demolished since 1960. Most of these losses had taken place in two of the larger black communities, Turners Station and Towson, and expulsive zoning was a significant factor in both places.

Turners Station is in an industrial area of Baltimore County and contained residential areas housing mainly factory workers. These areas were in existence at the time zoning was adopted by the county in 1955. The white residential area was zoned residential while the black residential area, consisting mainly of apartments, was zoned industrial. In 1966, the 244 black families there were displaced, the housing they had occupied was demolished, and the area was redeveloped for industry. Because no relocation housing in the county was available, most displacees were forced to move into the city of Baltimore.

In Towson, where one section of the black residential area was zoned for business and the other for industry, the number of black-occupied homes was being steadily reduced by commercial development and by condemnation by the county for new public buildings. By 1970, Towson's 1960 black population of 610 had been reduced by about one-third. In four other black communities in the county zoned for business or industry, population had also declined because housing could not be added or replaced.

EL PASO, TEXAS

The persistence of expulsive zoning's effects is illustrated by the case of El Paso. In 1975 I was retained by the Mexican-American Legal Defense Fund to carry out, for *Alvarado* v. *Independent School District of El Paso,* a housing-related study similar to that undertaken in *Swann.* I found then that the barrio that stretched along the city's southern edge was interspersed with commercial and light industrial uses and was zoned industrial. At that time, this condition did not appear to be a significant factor in the school desegregation case.

In June 1986, in an article about the barrio in El Paso, "Displacement Forum," noted that,

> For decades the M1 (light manufacturing) zoning has inflated land values, promoted commercial encroachment, and allowed chaotic land uses leaving the predominantly residential community in nonconforming status.[47]

The article described the constant pressure to convert the entire barrio into a commercial and tourist area, and pointed out that the barrio had lost half of its population in the last 15 years. Residents are currently organizing to resist the change by having the area rezoned to residential.[48]

DETROIT, MICHIGAN

The most recent example I have encountered of expulsive zoning is from a study that began in the fall of 1986. The issue centers around the impacts of a scrap yard on a black neighborhood just northwest of downtown Detroit. The few facts that have emerged to date are that (1) the area has been a black residential neighborhood for at least 25 years; (2) the area has been zoned industrial for at least 25 years; (3) the scrap yard is leaking toxic PCBs into the surrounding neighborhood; and (4) tests conducted on neighborhood residents reveal the presence of PCBs in their blood. A more precise chronology of events remains to be determined.

SUMMARY AND CONCLUSIONS

The adverse impacts evident in these 12 cases of expulsive zoning vary widely. They include environmentally blighting nuisances, displacement, and life-threatening hazards. This diversity suggests that a more extensive national study of expulsive zoning would not be likely to yield more consistent findings. However, the evidence to date does appear to support three significant generalizations. First, as illustrated most vividly by the case of Detroit, the magnitude and severity of adverse impacts are not necessarily proportional to the scale of intrusion or the extent of displacement. A single intrusive use can sometimes have disastrous effects. Second, the blighting and disruptive effects of expulsive zoning grow, rather than diminish, with the passage of time. Finally, expulsive zoning is not merely an historical remnant of a racially unenlightened past, but a current practice that continues to threaten, degrade, and destabilize black and other minority neighborhoods.

If these examples are isolated instances in local land use regulation, then expulsive zoning is merely an unfortunate curiosity whose overall impacts on low-income minority residential areas may be of minimal significance. If, on the other hand, expulsive zoning has been a widespread and common practice, then many of the neighborhoods in which blacks and other minorities live have been systematically denied the protection that the Court in *Euclid* found so important and that has been commonplace in white neighborhoods.

The readily observable mixed-use conditions, so common in low-income black neighborhoods, appear to support the latter hypothesis. The fact that none of the places discussed above, with the exception of Mount Laurel, became the subjects of study for reasons relating to zoning adds weight to that hypothesis. All were discovered in the course of investigating some other form of racially discriminatory public action; and in each case expulsive zoning was found to be one among a number of such discriminatory practices engaged in by local government in those jurisdictions. These circumstances strongly suggest that a study directed at uncovering instances of expulsive zoning would confirm that the practice has been widespread.

Whether or not judicial relief from these practices may be available is an important threshold question whose legal and practical implications are beyond the scope of this chapter. The decision in *Garrett v. Hamtramck* and the court-approved settlement in *Clark School Urban Renewal Committee* v. *Romney* are promising. They seem to suggest implicit recognition by those courts of the discriminatory nature and effect of expulsive zoning. Perhaps they can provide a base from which to seek relief in analogous situations such as those in Mount Laurel, Detroit, El Paso, and Alexandria.

If expulsive zoning is found to be a violation of equal protection—and in some cases of due process as well—then other questions arise about the nature and possible sources of relief. Does the replacement of expulsive zoning by appropriate residential zoning constitute adequate relief? If expulsive zoning is replaced with appropriate residential zoning, can blighting, but nonhazardous, uses established under the earlier zoning be terminated? If so, must offending local governments bear the costs of necessary relocation or other losses?

Are residents of areas blighted by expulsive zoning entitled to compensation for any harm suffered as a result? These and similar questions clearly warrant further exploration.

More immediately, there is a need to know how widespread the practice of expulsive zoning has been and continues to be. Beyond this there is a pressing need for a better understanding of the nature and extent of its impacts. While the situation revealed in Detroit may be an isolated case, junkyards are a common feature of expulsively zoned black neighborhoods, and junkyards have been frequently found to be disposal sites for toxic materials. We may yet discover that exposure to hazardous wastes is one more burden disproportionately imposed on black neighborhoods by the racially discriminatory implementation of land use regulations.

It is feasible to determine the existence of expulsive zoning locally, as I have done, by systematically comparing a time series of contemporaneous zoning maps with aerial photographs and maps of population distribution by race. Assembling such information nationally would be a substantially more difficult task. However, a study of a sample of long-established black neighborhoods in 10 to 15 major cities would be a manageable and informative undertaking.

In the interim, planners and others who administer local zoning could, and should, identify every instance of expulsive zoning. A simple on-site visual survey, or in some cases reference to a land use data bank, would quickly reveal the existence of any potentially hazardous intrusive uses. These should be investigated and steps taken to abate any such uses in accord with appropriate zoning revisions. Such measures could eliminate yet another vestige of minority second-class citizenship by extending to all neighborhoods the level and quality of regulatory protection for the residential environment that has routinely been provided to white neighborhoods, through zoning, for over 60 years.

NOTES

1. Yale Rabin, "The Roots of Segregation in the Eighties: The Role of Local Government Actions," in *Divided Neighborhoods: Changing Patterns of Racial Segregation in the 1980s,* Gary Tobin, ed. Sage Urban Affairs Annual Review, vol. 31, 1988, pp. 208-226.

2. Thomas Logan, "The Americanization of German Zoning," *Journal of the American Institute of Planners,* vol. 42, no. 4 (October 1976): 377–381.

3. B. Antrim Haldeman, "The Control of Municipal Development by the Zone System and its Application in the United States," *Proceedings of the Fourth National Conference on City Planning* (Boston, Mass.: University Press, 1912), p. 175.

4. Benjamin C. Marsh, *An Introduction to City Planning: Democracy's Challenge to the American City* (New York, N.Y.: 1909, p. 9, Arno Press reproduction of the original edition. New York, N.Y., 1974.)

5. Marc A. Weiss, *The Rise of the Community Builders: The American Real Estate Industry and Urban Land Planning* (New York, N.Y.: Columbia University Press, 1987), pp. 81–82.

6. Marsh, "Some Reflections" (page is unnumbered).

7. Haldeman, "The Control of Municipal Development," p. 178.

8. Ibid., p. 179.

9. Marsh, *An Introduction to City Planning,* p. 10.

10. Ibid., p. 129.

11. Haldeman, "The Control of Municipal Development," p. 177.

12. Ibid., p. 185.

13. Seymour Toll, *Zoned American* (New York, N.Y.: Grossman Publishers, 1969 p. 158).

14. Ibid., p. 150.

15. Ibid., p. 202.

16. Lawson Purdy, in discussion of Robert Whitten, "The Zoning of Residence Sections," *Proceedings of the Tenth National Conference on City Planning,* St. Louis, Mo., May 27–29, 1918, p. 41.

17. Toll, *Zoned American,* p. 150.

18. Ibid., p. 148.

19. The zoning envelope is the potential development capacity created by the ordinance, as calculated from the areas available for development, and the height, floor area ratio, and density limits permitted.

20. W. Phillip Shatts, "The Relation of Zoning to Land Values," in *Urban Blight and Slums: Economic Factors in their Origin, Reclamation and Prevention,* M.L. Walker, ed., (Cambridge, Mass.: Harvard University Press, 1938), p. 162.

21. Ibid., p. 166.

22. Ibid., p. 162.

23. Benno C. Schmidt, Jr., "Principle and Prejudice: The Supreme Court in the Progressive Era. Part 1: The Heyday of Jim Crow," *Columbia Law Review,* vol. 82, no. 3 (April 1982): 452.

24. C. Vann Woodward, *The Strange Career of Jim Crow* (New York, N.Y.: Oxford University Press, 1957), p. 75.

25. Jack T. Kirby, *Darkness at the Dawning: Race and Reform in the Progressive South,* (Philadelphia: Lippincott, 1982), p. 4; *see also* Arthur Ekirch, Jr., *Progressivism in America* (New York, N.Y.: New Viewpoints, 1974), pp. 111,112.

26. Roger L. Rice, "Residential Segregation by Law, 1910–1917," *The Journal of Southern History,* vol. XXXIV, no. 2 (May 1968): 184; *see also* Norman Williams, Jr., "Racial Zoning Again," *American City,* Nov. 1950, p. 137.

27. Schmidt, "Principle and Prejudice," pp. 498–524; *see also* Rice, "Residential Segregation," pp. 179–199; Woodward, "The Strange Career," pp. 85, 86; and Charles Johnson, *Patterns of Negro Segregation* (New York, N.Y.: Harper and Row, 1943), pp. 173–176.

28. Rice, "Residential Segregation," p. 196.

29. Raymond A. Mohl, "Race and Space in the Modern City: Interstate 95 and the Black Community in Miami." Paper presented at the annual meeting of the Organization of American Historians, Reno, Nevada, March 24, 1988, p. 26.

30. Norman Williams, Jr., "Racial Zoning Again," p. 137.

31. Woodward, "The Strange Career," pp. 83–87.

32. Ibid., p. 86.

33. Garrett Power, "Apartheid Baltimore Style: The Residential Segregation Ordinances of 1910–1913," *The Maryland Law Review,* vol. 42, no. 2 (1983): 289–328.

34. Barbara J. Flint, *Zoning and Residential Segregation: A Social and Physical History: 1910–1940.* Unpublished Ph.D. dissertation, Faculty of Social Science, Department of History, University of Chicago (December 1977): 133–134.

35. Garrett Power, "The Unwisdom of Allowing City Growth to Work Out its Own Destiny." Unpublished paper, Baltimore, 1985, pp. 7–22.

36. Garrett Power, "The Development of Residential Baltimore, 1900–1930." Paper presented at the Chancellor's Colloquium, University of Maryland, Baltimore, March 3, 1986, p. 17.

37. St. Louis Plan Commission, "Urban Land Policy," October 1936, pp. 18–20.

38. Ibid., pp. 18–20.

39. *Garrett* v. *Hamtramck,* 335 F. Supp. 16, 27 (1971).

40. *Garrett* v. *Hamtramck,* 394 F. Supp. 1151, 1157 (1975).

41. Yale Rabin, "Discrimination in the Public Use, Control, and Development of Land in Selma, Alabama." Unpublished report to the NAACP Legal Defense Fund, February 1970.

42. Urban Consultant Associates, "Housing Conditions and Neighborhood Analysis: A Part of the Workable Program of Selma, Alabama," October 1961, statement accompanying map preceding p. 7.

43. *Clarke School Urban Renewal Project Committee* v. *Romney,* Order of Dismissal, March 14, 1972.

44. Hammer, Siler, George Associates, "Final NEA Study Report to the City of Alexandria," Virginia, March 26, 1976, p. 4.

45. Ibid., p. 12.

46. U.S. Commission on Civil Rights, "Demographic, Economic, and Social Characteristics of Baltimore City and Baltimore County," transcript, Hearing Before the U.S. Commission on Civil Rights, Baltimore, Maryland August 17–19, 1970. (Washington, D.C.: Government Printing Office), p. 499.

47. Low Income Housing Information Service, "Displacement Forum," vol. 1., June 1986, p. 2.

48. Ibid., p. 2.

5

Planning and Zoning

Peter L. Abeles

Of all the modern industrialized nations, the United States is the only one that began with what originally seemed to be an endless supply of land. In fact, it was this seemingly unlimited supply of land that was one of the main reasons for the continuous immigration that eventually used up so much of the land. One of the important foundations of this country was that everyone was free to do what he wanted, partly because of the abundance of land. And that freedom certainly included control of the use of one's own land.

In retrospect, it seems strange that in a very short time frame, 60 years, the use of land would change from one of almost absolute personal freedom to the current situation where land use is controlled, to a large degree, by local government.

When the first settlers arrived from Europe, they brought some amount of public regulation over how land was to be used. The legal concept was enshrined in the law of nuisances. Simply stated, that legal principle prevented one landowner from using his or her land in ways that would interfere with the productive use of a neighbor's land. For some 300 years that concept was the major public tool of land use regulation.

By the end of the nineteenth century there was a sudden, dramatic departure from the well-established ways of determining how land was to be used. Until then, a landowner had almost unlimited control over the present and future use of his land. Then, in just about a decade, in response to new problems resulting from urban growth, local governments started to control land by regulating its use. With the Supreme Court's decision in *Village of Euclid* v. *Ambler Realty Co.* in 1926, a dramatic change occurred in how the use of private land could be regulated. During the 60 years since *Euclid,* this change brought other fundamental changes to the way Americans live and work. Indeed, *Euclid* helped to change the structure of American society. During the last 60 years, this legal concept has become complex and, more importantly, zoning has come to play a vital role in the social, political, and economic lives of all the people it affects.

While the *Euclid* controversy started out as a planning problem, it ended up as a legal matter. Therefore, it is natural that an evaluation of the legacy of *Euclid* is most often conducted in a legal setting. To add another dimension to understanding zoning, this chapter will look at the subject from the perspective of planning.

In the beginning of this century, zoning was a fairly simple planning and legal tool. A look at the zoning ordinances before the 1920s shows that zoning was the process of dividing a community into a set of simple zones in which certain land uses were either prohibited or allowed. Today, a glance at any local newspaper will turn up a significant number of articles about events that hinge on zoning and an almost endless number of other controls over land. What has occurred during the 60 years since *Euclid* is a change from zoning as a tool to regulate life in an increasingly complex physical setting to an aspect of the police power that affects a multitude of important human events.

In reality, zoning sharply divides the producers and consumers of land uses. It is a continuous source of local political warfare. It often creates two or more widely opposing groups among people who have most other things in common.

Zoning is no longer a simple tool for separating the work place from the home. Zoning now includes regional housing needs and indirect taxation, provision for scenic vistas and conservation of special habitats, among a host of current applications. Many of these new zoning issues have only the remotest connection to the division of a community into districts that would preserve the health, safety, and welfare of the local inhabitants.

This chapter attempts to describe from a planner's perspective how this occurred. It attempts to show why zoning is so important to the post-*Euclid* world of suburban America, and how zoning as a legal tool has come to benefit principally suburbia. It will outline how the three types of settlement in America—urban, rural, and suburban—have developed since *Euclid,* and how that change has taken zoning as the major tool of planning away from the city where it began, to the suburbs, its real home.

Our principal tools will be those of planning. We will focus on the impact that land use and economic changes have had on the American landscape, as well as the effect those changes have had on zoning. In the process we will see that a great conflict has emerged between urban and suburban America in the use of zoning since *Euclid.* This land use conflict concerns where the poor and the working classes should live.

Today planning is carried out in all of the 50 states. Any major urban or suburban setting has some form of zoning and related planning powers. Most of these powers have a common ancestor in the Model Planning Act of 1927 promulgated by the U.S. Department of Commerce.

A premise of this chapter is that the impact of zoning on a community relates to where that community is in terms of its growth and economic development. This chapter looks at zoning in communities with approximately the same development cycle as Euclid, Ohio. The future impact of zoning in the West and Southwest may be different from that of the Midwest and the East. The chapter concludes that zoning has a very limited role in the older major cities of the country, a conclusion that may not apply to some of the newer American cities that have recently developed out of new economic activities such as oil, gas, and defense technologies.

ONCE EUCLID: NOW NEW JERSEY

As brilliantly described in the six-volume series *American Planning Law: Land Use and the Police Power* by Norman Williams, Jr., the actual application and use of zoning and related powers varies widely from state to state. Williams points out that there are two leading zoning states as measured by the number of reported cases in this field, California and New Jersey. New Jersey has the highest concentration of population per land area of the 50 states, and because of that, zoning as a legal concept has bloomed in the Garden State. Therefore, for most of the practical examples in this chapter, New Jersey will provide the cases.

In the briefest terms, these are the reasons why New Jersey has become a primary zoning state. Even with its limited land area, New Jersey has more than 500 independent municipalities. Each one, given the zoning powers created by the state, often views itself as an independent dutchy not unlike Germany in the days before Bismarck.

From its earliest days, New Jersey was both an industrial power and a major agricultural state because of its waterways. With Ellis Island conveniently located near the northern end, each wave of immigration brought to the state a goodly representation of the entire immigration stream. Depending on the Old World skill of the immigrant group, they settled in the communities that had a ready market for their skills and among people who could speak their language. As a consequence of its central position along the north–south axis of the eastern seaboard, New Jersey has always enjoyed being part of the mainstream of economic growth and change (with the sad exception of some of its older major cities). As a ready land reserve for the outgrowth of New York City, major new income groups have settled in the state. This tremendous diversity of people, income groups, and economic activity has given rise to a great competition for the limited land resources of the state, hence the rise of New Jersey as a primary zoning state.

MAJOR LANDMARKS OF PLANNING AND ZONING

Along the historical road of planning and zoning, three major landmarks appear.

The first landmark is that zoning is principally a planning tool for the issues that face suburbia. While zoning was invented for the emerging problems of the city, it has little relevance 60 years later to the planning problems of older cities and towns. While the city is and has been the location of many of the social and economic problems of modern America, zoning as a legal tool has had little impact on these problems in the city. It is suburbia that is the beneficiary of zoning.

The second landmark is that as a result of the powers of zoning, it has been used extensively to create or maintain exclusionary communities. This feature of zoning explains both its popularity and its greatest dilemma. From the very first zoning ordinances and master plans, the purpose of zoning was to maintain the community pretty much as it had been. Either by implication or direct statement, a goal in most suburban zoning plans is to exclude certain groups of people from certain neighborhoods or from the entire community. This exclusionary aspect of zoning has and will have a tremendous impact on the American economy. Before zoning became important in the regulation of land use, people had always been able to move wherever new employment opportunities were created. With the introduction of zoning as an agent of exclusion, this mobility has declined and will continue to decline. The full economic and social impact of this change is still far from understood.

The third landmark is the use of zoning to prevent further suburban growth based on environmental and land preservation goals. The most recent manifestation of this use of zoning power is to create land for the conservation of agriculture. Yet historically, the principal method of growth for both the city and the suburb was through the use of agricultural land and vacant areas at the outer edge of development. A serious question now is whether the pattern of American development, with its benefits to a wide spectrum of society, can continue if no relatively inexpensive source of land is available.

A PLANNER'S TOOLS

Planners are concerned with providing direction for future growth and internal change for a community. The foundation of planning is the goal or objective of the client community. While zoning is the focus of this chapter, the land use tools of planning include more than zoning. A true list of planning powers covers a wide range of legal and budgetary tools including condemnation, capital budgeting, landmarks preservation, the official map, Sections 201 and 208 of the Water Quality Act, federal and state housing programs, Urban Development Action Grants, and other regulatory acts. Traditional planning, however, relies on three major tools: zoning, subdivision, and site plan. While in the ordinary day-to-day practice of planning this triumphant process is often so intermingled that it is difficult to distinguish one tool from the other, they are in fact very different tools and each has its own history.

Historical Reasons for Zoning

Long before there was planning, there was zoning. The idea of dividing the city into districts for public welfare goes far back in time.

We received from our European ancestors the concept of separating the dense and highly developed parts of the city into districts. The primary purpose of such separations was to prevent the spread of fire and disease. Once the building of cities progressed from the days of the city as a fortress or the seat of royalty to the days of the city as the location of commerce, trade, and industry, then society determined by rude experience that land uses like gunpowder factories and tanneries should be kept at the edge of town. Even if the local slaughterhouse was not the cause of death and disease, it still did not smell particularly good. Its removal to a separate district became expected. A more recent example of such regulation comes from the early days of New York. While dairy cows were acceptable on Broadway, pig farms had to remain out in the country north of Canal Street.

Before the advent of ductible iron pipe and public fire fighters, it was difficult if not impossible to stop a serious urban fire. Countless urban conflagrations brought forth the idea of fire regulations. These regulations usually contained two important features. First, in some zones like the center city, buildings had to have roofs that would not easily ignite. Second, there had to be sufficient space between certain types of buildings to reduce the spread of fire. From fire rose the phoenix of dividing the city into zones.

The Development of Subdivisions

The second major tool of American land use practice came out of the concept of maintaining the value of property by ensuring adequate access to the land. Over the centuries, the European landscape developed hundreds of farm roads. Wherever lots were required to meet the needs of urban growth, the lots came out of farm parcels with adequate road frontage. For the most part, the American landscape did not develop such a gradual infrastructure. In the days before mass immigration, the lack of access to land did not really matter. Then the concern was to protect land for farming. In the process of creating new farms out of wilderness, the legal process called subdivision developed. New farm land could not be created if it did not have the essential public access to maintain its value.

The first American cities grew like their European counterparts, by dividing land along the simple road system that led from town to farm. The early centers such as Washington, New York, and Philadelphia had the street and subdivision patterns of their European origins. Once the immigrants started showing up in masses, a new and more efficient method of creating land suitable for development had to be developed. The grid pattern was one such method. With this process of land division and the concern that it be highly effective came the concept of subdivision controls.

Site Plan Review

By the turn of the century, Americans had accumulated enough public wealth to indulge in the aesthetics of cities. America's emerging upper classes had become painfully aware of the aesthetic difference between the rough and tumble American city, with its endless profusion of cheap immigrant housing, factories, gas works, and rail yards, and the majesty of the imperial cities of Europe such as Vienna, Paris, and London. The great Chicago World's Fair of 1893 was the first illustration of what could be done in an American city given the application of taste and great wealth. From that inspirational event was born the City Beautiful movement. This architectural movement founded the concept of land use control for aesthetic reasons.

While planners wanted to make the future visually nicer than the past, the courts looked with disfavor on the direct use of the police power for that purpose. Fairly late in the development of land use regulations, the tool of site plan review was developed to provide some amount of control based on aesthetic considerations. Originally, the tool was designed to provide a comprehensive check on whether a development proposal met all local zoning and subdivision standards. In addition, the result was a planning tool that allowed some control over more than just the use of land; it was a method that allowed control over how a project would look.

One of the certain things about planning is that there is never a plan to which everyone agrees. For each master plan or its implement-

ing device—zoning—there are planning alternatives. In most cases, the differences in opinion deal with how land should be used and, therefore, its economic value. Usually, the sides embroiled in this debate are the community and the developer.

These disputes have given rise to a group of planners whose professional task is to counter the master plan. Since it is understandably rare for the community to change its mind or plan, the arena for judgment on whether the plan is correct is the courtroom. By virtue of their exposure to court, this group of planners looks at zoning and other land use controls as lawyers do. Today zoning is no longer just a tool of planning, it is a legal concept subject to test in the courtroom.

MODERN ZONING AND THE CITY BEFORE *EUCLID*

Today, zoning and other land use controls are associated with controlling suburban development. Yet the reality is that American zoning was invented for the city.

After the Civil War came the great period of American city building. As with today's suburbs, that development process brought a number of major problems. Zoning and planning evolved as the reaction to some of these problems. Of all the issues confronted by the expanding city of that time, three were to play a major role in the search for new solutions that culminated in the birth of American planning and zoning: the economic and social shock that allowed rapid urban growth, municipal corruption, and the influence of the scientific method.

Until the end of the Civil War, urban growth and change had been a slow and gradual process. Suddenly, industrialization, rapid economic growth, and its related waves of immigration resulted in cities that were under constant strain and conflict due to rapid land use changes. For example, in New York City (the city that had the first zoning regulations), the retail center of the city had to rapidly move from 14th Street to the 20s and 30s and finally to Midtown and Fifth Avenue in the space of 100 years. The forces that created this movement were the need for industrial space and the related land needs for immigrant housing. As retail land values were diminished by these land use movements, there was a perceived need to deal with this constant change in land use and land value.

Dramatic land use changes not only affected commercial land values, they also created social problems for the middle and upper classes. As the waves of immigrants washed up on the doorsteps of the cities, they often lapped at the edges of established neighborhoods. This was before the middle class had the alternative of suburbia and thus something had to be done. The solution was to create residential districts in which it was impossible to introduce immigrant housing. That type of early use of planning is evident in the *Euclid* decision where Justice Sutherland wrote about the danger of apartment houses.

It is at this time also that long-term financing for residential development began to be a reality in the real estate economy. One of the early problems faced by mortgage lenders was the rapid change in land use and the potential for major declines in real estate values in many parts of a rapidly changing city. Zoning was quickly seen as having an additional important function; it helped to ensure neighborhood stability and therefore provided the basis for sound long-term lending.

The growth of the American city brought prosperity not only to many of its residents and builders, but it also brought great opportunities for municipal corruption. The ever-growing city needed new public buildings, waterworks, streetcar systems, and streets.

Demand for all types of buildings raised the value of any required permit or approval. This was the period of Boss Tweed and the use of political power based on controlling the votes of the vast number of new immigrants. In due time, the excesses of this process brought forth the municipal reform movement. This movement had as its cadre the old urban elite and the newly educated upper middle class. This was also the time when the assumed powers of "science" became accepted. One of the new "sciences" was the science of government. While it started in England and Germany, it was quickly brought to the United States. Planning for city development had already been part of the German science of municipal government. The reform movement incorporated the concept of planning as part of the scientific response to municipal corruption.

Linking zoning with science also was to be a very important step in providing the necessary legal foundation for planning. Science always has been accorded the qualities of accuracy and fairness. In the days of the law of nuisance method of planning, the nuisance event actually had to occur before the land regulators could step in and separate certain activities. Before planning and zoning could take on the role of land regulator in a societal setting of laissez-faire, one very major problem had to be overcome: how to make sure that the planners were right in their comprehensive land use decisions. How were the public and landowners to know that the proposed zoning was right, *before the facts* occurred? Since planning and zoning were simply part of the emerging new order of a scientific world, the results would be fair and accurate.

The other side of the reform movement was the call for social justice. The teeming tenement house, the working conditions of the poor, and the health and education of the immigrants all were translated into calls for social reform. Better housing and better neighborhoods were part of the agenda of the reforms.

While the events described above were taking place in every major American city, the turning point occurred in New York just before World War I.

A young attorney by the name of Edward Bassett had been employed by New York's underground transit system. He was part of a group of young reformers who concluded that the science of planning could help solve the social ills of the day. His next municipal assignment was to prepare a zoning resolution for New York.

Anyone living in New York at the turn of the century must have had a fearful vision of what the outcome would be of building new sections of the city to house the masses of immigrants if the density of 400 dwelling units per acre and 80 to 90 percent ground coverage continued. Bassett's job was to develop regulations to solve the worst aspects of this problem.

By 1916, Bassett had produced the first major American zoning ordinance. On paper it seemed to be a solution to the social and physical problems of the city. By dividing the city into zones and regulating the building type in each zone, Bassett assumed that some of the emerging urban problems could be managed.

Before streetcars and subways, the city was limited by how far people could move about on foot or by horse in a reasonable period of time. The typical form of the pre-1870 city was between four and eight miles in diameter. In order to maximize that limited area, development occurred at 20 to 70 housing units to the net acre.

With the introduction of rail transport and all-weather vehicles came a major expansion of city size and, at the same time, a radical reduction in the typical urban density. The speed of movement tripled, from an average of three miles per hour to ten. The same number of people and urban activities could be accommodated, but at much lower density of development. At the same time, a new form of housing emerged. One- to four-family houses on small lots replaced the mass housing of the tenements. The result was a reduction in density from the old inner city of 20 to 70 dwellings per acre to 7 to 20 dwellings per acre on the former farm land at the edge of the city. This was the beginning of suburbia.

As suggested by Table 5.1, the end of this period coincided with the end of the major expansion of the American city. And it was just about this time that New York City adopted its zoning resolution and the U.S. Supreme Court decided *Euclid*.

The dimensions of the older American city were just about complete. If one goes to the boundary of these cities today, the housing is what was built in the 1920s. Some further changes did occur, but these were limited areas built in the 1930s because of the Depression.

With a few exceptions, most large cities undertook the planning and zoning process at the very same time that they had come to the end of their long period of growth. Until the 1930s the city expanded by annexation as the rail lines expanded outside the city. The expanding city, flush with tax dollars, promised public water and sewer service, fire and police protection and other benefits of merging with the great and growing city.

The Depression put an end to this type of growth. Cities ran out of money. Providing services to the new annexations had been funded on what seemed like an endless growth of new taxes and ratables. After 1929, cities soon found themselves with declining

Table 5.1. The Population of Major American Cities, Civil War to Present

City	Year							
	1860	**1880**	**1900**	**1920**	**1930**	**1940**	**1960**	**1980**
New York	1,174	1,478	3,347	5,620	6,930	7,454	7,781	7,071
% Change		26%	123%	63%	23%	8%	4%	−9%
Philadelphia	565	847	1,290	1,823	1,950	1,931	2,002	1,688
% Change		50%	53%	41%	7%	−1%	4%	−15%
Baltimore	212	332	505	733	804	859	939	786
% Change		57%	52%	45%	10%	7%	9%	−16%
Boston	177	362	560	748	781	770	697	562
% Change		104%	54%	33%	4%	−1%	−10%	−19%
New Orleans	168	216	287	387	458	494	627	557
% Change		29%	33%	35%	18%	8%	27%	−11%
Cincinnati	161	255	325	401	451	455	505	385
% Change		58%	27%	23%	12%	1%	11%	−23%
Buffalo	81	155	352	506	573	575	532	357
% Change		119%	64%	34%	6%	1%	−8%	−40%
Louisville	68	123	204	234	307	319	390	298
% Change		81%	66%	15%	31%	4%	22%	−24%
Washington	61	147	278	437	486	663	763	638
% Change		141%	89%	57%	11%	36%	15%	−16%

Note: Data are rounded and presented in thousands.
Source: United States Census. Selected cities were among the 10 largest in 1860.

ratables and taxes, and operating costs that did not decline. Even while people were out of work and their landlords went into tax arrears, the sewage plants still had to be operated and the schools had to educate the children. The ever-growing supply of tax dollars and the golden age of urban expansion ended.

With some exceptions, American cities were built to last. The typical building material was masonry and that allowed buildings of four, five, and even eight stories. This type of structure allowed the builder to maximize the number of living units on a minimum amount of scarce ground. Even where wood was the ma-terial of choice, high-density buildings were produced. By the time Jacob Reiis and other reformers had described the life-threatening aspects of tenements, the immigrants had already filled this housing to capacity and the process of supply and demand kept them full.

In order to sustain the high density associated with the great immigrant cities, the public infrastructure had to be built to support great loads. No longer could streets be simple grad-ed dirt roads. To support the teeming life, the city streets required a good subbase and a durable layer of cobblestones. Underneath these streets extensive, permanent water and sewer systems had to be built. On top of the streets were trolley lines and, in the largest of the cities, great underground rail systems. As a result of endless demand for new housing and new technology, the key physical elements of the city had become cast in concrete. Substantial physical rearrangement of the city was no longer as easy as it had been after the fires and disasters of earlier eras.

For planning and zoning to be a meaningful public process, one of two essential physical conditions is necessary. First, the economic, social, and physical conditions must allow the reuse of land or, second, new unimproved land must be available. By the time of *Euclid,* neither of these two conditions existed within the boundaries of the older cities. One could make endless great plans for the city, but the major planning tool of zoning was no longer effective because there was no major supply of new land.

While the cities were finding themselves locked into a physical setting that limited their ability to solve problems, the suburbs were just beginning their great periods of growth. Zoning really arrived too late to have much of an impact on the cities. The great American cities (with the exception of the newcomers of the West and Southwest) had completed the process of both physical and population expansion by the time zoning arrived.

ZONING IN RURAL AMERICA

Until very recently, zoning played no important role in regulating land use in rural America. Yet it was rural America and the changing economics of agriculture that had profound effects on the history of American zoning.

The first effect was due to the shift in America's farming population. Half of the population lived in rural America until about 1910. After the Civil War, however, the farmer began to get out from behind the horse-drawn plow and into the driver's seat. At the same time, commercial fertilizers and the land grant colleges radically increased the productivity of farms and farmers. Fewer farms fed more city people. New employment opportunities in the growing cities absorbed the population that agricultural changes forced off of the farm.

Some of the farms forced out of agriculture for economic reasons adjoined expanding cities. Often the early farms were quite small, and especially in the Northeast, established on marginal ground. Farmers began to see housing as the last good crop for their land.

This method of expansion continues even today. Suburban growth now is usually at the expense of farm land. As a result of this continuing shift in land resources, a major new issue has entered the arena of planning conflicts. The conservation and protection of agricultural land is now an important method of restraining suburban growth.

ZONING IN SUBURBIA

In the mid-1920s, at the historical origins of zoning, the concept seemed simple. By dividing a community into a series of zones, important issues of health, safety, and welfare could be resolved. By keeping an industrial plant away from homes, the future of the homes is secured. The same result can be achieved by keeping homes from moving into an industrial zone. Not only can we hope to increase the usefulness of the homes by keeping them out of industrial zones, but we can also prevent future problems if industry needs to expand at its location.

After reading a sample of traditional American zoning ordinances, anyone, including a visitor from outer space, would reasonably conclude that the basic purpose of zoning is to protect private property and that protection will in some way contribute to the public good. In rarer instances, it may be possible to find a connection between the separation of land uses and public health. While less common today than in the era of gas works and asbestos factories, there are some occupational hazards where the separation of various land uses contributes to the public welfare. But we can look more closely at the rationale of zoning as it changed over the last century.

Suburban Growth: 1870–1929

During the period 1870–1929, suburban America grew quietly. It was still necessary to have agriculture close to the city, and to supply the daily needs of the city a very extensive rail system was developed. The same trains that provided the food supply to the city set the stage for suburban growth.

In the best parts of the city, the upper class, with its great houses and newfangled apartment houses, had first choice of land resources. At the other end of the economic scale was the endless need for land to support cheap housing for the masses. It did not take the building industry long to figure out that the daily milk train would get the newly burgeoning middle-class housing consumers to the countryside. The age of the commuter was born. Farm land was cheap and the cost of development was low. A private well and septic system were just as good as the expensive public systems of the city. Except for public education, there was little else that had to be provided out of local real estate taxes. The only physical limitation to further suburban development was the poor roads between home and the railway station and therefore suburbia stayed fairly close to the station at first.

This first period of suburban development is associated with the birth of American planning and zoning. One would expect the early days of such a new process to be difficult. In hindsight, these were the carefree days for planning. From a planning perspective, these were the days to invent the suburbs. Garden City on Long Island and Radburn and Llewellyn Park in New Jersey were designed as models of living in the new automobile age. While the reported cases of that day gave some hint of the future dilemma of American planning, the fair and equitable distribution of land and housing was a nonissue.

The day-to-day local zoning battles were over the details of growth. The important issues dealt with the placement of schools, gas stations, and the occasional apartment house so as not to affect adversely the value of new single-family homes. What is important to remember is that like the school that was to serve the new homes and the gas station that was for the local cars, the apartment house proposed for down the street was intended for white, middle-class Americans.

Zoning and suburban America grew together. More zones were invented. From the simple one- or two-family zone of the 1920s' ordinances, it was soon found that one could somehow find a difference between a single-family house on a 5,000-square-foot lot and one that was on a 7,500-square-foot lot. Based on an earlier need to have side yards for fire prevention, zoning ordinances provided endless details regulating all aspects of suburban housing production. Until World War II, zoning, for all of its growing complexity, was still a method to regulate the use of land and affect its economic value.

In the process of using the tools of land control, it was soon found that the combination of zoning, subdivision, and site plan review had the power of determining who could live where.

By itself, zoning was limited in its final effects. The zoning power allowed local planners to determine which areas should be used for single-family housing and which should be used for garden apartments. Subdivision regulations could determine the size of the lot. Given the economics of residential development, there is usually an economic relationship between the size of a lot and the value of the house to be built on that lot. Site plan review would add the final touch to the planning process. Taken all together, the three tools of land use control contributed to what has always been the agenda of suburban planning, the determination of who will live where.

Race, Class, and Conservation Politics at the Time of *Euclid*

America, by virtue of its industrial might, its geographic isolation, and its good timing in entering World War I, had become a world power. The country never experienced the economic ravages of war. The fortunate combination of great immigration and seemingly endless land and natural resources allowed this country to achieve a long period of prosperity.

At the outset of zoning, concerns about racial separation were often a direct part of the planning process. For decades before the *Euclid* decision, there was ghastly racial violence in this country. Lynch mobs were common, and a large number of black soldiers were executed by the Army in the course of one of the border wars. Race and fears related to race were very much part of the American scene during the early period of zoning. This is clear in such planning efforts as the plan for Atlanta, which established its zones not on land use but on the skin color of the proposed inhabitants.

Racial segregation was accepted by the pre-Depression society and economy. There were plenty of jobs for people at the bottom of the economic pyramid. The white urban families needed household help; the booming con-

struction industry needed a growing supply of laborers.

The widespread acceptance of a fairly demarcated class society was both a result of the country's European heritage and the Industrial Revolution. The new immigrants came from a world in which one's class usually was preordained. The economic prosperity of the country gave the working classes hope for change. Since that hope was far more than what had been possible in the old country, there was widespread acceptance of American class structure.

The physical conditions of the times facilitated this world of divided classes. For the very rich there were carefree city districts where a foreign face or sound was uncommon. Park and Fifth Avenues, Sutton Place, and Gramercy Park were products of this age. For the upper and middle classes who wanted a quieter setting, the countryside and the new suburbs offered an alternative. The rail system provided excellent transportation, yet it was expensive enough to provide an economic barrier to the poor.

New housing still was being provided for the poor in the city. The "old law" tenements with their inhumane qualities now were technically illegal, but the "new law" housing for the poor was being provided in the city. The new building regulations added a measure of light and air to the apartments, but still allowed a high enough density to make it economically feasible to reuse older and less desirable parts of the city.

Many of the urban conditions that are considered to be major social problems now were accepted as part of the natural process of urban development before *Euclid*. Until the shattering experience of the Depression, America was a country of self-sufficiency, confidence, and conservatism. There seemed to be no limit to the iron, coal, oil, lumber, and other natural resources that the country needed to sustain its economic growth. Combined with the inventiveness and energy of its people, the natural wealth and accumulating capital made the United States a first-rank industrial state.

The results of the country's growth strengthened the conservatism of the period. For the expanding middle class, the American dream was coming true, especially as it related to housing. Cheap labor, an endless supply of lumber and building materials, low interest rates, and a seemingly constant supply of land made the dream house a reality.

When planning conflicts did occur, they seemed benign compared to urban conditions. For example, if overbuilding on steep land resulted in soil erosion, that was a small price for growth. Since industrial uses were chained to rail sites, there was minimum conflict with new residential growth.

The early days of zoning coincided with economic good times. Today, many of the conflicts that zoning is intended to resolve are related to economic disruptions and social inequities. In the period before *Euclid* that was not the case.

Building at the Time of *Euclid*

Other factors made real estate development highly effective at the time of *Euclid*. Mortgage money was available, although the payment periods were short and most ended with balloon payments. To build quickly and cheaply, a whole new construction method, the frame house, was invented. Building roads and utilities on farm land was quick and relatively inexpensive. New roads and utilities accelerated and strengthened the process of annexation. Enterprising developers often convinced municipalities eager to expand to undertake the cost of these improvements. By 1921, at the urging of American farmers, the federal government got into the road business. With 50 percent federal financing, road building began in earnest.

During this period, planners developed theories of appropriate land use. If anything can be described as the central core of planning theory, it is this idea that there is a certain hierarchy of land uses. Accordingly, the main goal of planning is to ensure that in the process of growth and change, land uses follow each other in their proper order. If this order is not correctly followed, then planning theory predicts certain types of land use will have an adverse impact on other land uses.

Planning established that the basic criterion for a well-planned community was the large single-family home. The hierarchy then proceeded through ever-decreasing residential lot sizes to various types of multifamily housing. It ended with a variety of industrial and commercial uses. Based on limited observation and almost no science, planners determined that various conflicts would develop between land uses if the uses were placed on the landscape out of proper rank order. Other problems would be generated by the improper placement of certain types of streets and traffic patterns on adjacent land uses.

The principal source of this planning theory was practical real estate experience. Based on consumer preferences, the real estate analysts found that land values increased or decreased based on changes in and interrelationships among various types of land uses. There was no further scientific explanation for such changes in land values other than market considerations. Nevertheless, planners assumed that if current consumer preferences determined land values, then these land values could be used to determine what was good and bad land use.

While 60 years have passed since *Euclid*, much of planning and zoning is still based on these early planning concepts. And there is very little more scientific evidence today for the concepts of proper land use. It is still common to find local master plans that carefully detail how various residential areas of different lot sizes should be separated from each other. More often than not, municipal planning assumes that multifamily housing is, by the nature of the land use, less desirable than single-family housing.

Suburban Zoning: A Summary

The question that comes to mind is why zoning was invented at what now appears to be one of the best of times in land development. There are two broad answers: One comes from the case law of the period, the other out of municipal history.

This period was marked by a process that was until quite recently singularly American. A whole new class of people established a new way of life in the suburbs. For the first time in western history, a large and growing segment of the population could own a house and land. It took another 50 years before the same type of physical and social development was to occur in Europe.

For those who had not made much economic progress and still lived in the tenements, there were always new examples of people who left a cold water flat and moved to a house with light and air and land. Zoning as a planning tool and a legal concept was intended to ensure that this achievement of home ownership and property value would remain. The basic purpose of zoning, and its related planning tools, was to maintain and defend the new American Dream.

In the city, the planning and zoning issues were not ones of protecting the newly built areas. Planning was concerned with ensuring the continuation of the city's rebuilding process. In order to reuse the land in built-up areas, the planning process had to deliver, through zoning, new land uses that supported a major increase in land values. Without that benefit, the private sector's reuse of older and deteriorating areas was impossible.

In rare situations where the housing and related social needs of the poor were acknowledged, a simple solution appeared in the development ideas of that time. As early as 1860, one of the roles of the new suburb was to provide a convenient, healthy environment for housing the lower class. Housing experts of that day believed that the ills of the urban slum were a function of its population density and its building types. What was required was a new physical solution to low-income housing.

At the very time that these concerns were raised, the new light rail technology of the trolley came into use. This transportation made large new land areas at the city's outer edge accessible. An example of this was the development of large quantities of housing for the working class in an area of the Bronx called South Morrisania, now more commonly called the South Bronx. As long as it was possible to obtain adequate amounts of farm land for inexpensive housing, it looked as if the problems associated with slum housing would disappear in the natural course of events.

It is interesting to speculate what might have happened if this urban development process had continued after 1930. With the end of this era came an end to private sector production of what would be called moderate-income housing today. Conceivably, enough housing might have been produced then so that today's housing shortages might not be so critical. Housing supply did work well when the city's growth was unrestricted by the availability of new land.

SOCIAL CHANGES AND ZONING: 1930–1950

Two major developments occurred in the two decades after *Euclid,* but zoning did not really respond to those changes until after 1950.

The Great Depression and World War II gave rise to the major social changes that influenced zoning in this period—an increasing demand for food and agricultural products like cotton had a devastating impact, especially on small farms. For black farm laborers in the South, it meant the end of a way of life that had persisted since emancipation.

The Great Depression

For the cities, the Great Depression was a period of retrenchment and disinvestment. For the first time in decades, American cities faced a period of no growth or even contraction. Major physical and social problems of the city, which had been hidden by the forces of growth and demand, now became visible. Their visibility was increased because the problems now affected not just a small part of society but larger numbers of people. As people could not meet their rent bills, vacancy signs appeared. With increased vacancies came municipal tax arrears and foreclosures on housing that had so recently been part of the economic success of the city.

The process of city development came to a virtual halt. Annexation and expansion, which had been so much a part of local housing needs, could no longer be met by building the next new neighborhood at the outer edge of the city. For the first time in memory, families without food or shelter looked to local government for help. Local government found itself with the irreconcilable problems of increased demand for social and physical solutions at the same time as its tax base was declining.

For the labor movement, the bad times meant that its time had come. No longer were there jobs available, nor would the demand of an expanding economy protect those who had jobs. With nothing much to lose, American workers finally joined the union. In doing so, the long-ignored social message of the labor movement finally was heard. Jobs by themselves were not enough; workers were entitled to a fair share of the economic pie. The new union members dreamed of, and later would expect to achieve, a single-family house in a nice subdivision to go with the car in every garage and the chicken in every pot.

Along with the idea of an economic fair share came another concept, a social fair share. The acceptance of a class society that had persisted in pre-Depression America was eroded by both the labor movement and the notion that the upper class was responsible for the Great Depression. After all, why would well-born stockbrokers jump out of windows? Why would prosperous companies suddenly close their doors? The message was clear: The people and the class that had run the country had created the current economic disaster.

The new politics of the Democrats, both in Washington and in city hall, supported the notion that something was wrong with America. The introduction of radical social and economic programs like the Works Progress Administration, Federal Housing Administration, and National Recovery Act supported the idea that the old system had broken down. If this was not enough evidence, then the Democratic Party was there to assign the blame.

The Second World War

World War II set in motion profound structural changes in American society. It gave impetus to the civil rights movement. Although the civil rights movement had started long before the war, the manpower shortages of wartime brought blacks into the great crusade. While blacks were separate in the military until after the war, the fact that many blacks paid the full measure for their country was finally recognized by the government in the antidiscrimination order of President Harry Truman. While social and physical segregation was still very much alive, the seeds of its destruction had been planted.

Another important change occurred on the home front. Women entered the labor force as part of the war effort. Rosie the riveter discovered that she not only could do the work but also could bring home a paycheck.

When the war ended, one of the most pressing national needs was housing. While some tentative government housing programs had started during the New Deal years, they were limited to a few cities, directed at the poor, and designed to stimulate the Depression economy. The war brought the housing industry to a dead stop.[1]

Until the postwar housing shortage, housing had never been a major governmental activity. After the war, however, the housing needs of the returning veterans and the pent-up civilian demand made that a different matter. It was no longer just social reformers crying out for housing for the poor; it was everyone's sons and daughters who needed housing. This broadly based appeal brought about the first massive government intervention in the housing market. The creation of these middle-class government housing programs provided the foundation of rapid suburban growth and the decline of the older city.

THE GOLDEN AGE OF SUBURBIA: 1950–PRESENT

As soon as the good war ended the cold war began. One consequence was national concern about the defense of the continental United States. It was national policy that an interstate road system was essential to the national defense. What followed was a decade and a half of intensive road building funded in large measure by the federal government. The resulting federal highway program gave birth to the great period of suburban development.

The City's Aging Industrial Base

The Allies' victory over Germany and Japan set the stage for their economic revival and, in part, the demise of America's industrial base. America's postwar largess enabled the former enemies to rebuild their industrial base to the most modern standards. In contrast, most of America's aging industrial base in 1950 was in or close to its cities. By the 1960s, America would discover the impossibility of competing in the international marketplace with an industrial base that was 30 years older than that of its former enemies. Some urban industries, like the New England shoe industry and the Midwest steel industry, would eventually all but disappear.

By the 1950s, American industry, in order to survive, found it necessary to leave the outmoded city plants to set up new facilities along the interstate highways. The suddenness of this economic event left behind empty industrial buildings in the city and a large number of people with limited skills and decreasing economic prospects.

The new jobs that were created by this shift in the industrial base occurred in the postwar suburbs. Because of residential zoning restrictions, however, many of the people who had these types of jobs could no longer get to them. The city came to have a large number of people locked into a stagnant and depreciating housing supply who were also separated from new employment opportunities.

The Civil Rights Movement and White Flight

The civil rights movement became a reality in the 1960s. By condemning the deteriorated housing of the poor and the existence of urban ghettos, the civil rights movement brought to national attention what had always been accepted as the way things were.

In one decade, the city of Newark, New Jersey, changed from a white, middle-class city to one where the majority was black and poor and surrounded by empty old factories. In the course of that dramatic shift, millions of dollars in hard-earned property values disappeared. In the Bronx, New York, the sudden flight of middle-income Jews from the Grand Concourse to the brand new government-assisted housing at Co-op City set in motion a population movement that was to devastate the Bronx.[2] At the same time, migrants from the South and Puerto Rico were looking for a new place to live. The social and physical effect was devastating. Once the process of population change had started with the Grand Concourse, it spread to most of the other ethnic communities of the Bronx.

In its flight from the city, white America saw the physical results of rapid population movement caused by social and economic change. What compounded the fear was the fact that for many of them the move to suburbia required all of their economic resources. Anything that reduced or could possibly affect the economic value of their new home or neighborhood was potentially devastating. For white city dwellers who lived amid the social changes, these rapid events accelerated the flight to suburbia.

Having acquired a new suburban house and mortgage, the new suburbanite wanted to ensure that such dramatic neighborhood changes would not happen again. One of the most effective methods to ensure stability was to con-

trol the housing costs of the next subdivision. It was assumed that if the next subdivision was priced at the same or even higher level than the last development, then the next group of neighbors would be the same kind of people. That type of market control was established by planning: Zoning had become the Maginot Line of suburbia.

The Independence of Suburbia

The growing suburbs found that they could thrive without annexation. They found themselves capable of self-government. The increasing local tax base provided the economic resources for increasing local services. An array of federal New Deal-like programs helped to provide some of the public works necessary for suburban growth.

While a real separation was occurring between the city and the suburbs, they were still tied together by the location of most of the region's employment. The suburban wage earner still took the 7:45 a.m. to the city and the 5:15 p.m. back home.

Everybody Gets a Car

In the first stages of suburban development before 1950, homes were built on small lots close to transportation. Once an extensive road system was put in place and it became possible to drive to the train station there was no stopping suburban development. As the car became the connecting link between home and work, new homes were built on larger lots. Not only did the lots grow in size, but the suburban population exploded.

The New Jersey counties of Bergen and Essex are a part of the inner ring of counties around both New York and Newark. Parts of these two counties closest to the Hudson River experienced much of their growth before *Euclid.* These two counties have been tied to the principal cities by both rail and ferry services.

But northern Bergen and western Essex grew after *Euclid* because of the automobile. They grew because road building was now the new method for suburban growth. Tables 5.2 and 5.3 tell that story in numbers. The tables present the population statistics for selected communities in both counties divided between those that developed as railroad towns and those that, later on, had their major period of growth based on the developing highway system.

Furthermore, for those who had an income, there was capital available for mortgages. If you qualified, you got a 3 percent mortgage for a single-family home that cost less than 25 percent of your income.

The After-Effects in the City

While a significant number of Americans were benefiting by the expanding suburbs, large numbers were left behind. For the minorities

Table 5.2. Population Growth (*persons per sq. mile*) in Selected Municipalities: Bergen County, N.J., 1910–1980

Town	Developed During the Railroad Era Years							
	1910	1920	1930	1940	1950	1960	1970	1980
Englewood	2,005	4,153	6,359	6,774	8,226	9,306	8,923	8,465
Garfield	4,863	6,922	10,621	10,016	9,839	10,448	10,999	9,573
Hackensack	3,513	6,310	8,774	9,385	10,435	10,900	12,860	12,871
Ridgefld Pk	2,350	3,063	3,844	4,028	4,283	4,536	4,996	4,549
Ruthford	2,710	3,392	5,327	6,596	6,697	6,218	7,312	6,810

Town	Developed During the Highway Era Years							
	1910	1920	1930	1940	1950	1960	1970	1980
Fairlawn	0	0	2,139	3,238	8,530	13,008	13,586	11,510
New Milford	175	707	913	1,148	2,145	6,170	6,839	6,027
Northvale	0	452	409	414	520	1,033	1,849	1,802
Paramus	0	0	946	1,317	2,239	8,299	10,136	9,455
Rivervale	107	208	311	397	607	2,006	3,175	3,389

Source: United States Census, 1910 to 1980.

**Table 5.3. Population Growth (*persons per sq. mile*) in Selected
Municipalities: Essex County, N.J., 1910–1980**

Town	Developed During the Railroad Era Years[a]						
	1910	**1920**	**1930**	**1950**	**1960**	**1970**	**1980**
Bloomfield	2,791	4,078	7,051	7,708	9,131	9,641	8,850
Essex Fell	340	460	858	1,128	1,244	1,672	1,955
E. Orange	8,643	12,678	17,005	17,236	19,835	18,868	19,256
Montclair	3,476	4,647	6,777	7,085	6,956	7,104	6,181
W. Orange	907	1,287	2,010	2,364	3,297	3,613	3,265

Town	Developed During the Highway Era Years[a]						
	1910	**1920**	**1930**	**1950**	**1960**	**1970**	**1980**
Cedar Grove	535	707	1,065	1,783	N.A.	3,463	2,800
Livingston	73	80	248	709	1,652	2,152	2,003
Milburn	372	463	860	1,456	1,880	2,109	1,954
N. Caldwell	205	161	514	1,614	1,436	2,322	2,011
Roseland	136	170	296	564	783	1,244	1,489

a The year 1940 was deleted for reasons of space.
Source: United States Census, 1910 to 1980.

and those with limited incomes, the aging city with its declining economic base and growing housing problems was still home.

For the cities, these years brought major changes. The "housing problem" and its location, the slum, became part of the cities' official agendas. While poor housing conditions had been present in the pre-*Euclidean* industrial city, it was in this period of economic decline that the solution was recognized clearly as a major municipal responsibility. Whereas the period had started with the most tentative federal housing programs, the end of the period was marked by massive federal and state participation in housing.

Because of the war-related housing shortages, a large number of cities had already instituted rent control. In most localities this control ended with the war, but in a few cities it continues today, thus adding a major impediment to the process of urban rejuvenation.

During the 1950s and 1960s, retail and service land uses were predominantly an inner city function. Now the urban growth in these land use sectors had come to an end. The downtown area was unable to maintain a rate of expansion large enough to reuse outdated urban land. At the same time, the suburban shopping center was following the highways to the suburbs.

Before 1950, there was a movement of economic and ethnic groups around the city as families moved up the economic ladder. For most major ethnic groups, there were a number of different and usually newer neighborhoods to which one could move in accordance with one's improving economic status. This was part of the built-in pre–World War II renewal process. But after 1950, the visibility of the social problems in the city and the availability of the suburbs ended this self-renewal.

SUBURBAN HOUSING: 1950 TO THE PRESENT

By the 1950s, inner counties such as Bergen and Essex were used up. The next major move was beyond the suburban areas that were both adjacent to the old inner city and serviced by a rail connection. In New Jersey, the move was to Middlesex, Morris, and Mercer counties. Before World War II, these three counties had a very limited connection to the New York metropolitan center. Middlesex had been largely agricultural with some low-value industry. Morris was also agricultural but had a fair number of larger estates. Mercer had the state capital, farming, and Princeton University.

Table 5.4 illustrates the rates of growth that occurred—and still continue—in these three counties.[3] To provide some perspective on the current rates of development, data for the preceding decades have also been included. To simplify the tables, only the larger, nonurban municipalities have been included. The numbers also indicate the population changes for the first group of suburban communities of the inner ring. Then it adds those communities that changed from farm to suburb in the space of a decade after the war.

Suburban Housing for the Common Man

During World War II, a residential builder named Arthur Levitt had a contract for war housing. Both skilled labor and construction

Table 5.4. Population Growth in Mercer, Morris, and Middlesex Counties, N.J., 1910–1980, Selected Municipalities

Mercer County Town	Area (Sq.Mi.)	1910	1920	1930	1940	1950	1960	1970	1980
East Windsor	15.60	941	733	922	845	1,284	2,298	11,736	21,041
Ewing	15.13	1,889	3,475	6,942	10,146	16,840	26,628	32,831	34,842
Hamilton	39.38	7,899	14,580	27,121	30,219	41,156	65,035	79,609	82,801
Hopewell	58.00	3,171	3,249	3,907	3,728	4,731	1,928	10,030	10,893
Lawrence	21.87	2,522	3,686	6,293	6,522	8,499	13,665	19,567	19,724
Princeton	16.25	1,178	1,424	2,738	3,251	5,407	10,411	13,651	13,683
Washington	20.70	1,090	1,161	1,347	1,365	1,843	2,156	3,311	3,487
West Windsor	26.84	1,342	1,389	1,711	2,160	2,519	4,016	6,431	8,452

(continued)

Table 5.4 (*continued*)

Morris County Town	Area (Sq.Mi.)	1910	1920	1930	1940	1950	1960	1970	1980
Chester	28.90	1,251	1,195	1,453	874	1,297	2,107	4,265	5,198
Denville	12.70	0	1,205	2,162	3,117	6,055	10,632	14,045	14,380
Hanover	10.80	6,228	8,531	2,516	2,812	3,756	9,329	10,700	11,846
Jefferson	41.20	1,303	1,226	1,254	1,548	2,744	6,884	14,122	16,413
Kinnelon	19.05	0	0	428	745	1,350	4,431	7,600	7,770
Montville	18.97	1,944	1,515	2,467	3,207	4,159	6,772	11,846	14,290
Mount Olive	30.06	1,160	1,008	1,235	1,526	2,597	3,807	10,394	18,748
Randolph	20.88	2,307	2,509	2,165	2,160	4,293	7,295	13,296	17,828
Rockaway Twp	42.35	4,835	3,506	3,178	2,423	4,418	10,356	18,955	19,850
Roxbury	21.46	2,414	2,976	3,879	4,455	5,707	9,983	15,754	18,878
Washington	45.12	1,900	1,779	1,615	1,870	2,147	3,330	6,962	11,402

Middlesex County Town									
Middlesex	3.45	0	1,852	3,504	3,763	5,943	10,520	15,038	13,480
Monroe	41.80	2,238	2,625	2,894	3,034	4,082	5,831	9,138	15,858
Piscataway	18.90	3,523	5,385	5,865	7,243	10,180	19,890	34,418	42,223
Somerville	16.60	5,786	7,181	8,658	8,186	10,338	22,553	32,508	29,069
So. Brunswick	41.00	2,443	2,206	2,758	3,129	4,001	10,278	14,058	17,127
Woodbridge	23.10	8,948	13,423	25,266	27,191	35,758	78,846	98,944	90,074
E. Brunswick	22.20	1,602	1,857	2,711	3,706	5,699	19,965	34,166	37,711
Madison	31.31	1,621	1,808	2,566	3,803	7,366	22,772	48,715	51,515
Raritan	30.65	2,707	5,419	10,025	11,470	16,348	44,799	67,120	70,193

Source: U.S. Census, 1910 to 1980.

time were limited, so Levitt invented a new method of housing production. His new methodology reduced both building time and cost. What worked in wartime could also work for peacetime housing needs. The country understood that whatever it took, it was essential that the postwar housing needs were met. It was also assumed that in shifting from a wartime to a peacetime economy, the possibility of another depression existed. Since memories of that awful period were still fresh in the country's mind, no one, especially the political party in power, wanted to repeat that devastating experience.

Government Financing

The combined pent-up demand from the war and depression years led to massive federal participation in providing housing. While the birth of the Federal Housing Administration dates back to the National Housing Act of 1934, it grew up after the end of World War II. Under an expanded FHA housing program, a qualified civilian almost was assured of a mortgage. For the veteran, a parallel housing program was started under the G.I. Bill.

The FHA and the Veterans Administration had two housing programs, one for single-family housing, the other for multifamily rental housing. Both forms of housing were desperately needed. Millions of families were living doubled-up or in temporary housing. For the single-family home buyer, the federal housing programs provided insurance for the housing loan. The heart of the federal program reduced the home buyer's monthly payment to a minimum amount. Secondly, the government required that its loans be self-liquidating. Where before the war most single-family home loans were for short periods of time with a tough balloon payment, now there was a loan program that brought housing within the reach of large numbers of people. The government housing programs were so effective that soon private lenders had to provide very similar terms.

Early in this period, the explosion of the housing industry overcame the backlog of demand by veterans and civilians. Once this process of building affordable housing began, however, it never stopped. It was a case of success breeding more success. While most planners and social commentators ended up hating

the new suburban dream, Americans voted with the moving van for this housing solution. Until temporarily stopped by the recession of the 1970s, the process of building the suburbs has continued as the principal method of providing housing for this country's expanding middle class.

Multifamily Housing

Not all veterans or civilians could afford a single-family home. Some needed less expensive rental housing. Massive financing for developers at very favorable rates, and the general acceptance/acknowledgement of a housing crisis made the large-scale production of inexpensive rental housing possible.

Some 50 years earlier, English planners had started what was known as the New Town movement. Out of that concept came the garden apartment. During the 1920s and 1930s, this low-density housing innovation designed for suburban development was tried in a few American settings. In the 1950s, as a good solution to the postwar housing crisis, its day arrived. Until the garden apartment appeared, most suburban multifamily housing had been in the form of a modified city tenement or apartment house. By association with urban social problems, multifamily housing was often rejected by the local town fathers. In fact, this problem showed up in *Euclid*.

The garden apartment, with its modest height and density (from 12 to 22 units per acre) was the solution for providing rental housing for the veterans. Because it would house G.I.s and because it looked pretty good compared to other forms of higher density housing, the garden apartment was acceptable to town fathers.

The federal multifamily housing programs did bring a large number of less than affluent people to the suburbs. After the great rush to produce veterans' housing was over, the new single-family home owners, who by now had also become the town fathers, decided that no more of such housing would be needed. That reaction toward postwar multifamily housing was one of the starting points for exclusionary zoning.

In order to meet the postwar housing demand, vast new land areas for the new suburbs were needed. While many of the 1930s-vintage suburbs still had some vacant land, those sites were not enough for the production of large numbers of new housing units. Also, the land had to be inexpensive to meet the economic constraints of both the buyer and the FHA and VA housing programs. Consequently, rural townships were invaded by developers looking for unimproved, inexpensive land for new, moderately priced subdivisions.

With the rapid expansion of the regional road systems, large areas of rural land were brought into the development cycle. Equally important, local planning officials were willing to support the construction of the infrastructure necessary for growth.

For the last time in the development process, the farmers and their local friends were in charge of local planning and zoning. If a builder wanted to pay a farmer $500 or $1,000 per acre, that made sense to the farmer on the planning board. If that land were used for farming, it could take 10 to 20 years to get the same rate of return from that same acre. It also probably helped that the proposal was for housing for the veterans. The result was that large amounts of suitable land were zoned for development. With the large amounts of land came low land costs and inexpensive housing.

Shopping and Services Leave the City

As in the previous period of suburban growth, local retailing and services did not immediately follow the migration out of the city. By the 1960s, when these droves of new suburban home owners tried to drive into the old retail area downtown they found that there was no place to park. This inconvenience helped to bring about the suburban retail explosion that in turn accelerated the decline of the center city. With federal and state governments creating new highway interchanges, the conditions existed for the creation of shopping centers.

Once the process had started with people and retail services, then other major businesses followed to the suburbs. At first it was access to the highway system and the labor force that led to the move out of the city. This led to the suburbanization of light manufacturing, distribution, and similar land uses. It became increasingly difficult and expensive to obtain a reasonable site in the old city for the more extensive land uses. The land use limitations of the city pushed such economic activity out to the suburbs. Then intensive economic activities moved. Finally, when no reasonably priced land was left in the city, the most traditional city land uses, the front and back offices, began the move as well.

Consequences for the City

While planners in the suburbs were struggling with the problems of growth, planners in the city were concerned with the process of decline. While some cities in the South and Southwest would still have an era of growth, the older industrial cities faced decades of dealing with a new problem—retrenchment.

Once the middle class and many of its supporting institutions moved out of the city, lower income groups moved into the empty housing and neighborhoods. By the late 1950s and early 1960s, this process had changed the face of many older cities. And while the older cities were in a major decline, it was not until New York's fiscal crisis in the mid-1970s that people were willing to acknowledge that fact.

It may be true that cities stagnated during the Great Depression, but the postwar period marked the first time in the history of urban America that the city actually declined. During this same period, the suburbs achieved growth and their own political power.

The Invention of Urban Renewal

The postwar city problems were viewed by planners and political leaders as temporary in nature and subject to change through active planning intervention. For the first time since *Euclid,* a major new planning concept and program was introduced into the urban development process. To treat the problem of urban decline, a new planning tool—urban renewal—was invented. A fundamental premise of urban renewal was that significant growth could be reintroduced in the older city.

The origin of urban renewal was the planning theory that if certain physical conditions and problems could be removed, then city growth could be reestablished. The original objective of the renewal process was to save the old urban retail center. Planners believed that by providing enough parking and amenities, the shoppers would come back.

While the shoppers rarely came back, the concept of getting the federal government to bear the largest financial burden of the city's renewal was established. In short order, the concept of renewal was expanded to treat the decline in urban housing. Major residential projects involving blocks of buildings and hundreds of families were conceived. The objective was to replace old housing with new housing. In order to have new types of residential land uses for the newly cleared land, a variety of new federal and state housing programs were established.

Twenty years after the urban renewal process was started, it was stopped. While some showpiece projects did produce results, the overall experience of urban renewal was failure. Hindsight suggests that it could not succeed without the essential ingredient for housing growth: economic demand. Urban growth based only on government-sponsored activity was impossible.

During the urban renewal episode, one key question never seemed to be asked about the viability of residential renewal. Where were the employment opportunities for the people about to be housed in the urban renewal areas? It was assumed that the right location for rebuilding worn out neighborhoods was the same location for employment.

A good reason for not questioning this assumption was obvious. What other residential areas would accept those groups of people displaced in the process of tearing down the slums? But if jobs were moving out of the city, did not that also require moving city people out to suburbia?

Had this essential question about the relationship of housing and jobs seriously been explored, the answer would have been to move the slum dwellers to the suburbs. Instead, planners hoped that some of the jobs for those people would remain and that other jobs would return to the city. Most of the new sources of employment, however, would not be in the city, but in suburbia along the major highways.

Until the 1950s, the planning process had been connected closely to zoning. While zoning had at times directed the use of land outside of economic realities, by and large zoning had been responsive to the requirements of the marketplace. In the case of urban renewal, planning solutions not connected to economic reality often were introduced. Earlier, the city had survived the problems of physical obsolescence because new neighborhoods were created for various groups as economic conditions changed.

Effective answers to the city's problems were missed for two reasons. First, planners were unable to understand or accept the economic changes that had occurred in the urban and suburban landscape. The fundamental redistribution of employment opportunities was not recognized for a number of decades. Second, part of the solution to the city's problems would have required the creation of large-scale residential development at the edge of the city. At the very time the city had the greatest need for this traditional growth process, it was no longer possible. The rise of suburban political power had made exclusionary zoning a permanent factor in determining regional land use.

THE MAJOR PROBLEMS OF ZONING

Sixty years have passed since zoning came of age in *Euclid*. Until about 30 years ago, the focus of zoning was the attractive process of growth. Within the last two decades, zoning has become deeply involved in the more difficult and far-reaching problem of restraining growth and change.

The most obvious current problem of zoning is its use as a means of social and economic exclusion. As discussed, growth in the United States has been associated with the free movement of people and employment at the edge of development. This traditional process seems to be essential for both social and economic growth, and it is now halted, or at least seriously hindered, by the advent of exclusionary zoning.

The stated reasons why planning and zoning are being used to prevent growth are the following: (1) to preserve agriculture, (2) to provide for very low density suburban development, and (3) to save some environmentally sensitive land areas. What is not stated, perhaps because the implications are not understood, is what these zoning restrictions will

mean to future regional social and economic growth.

The cities, both large and small, will continue to pay the price of the suburban zoning. In fact, these suburban zoning problems may eventually compound the inner city's social, economic, and racial problems.

Exclusionary Zoning in Englewood, New Jersey

The exclusionary problems inherent in the zoning powers were recognized from the very beginning. In fact, in some of the early zoning ordinances, the power to zone was used to divide the community into separate racial areas. It was not until the great suburban rush of the 1960s, however, that the less visible exclusionary aspects of zoning emerged as major political and planning issues. While the problems of exclusionary zoning were confronted in a number of states, it was in New Jersey that the exclusionary zoning debate became a major political issue, and the courts became major forces in this conflict.

One of the watersheds of exclusionary zoning occurred a few miles west of New York City in Englewood, New Jersey. Englewood has a history that goes back to colonial farming, but as a suburb it took shape in the 1920s as a railroad commuter town and summer resort of the wealthy. A small black neighborhood developed in a corner of town just west of the railroad tracks. In the 1950s, the last large empty areas were filled by white middle-class migrants from the city. The newcomers included Democrats looking for a way to overthrow the established Republican rule. They made a pact with the old black community; they promised better housing in exchange for coming out to vote Democratic.

The Democrats won and proceeded with a state and federally assisted housing program. While some of this seemingly radical program was based on practical politics, the civil rights movement was present in both spirit and numbers.

For both political and civil rights reasons, the housing coalition of blacks and whites determined that part of the housing program had to be in an area that was traditionally white. The town already owned the land, but it was zoned for single-family homes just like the rest of the neighborhood. What was needed was a zoning variance to allow the construction of multifamily housing.

A black, nonprofit housing sponsor leased the land from the city. For 13 long nights of hearings, the application for the variance was opposed by a neighborhood group. From this contest arose the case of *Greater Englewood Housing Corp.* v. *DeSimon*.[4]

GEHC won and built more than 140 low- and moderate-income apartments. The New Jersey courts found that included in the concept of special reasons for a variance was the affirmative obligation to use zoning to break down the very same racial ghettos zoning had helped to create.

Perhaps encouraged by the GEHC case, three more exclusionary zoning cases followed in short order. Each of them was brought by people who had a direct relationship to the civil rights movement.

Suburban Action Institute and Mahwah, New Jersey

The Suburban Action Institute tested the exclusionary zoning policy of Mahwah, a growing north Jersey town.[5]

Mahwah was chosen partly because it had a very large Ford Motor Company plant. The issue was whether the town could use zoning to keep low-cost housing for the factory workers out of the town. Fifteen years after the case was brought, it was resolved in favor of low-cost housing, but by that time the plant

had closed because of economic changes in the automobile industry.

The Suburban Action Institute suit raised the now-traditional exclusionary zoning arguments. What was not raised in court was the effect of Mahwah's zoning on housing in New York City, where most of the Ford workers lived. Then, as now, planners did not see the other side of exclusionary zoning: its effect on the older city that must continue to provide housing for those excluded from the economic opportunities of the suburbs.

Madison Township, New Jersey

In central New Jersey, the Suburban Action Institute joined a major residential builder in attacking Madison Township for exclusionary zoning.[6]

By the early 1970s, Madison Township had just finished a period of tremendous growth that had started in the late 1950s. Most of that growth had been in the form of moderately priced, single-family homes and large numbers of inexpensive garden apartments. Madison's growth was typical of postwar suburbia. By the time Suburban Action sued, taxes were increasing, schools were on double sessions, and traffic had become impossible.

Since the growth had occurred under one political party, the other party correctly decided that the way to win an election was to advocate a closed-door zoning policy. They won the election.

The *Madison* case added two new concepts to the body of exclusionary zoning law. The *Mahwah* case had already dealt with the fact that local zoning kept the people who were working in town from living there. *Madison* took the employment issue a step further: There were increasing employment opportunities in the geographic region around Madison, and lower income workers living in the older cities of the region could not take advantage of the opportunities because, due to local zoning, there was no adequate housing for them. In addition to the concept of fair access to regional employment, the *Madison* case developed the concept of regional housing needs. This in turn would become a major issue in the subsequent *Mount Laurel* cases.

Until the *Madison* decision, the municipality almost always had the last word in a zoning battle. If the fight found its way into court and the town lost, the court's legal remedy was to order some form of rezoning. In the process of rezoning, it was understandable if the defeated town decided to apply the economic benefits of rezoning to a favorite landowner who had had the good sense not to sue the town. The court, in *Madison,* recognized that this favoritism would, in all likelihood, discourage future exclusionary lawsuits. Therefore, in a footnote to the *Madison* decision, the court suggested the application of what has become known as the "builder's remedy."

This "builder's remedy" footnote held out the promise of economic benefit to the zoning plaintiff. If a plaintiff won an exclusionary zoning case, and if there were no conditions that prevented his land from being used for housing, then the town was obligated to rezone the developer's particular parcel of land. For the first time in the zoning wars, substantial economic incentive was added to the exclusionary zoning battle.

The *Mount Laurel* Cases

The best known of the exclusionary zoning cases in New Jersey took place in Mount Laurel Township in Burlington County.[7] In light of the importance of this case, this book might well have been called "From *Euclid* to *Mount Laurel.*" Sixty years after the exclusionary problem clearly had been identified in *Euclid,* the New Jersey Supreme Court, in three separate decisions, first clearly stated the problem,

then required a solution, and finally stepped aside to abide by the power of local politics.

Mount Laurel started to bloom in the 1960s as people left Camden and Philadelphia. What had been a farming community suddenly became a series of massive planned unit developments and large subdivisions of small, inexpensive homes. One of the few presuburban settlements in Mount Laurel was a small black neighborhood that dated back to the Civil War.

Planning for the perfect new suburban world in Mount Laurel did not include a small parcel zoned for a black-sponsored, government-assisted housing development. The black community decided that it needed some new housing to meet its own modest needs for growth. Rejected by the local township leaders, the black leadership turned to the office of Camden Legal Services. What started as a case that could have been settled by a small variance for 100 housing units turned into the landmark case known as *Mount Laurel I.*

Mount Laurel I ended with a decision by the New Jersey Supreme Court that required all developing communities to make a voluntary effort to meet local housing needs for low- and moderate-income families. The number of units was to be decided by a local housing plan. A town's zoning plan would be in compliance if the zoning provided a reasonable opportunity for conventional or government-assisted housing. No local affirmative action to provide such housing was required.

Mount Laurel's compliance with the decision was an affront to the court. A small parcel of land behind a shopping center was rezoned for multifamily housing. It was known that the owner of the land, which had previously had good industrial zoning, was not interested in such a use and was certainly not interested in building low-income housing. On a parcel of wet land, intended for a private bird sanctuary, the township established a zone for a sub-division of inexpensive small lots. In due course, the plaintiff went back to the courts for further remedy in what became known as *Mount Laurel II.*[8]

In deciding *Mount Laurel II,* the New Jersey Supreme Court included all of the large number of exclusionary zoning cases that were awaiting appeal. The result was a zoning revolution.

The court ordered all municipalities located in areas of the state that were designated as growth areas to fulfill an immediate obligation to provide opportunities for low- and moderate-income housing. A state agency would define those growth areas. To expedite the time-consuming process of zoning litigation, a special three-judge court would be established. The instruction to this court was to move all exclusionary zoning cases as quickly as possible. The special court would, in turn, establish a methodology for computing each municipality's "fair share" housing obligation. The court also accepted the fact that very little low- and moderate-income housing would be built by public action.

Several years before *Mount Laurel II,* the federal government had removed itself from the business of providing low-income housing. Therefore, the court provided the "builder's remedy" to any builder who was willing and able to build low-income housing. The rule of thumb for the number of low-cost units became 20 percent of the total development. For the suburban community, there was almost no defense now to an exclusionary zoning suit.

For a few short years after *Mount Laurel II* it seemed as if the zoning clock had turned back to 1950. The decade preceding *Mount Laurel I* had been a time of limited residential building. Two oil crises and one major recession followed by inflation had reduced New Jersey residential development to a crawl. For most

of the 1970s, housing production had been limited by both market conditions and restrictive zoning.

When the 1980s brought an end to the housing recession, the pent-up demand was there for a housing boom if the land and necessary infrastructure could be obtained. The builder's remedy initiated a major era of new development proposals. When the builder's remedy was combined with very strong market demand and falling interest rates, the result was a flood of more than 140 cases before the special court.

The builder's remedy proved to be the poison pill of *Mount Laurel II.* Under the fair share methodology developed by the courts, towns that had never previously even considered a few units of lower income housing found themselves obligated to accommodate hundreds of such units. What was even harder for the towns to swallow was the fact that for each unit of lower income housing, a builder would also be allowed to build four units of conventional housing to pay for the below-market units. For a time, the impending result seemed like a recreation of the postwar housing boom.

For about a decade, local planning and zoning had focused on limiting new growth. Suddenly, new growth was not only possible but probable. From the point of view of the municipality, the fact that the builder could pick the site for the new housing, unless it was an unreasonable one, made matters even worse. It was not only an insult to the concept of home rule, but it also brought about a political reaction from the established neighborhoods adjacent to the proposed developments.

The State Legislature Responds

Given the political issues of home rule and reaction by the establishment, the fallout from *Mount Laurel II* was substantial. The New Jersey legislature proposed a constitutional amendment that would take the courts out of land use issues. Two members of the New Jersey Supreme Court, including the Chief Justice, were up for reappointment. Unless the court was willing to retreat from its active participation in the zoning field, the reappointment of the two justices was very much in doubt. The amendment was not passed.

In 1985, the New Jersey Legislature proposed legislation to take zoning out of the courts and return it to the political process.[9] As a wag suggested, when it appeared that the builders could and would solve the lower income housing problems through the economic incentives of *Mount Laurel II,* it was decided to bring the problem back to government and the housing bureaucracies.

A statewide Affordable Housing Council was established. Its job is to oversee the adoption of locally sponsored housing plans. If a builder or landowner finds fault with the locally inspired plan, the council will provide mediation. Only when all such governmental efforts fail can the matter be litigated. Furthermore, the assurance of a builder's remedy has disappeared. It is worth noting that since the New Jersey Supreme Court approved the legislature's new approach to zoning and the court's retreat from the zoning wars, virtually no new *Mount Laurel* cases have been started.

One of the first actions taken by the Affordable Housing Council was to reexamine the methodology of preparing fair share housing plans. In the new plan adopted by the council, two important changes have occurred. These changes suggest the future course of the exclusionary zoning debate under the council's mandate.

For the older suburban counties that mostly have completed the development process, the council has adopted high fair share numbers. While it is true that large numbers of jobs exist in these communities, it is also true that there is virtually no land available for new housing production. Only very expensive or high density housing can compete successfully for the little land that remains vacant in these older suburbs.

For the emerging suburban areas that have just started the process of growth, the council allocated very low fair share numbers. The formula adopted by the council uses existing employment as a major factor in determining a locality's fair share. A principal reason for this is that at the outer fringe of suburbia, employment still is not fully developed. Yet it is precisely in these communities that large and inexpensive land is available for realistic private sector housing solutions. It is also here that most of the new jobs will be created. Under the rules of *Mount Laurel II,* most of the lower income housing would have been produced in the areas just starting their major growth. Under the new rules, the housing obligation was shifted to the older suburbs. While it may not have been intentional, the result will be a reversal of the basic concepts of *Mount Laurel II*—to produce large amounts of low-cost housing in areas that have the land resources for it.

The conclusion that can be drawn from almost 15 years of *Mount Laurel* battles is that, for the present at least, a major reversal of the exclusionary effects of zoning is unlikely. Zoning is no longer a simple method of regulating land use; it is now a part of the political process.

After the experience of the *Mount Laurel* cases, some conclusions can now be drawn. Zoning is no longer a simple means for implementing good land use planning. Zoning has become very important in determining who lives where. The political fallout from *Mount Laurel II* strongly suggests that the exclusionary aspects of zoning are too important politically to leave them to control by the courts or the planning process.

The economic and social consequences of maintaining exclusionary zoning never have been addressed seriously. The reason for this lack of concern lies in the fact that zoning, from its very beginnings, was always a local matter. Zoning is almost always confined in its application to the smallest part of a region, the individual municipality. Its regional impact is regarded as invisible. In the case of New Jersey, except for institutions such as the Suburban Action Institute and Camden Legal Services, the broader issues of local zoning do not have a regional constituency. Given the political support for the concept of home rule, this condition is unlikely to change in the foreseeable future.

It is possible to suggest some of the problems that will intensify as a result of the local nature of zoning.[10] The process of shifts in employment, particularly for lower income families, that started in the 1930s continues. More and more new employment opportunities for lower income people are developing at the outer fringes of suburbia. Much of that new employment is associated with the regional and interstate highway systems just being completed. Without an adequate supply of people for those jobs, that new economic growth will be retarded. Due to the lack of affordable housing in those areas, many people will miss out on these economic opportunities, creating a future generation of the unemployed and the poorly housed.

PRESERVATION OF OPEN SPACE

Exclusionary zoning has become widely recognized as the major social and political zoning issue of the last 20 years. The preservation of undeveloped land and farm land is a more recent zoning issue. While there may be no direct relationship, it does seem that preserva-

tion and environmental issues were discovered at the height of the civil rights movement.

In places like Montgomery County, Maryland, a suburb of Washington, D.C., and Middlesex, Monmouth, and Mercer counties in central New Jersey, major planning efforts are underway to prevent further use of land for suburban expansion.

These planning efforts appear in a number of guises. In recent years, the preservation of agriculture has become one of the most popular manifestations of this type of zoning.[11] Where there is no meaningful agriculture to preserve, large-lot zoning, typically of five, ten, or more acres per housing unit, is used. While floodplain, wetlands, steep slope, and other similar environmental regulations may have some legitimate public purposes, regulating land use for environmental purposes like these often is used simply to reduce new suburban growth.

Where communities are afraid of or have been losing exclusionary zoning battles, zoning for open space is often introduced as a final defense against the consequences of providing socially balanced residential land use plans. In one hard-fought case after *Mount Laurel, City of Newark* v. *Township of West Milford,*[12] defense against its housing obligation was that most of its land area was used to provide a watershed area and hence that the regional land use obligation would conflict with development.

Of all the techniques to preserve open space, agricultural zoning is now becoming the most popular. While courts have upheld large-lot zoning in such cases as *Colts Neck,*[13] the problem with the large-lot method of land preservation is its constant exposure to legal attack on the basis that it is confiscatory or discriminatory. Where there is no demand for expensive housing on large lots, this method of controlling development is hard to defend.

On the other hand, agricultural preservation

can cover much larger land areas and can be established on an existing use of the land, the residual agriculture within the proposed zone. Even if local agriculture is declining, it can always be argued that it will get better.

Two different methods have emerged to preserve agricultural land. For the last decade, state and county governments have been experimenting with the acquisition of development rights to farmland by direct purchase. As one can imagine, this method has not met with much success. The basic flaw in this system of conserving farmland and preventing growth is that it requires large amounts of taxpayers' money. Transfer of development rights, or TDRs as they are commonly called, through the power of zoning is becoming the major means of conserving open space or limiting growth, depending upon one's point of view.

The TDR concept works this way: The area that is to be conserved for agriculture or open space is defined as a "sending zone." Within a sending zone, each acre or other unit of land is allocated a certain number of development rights. The owner of development rights, whether farmer, builder, or investor, has the right to build housing in an area designated as a "receiving zone." In a receiving zone, the plan provides for two development alternatives. One alternative allows for development without the use of a TDR; the second alternative provides for the same land use but at a greater density of development with the use of the TDRs. The theory is that owners of farmland can share in the economics of suburban growth, but that growth would take place on land that is not to be preserved as open space.

This spreading of the wealth of development was designed to meet some of the major legal and political problems of using zoning to prevent growth. Zoning farmland for uses that would never be needed or for very large lots often sets the stage for a confiscatory zoning suit. Under TDR zoning, those problems could be overcome if the planning for the receiving zone makes it reasonably valuable. To create that kind of potential value in a receiving area, the essential planning ingredient is some form of high-density development. If a significant number of TDRs are needed, and there are not a large number of TDRs available, then the farmers' TDRs have a great deal of value. To create a valuable receiving area, however, involves the kind of higher density zoning that many conservation-minded suburbanites want to prevent in the first place. As of this date, that contradiction in the preservation of land has not been solved. The reasonable expectation is that planning and zoning will be used to find additional ways to conserve vacant land at the edge of the newest suburbs.

It is unlikely that much of that conserved land will be used for agriculture in the long run. If farmers in the Midwest cannot make a living, it is unlikely that the remaining farmers on the edge of suburbia will be able to survive. Therefore, the long-term result, assuming an effective method is found to prevent development, will be large vacant green areas defining the boundaries of urban regions.

It would seem that everyone—citizens, politicians, and planners—would be happy with such a result. The concept of greenbelts and other forms of permanent open space was a central idea in the new town movement and early suburban design efforts. The possibility of large urban regions surrounded by open fields and forests has to be a suburban planner's dream. Even the farmer, bought out of a tough and unprofitable business, should be satisfied with a zoning program that turns corn fields into greenbelts.

Yet this apparently wonderful planning

concept may be the cause for very serious urban problems in the future. The history of American urban development has been one of constant expansion. Through the process of expansion, the American economic system has been able to provide housing and employment opportunities for a very wide range of population groups. In fact, recent planning history suggests that when expansion was cut off by suburban zoning, the supply of affordable housing near expanding employment opportunities was inadequate.

The American economy developed in a climate of optimum choices for land use. It may well be that under the guise of conservation, the suburbs may finally be able to shut their doors. In doing so, the land preservation movement may hurt the city and the older suburbs.

The very serious social and economic problems of the American city that developed just after *Euclid* persist today. While there may be a number of contributing factors, it does seem certain that a major cause is the disruption in the process of city growth. It is the point of view of this writer that the use of suburban zoning was a major factor in that disruption.

Planners are responsible for another factor in the decline of the city. By the use of large-scale government housing programs, the social problems of the poor were compressed and compounded. By providing very badly needed housing in the center of aging cities, planners also locked people into areas least likely to provide new employment opportunities.

The last decade has seen a reversal in the economic fortunes of the older city. Boston's Waterfront and Back Bay neighborhoods and New York's Midtown and West Side are bright examples of the dramatic change of events. Yet the city's new-found vitality is compounding the problems of those city dwellers who have not made it. As the affluent rediscover the city, they have started to displace the poor. This most recent urban process of change, gentrification, has two effects. First, it erodes the limited housing resources of the lower income groups. Second, it is producing the urban renewal that government could not produce.

Today, neighborhoods such as New York's Lower East Side, the historical first home of the immigrant, have become battlegrounds for the limited amount of housing. One very dramatic manifestation of these events is the rise of a whole new social group, the homeless. For the first time in the history of the American city, there is not even enough substandard housing to go around.

There is still a shortage of city land for new employment opportunities. The constant rebuilding process of the inner city at increasing densities is a manifestation of this problem. For reuse of land to be economically viable, it must be used for more lucrative uses. This seldom produces the kinds of jobs needed by those at the bottom of the economic ladder. As New York's garment industry is displaced by high-rise office buildings, for example, the traditional jobs for new immigrants are replaced by jobs for children of the middle class who migrate to the city after college.[14]

If land use can be used to understand current social and economic problems, then, in theory, land use should be part of the solution to these problems. This chapter suggests that the social and economic mobility that was part of life before *Euclid* may well be what is required to treat some of the long-standing problems of the American city. It is no longer within the power of the city to influence the use of land beyond its borders. The power to zone is, and has been since *Euclid*, reserved for the suburbs.

There is no question that zoning has made a significant contribution to those fortunate enough to have moved to suburbia. For the city, however, the place for which zoning was originally developed, zoning has played an unforeseen role. Instead of solving the physical, social, and economic problems of the city, zoning appears at age 60 to be a major factor in its problems.

NOTES

1. One exception during the war was the construction of Oak Ridge, Tennessee. In order to concentrate the development of atomic research, the government built Oak Ridge with 5,000 mobile homes, 9,600 prefabricated dwellings, and barracks. It may have marked the high point for the conventional housing industry.

2. Co-op City was a nonprofit, "do good" housing effort designed to give new cheap housing to an established community. It worked so well that it emptied a good part of the Bronx.

3. These three counties have been the scene of most of the New Jersey zoning cases in the last two decades.

4. *Greater Englewood Housing Corp.* v. *DeSimon*, 56 N.J. 428, 267 A.2d 31 (1970).

5. *Urban League of Essex Co.* v. *Township of Mahwah*, N.J. Super. Ct. Bergen County Law Div. Docket No. L–17112–71 (1984).

6. *Oakwood at Madison, Inc.* v. *Tp. of Madison*, 72 N.J. 481 (1977).

7. *So. Burlington Cty. N.A.A.C.P.* v. *Tp. of Mount Laurel*, 67 N.J. 151 (1975) [hereinafter *Mt. Laurel I*]; *So. Burlington Cty. N.A.A.C.P.* v. *Mount Laurel Tp.*, 92 N.J. 158 (1983) [hereinafter *Mt. Laurel II*].

8. 92 N.J. 158 (1983).

9. Fair Housing Act, N.J.S.A. 52: 27D-301 et seq.

10. One should not believe that if zoning were delegated to the county level it would necessarily change this situation. For example, Mercer County, which includes the older city of Trenton and some of the state's wealthiest suburbs, does not have direct zoning powers. Instead, the county currently has a planning policy to slow suburban growth by restricting development of new sewer service. It achieves this by using section 208 water management powers.

11. See, e.g., *Orgo Farms and Greenhouses, Inc.*, v. *Township of Colts Neck*.

12. *City of Newark* v. *Tp. of West Milford* (Super. Ct. of N.J. Docket No. L–25413–77PW (1980)).

13. *Orgo Farms and Greenhouses, Inc.* v. *Township of Colts Neck*.

14. One interesting sidelight to this struggle is the use of the *Mount Laurel* concept to hold onto the little that is left. In *Asian Americans for Equality* v. *Koch* (492 Super. Ct. N.Y. 2nd Dept. 837 (1985), lower income minorities are insisting that their housing needs be included in any new market–rate housing within the Chinatown community.

6

Euclid and the Environment

Earl Finbar Murphy

THE MEANINGS OF ENVIRONMENT

Euclid and the environment do not present together the likeliest of topics. The terms "environmental protection" and "environmental law," have been seen as inventions of the 1960s.[1] How then could the word environment relate to a 1926 decision of the United States Supreme Court,[2] other than through the most extreme use of analogy? Perhaps deciding how the word environment has been used, and might be used under the *Euclid* decision, could offer some help.

Defining words starts with dictionaries. In the dictionaries' definitions, the word "environment" tantalizes more than it satisfies the investigator's curiosity. Usages make the word expansive in meanings. And usage is what determines the choice of meaning that has to be made in discussing *Euclid* and the environment.

The word environment first appears in the English language at the end of the Elizabethan Age in an attempt to translate from Plutarch the word *perielefsis.*[3] As such, the translator might as well have used a word well known to Geoffrey Chaucer and other fourteenth century authors, "environs," since its long-established derivation from the Latin meant "coming around," "circling," or "surrounding" in the same sense as Plutarch's Greek word.[4] The objectifying suffix, "-ment," only emphasized the action of surrounding or environing.

Whatever the early purpose for devising the word, however, "environment" had been launched into the English language, a language whose development has been often crossed with other ambiguities. Justice Sutherland himself in *Euclid* uses the word when he talks about "a more favorable environment in which to raise children."[5] What possible meaning might he have had in mind and what, subsequently, has been done in law with the word?

The word, in accordance with its ancient meaning, can include everything which surrounds a human being individually or which encompasses all of humanity collectively.[6] Often, in law, the word still is used that way. Lawyers and planners speak of a natural environment. They also talk of a built environment with which environmental law has to deal.[7] Lying somewhere between the natural and the built, the polluted environment in this usage becomes an object of rehabilitation or pollution prevention.[8]

Used in such general fashion, the word environment too often threatens to become a synonym for the universe in which humanity lives and for the human institutions surrounding the individual human being.[9] Such an encompassing employment has a value in establishing connections and refuting claims of autonomy.[10] For purposes of talking about *Euclid* and the environment, however, some narrowing in the usage must be made.

By the late nineteenth century, the word had taken on a narrower and more particular meaning, being akin to the scientific word *ecology*.[11] When so used, "environment" became the whole complex of natural forces that acted upon an individual organism or an ecological community so as to determine their form and survival.[12] Environment, so employed, is less than the universe. In this application, the word focuses on the carrying capacities supporting ecosystems.[13] Even so, how can the word environment be related more particularly to such matters as land use planning and zoning, that is, to the spatial allocation of physical objects in nature by legal means allowing, restricting, or mandating their allocation? At least this much specifically is required in order to talk simultaneously about *Euclid* and the environment.

In this regard, Aurelio Peccei has said,

> The land space has to be comprehended with the entire natural endowment pertaining to it—climate, the soil, water, plant and animal life, and also mineral and fossil deposits, but chiefly the biological part of our planet which pertains to that land space. . . . The land space of the world should be envisioned together with the elements which make it fit for human existence over time. . . . Therefore, that land must be strongly defended against any waste, any mismanagement, so as to preserve as much as possible, and possibly improve, the carrying capacity of the planet.[14]

The goal of land use planning and zoning for environmental purposes is enunciated clearly in this passage. No contradiction exists, either,

between this goal for controlling human use of land and what is permitted by *Euclid* to those legally charged with land use control and zoning.

Justice Sutherland in *Euclid* indicated a willingness to believe that neighborhoods, indeed entire towns, could adversely be affected by the uncontrolled location of industries, businesses, multifamily dwellings, and different, otherwise economically useful activities. If zoning could prevent this harm, then he thought it capable of being constitutional.[15] Nothing is present in his line of argument that would indicate his opposition to an environmental land use planning that would prevent or reverse

> . . . the eating up of open land through expanding urbanization, and environmental deterioration because of the growing megalopolitan systems, . . . [through] measures of environmental control and protection, distinguished according to zones of increasing human intervention in the natural environment.[16]

The land use planner perhaps most associated in the United States with the idea of land suitability in planning has been Ian McHarg.[17] In his view,

> Nature as a creative, interacting process in which man is involved with all other life forms is . . . the best approximation of the world . . . and the indispensable approach to determining the role of man in the biosphere. It is indispensable also for investigation, not only of the adaptations which man accomplishes, but of their forms.[18]

For McHarg, people in communities did their best environmental "planning" when town and country formed a single social and economic unit, constituting "the vernacular architecture and urbanism of earlier societies and primitive cultures."[19] Complete integration of this kind is not possible in the modern megalopolis, he admits. But nature can still be preserved—or brought into—the urban agglomerations through careful environmental planning, requiring an ecological model of the megalopolis.

> Such a model would identify the regional inventory of material in atmosphere, hydrosphere, lithosphere, and biosphere, identifying inputs and outputs, and both describe and quantify the cycling and recycling of materials in the system. Such a model would facilitate recognition of the vital natural processes and their interdependence which is denied today. Lacking such a model, we find it necessary to proceed with available knowledge.[20]

Ian McHarg has selected water as the natural element—failing the perfection of his ecological model—around which he would organize his environmental planning. Avoiding floodways. Building lightly in floodplains, if at all. Avoiding building on steep gradients or on friable hillsides. Not draining wetlands. Saving open space for agriculture, even within the urban built environment. Protecting aquifers. Not building on beaches. These constraints and objectives constitute his planning specifics under his centralizing water conception. Still, McHarg thinks environmental planning is insufficient when it is limited even in this way.

> This conception is still too bald; it should be elaborated to include areas of important scenic value, recreational potential, areas of ecological, geological, or historic interest. Yet, clearly, the conception, analogous to the empiricism of the farmer, offers opportunity for determining the place of nature in the metropolis.[21]

Justice Sutherland drew his concerns more legalistically and with less scientific knowledge. Still he was just as concerned about what values could be protected constitutionally concerning land. If the public authorities, through the police power, wanted to assume some of the responsibility that otherwise would be left to private or public nuisance actions, Sutherland believed that the public authorities would not be blocked across the board from such an initiative.

> There is no serious difference of opinion in respect of the validity of laws and regulations fixing the height of buildings within reasonable limits, the character of materials and methods of construction, and the adjoining area which must be left open, in order to minimize the danger of fire or collapse, the evils of overcrowding, and the like, and excluding from residential sections offensive trades, industries, and structures likely to create nuisances.[22]

These were accepted givens in 1926. For all the adversaries in *Euclid,* such conclusions were part of the tradition of the common law, even before Justice Sutherland on behalf of the United States Supreme Court began to address the constitutionality of the *Euclid* ordinance. Going from traditional limitations to accepting the recommendations of a land suitability planner, like Ian McHarg, who wants to plan the city in a way "analogous to the empiricism of the farmer," might not have been hard for Justice Sutherland, who thought he had justified the zoning by his homely, rural image of "the pig in the parlor."[23]

Ian McHarg, for whom "the distribution of open space must respond to natural process . . . [in] any metropolitan area,"[24] has been much taken with the ideas of the legal theorist Clarence Morris, who worked with him for many years in lectures for landscape architects.[25] Morris's ideas, which long antedate the National Environmental Policy Act and the net of environmental impact statements descending from it, are particularly relevant to someone doing environmental planning.

> Nature's integrity will be furthered if a presumption in favor of the natural casts a burden of proof on those who propose to disturb nature—a burden to establish affirmatively that the change should be made. In other words, the natural should not be dislocated on whim or without forethought about the harm that might ensue. He who proposes dislocation must justify it in advance. . . . What is the sounder alternative when a proposal is put forward to intrude drastically on nature absent reasonable foreknowledge of what is likely to ensue? Whoever plans to dump quantities of waste, kill myriads of pests, or uproot acres of natural growth should customarily have to make the case that sound reason warrants disturbing nature. . . . The presumption in favor of the natural should not be only a debating stance against those who propose change; it calls for legal action developing safeguards affirmatively creating nature's legal rights . . . backed up by policemen, inspectors, and judges.[26]

At a time when citizens' suits, environmental impact statements, the Environmental Protection Agency, and most federal environmental statutes did not exist, these words can only seem prophetic to an environmental lawyer.[27]

One can also understand why the environmental planning of Ian McHarg today is called impact zoning. This kind of planning is associated in the public mind with the environmental statement as well as with traditional land control techniques.[28] In making this association, the determination of precisely what it is in the environment that is to be protected may

be more discoverable. But perhaps only *just* discoverable.

In environmental planning, as in conservation biology or anything else involved with living and/or renewing resources, an answer rarely exists that is "both simply and politically appealing." The natural environment is a complex, nonlinear system unloved by engineers, economists, politicians, and others looking for the "bottom line" borrowed from accountancy.

> Therefore, the quest for a simple bottom line on such issues as stability, extinction thresholds, effects of atmospheric pollution, effects of overharvesting or species introductions, effects of eutrophication, etcetera, is a quest for a phantom by an untrained mind. Qualification of generalizations is inherent in the subject matter of biology. . . . It benefits no one to be defensive about the "bottom line" issue.[29]

Keeping in mind the unavoidable uncertainties in environmental planning, therefore, one can understand the unhappiness of real estate, building, banking, contracting, and other developmental types. Too often, they have received as bland assurance governments' claims of only wanting "to encourage environmentally sound land use practices by requiring developers to account for environmental values in project design and site layout."[30]

California and Washington are two states which have integrated zoning and environmental impact reports. It is the distinction of these jurisdictions to apply environmental impact control to private land development.[31] California's laws are exemplary of this approach in the extent and complexity of their provisions, with the legislature making repeated returns to the legislation since 1970 in order to "clarify" its provisions.[32] But the requirement of a report on environmental impact is required from every person obtaining a land-related permit from a state agency, including such permits as are required under a local zoning ordinance.[33]

The legislature does offer some mitigation.

> If a parcel has been zoned to accommodate a particular density of residential development . . . and an environmental impact report was certified for that zoning . . . action, the application of this division . . . shall be limited to effects upon the environment which are peculiar to the parcel . . . and which were not addressed as significant effects in the prior environmental impact report.[34]

Ian McHarg himself would take no exception to this. He particularly would not since the statute makes it clear that even such limited mitigation does not apply if the proposed use of the parcel would have off-site effects on the environment not covered in a previous environmental impact report.[35] Generally, however, the environment in California is protected by a requirement of environmental impact reports, or some functional equivalent, where a proposed land use is contemplated requiring a permit in an omnipresent permit atmosphere.

And what in California is that environment?

> "Environment" means the physical conditions which exist within the area which will be affected by a proposed project, including land, air, water, minerals, flora, fauna, noise, objects of historic or aesthetic significance.[36]

The emphasis, though not the entirety, of the definition is upon elements in nature. This is reinforced by language elsewhere in the statute, particularly in the sections that were among the earliest adopted. These say:

> It is necessary to provide a high-quality environment that at all times is healthful and pleasing to the senses and intellect of man.
>
> There is a need to understand the relationship between the maintenance of high-quality ecological systems and the general welfare of the people of the state, including their enjoyment of the natural resources of the state.
>
> The capacity of the environment is limited, and it is the intent of the legislature that the government of the state take immediate steps to identify any critical thresholds . . . and take all coordinated actions necessary to prevent such thresholds being reached.[37]

In other original language, however, a mix of content appears in the definition for environment. Ambiguity is present when the policy of the state is said to be to:

> Take all action necessary to provide the people of this state with clean air and water, enjoyment of aesthetic, natural, scenic, and historic environmental qualities, and freedom from excessive noise.[38]

Not content with their labors in 1970 and 1972 in defining environment for purposes of controlling impact upon it, the legislature returned to their labors in 1979 and declared that all of the work would have to be done "while providing a decent home and satisfying living environment for every Californian."[39] As if the original ambiguity concerning the legislative meaning of environment had not been enough, this was an added fillip.

Often when the term "living environment" is used, it applies to life forces, either organisms that live and die or physical elements needed to sustain that life. The living environment is a part of the renewing environment, juxtaposed to the stock resources in nature that cannot be renewed or that renew themselves only in eons of geologic time.[40] The California legislature, though, clearly is *not* so using the term.

Because of the rich capability of language to mean all things at once, "living environment" in this statutory amendment embraces the built environment, as well as social institutions. The home is a structure—as well as a social definition of family. The living environment in California is the physical structure and infrastructure humanity builds—as well as the social institutions of community, workplace, leisure, neighborhood, and much else. Ambiguity, even in California, is here reintroduced—or, perhaps, merely preserved—in the meaning of "environment."

The use Justice Sutherland in *Euclid* made of the word environment is very much at home with the kind of ambiguity that California has kept weaving in to environmental planning, impact zoning, and the imperative of an "environmental" kind of decision making.[41] What can be gleaned from his words? What is to be drawn from the cases that he chose to quote about his meaning of the word environment?

Justice Sutherland stressed quiet and freedom from industrial and street noises. Open space, good air, grass, and trees were in his mind. Buildings were best dispersed so that these good things were possible. Disease from crowds, illness caused by the discharges of industry, derelict loiterers, heavy truck traffic through streets, malodors, vermin—these were risks incident to industry and commerce, as his quoted cases saw it. Risks like these could be zoned out of residential districts, said Justice Sutherland and his carefully culled authorities, in order to "preserve a more favorable environment in which to rear children."[42]

The emphasis, but not the entirety, of Justice Sutherland's definition of "environment" was upon the built environment. But the natural environment was present also, else the openings called for in residentially zoned districts could not provide the air, sunshine, and greenspace that his language implied would be present. Clearly, Justice Sutherland did not see his single-family homes set down in a concrete jungle of paved-over space.[43] His language made his meaning plain when he referred to "the free circulation of air," "the sun which . . . would fall upon the smaller homes," the "privilege of quiet and open spaces for play, enjoyed by those in more favored localities," and "the advantage of the open spaces."[44] Justice Sutherland was no stranger to nature, nor to what today would be called "environmental elements" in land use planning and zoning.[45]

THE ENVIRONMENTAL AND THE AESTHETIC CONSIDERATIONS

Were *Euclid* and its companion case, *Gorieb* v. *Fox*,[46] important because they contributed to "the progress of urban planning and beautification?"[47] If so, what is "beautification?" Is beautification different from environmental planning? If it is, does *Euclid* represent an endorsement of that beautification? In short, is environmental planning just another way to say aesthetic zoning? Or are they concepts that are essentially different, however often a particular planning action might be both environmentally protecting and aesthetically pleasing?

One doubts that Justice Sutherland himself saw his decision as constitutionally justifying restrictions on private property use simply to carry out a public entity's idea of beautification. The view that "neither aesthetic reasons nor the conservation of property values nor the stabilization of economic values . . ., singly, or combined [are] sufficient to promote" traditional police powers restricting the use of private property would have seemed unexceptional to Justice Sutherland.[48] In his own time, aesthetic considerations, "while not wholly without weight, did not of themselves afford sufficient basis for the invasion of property rights."[49] Courts then regarded as unreasonable restrictions in a zoning ordinance that should destroy the greater part of a private property's value "simply to enhance the beauty of the village as a whole."[50]

Interestingly enough, however, some courts, as well as some dissenters, subsequently did find in Justice Sutherland's words a justification for aesthetic zoning. The Georgia Supreme Court, citing *Gorieb*[51] as authority, has declared that an "ordinance would not be an unwarranted exercise of police power based on aesthetics alone."[52] Because of the elasticity of the police power in *Euclid,* the Ohio Supreme Court has said "both zoning and nuisance issues have implied that there is a governmental interest in maintaining the aesthetics of the community and have recognized [aesthetics'] role in the exercise of the police powers."[53] Dissenters have had even less difficulty in seeing *Euclid* as having given "legal recognition to architectural and aesthetic considerations," at least as far as "certain dicta of Justice Sutherland" are concerned.[54] Still another dissenter sees in *Euclid,* along with some other cases, authority for both the promotion of aesthetics and environmental protection in public control of private land use.[55]

Rightly or wrongly, therefore, in many minds *Euclid* is regarded as allowing the implementation of public ideas of beautification at private expense, of confirming the constitutionality of aesthetic zoning, and of assimilating environmental and aesthetic considerations. The example of the California statutory definition of environment includes "objects of historic or aesthetic significance," which seems to go beyond preserving some natural, scenic landscape.[56] This view is reinforced when the same legislature seems to find

a difference existing between "aesthetic, natural, scenic, and historic" and yet lumps them all under the rubric "environmental qualities."[57]

The *American Law Reports,* a series of commentaries having great authority with practitioners on leading American cases, has said in this regard,

> In view of the current public concern for the quality of the environment, including its beauty, the validity and construction of zoning ordinances regulating the architectural style or design of structures has become a subject of considerable importance.[58]

This comes perilously close to conflating environmental zoning with aesthetic zoning and the architectural possibilities of the built environment with the physical conditions of the natural environment. If this is simply all part of a general movement away from "the almost universally accepted view that a zoning ordinance based solely or predominately on aesthetic considerations was necessarily invalid,"[59] then perhaps this also bodes well for environmental planning and zoning. Yet, even if this were true for current legal developments, aesthetic and environmental planning and zoning do not contain necessarily the same subject matter.

Efforts have been made to gloss over the distinctions. "'Aesthetic' regulation . . . is regulation that bears upon the visual character of the physical environment."[60] The author, though, then goes on to include within aesthetic regulation not only architectural form, junkyards, sign control, and historic preservation but also setback and side yard requirements, height limitations, and fence control.[61] With only a little effort, it seems, the aesthetic can be made as universal as the environmental in planning and zoning land use control. But there is little help in that kind of linguistic imperialism. Far narrower meanings are needed.

Lewis Mumford, the historian of cities, said,

> Until our own day human culture as a whole developed in an organic, subjectively modified environment . . . . In a confused unfocused way the criteria of life prevailed everywhere and man's own existence prospered or failed in so far as a balance favorable to life was preserved among all organisms. . . . Man lived in active partnership with plants and animals for whole geological periods.[62]

For Mumford, both human biology and the environment of life enfolded aesthetic preconditions within the life processes.

> Long before man himself became conscious of beauty and desirous of cultivating it, beauty existed in an endless variety of forms in the flowering plants; and man's own nature was progressively altered, with his increasing sensitiveness to sight and touch and odor, through his further symbolic expression of beautiful form in his ornaments, his cosmetics, his costume, his painted and graven images: all byproducts of his enriched social and sexual life. In this sense, we may be all "flower-children."[63]

In this fashion, aesthetics may be biological. Human attitudes toward the environment may originate, as a result, in humanity's self-conscious segregation from other life-forms in paleolithic time.[64]

But what does that mean for someone concerned with the legal problems of something called environmental planning and zoning? If Mumford is right, he is right at a very deep level of human feeling, the sort of bio-socio-physico fundament that empowers human aspirations. But that lies at an immeasurable depth below the operational difficulties of planners, lawyers, politicians, and business people. Perhaps that is why Mumford so often expressed a despair over humanity's ability to continue to exist in harmony with its own nature and the natural environment while living in a society dedicated to urban technology.[65]

THE ENVIRONMENT: NATURAL AND BUILT

Simplification in what is meant by environment runs into the roadblock of what humanity means by nature. Much of what is seen today as natural is really a built environment, as man-made as any artifact that can be held in the hand and sold as a commodity. The moors of the Brontë sisters are the result of ruthless deforestation for charcoal production, with the heather representing a stage in the forests' return.[66] But who wants the return of the forest in place of the heather-covered moors?

A commonplace tells us that the most natural-seeming parks, such as New York's Central Park, are purely products of human ingenuity. Fredrick Law Olmsted, Sr., as well as other nineteenth century American park builders, acted "to form picturesque scenery through abrupt variations of surface . . . [with] a good deal of rock brought with cost from a distance, or of artificial rock made of materials brought from a distance."[67] They might have preferred a locale with more rolling terrain with which to start, but they were not limited in their designs by the flatlands.

The nineteenth century parks, vast in dimension, owe their inspiration to the eighteenth century English garden.[68] Such landscape architects as Capability Brown hoaxed the eighteenth century public into seeing these prospects as natural when they were in every sense a product of human imagination and labor.[69] At the same time, as a partial result of the "scientific revolution in agriculture" carried through by Arthur Young and others in the same eighteenth century, the open field system of agriculture inherited from medieval England was replaced deliberately by a new kind of "nature."

The small fields, enclosed by hedgerows, were the product of a new, later eighteenth century technology, as artificial as anything that produced crops could be.[70] Yet when technology changed again in the mid-twentieth century and "the overmature and obsolescent but delightful eighteenth century landscape" was "grubbed up, leaving . . . a starkly utilitarian panorama," many regretted this loss of the "natural" English landscape.[71] The open fields of the Middle Ages, the hedgerows introduced in the eighteenth century, and the open sweep for heavy farm equipment today are equally no part of "nature's England."

The built environment, therefore, lies intimately intermingled with what people casually call a natural environment. This turns out to be a common attitude whether they are talking about rural areas, hunting grounds, forests, or many water bodies. Still, even in this instance, what is truly innate in nature can be sorted out from what humanity did to "enhance," or otherwise change, the natural to the pseudo-natural, however more beautiful human beings may regard the altered landscape.[72]

The planner Patrick Geddes, who began his career as a botanist, made plain the interrelationship of the natural and the invented in the human environment. His work drew on the English garden past when he planned cities. His plans were congruent also with the Garden City concepts of his time. Both presaged the environmental planning of planners such as Ian McHarg.[73] Indeed, McHarg's "water-centered" planning draws from Geddes's view that would plan the "Valley Section, the human landscape from river source to sea."[74] The entire region of human settlement, according to both Geddes and McHarg, should be planned around the water, an environmental sort of planning that starts with minimum regard for any built environment and with full knowledge of just what nature has provided the planner for work space on the land. Since at least Geddes's time, city and/or regional planning without any regard for nature, as well as the built environment, has not been possible.[75]

Ideas of such environmentally oriented planners as Geddes were already common coin among city planners by the time of *Euclid.* In 1926, but preceding the decision, the secretary of the American Civic Association and the Federated Societies of Planning and Parks had asserted that "the progress of zoning laws during the past 10 years has been little short of marvelous" and that "the weight of the evidence is increasing each year that the law is developing with the needs of the communities."[76] Harlean James based the development of her ideas about zoning upon what she regarded as a well-established process in environmental planning that had been fully accepted by the associations of which she was executive.

By that time, she claimed, American planning had started three-quarters of a century earlier with the work of the American horticulturist and city and park planner, Andrew Jackson Downing.[77] "[D]uring the latter half of the nineteenth century gathering strength and wide influence . . . was the growing interest of the American people in their native landscape. . . ."[78] As Harlean James explained the development, "The history of city planning in the United States began to take conscious shape in the late years of the nineteenth century and to flower into reports during the early years of the present century. . . . Every year since [1911, the year of the National Conference on City Planning] has seen new reports, mounting in number and in magnitude of scope and detail of basic data."[79] The second century of the United States, which had begun in 1876, had been for her a time when "we have begun to extend public control over privately owned land when it could be clearly shown to the courts that such control was in the interests of the health, safety, morals or general welfare of the community as a whole."[80] Any different outcome in *Euclid* doubtless would have been regarded by her as a stunning reversal of decades of American history.

Environmental planning had been very much a part of this American movement, as much so as the English developments, with the origins of both being traceable as far back in direct line to the 1840s.[81] "The cardinal conception of modern city planning is that all of its parts . . . be designed for an entire community . . . . Only thus can organic unity be secured. . . . [T]he comprehensive planning of great cities should be placed in the hands of the few planners who have demonstrated that they 'have the magic to stir men's blood.'" Anything else is for "lesser men."[82]

Plainly, the location of streams, the determination of open spaces, the use of zoning to preserve "the winding course of a wooded stream," or of planning to create "the pleasant green of an artificial parkway" were all a part of how to deal consciously with cities on a comprehensive scale.[83] Zona Gale for the American Civic Association in 1913 had urged every town to be a garden town, to clean up, to provide for disposal of trash, "to get into the current of the new understanding that the conservation of physical and moral life is largely economic, and that its enemy is . . . bad economic and social and other physical condi-

tions."[84] The result was that, even before the decision in *Euclid,* Americans

> already, as a people . . . have created a fairly comfortable environment; but that has been done carelessly. . . . In the future *we must plan ahead* and make the best possible use of land, both rural and urban, if we are to maintain or improve the comfortable standards of living which we have set up. We need a Statement of our Land Assets and Liabilities. We need an analysis of our Resources. We need Comprehensive Plans for the best use of our land, both publicly and privately owned. These are not grandiose schemes which it is impossible to formulate.[85]

As references to comprehensive planning became the kind of talk that Americans could hark to, the role of the environment had become integrally a part of planning's foundation years before Herbert Hoover became president.[86]

The environment that was taken into consideration might be natural, or it might be a built environment made to look as if it were natural.[87] In either case, this was not the same thing as the planning that dealt with paving, or building structures for work or residence, or other constructions that unambiguously composed the built environment. This distinction has been recognized by developers of cities and parts of cities from the mid-nineteenth century to the present, even though architects such as Louis Sullivan claimed that they had a "natural" architecture embracing the structure and its background.[88] Nevertheless, what had become clear among planners by the time of *Euclid's* decision in 1926 was the important role that nature played—or ought to play—in planning and zoning. Anything else would be either a hit-or-miss mosaic or the butchery by a ready-made zoning law of a city's existing environment.[89]

THE METROPOLITAN EXPERIENCE IN ENVIRONMENTAL PLANNING PRIOR TO 1926 IN THE UNITED STATES

The Cleveland metropolitan area by the early 1920s was certainly familiar with a variety of environmental planning. The writing of Stanley L. McMichael, a local Cleveland real estate man, makes this plain. Formerly the secretary of the Cleveland Real Estate Board and an authority on leases, McMichael was conversant with the opinions of developers and the financiers of urban development[90] and his opinions are not those of theory alone. They are drawn, instead, mostly from what had happened in contemporary cities, particularly Cleveland. Environment to him represented something that no city planner could ignore, even if that planner should often see the natural environment as something to be overcome as well as worked with by city plans and zoning ordinances.

McMichael favored zoning. He especially favored what later came to be called the Euclidean type of zoning. He preferred imposing zoning "while a city is still small in size" and of "practical necessity . . . done under the police power of the state without compensation to owners."[91] Indeed, his writing on zoning, without mentioning any cases or any ordinance except New York's, seems to be dealing with the particular facts that led to *Euclid.* In any event, he is insistent that zoning helped urban growth, was an assistance to municipal revenues, and increased residential values by stopping "promiscuous growth."[92]

As someone who was interested in the development of major cities and in maximizing real estate values for land owners within those cities, environment had to be important to Stanley McMichael. First for him were the environment's faults:

> Hills, deep ravines, rough and irregular surfaces, form one kind of fault, while water surfaces, such as rivers, creeks, swamps, lakes and harbors, form another. . . . The control which a stream exercises, to limit and restrain the growth of a city to the side upon which is located the point of origin depends on width and depth of the stream, the comparative area, topography, and natural advantages of the sites on the two sides of the river, and speculative enterprise."[93]

What might be the environmental advantages? Why, often the faults themselves! Faults for business development were to other people on other occasions the chance to "view pretty lakes, rivers or parkways."[94] The chance for environmentally good things abounded in the city. Trees should be "planted in order to provide shade over the sidewalks and . . . [to] add an element of forest beauty that attracts most people."[95]

Natural environment was important in McMichael's urban views. He was even aware of how much value could be placed upon being in business on the shady side of the street, or the effect of wind direction and velocity, or the business effect of street dust.[96] Perhaps most interesting of all for one writing in the early 1920s, he was convinced that airplane travel would be the way of the future and that airfields had to be located with particular environmental care.

> Four principal things must be observed by the city which desires to place itself on the air map of the country: 1.—The position of the field must bear some definite reference to the main aerial routes. 2.—It must be so located and of such size that it cannot be hemmed in by future building operations so as to hinder flight and

landings. 3.—It must, if possible, be susceptible of expansion. 4.—It should be situated close to transportation facilities and water supply. . . . The ground should be firm under all weather conditions. A light, porous soil, with natural drainage, and covered with close cropped grass is preferred. . . . The surrounding country should, if possible, afford opportunity for forced landings, in the event of engine trouble in taking off. . . . With the development of the helicopter type of airplane, which rises or descends vertically from a given point, it is within the realm of possibility . . . [to] land directly on top of [an] office building. . . . When the automobile first came into use, no one could visualize the revolution in city life that it was to bring. Time only will tell the story of the effect of the airplane.[97]

But for airplanes, automobiles, differing land use districts, or whatever else pertained to urban life, environmental planning and zoning had to be taken into account because this was what a pragmatist like Stanley McMichael saw happening all around him in the early 1920s.[98]

In summary, therefore, by 1926 the United States had known the planning of cities in terms of their natural features, with the consequent enhancement of their residents' environment. For more than eight decades before *Euclid,* a kind of environmental planning had been emerging. This particularly had been the case with the new western cities in the United States after the Civil War and with the widespread adoption of the City Beautiful concept after 1892.[99] The country had initiated the experience of the regional planning of metropolitan areas in the 1880s, focusing from the beginning on such environmental matters as water supply, sewers, and parks.[100] Zoning that included both natural and built environmental considerations had been in practice for

at least a decade before 1926 and had been known conceptually even earlier.[101]

Maybe purists like Sir Walter Scott in his 1820 attack on the term "landscape gardening," disliked the idea of mixing natural and man-made elements in a program of environmental enhancement. But the pragmatists had accepted environmental planning, zoning, and development for urban regions as part of an "urban landscape garden" almost from the time Sir Walter had denounced the combination.[102]

Furthermore, all of this knowledge and experience had long been known in Cleveland. Much of it already was in place in 1926—in Cleveland-area ordinances, in the statutes of Ohio enabling the ordinances, in the advertisements of local real estate companies, and on the ground throughout the Cleveland metropolitan region.[103] One wonders if a different outcome in the United States Supreme Court in *Euclid* would have produced much undoing of all this at the business level. One can doubt that the Cleveland urban landscape subsequently would have developed much differently than it was to do under *Euclid,* given the business views expressed by Stanley McMichael.

THE ENVIRONMENT IN THE *EUCLID* LITIGATION: THE OPINION OF THE TRIAL COURT

Having said all this, are any environmental concepts reflected in the *Euclid* decision? The answer is yes, not only in some of the references already noted in the opinion of Justice Sutherland but also in the opinion of the lower court and in the briefs of counsel for both the village of Euclid and the Ambler Realty Company. The environment had been very much present from a time prior to the adoption of the zoning ordinance in 1922 by the village of Euclid. The preamble makes this clear. The drafter of the ordinance, in recounting the factual predicates, included the inadequacy of the sewer and water systems for industry and the prevention of congestion in a scattered and still rural village.[104]

From the opinion of the lower court, we know that these two allegedly significant references to the environment in the zoning ordinance of the village of Euclid had been pointed out to the trial judge. The one reference had been to "the entire area of the village, comprising . . . now largely farm land," with the ordinance having "an aesthetic purpose . . . to make this village develop into a city along lines now conceived by the village council to be attractive and beautiful . . . [by] prevent[ing] congestion. . . ." The other reference had cited the ordinance's allegation of "the inadequacy of the present water supply of the village of Euclid."[105]

Although accepting all these allegations as facts truly pleaded, the court had been utterly unimpressed. The trial judge had swept them away as inadequate justifications for the invocation of the police power to restrict the use of property from being used for otherwise legitimate purposes desired by the private land owner.[106] In response, James Metzenbaum, the drafter of the Euclid ordinance, first chairman of the Euclid Zoning Board of Appeals, and the village's lawyer in zoning litigation, concluded:

> Here was the undoing of all the efforts of the men and women who had preached and sincerely believed in the very necessity of zoning in order to safeguard the public welfare. This decision was a challenge to American citizenry.[107]

The desire of the village of Euclid to preserve its open space character, to maintain slow growth, and to *not* develop as an industrial suburb of Cleveland had been regarded by the trial court as nothing much more than passing fancies. In any event, the trial judge had regarded them as fancies constitutionally unrealizable. Insofar as any assertions had been made that these aspirations related to "the maintenance and preservation of the public peace, public order, public morals, or public safety," the assertions were merely "false pretenses."[108] Furthermore, the amenities from the existing natural environment that the village of Euclid had wanted would simply have transferred industrial activity "to other unrestricted sections of the Cleveland industrial area."[109]

On this point, the court probably was aware of the consequences of similar no-growth zoning ordinances in communities ringing Cleveland that Harlean James and other planners already had been lamenting.

> But it is one thing to zone a metropolitan region with the purpose of making the best use of the land from the point of view of the entire region, and it is quite another thing to permit each city and town in the region to adopt zoning regulations which may protect one district at the expense of another. Mr. Ford [George B. Ford, a prominent contemporary planner] cites the instance in which "a number of cities and towns around Cleveland have been adopting stringent building zone ordinances which often exclude all industry and severely limit the spread of business. In other words, they have zoned against the city of Cleveland which will thus be obliged to provide common, economic facilities for the surrounding communities." . . . The metropolitan region is not unlike a network of cells of different sizes and shapes all gradually enlarging their circumstances until at certain points two, or even three, cells overlap. The futility of trying to zone these separate cells as though they were isolated will readily be apparent.[110]

Furthermore, the trial judge described the network binding the village of Euclid to greater Cleveland. He listed the interstate trunk rail lines, the main highways, the business character of Euclid Avenue (one of the main highways) from downtown Cleveland right through Euclid, the location of the property at issue in proximity to all of these, and the fact that "Euclid is a suburb of the city of Cleveland and a part of its great metropolitan and industrial area." On these bases, the judge implied that the village of Euclid would not succeed in its rural-preservation efforts, even if they were constitutional.[111] If Judge Westenhaver were still around after World War II, when the site at issue was developed as a Fisher Body plant of the General Motors Corporation (now GMC's Inland Division), one can be sure he gave the receipt of such information a knowing wink of expectation fulfilled.[112]

As to the issue of water supply, the village believed that its water supply system was inadequate to handle more industry than it already possessed, if service to residential users was to be maintained.[113] At the trial, the village offered a "large volume" of evidence "relating to the inadequacy of the present water supply of the village of Euclid."[114] The *amici* brief filed for the National Conference of City Planning, the National Housing Association, and the Massachusetts Federation of Town Planning Boards before the United States Supreme Court returned to the subject. The *amici* brief asserted the need for large volumes of water under high pressure to meet the fire hazards posed by industry, the increased size of water mains needed, the need to determine well in advance of industrial growth the size of the "feeder main extension," and the inflexibility of water distribution structures already in place.[115] The Supreme Court, however, made no mention of any inadequacy of water supply and the trial court called it immaterial testimony because:

> Manifestly, the police power of the village to legislate in the interests of the public health or public safety cannot be enlarged by its failure or refusal to perform its fundamental duty of providing an adequate water supply.[116]

This conclusion might surprise an urban planner in the 1980s. Yet the attitude of the trial court was in accord with the then prevailing rules in the 1920s concerning water supply.

Possibly the then Ohio statutes concerning the powers and duties "possessed by, and incumbent upon" villages supplying water within their limits to consumers required the village to supply water as demanded.[117] While the statutes are clear that a village "may" supply water beyond its corporate limits[118] or "may" contract to sell water to another contiguous village,[119] no such precatory language can be found concerning the village's duty, when engaged in a municipally owned water service, to supply its own villagers with water. Furthermore, villages having municipal water services had been delegated draconian tax, assessment, collection, and lien powers, so that a village "shall look directly to the owner of the property for . . . the water rent [for water] supplied with one hydrant or off the same pipe."[120] As a result of the then Ohio state statutory scheme of village enabling acts concerning water supply, it seems possible that the village of Euclid *could* have charged the Ambler Realty Company or its tenants or successors the costs of supplying the water for *any* potential use; therefore, the village *had* to supply the water on demand.

But whatever the Ohio statutes' empowerments and mandates, the general rule at that time for both private water companies and municipal water suppliers was set forth by John Dillon, the leading authority on municipal corporations for decades after the Civil War:

> The organization supplying water is under *a duty to consumers to supply* the water . . . *impartially to all reasonably within the reach of its pipes* . . . . The public character of the service, the obligation of the municipality to perform its duty towards all inhabitants without discrimination . . . *must be exercised without discrimination* between persons similarly situated. . . .[121]

Since Euclid already had industry that it was supplying water (and intended to have more), there existed users similarly situated to any industrial users who might be located on the site owned by Ambler.[122]

Furthermore, *Ruling Case Law,* the then most highly regarded American legal encyclopedia, went beyond even John Dillon. It asserted that a municipality

> assumes a public duty to be discharged for the public benefit; a community service commensurate with the offer of providing a service system which will be reasonably adequate to meet the wants of the municipality not only at the time it began to service but likewise to keep pace with the growth of the municipality, and gradually to extend its system as the reasonable wants of the growing community may require.[123]

As *Ruling Case Law* saw it, Euclid, at best, would have to phase in an increase in its water service. As a municipal water supplier, Euclid lacked the power to deny water service on the basis of an inadequacy that had no plan and no schedule for remedying any water deficiency.[124] Any landowner in the village wanting water supplied, and being willing and able to

pay for it, could have enforced this right to water in *mandamus.*[125]

Environmentally appealing as the inadequacy of a water supply might have been to insurance underwriters, water engineers, planners, and the village council of Euclid, the excuse was an invalid one in traditional law and, perhaps, under the Ohio statutes. In the late twentieth century, of course, a moratorium on municipal growth based on the inadequacy of water supply will be sustained if the court—as the trial court did in *Euclid*—believes that the water supply is inadequate.[126] This legal recourse seems not to have been available in the 1920s. The absence of such a legal rule may explain why the opinion of Justice Sutherland chose to remain silent on the subject.

THE ENVIRONMENT IN THE *EUCLID* LITIGATION: THE OPINION OF COUNSEL

With so much of environmental concern in the work of the trial court—even though unimpressive to the trial judge who thought zoning on the basis of race and national origin made more sense[127]—one understands that environmental material had to have appeared within the briefs of counsel. James Metzenbaum for the village and Alfred Bettman for the *amici* used such material and, perhaps paradoxically, so did Newton D. Baker, counsel for the Ambler Realty Company. The natural as well as the built environment were present in their arguments, as one would anticipate from the evidence offered to the trial court and the motives that caused the village council of Euclid to adopt the kind of zoning ordinance that it did.

James Metzenbaum in drawing the ordinance was interested in preserving the open spaced, rural character of the village, in preventing congestion, and in working within the limitations of the existing systems of water supply and drainage. He tells us that at the trial in federal court "typewritten volumes" of testimony were taken, much of it "the facts pertaining to the specific land in question" as well as to "the basic philosophy of zoning."[128] Under the latter rubric in his treatise he included much that would be regarded as environmental in character: open space, dispersed structures, sunlight, fresh air, trees and flowers, parks, unpolluted air and water, all of which he asserted are needed in order to prevent "blight."[129]

Indeed, reading the material in Metzenbaum's later treatise on zoning law makes it evident that he drew upon his arguments in both the trial court and the Supreme Court. Much of the treatise probably came from the first two briefs filed with the United States Supreme Court and, most probably, from his first argument before the Supreme Court.[130] But that argument had not gone well, as James Metzenbaum knew.[131] Not surprisingly, therefore, by the time he got to his third brief in the case, his arguments had become terse, legalistic, with heavy use of string citations, and with no attention to environmental matters as such.[132] The references to the environment were left to Alfred Bettman in his brief for the *amici* at the late stage of the appeal.

Alfred Bettman, himself, believed strongly in what he called "the fact bases of zoning." Focusing on the built environment, these fact bases nevertheless included the natural environment and tied its preservation closely to the police power. In 1925 he had asserted,

> A zone plan finds its scientific as well as its legal justification in the fact that it represents the product of a studied design for the promotion of the public health, safety, convenience, prosperity, and welfare, and that he who made the design kept these purposes in mind throughout the work and laid out his zones and

his regulations in accordance with recognized principles of public health, safety, and so on.[133]

So important were open spaces and the preservation of natural or rural landscapes to Bettman that he personally wanted cities to have extraterritorial zoning powers so as to enable them to preserve "large open development zones" outside their city limits.[134] The value of *Euclid* that he recalled most strongly later was that "the suburban community is not required to merge its welfare completely in that of the metropolitan region," which to him was "salutary and refreshing."[135]

Reference has already been made to Bettman's discussion of why the availability—or nonavailability—of water supply ought to have been allowed consideration in zoning.[136] Bettman, in his brief, also cited and relied heavily on the arguments of Stanley McMichael on behalf of zoning in the Cleveland area that already have been considered here.[137] But more significant than either of these Bettman arguments for Justice Sutherland's ultimate opinion—notably the Justice's references to "preserving a more favorable environment in which to rear children," "depriving children of the privilege of quiet and open spaces for play,"[138] perhaps even the comparative imagery behind the "pig in the parlor" simile[139] —are other elements in Bettman's brief.

Alfred Bettman began this important section of his brief with the flat assertion, "Zoning is not for aesthetic purposes."[140] Judge Westenhaver's crack that, "The blighting of property values and the congesting of population, whenever . . . certain foreign races invade a residential section,"[141] had an effect on Bettman's argument. "An artist might prefer the slovenly streets of Naples to the neat American suburb."[142] But no zoning would be justified that sought to meet such an artist's tastes in "the artistic or the beautiful."[143] No, indeed!

> Zoning does aim to improve the good order of the cities, that is the general orderliness. . . . The essential object of promoting what might be called orderliness in the layout of cities is not the satisfaction of taste or aesthetic desires, but rather of the promotion of those beneficial effects upon health and morals which come from living in orderly and decent surroundings. . . . [T]he man who seeks to place the home for his children in an orderly neighborhood, with some open space and light and fresh air and quiet, is not motivated so much by considerations of taste or beauty as by the assumption that his children are likely to grow mentally, physically, and morally more healthful in such a neighborhood than in a disorderly, noisy, slovenly, blighted, and slumlike district. This assumption is indubitably correct. . . . Disorderliness in the environment has as detrimental an effect upon health and character as disorderliness within the house itself. . . . [T]he conditions outside the house affect the conditions within the house, as for instance the noise of industrial traffic . . ., and the light and air conditions outside. . . . Zoning has . . . this purpose of promoting public health, order, safety, convenience, and morals by the promotion of favorable environmental conditions in which people live and work; which is something very different from aesthetic in the sense of pleasing to the eye or satisfying to artistic cravings.[144]

So, there it is: Zoning promoted favorable environmental conditions. For Bettman, it was for the benefit of all people. For Justice Sutherland, it was primarily for the benefit of children. But in any event Justice Sutherland had taken up Bettman's argument that zoning provided at least children with an environment that could be quiet and sunny with fresh air, open space, and room to play. Justice Sutherland had dropped the negative pejoratives of Bettman, but he had picked up in his opinion what was positively important. As for imagery, Bettman talked about "putting the furnace in the cellar rather than in the living room."[145] Justice Sutherland may have picked up the comparison as keeping the pig from the parlor.

For Bettman, the point was that he had influenced some of the content of the opinion. Precise quotation and precise use of simile were not what he had wanted. In essence, zoning for environmental purposes had moved from Bettman's brief into Justice Sutherland's opinion. That was enough for Alfred Bettman.[146] As a result, Newton D. Baker, the lawyer who had won at the trial level and had "won" after the first hearing before the Supreme Court, became the loser. But Baker also had not been indifferent in his brief concerning the environment. Bettman's environmental arguments were the ones that ultimately had convinced the majority of the Supreme Court. Baker's losing advocacy, nevertheless, had possessed two strong environmental components, even though the Court finally was unpersuaded by them.

Baker had argued that Euclid's zoning ordinance "erects a dam to hold back the flood of industrial development and thus to preserve a rural character in portions of the village which, under the operation of natural economic laws, would be devoted most profitably to industrial undertakings."[147] Considering the later industrial development of the site at issue, as well as the later industrialization of Euclid (albeit after 1940),[148] Baker seemed to have had a sure grasp of what the village council wanted to accomplish environmentally, why they had turned to zoning to fulfill their objective, and why the effort likely would fail "as an arbitrary attempt to prevent the natural and proper development of the land in the village."[149] Only Baker's client, he claimed, "would simply be required to sit still and see the normal industrial and commercial development diverted" from itself to others.[150]

Baker, the old municipal reformer and the man who had earned at the time of his death the epithet "the ideal public servant,"[151] conceded much as being traditional law for municipal control over the environment, natural and built, under the police power. After all, as mayor of Cleveland he had completed Daniel Burnham's City Beautiful design of the Cleveland Mall and had supported the Emerald Necklace of parkland around Cleveland.[152] His views were not quite so antiquated as Alfred Bettman thought—"about as appropriate to twentieth century cities as electric traffic control would have been to a wilderness crossroads in the time of President Washington."[153] In his brief, Baker had claimed:

> That municipalities have power to regulate the height of buildings, areas of occupation, strengths of building materials, modes of construction, and density of use, in the interest of the public safety, health, morals, and welfare are propositions long since established; that a rational use of this power may be made by dividing a municipality into districts or zones, and varying the requirements according to the characteristics of the districts, is, of course, equally well established. . . . In every ordered society the State must act as umpire to the extent of preventing one man from so using his property or rights as to prevent others from making a correspondingly full and free use of their property and rights. . . . Accordingly, the so-called police power is an inherent right on the part of the public umpire to prevent misuses of property or rights which impair the health, safety, or morals of others, or affect prejudicially the general public welfare. The

limitations imposed on the police power . . . are inherent in the ownership. . . . I always know when I buy land, that I may not devote it to uses which endanger the safety, health, or morals of others or make its use a common nuisance to the prejudice of the public welfare.[154]

This certainly is no argument for an absolute right of private property nor advocacy for a fee simple absolute stretching from Heaven to Hell and all points in between. Baker also did not in his argument simply affirm common law actions of nuisance or classical equity's prohibitory injunctions as the sole process controlling land owners in their property uses. Instead, Baker extended a full recognition to the municipal administrative agencies to set standards, control permits, zone land, and enforce regulations both administratively and through judicial proceedings. For these reasons, Baker had to be insistent in his theory of the case that the village of Euclid was zoning merely for "taste" determined by a group of officeholders who subjected private property to their whimsy.

> [T]here are few unlikelier places to look for stable judgments on such subjects than in the changing discretion of legislative bodies, moved this way and that by the conflict of commercial interests on the one hand, and the assorted opinions of individuals, moved by purely private concerns, on the other.[155]

This kind of argument forced Alfred Bettman to meet him at an oblique angle. Bettman agreed with Baker that aesthetics ought not to be a constitutionally approved basis for zoning. Bettman then proceeded with the argument that zoning in the Euclid situation was not for aesthetic purposes at all.[156]

EUCLID, THE ENVIRONMENT, AND THE POLICE POWER: THE CHOICE

Given Baker's view of the proper exercise of the police power by municipalities, Baker had insisted that "mere questions of taste or preference" could not be given constitutional protection. The village's preference to remain rural had "no other basis than the momentary taste of the public authorities." In their theories, Bettman and Baker came out close to the same position.[157]

Assume that a person had bought land, knowing that traditional public policies could be enforced upon it. Assume further that these traditional public policies would be enforced in a manner to substantially reduce the land's value without public compensation and to accrue much of its value to other person's private advantages. Both Alfred Bettman and Newton Baker, under these assumed legal/factual conditions, would have agreed that this buyer's rights always had been constitutionally subject to just that scope of the police power. Further, both also would have agreed with Baker's following assertion,

> Even if the world could agree by unanimous consent upon what is beautiful and desirable, it could not, under our constitutional theory, enforce its decision by prohibiting a land owner, who refuses to accept the world's view of beauty, from making otherwise safe and innocent uses of his land.[158]

Where Bettman parted company from Baker was in his disbelief that the zoning ordinance of Euclid did not "otherwise" direct itself to setting forth "safe and innocent uses of land" that had nothing necessarily to do with beauty. Bettman thought the ordinance contained weaknesses. Permitting industrial development on the contested site seems not to have been to him a bothersome prospect and,

therefore, beauty could not have been for him either the factual or the constitutional basis of the ordinance.[159]

But Baker, given his theory of the case, had to cling to beauty as the ordinance's purpose of attainment—an unconstitutional purpose, as conceded by Bettman. Once Justice Sutherland's attention, however, had been directed elsewhere by the Bettman brief, much of what was in Baker's own argument would have become persuasive, paradoxically, to the justice that the Euclid ordinance was constitutional in its exercise of the police power by a municipality over private property. In Baker's own words, the ordinance then became—to paraphrase, but not to distort, his argument—"a rational use of power by dividing a municipality according to existing characteristics into zones."[160]

Newton Baker, in an earlier lecture at the University of Virginia, had set forth an excellent series of arguments that might have justified the view of the police power taken by Justice Sutherland in *Euclid.*

> [T]he definition of the police power . . . has been steadily expanded, until it no longer is limited to the safety of the people in the old sense of their safety against the perils of fire, flood, and disease, but includes an indefinite and indefinable element of the general public welfare, which the legislature undertakes to determine and which the courts have shown an increasing disposition to sustain. Thus we have come to have what is called a sociological interpretation of the law and the guaranties of the Fifth Amendment [he probably later would have included the Fourteenth Amendment as well] yield more and more, as a bulwark of the individual right of liberty and property, to a legislative and judicial determination of the paramount social need which grows out of the changed conditions under which men now live and work. . . .[161]

Everything within the Constitution of 1787, he argued, had been subjected to change and the change was continuing, without any end in sight.

> [T]hat . . . which the framers of the Constitution would have regarded to be purely private rights have been analyzed and discovered to contain ingredients of public obligation. . . .[162]

The discovery, as Baker's argument in *Euclid* indicated, was not entirely an unwelcome one to him. He justified this change, and his acceptance of much of the change, by an appeal to Woodrow Wilson, who was

> wont to say that institutions are profoundly affected by current theories of physical science; that the Constitutional Fathers had reflected the Newtonian physics . . . [so] that the so-called checks and balances are the political analogue of that great equivalence of forces by which . . . the solar systems are kept steady in their courses in space. Our later attitude toward the Constitution, Wilson plainly regarded as a reflection of the Darwinian hypothesis, involving growth and change through progressive adaptation.[163]

With views such as these, one can see that Newton Baker could not adopt the simplistic view that any restriction, regardless of public purpose, imposed on the Ambler Realty Company was unconstitutional.

Alfred Bettman and Newton Baker were very similar in their careers as well as in many of their opinions. Both began their public activities in the municipal reform movement in Ohio—Bettman in Cincinnati, Baker in Cleveland.[164] Both were nationally active in public welfare organizations,[165] both were adjunct lecturers at universities,[166] and both left behind outstanding national reputations at their respective deaths. John Lord O'Brian called

Bettman's work on *Euclid* a "great pioneering service,"[167] while Justice Oliver Wendell Holmes called Baker "the outstanding lawyer of his generation."[168] Where they most decidedly parted company was in that Bettman held Jeffersonian Democracy and early nineteenth century laissez-faire political philosophy in very low regard, while Baker purported to be a Jeffersonian Democrat.[169]

Baker's Jeffersonianism, however, was not the same as that of his friends Herbert Hoover and John W. Davis, to name just two contemporaries with whom he thought he shared his views. Justice Harlan Fiske Stone, one of the majority in *Euclid,* had been asked to review a manuscript of Herbert Hoover's that dealt with Jeffersonian Democracy. Stone did so with candor.

> I like the Jeffersonian state better, but I have to recognize that because I live in a highly industrialized modern state, in order to make the system work, I have to suffer restrictions on individual liberty which Jefferson would probably have regarded as intolerable.[170]

In all candor also, once Alfred Bettman had directed Justice Sutherland away from any aesthetic basis for zoning, a view like Justice Stone's may have led to Justice Sutherland's own pronouncement on changed conditions:

> Until recent years, urban life was comparatively simple; but with the great increase and concentration of population, problems have developed, and constantly are developing, which require, and will continue to require, additional restrictions in respect of the use and occupation of private lands in urban communities. Regulations, the wisdom, necessity and validity of which, as applied to existing conditions, are so apparent that they are now uniformly sustained, a century ago, or even half a century ago, probably would have been re-

jected as arbitrary and oppressive. Such regulations are sustained, under the complex conditions of our day, for reasons . . . which . . . would have been condemned as fatally arbitrary and unreasonable. And in this there is no inconsistency, for while the meaning of constitutional guaranties never varies, the scope of their application must expand or contract to meet the new and different conditions which are constantly coming within the field of operation. In a changing world, it is impossible that it should be otherwise.[171]

Both the statements of Justices Stone and Sutherland set forth views on the Constitution with which Newton Baker, explaining why an eighteenth century organic act could survive and remain admirable in its second century, would have agreed.[172] That was true, even if Newton Baker, as advocate and abstract Jeffersonian Democrat, would not.[173] And this probably is the reason why Baker did not follow his friend Herbert Hoover out of the Democratic party or his friend John W. Davis into the Liberty League.

Euclid, Alfred Bettman asserted, had represented an effort "seeking to destroy the zoning movement."[174] James Metzenbaum claimed suit had been brought by property owners who had refused offers of compromise, insisting on "the right to go entirely unregulated and completely unrestricted."[175] They lost.

Thereafter, "the municipalities of this country might feel themselves free, within the bounds of reasonable and proper limits, to so zone and regulate their territories, that conditions in the future might be livable and tolerable."[176] The Supreme Court in 1928 then took, as James Metzenbaum put it,

an opportunity to practice the reservation which it specifically and purposely retained to itself in the Euclid Village decision, wherein, in effect, the Supreme Court had said that al-

though it gave its validation to the fundamental theory and philosophy of zoning, yet it did not thereby intend to grant a blanket endorsement of every situation of zoning, because if and when a situation would be presented wherein zoning had been employed for an unwarranted purpose or in an unreasonable manner, the court would not approve thereof but would exercise the right to declare the same unconstitutional.[177]

What the Supreme Court, writing through Justice Sutherland, had accomplished for zoning in the years 1926 through 1928 in *Euclid,*[178] *Gorieb* v. *Fox,*[179] and *Nectow* v. *City of Cambridge,*[180] proved more important than contemporaries could have realized. As a leading basic text in property law puts it,

After *Nectow,* the Supreme Court went out of the zoning business for nearly half a century, leaving the policing of zoning laws to state courts. . . .[181]

The victory in *Euclid* by James Metzenbaum and Alfred Bettman over Newton Baker helped form America's land use for the rest of the twentieth century. Lawyers' work proved significant, even if subordinate to long-established cultural and economic forces that ran more in the direction of Metzenbaum's and Bettman's arguments than those of Baker, "the outstanding lawyer of his generation."

ZONING FOR THE ENVIRONMENT AND EUCLID SINCE *EUCLID*

Whether or not recusancy on the subject of zoning was a wise course for the Supreme Court to have chosen, that was the choice, thereby making *Euclid* a very important case. Clearly, *Euclid* in its own terms supports zoning for environmental purposes. *Euclid* allowed for protecting open space; low-density development; slow (maybe even no) growth; and protecting air and water quality and topography, following and assuring natural ground cover. The objectives in planning (and later in zoning) of a Patrick Geddes and an Ian McHarg, those whose ideas are most notably associated with environmental planning for conserving the natural environment,[182] could later be achieved under the authority of *Euclid.*

This environmental type of planning, of course, recently has been attacked widely as that of "utopians" who dispersed the city, scattering it in urban sprawl because "their attitude to urban life [is] morbid and biased and their influence . . . malign."[183] Others, also recently, have denounced this planning as too clustered and too preservative of "open space [that is] marshy, steeply sloped, or otherwise unusable."[184] But the criticism cannot dismiss an historical experience. Whether either—or neither—group of critics is right, one fact they do establish: the pervasive impact of environmental planning for both nature preservation and human "life quality."[185]

It is known that the site at litigation in *Euclid* was eventually developed industrially and that many planners thought it ought to have been so developed. Euclid later became an industrial city, as predicted and as feared. The Euclid zoning ordinance had imperfections.

Yet the Euclid zoning ordinance *was* designed to preserve the open character of a rural village when adopted in 1922. And the village of Euclid *did* preserve its rural character until the Second World War.[186] What overwhelmed the village proved to be the introduction of, first, defense industries for the war and, second, the interstate highway system's freeways after the war. Local zoning could not have kept either out—assuming that patriotic sentiment had been absent as to the first or motorists had not wanted freeways as to the second. Neither presumably ever was the case. Any urban environmental planner who had a gen-

eration's success, where a rural village that *meant* to stay rural, *stayed* rural, would be regarded as a great success today.

Ultimately, what happened? Well, later events had much in store for Euclid. Nor is history closed for what is now a small city of about 60,000 residents.

In 1986, Euclid had been 99 percent developed, possessing 151 industries, which was more than any other industrial suburb of Cleveland in Cuyahoga County. Industrial diversity is Euclid's current strength, though its industrial employment peaked in the late 1960s.[187] The new freeways are its industries' main means of transportation. Euclid has come a long way from being a rural center for grape culture.[188]

Euclid Avenue remains a major business street, lined with apartment houses and commercial establishments that are suffering some "blight." Euclid is now buffered from Cleveland as Euclid Avenue crosses into Euclid by large institutional construction along the boundary. This has become a common phenomena for Euclid Avenue. In the early 1920s, part of it was still Millionaires' Row. Throughout its length, Euclid Avenue since those days has been saved from blight by such institutional structures as universities, clinics, senior citizens' apartments, and other similar public uses. Public construction and joint rehabilitation efforts by the cities of Cleveland and Euclid have kept the street commercially sound.[189] The topography south of Euclid Avenue in Euclid has confined commercial development to a narrow strip between the avenue and a steep incline, back of which the main residential district for detached private homes in Euclid has maintained its value.[190]

A history also has been experienced specifically for the site that was at issue in *Euclid.* Shortly after World War II, General Motors built a body plant on it. The plant formerly did heavy work, but now does mostly cut-and-trim for car interiors. This work is labor intensive and is in stiff competition with other GM plants, as well as with non-GM manufacturers. At the initiative of GM, the city of Euclid has assisted in setting up a state-authorized urban jobs and economic development zone "for the purpose of facilitating . . . expanded growth for commercial or economic development."[191] A review of what the Ohio statute requires in the form of existing economic suffering before a zone can be created shows how advanced in age Euclid is as an industrial city—and maybe the rightness of those long-ago village planners who had tried to stay rural.[192]

Although Euclid has maintained its economic health perhaps better than other industrial communities in the northeast Ohio quadrant, Euclid's economic activities have shrunk. Empty factory buildings exist. Development now consists not in covering rural open space with factories but in remodeling or razing such empty buildings for new construction. The new economic zone stretches from the Cleveland border along Euclid Avenue to Babbitt Road, then north to Chardon Road, and back to the Cleveland line, including within it the two rail lines and U.S. Route 2/Interstate 90 for industrial service purposes.[193] Today, the condition of Euclid is that of any small American industrial city caught in national and world markets that continuously buffet it.

The late 1980s present a development picture that the Euclid planners of the early 1920s might deplore. But they would argue that events produced circumstances beyond any planning and zoning powers available in Warren Harding's Ohio—or beyond *any* powers of *any* planners who were *any* where in the world in 1922. Each age can only take care of itself. The Euclid planners of the early 1920s could

claim to have done better because—through prescience, luck, or good administrators who served as the "conscience" of the zoning laws[194]—Euclid stayed rural for almost 25 years after these planners' ordinance was adopted.

Certainly the development people in Euclid are happy with the ordinance today. The director of Euclid Community Development has said,

> As a native of Euclid—as well as someone professionally involved in planning its contemporary economic development—I am proud of Euclidean zoning. Our zoning ordinance and its plan are what I use to promote Euclid for development when competing with other local municipalities for business.[195]

Those planners back in 1922 could not have been better pleased than by that viewpoint of their work more than six decades later.

But, then, perhaps all of what happened was fate, nature's ultimate intrusion into human affairs. Or perhaps all of it, even the most seemingly natural parts of the planning in the village of Euclid, was a human invention. Either way, when one talks about planning, perhaps the best commentary of all is that provided by Virgil: *Inventas aut qui vitam excoluere per artes.*[196]

On the other hand, Virgil never knew a decision like *Euclid* that could have made zoning "now a central task of local government, a major consumer of a property lawyer's energy, and an important force in shaping our physical environment, our income distribution, and our politics."[197] By descent from *Euclid,* urban planning and zoning have become major productive forces in society, as artful and profitable a couple of inventions as human artifice could devise.[198]

Maybe planning ought to have left alone the

urban environment. In his 1925 presidential address to the American Sociological Association, Robert E. Park claimed that:

> . . . a slum . . . is an area of casual and transient population, an area of dirt and disorder, "of omissions and of lost souls." These neglected and abandoned regions become . . . our ghettos [for poor immigrants to the city], and sometimes our bohemias, . . . where artists and radicals seek refuge from the fundamentalism and Rotarianism, and, in general, the limitations and restrictions of a Philistine World.[199]

But, as Virgil indicated, people can extract almost anything they desire out of their environment. And, just maybe, if Virgil is right, planning and zoning may produce good results both for people and their natural and built environments.

Yet, whatever the rightness of Virgil, the United States Supreme Court has said that it is constitutional for states and local governments to regulate the environment by way of zoning law,[200] thereby combating any "undesirable secondary effects" that business may produce in the zoned area.[201] For a lawyer, perhaps this legal conclusion is all that need be known. But even under this restricted professional view, the points in lawyers' arguments about the environmental content of zoning will continue to involve issues raised in, and around, the *Euclid* litigation. These issues, as well as the still-pervasive cultural attitudes that impelled the village of Euclid to adopt its "Euclidean" zoning, will go on providing much of America's law work about its land use.[202]

NOTES

1. F. Trelease, *Cases and Materials on Water Law,* 3rd ed., (1979), p. xv.
2. *Village of Euclid* v. *Ambler Realty Co.,* 272 U.S. 359 (1926).
3. *Oxford English Dictionary* 3 (1933), p. 231. Entry for "environment." The English translator was Philemon Holland, "the translator-general in his age," *Chamber's Biographical Dictionary* (1962), p. 655 entry for Philemon Holland.
4. *Oxford English Dictionary,* p. 230, entries for either the verb or the noun. The modern Greek word for environment is *perivallon,* while *elefsis* announces the arrivals of airplanes.
5. *Euclid* v. *Ambler,* p. 394.
6. "The aggregate of all the external conditions and influences affecting the life, development, and ultimately the survival of an organism," N. Landau and P. Rheingold, *The Environmental Law Handbook* (1971), p. 481.
7. Both the city and the countryside have become a total, man-made system, an environment that humanity shapes and can reshape to a better result for the maximization of human potential. C. Doxiadis and J. Papaioannou, *Ecumenopolis* (1974), p. 320.
8. G. Leinwand, *Air and Water Pollution* (1969), pp. 34–46. See the story of the anthropologist offended by the pollution of human excreta in jungle villages who still "reflected on the sort of civilization that could spend so much time and money to fight one kind of pollution while almost completely neglecting another kind." E. Edelson and F. Warshofsky, *Poisons in the Air* (1966), pp. 114–116.
9. Conversely, there is also the narrow definition of environment used in the classic, L. Henderson, *The Fitness of the Environment* (1913), pp. 61–63, which confines the meaning to certain physical properties necessary to support life in the universe.
10. C. Merchant, *The Death of Nature* (1980), p. 293.
11. M. Nicholson, *The Environmental Revolution* (1970), pp. 22–32, shows how this development between ecology and this meaning of environment developed in tandem, eventually replacing, as the previously employed word of choice, "conservation."
12. This is a paraphrase taken from *Webster's Third New International Dictionary* (1970), p. 760, entry for "environment," 2nd def.
13. R. Arvill, *Man and Environment,* rev. ed. (1969), p. 163.
14. Peccei, "Land Policy: A Global Outlook," in *Second World Congress on Land Policy, 1983,* eds. Cullen and Woolery (1985), pp. 7, 10–11. He adds, "Also, it must be considered with the human artifacts, those already existing and those that will be built in the future."
15. *Euclid* v. *Ambler,* pp. 391–394, for the adverse effects. *Id.,* pp. 395–397, sustaining the tentative constitutional character of the decision rather than judging the consti-

tutionality of any particular provisions within the Euclid ordinance.

16. Psomopoulos, "The City of the Future," in *Second World Congress,* pp. 91, 111.

17. Phillips, "The Impact of Impact Zoning," *Urban Land* vol. 45, no. 3 (1986): 34–35.

18. McHarg, "Values, Process, and Form," in *The Fitness of Man's Environment,* Smithsonian Annual II (1968), pp. 208, 210.

19. McHarg, "Man and His Environment," in *The Urban Condition: People and Policy in the Metropolis,* ed. Duhl and Powell (1963), pp. 44, 50.

20. McHarg, "The Place of Nature in the City of Man," in *Challenge for Survival: Land, Air, and Water for Man in Megalopolis,* ed. Dansereau (1970), pp. 37, 48.

21. *Id.,* 51.

22. *Euclid* v. *Ambler,* p. 388.

23. *Id.* "A nuisance may be merely a right thing in the wrong place—like a pig in the parlor instead of the barnyard."

24. I. McHarg, *Design with Nature* (1969), p. 65. He also sets out here his view of water, as central to land suitability planning. *Id.,* pp. 55–65.

25. *Id.,* p. 125, where he refers to the significance that the ideas of Clarence Morris had for him. McHarg also cites frequently, as influential in the formation of his own ideas, the work of Lawrence Henderson, *supra* n. 9.

26. Morris, "The Rights and Duties of Beasts and Trees: A Law-Teacher's Essay for Landscape Architects," *J. of Leg. Ed.* 17 (1964): 185, 190. He states that the article was an outgrowth of his participation over several years in "an ongoing series of lectures," during which he made the statements later contained in the published article. *Id.,* p. 185, note. Therefore, one cannot know just when Morris formulated these forward-looking ideas.

27. One thinks particularly of *Scenic Hudson Preservation Conference* v. *Federal Power Commission,* 354 F.2d 608, 620 (2nd Cir. 1965), *cert. den.,* 384 U.S. 941 (1966), "This role does not permit [the decision maker] to act as an umpire blandly calling balls and strikes for adversaries appearing before it"; *Calvert Cliffs' Coordinating Committee* v. *AEC,* 449 F.2d 1109, 1118 (D.C. Cir. 1971), ". . . environmental issues [must] be considered at every important stage in the decision-making process concerning a particular action—at every stage where an overall balancing of environmental and nonenvironmental factors is appropriate and where alterations might be made in the proposed action to minimize environmental costs." Morris also urged "surrogates for protecting birds, flowers and ponds," Morris, *supra* n. 26. 191, predictive of Justice Douglas's view in *Sierra Club* v. *Morton,* 405 U.S. 727, 741 (1972), see

C. Stone, *Should Trees Have Standing? Toward Legal Rights for Natural Objects* (1974).

28. Phillips, "The Impact of Impact Zoning," pp. 34–35, ". . . impact zoning is the mapping and analysis of detailed environmental and social data. . . ."

29. Soulé, "Conservation Biology and the 'Real World,' " in *Conservation Biology: The Science of Scarcity and Diversity,* ed. Soulé (1986), pp. 1, 7.

30. D. Brower, C. Carraway, T. Pollard, and C. Propst, *Managing Development in Small Towns* (1984), p. 141. Especially when, ". . . local requirements for environmental reports generally include a discussion of the environmental impacts of proposed development, measures to mitigate adverse environmental effects, alternatives to proposed actions, relationships between short-term uses of the environment and long-term environmental productivity, and irreversible environmental changes." *Id.*

31. *Environmental Protection: Law and Policy,* eds. Anderson, Mandelker, and Tarlock, pp. 788–789. Both California and Washington statutes (but especially the California) received particular resonance from broad judicial interpretations, subsequently and substantially accepted by their respective legislatures. *See Friends of Mammoth* v. *Board of Supervisors,* 8 Cal. 3d 247, 104 Cal. Rptr. 761, 502 P. 2d 1049 (1972) and *Polygon Corp.* v. *City of Seattle,* 90 Wash. 2d 59, 578 P. 2d 1309 (1978).

32. *West's Cal. Ann. Codes, Public Resources,* secs. 21000–21193. The California Coastal Act also is pertinent in this regard for the land lying under its jurisdiction. *Id.,* secs. 3000–3082.23. This later act, too, has had repeated revisitations since its initial enactment—also in a simpler form, at first—in 1976.

33. *Id.,* sec. 21065(c), added by Stats. 1972, c. 1154, p. 2271, sec. 1. *See Plan for Arcadia, Inc.* v. *Arcadia City Council,* 42 Cal. App. 712, 117 Cal. Rptr. 96 (1974).

34. *West's Cal. Ann. Codes, Public Resources,* sec. 21083.3(a). It has broader mitigating features than the one quoted in the text.

35. *Id.,* particularly the language added by Stats. 1984, c. 440, sec. 1. Somewhat similar mitigating provisions for single-family residences and certain certified urban areas that exclude them from certain controls of the coastal zone commission are in *Id.,* secs. 30610–30610.5.

36. *Id.,* sec. 21060.5, added by Stats. 1972, c. 1154, p. 2271, sec. 1.

37. *Id.,* sec. 21000(b), (c), and (d), respectively. The other subsections do not introduce other content to the use of the word environment.

38. *Id.,* sec. 21001(b). Other subsections bring in the need for "man and nature [to] exist in productive harmony to fulfill the social and economic requirements of

present and future generations." *Id.,* (e), and government "to consider qualitative factors as well as economic and technical factors and long-term benefits and costs, in addition to short-term benefits and costs and to consider alternatives to proposed actions affecting the environment." *Id.,* (g).

39. *Id.,* sec. 21000 and sec. 21001(d), as added by Stats. 1979, c. 947, pp. 3270–3271, secs. 4 and 5.

40. E. Murphy, *Governing Nature* (1967), p. 9; E. Murphy, *Man and His Environment: Law* (1971), p. 117, drawing on the ideas of Charles Fourier, see C. Fourier, *Harmonian Man,* ed. Poster, trans. Hanson (1971), pp. 30–47. The distinction between "flow" and "stock" resources is drawn from the writings of S. Ciriacy-Wantrup, *Natural Resource Economics: Selected Papers,* eds. Bishop and Anderson (1985), p. 211.

41. The California legislature is emphatic about the imperative. "Every citizen has a responsibility to contribute to the preservation and enhancement of the environment," *West's Ann. Cal. Codes, Public Resources,* secs. 21000 (e); and, "The Legislature further finds and declares that it is the policy of the state to . . . ensure that the long-term protection of the environment shall be the guiding criterion in public decisions." *Id.,* sec. 21001 (d).

42. *Euclid* v. *Ambler,* p. 394. Also see his discussion of state cases. *Id.,* 392–394.

43. This is made very clear in his description of apartment houses among detached residences as "mere parasites." *Id.,* pp. 394–395.

44. *Id.,* p. 394. Insights into the private attitudes of Justice Sutherland concerning the environment are offered in *George Sutherland: Proceedings of the Bar and Officers of the Supreme Court of the United States in Memory of George Sutherland* (1944). His favorite poet was Dante Gabriel Rossetti, Stephens, "Remarks," *Id.,* pp. 17, 42. "[H]is memory harked back to his early days in Utah, under its territorial form of government, when its problems and those of the miner and of irrigated lands and of government land patents were all about him," Rigby, "Remarks." *Id.,* pp. 47, 53. "His later practice of the law in a pioneer community brought him . . . extensive trips on horseback over the mountains," Hughes, "Remarks." *Id.,* pp. 75, 77–78. Chief Justice Stone, who had called his opinion in *Euclid* one of several opinions of Sutherland that "are illuminating examples of the application of constitutional principles to new situations," Stone, "Remarks." *Id.,* pp. 101, 108, commented upon Sutherland's life "as a child in the mining camps of Montana and Utah" and his "country law practice in a western pioneer community." *Id.,* pp. 108–109. Too much ought not to be made of this;

nevertheless, this experience and viewpoint were an inherent part of Justice Sutherland's worldview.

45. *Public Planning and Control of Urban and Land Development,* 2nd ed., ed. Hagman (1980), pp. 1,172–2,279.

46. 274 U.S. 365 (1927).

47. Reinhardt, "Mr. Justice Sutherland," *U. of Kans. City L.R.* 12 (1943): 42, 49.

48. *Soble Construction Co.* v. *Zoning Hearing Board of East Stroudsburg,* 16 Pa. Comm. 599, 607, 329 A. 2d 912 (1974).

49. *State Bank & Trust Co.* v. *Village of Wilmette,* 358 Ill. 311 (1934).

50. *Downey* v. *Village of Kensington,* 257 N.Y. 221, 231 (1931), being the unanimous decision of the New York Court of Appeals of which Benjamin Cardozo was chief judge. Such unanimity from what then was arguably the most distinguished court in the United States indicates the traditional view of not allowing restricting the use of private property for purely aesthetic reasons.

51. *Gorieb* v. *Fox, supra* n. 46.

52. *City of Smyrna* v. *Parks,* 240 Ga. 699, 705, 242 S. E. 2d 73 (1978). The court then adds, "provided there is a reasonable relationship between the regulation and the legitimate purposes of regulations, as enunciated by the legislature." Chain link fences could thus be outlawed if the local government decided that "in the minds of many such fences are associated with commercial and even prison usages." *Id.,* p. 706. The court will not "reassess" this local decision based on local attitudes, *Id.,* pp. 705–706.

53. *Village of Hudson* v. *Albrecht, Inc.,* 9 Ohio St. 3d 69, 72, 9 Ohio O. Rep. 273, 458 N. E. 2d 852 (1984); *app. dis.,* 467 U.S. 1237 (1984). The dissent vigorously asserts that *Euclid* "was never meant to be a vehicle to enforce the personal taste of one or another. The purpose was to allow for the controlled and orderly growth of cities. There are many legitimate interests which should be protected by zoning. Aesthetics alone is not one of these." *Id.,* 75. The dissent insists, however, that the majority opinion does not stand for the proposition "that aesthetic considerations alone will not justify zoning restrictions." *Id.*

54. *Ben Lomond, Inc.* v. *The City of Idaho Falls,* 92 Idaho 595, 448 P. 2d 20 (1968).

55. *Sarasota County* v. *Barg,* 302 So. 2d 737 (Fla. Sup. Ct., 1974).

56. *West's Cal. Ann. Codes, Public Resources,* sec. 21060.5.

57. *Id.,* sec. 21001 (b).

58. Ghent, "Annotation: Validity and Construction of Zoning Ordinance Regulating Architectural Style or Design of Structure," 41 *A.L.R.*3d 1397, sec. 2a (1972). With *A.L.R.*'s usual care, *Euclid* is not cited for this proposition.

Euclid is cited, however, as the case that made possible *any* decisions upholding the constitutionality of zoning.

59. *Id.*

60. Bufford, "Beyond the Eye of the Beholder: A New Majority of Jurisdictions Authorize Aesthetic Regulation," *U. of Mo. K. C. L. R.* 48 (1980): 125, 127.

61. *Id.*, Judge Bufford asserts, "One may confidently predict that . . . a court faced with the issue of the validity of aesthetic regulation today would approve it. . . . Thus, if beauty has not become queen, neither is she any longer a pauper in American law, always needing the help of other interests to entitle her to protection." *Id.*, p. 166. He does not cite, however, the *Euclid* case for this proposition. *Id.*, pp. 128–129.

62. L. Mumford, *The Myth of the Machine: The Pentagon of Power* (1970), pp. 380–381.

63. *Id.*, pp. 381–382. This follows a long discussion about the significance of "the explosion of flowers" in the Age of Mammals. "Efflorescence is an archetypal example of nature's untrammeled creativity. . . . Biological creativity and the aesthetic creativity that so often accompanies it exist for their own sake and transcend the organism's earlier limitations." *Id.*, p. 381.

64. G. Bateson, *Steps to an Ecology of Mind* (1972), pp. 494–505.

65. L. Mumford, *The City in History* (1961), p. 567. "Our civilization is faced with the relentless extension and aggrandizement of a highly centralized, superorganic system, that lacks autonomous component centers capable of exercising selection, exerting control, and above all, making autonomous decisions and answering back. The effective response to that problem, which lies at the very heart of our future urban culture, rests on the development of a more organic world picture, which shall do justice to all the dimensions of living organisms and human personalities."

66. The same has been said of the Highland grouse country, "with their constant over-burning of heather and persecution of predators . . . [they] were crudely and heavily managed. . . . The regime for the Highlands was largely escapist in its objects, and sportsmen, artists, poets, and tourists agreed in not seeing what they did not want to see, . . . in the natural scene . . . rapidly degrading the vegetation and scenery. . . ." M. Nicholson, *The Environmental Revolution* (1970), p. 152.

67. F. Olmsted, Sr., *Civilizing America's Cities*, ed. Sutton (1971), pp. 199–200. His justification is the use of park "spaciousness" to enhance public enjoyment. *Id.*, p. 262.

68. R. Foglesong, *Planning the Capitalist City* (1986), pp. 91–93.

69. *Id.*, p. 91, citing David Harvey for the "pure hoax"

charge and Raymond Williams for the "discovery" of rural landscape by the eighteenth century upper classes.

70. J. Harte, *Landscape, Land Use and the Law* (1985), p. 2. Richard Foglesong attributes this to "the emergence of capitalist forms of agriculture," Foglesong, *Planning the Capitalist City*, p. 91.

71. M. Nicholson, *The Environmental Revolution*, p. 157, for the "overmature" quote and Harte, *Landscape, Land Use*, p. 2, for the "grubbed up" quote.

72. P. and P. Goodman, *Communitas* (1960), pp. 50–51. "Urban beauty does not require trees and parks." *Id.*, p. 50.

73. P. Geddes, *Cities in Evolution*, rev. ed. (1949), pp. 147–148, 190–192, indicates his debt to predecessors and contemporaries like Ebenezer Howard and Sir Raymond Unwin. As to his beginnings as a botanist, *Id.*, pp. 231–232.

74. Tyrwhitt, "Introduction," in Geddes, *Cities in Evolution*, p. xv. The book was first published in 1915, based on an unpublished draft written in 1909–1910. *Id.*, p. ix.

75. Wurster, "Framework for an Urban Society," in *Goals for Americans, The Report of the President's Commission on National Goals and Chapters Submitted for the Consideration of the Commission* (1960), pp. 225, 244–247. Catherine Bauer Wurster, however, regarded "the physical environment" as "indivisible" with the natural and built environments forming "the same organic system." *Id.*, p. 245, but with a need to "focus on the house and the neighborhood, instead of the big framework." *Id.*, p. 246, because "the physical environment plays a dynamic role in human enterprise and welfare." *Id.*, p. 225.

76. H. James, *Land Planning in the United States for City, State and Nation*, p. 247 for "marvelous progress," p. 245 for "developing law" (1926). This book is Volume IX in the *Standard Course in Real Estate* outlined by the Joint Commission of the National Association of Real Estate Boards and the Institute for Research in Land Economics and Public Utilities as well as in the Land Economics Series, edited by Richard T. Ely. *Id.*, pp. iii and i, respectively. This is noted simply to show the common character of the ideas expressed in what was regarded at that time as a fairly basic text.

77. Foglesong, *Planning the Capitalist City*, pp. 92–94, on the work and influence of Andrew Jackson Downing.

78. James, *Land Planning*, p. 48.

79. *Id.*, pp. 70–73. She briefly outlines the views, "a rough outline of the dominating ideas," of leading American planners from the years 1901 to 1911 on these pages.

80. *Id.*, p. 83.

81. Foglesong, *Planning the Capitalist City*, pp. 92–94. His-

tory being a river that goes back endlessly to remote sources, one has to qualify these origins by talking of the "direct development" of ideas; but, even so, the 1840s are *not* the beginning of these ideas.

82. H. James, *Land Planning,* pp. 83–84.

83. *Id.,* pp. 84–89. Natural environment is important to her description of planners' thinking. "It will be seen clearly that all the physical features of the city must be considered as interrelated. Water and sewer levels dictate the layout of building lots for homes. . . . It is usually possible to use a sloping wooded area to excellent advantage. . . . The problem of providing building lots of uneven elevation with water at proper pressure and sewers with sufficient gravity flow can usually be met. . . . In practice, however, beautiful wooded slopes too frequently are denuded of their trees, stripped of their top soil and terraced into clay strips . . . and the whole area developed into an ugly, bare expanse. . . ." *Id.,* 87–88. Nothing could make clearer than this quotation that importance already had been assigned to the natural environment by planners as of 1926.

84. Z. Gale, *Civic Improvement in Little Towns* (1913), discussed in James, *Land Planning,* pp. 76–77.

85. James, *Land Planning,* p. 416.

86. Interestingly enough, Herbert Hoover, as United States secretary of commerce, had picked up on Patrick Geddes's idea of planning in terms of entire river systems, calling for an inventory of the resources of inland waters. "For generations, we have driven our energies in the development of land. . . . We have done comparably little with our water resources. To-day we must speed the development of our water in its aid to the land. . . . This will test our vision and our statesmanship." *Id.,* pp. 373–376. Rivers, at the federal level, have retained their charm as a focus for planning to this day, 7 CFR 621 (1988), River Basin Investigation and Surveying, and 18 CFR 701 (1988), Water Resources Council.

87. Olmsted, *Civilizing America's Cities,* pp. 206–207, but the same mix can be found anywhere else in this book of his collected writings. See also Foglesong, *Planning the Capitalist City,* p. 115.

88. Foglesong, *Planning the Capitalist City,* pp. 68, 133.

89. James, *Land Planning,* pp. 84 and 238–239, respectively.

90. Nelson, "Endorsement," in S. McMichael and R. Bingham, *City Growth and Values* (1923). Herbert U. Nelson was the secretary of the National Association of Real Estate Boards and he says that this book has been published with the approval of the association. See the authors' Foreword, where they say: "Years of study and observation have been crystallized in this effort to visualize the modern city, and the elements of its growth," and then note the occupations of those whom they thank for advice and information. See also S. McMichael and R. Bingham, *City Growth Essentials* (1928); S. McMichael, *How to Operate a Real Estate Business* (rev. ed., 1972); and S. McMichael and P. O'Keefe, *Leases* (6th ed., 1974).

91. McMichael and Bingham, *City Growth Essentials,* 1st citation, pp. 321 and 326, respectively.

92. *Id.,* p. 322. His discussion on zoning is *Id.,* pp. 315–327. There is an implicit reference to *Buchanan* v. *Warley,* 245 U.S. 60 (1917). *Id.,* p. 326. Robert Bingham probably wrote much of the legal material, though the dominant voice throughout the book is that of Stanley McMichael.

93. *Id.,* pp. 34–35. Elsewhere, rivers and other water bodies are referred to by him as the geographical factor that determined the success of a city economically. *Id.,* p. 24–25, and that the same is true for many cities located in the foothills of mountains. *Id.,* p. 27. He is never quite certain what is a "fault" unless no one has been able to make money from some particular natural condition.

94. *Id.,* p. 173.

95. *Id.,* p. 105.

96. *Id.,* pp. 105–106. He speaks of the value of open space, spacious layouts, light and air, quiet, plottage of lots in terms of topography, and so forth. *Id.,* pp. 107–109. "Many a merchant, just going into business, has 'bet wrong' on the weather and has had the struggle of his life to pull through, if he succeeded at all in doing so." *Id.,* p. 97. Rain, ice, sunshine, dust, and wind are referred to over and over again as climatological factors so affecting urban business life that city planning cannot ignore them.

97. *Id.,* pp. 290–292. Bear in mind that this was written before 1923.

98. *Id.,* pp. 345–348.

99. Foglesong, *Planning the Capitalist City,* p. 199, who conflates the building of the new western cities in the United States and City Beautiful reconstructions.

100. James, *Land Planning,* pp. 249–251.

101. *Id.,* p. 85. She dates the origin of zoning in the United States from 1901. The historical development of the idea of zoning in the United States is recounted in *Land Use Planning,* 3rd ed., Charles M. Haar (1977), pp. 185–187. Zoning, contemporaneously with *Euclid,* was regarded as a way to assure cities' light, pure air, open space, N. Baker, *Legal Aspects of Zoning* (1927), pp. 35–38, unpolluted water, parks, vistas, and beauty. *Id.,* pp. 14–15. The book is substantially a reprint of a series of articles published in the winter of 1925–1926. *Id.,* "Acknowledgements," and seems uninfluenced by *Euclid.*

The author is Newman Baker and not, of course, Newton Baker.

102. Olmsted, *Civilizing America's Cities,* p. 180, citing Scott, *Quarterly Review* (1820), p. 303. Frederick Law Olmsted, Sr., delivered his paper in 1893, so Sir Walter Scott's remarks were not so remote to that audience as they may seem today.

103. McMichael and Bingham, *City Growth Essentials,* 1st and 2nd citations. The city of Cleveland did not adopt a zoning ordinance until 1929, when it was approved by a citywide referendum "after a sharply contested referendum campaign in which the voters were informed and schooled upon the subject," J. Metzenbaum, *The Law of Zoning,* 1st ed. (1930), p. 392.

104. J. Metzenbaum, *Law of Zoning,* p. 336. The entire ordinance is at *Id.,* pp. 335–352; the *Euclid* opinion of the Supreme Court, *Id.,* pp. 454–496; and the *Euclid* controversy from the consideration of the ordinance through the decision of the Supreme Court, *Id.,* pp. 108–122. Even in the three-volume second edition (1955), James Metzenbaum focused his book upon the *Euclid* litigation. The work was updated by L. Ratner until 1969.

105. *Ambler Realty Co.* v. *Village of Euclid,* 297 F. 307, 309 for "farmland," 316 for "aesthetic purpose," and 308 for "water supply" (N.D. Ohio, 1924). From the tone of the opinion, Judge Westenhaver accepted the stated purpose of the village council as their true purpose, accepted the water supply as inadequate, and accepted that the village still was, and wanted to remain, an uncongested, open spaced community.

106. *Id.,* pp. 316–317. "My conclusion is that the ordinance . . . is unconstitutional and void; that it takes plaintiff's property, if not for private, at least for public, use without just compensation; that it is in no just sense a reasonable or legitimate exercise of police power." *Id.,* 317.

107. J. Metzenbaum, *Law of Zoning,* p. 112. In 1923, the Euclid ordinance had been unsuccessfully attacked in state court, presumably the Cuyahoga County Court of Common Pleas. *Id.,* 109 (no citation), and James Metzenbaum seems annoyed that the new plaintiffs "had chosen to ignore the state tribunals and had hailed zoning before the bar of the federal court." *Id.,* p. 111.

108. *Ambler* v. *Euclid,* p. 314. The trial judge asserted, in support of his view of the ordinance's objectives as passing fancies, "If police power meant what is claimed, all private property is now held subject to temporary and passing phases of public opinion, dominant for a day, in legislative or municipal assemblies." *Id.*

109. *Id.,* p. 316. The trial court, as another matter, was also most unimpressed with the authority of *Hadacheck*

v. *Sebastian,* 239 U.S. 394 (1915), as being "somewhat extreme on the facts," *Id.*

110. James, *Land Planning,* pp. 253–254. Her imagery of the cell in urban regional growth is not contemporary with the planners of her time, but it is predictive of the later work of geographers, planners, and demographers, *see* C. Doxiadis, *Ekistics* (1968), p. 133, discussing the 1933 work of Walter Christaller, as well as Doxiadis's own views. *Id.,* p. 244; and B. Berry, *Megalopolitan Confluence Zones* (1971), p. 2.

111. *Ambler* v. *Euclid,* pp. 308–309. He is even uncertain whether the village's purposes would sustain the taking of this property under a condemnation proceeding in eminent domain. *Id.,* p. 316.

112. *Property and Law,* 2nd ed., eds. Haar and Liebman (1985), p. 1098. Knowing this, I stated at a roundtable on Alfred Bettman at the First National Conference on American Planning History (March 13–15, 1986) that the village of Euclid may have intended to warehouse the land for future industrial development by classifying it under a use that meant in practical terms no development could occur until reclassification. Peter Marcuse thought this anachronistic as a planning or zoning purpose in that era. Now knowing more, I know that Professor Marcuse was right. I am indebted to Laurence Gerckens, "Alfred Bettman on *Euclid:* Letters from the Bettman File, 15 September 1924–22 May 1925," *Proceedings,* Society for American City and Regional Planning History (1986): 5–25.

113. Euclid Village Ordinance, Preamble, in J. Metzenbaum, *Zoning Law,* pp. 335, 336. During the years of the *Euclid* litigation, the village of Euclid was expanding its water, sewer, and drainage services, having begun the expansion in 1921, *Euclid, A Proud Past, A Proud Future,* A7 (n.d., c. 1983).

114. *Ambler* v. *Euclid,* p. 308.

115. Brief of Alfred Bettman in *Euclid* v. *Ambler* received at the Court October 11, 1926, pp. 108–112. "Absolutely, the design of the water distribution system for fire protection and for domestic and manufacturing consumption is dependent on a definite plan for the use of property and on the height and bulk of buildings." *Id.,* p. 112. Most of the material on this point is taken from the *Fire Prevention Year Book* of the Baltimore, Maryland, Underwriters and National Agent (1925). *Id.,* p. 108. It, in turn, quotes from water engineers, particularly a Mr. Siems, experienced in planning municipal water systems, *Id.,* p. 111. The above quotation seems to be from him.

116. *Ambler* v. *Euclid,* p. 308.

117. Villages supplying water were given the same power as directors of public services in cities that sup-

plied water, *General Code of Ohio* (Page, ed.), sec. 4261 (1921). Also, "All municipalities shall have the general powers . . . to provide for a supply of water . . . and to prevent unnecessary waste of water, and the pollution thereof." *Id.,* secs. 1316 and 1319, which must be read together.

118. *Id.,* sec. 3966.

119. *Id.,* sec. 3971.

120. *Id.,* sec. 3958.

121. J. Dillon, 3 *Municipal Corporations,* 5th ed., sec. 1317, 2204 (1911), his emphasis. He also says, "So far as the consumption of water . . . is concerned, it is immaterial to the consumer whether the supply be furnished by a municipality or by a private service corporation. As a general rule the obligations to the consumer are the same in either case." *Id.* Dillon's fame once was such that his name, along with those of such legal luminaries as Bracton and Blackstone, is cut in granite on the facade of the Ohio State University College of Law.

122. J. Metzenbaum, *Law of Zoning,* p. 336, concerning the existence of industry and the desire for more in Euclid—but not on Ambler's site. *Id.,* pp. 110–111.

123. *Ruling Case Law,* vol. 27, sec. 28 (1920): 1409. Municipal water suppliers were under the same duties as private companies holding franchises to supply water. *Id.,* sec. 27, p. 1408.

124. *Id.,* sec. 29, pp. 1409–1411.

125. Dillon, *Municipal Corporations,* sec. 1317, 2209.

126. *Land Use Controls,* eds. Ellickson and Tarlock (1981), pp. 841–842. They call for "interim zoning" to be used during the moratorium; and it may have to be limited to a "reasonable" time; but, otherwise, they see no problem. Perhaps this is only a modern extrapolation of the concepts of "reasonableness" set forth on denial of a water supply on a consumer's demand by a municipal water supplier in 27 *R.C.L.,* vol. 27, sec. 29, pp. 1409–1411.

127. *Ambler* v. *Euclid,* pp. 312–313.

128. J. Metzenbaum, *Law of Zoning,* p. 112.

129. *Id.,* p. 123, where the heading "The Philosophy of Zoning" appears and *Id.,* pp. 123–129, where he set forth what he meant by it.

130. *Id.,* p. 114. "Because this was the first occasion upon which zoning had been presented to the Supreme Court, it became necessary first to set forth and explain the philosophy, the theory and the fundamentals of zoning . . . and so that the benefits, purposes, and the growth of zoning might be adequately set forth."

131. *Id.,* p. 116. "[T]here was an apparent flush of victory among the opposition and a fully recognized feeling thereof, within the mind of the writer as well."

132. *Id.,* p. 121, where he refers to his third brief, and *Euclid* v. *Ambler,* pp. 367–370, where the brief appears.

133. A. Bettman, *City and Regional Planning Papers,* ed. Comey (1946), pp. 44, 47. This paper first appeared in *City Planning,* vol. 1, no. 2 (July 1925): 86–93.

134. *Id.,* p. 80.

135. *Id.,* p. 56. He did admit, however, that "the attorneys of the realty company had a valid idea in their emphasis upon this metropolitan factor, though they pushed this factor beyond its just deserts . . .". The paper was a memoir, Bettman, "The Decision of the Supreme Court of the United States in Euclid Village Zoning Case," *Univ. of Cincinnati L. R.* 1 (1927), pp. 184–192. He spends much of his time considering future consequences, A. Bettman, *City and Regional Planning Papers,* pp. 55–57, that seem predictive of what Justice Sutherland was to do later in *Nectow* v. *City of Cambridge,* 277 U.S. 183 (1928).

136. Bettman, *supra* n. 115. His brief is included in A. Bettman, *City and Regional Planning Papers,* p. 157–193. However, the material in the brief, "a few illustrative documents," that concern the environment and water are omitted in this reprint. *Id.,* p. 182.

137. *Id.,* p. 180; McMichael and Bingham, *City Growth Essentials,* 1st citation.

138. *Euclid* v. *Ambler,* p. 394.

139. *Id.,* p. 388.

140. Bettman, *supra* n. 115, p. 28, and A. Bettman, *City and Regional Planning Papers,* p. 172.

141. *Ambler* v. *Euclid,* p. 313. The judge states that this is "so well known as to be within the judicial cognizance."

142. Bettman, *supra* n. 115, p. 29; A. Bettman, *City and Regional Planning Papers,* p. 172.

143. Jane Jacobs might have agreed with this artist on how to "plan" a city, J. Jacobs, *The Economy of Cities* (1969), pp. 222–223, 243–244, 250–251.

144. Bettman, *supra* n. 115, pp. 29–30; A. Bettman, *City and Regional Planning Papers,* pp. 172–173. Bettman would have understood the stress in the 1980s on the maintenance of a good internal environment as well as a good external environment. See R. Banham, *The Architecture of the Well-Tempered Environment,* 2nd ed. (1984), pp. 296–304.

145. Bettman, *supra* n. 115, p. 29; A. Bettman, *City and Regional Planning Papers,* p. 172. He called the furnace, the kitchen range, and the shop for home repairs the "industrial features of the house."

146. A comparison of Bettman's language with that of Justice Sutherland, *Euclid* v. *Ambler,* p. 394, shows an unavoidable similarity. Perhaps Justice Sutherland's background made him prefer the pig-parlor-barnyard

analogy. *Id.,* p. 388, to "the furnace in the living room" or "the gas range in the sleeping room," Bettman, *supra* n. 145.

147. *Euclid* v. *Ambler,* p. 371.

148. Euclid "remained largely rural, noted chiefly for grapes, until after 1940, when there was a rapid industrial and urban growth. Manufacturers now include [except as affected by the general decline in industrial activity in Ohio's northeast quadrant since 1981] airplane parts, castings, brass and copper goods, electrical and welding equipment, and road machinery," 4 *Encyclopaedia Britannica,* 15th ed., vol. 4 (1986), p. 590.

149. Haar and Liebman, *Property and Law,* p. 1098; *Euclid* v. *Ambler,* p. 373.

150. *Euclid* v. *Ambler,* p. 372.

151. Hostetler and Chesnut, "Memorial," 24 *ABAJ* 732, 733.

152. C. Cramer, *Newton D. Baker* (1962), p. 53. The Mall was "a spacious development with buildings around trees and grass." For the condition of the parks after Baker's two terms as mayor, see Herrick, "Cleveland," *Encyclopedia Americana* 7 (1918), pp. 91, 96, and the references in W. Rose, *Cleveland: The Making of a City* (1950), accessed through the index under "parks."

153. A. Bettman, *City and Regional Planning Papers,* p. 53. Bettman is using in sarcastic fashion an image employed by Newton Baker about a "lumbering coach" in 1789 delivering the Washington family (that of Augustin, not George) to the inn at Warm Springs and how complex life had become in the modern age of technology even though the United States still was under a constitution becoming operational in that year, N. Baker, *Progress and the Constitution* (1925), pp. 33–34.

154. *Euclid* v. *Ambler,* p. 373, "municipalities have power"; p. 375, "every ordered society" and "police power inherent in ownership."

155. *Id.,* p. 376.

156. A. Bettman, *City and Regional Planning Papers,* pp. 191–192, though aesthetic considerations could be "auxiliary" to other independently and traditionally based exercises of the police power. Bettman retained the importance in his view of both the built and natural environmental bases of zoning in order to prevent "blight," but the aesthetic seems genuinely not regarded by him as a basis by itself for zoning. *Id.,* pp. 99–107, and particularly his "Draft of an Act to Zone Highway Protective Areas," sec. 2, *Id.,* pp. 244–246. How either he or Baker would have responded on whether or not to allow aesthetics alone to justify the exercise of the power of eminent domain is hard to say. Both, probably, would have thought it constitutional.

157. *Euclid* v. *Ambler,* pp. 373–374.

158. *Id.,* p. 376.

159. A. Bettman, *City and Regional Planning Papers,* pp. 50–51.

160. *Euclid* v. *Ambler, supra* n. 2, p. 373.

161. N. Baker, *Progress and the Constitution,* p. 56. No one in the litigation referred to Baker's book on the United States Constitution. Bettman, however, seems to have been familiar with it, *supra* n. 153. Also, in his rhetoric in his brief, Bettman says, "Zoning has . . . this purpose . . . by the promotion of favorable environmental conditions in which people live and work," A. Bettman, *City and Regional Planning Papers,* p. 173. Perhaps, however, this was language common to all at that time.

162. N. Baker, *Progress and the Constitution,* p. 59.

163. *Id.,* p. 8. Neither Wilson nor Baker in this regard invoked the influence of the then contemporary ideas of Albert Einstein that, already in their day, were impacting on popular views of law, social science, society, and other topics outside the discipline of physics, R. Clark, *Einstein: The Life and Times* (1971), pp. 237–254. That different imagery might have strengthened both Wilson's and Baker's views of a constitution unhinged from checks and balances. But there are strong intellectual reasons why post-Darwinian legal theorists could not accept Einstein's relativity within their canon of professional values, L. Kalman, *Legal Realism at Yale, 1927–1960* (1986), pp. 14–16.

164. O'Brien, "Foreword," in A. Bettman, *City and Regional Planning Papers,* p. xv. C. Cramer, *Newton D. Baker,* pp. 39–45.

165. Bettman concentrated on planning organizations, but he also worked on the Wickersham Commission and the Cleveland Crime Survey, O'Brian, "Foreward," *supra* n. 164, p. xviii. Baker was a member of the Wickersham Commission, C. Cramer, *Newton D. Baker,* p. 188. Baker worked in the National Consumers' League, despite Florence Kelley (its general secretary) having a "Marxian criticism of production for private profit and her desire for national regulatory legislation." *Id.,* p. 192, the United States League of Nations' Association. *Id.,* p. 240, and what Baker called "the other 3,561 organizations." *Id.,* p. 266.

166. Bettman lectured at Harvard University and the Massachusetts Institute of Technology, O'Brian, "Foreword," *supra* n. 164, p. xvii; Baker taught at Cleveland Law School (now the Cleveland State University Law School) and Cleveland College (now part of Case Western Reserve University), C. Cramer, *Newton D. Baker,* p. 197.

167. O'Brian, "Foreword," *supra* n. 164, p. xv. Bettman

was also the man most responsible outside Congress for the District of Columbia Redevelopment Act of 1945, 60 Stat. 790, D. C. Code 1951, secs. 5–701–719, O'Brian, "Foreword," p. xvii; Comey "Preface," in A. Bettman, *City and Regional Planning Papers,* p. ix. For Bettman's own views on the legislation, see *Id.,* pp. 111–133. This made *Berman* v. *Parker,* 348 U.S. 26 (1954), possible. Thus, how to be certain about Bettman's response to purely "aesthetic" bases for the exercise of eminent domain is difficult, *supra* n. 156.

168. C. Cramer, *Newton D. Baker,* p. 186. Baker's career as United States secretary of war during World War I, of course, gave Baker far more fame than Bettman ever had received in his lifetime.

169. A. Bettman, *City and Regional Planning Papers,* p. 53. C. Cramer, *Newton D. Baker,* p. 276. Public personalities in the mid-1930s were very much involved over whether Jefferson would or would not have supported the New Deal, *Id.,* see particularly, W. Harbaugh, *Lawyer's Lawyer: The Life of John W. Davis* (1973), pp. 255–256. Although Davis called Jefferson "my idol," *Id.,* p. 520 (with which Baker shared the opinion, C. Cramer, *Newton D. Baker,* p. 197), Davis's view of Jefferson's philosophy was scarcely profound, Davis, "Thomas Jefferson" in H. Green, *The Life of John W. Davis* (1924), pp. 285–290.

170. C. Cramer, *Newton D. Baker,* pp. 263–264.

171. *Euclid* v. *Ambler,* pp. 386–387. Since Stone "shook his convictions," McCormick, "A Law Clerk's Recollections," *Columbia L. R.* 46 (1946), pp. 710, 712, Stone's views are pertinent to Sutherland's opinion in *Euclid.*

172. N. Baker, *Progress and the Constitution,* pp. 153, 159.

173. C. Cramer, *Newton D. Baker,* p. 260.

174. A. Bettman, *City and Regional Planning Papers,* p. 51.

175. J. Metzenbaum, *Law of Zoning,* pp. 110–111.

176. *Id.,* p. 121.

177. *Id.,* p. 242, referring to *Nectow* v. *City of Cambridge.*

178. *Euclid* v. *Ambler.*

179. *Gorieb* v. *Fox.*

180. *Nectow* v. *City of Cambridge.*

181. Dukeminier and Krier, eds., *Property,* 2d ed. (1988), p. 1128.

182. Mumford, "Introduction," in I. McHarg, *Design with Nature,* p. viii, clearly establishes the connection between these two environmental planners of different generations.

183. E. Morgan, *Falling Apart: The Rise and Fall of Urban Civilization* (1977), p. 210, citing Jane Jacobs. Ian McHarg is not mentioned, but Lewis Mumford is, so one must conclude McHarg's work partakes of these qualities too. Elaine Morgan has her own—but equally vigorous—reasons for rejecting their work.

184. Phillips, "Impact of Impact Zoning," p. 35.

185. *The Unfinished Agendas: The Citizen's Policy Guide to Environmental Issues, A Task Force Report by the Rockefeller Brothers Fund,* ed. Barney (1977), p. 26.

186. "Euclid," *supra* n. 148. Within less than 40 years after World War II, the amount of land in agricultural use in Euclid was zero, "Euclid Community Profile," Ohio Department of Natural Resources, Land Use/Land Cover (1981).

187. Interview with Paul F. Oyaski, director, City of Euclid Department of Community Services and Development, September 25, 1986, by the author. See "Suburban Cuyahoga County Industrial Buildings Summaries," in 1986 Regional Planning Commission Analysis, 1984 Auditor's Data.

188. *Euclid Comprehensive Annual Financial Report,* for the year ending December 31, 1985 (1986), pp. 69–78.

189. "Report on Euclid Avenue Investment," City of Euclid, Department of Community Services and Development, December 23, 1985. Euclid Avenue in the 1920s has been described as the "fashionable vector" for Cleveland, J. Barnett, *The Elusive City* (1986), p. 108. It is still a "vector."

190. Interview with Mr. Oyaski, *supra* n. 187.

191. The quoted language is from the enabling statute for joint economic development zones, Ohio Revised Code, 715.69, which best summarizes the legislative purpose of all this development assistance by municipalities in Ohio. "Enterprise Zone Designation," City of Euclid Department of Community Services and Development, August 12, 1986, describes the urban jobs and enterprise zone under Ohio Revised Code, 5709.61–5709.66 (which is far more detailed enabling legislation than that for joint enterprise zones), which the city of Euclid has created today for an area that included the site of the litigation in the *Euclid* case.

192. Ohio Revised Code, 5709.61 and 5709.62. See City of Euclid, "Enterprise Zone" brochure (n.d., October 1986 actual issue). The Cuyahoga County Commissioners approved the zone and it was advertised October 22–29, 1986, at the Cleveland International Trade Fair. A joint zone with the city of Cleveland had been sought but had proved unachievable within available time limitations. Interview with Mr. Oyaski, October 22, 1986.

193. Interview with Mr. Oyaski, *supra* n. 187. The main form of transportation used today by industry in Euclid is motor freight using the freeways. The railways generally are used for the heaviest, roughest, and least urgent freight. The two railways today are the Norfolk & Southern Railway System and the Conrail System. See also "Enterprise Zone Designation," *supra* n. 191. The city

of Euclid currently is classed as being among the Cleveland suburbs having "higher numbers of low reusability buildings," 1986 Regional Planning Commission Analysis, Industrial Building Inventory, p. 27 and Table VII, p. 29.

194. The "conscience of zoning" concept is from Hepler, "For Planning Practitioners," *Res Gestae* 30 (1986), p. 127.

195. Interview with Mr. Oyaski, *supra* n. 187. Mr. Oyaski says, "The zoning is still pretty much intact," letter to the author, September 25, 1986. See *Euclid, supra* n. 113, A7, for the city's own positive view of the *Euclid* decision. The village of Euclid having expanded its water, sewer, and drainage services in the 1920s, later dubbed itself "Euclid, the City of Services." *Id.* This seems to establish the truthfulness of the village of Euclid's claim that it had inadequate water supplies in the years 1922–1925, at the least. One needs to recall that the administration of Mayor Charles Zimmerman, 1921–25, under which so many improvements were initiated, was a reform mayoralty. *Id.,* p. A8.

196. *Aeneid,* book VI, line 663. Charles Saint-Beuve asserts that this says, "Civilization, *life,* as we know it, is something learned and invented. This we must never forget," (his italics), J. Russell, *Paris* 2nd ed. (1983), p. 38. The best I can get Virgil to say is, "Consider that which can be drawn out of life through the arts." The line, which is from a statement of Anchises in the Underworld, has long presented textual problems because *vitam excoluere* probably means more a drawing forward of (more than a drawing from) life by the arts, see *Aeneid* (Page, tr. and ed., 1894) and *Aeneid, Book VI* (Fletcher, tr. and ed., 1968), book VI, line 663, notes.

197. Haar and Liebman, *Property and Law,* p. 1089. After 1926, zoning ordinances became almost universal (with the notable, but now only partial, exception of Houston) in the United States. In the 1980s the pressure is present for regional metropolitan planning and zoning arrangements, some imposed as a state constitutional requirement, *Southern Burlington County NAACP v. Township of Mt.*

Laurel, 92 N.J. 158, 456 A. 2d 390 (1983), with a call for "the need for state governments to 'take back' the zoning power," particularly in order to deal with perceived statewide and regional environmental problems that local planning and zoning arrangements cannot—or will not—adequately solve, *Basic Property Law,* 3rd. ed., eds. Browder, Cunningham, Julin, and Smith (1979), pp. 1120–1124. All of these issues, of course, were pregnant in *Euclid,* H. James, *supra* n. 76, 251–262, particularly the remarks of George B. Ford about the Cleveland region. *Id.,* pp. 251–252, and the material on "regional planning and open spaces." *Id.,* pp. 257–258; and A. Bettman, *City and Regional Planning Papers,* p. 56. See also Michelman, "Localism and Political Freedom," in *The Land Use Policy Debate in the United States,* ed. de Neufville (1981), pp. 239–243.

198. Foglesong, *Planning the Capitalist City,* p. 233. This is a structural Marxist analysis of American city planning whose purpose is to assist "The left . . . to liberate society from the dead weight of deference to market principles." *Id.,* p. 256; but in the interval, the role of private wealth must be recognized as such a productive force. *Id.,* p. 257. A Marxist critique of zoning conditions that were contemporaneous with *Euclid* is made in Boyer, "National Land Use Policy: Instrument and Product of the Economic Cycle," in *The Land Use Policy Debate,* pp. 109, 117–120.

199. Park, "The Urban Community as a Spatial Pattern and a Moral Order," in *The Urban Community,* ed. Burgess (1926), pp. 3, 6. He implied, in addition, that slums are the environment from which the poor urban immigrants extract the means for their personal successes, so that slums possess that advantage as well.

200. *Larkin* v. *Grendel's Den,* 459 U. S. 116, 121 (1982).

201. *City of Renton* v. *Playtime Theatres, Inc.,* 475 U. S. 41 (1986).

202. Laitos, *"Land Use Planning,"* in *Natural Resources Law,* ed. Laitos (1985), pp. 900, 903–907, makes these points in relation to *Euclid* as part of his view concerning the "several consequences [that] flow from the backward nature of planning." *Id., Teachers Manual* 273 (1985).

7

Legislating Aesthetics: The Role of Zoning in Designing Cities

Michael Kwartler

THE CITY AS COMMONS

Freedom is the recognition of necessity. [HEGEL]

The biologist Garrett Hardin presents a convincing argument in treating the environment as a commons. In his paper "The Tragedy of the Commons" he describes the overexploitation of the commons, or in our case the city, by its citizens.

> Finally, however, comes the day of reckoning, that is, the day when the long-desired goal of social stability becomes a reality. At this point, the inherent logic of the commons remorselessly generates tragedy.
>
> As a rational being, each herdsman seeks to maximize his gain. Explicitly or implicitly, more or less consciously, he asks, "What is the utility *to me* of adding one more animal to my herd?" This utility has one negative and one positive component.
>
> 1. The positive component is a function of the increment of one animal. Since the herdsman receives all the proceeds from the sale of the additional animal, the positive utility is nearly +1.
>
> 2. The negative component is a function of the additional overgrazing created by one more animal. Since, however, the effects of overgrazing are shared by all herdsmen, the negative utility for any particular decision-making herdsman is only a fraction of −1.
>
> Adding together the component partial utilities, the rational herdsman concludes that the only sensible course for him to pursue is to add another animal to his herd. And another . . . . But this is the conclusion reached by each and every rational herdsman sharing a commons. Therein lies the tragedy. Each man is locked into a system that compels him to increase his herd without limit—in a world that is limited. Ruin is the destination toward which all men rush, each pursuing his own best interest in a society that believes in the freedom of the commons. Freedom in a commons brings ruin to all.[1]

The utilitarian calculus used by the herdsman requires him to downgrade the negative effects created by his activities because they are shared by all. The underlying assumption of this calculus is that the herdsman has unlimited rights to the commons. There is no mention of countervailing obligations that would avert the imminent tragedy of the commons. The U.S. Constitution is notably reticent regarding the obligations inherent in the ownership of private property. With the exception of the police powers broadly defined in the Preamble, all other references to property refer to the rights of the owner. Government interference or regulation of the use of property, except in those special circumstances when the public health, safety, and welfare are adversely affected, was for all intents and purposes implicitly forbidden. The Common Law of Nuisance, the elusive power of social pressure, and the enlightened self-interest of the marketplace were deemed sufficient to guide the development of American cities. The late eighteenth century machinery of liberal economics in turn reduced the traditional ethical, political, and social values inherent in land ownership to that of an economic commodity as it did of all things, including human labor. The free use and manipulation of urban land was the signpost of an urbanizing America in the nineteenth and early twentieth centuries.

The concept of obligations to the community or commons in the case of our cities was relegated to the laissez-faire world of Adam Smith's "invisible hand" wherein the individual who "intends only his gain" is "led by an invisible hand to promote . . . the public interest."[2] In Smith's simpler world where a large productive unit might have had 15 persons, many of whom were family members, this might have been true. When Smith wrote, his world of small workshops was beginning to be displaced by the larger scale and anonymity of the factory system and the institution of the limited liability corporation. By the middle of the nineteenth century American cities were expanding rapidly, urbanizing rural land while simultaneously increasing the intensity of use of previously urbanized land.

By World War I, our older cities had an-nexed virtually all the land that defines their current boundaries. This accelerated growth took place without significant governmental intervention, the exception being the tenement laws enacted in the largest cities, occasional limited height districts, and building and fire codes. The design of the form of our cities was carried out primarily by lawyers and surveyors and municipal engineers who, in the process of laying out the gridded street systems, subdividing the blocks into lots and determining the size and location of infrastructure, probably had very little understanding or appreciation of the design implications of their decisions. Issues of land use, functional relationships, traffic and transportation, density, and building form and design were determined by the rationale of the free market.

In many ways the free market in development was reasonably rational. The economic activities of the city, commerce and manufacturing, for reasons of economic and functional efficiency, tended to locate in proximity to each other. The better sort of residential development tended, by economic power and social pressure, to be in exclusively domestic environments. Nonetheless, the nineteenth century city presented an image evoked in the literature of the period of chaos, congestion, and disease. Urban residential and commercial densities in New York City in the nineteenth century, for example, were among the highest in the history of urbanization. The skyscraper, the combined manifestation of a free market in land and a new building and transportation technology, got taller and taller in an effort to get its day in the sun. The skyscraper was developed in response to the functional demands of proximity, the maximization of profits, and the amortization of high land costs. The darkened and congested streets of our burgeoning central cities were the result of unregulated urban development.

Notwithstanding the free market, the City Beautiful movement, a derivative of French Beaux Arts planning, inspired large-scale urban design plans during its period. The most notable example was the Chicago Plan of 1909 by Daniel Burnham. The plan presented an image of a rebuilt Chicago along the lines of Baron Haussmann's Paris. While the municipality could, through eminent domain, condemn land for the envisioned boulevards and parks, it lacked the ability to impose its design controls on private property without the wholesale condemnation and purchase of private land and buildings. This traditional European autocratic approach was clearly anathema to the American zeitgeist of the times and probably beyond the budgetary capabilities of Chicago. Clearly the common law of nuisance was ineffective to deal with the new metropolitan reality because in most instances it was not anticipatory. Indeed, so was the ability of the free market to socialize development. The "invisible hand" had lost its punch. A broad application of the police power was invoked to deal with the emerging urban reality.

The Commons Zoned: The 1916 New York City Zoning Ordinance

The development and adoption of zoning was the single most potent legislative response to the lack of adequate controls on urban development in lieu of the drastic actions outlined above. On February 27, 1913, the Board of Estimate and Apportionment of the City of New York adopted a motion proposed by the president of the Borough of Manhattan to create the Heights of Buildings Commission, which developed the United States' first comprehensive zoning resolution. The motion read as follows:

> Whereas there is growing sentiment in the community to the effect that the time has come

when effort should be made to regulate the height, size, and arrangement of buildings erected within the limits of the City of New York, in order to arrest the seriously increasing evil of shutting off light and air from other buildings and from public streets, to prevent unwholesome and dangerous congestion both in living conditions and in the street . . . .[3]

Testimony submitted to the commission by architects, landscape architects, businessmen, insurance companies, real estate companies, and good government groups were unanimous in their support of regulations that would direct the spatial organization of urban activities and the density and form of the buildings. Ernest Flagg, architect of the Naval Academy at Annapolis and the Singer Building and model tenements in New York City, spoke in favor of zoning as the representative of the New York Chapter of the American Institute of Architects.

> It seems to be generally conceded that something must be done to limit the height of buildings. We are learning by experience that streets designed for a city of four or five stories high cannot be made to serve properly for one, two, or three times that height.

He then proceeded to outline the advantages and disadvantages of high buildings, concluding

> . . . that a plan which will prevent overcrowding while still permitting the erecting of high buildings is the best one to adopt. If such a plan can be found, why is not the problem solved, for what more can be desired than to avoid the evils while retaining the benefits of high buildings.[4]

Similarly, businessman Simon Bretano speaking for the Fifth Avenue Association stated in testimony before the Building Heights Commission:

> ...that it is no longer a universal opinion that a building of unrestricted height is necessarily the final form of construction in the City of New York for the purpose of conveniencing the needs of modern life or business, or that its relations to the economy of the city is such as it was a short time ago believed to be by almost everyone.[5]

In 1916, the City of New York adopted the first comprehensive zoning ordinance in the United States. The ordinance regulated the density and location of urban activities as well as the form of the buildings. The device of choice was districting, a European planning concept that caught the imagination of the country's progressive-minded urban activists and professionals. Although employed in numerous American cities, districting never had been comprehensively applied to the entire area of a municipality before the 1916 ordinance. Districting, the rational distribution of land uses and density, organized the activities of the city into discrete areas reflecting the application of the factory mode of production wherein the production process was atomized into its component parts, rationalized, and reassembled into a more efficient process. Cities were similarly dissected into component parts and reorganized, to the degree possible, into a coherent and efficient whole.

Districting was anticipatory. Through both analysis and experience, future land use conflicts were identified and then resolved through the spatial segregation of apparently incompatible land uses. This was accomplished by the mapping of the Use Districts. The 1916 Ordinance lists nine Use Districts: a residence district, four retail districts, two business districts, one manufacturing district and an unrestricted district allowing all uses. Each Use District was an exclusivity with the residence districts limited solely to residential use. In addition, there were Height and Area Districts that regulated the form and density of new development within the Use Districts. Every piece of real property in the city was governed by this mapping triumvirate. Supplementing the maps was a text that outlined the police power purpose of the regulations, defined terms, and detailed the district regulations and administrative procedures. The regulations were administered as-of-right by the Department of Buildings, which reviewed all new buildings for compliance. The application of the New York law was widespread as it defined the structure and substance of subsequent zoning ordinances. Justice Sutherland, writing 10 years later for the majority in *Village of Euclid* v. *Ambler Realty Co.,* acknowledged the origins of the village of Euclid's zoning ordinance by citing the substantive work done by the Building Heights Commission preceding the adoption of the 1916 New York Zoning Ordinance.

> Zoning has received much attention at the hands of commissions and experts, and the results of their investigations have been set forth in comprehensive reports.[6]

The majority opinion in *Euclid* recognized the impasse of the "tragedy of the commons" regarding unrestricted urban development. The unrestricted use of the commons would need to be restrained if the commons itself was not to be exploited to ruination and depletion. Writing for the majority Justice Sutherland stated that:

> Building zone laws are of modern origin. They began in this country about 25 years ago. Until recent years, urban life was comparatively simple; but with great increase and concentration

of population problems, have developed, and constantly are developing, which require, and will continue to require, additional restrictions in respect of the use and occupation of private lands in urban communities. Regulations, the wisdom, necessity and validity of which as applied to existing conditions, are so apparent that they are now uniformly sustained, a century ago would have been rejected as arbitrary and repressive. Such regulations are sustained, under the complex conditions of our day, for reasons analogous to those which justify traffic regulations.[7]

In Sutherland's eyes, unrestrained urban development was destructive to the interests of all landowners. The overexploitation of the urban commons by individuals was producing problems that were to be absorbed by the community as a whole recreating, in more complex terms, Hardin's herdsman's dilemma. Zoning, particularly the concept of physically bounded districts, was deemed a viable solution to the potential "city as commons" tragedy. The simple fact of the recognition of the impending ruination of the urban commons was significant in the choice of zoning as the legislative technique of choice. The ability to, or at least the sense that one can anticipate land use problems and conflicts, is at the conceptual core of traditional zoning.

But what was lost in the trade for predictability and certainty? Obviously, the developer and architect now had a partner in the development and design process. Unlike the prezoning days of American urban development when the developer and architect virtually were free to determine the uses to be contained within the proposed building, the intensity of the use of land, and the form and details of the building, the development now was to be shaped by a public-private partnership. By instituting zoning, the municipality

had acknowledged its interest in the development of privately held urban land. The types of uses to be housed and the density and the form of the building, but not its architectural details and style, were determined by the zoning ordinance as a function of a site's location and its size. The loss of a degree of freedom of choice was compensated for by the relative predictability of what could and might be built on adjoining sites thereby protecting the public and the investments of individual property owners. Furthermore, the attributes which made the city or commons desirable could not, with certainty, be appropriated by any individual developer. At its best, zoning fits the axiom that "the whole is more than the sum of the parts."

Despite its rigidities, Euclidean zoning has many virtues. Its structure and substantive regulations allow for development predictability, certainty, and administrative accountability and objectivity. Euclidean zoning is accountable because its rules are explicit and inflexible. The clarity and consistency of the rules allow for the objective review of each individual project as-of-right. The reviewer has virtually no discretion in administering a Euclidean ordinance. The development either complies or does not comply. Paradoxically, as we shall see, it is exactly this virtue that its critics point to as its conceptual flaw.

In a sense, zoning attempts to legislate the utilitarian dictum: "The greatest good for the greatest number." Notwithstanding the clarity of purpose of the dictum, the dictum is, as others have pointed out, mathematically impossible. One cannot maximize two variables in the same equation. (Note: maximization is not to be confused with optimization, which can be achieved through linear regression analysis, for example.) In one case, maximization of individual freedom of choice, as we have seen in Hardin's example, ultimately is contradictory to the promotion of the greatest good and similarly the promotion of the "good for the greatest number" may be at the expense of the individuals whose "good" is not served or at least compromised. Since the formula is a mathematical and practical impossibility, it behooves us to explore the location of the boundary line, fuzzy as it may be, between the public interest and private interest in the design of an urban building. This may be restated as the degree of intrusiveness of the public regulation of private property given First, Fifth, and Fourteenth Amendment protections.

This is even more true, given that zoning in New York City and elsewhere was not ostensibly aesthetically based. Architect Thomas Hastings of Carrère and Hastings, architects for New York's Grand Central Terminal, specifically dealt with the issue of an aesthetically driven zoning ordinance:

> Where I believe we American architects so often make a mistake is that we present our case as an appeal for aesthetic consideration and for the general appearance of the city. In my opinion, it is not a question of art, but of sanitation and of justice and of law . . .
>
> . . . I do not believe that the aesthetic argument will do any good. A city will look well if the conditions imposed upon architects are reasonable. I do not believe in the idea that for the sake of beauty we should look for any uniformity of belt courses or cornices on buildings.[8]

Hastings attempted to define the boundary between city design and building design. In zoning terms, this might be defined by the limits of the public interest in a private matter: the design of a building. For Hastings, the design of a building included determining its use, its form, and its articulation and individuation from adjacent structures within a broader institutional construct. With the exception of the form that would, in part, be determined by zoning, all other aspects of a building's design remained with the architect. This scheme apparently was not only acceptable but encouraged by Hastings. Flagg viewed zoning as the reasonable distribution of rights and obligations when building in central cities. Design freedom was apparently a nonissue to these master architects. In subsequent sections, we will examine traditional and nontraditional zoning techniques relative to the Hastings schema.

ZONING AND CITY DESIGN

There are intentional and unintentional towns. St. Petersburg is an intentional town. [DOSTO- EVSKI]

The European monumental tradition of city design makes no distinction between the architecture of buildings and city design. City design is architecture and vice versa. Although conceived to some degree with the rationalization of urban functions (e.g., Leonardo's multilevel street systems for ideal cities), the primary purpose of the European monumental tradition was to impose a sense of visual order on the city through the application of formal design conventions, many of which derived from Renaissance painting. The distinction between city and building design, so fundamental to our evaluation of the proper role of zoning in American city design, is of no relevance in a tradition that treats streets and cities as idealized architectural set pieces. The intentional city, in this context, often was approached as a huge idealized architectural project whose ultimate form was predetermined by a carefully elaborated set of plans, drawings, and specifications. The physical master plan is the contemporary manifestation of this tradition. In the American context, Jonathan Barnett has defined urban design as the art of designing cities without designing all the buildings.[9] First, Barnett suggests that the art of designing cities must include its most visible component—the city's constituent buildings—and second, that there are and should be methods to design cities without designing each building. His definition is consistent with American concepts of property and cultural pluralism and pragmatic in its understanding that no central authority is capable of designing all the city's buildings nor is that capability desirable. This view holds that city design is contingent or dependent on or conditioned by something else rather than idealized. For our purposes, the intentional city is the idealized city in which the building forms are predetermined while the unintentional city is the contingent city. While both represent concepts of city design, they are based on different premises.

Kevin Lynch describes the contingent nature of a city as a place:

> . . . which is perceived (and perhaps enjoyed) by millions of people of widely diverse class and character, but it is the product of many builders who are constantly modifying the structure for reasons of their own. While it may be stable in general outlines for some time, it is ever changing in detail. Only partial control can be exercised over its growth and form. There is no final result, only a continuous succession of phases. No wonder, then, that the art of shaping cities for sensuous enjoyment is an art quite separate from architecture or music or literature. It may learn a great deal from these other arts, but it cannot imitate them.[10]

This assertion that the art of designing cities is separate from architecture is a distinctly American observation based on American tra-

ditions and attitudes. If Barnett and Lynch are correct, then where does one draw the line between civic design and architecture in the context of zoning as a technique to guide the development of the form of the city?

Urban Building Blocks: Replicability and Redundancy

The physical building blocks of a city are the specific geography of the site, the street and open space system, the blocks and the lot divisions, and the building types which give three-dimensional form and meaning to these structures. Traditional zoning defines the form, density, and use of the thousands of anonymous buildings that make up a city and its districts. In that sense, zoning builds on the idea that cities are conventionalized environments that communicate to the city dweller through the repetition of design conventions on an urban scale. An urban convention may be the clear distinction between public and private space, as defined by building walls, the hierarchical street system of the Arab city, the stoop of the New York row house, or the freestanding, axially sited public building of the Baroque era.

Cities are models of perceptual redundancy, a time-honored method of importing information to the uninitiated. The redundancy includes the grid of blocks and streets and the redundancy of the form of the street space defining buildings. The building form that is repeated is the replicable model or type. It traditionally has resulted from social, economic, and aesthetic concerns and has evolved over time. The replicable model is the building block of the city. The Amsterdam canal house, the Georgian row house, the New York brownstone, the loft building, and the highrise office building are examples of building types.

One should note that not all urban buildings possess the necessary virtues that allow them to become successful replicable urban models. Some buildings are one of a kind and are not replicable. The Seagram Building in New York City, the model for the 1961 Zoning Resolution, is one such building. Its apparent replicability is denied by the specificity of its site design. The masonry palazzo-style Racquet Club fronting the Seagram Building across Park Avenue and the prismatic bronze and glass Seagram Building with its flat granite plaza is an architectural set piece. The two buildings are mutual foils. Attempts to replicate the Seagram Building without the Racquet Club and the expanse of Park Avenue have proven disastrous.

Amsterdam also illustrates this point: Its replicable model, the canal house, is virtually the sole building type in the city with the exception of public institutions, warehouses, and churches. The form of the canal house is repeated ad infinitum, lining the concentric rings of the city's canals. Most people would agree that Amsterdam is a wonderful and liveable city although its individual buildings are not architectural set pieces. That is not to say that all the canal houses are either identical or undifferentiated. The differentiation or individuation results from the distinctive architectural treatment of each house. The roof line, window and door size and treatment, ornamentation, and the interior planning all are a function of the architect's ingenuity in working with the type: the canal house.

Similarly, New York's residential Park Avenue is a good contemporary illustration of the role of zoning. In this instance, the 1916 ordinance created the standardized building envelope in which the type, the apartment house, evolved and developed.

Some time ago, a student of mine[11] undertook an exercise formulated to isolate the urban design and architectural conventions of this highly imageable street. The student's method was simple. Montaging photographs of an entire section of Park Avenue, he selectively began to strip the buildings of their architectural features. First the varying building materials were neutralized, then architectural band coursing was removed, then detail articulations such as window moldings were removed, leaving only punched windows and entries. Finally the windows and entries were removed. What was left were boxes, all of approximately the same height on parcels representing multiples of the original parcelization of New York. The gross form of both the individual building and the street as a whole was the handiwork of the Height and Area Districts. These buildings are representative of both the pre-war apartment building type and the urban convention of street-defining building walls. Without designing each building, the street itself was designed.

Park Avenue exhibits the power of zoning as an instrument of city design. The role of the architect was twofold: the evolutionary development of the type (in this case the apartment house) in response to the market, social conventions, and building technology, and the individuation of the building through the manipulation of architectural conventions and details. Simultaneously, Park Avenue is both a unified place and a collection of distinctive buildings designed in a variety of styles. The Park Avenue apartment building was not legislated by zoning, rather the 1916 Zoning Ordinance provided the context—in this case a residential use district and a loose-fitting envelope in which the type was relatively free to develop in response to architectural and marketing requirements. Park Avenue illustrates the idea of civic design legislation that is contingent in the meaning of the word mentioned earlier. The ordinance did not legislate the building type but rather designed the public space of the street—the unintentional by-product of the Height and Area Districts.

EUCLIDEAN ZONING: STRUCTURE AND SUBSTANCE

I meant what I said
And I said what I meant
an elephant's faithful 100 percent.

[DR. SEUSS, *HORTON HEARS A WHO*]

Euclidean zoning is a term of art, which includes all traditional zoning ordinances that are based on the New York districting plan of 1916. The Euclid, Ohio, zoning ordinance was its progeny—in structure. The content or the substantive regulations concerning the types of districts, and their attendant regulations for Euclid, Ohio, were, as logic would dictate, attuned to the village of Euclid and were not a literal translation of New York's substantive regulations. In zoning terms, the structure rather than the substance was replicated.

Virtually all Euclidean ordinances adopted New York's system of mapped Use, Height, and Area Districts and supporting text which described the uses allowed in each district, the height and building bulk or form controls, and the area regulations regarding yards and courts. The number of Use Districts, and the number, type, and degree of Height and Area Districts and controls, of course, varied from municipality to municipality.

The structure of Euclidean zoning is prescriptive and as-of-right. Prescriptive zoning has its equivalent in Mosaic Law in the sense that it is based on absolute prohibitions unequivocally written as "Thou shalt not . . . ." Certain uses are prohibited from specified districts, building street walls cannot exceed a certain maximum height, towers may not exceed a fixed percentage of the lot area, and so forth. The prohibitions are applied uniformly in all similar situations without exception. The prescriptive structure of Euclidean zoning requires, by definition, that all potential con-

flicts regarding use, building form, and density be resolved internally in the ordinance itself. A districting system, for example, resolves potential land use conflicts by excluding one or the other conflicting land use. In terms of building form, the usual trade-offs and accommodations that are typical of an architectural design process are similarly resolved in the ordinance rather than on the architect's drawing table, thereby limiting and in many cases strictly delimiting the architect's choices. The degree to which the design conflicts or choices are internally resolved as well as the reasonableness of the regulations are issues of substance to which we will return later. In essence, Euclidean zoning anticipates conflicts or choices, identifies them in the abstract, reduces them to a limited number of generic cases, and then proceeds to resolve them in the body of the ordinance. The combination of the prescriptive text and maps ensures predictability and certainty.

Use Districting

The system of Use Districts is the structural core of Euclidean zoning. Use Districts are exclusive rather than inclusive. They are organized from the most exclusive to the most inclusive. In Euclidean zoning, the area of single-family detached houses is designed to be the most restrictive and hence most exclusive zone. This undoubtedly reflects the importance placed on the domestic environment by nineteenth century reformers. Frederick Law Olmsted, arguing for planned domestic suburbs, emphasized that:

> It would appear, then, that the demands of suburban life, with reference to civilized refinement, are not to be a retrogression from, but an advance upon, those which are characteristic of town life, and that no great town can long exist without great suburbs. It would also appear that whatever element of convenient

residence is demanded in a town will soon be demanded in a suburb, so far as is possible for it to be associated with the conditions which are the peculiar advantage of the country, such as purity of air, umbrageousness, facilities for quiet out-of-door recreation and distance from the jar, noise, confusion, and bustle of commercial thoroughfares.[12]

In similar language, Justice Sutherland rationalized the virtues of Euclid's Use Districting, prohibiting apartment houses in Residence Districts:

> With particular reference to apartment houses, it is pointed out that the development of detached house sections is greatly retarded by the coming of apartment houses, which has sometimes resulted in destroying the entire section for private house purposes; that in such sections very often the apartment house is a mere parasite, constructed in order to take advantage of the open spaces and attractive surroundings created by the residential character of the district. Moreover, the coming of one apartment house is followed by others, interfering by their height and bulk with the free circulation of air and monopolizing the rays of the sun which otherwise would fall upon the smaller homes, and bringing, as their necessary accompaniments, the disturbing noises incident to increased traffic and business, and the occupation, by means of moving and parked automobiles, of larger portions of the streets, thus detracting from their safety and depriving children of the privilege of quiet and open spaces for play, enjoyed by those in more favored localities—until, finally, the residential character of the neighborhood and its desirability as a place of detached residences are utterly destroyed.[13]

The advent of the bourgeois nuclear family, for whom the home was seen as a refuge against the vagaries and brutality of the capitalist city,[14] clearly influenced the exclusivity of the residential district. In an urban environment where very little was predictable except change, the urban residential district offered by comparison a controlled and predictable environment. Furthermore, the traditional European concept of urban space as a public living room of sorts ran counter to the prevailing post-Civil War thought. Urban public space became a threatening spectacle of lower-class behavior. The positive values generally associated with the street and square and public life took on negative associations. Uses formerly associated with public space became internalized in the house. This was a grand departure from the historical city where, with the exception of nuisances per se which by definition were prohibited from locating in a populated quarter, land uses were stratified vertically rather than horizontally.

The districting concept, when effective, reorders the idea of the traditional European city by surgically separating urban activities that once had coexisted in the same space. In older cities such as New York, the traditional European pattern of mixed uses was already out of favor by the end of the nineteenth century. The pattern of segregated land uses already was advanced with the market playing a significant role in rationalizing the use of urban land. Manhattan's Upper West Side in 1913 already was a restricted residential neighborhood of brownstones and avenue-fronting apartment houses.[15] Retail shopping was restricted to the interior north–south avenues (Broadway, Amsterdam, and Columbus avenues) while the perimeter streets, Riverside Drive and Central Park West and West End Avenue were exclusively residential.

The 1913 commissioner's report acknowledged this market-driven ad hoc districting:

Every city becomes divided into more or less clearly defined districts of different occupation, use, and type of building construction. We have the central office and financial district, loft districts, apartment house and hotel districts, tenement house districts, private dwelling districts. The character of building appropriate for each district is of course dependent on the character of occupation and use in that particular district. A comparatively high degree of concentration is believed to be important for the facilitation of business in the office and financial district. Certain trades and industries require structures of unusual size or shape. The demand for housing varies with the differing taste and necessities of the inhabitants of the city. There is a demand for hotels and apartment houses as well as for single-family dwellings. Moreover, advantage of location and the resulting enormous difference in land values tend strongly toward differentiation in the character and intensity of use and this and other social and economic factors tend toward a natural segregation of buildings according to type and use. The city *is* divided into building districts. We believe that these natural districts must be recognized in any complete and generally effective system of building restriction.[16]

In the case of the Upper West Side, Use Districting legitimized practice.

By the time of the First World War, mass transit and suburban railroads, escalating automobile ownership, the scale of American businesses, advances in communications, and a host of other innovations made districting possible. Cities were less spatially bounded than they ever were because of the apparent conquest of time by technology. Furthermore, organizational specialization, be it industrial or commercial, legitimized the development of discrete districts in which the backward and

forward production and organizational linkages of the district's activities were rationalized.

Zoning use districting probably has been given too much credit in determining the initial form of our suburbs and cities. The process already was well underway after the Civil War in both the suburbs and the central cities. Sutherland's judicial support of the sanctity of the single-family house—the residence district from the "coming of the apartment house"—reasonably can be interpreted as the legitimization of his own values and his attitudes toward the working classes, the people who lived in rented apartments. At best, districting legitimized the then-prevailing attitudes of the affluent classes that were manifested by the market and planning ideology. Judge Westenhaver best summed up these attitudes in his lower court decision:

> [The object of the ordinance was] to place all the property in an undeveloped area of 16 square miles in a straitjacket. The purpose to be accomplished is really to regulate the mode of living of persons who may hereafter inhabit it. In the last analysis, the result to be accomplished is to classify the population and segregate them according to their income or situation in life. The true reason why some persons live in a mansion and others in a shack, why some live in a single-family dwelling and others in a double-family dwelling, why some live in a two-family dwelling and others in an apartment, or why some live in a well-kept apartment and others in a tenement, is primarily economic. It is a matter of income and wealth, plus the labor and difficulty of procuring adequate domestic service. Aside from contributing to these results and furthering such class tendencies, the ordinance also has an aesthetic purpose; that is to say, to make this village develop into a city along lines now

conceived by the village council to be attractive and beautiful.[17]

Use Districting is fundamental in determining the character of urban areas. It is the activity that determines the character of an urban area rather than the buildings. Buildings often outlive their initial purpose and are adapted to new activities which redefine the character of the district. Soho in New York City or Lowertown in St. Paul, where turn-of-the-century manufacturing buildings have been converted into apartments and fashionable shops, are recent examples of this phenomenon. When referring to sections of the city, urban dwellers invariably will refer to the activity when describing an area rather than the buildings, e.g., the Flower District, Garment District, Theater District. The Use Districts essentially canonized the prevailing activities and undoubtedly served to protect them against the infiltration of new displacing activities. This is not necessarily undesired as experience has shown that the competition for urban space, if solely determined by sheer economic muscle, creates problems and conflicts, the burden of which the public ultimately must bear.

The content or substance of the Euclidean ordinance similarly varied from locale to locale and was based on existing conditions. This fact was recognized by Sutherland who wrote in regard to the appropriateness of each zoning ordinance of its locale:

> The ordinance now under review, and all similar laws and regulations, must find their justification in some aspect of the police power, asserted for the public welfare. The line which in this field separates the legitimate from the illegitimate assumption of power is not capable of precise delimitation. It varies with circumstances and conditions. A regulatory zoning ordinance, which would be clearly valid as ap-

plied to the great cities, might be clearly invalid as applied to rural communities.[18]

For that reason, the substance of a Euclidean ordinance is not easily replicable, it is city specific. The New York ordinance is a case in point from which one may generalize as it became the model for zoning ordinances of its generation.

The 1916 Height and Area Districts

The content of the New York City 1916 Zoning Ordinance was absolute and abstract. In addition to the spatial distribution of land uses, density was controlled by the Height and Area Districts. Each lot in the city had a maximum density that could be realized if the zoning envelope entirely was filled out. The envelope was defined by a maximum street wall height, based on a multiple of the width of the fronting street and a sky exposure or angle of light plane defined by a line drawn from the center of the street and intersecting the maximum allowable street wall height. This inclined plane intersected the Area District requirements for yards completing the envelope. Towers of 25 percent lot coverage or less were allowed to penetrate the sky exposure plane. The system of maximum street wall heights was proportional rather than numerical, honoring a traditional method of regulating building heights. It also was consistent with traditional architectural proportional building design systems. The zoning envelope defined the limits of the public's interest in the design of a building on private property. The building might take any configuration within the boundaries of the envelope which safeguarded the light and air to the street and adjoining properties. The 1916 Zoning Ordinance was contingent; it did not legislate a building type but rather defined the acceptable use or activity and a spatial envelope leaving the market place and the architects' ingenuity to develop the building type.

In terms of the commons analogy, zoning's sky exposure planes limited the exploitation of the urban commons by the new building. The Height of Buildings Commission's assumption was one of equity:

> The restrictions recommended are designed to secure as much light and air, relief from congestion and safety from fire as is practicable under existing conditions as to improvements and land values. In place of proving a menace to existing values, they will tend to prevent future serious injury to such values.[19]

The Height and Area District regulations were inflexible regardless of the size of the lot, its orientation, and in most cases, the surrounding built context and topography. The Ordinance was absolute in the sense that the dimensions such as those for yards and proportions for street walls and sky exposure planes were invariable. It was also abstract in that it took little account of localized conditions with the exception of site size. Design flexibility increased as the site size increased. It was consistent with Euclidean zoning's concern for resolving boundary conflicts—those conflicts that occur at the property lines between public and private realms. The larger sites allowed for greater design choice.

This fact reflects the other contingent aspect of the 1916 ordinance (the other being its nontypological zoning envelope) and is realized by the greater variety of building forms on large sites in New York. The Empire State Building, Rockefeller Center, and the blockfront twin tower apartment buildings fronting Central Park are but a sample of the numerous distinguished buildings and the variety of building types that were developed during the almost 50 years that the 1916 Zoning Ordinance was

in force, giving testimony to the "reasonableness" of the ordinance.

Notwithstanding the broad powers to form development (Height and Area Districts), Euclidean zoning did not attempt to change fundamentally the lot-by-lot development of America's older cities but rather attempted to harness it as did the earlier New York City Tenement Acts that created unified rear yards by requiring identical yards for each development. Large-scale assemblage of land for a single development was rare in developed cities. Rockefeller Center was an exception to the rule. The European urban design legacy which treated entire streets as architectural objects was anathema to the turn-of-the-century American development practice. Thus, Burnham's attempt to transform Chicago into the Paris of the prairie failed because it ran counter to the traditions of American urban development and private property. The individual lot was and still is the traditional focus of American urban development. Therein lies the dilemma. Can the thousands of landholding individuals making development decisions in their own economic self-interest, according to their own aesthetic preferences, be collectively harnessed to create, over time, an imageable and coherent block, street, district, and city without sacrificing constitutional values?

It was in this arena that Euclidean zoning had its greatest impact on the form of our cities. The Height and Area Districts determined the form of the city. These regulations not only determined the density of the proposed buildings but also influenced the form or volumetric configuration of buildings particularly when the development potential was fully utilized. New York's Euclidean Height and Area Districts, imperfect and unintentional as they were, demonstrated the urban design potential of zoning. Over time, buildings constructed on individual lots in conformance with the

Height and Area District regulations ultimately filled out entire streets and avenues.

While the buildings constructed under the 1916 ordinance might have been departures from earlier urban buildings, the aggregate ensemble of these buildings nonetheless adhered to traditional urban values that were both implicit and unintentional in the ordinance. The buildings continued the time-honored practice of street walls built at the street line, defining the public space of the street. Furthermore, the street walls were continuous, creating continuous building walls composed of multiple buildings. The Park Avenue diagrams discussed earlier illustrate this phenomenon. The combined effect of the sky exposure planes and the tower regulations, in typical development situations, required high coverage buildings if the maximum development potential was to be attained on a site that generally meant building to the street line. The effect of the 1916 Ordinance was to subordinate each building to that of the ensemble of buildings lining and defining the public space of the street—the streetscape.

Central Park West, Riverside Drive, and Fifth Avenue in Manhattan and the Grand Concourse in the Bronx, to name but a few, all are visually coherent or imageable streets that owe their form to the 1916 Ordinance. The buildings that line these streets are designed in a variety of architectural styles. They maintain fairly consistent street walls in both location and height with the upper portions of the larger developments set back in conformance with the sky exposure planes and tower regulations. The vividness of these streets rivals in its own way the best European examples of autocratic large-scale development and unified architectural design without designing, in a traditional sense, the architecture of the buildings in the context of a predetermined master plan.

The 1961 New York City Zoning Resolution

In 1961, New York City adopted a new zoning ordinance which was based on the Euclidean structure but not the substance of the 1916 Zoning Ordinance.

The 1961 Zoning Resolution had its origins in the utopian visions of the Modern Movement which were codified in CIAM's (Congres Internationale D'Architecture Moderne) Athens Charter and the more pragmatic *Plan for Rezoning the City of New York.* [20] The Modern Movement's vision of the twentieth century city, although all too easy to dismiss today, nevertheless had its virtues. As with most nineteenth and twentieth century urban reform, it was a reaction to the chaotic, speculative, unplanned, unhealthy, dark, squalid, and sordid cities of the nineteenth century. Modernism's critical analysis of the capitalist city led to the utopian approach that treated the existing city as a tabula rasa. The resulting discontinuities between new and old were seen as a minor inconvenience that was to be tolerated until the vision was realized. The 1920s European utopian imagery of a rationalized city structure of discrete land uses, located in super blocks and defined by a coherent street system containing freestanding prismatic towers, glittering in parks filled with the healthful benefits of air and sunlight and vegetation, was the intellectual and formal antecedent of the 1961 Zoning Resolution.

The physical form of the city was to be turned inside out. The nineteenth century capitalist city, continuing the pattern of earlier urban development, was composed of buildings fairly consistent in height and, most importantly, interconnected street walls that defined the public space of the street, while the modernist approach reinterpreted the building as an object sitting in space. The 1950 *Plan for Rezoning the City of New York* blandly described this dramatic reversal of urban form in the section dealing with "angle of light obstruction" regulations. It was argued that the regulations would free the architect to design better buildings instead of "merely filling the (zoning) envelope," and "that the architectural ingenuity encouraged by the new regulations are believed to be more than adequate recompense for any loss of cornice uniformity (in either height or location)." All of this was justified by the new regulations producing:

> First (buildings) that are more economic to build. Second it will be possible to get light and ventilation into side windows. Third, in blocks developed under these regulations, more sunlight will come into the street over the lower portions of buildings.[21]

Nowhere is urban aesthetics or good city form mentioned. Although completed three years before the adoption of the 1961 Zoning Resolution, the Seagram Building, by Ludwig Mies van der Rohe, played a significant role in giving tangible expression to the new urban form. This pristine and elegant bronze-clad building, although built in conformance with the 1916 Zoning Ordinance (its tower covers only 25 percent of the lot area rather than the 40 percent coverage allowed by the 1961 Zoning Resolution) was suggesting the future by example in its provision of a publicly accessible open space—a plaza. The success of this design was compelling, and reinforced the architectural community's belief in the Modern Movement with its formal design theories, if not its underlying social program. Furthermore, it appeared that this distinctive building and its plaza constituted a replicable model. The Height and Setback regulations of the 1961 Zoning Resolution, in effect, legislated this building type. The approach was typological and was fraught, as we shall see, with all the problems inherent in legislating a building type.

The as-of-right sections of the 1961 Zoning Resolution were administered by the New York City Department of Buildings. The statutory basis for the as-of-right review was a series of regulations that prescribed the density, use, site planning, and form of the building. An incentive, new to New York's zoning, was built into the system. In residential districts higher density was awarded those developments that minimized lot coverage by constructing low coverage towers.[22] In the highest density residential districts and the central business districts a bonus of additional density and/or floor area was awarded the development for providing a publicly accessible, on-site open space—a plaza and/or arcade.[23] All of this was to be done as-of-right and was nonnegotiable, done in conformance with the absolute dimensional standards prescribed in the regulations.

Floor area ratio (FAR) was introduced to control density in commercial buildings and building volume in both residential and commercial buildings and therefore capped densities for any given site and the city as well. Each square foot of land in New York City was given a maximum development potential that could only be exceeded by the provision of a plaza and or arcade and which, if fully complied with, increased the basic maximum FAR by 20 percent.

This was a dramatic change from the 1916 Zoning Ordinance which controlled density and floor area indirectly through the combination of lot size, Height and Area Districts, tower coverage, building technology, and the marketplace. The result of the indirect control of density in Midtown, for example, was higher densities on large sites—the Empire State Building, occupying most of a full city block, has an FAR of 30.1—and lower densities (10–12 FAR) on smaller sites where the combination of street wall height, setback, and tower requirements practically precluded large, dense structures. The resulting population density was far less in practice than it would have been in theory due to the variable lot sizes and the difficulties inherent in assembling larger sites. (Theoretically 55 to 77 million inhabitants could have fit within the 1916 zoning envelope, assuming full build out, which in practice was impossible.)[24]

The flaw in the 1961 Zoning Resolution was not the as-of-right prescriptive nature of the ordinance (which worked all too well in achieving its implicit urban vision) or the piecemeal nature of its control over development—that is development parcel by development parcel.[25] The former was the traditional format of zoning while the latter the traditional form of property regulations (with the exception of urban renewal).

The flaw in the regulations was that they tended to produce virtually the same building and bonused plaza and/or arcade (arcades rarely were built because the bonus was undervalued compared to the plaza bonus—3 to 1 versus 6 to 1—and costlier to achieve) on every site. The result in this case *did* match the intentions, but the urban critics didn't like what the buildings looked like—they were banal architecture. Similar to the Park Avenue apartment houses discussed earlier, the new buildings were decorated versions of the legislated model or type. The zoning envelope and the building tended to be isomorphic, regardless of context and orientation.

It is telling that the critics focused on the banality of the Modernist building designs and the prescriptive as-of-right regulations rather than the fundamental question regarding the appropriateness of either the vision of an ideal city of freestanding towers or the typological approach to urban zoning which in practice

produced an urban landscape of grinding uniformity.[26] The inherent rigidities of as-of-right prescriptive zoning were common to both the 1916 and 1961 regulations. While the structural flaw of prescriptive zoning was common to both, it was the substance and content of the 1961 regulations that were the issue. Whereas the 1916 zoning envelope was loose, spatial, and nontypological (its concern being the quality of the street space), the 1961 zoning envelope was tight and typological. It literally attempted to legislate not only a single building type to the exclusion of all others but, more grandiosely, attempted to legislate the physical master plan of the ideal city of the future. The ordinance treated the entire city, in European fashion, as an architectural design defying Kevin Lynch's observation that the art of city design is different from the art of architecture.

The structure of Euclidean zoning is essentially neutral concerning building and city form (one could contemplate mixed-use Use Districts). It is given form by the substance of the regulations. The critics' arguments missed the mark; the issue was not the quality of individuation of an architectural form, which was more an issue of prevailing architectural taste, building economics, and marketing, but rather the implicit values and inflexibility of the 1961 regulations. The vision itself was wrong and ultimately antithetical to New Yorkers' sense of urbanity. What is most revealing is that the substantive regulations under the two ordinances regarding height and setback that grew out of the desire to ensure adequate light and air to streets and buildings could produce such divergent urban and building forms.

The freestanding towers of Sixth Avenue are approximately the same density (FAR of 18) and provide the same amount of daylight as the earlier setback "wedding cake" and tower and base buildings that line Madison and Park avenues. Clearly, building and city form are value sensitive. Ultimately, the abstractions of light and air, minimizing congestion, and so forth, must be translated into substantive regulations that cannot but reflect the cultural values and aesthetic preferences of the times, all other things being equal.

SETTING THE STANDARD

What a human being can adjust to no one should have to live through. [GUSSIE SINGER]

Euclidean zoning always has been presented as having two significant virtues:
- Design neutrality, and
- Standards and criteria empirically and objectively based.

The issue of design neutrality has been dispelled in the preceding discussion. All zoning standards ultimately have aesthetic implications whether intentional or unintentional. The variable is the degree and type of specificity of the regulations.

The standards question should be looked at in terms of the substantive basis, if any, for the standard and the ease of administration of the standard.

As has been demonstrated, the simplicity and relative lack of ambiguity of Euclidean zoning allowed an architect and client to determine easily the zoning parameters for a particular site. The resulting scheme could, with the same ease, objectively be reviewed by a buildings department plan examiner for conformance to the regulations. There was almost no exercise of discretionary judgment in reviewing the scheme. The review was ministerial, based on absolute if not abstract standards. If there is a virtue in prescriptive as-of-right zoning, it lies in the consistency of its application and its strict adherence to the equal protection and procedural due process values of the Constitution.

Standards: The Use District

This leaves us with the substantive due process question, or how the standards are determined and whether they do, in fact, protect the public health, safety and welfare. Let us begin by examining the use districting of Euclidean zoning, first in terms of the exclusion of nonresidential uses from residential districts and, second, the exclusion of apartment houses from some residential districts. Later we will return to the origin and bases of the light and air standards. Justice Sutherland clearly outlines the rationale for the first case:

> The decisions . . . agree that the exclusion of buildings devoted to business, trade, etc. from residential districts, bears a rational relation to the health and security from injury of children and others by separating dwelling houses from territory devoted to trade and industry; suppression and prevention of disorder [later on referred to as nervous disorders—author's note]; facilitating the extinguishment of fires, and the enforcement of street traffic regulations and other general welfare ordinances; aiding the health and safety of the community by excluding from residential areas the confusion and danger of fire, contagion, and disorder, which in greater or less degree attach to the location of stores, shops and factories. Another ground is that the construction and repair of streets may be rendered easier and less expensive by confining the greater part of the heavy traffic to the streets where business is carried on.[27]

With the exception of noxious and harmful industrial land uses such as tanneries, stockyards, refineries, and the like that traditionally have been excluded from residential areas under the common law of nuisance per se, the exclusion of other land use activities such as business, trade, and so forth from residential areas certainly is arguable.

The exclusion of industrial land uses from residential districts easily is supportable on the basis of actual objective documentation and experience with industrial activities. As with all land uses that have negative impacts, anticipatory land use legislation can take two approaches vis-à-vis locational standards; the noxious uses can be segregated physically or they can be required to internalize their negative aspects by adhering to specified performance standards. Euclidean zoning adopted the former approach probably because of the availability of space, the accessibility offered by mass transit and the automobile, and the relative simplicity of its administration.

The districts legislate homogeneity in residential areas to the exclusion of business, commerce, and trade. Residential districting can be ascribed to a consensual and acculturated sense of urban order and the value placed on the home environment by American bourgeois society discussed earlier. The exclusion being discussed here is absolute while the harm created by the inclusion of business and trade in residential districts is one of degree. Euclidean use districts are absolute in their exclusion and are not sensitive to issues of degree.

The potential harm described by Sutherland is supported neither by experience nor empirical data. At best, residential districting represents the social preferences of the lay public and professionals. Virtually every Old World city mixed business, trade, and residential living quarters. As tourists, we flock to these cities to vicariously experience their urbanity and civility.

Greenwich Village in New York City still functions as a traditional mixed-use neighborhood. Many commentators have held it up as the quintessential urban neighborhood[28] that might serve as a model for the development of other urban neighborhoods. Greenwich Village exhibits all the charms and character of a traditional European quarter, a character that the current diverse population finds attractive. For many it is a highly desirable place to live, work, and raise children.

One can only surmise that the traditional mixed-use neighborhood and homogeneous Euclidean residential district represent different values and preferences. In each case, the individual calculus used to assess the advantages of the environment is based on the values used in the calculus. The public life of the streets in Greenwich Village easily could be seen as good by some and bad by others. Similarly, the easy access to virtually all the daily necessities of life is evaluated against the quiet of strictly residential enclaves. In either case, the discussion of single-use or multiple-use districts is not an aesthetic issue in the sense of museum aesthetics but rather of consensual cultural values regarding urban order.

Problems associated with the gross grain of the Use District net were dismissed by Justice Sutherland, who wrote:

> The inclusion of a reasonable margin to insure effective enforcement will not put upon a law otherwise valid, the stamp of invalidity. Such laws may also find their justification in the fact that in some fields, the bad fades into the good by such insensible degrees that the two are not really capable of being readily distinguished and separated in terms of legislation. In the light of these considerations we are not prepared to say that the end in view was not sufficient to justify the general rule of ordinances although some industries of an innocent character might fall within the proscribed class.[29]

Obviously, what is one person's order or good is another person's disorder or bad. By analogy, imagine a desk overflowing with books, papers, and other paraphernalia. The desk user sees order on the desk while the outsider sees chaos. Furthermore, as noted earlier, the 1916 Building Heights Commission freely acknowledged that the Use District adhered to development patterns already in place, replacing "planning objectivity" with the standards of the marketplace and the social and economic values they represented.

The issue of empirically derived standards for use districting is carried from the sublime to the ridiculous in Sutherland's support of the exclusion of apartment houses from residence districts.[30]

Putting aside the presumed validity of class segregation and the role of home ownership in determining economic status and social stability, there remains a double standard at work. Children in detached-house residential districts are to be accorded the full force of the law to create an environment perceived to be beneficial and salutary for child development. The same protection is not afforded children in apartment houses. In fact, one wonders, given the omission, whether Justice Sutherland knew children were raised in apartment houses.

Giving the good Justice the benefit of the doubt, he may have been generalizing from his own limited experience with tenements and their occupants. It also was not unusual for individuals to subscribe to a Spencerian form of environmental determinism. Reformers from the early days of housing reform through the heyday of urban renewal believed the tenement buildings themselves, the high densities, and sunless apartments bred the social and physical pathologies associated with slum dwellers.[31] For example, the high incidence of tuberculosis, long associated with the tenement apartment house by inferential evidence, has been shown to have been caused by the type of work being done at home (Bohemian cigar makers had a particularly high incidence of tuberculosis, we now know, primarily as a result of diet, sanitary habits, and the ingestion and inhaling of tobacco dust). The lack of sunlight to the workers was not confined to the tenement sweatshop but also was experienced by factory workers in loft buildings and office workers in buildings located in the darkened commercial canyons of the older central cities suggesting a causal relationship between the workers' incidence of illness and the lack of sunlight.[32]

One can only assume, as had Judge Westenhaver, that use districting in the clear absence of objective empirically derived planning and public health criteria was a proxy for the social values of those with the political muscle to legislate their sense of urban order.[33] Use districting under most circumstances represents a socially rather than an objectively determined use of urban space. In city design terms, it is an open choice, as both Greenwich Village and the exclusive residence district have proved to be workable models for city design either singly or in combination. Use districting is a design decision of the highest order as it is the structure that supports and is supported by the buildings.

As with the Use Districts, the Height and Area District regulations also were administratively objective. Either the proposed building conformed to the zoning envelope or it didn't. As with the Use Districts discussed above, control of density and the form of the building were in most instances practically and culturally determined. The light and air provisions of New York's two zoning ordinances illustrate this point.

Light and Air

The sky exposure planes of the 1916 and 1961 New York zoning regulations are practically and culturally based. They do not reflect in any way minimal but rather socially and politically acceptable daylighting standards for New York's streets and buildings. The Building Heights Commission acknowledged the practical origins of the daylighting standards represented by the Height and Area Districts:

> In recommending restrictions we have necessarily been limited by existing conditions as to improvements and land values in the office and financial district. Were it not for the existence of many tall buildings, other and more nearly ideal restrictions could be imposed. The restrictions recommended are designed to secure as much light and air, relief from congestion and safety from fire as is practicable under existing conditions as to improvements and land values. In place of proving a menace to existing values they will tend to prevent future serious injury to such values.[34]

Retained to design the new daylight regulations for Midtown, the consultants (Kwartler/Jones) examined the daylighting and planning literature for empirically derived daylighting standards. Much of the literature came out of the public health movement and its research into the beneficial aspects of daylighting. Upon reflection, the consultants found much of the research scientifically naive and causal at best and political advocacy at worst. Conversations with staff at the Atlanta Center for Disease Control, the successor to the public health movement, regarding minimum daylighting level to maintain physiological well being, suggested daylighting levels slightly above that of a medieval dungeon.

Euclidean zoning posits minimum standards to protect the public health, safety, and welfare. In regard to daylight, even the worst canyons of Manhattan registered significantly above the physiological minimum. Daylight-

ing standards are clearly a function of habituation, acculturation, and the hard practicalities of development economics, building marketability, and the layout of the city's streets and blocks. The absoluteness of the ratios and the pseudo-science of the sky exposure planes reveal a fatal flaw.

Can one, with any conviction and certainty, suggest that a 30-foot rear yard is so much better for us than one 29 feet deep, or that the sky exposure plane of 45 degrees is sufficiently better for our well-being than one of 46 degrees? Of course not!

The consultants' analysis of the 1916 and 1961 daylighting standards indicated elasticity in the daylighting performance of building in Midtown. Using the Waldram Diagram, an internationally accepted graphic indicator of daylighting performance, the consultants evaluated representative building "types" for their daylighting performance. Analysis revealed that daylight performance under both sets of prescriptive regulations (1916 and 1961) was fairly consistent but that the performance of the building "types" was elastic. Seventy degrees (the angle formed by a line drawn from the centerline of the street to the top of the street wall) was the typical height of street walls in Midtown Manhattan. The consultants found that the daylight performance of building "types" might be as high as 80 percent and as low as 66 percent of the skydome above 70 degrees, the typical street wall height, left unobstructed. The average area of the sky dome left unobstructed above 70 degrees was 75 percent.[35]

The absolute and abstract sky exposure planes of both the 1916 and 1961 regulations proved in practice to produce buildings with a range of daylight responses. In other words, the sets of sky exposure planes did not produce a uniform daylighting response. The noncomplying 46 degree sky exposure plane would have fallen within the permissible range of daylighting performance described earlier. Furthermore, as we have seen, the daylighting standard was consensually determined. It was the practical "best."

We can conclude that the absoluteness of the Euclidean numerical and graphic standards obscures the fact that they are value-based standards. The purported objectivity of Euclidean zoning paradoxically results from the absoluteness of the standards. Administrative objectivity of the standard has obscured the value basis of the standard that is being evaluated.

The Rise of Discretionary Review and the Failure of 1961's Prescriptive Zoning

Less than 10 years after the adoption of the 1961 Zoning Resolution, disaffection with the concrete results of the idealized utopian vision set in. The common wisdom of then and today was that the rigidities resulting from the abstraction and absoluteness of the 1961 Resolution forced the architects and developers to fill the freestanding tower form resulting from the right zoning envelope and thus maximize floor area, density, and profits. This was and is incompatible with the best efforts of architects and urban designers to produce good architecture and good city form. In fact this had been the case under the 1916 Zoning Ordinance, under which the zoning envelope was similarly filled as evidenced by Lower Manhattan and the "wedding cake" or setback structures of Midtown. The difference between the 1916 and 1961 regulations was that the 1916 Ordinance's envelope was loose and could be filled by a variety of drastically different building forms (setback, tower and base, setback slab, and freestanding).

This wisdom, while most often heard from architects and urban designers, was also expressed with great regularity by the developers, bankers, community representatives, and other professional, lay, and governmental constituencies. They posited that the 1961 Zoning Resolution legislated building and city form and that its singular vision was too restrictive and left little room for genuine architectural design quality and innovation. The result was cookie-cutter building that was often ugly and sterile, set in an ill-considered and barely usable public open space that often was neglected. These same buildings also appeared to be insensitive to older buildings that formed the physical context, resulting in visual dissonance. Furthermore, the buildings when taken in the aggregate did not appear to support urban life, particularly traditional street-related public life, but rather seemed to produce an antiurban or minimally a-urban environment of independent structures reminiscent of our worst nightmares of the chaotic suburban strip, but at urban densities.

For the moment, let us put stylistic controversy aside and assume the AT&T Building, executed in the postmodern style, is an exemplary high-rise structure. The same design realigned in a plaza on Sixth Avenue—let us say the Exxon Plaza—in all probability would satisfy neither the architect nor the chorus of critics. The issue is not the design quality of the architectural object per se but rather the type of urban values embodied in the zoning resolution. The free-standing tower in the plaza, be it the unrelenting slab of the Exxon Building or the highly articulated AT&T tower, is a-contextual, and ultimately destructive of the traditional urban form of New York.[36]

As evidenced above, the replicable model, the freestanding tower in an open space or plaza, proved in practice not to be particularly successful. In the effort to provide usable public open space in New York on private property, and light and views to and from new buildings, the 1961 Resolution managed to throw the baby (traditional urban street-defining buildings) out with the bathwater (the lack of usable open space at grade and light and air). As noted earlier, the Seagram Building turned out not to be a replicable building type, probably because it was viewed as something other than the piece of contextual urban design it was. The Seagram Building demanded the masonry counterpoint of the florentine Racquet Club across the street to function as a foil to the glass walls of the tower. The reflection of the masonry facade across the street in the continuous glass wall of the lobby is as much a part of the design of the Seagram Building as the original low-rise street wall buildings that framed it and the plaza. When another plaza and tower was to be built on the cleared site to the south, public pressure was exerted on both the architect and developer to include a low-rise street wall in their development to continue to define the space created by the Seagram Building. The Seagram Building worked in part because it broke with the urban design conventions of the 1916 Zoning Ordinance and Park Avenue. It was a dissonant note in the landscape of Park Avenue, a one of a kind site-specific building. Unfortunately, the 1961 Resolution had only one model in mind. When the tower and plaza model failed, the Height and Setback regulations of the 1961 Resolution failed with it.

The model failed in many other ways. The loss of retail continuity at the street and the proliferation of plazas and towers that appeared diminished the potential attractiveness of each development. The seemingly endless row of plazas on Sixth Avenue was apparently too much of a good thing. The streetscape was being irreparably wrenched apart.

The nature of our property relationships requires developers to avail themselves of all the

Zoning Resolution offered without regard to the developments on adjoining blocks or lots. The plazas were located only where development activity occurred and not necessarily where a plaza might have been both useful and appreciated, making the operations of the 1961 Resolution contingent on the activities of the marketplace, thereby undermining the coherence of the utopian vision. Le Corbusier's utopian scheme for urban order based on the high-rise, high-density tower in the park, zoned land uses, and rationalized road systems was ultimately a traditional physical master plan. Physical master plans, such as the "Plan Voisin" envisaged by Le Corbusier for Paris,[37] were not contingent and as such required the steady hand of the despot to achieve rather than the 40 to 60 years of market-motivated building by individual developers that is characteristic of the private real estate market in New York City.

It undoubtedly is clear to the reader that the litany of the 1961 resolution's shortcomings could fill a book and in fact has.[38] But if the 1961 Resolution had these perceived shortcomings, what could be done to ensure that New York would be the beneficiary of well-designed buildings that when viewed as an ensemble would create the good urban environment? The answer the critics said was simple—relax the zoning regulations that tied the hands of the designers and good architecture and good city form would flow as surely as the East River flows under the Brooklyn Bridge.[39]

The idea that "good" architecture and "good" city form are equivalent has not been borne out in practice, as witnessed by the close packing of the monumental AT&T and IBM buildings on Madison Avenue, nor has the notion that good architecture will result in good urban form been borne out. Nonetheless, the idea was seductive and served to deflect the physical planner's concerns from the environmental quality of the public streetscape to that of shaping individual buildings.

The design community suggested that their buildings be exempt from the conventions (the tower in the plaza) required by Height and Setback regulations of the 1961 Zoning Resolution. But on what basis should the Height and Setback regulations be waived? Rather than comprehensively reevaluate the value system and structure of the 1961 Resolution, the City Planning Commission opted for regulatory techniques designed to deal with development pressures as they arose on a case-by-case basis, thereby recognizing the contingent nature of development in New York City. In order to overcome the rigid abstractions and absolute numerical standards of the as-of-right tower in the park prescriptive regulations of the 1961 Resolution, the commission moved to expand the bonus concept or the idea that zoning might, if properly done, go beyond restricting a harm to conferring a good.[40] This was to be achieved by manipulating the substantive and procedural rules of the zoning resolution. As a legislative body, the City Planning Commission could waive the rules, reduce rules to the bare minimum, create flexible or contingent rules, redefine the rules, and relax the process.

The City Planning Commission's Counsel's Office, its related Office of Technical Controls, and the Manhattan Office of City Planning were the other activists in the development, evolution, and administration of incentive zoning by negotiation. Incentive zoning had its origins in the 1961 zoning resolution. The shift from as-of-right incentive zoning to the process of incentive zoning by negotiation was revolutionary. The development of zoning text from the Urban Design Group's (UDG) proposals, its interpretation during the negotiation between Department of City Planning and the development team, and the certification of the applicant's project were performed in collaboration with the UDG. The constitutional validity of the concept of "discretionary incentive zoning" was successfully navigated by Department of City Planning Counsel Norman Marcus, who later went on to coedit a book championing negotiated incentive zoning[41] and the inclusion of aesthetic control of building design as a logical extension of the police power.

The entire concept, as Weaver and Babcock have noted, found its origins in the discretionary zoning techniques, floating or conditional zones, including Planned Unit Developments (PUDs), which were developed in the suburbs and sustained by the courts to control burgeoning development after World War II.[42] Discretionary zoning's perceived success was in its ability to tie the piecemeal and ad hoc development of land to larger planning concerns while sensitizing a development's response to the specifics of site and program.

The Discretionary Years: Special Districts and Special Permits

Two vehicles were used that allowed the New York City Planning Commission to waive or modify, in part or wholly, the underlying abstract and absolute regulations: the Special Districts that were mapped for specific areas, and Special Permits, which applied when the use, size, or location of one development lot met certain objective criteria. Both involve discretionary review procedures requiring, in varying degrees, a process of negotiation between the public and private sectors.

The importance to New York City of the concept of negotiated incentive zoning techniques to deal with the site-specific complexities of development and the uniqueness of the area is manifest in the 31 Special Purpose Districts and the 54 Special Permits. Special Permits and Special Districts have two things in common—the use of discretion in determining a new development's conformance to the zoning standard and a floor area bonus for the provision of a public amenity. The waiver and/or modification of the underlying height and setback regulations and the incentive bonus proved to be very popular with developers, architects, public officials, and the concerned public.

In physical design terms, the commission's special district discretionary regulations pursued three paths simultaneously: conservation of the traditional physical fabric of the City through the reiteration of the conventions which created that fabric (e.g., Fifth Avenue); the design of new conventions to which adherence could be evaluated with reasonable objectivity (e.g., Lincoln Square at Lincoln Center); and the negotiation of new conventions in a public design review process that had few if any objective criteria for evaluating the results (e.g., Theatre District). Of the three types of Special Districts, accountability and certainty were strongest in the first, diminished to some degree in the second, and virtually absent in the last type. All types of Special District generally required a lengthy administrative and public review process.

The Special Permits, sometimes called floating or conditional zones, on the other hand, were not mapped and were not designed to protect or advance the unique qualities of a particular area. They fell into three categories: those that applied to unique uses such as public facilities (court houses, bus terminals, heliports, etc.); those that applied to specific types of locations (developments over railroad yards, sites opposite parks of three acres or more, sites adjacent to landmarks using development rights transfers); and those that applied to specific and often unique development sites meeting stated criteria. The

main criterion in the third category consisted generally of size, such as commercial developments extended into more than one block, large-scale residential and community facility developments, and Section 74–72, which was operative for Midtown blockfront sites having a minimum lot area.

The first type of Special Permit was designed in the historic tradition of waiving underlying urban conventions for what, in most cases, were important public institutions. Historically, not only was the architecture of the institution intentionally different from that of the context but the site planning also frequently was unconventional and complemented those structures as exceptions to the rule. This approach has its antecedents in historic cities.

The second type of Special Permit was location-specific and hence predictable to some degree. It applied to sites that presented unique design problems that were difficult to anticipate in the abstract. Buildings adjacent to or over a landmark required the proposed structure be responsive to the landmark. Developments over railroad rights-of-way also created unique design and planning considerations.

It was the third type of Special Permit that created the most difficult problems for the planning commission in urban design terms. With criteria written in the most nebulous yet well-meaning prose, objectivity, accountability, and certainty and predictability lost whatever meaning they may have had. Until the adoption of the new Midtown regulations in 1982, the desirability of this type of special permit was, for example, reflected in its growing use in Midtown Manhattan. As-of-right buildings accounted for 100 percent of all floor area built in the period 1960–1964; 87 percent in the period 1965–1969; 36 percent in the period 1970–1974; 14 percent in 1975–1979; and zero percent in the period 1980–1982. Essentially, the as-of-right system of preregulation described earlier had gone unused for almost 10 years in Midtown and was moribund.

Tailored to ease the development of relatively small sites, Section 74–72 of the 1961 Zoning Resolution merely required a certain size site with a blockfront configuration to qualify. It was, of course, amended frequently to accommodate specific developments.

When coupled to the new array of interior public spaces and the renewed taste for buildings that rise directly on the street, it proved to be the most popular show in town.[43] The bonusable exterior public spaces were internalized[44] and rationalized as a good thing for the obvious reason that the new building, if it were to be marketable, had to cover a considerably higher proportion of the zoning lot than the as-of-right prescriptive tower provisions allowed.

The process of tailoring special permits to the needs of particular developments is endemic to the 1961 resolution and resulted from its rigid form of preregulation and its origin in a specific and singular vision and everyone's delight in the negotiation process. Section 74–72 of the 1961 Resolution allowed the City Planning Commission to modify the height, setback, tower, and coverage requirements for what was construed to be superior design.[45] This generation of special permit buildings—of which the new AT&T and IBM Buildings are probably the best known—caricatured the renewed interest in "context."

The public streetscape-defining attribute of the earlier street wall buildings resulting from the 1916 Zoning Ordinance was, as we have seen, achieved unintentionally by its system of Height Districts. In practice, Section 74–72 ultimately legitimized the practice of placing very tall freestanding towers or slabs of repetitive and standardized floors up to the street line (AT&T, IBM, and I.M. Pei's 490 Park Avenue).

These buildings have street walls with a vengeance! They bear little relationship to the heights of adjacent street walls, create low lighting levels in the street that harken back to prezoning days, and create wind effects on the public space of the street adjacent to those sheer towers that at best are uncomfortable and at worst dangerous.[46] Objective environmental and sensory criteria (one might even say common sense) were discarded for what appeared to be good architecture. In the most profound sense, the Department of City Planning and City Planning Commission found themselves in the awkward position of legislating architectural taste. The developers quickly learned that noted architects, like designer labels, provided a veneer of aesthetic chic and cachet. The fine line between designing buildings and designing cities disappeared while the two activities merged into one. The public's interest in a private design was dramatically expanded. The City Planning Department's role expanded to that approximating an architectural review board or landmarks commission. No longer concerned merely with issues of civic design, the planning commission with its increased degree of intrusiveness in building design, moved from legislating cultural values (civic design) into the more problematic and abstract arena of legislating beauty (architectural design).

By what criteria can some buildings be rejected and others approved? John J. Costonis, in his well reasoned article for the *Michigan Law Review*, "Law and Aesthetics: A Critique and a Reformation of the Dilemmas," forcefully argues that abstract beauty in this country is not a sustainable legal doctrine although it is certainly a sustainable aesthetic philosophy. He states:

Aesthetic policy, as currently formulated and

implemented at the federal, state, and local levels, often partakes more of high farce than the rule of law. Its purposes are seldom accurately or candidly portrayed, let alone understood, by its most vehement champions. . . . Its indiscriminate, often quixotic demands have overwhelmed legal institutions, which all too often have compromised the integrity of legislative, administrative, and judicial process in the name of beauty.[47]

By 1980, discretionary zoning, with particular emphasis on Midtown Manhattan, seemed to be out of control. As noted, the environmental effects of the new generation of negotiated buildings often harkened back to the worst excesses of prezoning days. The special permit process was time-consuming and unpredictable. The city planning department staff, community, and planning commission reviews were conducted in the absence of any standards other than those of stylistic preference and political agendas. In a rare show of unanimity, the developers and good government groups suggested that the discretionary approach be abandoned for more accountable and predictable zoning regulations.

In 1980, Kwartler/Jones was retained by the City Planning Commission to develop new Height and Setback regulations for Midtown.[48] The consultants' analysis of the array of pragmatic and conceptual issues suggested that neither the structure of administrative discretion exercised through the lengthy special permit process nor the simple as-of-right structure of prescriptive preregulation characteristic of the 1961 Zoning Resolution was workable any longer. The former, in addition to being time-consuming, had virtually no substantive basis for decision making, while the latter's typological approach that resolved almost all design decisions within the regulations themselves, proved in practice to be a-

urban (antithetical to the city's traditional urban form) and unresponsive to the changing nature of development in Midtown. While the 1916 as-of-right prescriptive Zoning Ordinance, with its focus on the daylighting and the quality of the public space of the street and its nontypological approach to regulation, proved to be a valuable construct that informed the consultants' response to the issues, it too was incapable of responding to the complexities of development in Midtown in the 1980s.

Given the City Planning Commission's interest in an as-of-right Building Quality System, a variation of Housing Quality Zoning (HQZ) developed for the Mayor's Urban Design Council in 1974 and adopted by the Board of Estimate in 1976,[49] the consultants proceeded to investigate the applicability of the structure of HQZ to the Midtown issues.

Briefly, HQZ is a performance system that recognizes that zoning cannot successfully predetermine the appropriate building form or building type in the abstract but is contingent on a variety of factors including site size and configuration, orientation, context, building program, building technology, and architectural design values. As such it is the antithesis of the typological approach of the 1961 Zoning Resolution. Too many forces and actors are involved in the creation of the model or replicable building type for zoning to predetermine in the abstract.

In a legal context, zoning can at best represent the public interest in the development of the type or model by private individuals acting in their own perceived interest. The public interest embraces the need to protect the environmental quality of the locale—in this case, Midtown Manhattan. This meant the clear enunciation of public policy regarding environmental quality in Midtown. For the developer, it represented positive obligations to the commons.

More specifically, by definition performance systems are contingent as they assume a multiplicity of "right" answers. The performance structure of Housing Quality Zoning was admirably suited to this purpose because it clearly distinguished between the implicit goals and practices of architectural design (building quality) and zoning as civic design (environmental quality). Civic design achieved through zoning, if it is to take seriously the First Amendment guarantee of freedom of expression, recognizes the pluralist context of architectural design in America.

Nonetheless, zoning must by definition make aesthetic judgments at the gross level of building form although, as Stephen Williams has noted:

> . . . aesthetic judgements often present the type of problem that Professor (Buckminster) Fuller described as "polycentric." Polycentric problems arise when three factors coincide: (1) a multiplicity of possible solutions; (2) an interdependency of relevant factors so that the outcome as to one feature of the problem will affect the outcome as to the other features; and (3) a multiplicity of relevant factors that makes it difficult to trace one solution's superiority to any particular attribute or combination of attributes.[50]

Performance zoning attempts to deal with this issue of polycentricity by specifically recognizing the contingent nature of the first two factors and their resolution in the third. This assumes that the multiplicity of factors can be reduced to a manageable number and that the attributes in combination can be said to be representative of environmental quality. The standard for delimiting the public interest in private design decisions is found in the legal

context of procedural and substantive due process. This is similar to the conceptual approach to design outlined by Christopher Alexander in his *Notes on the Synthesis of Form*[51] and often referred to as "fit"—whereby a building design, program, and context are made isomorphic.

The performance structure of HQZ does just that. The system is composed of desirable attributes that are empirically and consensually based and which are clearly described as goals to be achieved: for example, street wall height, street wall length, building height, sunlight on site, sunlight off site, and ground floor activity.

The performance criteria for each attribute are established. Each attribute is given a numerical value reflecting its social desirability, the degree of economic effort to achieve it, and its importance in the building design process (some decisions are more important than others as they set the context for the next level of design decisions). This is then followed by a numerical formula for evaluating conformance to the standards for the particular attribute, which allow for partial compliance. Finally, there are directions for special conditions. In this formulation, the goal to be met is consensually subjective while the performance system of measuring or evaluating goal compliance is objective as in Euclidean as-of-right zoning.

The numerical sum of all the attributes is 100 points. Environmental quality is considered to be achieved when a design accumulates 85 points. Environmental quality is defined as a statistical probability. HQZ assumes that virtually any combination of attributes, scored as to performance and adding up to 85 points, will mean a building has achieved a desirable level of quality. Quality is expressed in equivalencies rather than abstract absolutes and is literally contingent on the project's context. The system not only allows for trade-offs but requires them. Each attribute interacts with the others through a series of design iterations until the building "fits" the situation represented by a minimally complying score of 85 points. The passing score of 85 points and point values for the attributes ensure that the primary attributes cannot be totally ignored.

It was further realized that any architectural design problem would have either direct or implied conflicts and contradictions. In past zoning ordinances these were rationalized beforehand. These conflicts are the meat and potatoes of a design problem. They intentionally were built into the program to allow resolution on a site-by-site basis by the architect and client. What would seem appropriate in one situation might be less than desirable in another. No two buildings had to emphasize the same areas to achieve the passing score of 85 points. Those involved in the design of a building could instead pick and choose their emphasis. The system allowed for a localized design response which encouraged both freedom of expression and contextual fit. It could be called an existential approach to zoning. Jonathan Barnett put it another way when he observed:

> There are more possible quality design elements than any one building would be expected to include, thus recognizing that design is always a series of choices—that circumstances alter cases, and you can't win 'em all. Sometimes, one objective can be achieved only at the expense of another. The architect can choose appropriate design elements in relation to the existing neighborhood, the shape of the site, the topography, and so forth, instead of adapting the needs of his client to a single stereotype. [Or the tastes of the reviewing urban designers and community groups in a negotiated design—author's note.][52]

Performance zoning is zoning's response to Milton's dictum "Reason is Choice."

Relevant aspects of HQZ's Neighborhood Impact Program were selected for inclusion into the Midtown performance zoning regulations. In addition, daylighting procedures to objectively evaluate each building's daylight performance were developed using the Waldram Diagram mentioned earlier to ensure that the streets and building interiors of Midtown were adequately lighted and that the streets were perceptually open. A subcategory was building surface reflectivity which encouraged the use of light-colored reflective materials to both compensate for an incremental reduction in daylighting and to enhance the brightness of Midtown streets and building interiors.

The zoning standards for the Midtown performance regulations were derived from the Midtown environment. The preferred street wall length and height, for example, were statistically derived and based on the street district, the contextual locus of the development site, and included the buildings along the street on which the proposed building would front. The daylighting standard was formulated from an analysis of existing daylight conditions mentioned earlier. The standard reflected the pedestrian's expectation of daylighting, which was based on the common law principle of a "continuing expectation" similar to the right enjoyed under the English "Law of Ancient Lights." In all cases, the level of performance could be evaluated objectively by a ministerial review for compliance as is required if the regulations are to be administered fairly.

The consultants' proposal was modified during the public review process, before finally being adopted. Numerous buildings have been built since the new Midtown regulations were adopted in 1982. They exhibit a variety of forms and styles and are in most instances site specific rather than prototypical. If these buildings are representative of the buildings that can be built under the Midtown regulations, then the two apparently mutually exclusive goals of marrying the virtues of discretionary and as-of-right zoning have been reasonably met. The new regulations avoid both the sterile abstractions of prescriptive zoning as well as the indiscriminate use of discretion characteristic of negotiated zoning; they also do not legislate a building type. Most importantly, the boundary that defines the public interest in the design of a private building has been clearly drawn at the level of civic rather than architectural design. The public's interest is limited to the relationship of the gross form of the new building to its neighbors, its street level use, and its daylighting performance. In fact, the system is not biased toward tall, thin towers or lower, bulky "wedding cakes." Both building types and appropriate building forms are complying forms, as are countless others not yet conceived.

CONCLUSIONS

The major components of New York City's zoning resolution, the districting of use, density, and site planning and building form all have strong aesthetic implications if one assumes city form has aesthetic content, e.g., "Paris is a beautiful city." The first two components guide, if not determine in the rough, the location of the residential areas, local shopping streets or districts, and commercial and manufacturing areas. The separation of uses is objectively justifiable under the police power in the case of a nuisance per se where the physical harm is apparent, for example. But separation of uses becomes less compelling when the harm reflects a social and economic policy, for example, mixed-use neighborhoods versus the exclusively residential neighborhood of single-family detached houses.

Similarly, density has aesthetic implications because it dictates not only the building volume that will be perceived by the public but also the volume of people that will use the streets, infrastructure, shops, and cultural institutions. Historically, high density was associated with cities for reasons of economics and proximity. Furthermore, density, as with the separation of uses, has no absolutes until public health issues, such as epidemics resulting from inadequate sanitary and fresh water infrastructure, manifest themselves. Low density is not necessarily better than high density, as the high-density cities of Europe testify (Paris and Rome: 300 to 400 persons per acre). Low density produces one kind of physical environment, high density another for the obvious reason of building volume. High density is contingent on a host of other factors that may or may not make it possible, including cultural adaptation. Jane Jacobs has noted that yesterday's unmanageable cities become today's ideal cities in terms of size and density.[53] Obviously Midtown would not be Midtown at an FAR of 2.

Density regulations always manifest themselves in building volume which is not always directly related to population density. Soho, the city's former manufacturing district with its cast-iron buildings, used to be virtually empty of people, but now is teeming with residents and visitors.

The height and setback regulations both configure the use to be contained in the new building and the building volume generally measured in FAR (a measure of total floor area which assumes a building volume based on minimum floor-to-floor heights and more directly limited by the population density regulations). These regulations give form to the density. Let us call it perceptual density as distinct from FAR and population density.

A few examples will help explain this point. A typical 17- to 20-story freestanding high-rise apartment house built in an R6 district (e.g., Co-op City) in accordance with the as-of-right regulations of the 1961 Zoning Resolution has the same density as the four- and six-story perimeter block configuration of Phipps Houses in Sunnyside, Queens, designed by Clarence Stein in 1938. The difference is that Phipps Houses covers approximately 43 percent of its lot while the tower/slabs of Co-op City cover approximately 15 percent of their lot. Furthermore, Phipps Houses is a perimeter block building—it defines a completely enclosed interior courtyard, while the Co-op City tower/slab sits in the middle of its lot. Both developments are constructed at R6 density of 100 to 120 persons per acre and an FAR of 2.4.

In Midtown, the so-called wedding cake buildings constructed under the 1916 regulations are approximately equivalent in FAR to the newly constructed AT&T and IBM buildings and the earlier as-of-right tower and slab buildings which line Third, Park, and Sixth avenues in Midtown (Exxon, etc.) In fact, their lot sizes are virtually identical, 30,000 to 35,000 square feet in the case of both the wedding cake Look Building and the freestanding AT&T Building, which are within blocks of each other on Madison Avenue. The physical density (floor area) is the same but the Look Building is approximately 300 feet tall while AT&T is more than twice that height. Clearly, as the two examples illustrate, the size of the lot, the form of the building, the height of its street wall, if any, and the building's siting not only produce different sensations of perceived density but, when replicated by the hundreds, a different perception of density and place in the city—in fact different cities.

From this discussion, it should be clear to the reader that the abstractions of use and density can be configured in ways that will produce dramatically different sensory environments. Assuming for a moment a rational and objective reason for the spatial distribution of uses and maximum densities components, we are left with the choice of how to give form to use and density. The choice is clearly an aesthetic one even assuming there might be functional and economic reasons for the form. Functional determinism of urban form is a poor argument for two reasons. The first is that cities are more than instrumentalities of economic and functional determinism. The second calls into question the idea of functional determinism as evidenced in the dramatically different engineered designs of the rocketry, satellites, and space capsules of the Soviet Union and the United States. After all, even engineers have aesthetic preferences.

If aesthetics, expressed as cultural values, is a major component of city form, the overriding conceptual issue is the legitimate legal basis for intentional aesthetically based zoning legislation. The constitutional safeguards regarding freedom of expression, property rights, and the procedural and substantive due process values embodied in the First (freedom of speech/expression) and the Fifth and Fourteenth (taking of property, equal protection and procedural due process) amendments are complicated further in practice by the cultural context of a pluralist society.

The indiscriminate use of discretion and its questionable results as applied to Midtown and elsewhere in the city might lead us to the argument that aesthetics have no place in zoning. But as we have seen, zoning and aesthetics are inextricably bound together. Rationalizations that zoning is merely an instrument to protect ourselves from harming each other is sophistry at its worst.[54] On the contrary, one must agree with John Costonis's assessment of the issues:

> I do not agree that the aesthetic enterprise is inherently repugnant to sound legal or social values. But I am persuaded that its second-generation problems, those relating to its actual effects rather than to its ostensible goals, confirm that aesthetic policy making and jurisprudence must be disciplined by the courts and legislatures if the rule, rather than the pretense, of law is to govern. My recommendations reduce to the single prescription that, consonant with appropriate institutional constraints, legislatures and courts should take a much harder look at these demands than they do at present. Legislatures should insist that they reflect values that are reasonably representative of communitywide sentiment; that their implementation falls within the capabilities of the agencies designated to administer them and are thus not unduly vulnerable to subversion, and that they be confined by standards intelligible to property owners, the foregoing agencies, and reviewing courts. . . . Formulated in terms of the foregoing triad of constitutional values (vagueness due process or standards, substantive due process and freedom of expression), each [proposal to legislate aesthetics] traces to the challenge of specifying the harm aesthetic regulation seeks to forestall and of ensuring that these values are not compromised in an attempt to prevent the harm.[55]

Implicit in the Costonis argument is the recognition of environmental change. It translates into zoning as a program for regulating change that is reasonably representative of communitywide sentiment or perceptions. Implicit in aesthetics, sentiments, perception, and cultural values is the concept of beauty. Aesthetic theory aimed at defining beauty has been a favorite cultural activity of civilization for thousands of years. In the past, one theory has tended to dominate the cultural life of a period only to be recast as the society changes. Rather than having the force of law (e.g., zoning), each was culturally enforced by an aesthetic orthodoxy as manifest in a national style of the ruling class. The autocratic nature of such societies is at odds with our pluralistic society. In our social context, it is not only incumbent on us to determine community settlement but also to come to grips with beauty in regard to legislation. Put another way, what concept of beauty can be sustainable and justifiable constitutionally, while simultaneously having perceptual credibility in a pluralistic context?

While Costonis primarily is concerned with the "beauty question" as it pertains to historic preservation, the issues he discusses are relevant to aesthetically based zoning, although to a lesser degree. The "beauty question" is far less problematic when one shifts from landmark structures and landmark districts based on museum aesthetics to the design of city form. The fundamental difference between city design and historic preservation is a matter of the degree of intrusiveness of the legislation on private property and freedom of expression. First, generic as-of-right zoning as defined in this chapter is unlike historic preservation because its concerns are more narrowly drawn, for example, zoning should not be concerned with architectural style. Furthermore, the aesthetic component in zoning is culturally based and builds on consensual community values obviating the beauty question. For example, aesthetically based zoning could and has been used to make each place or community in the city more of what it is in order to avoid homogenizing the city as modernist practice has tried to do. The issue as to whether the place is beautiful or not is irrelevant: for example, Times Square and the honky tonk associated with it. If a city composed of unique and identifiable places and communities is desired by public consensus, the rough outlines of the appropriate urban form can be regulated by zoning, still leaving room for a broad spectrum of design responses. Zoning designed as an instrument of civic design becomes the context in which buildings are designed and individuated as demonstrated in the Park Avenue example.

To amplify the point, the definition of beauty must relate directly to the way in which we perceive the world around us physiologically and psychologically. It must recognize the constitutional and psychological values embodied in freedom of expression by encouraging a diversity of design responses while simultaneously defining the level of unacceptable environmental dissonance. The definition of beauty must be resolvable into objective methods and standards that can be uniformly applied and periodically reviewed, and be responsive to the contingent nature of development vis-à-vis individual private property rights. It is worth repeating again that the definition of beauty must be inclusive rather than exclusive—that is, representative of community sentiment, but limited by a clear understanding of the public interest in the development of a piece of private property.

Structurally generic as-of-right zoning should be capable of equitably balancing the forces of change with the forces of stability. This is a particularly thorny issue in New York City as there is no ostensible overall physical master plan for development nor has a consensus for one developed. In New York City, the history of planning is synonymous with the history of zoning. Zoning not only precluded planning (the planning commission was established in 1938—22 years after the first zoning resolution) but is planning in New York City

with the exception of urban renewal and the vague "plan" produced in the late sixties.[56] New York City has resisted the pull of traditional planning with its physical and/or policy plans. The idea of the mandatory plan was promulgated by the courts in response to the abuse of discretionary power. On balance the "plan" has been a failure in controlling these excesses whether in the suburbs or in the cities. [Note: Every time New York City's zoning resolution is amended, the plan is amended simultaneously making a mockery of both planning and zoning.] Weaver and Babcock are right when they suggest:

> At the very least, however, if this placebo is to be administered in place of real medicines, cities should be exempted from the treatment. Mandatory planning as it relates to cities is an unnecessary interference with the urban land use process . . . nor is it [the plan] a cure adopted to the problems that cities do have. The complex problems of maintaining and redeveloping a major city are not likely to be much helped by the development of long-range goals, broad policies, or detailed future land use maps, which is what most mandatory planning legislation mandates. City planning for a city demands a rather different orientation.[57]

They suggest that planning for major cities be reoriented so that it begins by answering the questions:

• What *must* we do today to deal with currently perceived problems?

• What, given our current resources and the present demands on them, can we expect to do tomorrow to deal with the problems and concerns we now foresee?

• If nothing unexpected happens, what might we want to do in the future to avoid problems that a continuation of current trends is likely to produce?

• Given all our answers to all the previous questions, where will the city be in five or ten years, and how acceptable will that be?[58]

This articulates an approach to planning and zoning that recognizes the contingent nature of urban development and offers a method for contextualizing short-term decisions while recognizing that these cumulative decisions ultimately give form to the city. Given the failures of the rigidities of the Euclidean prescriptive zoning and its crude and simplistic system of preregulation which attempts to resolve all design issues in the body of the regulations regardless of the complexity and uniqueness of each situation, and the failures of the discretionary approach which in its ad hoc nature sacrifices standards and a longer term policy context, zoning regulations demand a structure that will incorporate the positive aspects of both approaches in an easily administered generic as-of-right system. Conceptually, such a structure has to recognize that: Zoning is a powerful technique with which to design the form of our cities; standards are relative and not absolute and tend to be culturally based; the process of design of a particular building involves contradictions, conflicts, and mutual exclusivities that cannot be resolved in advance in the body of regulations (an explicit rejection of the typological approach); and good city form is the result of the orchestration of many factors. Furthermore, recalling Dostoevski's Underground Man admonition that man's "most advantageous advantage" is free choice and Milton's definition of reason as "reason is choice," the structure for zoning must be existential—that is, responsive to the fact that we never really know. As-of-right generic performance zoning with its contingent structure meets these criteria.

AUTHOR'S NOTE

I would like to thank John Costonis, Eric Bregman, Kathleen Kelly, and Dennis Ferris for their insights, comments, and editorial assistance in the preparation of this chapter.

NOTES

1. Garrett Hardin, "The Tragedy of the Commons," *Science* 162 (December 13, 1968): 1245.

2. Adam Smith, *The Wealth of Nations* (New York, N.Y.: Modern Library, 1937), p. 423.

3. *Report of the Heights of Buildings Commission* to the Committee on the Height, Size and Arrangement of Buildings of the Board of Estimate and Apportionment of the City of New York. New York City, 1913, p.1.

4. Ibid, p. 223.

5. Ibid, p. 192.

6. *Village of Euclid* v. *Ambler Realty Co.,* 272 U.S. 365, 394 (1926).

7. Id. at 386.

8. *Report of the Heights of Buildings Commission,* p. 234.

9. Jonathan Barnett, *An Introduction to Urban Design* (New York, N.Y.: Harper Row, 1982), p. 60.

10. Kevin Lynch, *The Image of the City* (Cambridge, Mass: MIT Press, 1960), p.2.

11. Jim Lancancellera, "Park Avenue: An Elemental Study of Urban Form," (Masters thesis, RPI, School Architecture, August 1985).

12. S.B. Sutton, ed., *Civilizing American Cities: A Selection of Frederick Law Olmsted's Writings on City Landscapes* (Cambridge, Mass.: MIT Press, 1971), p. 295.

13. *Euclid,* at 394.

14. Richard Sennett, *Families Against the City: Middle Class Homes of Industrial Chicago* (New York, N.Y.: Random House, 1970).

15. Donald G. Presa, "The Development and Demise of the Upper West Side Row House: 1880–1980," New York Neighborhood History Project, Columbia University, New York.

16. *Report of the Heights of Buildings Commission,* p. 67.

17. 297 F. at 316.

18. *Euclid,* at 387.

19. *Report of the Heights of Buildings Commission,* p. 58.

20. Harrison, Ballard and Allen, *Plan of Rezoning the City of New York* (New York, October 1950).

21. Ibid, pp. 47–48.

22. Section 23–14, "Minimum Required Open Space Ratio and Maximum Floor Area Ratio in R1 Through R9

Districts," *New York City Zoning Resolution* (New York, 1961).

23. Ibid, Sections 13–16, "Floor Area Bonus for Plaza," 23–17, "Floor Area Bonus for Plaza Connected Open Area," 23–18, "Floor Area Bonus for Arcades."

24. Stephen Zoll, "Superville," *Massachusetts Review,* Summer 1973, p. 480.

25. Barnett, *Introduction to Urban Design,* p. 60.

26. William S. Paley, *The Threatened City: A Report on the Design of the City of New York by the Mayor's Task Force* (New York, 1967).

27. *Euclid,* at 391.

28. Jane Jacobs, *The Death and Life of Great American Cities* (New York, N.Y.: Vintage Books, 1963).

29. *Euclid,* at 388–389.

30. Id. at 394–395.

31. *Berman* v. *Parker,* 348 U.S. 26 (1954), and James Ford, *Slums and Housing* (Cambridge, Mass.: Harvard University Press, 1936).

32. *Report of the Heights of Buildings Commission,* pp. 242–243.

33. 297 F. at 316.

34. *Report of the Heights of Buildings Commission,* p. 58

35. Michael Kwartler and Raymond Masters, "Daylighting as a Zoning Device for Midtown," *Energy and Buildings* 6 (1984): 181–184.

36. Paul Goldberger, "On the Rise," *New York Times,* 1983, p.3.

37. Le Corbusier, *Oeuvre Complet 1910–1929* (Zurich: Editions Ginsberger, 1937), pp. 109–119.

38. Bernard Siegan, *Land Use Without Zoning* (Lexington, Mass.: D.C. Heath and Co., 1972); *see* Chapter 7, "Publishers, Pop Architecture and Minorities."

39. Der Scutt, "Letter to the Editor," *Oculus,* February 1981, p.3; and Andrew Stein, "Hearing on Midtown Development," July 17, 1979, comments by Donald Elliot, p. 6.

40. Norman Marcus and Marilyn Groves, eds., *The New Zoning* (New York, N.Y.: Praeger, 1970), pp. xvi–xxii.

41. Ibid.

42. Clifford L. Weaver and Richard F. Babcock, *City Zoning: The Once and Future Frontier* (Chicago, Ill.: Planners Press, 1979), p. 14.

43. Kwartler/Jones and Davis, Brody and Associates, *Zoning Regulations Study; Midtown Development Project—Final Draft* (New York, N.Y.: June 1980), pp. A30 and A107.

44. New York City Zoning Resolution, Section 12–10.

45. New York City Zoning Resolution, Section 74–72.

46. Morrison Hershfield Limited, *Pedestrian Level Wind Assessment on Lincoln West Development,* June 1984.

47. John Costonis, "Law and Aesthetics: A Critique and Reformation of the Dilemmas," *Michigan Law Review* (January, 1982), p. 356.

48. Midtown Development Study Task Force Meeting, June 26, 1979, and memorandum to Richard Bernstein from Norman Marcus, June 27, 1979.

49. Charles Reiss and Michael Kwartler, "Housing Quality Zoning Puts Human Scale into Residential Zoning," *Planners Notebook,* vol. 4, no. 6 (December, 1974).

50. Weaver and Babcock, *City Zoning,* p. 298.

51. Christopher Alexander, *Notes on the Synthesis of Form,* (Cambridge, Mass.: Harvard University Press, 1964), Chapter 5, "The Self-Conscious Process."

52. Barnett, *Introduction to Urban Design,* p. 222.

53. Jane Jacobs, *The Death and Life of Great American Cities,* pp. 103–104.

54. Jacob Ukeles, *The Consequences of Municipal Zoning* (Washington, D.C.: Urban Land Institute, 1964) p.22.

55. Costonis, "Law and Aesthetics," pp. 360–361.

56. New York City Planning Commission, *Plan for the City of New York* (Cambridge, Mass.: MIT Press, 1973).

57. Weaver and Babcock, *City Zoning,* p. 261.

58. Ibid, p. 264.

Zoning and the Courts: A Steady Legal Legacy?

Some of the most interesting writing about zoning is found in the numerous judicial opinions about it. In the state courts, the arguments are frequently about interpretation of words in a local ordinance or whether the local ordinance exceeds the boundaries set forth in state enabling legislation. The judicial literature of zoning is richest, however, in its consideration and discussion of the essential balance between public and private rights, framed against the ambiguous yet majestic phrases found in federal and state constitutions. And, over time, the judicial mark on the substance of zoning has been as pronounced as that imprinted by legislative and executive bodies. Whether providing a definition for statutory "uniform district" requirements, or interpreting the meaning of "equal protection" in the context of a system that inherently differentiates between landowners, the courts have done far more than fill the interstices.

Landowners regularly invoke "due process," "equal protection," and "taking" to bolster their constitutional challenges to zoning. At base, these claims reduce to arguments about fairness: Is it fair for the government to infringe upon private property rights to protect the public interest? Is it fair for the government to ask *this* landowner to bear burdens to benefit the public? Judges ultimately answer these questions, not according to any fixed constellation of formulas, but by relying

on common sense honed by years of decision making in individual fact patterns.

In Chapter 8, "Judges as Planners: Limited or General Partners?", Jerold Kayden describes the traditional role of judges in reviewing local planning and zoning, and explains why the U.S. Supreme Court's 1987 *Nollan* v. *California Coastal Commission* decision may dramatically expand that role. Tracing its lineage back to *Village of Euclid* v. *Ambler Realty Co.*, he argues that *Nollan's* attempt to deny its patrimony is flawed, and that the decision ultimately will be less influential than private property owners had hoped, and public officials had feared.

Michael Wolf, in Chapter 9, "The Prescience and Centrality of *Euclid* v. *Ambler*," explores what he calls the "four seeds" planted in *Euclid*—exclusion of uses and people, anticompetitiveness, local parochialism, and aestheticism. Too often, he concludes, these seeds have borne "poisonous fruit" in the application of zoning since *Euclid*, although some recent state court opinions have helped steer zoning in a beneficial direction.

In Chapter 10, *"Euclid's* Lochnerian Legacy," Robert Williams, Jr., sees the reemergence of Lochnerian analysis of land use regulations, and wonders aloud whether this spectre has enervated the Supreme Court's ability to provide predictability and stability in its land use decisions. "Lochnerian" derives from *Lochner,* the name of a Supreme Court case; but its significance is in describing the Supreme Court's constitutional adjudication in the 1920s and 1930s, when it repeatedly struck down social and economic legislation inconsistent with the Court's own substantive views of contract and property. In the late 1930s, the Court abandoned the so-called *Lochner* approach and has since upheld socioeconomic legislation as long as it is reasonably related to a legitimate state purpose. Williams characterizes many of the Court's recent land use decisions as deviating from this test and reviving the *Lochner* standard.

8

Judges as Planners: Limited or General Partners?

Jerold S. Kayden

Since the advent of zoning, and especially since the U.S. Supreme Court's 1926 *Village of Euclid* v. *Ambler Realty Co.*[1] decision, judges have played a distinct, but secondary, role in the planning and zoning of American communities. The primary responsibility for crafting and applying zoning resides with the executive and legislative branches of local government. They do the heavy lifting: assembling statistics, conducting background studies, evaluating physical conditions, checking demographic and market trends, sniffing out the politics, consulting affected interest groups, setting objectives, preparing plans and maps, drafting the language, and adopting or amending the ordinance. The judicial branch gets into the act only when zoning is challenged in court by an affected party, and only to determine that the heavy lifting seems reasonable. Countless state and federal court opinions stress the narrowness of judicial oversight of local zoning actions. The consensus is unequivocal: Judges are not super-planners, free to substitute their own views for those of local officials as to what constitutes good planning.

This 60-year-old settled doctrine of narrow judicial review has been called into question by a 1987 U.S. Supreme Court opinion, *Nollan* v. *California Coastal Commission.*[2] That case arguably requires judges to scrutinize more carefully the justifications offered by planners in support of land-use regulations abridging private property rights. Some commentators have anointed *Nollan* as a major victory for owners of private property, and a major setback for government land-use planning and regulation. Other observers bracket the case, claiming it has no applicability to typical land-use regulations such as zoning.

This chapter explores the central question of whether *Nollan* represents a tidal change in the direction and level of judicial involvement in planning and zoning decisions, or whether the opinion may be harmonized with settled doctrine. First, the chapter traces the guidelines for reviewing zoning that were set forth in *Euclid* and followed over the next 60 years by state and federal courts. Second, the chapter analyzes *Nollan* and compares it with the *Euclid* approach. Third, the chapter offers suggestions about the impact *Nollan* should have on judicial participation in local planning and zoning.

223

THE *EUCLID* STANDARD

Since *Euclid,* judges have subjected zoning to a remarkably consistent constitutional test whose essential touchstone is a lenient standard of reasonableness. The typical zoning dispute pits property owner against local government. Following the recommendation of local planners, a zoning board or city council will vote on text or map changes affecting the entire community or a specific area of it. Prevented from using land in a certain way, or upset over what is permitted on a nearby property, a landowner or neighbor will allege that the change violates at least one of three constitutional clauses: Due Process, Equal Protection, or Just Compensation.[3]

The plain words of these constitutional provisions provide little guidance to judges about how they should review local zoning actions. The Due Process Clause states that persons may not be deprived of property without "due process of law."[4] The Equal Protection Clause guarantees individuals "the equal protection of the laws."[5] The Just Compensation Clause commands, ". . . nor shall private property be taken for public use, without just compensation."[6] Forced to give practical content to these majestic but ambiguous phrases,[7] judges have developed operational tests to assess the constitutionality of zoning. Although zoning opinions have imbued each clause with a distinct personality, Due Process[8] and Equal Protection[9] nonetheless belong to one analytical family, while Just Compensation belongs to another. And, as opinions from *Euclid* to the present (excluding *Nollan*) make clear, it is Due Process and Equal Protection, not Just Compensation, that constitute the central pegs for judicial inquiry into the planning rationale for a zoning decision. In contrast, the Just Compensation Clause focuses predominantly on whether government regulation has effected a taking of private property through severe diminution of its value or through physical invasion by the public, without regard to how sensible the underlying planning rationale may be.

Because *Euclid* initiated judicial participation in planning and zoning and laid the groundwork for the basic Due Process-Equal Protection zoning test, it is worthwhile revisiting in some detail Justice Sutherland's opinion and thinking. Adopted in 1922, the zoning ordinance of Euclid, Ohio, divided the village into overlapping districts defined by use (U), height (H), and area (A) restrictions.[10] The U-1 district limited use of land primarily to single-family dwellings, while U-2 allowed two-family dwellings in addition to single-family, U-3 allowed apartment houses as well as U-1 and U-2 uses, U-4 extended to commercial uses, U-5 added warehouses and some light manufacturing, and U-6 permitted everything including heavy manufacturing.[11] The H-1 district limited buildings to two-and-one-half stories or 35 feet, H-2 to four stories or 50 feet, and H-3 to 80 feet.[12] The four area districts (A-1 to A-4) set forth minimum lot size requirements per dwelling unit, as well as rules regarding lot widths, front, side, and rear yards, and the like.[13] In sum, the Euclid zoning ordinance of the 1920s was not markedly different from many ordinances still in effect today.

Ambler Realty Company owned 68 acres of land in Euclid.[14] As mapped, the village's zoning restricted much of Ambler's property to U-2 (single- and two-family dwellings) and U-3 (apartments).[15] Claiming that the land was most suited for industrial use, and that the residential restriction caused a substantial financial loss,[16] Ambler attacked the ordinance as a deprivation of liberty and property without due process, and as a denial of equal protection.[17] The *Euclid* opinion made no reference to the Just Compensation Clause at all.

In a six-to-three vote, the Court upheld the basic constitutionality of zoning against Ambler's facial challenge, even as it left for another day the resolution of individual challenges to zoning's impact on specific parcels of property.[18] Comforted by the view that, in its use districting and especially in its exclusion of industry from residential areas, zoning merely systematized the common law of nuisance, the Court could conclude that landowners were not really losing any property right to which they were previously entitled.[19]

Although the Court made several linguistic passes at the Due Process-Equal Protection zoning standard for judicial review, one key passage has influenced generations of subsequent land-use decisions and deserves full quotation:

> If *these reasons,* thus summarized, do not demonstrate the wisdom or sound policy in all respects of those restrictions which we have indicated as pertinent to the inquiry, at least, *the reasons* are sufficiently cogent to preclude us from saying, as it must be said before the ordinance can be declared unconstitutional, that *such provisions are clearly arbitrary and unreasonable, having no substantial relation to the public health, safety, morals, or general welfare.*[20]

Taken together, the linguistic formulations of "clearly arbitrary and unreasonable" and "no substantial relation to the public health, safety, morals, or general welfare" suggest two basic requirements for constitutional zoning under Due Process and Equal Protection. First, zoning must promote goals related to or identifiable as health, safety, morals, or general welfare (an "ends" question).[21] Second, zoning must promote these goals in ways that may result in their achievement (a "means" question). The true rigor of the Court's formulations cannot be ascertained, however, from

their phraseology. For example, the bare words do not reveal just how "substantial" the "relation" must be between zoning and the "public health, safety, morals, or general welfare," or for that matter what constitutes "clearly arbitrary and unreasonable" zoning.

In the word game of judicial writing, meaning frequently springs from concrete application in a specific context. In this case, illumination about the character of these formulations—and thus about the judicial role in planning and zoning—must be sought from an evaluation of the planning rationales actually relied upon by Justice Sutherland and his brethren in upholding Euclid's ordinance. A review of such rationales suggests an undemanding legal standard, an accommodating and deferential attitude toward local exercise of zoning, and a restrained judicial role.

Without evident independent analysis or discussion, the Court accepted the conclusions of commissions and experts (described in "Brandeis brief" fashion by appellant Euclid and amicus), and the emerging state court trend, that zoning was a reasonable exercise of public power.[22] To justify the salient feature of Euclid's ordinance—its segregation of residential, business, and industrial uses—the Court cited five rationales. *First,* zoning makes for "easier" deployment of appropriate fire apparatus.[23] *Second,* zoning promotes increased safety and security for home life.[24] *Third,* zoning decreases street accidents, especially involving children, through reductions in traffic and its resulting confusion.[25] *Fourth,* zoning decreases noise and other conditions "which produce or intensify nervous disorders."[26] *Fifth,* zoning preserves a more favorable environment in which to rear children.[27]

Treating the exclusion of apartment buildings from single- and two-family residential districts as a separate issue, the Court cited four additional rationales. *First,* apartment buildings discourage development of detached houses, and may thereby destroy an entire single-family neighborhood.[28] *Second,* an apartment building is a "mere parasite," taking advantage of open spaces and attractive surroundings.[29] *Third,* one apartment building breeds others, creating greater interference with light and air for the detached homes and bringing noise and traffic especially harmful to children.[30] *Fourth,* apartment buildings destroy residential character and desirability.[31]

Of course, care must be taken in examining *post hoc* the planning arguments made 60 years ago in support of zoning. Reasons seen as sensible then may no longer hold validity. That said, it should be noted that, if none of these planning rationales is foolish, they are hardly the stuff of compelling logic. The proffered reasons were meant to show two things: Zoning's goals fall within the ambit of the police power quartet of health, safety, morals, or general welfare, and zoning's specific hallmark mechanism of exclusive use districts rationally advances those goals. As to the first, while some of the goals cited by the Court (decreasing street accidents and noise, for example) are unambiguously identifiable as traditional health and safety goals, others (preserving exclusive single-family neighborhoods) are only tangentially related, if at all. Indeed, through the lenses of today's glasses, protecting single-family homes demonstrates a perverse bias for "haves" against "have-nots" (an inverted though historically unsurprising social and economic order preference), and if anything represents special, not general, welfare. The "mere parasite" metaphor causes modern-day opponents of exclusionary zoning to wince.

The Court was equally tolerant in its review of zoning's ability to accomplish the articulated goals. No one can dispute that zoning may advance the goal of fire safety. However, it is not hard to imagine more direct, more effective, and less involved strategies than zoning's total reordering of land-use patterns to fit fire-fighting needs (a strategy best analogized to the tail wagging the dog).[32] By the same token, traffic management approaches creating limited access streets (restricting truck traffic in residential neighborhoods) could equally well address problems of noise and safety.

Together, what these reasons amplify is the leniency of the Due Process-Equal Protection test for local exercises of zoning. Clearly, these are hardly the most compelling goals or the most effective methods, and that's the point. At base, the *Euclid* message to judges is simple: Do not substitute your views of planning for those of appointed and elected officials accountable through ballot-box democracy to the public. Absent some glaring irrationality or patently improper government purpose,[33] zoning is to be judged no differently than other exercises of the police power,[34] and thus is to be approved in almost all cases.

The *Euclid* opinion contains additional linguistic support for interpreting the "clearly arbitrary and unreasonable" and "substantial relation" formulations as adumbrating a lenient standard of judicial review. The Court repeated the familiar rule that, "if the validity of the legislative classification for zoning purposes be *fairly debatable,* the legislative judgment must be allowed to control."[35] Highlighting the "decided trend" of state courts,[36] the majority described their broad conclusion that excluding business uses from residential districts "bears a *rational relation* to the health and safety of the community."[37] The majority also quoted from a Louisiana Supreme Court opinion:

"If the municipal council deemed any of the reasons which have been suggested, or any other substantial reason for adopting the ordinance in question, a sufficient reason for adopting the ordinance in question, it is not the province of the courts to take issue with the council. We have nothing to do with the question of the wisdom or good policy of municipal ordinances. If they are not satisfying to a majority of the citizens, their recourse is to the ballot—not the courts."[38]

POST-*EUCLID* JURISPRUDENCE

In one grand gesture, the Supreme Court had resolved both the basic constitutionality of zoning and the judicial role in assessing planning and zoning justifications. As if to emphasize the completeness of its resolution, the Court (after a brief flurry of three opinions written by Justice Sutherland in 1927 and 1928)[39] delivered just one traditional zoning-style opinion over the next 50 years.[40] If *Euclid's* easy standard of review was ever in doubt, however, the 1927 and 1928 cases cemented its meaning.

In *Zahn* v. *Board of Public Works,*[41] a landowner challenged under Due Process and Equal Protection the application of Los Angeles's zoning that restricted its land to residential, not business, uses.[42] With the equivalent of a legal fly swatter, the Court, unanimously per Justice Sutherland, brushed aside this claim: "[I]t is impossible for us to say that [the city council's decision to zone the land residential] was clearly arbitrary and unreasonable. The most that can be said is that whether that determination was an unreasonable, arbitrary or unequal exercise of power is fairly debatable."[43] Thus, concluded the Justice, "In such circumstances, the settled rule of this court is that it will not substitute its judgment for that of the legislative body charged with the primary duty and responsibility of determining the question."[44]

Justice Sutherland's unanimous opinion in *Gorieb* v. *Fox*[45] was no different. There, the Court analyzed a Roanoke, Virginia, ordinance establishing setback distances from the street for placement of buildings on lots. Wanting to build up to the street line, a property owner attacked the ordinance under the Due Process Clause.[46] In upholding the ordinance, Justice Sutherland expressly relied on the same mode of analysis that he applied in *Euclid* and *Zahn*. Quoting verbatim his *Euclid* "substantial relation" formulation,[47] he once more observed that "[s]tate legislatures and city councils . . . are better qualified than the courts to determine" the need for such regulations, and that their conclusions should be upheld unless "clearly arbitrary and unreasonable."[48] He accepted the city council's justifications for its ordinance, justifications no different in quality and weight from those accepted in *Euclid.*[49] And he observed that lower court decisions on setback rules had been divided between those concluding that such laws "have no *rational* relation to the public safety, health, morals, or general welfare" and those finding that they had a rational relation, the position that Justice Sutherland herein adopted.[50]

Although the *Nectow* v. *City of Cambridge*[51] opinion (the fourth and final Justice Sutherland zoning opinion) overturned a local zoning decision, the *Euclid* standard was nonetheless reiterated in slightly different language. Here, one part of the landowner's parcel was restricted to residential uses, while the rest of it, and much of the surrounding land, was zoned business and industrial.[52] The landowner attacked the zoning under the Due Process Clause.[53] A master, confirmed by a judge, found, " 'I am satisfied that the districting of the plaintiff's land in a residence district would not promote the health, safety, convenience and general welfare of the inhabitants of that part of the defendant City, taking into account the natural development thereof and the character of the district and the resulting benefit to accrue to the whole City and I so find.' "[54]

Justice Sutherland expressly agreed with the lower court's formulation (linguistic differences notwithstanding) of his *Euclid* test: A zoning action must be upheld unless it " 'has no foundation in reason and is a mere arbitrary or irrational exercise of power having no substantial relation to the public health, the public morals, the public safety or the public welfare in its proper sense.' "[55] Thus, concluded the Justice, the express finding of the master that there was no such substantial relation to the police power quartet was "determinative of the case."[56]

Since *Euclid, Zahn, Gorieb,* and *Nectow,* zoning litigation under the Due Process and Equal Protection Clauses has become the province of state courts, with sometime forays by lower federal courts as well. Judges dutifully apply *Euclid's* "clearly arbitrary and unreasonable"-"substantial relation" test, even as they embellish it slightly with their own linguistic contributions. They continue to make two basic inquiries about the zoning at issue: Is the public purpose underlying it *legitimate,* and is the zoning a *reasonable* way to achieve that legitimate purpose? Thus, a map amendment whose sole purpose is to enable the proverbial mayor's brother-in-law to develop a more profitable office building would obviously fail the legitimacy test. A zoning measure meant to encourage open space, but which on its face and under all imaginable circumstances promotes greater development, would be an irrational way to achieve the purported open space purpose. The test tracks the prevailing Due Process-Equal Protection standard applied to all socioeconomic legislation and is commonly referred to as the "minimum scrutiny" test, because judges need only minimally scrutinize the reasoning behind legislation (as distinct from "strict scrutiny," where impingements of fundamental interests or suspect classes trigger the need to strictly scrutinize legislation).[57]

Culled from thousands of state and lower federal court opinions, land-use lawyers and planners can rattle off the legal boilerplate defining Due Process-Equal Protection judicial review of zoning in their sleep. Every presumption is to be made in favor of an ordinance's validity.[58] If its reasonableness is fairly debatable, then the judgment of the local legislative body must be sustained.[59] The burden is upon the challenging party to prove beyond a reasonable doubt that the zoning is invalid.[60] The zoning must be upheld unless it is without any rational,[61] reasonable,[62] conceivable,[63] or similarly described basis related to the public interest.[64] Whether the zoning authority in fact relied upon such basis in reaching its decision (or even whether or not such basis was argued at trial or on appeal) is irrelevant: If a justification is rational, then judges are precluded from lifting the veil shrouding the zoning decision to examine the motives of legislators.[65] Adding up the tests, zoning is presumed valid and will not be struck down unless the challenger proves beyond a reasonable doubt that it is not even fairly debatable that there is a conceivably rational basis for the zoning.[66] This is why judges look with a jaundiced eye at challenges to the planning justifications for a zoning action: One federal appeals court recently disparaged the case before it as "a garden-variety zoning dispute dressed up in the trappings of constitutional law."[67]

ENTER *NOLLAN*

At first glance, the Supreme Court's 1987 decision in *Nollan* v. *California Coastal Commission*[68] should have nothing to do with *Euclid* and progeny. *Nollan* involved a public physical invasion of private property authorized by a governmental agency, not a traditional zoning or similar land-use regulatory restriction. Furthermore, the Court decided the case under the Just Compensation, not the Due Process or Equal Protection, clause. Nonetheless, in language and in tone, the Court lobbed a bombshell into the field of land-use planning and zoning. Loaded principally in a footnote (recalling, albeit on a much lesser scale, that most famous of all Supreme Court footnotes, Footnote Four, from the 1938 *United States* v. *Carolene Products Co.* decision[69]), the bombshell is the notion that the time-honored *Euclid* standard of lenient judicial review of zoning (and other land-use regulations) is, has been, or should be, tougher.[70]

In its five-to-four majority opinion written by Justice Scalia,[71] the Court appears to command judges to ratchet up their level of scrutiny, and thus their level of participation, in the planning and zoning of American communities. The questions raised by the *Nollan* decision are manifold. Are land-use regulations abridging private property rights now meant to receive the same "intermediate scrutiny," a standard somewhere between minimum and strict scrutiny, that judges apply in cases of sex discrimination?[72] Has private property moved out of the rain and under that judicially defined umbrella protecting such Bill of Rights fundamental interests as speech, press, and religion? Does *Nollan* mean what it appears to say, and, even if it does, is it correct? In sum, should it be understood by judges, city planners, and landowners as fundamentally changing the legal landscape in which they operate?

The facts of the case are central to answering these questions, and to an evaluation of *Nollan's* ultimate impact. Mr. and Mrs. Nollan leased, with an option to buy, a small beachfront lot north of Los Angeles.[73] Most of the lot, anchored by a seawall, sat eight feet above

the beach.[74] The Nollans' existing 504 square foot bungalow, which they rented out to summer tenants, had seriously deteriorated to a point of uninhabitability.[75] Wanting to replace the bungalow with a new 1,674 square foot, three-bedroom house and attached two-car garage,[76] the Nollans applied to the California Coastal Commission, a state land-use regulatory authority, for a permit to demolish the bungalow and build their new house.[77] Under state law, a permit was required for all development, including the Nollans' replacement house, along the California coast.[78]

The Commission granted the permit, but subject to the condition that the Nollans provide a lateral access easement that would allow the public to walk north and south on the Nollans' private beach in front of their proposed house.[79] Since, under California law, the public owned the area up to the mean high tide line, the public at low tide could already proceed on dry sand up and down the coast without trespassing on the Nollans' beach. In the absence of the proposed easement condition, however, only swimmers would be able to proceed north and south at high tide. The Commission's permit condition solved the problem by converting from private to public a beach pathway some 10 feet in width running east of the high tide line all the way to the Nollans' seawall.[80] Individuals thus would be able to walk unimpeded along the coast between two public beaches, one-quarter mile to the north and one-third mile to the south of the Nollan property.[81]

In support of the proposed permit condition, the Commission made a number of factual findings. It found, for example, that the Nollans' replacement house would contribute to "a 'wall' of residential structures" preventing people "psychologically . . . from realizing a stretch of coastline exists nearby that they have every right to visit."[82] It also found that the house would result in increased private use of the coast which, along with other existing and proposed coastal developments, would "burden the public's ability to traverse to and along the shorefront."[83] Of the 60 other coastline developments approved in recent times, the Commission had imposed a similar lateral access condition on 43 of them.[84] Fourteen other developments had previously been approved without conditions, at a time when the Commission lacked administrative authority to impose them.[85]

The Nollans sued the Commission in a California trial court, alleging that imposition of the condition effected a taking of their property for public use without payment of just compensation, in violation of the Fifth Amendment's Just Compensation Clause.[86] Although the trial court ruled in favor of the Nollans, it based its decision on state law nonconstitutional grounds.[87] During the time the Commission appealed the trial court decision, the Nollans built their new house and purchased their property outright, without agreeing to or granting the lateral access easement.[88]

The intermediate state appellate court reversed the trial court and found for the Commission.[89] Among other things, it concluded that there was a sufficient relationship between the harm to public beach access created by the new house on the one hand, and the Commission's lateral access condition on the other, to justify the condition, even if the Nollans' new house alone had not created a need for additional beach access.[90]

The Court's Analysis

Reversing the California appellate court, the U.S. Supreme Court struck down the easement condition as a taking of private property in violation of the Just Compensation Clause.[91] Because this was a decision involving the Just Compensation, not the Due Process or Equal Protection, clause, one would expect the analysis to vary from the *Euclid* model. Indeed, the starting point for the Court's discussion implicitly recognized one significant difference relating to the nature of the land-use restriction under attack. Justice Scalia observed that the Commission could not have required *ex cathedra* the Nollans, continuing with their existing bungalow use, to provide the public easement, because that would constitute a " 'permanent physical occupation' " of private property by the public, the most extreme violation of settled takings law.[92] It would take from the Nollans, without compensation, one of the most essential sticks—the right to exclude others—from that bundle of rights known as private property. Thus, the "question becomes whether requiring [the easement] to be conveyed as a condition of issuing a land use permit" alters the analysis and the outcome.[93]

To answer this determinative question, the Court adopted and applied a constitutional test similar in wording and logic to *Euclid's* "*substantial relation* to health, safety, morals, or general welfare" test, namely that land-use conditions must "*substantially advance* legitimate state interests" in order to pass constitutional muster.[94] Thus, the Court employed the familiar two-part inquiry, asking whether the Commission's goals were legitimate (identifiable as members of the health, safety, morals, or general welfare quartet), and whether such goals were advanced by the condition.

As to the first, the majority simply assumed, without deciding, that the Commission's three asserted purposes—"protecting the public's ability to see the beach," "assisting the public in overcoming the 'psychological barrier' to using the beach created by a developed shorefront," and "preventing congestion on the public beaches," were legitimate.[95] Undoubtedly, Justice Scalia was willing to take this classic lawyer's "assuming arguendo" tack because he knew the condition would fail the second part of the test.[96]

Under that second part, the Court found that the Commission's asserted goal of preserving *visual* access to the beach was not advanced by the north-to-south *lateral* access condition.[97] The majority commenced its line of logic by asking whether the Commission could ban construction of the new house altogether. Given the assumed legitimate purposes, reasoned the Court, the Commission "unquestionably would be able to deny the Nollans their permit outright if their new house (alone, or by reason of the cumulative impact produced in conjunction with other construction) would *substantially impede* these purposes, unless the denial would interfere so drastically with the Nollans' use of their property as to constitute a taking."[98] Thus, concluded the majority, conditions serving the same legitimate purposes as those advanced by forbidding new construction altogether would by definition be constitutional.[99] And from the property owner's point of view, the conditions approach (as opposed to the ban) would at least allow for achievement of the primary objective of building the house. The Court enumerated three examples of acceptable conditions related to the goal of view protection: height and width limitations on the new house, a fence ban, and a "viewing spot" (a physical invasion) for the public located literally on the Nollans' private property.[100]

Having set the stage, the Court discounted any relationship whatsoever between the lateral access easement condition and the Commission's asserted goals:

> It is quite impossible to understand how a requirement that people already on the public beaches be able to walk across the Nollans' property reduces any obstacles to viewing the beach created by the new house. It is also im-

possible to understand how it lowers any 'psychological barrier' to using the public beaches, or how it helps to remedy any additional congestion on them caused by construction of the Nollans' new house.[101]

Classifying the Analysis

If this was the whole of *Nollan,* then all the fuss would be anticlimactic. No one—not the four dissenting justices in *Nollan,* not Justice Sutherland, not state and lower federal judges, and not land-use planners and lawyers—would disagree with the majority's overall constitutional theory that regulatory requirements imposed upon the Nollans must bear *some* relationship to a legitimate public goal whose realization was threatened by the Nollans' proposed new house. In *Euclid* itself, after all, it was Ambler Realty Company's (and other's) potential industrial use of property that threatened achievement of the village's legitimate public goal of safe and prosperous residential neighborhoods. Zoning's central mechanism of segregating nuisance-like activities from residential areas represented a reasonable way to advance that public goal.

There would be, and indeed was, disagreement over the *Nollan* majority's factual conclusion that there was absolutely no relationship. In his short dissent, Justice Blackmun lamented what he called the majority's " 'eye for an eye' mentality."[102] No one will accuse the Court of a comprehensive exploration of the Commission's position. The majority's predominant focus on the view blockage justification—the weakest of the three—demonstrates the power of a reviewing court to define the issue and predetermine the outcome. Surely one can question the Court's hypertechnical finding of no relationship, at least as to the congestion concern. After all, the Commission found specifically that the house, along with other developments, would result in increased private use of the shorefront.[103] And since the Nollans were replacing a small bungalow with a three-bedroom house, it is not exactly "impossible to understand" how that might be expected to generate more congestion on the public beaches north and south of their house. An easement along their beachfront would ensure easy access from one beach to the other in case one became overcrowded.

In dissent, Justice Brennan disagreed with the majority even on the visual access goal, claiming that loss of visual access *was* mitigated by the easement condition.[104] His assertion, however, that view blockage from "a phalanx of imposing permanent residences, including the [Nollans'] new home," would be reduced if people on the road and public beaches could see people walking along the coastline,[105] failed to blunt the majority's principal contention that view blockage *inherently* prevented people on the road from *seeing* the beach at all, let alone seeing people walking along it.[106]

Inventing A Heightened "Substantial" Standard: Nollan's Footnote Three

At bottom, the majority's factual conclusion of no relationship between the easement condition and the visual access goal is defensible, if not decisively so, and thus need not be read as undercutting the lenient standard of judicial review first established in *Euclid* and parroted by numerous state and lower federal court cases. Instead, it is completely superfluous language in *Nollan,* principally lodged in Footnote Three, that causes the major reverberations. As discussed earlier,[107] no land-use planner or lawyer ever imagined that the word "substantial," originally introduced vis à vis zoning in Justice Sutherland's *Euclid* opinion,[108] stood for a higher standard of review than that suggested by the words "conceivable," "reasonable," or "rational," adjectives used interchangeably in opinions of the U.S. Supreme

Court and lower courts to describe the necessary relation between means and ends.[109] Thus, *Nollan's* Footnote Three is worth quoting in full:

> Contrary to Justice Brennan's claim [in his dissent], our opinions do not establish that these standards [applied to Just Compensation Clause claims] are the same as those applied to due process or equal-protection claims. To the contrary, our verbal formulations in the takings field have generally been quite different. We have required that the regulation 'substantially advance' the 'legitimate state interest' sought to be achieved, *Agins* v. *Tiburon,* 447 U.S. 255, 260 (1980), not that 'the State *"could rationally have decided"* the measure adopted might achieve the State's objective.' [quoting Brennan dissent] quoting *Minnesota* v. *Clover Leaf Creamery Co.,* 449 U.S. 456, 466 (1981). Justice Brennan relies principally on an equal protection case, *Minnesota* v. *Clover Leaf Creamery Co., supra,* and two substantive due process cases, *Williamson* v. *Lee Optical of Oklahoma, Inc.,* 348 U.S. 483, 487–488 (1955)[,] and *Day-Brite Lighting, Inc.* v. *Missouri,* 342 U.S. 421, 423 (1952), in support of the standards he would adopt. But there is no reason to believe (and the language of our cases gives some reason to disbelieve) that so long as the regulation of property is at issue the standards for takings challenges, due process challenges, and equal protection challenges are identical; any more than there is any reason to believe that so long as the regulation of speech is at issue the standards for due process challenges, equal protection challenges, and First Amendment challenges are identical. *Goldblatt* v. *Hempstead,* 369 U.S. 590 (1962), does appear to assume that the inquiries are the same, but that assumption is inconsistent with the formulation of our later cases.[110]

The majority's earth-shaking conclusion

that the Just Compensation (sometimes called the Takings) Clause has always demanded an effectively *higher* level of judicial scrutiny into the relationship between means and ends is, simply put, based upon shoddy scholarship and misguided analysis. Straightforward legal detective work belies any claim that the verbal formulation "substantially advance a legitimate state interest" is any different than the verbal formulation used to describe the Due Process-Equal Protection standard applied to land-use cases. The "substantially advance a legitimate state interest" phrase is not only linguistically similar on its face to *Euclid's* "substantial relation to health, safety, morals, or general welfare," but not surprisingly is *directly traceable* to *Euclid* (a Due Process-Equal Protection, not a Just Compensation, case), via *Nectow* (a Due Process case).

Let's do the tracing. Justice Scalia correctly cited *Agins* v. *City of Tiburon*,[111] which announced a two-pronged disjunctive test for Just Compensation Clause analysis:[112] "The application of a general zoning law to particular property effects a taking if the ordinance does not substantially advance legitimate state interests, see *Nectow* v. *Cambridge*, 277 U.S. 183, 188 (1928), or denies an owner economically viable use of his land [citing *Penn Central*]."[113] Unfortunately, that is apparently the full extent of his research, making his claim that "the language of our *cases* gives some reason to disbelieve" ring disingenuously hollow. Had he pressed on—and the sweeping nature and future significance of his footnote made it incumbent upon him to do so—he would have realized that *Agins* itself (ironically a unanimous decision[114]) was based upon a false premise. *Agins* relied on *Nectow*—a Due Process, not a Just Compensation, case—as the exclusive source of its first prong, thereby mixing Due Process-Equal Protection apples with Just Compensation oranges. Indeed, the page in the

Nectow opinion to which *Agins* referred quoted *Euclid's* original "substantial relation" Due Process-Equal Protection zoning test.[115]

The circle is complete: As much as it may want to deny its patrimony, *Nollan* is a direct descendant of *Euclid*, via *Nectow* and *Agins*. Thus, there is no reason to believe—and Justice Scalia substituted bald assertion for precedential or logical evidence—that the word "substantial" means something different than what it meant in *Euclid, Nectow,* and every other state and federal zoning case issued in the intervening 60 years. Without rehashing earlier parts of this chapter,[116] it is clear that "substantial" is interchangeable with the other usual suspect adjectives of reasonable, rational, conceivable, and the like.[117] That is why *Penn Central Transportation Co.* v. *New York City*,[118] that landmark Supreme Court Just Compensation opinion upholding New York City's historic preservation law and saving Grand Central Terminal, could so easily say, "When a property owner challenges the application of a zoning ordinance to his property, the judicial inquiry focuses upon whether the challenged restriction can *reasonably* be deemed to promote the objectives of the community land-use plan . . . ."[119]

In dissent, Justice Brennan provided an additional argument against Footnote Three. In his own Footnote One, he invoked an entire line of Due Process-Equal Protection cases involving government regulation of private economic activities to demonstrate that, while the Court's "phraseology may differ slightly from case to case . . . [t]hese minor differences cannot, however, obscure the fact that the inquiry in each case is the same."[120] Justice Brennan commented that the majority's "narrow conception of rationality . . . has long since been discredited as a judicial arrogation of legislative authority."[121] The discrediting to which he referred occurred in the 1930s, when the

Court ended the so-called *Lochner*[122] era (named after a case), during which it routinely applied a heightened standard of review to strike down social and economic regulatory laws.[123]

Justice Brennan's citation of Due Process-Equal Protection cases (*Clover Leaf Creamery, Williamson, Day-Brite Lighting*) allowed Justice Scalia to introduce a red herring: to wit, that the three cases were not decided under the Just Compensation Clause. He is, of course, correct that they were not, but it does not follow *a fortiori* that the cases are inapposite. If the Just Compensation Clause is to be used to review the propensity of a government regulation to advance the public interest (a proposition to be examined later in this chapter[124]), there is nothing in the Clause, or in cases interpreting it, that implies that the "substantial relation"-"substantial advancing" standard should differ from that employed by the other clauses. Indeed, if one is to attribute any significance whatsoever to *Agins's* slight linguistic variation ("substantially advance a legitimate state interest") on the *Euclid-Nectow* "substantial relation to health, safety, morals, or general welfare" theme,[125] it suggests a partial borrowing ("legitimate interest") from the very formulation routinely used by modern Due Process-Equal Protection cases (including *Clover Leaf Creamery* and *Day-Brite Lighting*) that Justice Scalia rejected.[126]

Not unexpectedly, Justice Scalia was forced to disavow the nettlesome *Goldblatt* v. *Town of Hempstead*,[127] a Just Compensation case, precisely because it repeatedly relied on the basic approach of these Due Process-Equal Protection cases to articulate the appropriate standard (reasonableness) for reviewing planning justifications underlying the regulation of private property. Justice Scalia could only dispose of *Goldblatt* by disapproving it.[128]

Equally troubling to the majority position

is a Supreme Court case it failed to mention, the 1984 *Hawaii Housing Authority* v. *Midkiff*.[129] There, the Court decided that exercise of a government's power of eminent domain to break up large land estates, in order to eliminate market evils associated with land oligopoly, constituted a "public use" within the meaning of the Just Compensation Clause.[130] In determining the meaning of "public use" ("nor shall private property be taken for *public use*, without just compensation"), the Court explicitly found that public use and the constitutional requirements for exercise of the police power were "coterminous."[131] The Court then referred to *Clover Leaf Creamery* and other Due Process-Equal Protection cases—the very cases Justice Scalia asserted were irrelevant—to define the correct standard.[132] In unambiguous and familiar language, the *Midkiff* opinion announced, "When the legislature's purpose is legitimate and its means are not irrational, our cases make clear that empirical debates over the wisdom of takings—no less than debates over the wisdom of other kinds of socioeconomic legislation—are not to be carried out in the federal courts."[133] The Court upheld the Hawaiian statute because its purpose was legitimate and its means not irrational.

The apparent inconsistency of *Nollan* with *Midkiff* yields a bizarre, and plainly unintended, repercussion. If *Nollan's* heightened standard for reviewing exercises of the police power is to be taken seriously, then it also alters and heightens *Midkiff's* own "public use" test for exercises of the eminent domain power.[134] That peculiar boomerang occurs because *Midkiff* makes its definition of the "public use" limitation coterminous with the definition of the police power limitation. Changing one—and *Nollan* is the condition subsequent as *Midkiff's* chronological successor—changes the other. This unanticipated impact additionally illustrates the analytical tenuity of Justice Scalia's declarations.

Due Process-Equal Protection Versus Just Compensation Analysis

As demonstrated earlier in this chapter,[135] the tracing of roots for the "substantial advancing" test reveals its Due Process-Equal Protection origins. Until *Nollan* (and its promotion of *Agins's* disjunctive formulation to the big leagues), Just Compensation, as distinct from Due Process and Equal Protection, inquiry focused primarily, although not exclusively, on whether land-use regulations denied an owner economically viable use of property (the second prong of *Agins*) or authorized something resembling a physical appropriation of property by the public (such as a physical occupation), *without regard to the means-ends reasonableness of the regulation.*[136] Showing that the public purpose was illegitimate, or that the chosen regulation was an irrational way to achieve that purpose, was thought insufficient, standing alone, to prove a Just Compensation violation, although adequate to offend Due Process or Equal Protection. Indeed, a brief discussion in Justice Brennan's well-known *San Diego Gas & Electric Co.* v. *City of San Diego*[137] dissent underscored this very point. In a footnote, he speculated that a police power regulation not enacted in furtherance of health, safety, morals, or general welfare (violating the first prong of *Agins*), and denying economic viability (violating the second prong), might paradoxically not offend the Just Compensation Clause precisely because the requisite "public use" purpose had *not* been established.[138] Conversely, an otherwise reasonable land-use regulation nonetheless would be judged a Just Compensation loser if it denied the landowner economically viable use or authorized a physical occupation. Even the disjunctive *Agins* formulation corroborated this view, since

breaching the second prong, standing alone, violated the Just Compensation Clause.

A private property rights Supreme Court decision announced less than a year after *Nollan* exemplifies the conventional analytical approaches taken under the three clauses. In *Pennell* v. *City of San Jose,*[139] the Court upheld, under Just Compensation, Due Process, and Equal Protection, the constitutionality of a municipal rent control ordinance authorizing local hearing officers to weigh economic hardship to individual tenants in deciding whether to grant rent increases to owners of rental property.[140] In its six-to-two majority opinion,[141] authored by Chief Justice Rehnquist, the Court never cited *Nollan* nor discussed its "substantial advancing" test. Instead, the majority's Just Compensation inquiry concluded that "it would be premature to consider" the takings claim, because there was no evidence that the tenant hardship provision had ever been applied, and the hearing officer was not required to reduce the rent in any given instance.[142]

It was none other (who better) than Justice Scalia, in a concurring and dissenting opinion,[143] who correctly took the majority to task for the inconsistency of its conclusion with his (and the Court's) *Nollan* analysis. Never mentioning that case by name (perhaps artfully trying to avoid any tarnishing of its standing), he used *Agins* instead and convincingly demonstrated that the first prong ("substantial advancing") of its disjunctive formulation—the very prong animated and applied by *Nollan*—was necessarily ripe for application here, even if the second prong ("economically viable use") was not. After all, the property owner's basic contention, that "providing financial assistance to impecunious renters is not a state interest that can legitimately be furthered by regulating the use of property," went to the heart of the ordinance and did not depend on whether or how the tenant hardship provision would be used by the hearing officer.[144] In a telling analogy, Justice Scalia posited, "Suppose, for example, that the feature of the rental ordinance under attack was a provision allowing a Hearing Officer to consider the race of the apartment owner in deciding whether to allow a rent increase. It is inconceivable that we would say judicial challenge must await demonstration that this provision has actually been applied to the detriment of one of the [landlords]."[145]

The majority went on to examine the facial validity of the tenant hardship provision under Due Process and Equal Protection.[146] Like *Euclid* and progeny, the *Pennell* opinion adopted a deferential standard of reasonableness to explore San Jose's chosen regulatory means and ends. For its Due Process discussion, the Court analogized the rent control ordinance to price controls, and noted that the general objective of preventing excessive rent increases was a "legitimate exercise of appellees' police powers."[147] Rejecting the landlord contention that the specific goal of alleviating individual tenant hardship was not a policy the legislature could adopt, the Court described how "we have long recognized that a legitimate and rational goal of price or rate regulations is the protection of consumer welfare."[148] Because the ordinance assured landlords at minimum reasonable rent increases, the Court could conclude that it "represents a rational attempt to accommodate the conflicting interests of protecting tenants from burdensome rent increases while at the same time ensuring that landlords are guaranteed a fair return on their investment."[149]

Under Equal Protection, the Court again applied the traditional lenient test to find no violation. Referring to its immediately preceding Due Process discussion, the majority commented, "Here again, the standard is deferen-

tial; appellees need only show that the classification scheme embodied in the Ordinance is 'rationally related to a legitimate state interest.' . . . As we stated [in a previous opinion], 'we will not overturn [a statute that does not burden a suspect class or a fundamental interest] unless the varying treatment of different groups or persons is so unrelated to the achievement of any combination of legitimate purposes that we can only conclude that the legislature's actions were irrational.' "[150] Thus, asserted the majority, "In light of our conclusion above that the Ordinance's tenant hardship provisions are designed to serve the legitimate purpose of protecting tenants, we can hardly conclude that it is irrational for the Ordinance to treat certain landlords differently on the basis of whether or not they have hardship tenants."[151]

Although *Agins* and now *Nollan* are the principal cases expressly merging Due Process-Equal Protection inquiry into Just Compensation analysis, it nonetheless would be overstatement to suggest that they alone are responsible for analytical murkiness. For example, as much as *Goldblatt* supported the lenient interpretation of the "substantial relation" standard, and as often as it cited Due Process and Equal Protection cases, *Goldblatt* was nominally a Just Compensation case that nonetheless explored means-ends reasonableness of an ordinance. Although *Penn Central's* well-known Just Compensation framework highlighted as relevant factors the "economic impact of the regulation on the claimant and, particularly, the extent to which the regulation has interfered with distinct investment-backed expectations," and the "character of the governmental action,"[152] the Court also noted in passing the railroad company's concession that the objective of New York City's landmarks law was "an entirely permissible governmental goal" and that the restrictions were "appropriate means of securing [its] purposes."[153] Even the grandparent of all Just Compensation Clause cases, *Pennsylvania Coal Co.* v. *Mahon,*[154] though stressing diminution of value as the central inquiry, slightly muddied the waters with its impressionistic balancing of public interest against private loss.[155] Notwithstanding any ambiguities, however, none of these cases (in contrast to *Nollan* and *Agins*) suggested that a finding of no substantial relation, standing alone, would be enough to trigger violation of the Just Compensation Clause.

Does the Constitutional Peg Make A Practical Difference?

Is this discussion of interest only to scholars and legal technicians, little more than cerebral exercise for the land-use cognoscenti? Is not the real issue whether a regulation violates the seamless Constitution, and not upon which peg to hang one's hat? When all is said and done, does it really matter whether analysis is conducted under the Just Compensation, the Due Process, or the Equal Protection Clause? The answer is that it can matter. In *Nollan,* Justice Scalia's claim of difference arising from his placement of "substantial advancing" within the Just Compensation rather than Due Process or Equal Protection clause is proof positive that theoretical debates have practical consequences. Intentionally or not, he uses this distinction without a difference to invest "substantial" with a new meaning, and thus to invent and authorize application of a higher standard of planning rationality review than that used under either Due Process and Equal Protection.

The *Nollan* version of the Just Compensation Clause has a perplexing practical implication as well: It brings the award of just compensation into play even when there is no physical invasion and the diminution of property value

is nonexistent or *de minimus.* Whatever else a landowner may be entitled to upon winning a Due Process or Equal Protection case,[156] he or she is not entitled to Fifth Amendment just compensation. *Nollan* effectively makes judicial review of planning rationality under Due Process and Equal Protection precatory, because whenever a regulation fails to advance, let alone substantially advance, a legitimate state interest, it *a priori* violates the Just Compensation Clause as well. As such, the compensation web is spun into action (especially since the Court's *First English*[157] decision requiring payment of compensation for the period of time the regulation effected a taking) for any and all land use cases alleging usual constitutional infirmities.

The facts in *Nollan* obscure the possible peculiarity of this result. In *Nollan,* the condition "extinguish[ed] a fundamental attribute of ownership,"[158] namely the right to exclude others from one's private property. Indeed, this is so fundamental a right that a 1982 Supreme Court decision found that a government regulation authorizing the running of a television cable (less than one-half inch thick, 30 feet in length, and 18 inches above the building roof) through private property constituted a *per se* taking, without regard to diminution of value.[159] Thus, in its factual posture, *Nollan* involved a traditional violation (physical occupation) of the Just Compensation Clause.

But imagine a different Commission-imposed condition, one that equally failed to substantially advance the Commission's goal of visual access but not involving physical occupation. For example, what if the Nollans were required to paint on the street side of their house an ocean scene populated with flying porpoises? What if the Commission required that the new house be made of concrete rather than wood? Surely such conditions would fail to advance the Commission's goal of visual access and thus would violate *Euclid's* Due Process-Equal Protection standard. Does it make sense that these conditions also violate the Just Compensation Clause, with its creaky compensation machinery clanging into gear to require payment for the period of time that these regulatory conditions effected the taking?[160] What if the flying porpoises or concrete construction actually increased the value of the house?[161]

Unmasking the Real Relationship in *Nollan*

As discussed above,[162] Justice Scalia's decision to analyze the easement condition under the Just Compensation Clause initially made sense because the Commission's condition authorized a physical invasion of private property. But another reason stems from the clause's fundamental purpose, recited time and again by the Court, "to bar Government from forcing some people alone to bear public burdens which, in all fairness and justice, should be borne by the public as a whole."[163] Thus, no matter how legitimate the public interest and no matter how substantially that interest is advanced, i.e., satisfying the *Nollan-Agins* first prong test the Just Compensation Clause still looks askance at restrictions placed upon individuals whose activities (especially harmful ones) have no special relationship to or impact on the specific public interest underlying the regulation. A simple hypothetical illustrates this critical distinction. The California Coastal Commission wants to assure public awareness and appreciation of whales. Adopting a strategy of establishing branch whale exhibits along the coast, the Commission asks the Nollans to set one up on their front lawn. A worthy purpose and a mechanism that advances that purpose are nonetheless insufficient justification for asking the Nollans to run the show, absent some evidence that the Nollans' activities have a special relationship to or impact on the whales.

Ironically, *Nollan* was its own worst enemy. Its nominal reliance on one relationship (the *Agins* first prong linguistic formulation) masked its underlying concern with the other. Justice Scalia's real preoccupation resided with whether it was fair to saddle *these* property owners with the easement condition, not whether public access to the coast was a good thing (like saving the whales) or whether beach easements in general could help realize that goal (like whale exhibits). To show this second relationship, then, one must identify harms or needs generated by the Nollans' proposed house that would justify requiring them to contribute the easement.

Early discussion in *Nollan* tackled this issue by asking whether construction of the new house would "substantially impede" realization of the view access goal (a "substantial impediment" test should be added to the "substantial advancing-substantial relation" test).[164] If it would, the Court concluded, then a total ban on new construction, or by definition less drastic measures, would pass constitutional muster. In that the Commission found that the new house would harm visual access, the Nollans could fairly be asked to mitigate that harm. But since the Commission failed to articulate a public interest in lateral access, let alone present evidence that the new house would harm that public interest, the Nollans were unfairly burdened. Opined Justice Scalia, "unless the permit condition serves the same governmental purpose as the development ban, the building restriction is not a valid regulation of land use but 'an out-and-out plan of extortion.' "[165]

Familiar with numerous state court opinions reviewing mandatory subdivision exactions, land-use planners and lawyers would have little trouble recognizing and understanding the "substantial impediment" relationship of the *Nollan* analysis. Indeed, *Nollan* cited a passel of these state cases to support its approach.[166] For years, state courts have demanded the showing of some relationship between publicly imposed obligations and privately generated harms when evaluating regulations asking developers to make land dedications for streets and parks, cash payments in lieu of such dedications, and other provisions of desired public amenities and services. The theory is that developers and property owners should not be asked to shoulder a disproportionate share of public obligations more properly carried by taxpayers-at-large.

Under Due Process, Equal Protection, or Just Compensation umbrellas, courts have deployed a variety of phrases, including "rational nexus,"[167] "reasonable connection,"[168] "reasonable relationship,"[169] and "reasonably attributable,"[170] to describe the necessary relationship. The analyses commonly emphasize two factors: whether the proposed land use creates a need (or problem) that it should address, and whether the government-imposed requirement is proportional to the need (or problem) created. Like *Nollan,* state court decisions have engendered bewilderment among planners and lawyers over the stringency of judicial reviews (regardless of lenient linguistic formulations) and over the correct constitutional peg.[171] Justice Scalia may take some comfort from the complexities other courts have encountered in fashioning and applying tests for exaction-type land-use regulations.

Recasting *Nollan's* focus from the "substantial advancing" relationship to the "substantial impediment" relationship (stressing a property owner's propensity to impede realization of the public interest) may help interpret, if not reconcile, *Nollan* with *Euclid* and progeny. Perhaps Justice Scalia's call for *sub-*

stantial planning justifications is no more than empirical recognition that *selective* (picky-choosy) regulations impacting fewer individuals are inherently harder to justify than *comprehensive* (shotgun) ones. After all, as the comprehensiveness of a regulation increases, the burdened individuals enjoy increasingly offsetting benefits from those same restrictions placed upon others (upon neighbors, for example). Justice Holmes once described this phenomenon as the "average reciprocity of advantage."[172] Conversely, the more selective a regulation, the more detailed and specific the explanation must be to demonstrate how the individual has created a special problem justifying special treatment.

This issue had one of its best-known airings in the Court's 1978 *Penn Central Transportation Co. v. New York City* opinion, where Justices Brennan and Rehnquist squared off in disagreement over the comprehensiveness of New York City's landmarks preservation law.[173] Justice Brennan observed that, "[i]n contrast to discriminatory zoning, which is the antithesis of land-use control as part of some comprehensive plan, the New York City law embodies a comprehensive plan to preserve structures of historic or aesthetic interest wherever they might be found in the city. . . ."[174] Indeed, New York had designated over 400 landmarks and 31 historic districts by the time the law was challenged.[175] Acknowledging that landmark owners were more seriously burdened than non-landmark owners, just as Ambler Realty was affected more severely than surrounding owners happy with the permitted residential uses, Justice Brennan nonetheless was satisfied that the comprehensive nature of New York's program brought the owners sufficiently offsetting benefits to pass constitutional muster.[176]

Justice Rehnquist would calculate that "less than one one-tenth of one percent of the buildings in New York City" have been designated landmarks.[177] Wryly, he would say, "The owner of a building might initially be pleased that his property has been chosen by a distinguished committee of architects, historians, and city planners for such a singular distinction. But he may well discover, as appellant Penn Central Transportation Co. did here, that the landmark designation imposes upon him a substantial cost, with little or no offsetting benefit except for the honor of the designation."[178] On this spectrum, *Nollan* was very much a selective (picky-choosy) case, even though other homeowners along the coast had previously agreed to provide easements.[179] Thus, the Commission's attempt to justify its disparate treatment became at once more significant and difficult.

GAZING INTO THE CRYSTAL BALL I: BROAD VERSUS NARROW INTERPRETATION

Criticisms notwithstanding, *Nollan* is on the books. The interesting (some would say fundamental) question is whether it will dramatically expand the judge's role in evaluating planning rationales supporting traditional zoning measures. Lawyers for property owners, neighbors, local governments, and others will press their conflicting interpretations of the opinion in state and lower federal courts. Judges will put on their reading glasses, puzzle over the words, and through their reactions determine *Nollan's* ultimate impact on planning and zoning across the country.

One argument will take place over whether the opinion should be read to impose its higher level of judicial scrutiny to *all* land-use regulations (the "broad" interpretation), or just to similar facts, *i.e.*, government conditions or regulations authorizing physical occupations or invasions (the "narrow" interpretation). Between broad and narrow in-

terpretations lies an intermediate one: *Nollan* applies to all conditions, occupying or non-occupying, attached to government permission to develop land. Under this view, subdivision exactions, impact fees, linkage, and inclusionary zoning might be subject to the "substantial advancing" test. Surely, Justice Scalia's underlying concern with the fairness of saddling the Nollans with a government-imposed obligation unrelated to any harm generated by their activities would apply equally to non-occupying, as well as occupying, government conditions. However, arguments in favor of this intermediate interpretation are primarily derivative of arguments in favor of the broad or narrow interpretation.

The wording of the opinion belies the narrow interpretation. By its plain terms, the opinion undeniably ratcheted to a higher level the amount of judicial scrutiny to be accorded *all* land-use regulations. The majority stated without qualification that government "abridgement of property rights"—not just abridgements caused by physical occupations—must be justified as a "'substantial advanc[ing]' of a legitimate State interest."[180] And by definition, albeit in varying degrees, all land-use regulations, including traditional zoning, abridge property rights by telling owners what they may not do with their land. The sentence following the basic articulation of the rule provides additional linguistic evidence against the narrow interpretation:

[O]ur cases describe the condition for abridgment of property rights through the police power as a 'substantial advanc[ing]' of a legitimate State interest. *We are inclined to be particularly careful about the adjective where the actual conveyance of property is made a condition to the lifting of a land use restriction,* since in that context there is heightened risk that the purpose is avoidance of the compensation requirement, rather than the stated police power objective.[181]

By stating its inclination to be "particularly careful" about the adjective "substantial" when the "actual conveyance of property," such as an easement condition, is involved, the Court by implication reiterated that abridgements of private property *not* involving actual conveyance would be routinely subject to the basic "substantial" standard, although without the "particular care."[182] And Footnote Three sounded the death knell for equating boilerplate "substantial" with boilerplate "reasonable." If anything, the majority here may have complicated matters even more by creating a two-tier "substantial" standard, one for conditions involving actual conveyances of property, and one for all other abridgments of private property by government regulation.

Notwithstanding this linguistic conclusion, it is possible that lawyers representing cities and other public agencies will be able to persuade courts to adopt the narrow interpretation. Several arguments are availing. First, the broad interpretation finds its origin in what lawyers call dictum (a general rule of law stated in the opinion, but not essential to resolution of the case at hand), and not in the holding (the rule of law resolving the case at hand). Indeed, the actual facts of the case, and thus the decision itself, revolve around a regulatory condition of physical occupation, not a traditional zoning action or similar land-use restriction. Unlike a holding, dictum is not accorded the stature of binding precedent, and that principle has special resonance here. Adoption of the new standard for all land-use regulations, representing as it would a radical departure from settled doctrine, requires more evidentiary support than that provided from the linguistic sifting of a few phrases.

Second, the analytical approach of the opinion favors a narrow interpretation. What makes the majority's choice of the Just Compensation Clause for its analytical peg initially understandable (putting aside the issue whether the standard it articulated and applied was correct) is that *Nollan* factually does involve a public physical occupation, the most severe of traditional takings violations. As mentioned previously in this chapter,[183] the majority premised its entire discussion on the assumption that, had the California Coastal Commission approached the Nollans, with their existing bungalow use, and outright required them to provide a public easement, the Just Compensation Clause would be automatically violated because the easement would be a "'permanent physical occupation'" of private property.[184] Thus, continued the majority, the "question becomes whether requiring [the easement] to be conveyed as a condition of issuing a land use permit" changes the equation.[185] Clearly, the majority was not thinking about non-occupying traditional Euclidean zoning regulations or similar land-use restrictions as it went through its paces. Were a common zoning action under constitutional attack, it is uncertain at best that the Court would employ the *Nollan* analytical framework.

Indeed, the only major Supreme Court property rights abridgement case announced subsequent to *Nollan* supplies fertile ground for such speculation. As described previously in this chapter,[186] in *Pennell* v. *City of San Jose*, the Court examined the constitutionality of a municipal rent control ordinance under the Just Compensation, Due Process, and Equal Protection clauses. The majority did not once cite *Nollan*. Furthermore, despite Justice Scalia's explicit arguments to the contrary, the majority did not mention or apply the "substantial advancing" test to assess the ordinance's validity under the Just Compensation

Clause. Instead, a deferential *Euclid*-style review of means-ends relationships was conducted in that part of the opinion resolving Due Process and Equal Protection concerns.[187] The *Pennell* decision necessarily implies that the Court does not consider the *Nollan* test broadly applicable to all government restrictions abridging private property (as opposed to *Nollan*-type physical occupation conditions).[188] Without a narrow *Nollan* interpretation, *Pennell* stands for the mind-boggling proposition that, one year out of the gate, *Nollan's* overall suggestion of heightened scrutiny under the Just Compensation Clause now claims only two adherents (Justices Scalia and O'Connor, the *Pennell* dissenters), and thus has been *sub silentio* abandoned. Perhaps a future Supreme Court opinion will refer to *Nollan's* heightened substantial discussion much the same way Justice Scalia referred to *Goldblatt's* reasonableness discussion.

The indisputable ambiguity of *Nollan's* meaning and scope itself provides a third argument for the narrow interpretation. Upright since *Euclid,* the apple cart of judicial deference to public planning and regulatory efforts should be upset as little as possible without a clearer statement of intent from the High Court. The majority's dubious scholarship in Footnote Three and its questionable merger of Due Process-Equal Protection with Just Compensation inquiries, provide added force to this contention. Lower courts should exercise a limited degree of discretion before adopting an approach arguable in its conceptual legitimacy and muddled in the expression of its reach.

GAZING INTO THE CRYSTAL BALL II: THE PLAY OF *NOLLAN'S* "SUBSTANTIAL"

Whether the narrow or broad interpretation becomes the coin of the realm, the question

persists about what *Nollan's* "substantial" really means. As observed previously,[189] the application of "substantial" to the facts of *Nollan* sheds little light. Accepting, as one must, the majority's delineation of the record, there was no relationship at all, let alone a substantial one, between the Commission's visual access goal and its lateral access easement condition. Indeed, the Commission's condition would fail the lenient standard of *Euclid* and progeny. However, the Court did volunteer three hypothetical conditions that it said would meet its test of substantially advancing the presumed legitimate state interest of visual access: a fence ban, height and setback restrictions on the new house, and a viewing spot on the property for passersby. It is easy to understand how these three conditions advance the visual access goal. It is less easy to identify, however, what specific aspects qualify them as *substantially* advancing that goal. Indeed, short of a condition that unequivocally fails to advance the goal (such as the Commission's lateral access easement), it is hard to imagine a condition that *advances* the goal, but insufficiently to qualify as *substantially* advancing the goal.

A strategic colloquy between Justices Scalia and Brennan threw off only slight illumination. In an attempt to influence future readings by lower courts of the majority opinion, dissents sometimes will provide their own least damaging characterization of the majority. This risky strategy runs a danger of backfiring, however, because it invites a majority counterpunch explicitly rejecting the characterization. Justice Brennan's dissent attempted to color the Scalia opinion and precipitated such a counterpunch. Suggesting that "the [California Coastal] Commission should have little difficulty in the future in utilizing its expertise to demonstrate a specific connection between provisions for access and burdens on access produced by new development," Justice Brennan counseled that, "alerted to the Court's apparently more demanding requirement, [the Commission] need only make clear that a provision for public access directly responds to a particular type of burden on access created by a new development."[190] Justice Scalia was quick to retort, "We do not share Justice Brennan's confidence" that the Commission will be able to "avoid the effect of today's decision."[191] He powered his punch, "We view the Fifth Amendment's property clause to be more than a pleading requirement, and compliance with it to be more than an exercise in cleverness and imagination."[192]

Whatever it is, then, *Nollan's* "substantial" requires more than an exercise in cleverness and imagination, an exercise probably sufficient to meet the more lenient *Euclid* test. This much is predictable: Courts will neither accept, nor invent, planning rationales or goals that could have been, but were not, demonstratively relied upon by the government agency. Undocumented assertions will not substitute for hard evidence that planners and other public officials thought about what they were doing. It is plausible that trials will entail evidentiary battle royals over the likelihood that the challenged regulation will in fact advance the professed goals. Judges may no longer be satisfied that one credible expert witness is willing to testify as to the planning validity of a regulation. Instead, judges may hear several expert planners explain their underlying data and research methodologies and may weigh competing logics to decide which arguments are superior. A conceivably correct but inferior claim may no longer suffice, although one persuasive expert witness planner should still persevere over 12 unpersuasive ones. Further, courts may borrow tests from other areas of constitutional law to give content to the substantial advancing standard. For example, they may inquire whether there are

alternative government regulations, less restrictive upon the exercise of property rights than the challenged regulation, that might equally well accomplish the legitimate state interest (a "less restrictive alternative" test). They may also ask whether the regulations are "narrowly tailored" or "narrowly drawn," i.e., no broader than necessary to achieve the legitimate state interest. Or they may explore whether the regulations are "overinclusive" or "underinclusive."

GAZING INTO THE CRYSTAL BALL III: THE ROLES OF PLANNERS AND JUDGES

This outcome of greater judicial involvement constitutes a mixed blessing for planners and judges. For planning as livelihood, *Nollan* may be a shot in the arm, a "Planners Employment Act" drafted by the Court (particularly if the broad interpretation of *Nollan* gains favor). Much the way tax lawyers and accountants rejoice over periodic revisions of the Internal Revenue Code, planners may savor a newly discovered luster. Mindful of exposure to monetary damages for unconstitutional land-use regulatory measures—exposure made especially perilous by the strange alchemy of *Nollan's* analytical reliance on the Just Compensation Clause and *First English's* obligation under that Clause to pay compensation for the period of time that the offending regulation effects a taking[193]—wise public officials will requisition serious planning studies to guide and justify their decisions. Planners will be asked to establish and document connections (their stock in trade) between regulatory means and legitimate ends, and between privately created harms and publicly imposed abridgements of property rights. Written reports will supplement oral discussions. In short, formerly swathed in the protective clothing of presumed validity, the traditional ways that cities do their land-use regulatory business may no longer suffice.

Whether any of this will result in better planning, better zoning, and better communities, is another question. The debate rages between those who see the *Nollan-First English* combine as chilling the exercise of needed land-use regulatory authority,[194] and those who see it as reining in imperious and over-reaching regulators.[195] In an attempt to toe the constitutional line, will communities play it so safe that they resist taking legitimate and needed actions to protect their environments? Alternatively, will only unconstitutional conduct be curbed, resulting in fairer treatment of individual property owners and a system that imposes on the public-at-large those costs it should equitably bear? Will innovative land-use techniques such as linkage (where office developers are asked to contribute to housing and day care funds) and inclusionary zoning (where residential developers are asked to set aside units of affordable housing) be attacked as unfairly forcing property owners to bear a disproportionate responsibility for addressing society's ills unconnected with their activities?

More than any other group, judges will be put on the spot. Any lawyer worth his or her salt will frame attacks against run-of-the-mill zoning decisions, as well as attacks against *Nollan*-type conditions, with a call for heightened judicial scrutiny. In the face of continued uncertainty over *Nollan's* scope, judges will first have to decide whether the "substantial advancing" standard applies to the case at hand. If the conclusion is yes, then judges will enter the relatively uncharted terrain of measuring that murky standard against the choices of popularly elected officials and their planning experts.[196] As with most judicial interventions, age-old questions about institutional competence and technical expertise will arise. Will judges become contingent

planners, activated by the filing of lawsuits? Although they are not by training planners, *Nollan* challenges them nonetheless to participate more directly in the planning and zoning of American communities. How judges react to this challenge will determine the nature of their partnership with planners, and ultimately whether they shed their robes as limited partners to become general partners.

NOTES

1. *Village of Euclid* v. *Ambler Realty Co.,* 272 U.S. 365 (1926).

2. *Nollan* v. *California Coastal Comm'n,* 107 S. Ct. 3141 (1987).

3. The discussion in this chapter is limited to the federal constitutional standards for zoning found in the Due Process, Equal Protection, and Just Compensation clauses. Of course, a property owner or other interested party may allege legal defects with zoning arising from violations of state constitutions, state statutes, and local ordinances. Indeed, the importance of these challenges can rival, or even surpass, that of federal constitutional attacks. *See, e.g., Southern Burlington County NAACP* v. *Township of Mount Laurel,* 67 N.J. 151, 336 A.2d 713, *cert. denied and appeal dismissed,* 423 U.S. 808 (1975). However, because the Federal Constitution is the supreme law of the land, *see* U.S. Const. art. VI, state constitutions, state statutes, and local ordinances operate ratchet-like, expanding but never contracting, federal constitutional protections.

4. U.S. Const. amends. V, XIV. There are two Due Process clauses, one applicable to the federal government (in the Fifth Amendment), the other to the states (in the Fourteenth Amendment).

5. U.S. Const. amend. XIV.

6. U.S. Const. amend. V. The Just Compensation Clause is made applicable to the states through the Fourteenth Amendment's Due Process Clause. *See Chicago B. & Q. R. Co.* v. *Chicago,* 166 U.S. 226 (1897); *see, e.g., Keystone Bituminous Coal Ass'n* v. *DeBenedictis,* 107 S. Ct. 1232, 1240 n.10 (1987).

7. The second Justice Harlan wrote one of the more eloquent passages about the fluid meaning of the Due Process Clause:

Due process has not been reduced to any formula; its content cannot be determined by reference to any code. The best that can be said is that through the course of this Court's decisions it has represented the balance which our Nation, built upon postulates of respect for the liberty of the individual, has struck between that liberty and the demands of organized society. If the supplying of content to this Constitutional concept has of necessity been a rational process, it certainly has not been one where judges have felt free to roam where unguided speculation might take them. The balance of which I speak is the balance struck by this country, having regard to what history teaches are the traditions from which it developed as well as the traditions from which it broke. That tradition is a living thing. A decision of this Court which radically departs from it could not long survive, while a decision which builds on what has survived is likely to be sound. No formula could serve as a substitute, in this area, for judgment and restraint.

Poe v. *Ullman,* 367 U.S. 497, 542 (1961) (Harlan, J., dissenting). In *Euclid,* Justice Sutherland himself noted the inherent and necessary flexibility of meaning attached to the great constitutional provisions, how they "must expand or contract to meet the new and different conditions which are constantly coming within the field of their operation." *Euclid,* 272 U.S. at 387.

8. The type of Due Process discussed in this chapter is sometimes described as "substantive due process," because judges delve into the substantive reasonableness of a government action. This contrasts with so-called "procedural due process," where judges focus primarily on the fairness of government procedures such as provisions for a hearing or a statement of reasons, and other administrative protections.

9. The Equal Protection Clause is implicated when a property owner has been singled out for treatment different from others similarly situated, without a reasonable explanation connected to health, safety, morals, or general welfare for the difference in treatment. Equal Protection differs from Due Process primarily in its emphasis upon explanations that underlie disparate treatment of individuals or groups by government.

10. *Euclid,* 272 U.S. at 380.

11. *Id.* at 380–81. Each use district listed many other uses as well. For example, other U-1 district allowed uses included public parks, water towers and reservoirs, suburban and interurban electric railway passenger stations and rights of way, and farming, non-commercial greenhouses, nurseries, and truck gardening.

12. *Id.* at 381.

13. *Id.* at 381–82.

14. *Id.* at 379.

15. *Id.* at 382.

16. Ambler Realty asserted that, in industrial use, the land was worth $10,000 an acre, while in residential use, its value decreased to $2,500 an acre. *Id.* at 384.

17. *Id.* Ambler Realty also charged that the ordinance violated provisions of the Ohio Constitution. *Id.*

18. *Id.* at 397.

19. *Id.* at 387–88. The Court quoted the famous Latin nuisance maxim "sic utere tuo ut alienum non laedas," *id.* at 387, roughly translated, "use your property in such a way as not to injure another." Since no one had a right to conduct these uses under the common law, zoning did not deprive an owner of any preexisting property right.

20. *Id.* at 395 (citations omitted) (emphasis added).

21. This is probably the easiest-to-apprehend meaning of the "substantial relation" formulation. The goal of helping out a city councillor's brother-in-law by voting for a zoning change would be the proverbial illegitimate goal, and thus not related, let alone substantially related, to health, safety, morals, or general welfare. An ordinance may also lack a substantial relation to health, safety, morals, or general welfare if it is incapable under any circumstances of achieving its police power objective. It should be observed that Euclid was not the first case to employ the "substantial relation" formulation. *See, e.g., Mugler* v. *Kansas,* 123 U.S. 623, 661 (1887) ("If, therefore, a statute purporting to have been enacted to protect the public health, the public morals, or the public safety, has no real or substantial relation to those objects, or is a palpable invasion of rights secured by the fundamental law, it is the duty of the courts to so adjudge, and thereby give effect to the Constitution.")

22. *Euclid,* 272 U.S. at 391, 394.

23. *Id.* at 394.

24. *Id.*

25. *Id.*

26. *Id.*

27. *Id.*

28. *Id.*

29. *Id.*

30. *Id.*

31. *Id.*

32. Even back in the 1920s, firefighting did not require this sort of differentiation, except in central cities where high-rise office buildings were involved and in areas where high-risk heavy industrial uses were cheek-by-jowl with single-family residences.

33. Surprisingly, the goal of aesthetic quality was for many years considered an improper justification, standing alone, for exercise of the police power. Until the 1960s, billboard regulations undoubtedly adopted for

aesthetic reasons were nominally rationalized on grounds of promoting traffic safety, safely within the health, safety, morals, or general welfare quartet. After all, it could be argued, if a billboard did the trick, then the driver's eyes were not on the road.

34. For closely related exercises of the police power, *see, e.g., Hadacheck* v. *Sebastian,* 239 U.S. 394 (1915) (brick yards); *Reinman* v. *City of Little Rock,* 237 U.S. 171 (1915) (livery stables); *Welch* v. *Swasey,* 214 U.S. 91 (1909) (height restrictions).

35. *Euclid,* 272 U.S. at 388 (citation omitted) (emphasis added).

36. *Id.* at 390–91.

37. *Id.* at 391 (emphasis added).

38. *Id.* at 393 (quoting *State* v. *City of New Orleans,* 154 La. 271, 282–83 (1923)). Justice Sutherland also commented that "the inclusion of a reasonable margin to insure effective enforcement, will not put upon a law, otherwise valid, the stamp of invalidity." *Euclid,* 272 U.S. at 388–89. The Court had no trouble with the exclusion of industrial uses from residential areas, likening such uses to nuisances and citing cases where the Court had already approved their exclusion. The problem arose with exclusion of apartments and commercial uses from single-family residential districts, a question at "the crux of the more recent zoning legislation." *Id.* at 390.

39. *Nectow* v. *City of Cambridge,* 277 U.S. 183 (1928); *Gorieb* v. *Fox,* 274 U.S. 603 (1927); *Zahn* v. *Board of Public Works,* 274 U.S. 325 (1927); *see also State of Washington ex rel. Seattle Title Trust Co.* v. *Roberge,* 278 U.S. 116 (1928) (per J. Butler) (unlawful delegation of zoning power to neighbors).

40. *Goldblatt* v. *Town of Hempstead,* 369 U.S. 590 (1962). (technically unclear whether challenged dredging ordinance was part of zoning ordinance).

41. *Zahn* v. *Board of Public Works,* 274 U.S. 325 (1927).

42. *Id.* at 327.

43. *Id.* at 328.

44. *Id.* (citations omitted).

45. *Gorieb* v. *Fox,* 274 U.S. 603 (1927). Although the Court did not expressly refer to the Roanoke setback ordinance as a provision of the city's zoning law, it is probable that it was.

46. *Id.* at 608. The owner also alleged that the ordinance violated the Equal Protection Clause by fixing unequal distances from the street for different owners for erection of buildings. *Id.* at 607.

47. *Id.* at 610.

48. *Id.* at 608.

49. The justifications for the setback ordinance were that setbacks provide room for lawns, keep housing farther from the dust and noise of the street, add to the at-

tractiveness of the district, create a better home environment, reduce fire hazards, avoid cutting off light and air, and allow better visibility around street corners for automobiles. *Id.* at 609.

50. *Id.* at 609.

51. *Nectow* v. *City of Cambridge,* 277 U.S. 183 (1928).

52. *Id.* at 186.

53. *Id.* at 185.

54. *Id.* at 187.

55. *Id.* at 187–88. In another part of the opinion, the Court quoted verbatim the "substantial relation" *Euclid* formulation.

56. *Id.* It may be argued that the *Nectow* opinion utilized a more daunting standard than that suggested in *Euclid* to review the "as applied" challenge to a Cambridge zoning decision. Certainly, the Supreme Court displayed little deference to the decision of the highest court of the Commonwealth of Massachusetts which, ignoring the implications of the master's report, dismissed the landowner's claim. This may be contrasted with the Court's expressed deference to the views of the highest state court in *Gorieb:* "The highest court of the state, with greater familiarity with the local conditions and facts upon which the ordinance was based than we possess, has sustained its constitutionality; and that decision is entitled to the greatest respect and, in a case of this kind, should be interfered with only if in our judgment it is plainly wrong, . . . a conclusion which, upon the record before us, it is impossible for us to reach." *Gorieb* v. *Fox,* 274 U.S. at 609. The point is, however, that there was no evidence, at least as described in Justice Sutherland's *Nectow* opinion, to show how the Cambridge zoning in any way promoted the health, safety, morals, or general welfare.

57. *See, e.g., United States* v. *Carolene Products Co.,* 304 U.S. 144, 154 (1938) (exercise of police power will be upheld if any state of facts either known or which could be reasonably assumed affords support for it, but careful judicial scrutiny needed for infringements of fundamental rights and discrimination against discrete and insular minorities).

58. *See, e.g., Rousseau* v. *Building Inspector,* 349 Mass. 31, 35, 206 N.E.2d 399, 401 (1965); *LaSalle National Bank* v. *City of Chicago,* 5 Ill.2d 344, 350, 125 N.E.2d 609, 613 (1955).

59. *See, e.g., Montgomery County Council* v. *Scrimgeour,* 211 Md. 306, 312, 127 A.2d 528, 531 (1956); *LaSalle National Bank,* 5 Ill.2d at 350, 125 N.E.2d at 612;

60. *See, e.g., Veterans of Foreign Wars, Post 4264* v. *City of Steamboat Springs,* 195 Colo. 44, 49, 575 P.2d 835, 839, *appeal dismissed,* 439 U.S. 809 (1978); *Crall* v. *City of Leominster,* 362 Mass. 95, 102, 284 N.E.2d 610, 615 (1972). Courts some-

times employ slightly less daunting burdens such as by clear and convincing evidence.

61. *See, e.g., Caires* v. *Building Commissioner,* 323 Mass. 589, 594–95, 83 N.E.2d 550, 556 (1949).

62. *See, e.g., National Merritt, Inc.* v. *Weist,* 41 N.Y.2d 438, 443, 393 N.Y.S.2d 379, 383, 361 N.E.2d 1028, 1031 (1977).

63. *See, e.g., Cohen* v. *City of Lynn,* 333 Mass. 699, 705, 132 N.E.2d 664, 668 (1956).

64. *See, e.g., Doliner* v. *Town Clerk,* 343 Mass. 10, 14, 175 N.E.2d 925 (1961).

65. Of course, judges must assure themselves that an asserted purpose is the real one, and that it is not being used as a mask for illegitimate motivations. *See, e.g., Village of Arlington Heights* v. *Metropolitan Housing Dev. Corp.,* 429 U.S. 252, 268–71 (1977) (no evidence that zoning racially motivated). In general, the less fundamental the individual right, the more likely courts will accept at face value the asserted government purpose. *See, e.g., City of New Orleans* v. *Dukes,* 427 U.S. 297, 303 (1976) (ordinance prohibiting pushcart food sales in Vieux Carre district but "grandfathering" some operators upheld). Conversely, the more fundamental the individual right, the more likely courts will delve beyond the asserted purpose. *See, e.g., Schad* v. *Borough of Mount Ephraim,* 452 U.S. 61, 72–74 (1981) (zoning barring nude dancing and other live entertainment overturned); *Moore* v. *City of East Cleveland,* 431 U.S. 494, 499–500 (1977) (ordinance restricting grandmother from living with grandson overturned).

66. The test combines evidentiary and substantive standards that together stack the deck in favor of the government's zoning decision. To many, this is simply a long-winded way of stating that virtually any idiotic reason will carry the day in court, and that municipalities need not do any real planning at all.

67. *Coniston Corp.* v. *Village of Hoffman Estates,* 844 F.2d 461, 467 (7th Cir. 1988).

68. *Nollan* v. *California Coastal Comm'n,* 107 S. Ct. 3141 (1987).

69. *Carolene Products,* 304 U.S. at 152–53 n.4.

70. *Nollan,* 107 S. Ct. at 3147 n.3.

71. Justice Scalia's opinion was joined by Chief Justice Rehnquist, and by Justices White, Powell, and O'Connor. Justice Brennan, joined by Justice Marshall, wrote the major dissent. Justice Blackmun wrote his own dissenting opinion, and also joined Justice Stevens' dissent.

72. *See, e.g., Craig* v. *Boren,* 429 U.S. 190, 197, 204 (1976) (invalidating law establishing lower drinking age for females than for males under "intermediate scrutiny" standard).

73. *Nollan,* 107 S. Ct. at 3143.

74. *Id.*

75. *Id.*

76. *Id.; see also id.* at 3158 (Brennan, J., dissenting).

77. *Id.* at 3143.

78. *Id.* at 3143–44.

79. *Id.*

80. *Id.* at 3155 (Brennan, J., dissenting).

81. *Id.* at 3143. This assumes, of course, that all other properties have also granted lateral access easements to the public.

82. *Id.* at 3143–44.

83. *Id.* at 3144.

84. *Id.*

85. *Id.*

86. *Id.*

87. *Id.*

88. *Id.*

89. *Id.*

90. *Id.*

91. *Id.* at 3150.

92. *Id.* at 3145 (quoting *Loretto* v. *Teleprompter Manhattan CATV Corp.,* 458 U.S. 419 (1982)).

93. *Nollan,* 107 S. Ct. at 3146.

94. *Id.* at 3146–47, 3150.

95. *Id.* at 3147.

96. Thus, one may speculate whether the Court would have found the visual access goal a legitimate state interest had the Commission's condition indeed met the second part of the test by substantially advancing such a goal.

97. *Nollan,* 107 S. Ct. at 3147–50.

98. *Id.* at 3147 (footnote and citation omitted) (emphasis added). In this sense, the proposed use—construction of a new house—may be loosely analogized to traditional common law public nuisances (harmful, prejudicial, noxious uses injurious to health, safety, morals, or general welfare). *See, e.g., Mugler* v. *Kansas,* 123 U.S. 623, 668–69 (1887). Property owners simply have no preexisting right to use property in such as way as to injure others, in this case public passersby who might like to view the Pacific Ocean from the road. Thus, the new house may be banned, or, in the alternative, conditioned upon effective mitigation of the public injury.

The caveat "unless the denial would interfere so drastically with the Nollans' use of their property as to constitute a taking," although on the surface tautological, presumably referred to the requirement that landowners must be left with economically viable use of their property, no matter how legitimate the state interest or how substantially it is advanced by the regulation. *See Agins*

v. *City of Tiburon,* 447 U.S. 255, 260 (1980). Of course, it is questionable whether this guarantee of economic viability should apply when *all* uses of a given property, no matter what conditions are imposed, are harmful to the public. *See, e.g., Hadacheck* v. *Sebastian,* 239 U.S. 394 (1915). Does the Court really believe that property owners are entitled in all cases to some use of their property, even if that means a harmful one qualifying as a common law nuisance, and that when all use is taken, compensation must be paid? Lurking here are some fascinating questions about the definition of private property, questions only indirectly addressed in the *Nollan* opinion. *Compare Nollan,* 107 S. Ct. at 3146 n.2, *with Nollan,* 107 S. Ct. at 3160 n.10 (Brennan, J., dissenting).

99. *Nollan,* 107 S. Ct. at 3147.

100. *Id.* at 3147–48. If Justice Scalia's suggestion of a viewing spot on the Nollan property is to be taken seriously, then the decisive problem with the Commission's beach easement cannot be the fact that it is a physical occupation of private property.

101. *Id.* at 3149.

102. *Id.* at 3162 (Blackmun, J., dissenting).

103. *Id.* at 3144.

104. *Id.* at 3154 (Brennan, J., dissenting).

105. *Id.*

106. *Id.* at 3150.

107. *See generally supra* notes 57–67 and accompanying text.

108. *Euclid,* 272 U.S. at 395.

109. *See supra* notes 61–63 and accompanying text.

110. *Nollan,* 107 S. Ct. at 3147 n.3.

111. *Agins* v. *City of Tiburon,* 447 U.S. 255 (1980).

112. *See infra* notes 135–155 and accompanying text.

113. *Agins,* 447 U.S. at 260 (emphasis added).

114. The *Agins* nine included Justice Powell (author), Chief Justice Burger, and Justices Brennan, Stewart, White, Marshall, Blackmun, Rehnquist, and Stevens.

115. The *Agins* opinion offered no explanation for its substitution of the formulation "substantially advance a legitimate state interest" for the *Euclid-Nectow* "substantial relation to health, safety, morals, or general welfare" phrasing.

116. *See supra* notes 61–63 and accompanying text.

117. There is nothing even in *Agins* to hint that substantial meant something more than reasonable. If anything, the level of scrutiny the *Agins* Court actually applied to the Tiburon zoning regulation supports the lenient interpretation of the word. *See Agins,* 447 U.S. at 261, 262.

118. *Penn Central Transportation Co.* v. *New York City,* 438 U.S. 104 (1978).

119. *Id.* at 133 n.29 (emphasis added) (citing *Nectow*).

120. *Nollan,* 107 S. Ct. at 3151 n.1 (Brennan, J., dissenting).

121. *Id.* at 3153.

122. *Lochner* v. *New York,* 198 U.S. 45 (1905).

123. *See, e.g., Burns Baking Co.* v. *Bryan,* 264 U.S. 504 (1924); *Adkins* v. *Children's Hospital,* 261 U.S. 525 (1923).

124. *See infra* notes 135–179 and accompanying text.

125. *See supra* note 111 and accompanying text.

126. *See, e.g., Minnesota* v. *Clover Leaf Creamery Co.,* 449 U.S. 456, 461, 462 (1981) ("legitimate state purposes"); *New Orleans* v. *Dukes,* 427 U.S. 297, 303 (1976) ("legitimate state interest"); *Day–Bright Lighting, Inc.* v. *Missouri,* 342 U.S. 421, 424 (1952) ("legitimate end").

127. *Goldblatt* v. *Town of Hempstead,* 369 U.S. 590 (1962).

128. *Nollan,* 107 S. Ct. at 3147 n.3.

129. *Hawaii Housing Auth.* v. *Midkiff,* 467 U.S. 229 (1984).

130. *Id.* at 241–42.

131. *Id.* at 240.

132. *Id.* at 242.

133. *Id.* at 242–43.

134. The *Midkiff* equation of public use with police power limits suggests another equation. Under *Midkiff,* government need not make any greater showing to take property than to regulate it, as long as compensation is paid. For the owner, however, it is far from clear which exercise of power is more intrusive on property rights: the taking of property with compensation, or severe but constitutional regulation without compensation.

135. *See supra* notes 111–115 and accompanying text.

136. The most common land takings occur not through regulation, but through government exercise of its power of eminent domain. Usually, an entire parcel of land (and thus all the attributes of ownership, including the right of possession, the right to use land in noninjurious ways, the right to exclude others, and the right to sell or transfer property) is taken. Increasingly during this century, however, government has relied upon regulation to achieve public goals. In such cases, only part of the bundle of rights has been taken from the owner, and the complex question is whether what is taken is too much, thus demanding payment of compensation.

For the courts, "[t]he determination that governmental action constitutes a taking is, in essence, a determination that the public at large, rather than a single owner, must bear the burden of an exercise of state power in the public interest." *Agins* v. *City of Tiburon,* 447 U.S. at 260. This determination is easier said than done: "[T]his Court, quite simply, has been unable to develop any 'set formula' for determining when 'justice and fairness' require that economic injuries caused by public action be compensated by the government. . . ." *Penn Central,* 438 U.S. at 124.

137. *San Diego Gas & Electric Co.* v. *City of San Diego,* 450 U.S. 621 (1981) (Brennan, J., dissenting).

138. *Id.* at 656 n.23.

139. *Pennell* v. *City of San Jose,* 108 S. Ct. 849 (1988).

140. *Id.* at 853, 854.

141. Chief Justice Rehnquist's opinion was joined by Justices Brennan, White, Marshall, Blackmun, and Stevens. Justice Scalia wrote a decision concurring in part and dissenting in part, joined by Justice O'Connor. Justice Kennedy took no part in the consideration or decision of the case.

142. *Pennell,* 108 S. Ct. at 856.

143. Justice Scalia concurred with the majority's conclusion that the tenant hardship provision did not, on its face, violate the Due Process and Equal Protection Clauses. *Id.* at 859. He dissented from the majority's conclusion that the Just Compensation Clause challenge was premature, and he would have found that the hardship provision effected a taking of private property. *Id.*

144. *Id.* at 861. Consistent with his belief that the tenant hardship provision was ripe for examination under the *Nollan-Agins* substantial advancing test, Justice Scalia added, "Knowing the nature and character of the particular property in question, or the degree of its economic impairment, will in no way assist this [substantial advancing] inquiry. Such factors are as irrelevant to the present claim as we have said they are to the claim that a law effects a taking by authorizing a permanent physical invasion of property." *Id.* (citation omitted). Thus, at least insofar as the "substantial advancing" prong is concerned, the difference between facial and as applied challenges becomes muted. Conversely, intelligent judicial review of the economic impact of a challenged zoning action demands information about whether the property owner is able to obtain different, and more favorable, zoning treatment from government in the future, or about whether the challenged zoning is a final decision, and thereby properly ripe, for review. *See, e.g., MacDonald, Sommer & Frates* v. *County of Yolo,* 477 U.S. 340 (1986); *Williamson County Regional Planning Comm'n.* v. *Hamilton Bank,* 473 U.S. 172 (1985).

Justice Scalia was implicitly endorsing a triumvirate of Just Compensation tests: the *Penn Central-Agins* second prong economic impact tests, the *Loretto* permanent physical occupation test, and the *Nollan-Agins* first prong substantial advancing test. Violation of any one of the three would be enough to violate the Just Compensation Clause. For the record, Justice Scalia effectively misstated the *Penn Central* inquiry as looking to the "nature and

character of the particular property in question," when the *Penn Central* Court cited as relevant factors the nature and "character of the *governmental action.*" *See Penn Central,* 438 U.S. at 124 (emphasis added).

145. *Pennell,* 108 S. Ct. at 860 (Scalia, J., dissenting); *see also, e.g.,* Amicus Curiae Brief of the National Association of Home Builders *et al.* in support of Appellants, at 14–15. *Pennell* is not the only Supreme Court opinion to cast doubt on the *Agins* substantial advancing formulation of Just Compensation Clause analysis. In *Hodel* v. *Virginia Surface Mining & Reclamation Ass'n.,* the Court not only declined to discuss the *Agins* "substantial advancing" first prong, but also omitted it from its verbatim quotation of the disjunctive *Agins* test. *Hodel,* 452 U.S. 264, 296 (1981).

146. The majority defined the facial issue in terms of a challenge to the provision that the hearing officer may "consider" the hardship of the tenant in fixing a reasonable rent. *See Pennell,* 108 S. Ct. at 857. In two inscrutable footnotes, the Court commented that it was not evaluating "as applied" Due Process and Equal Protection challenges to instances where the provision actually forced landlords to subsidize individual tenants. *See id.* at 857 n.5, 858 n.7. Although this leaves room for speculation that the basic Due Process-Equal Protection analytical approach and standard might vary in an "as applied" context, there is nothing in this or other opinions to support such a view.

147. *Pennell,* 108 S. Ct. at 857 (footnote omitted) (citation omitted).

148. *Id.* at 858 (citations omitted).

149. *Id.*

150. *Id.* at 859 (citation omitted).

151. *Id.* The majority gave improperly short shrift, however, to the implications of its view that landlords, as a class, did not "cause" the tenant hardship: "We recognize, as appellants point out, that in general it is difficult to say that the landlord 'causes' the tenant's hardship. But this is beside the point—if a landlord does have a hardship tenant, regardless of the reason why, it is rational for appellees to take that fact into consideration." *Id.*

For Justice Scalia, this cause-and-effect mismatch was at the nub of his conclusion that the ordinance violated the Just Compensation Clause. Traditional land-use controls were justified, he described, on the theory that, but for the regulation, the owner's use of property would create a social harm. *Id.* at 862 (Scalia, J., dissenting). Here, he charged, landlords no more caused tenants to suffer individual hardship than grocers selling food or department stores selling clothes. *Id.* at 862. If this required relationship between burdens and benefits were severed, he cautioned, "there is no end to the social transformations that can be accomplished by so-called 'regulation.' . . ." *Id.*

152. *Penn Central*, 438 U.S. at 124. For the "character of the governmental action" factor, the Court gave the example of whether or not the government physically invaded private property. *Id.*

153. *Id.* at 129.

154. *Pennsylvania Coal Co.* v. *Mahon*, 260 U.S. 393 (1922).

155. *Id.* at 413–14.

156. The Court may invalidate the offending regulation. In addition, the individual may seek a monetary remedy for injuries through a Section 1983 federal civil rights action. *See* 42 U.S.C. Section 1983 (West 1981). What remains unclear is whether a person is better off asking for just compensation by bringing suit under the Just Compensation Clause, or by bringing a Section 1983 action for damages.

157. *First English Evangelical Lutheran Church* v. *County of Los Angeles*, 107 S. Ct. 2378 (1987).

158. *See Agins*, 447 U.S. at 262 (citing *Kaiser Aetna* v. *United States*, 444 U.S. 164, 179–80 (1979)); *Kaiser Aetna*, 444 U.S. at 176.

159. *See Loretto* v. *Teleprompter Manhattan CATV Corp.*, 458 U.S. 419 (1982). It is possible to distinguish *Loretto*, where the physical occupation of property was "permanent," *id.* at 434–35, 438, from the present case. In *Nollan*, the easement granted the public the right to pass and repass, but not to stop permanently. The *Nollan* Court did not address this distinction.

160. A stranger result is revealed in an illegal spot zoning case, where neighbors successfully challenge a zoning amendment affecting an adjacent parcel that benefits the adjacent owner but harms the neighbors. The neighbors challenge the zoning on the theory that the regulation does not substantially advance legitimate state interests. Are they entitled to compensation? Of course, the answer is no. Is the landowner entitled to it? After all, the ordinance does not substantially advance legitimate state interests and thus fails *Nollan*. Is it good enough to explain away this absurdity by saying that the benefited landowner is not the litigant, or that there is a taking, but that the landowner is limited to receiving a peppercorn's worth of compensation? In any event, neighbors alleging illegal spot zoning never cite the Just Compensation Clause, and instead sue under Equal Protection and Due Process.

161. One response is that the amount of compensation would be zero or *de minimus*. But that misses the point: The Just Compensation Clause is fundamentally de-

signed to secure owners their private property rights against onerous government regulations, no matter how rational or irrational the regulations may be.

162. *See supra* notes 92–93 and accompanying text.

163. *Armstrong* v. *United States*, 364 U.S. 40, 49 (1960); *see, e.g., First English*, 107 S. Ct. at 2388; *Penn Central*, 438 U.S. at 123. This may be characterized as the equal protection component of the Just Compensation Clause.

164. *Nollan*, 107 S. Ct. at 3147.

165. *Id.* at 3148. To Justice Scalia's credit, he is more consistent about the relevance and importance of this relationship than some of his colleagues. Several members of the *Nollan* majority subsequently dismissed this relationship, in the Equal Protection discussion of the San Jose rent control ordinance in *Pennell. See*, 108 S. Ct. at 859; *supra* note 151. More than anything else, it was this lack of relationship in San Jose's tenant hardship provision that rankled Justice Scalia. Since landlords did not create the tenant's economic hardship, any more than grocers selling food or department stores selling clothes created it, Justice Scalia thought it unfair to landlords to single them out for the subsidization of hardship tenants. For him, this was ultimately a circumvention of the democratic system of government. *See Pennell*, 108 S. Ct. at 863–64.

166. *Nollan*, 107 S. Ct. at 3149–50.

167. *See, e.g., Land/Vest Properties, Inc.* v. *Town of Plainfield*, 117 N.H. 817, 823, 379 A.2d 200, 204 (1977).

168. *See, e.g., Jordan* v. *Village of Menomonee Falls*, 28 Wis.2d 608, 618, 137 N.W.2d 442, 448 (1965), *appeal dismissed*, 385 U.S. 4 (1966).

169. *See, e.g., Call* v. *City of W. Jordan*, 606 P.2d 217, 220 (Utah 1979).

170. *See, e.g., Home Builders Ass'n* v. *City of Kansas City*, 555 S.W.2d 832, 835 (Mo. 1977).

171. This author is among many who have noticed the existence of, and lack of precedent for, a heightened scrutiny standard apparently applied by some state courts. *See, e.g.,* Kayden & Pollard, "Linkage Ordinances and Traditional Exactions Analysis: The Connection Between Office Development and Housing," 50 *Law & Cont. Probs.* 127, 127–28 n.3, 129–30 n.13 (1987).

172. *See Pennsylvania Coal*, 260 U.S. at 415.

173. *See Penn Central*, 438 U.S. at 133–35.

174. *Id.* at 132.

175. *Id.*

176. *Id.* at 133–35.

177. *Id.* at 147 (Rehnquist, J., dissenting).

178. *Id* at 138–39.

179. *Nollan*, 107 S. Ct. at 3144. In a footnote, Justice Scalia noted that the Nollans were not claiming that

they, as distinct from other coastal homeowners, had been singled out for special treatment. *Id.* at 3147 n.4. But, in the concluding paragraph of his opinion, Justice Scalia made clear his view that the Just Compensation Clause protects individuals against shouldering burdens more properly shared by the public: It would be unfair to impose the easement burden on "the Nollans (and other coastal residents)" so that the public at large would benefit. *Id.* at 3150.

180. *Id.* at 3150 (emphasis in original).

181. *Id.* (emphasis partially in original and partially added).

182. An alternate interpretation—that the Court would exercise no care at all when actual conveyance was not involved—is linguistically unpersuasive.

183. *See supra* notes 92–93 and accompanying text.

184. Whether the majority has correctly characterized the Commission's easement condition (authorizing the public to pass and repass, but not to linger) as a permanent, rather than temporary, physical occupation, is open to question. Furthermore, if the Nollans' *existing* use of their property (as a bungalow) itself substantially impeded the achievement of a legitimate state interest, would not a restriction, including a physical occupation, that substantially advanced realization of that same legitimate state interest, be acceptable under the very terms outlined in *Nollan? Cf., e.g., Block v. Hirsh,* 256 U.S. 135 (1921); *Hadacheck v. Sebastian,* 239 U.S. 394 (1915); *Mugler v. Kansas,* 123 U.S. 623 (1887). Thus, one can question *Nollan's* early assertion, prior to its subsequent finding of no relation between means and ends, that outright imposition of the easement on the Nollans' existing use would *a priori* constitute a taking.

185. *Nollan,* 107 S. Ct. at 3146.

186. *See supra* notes 139–151 and accompanying text.

187. *See Pennell,* 108 S. Ct. at 857–59.

188. Interestingly, an argument can be made that *Pennell* is a physical occupation case, and thus that *Nollan* should have applied here even under the narrow interpretation. Rent control ordinances in general, and the San Jose ordinance in particular, do authorize public physical occupations by forcing owners to permit needy tenants to physically occupy the owner's private property. If this interpretation is correct, then the *Loretto per se* taking rule might apply. *See Loretto* v. *Teleprompter Manhattan CATV Corp.,* 458 U.S. 419, 434–35, 438 (1982). The *Pennell* Court expressly declined to address this point, in the absence of a specific instance of lowered rent for a hardship tenant. *Pennell,* 108 S. Ct. at 857 n.5.

189. *See supra* notes 94–106 and accompanying text.

190. *Nollan,* 107 S. Ct. at 3161.

191. *Id.* at 3150.

192. *Id.*

193. *First English Evangelical Lutheran Church* v. *County of Los Angeles,* 107 S. Ct. 2378 (1987). Monetary liability would exist in any event under the federal civil rights act. *See* 42 U.S.C. Section 1983 (West 1981).

194. On the Supreme Court, Justice Stevens has been the most outspoken justice for this position. *See Nollan,* 107 S. Ct. at 3163 (Stevens, J., dissenting); *First English,* 107 S. Ct. at 2399–2400 (Stevens, J., dissenting).

195. *Cf. Nollan,* 107 S. Ct. at 3148 (referring to " 'extortion' ").

196. If judges ever find a violation, then they will have to decide whether their inquiry proceeded under Due Process and Equal Protection, or under Just Compensation, lines of inquiry. Monetary awards may depend on which analytical framework they choose. *See supra* note 156.

9

The Prescience and Centrality of *Euclid* v. *Ambler*

Michael Allan Wolf

The thing which hath been, it is that which shall be; and that which is done is that which shall be done; and there is no new thing under the sun.
ECCLESIASTES 1:9

Happy the youth in Euclid's axioms tried,
Though little versed in any art beside;
Who, scarcely skill'd an English line to pen,
Scans Attic metres with a critic's ken.
GEORGE NOEL GORDON, LORD BYRON,
"THOUGHTS SUGGESTED BY A
COLLEGE EXAMINATION" (1806)

The written judicial opinion, the lifeblood of the Anglo-American system of common law, on occasion is imbued by jurists, teachers, and scholars with the trappings and influence of symbol. There lies within the body of cases studied in nearly each American legal discipline one opinion from which the careful reader may perceive the dominant themes, the pervasive pattern of decision making, the extralegal underpinnings, or the operative vocabulary of the pertinent area of the law.

So, for example, the torts student struggles with Judge Benjamin Cardozo's daedal text in *Palsgraf*,[1] hoping to be rewarded with a fundamental appreciation of foreseeability. Every exercise of judicial review, the essential tool of constitutional litigation, is justified or criticized in Chief Justice John Marshall's terms, derived from his jurisprudential/political coup in *Marbury* v. *Madison*.[2] Justice Louis Brandeis, in his *Erie*[3] and *Chicago Board of Trade*[4] contributions, set the tone for generations of opinion writers and litigants immersed in federal choice of law and antitrust. To practitioners, students, and other interested parties, the names *Javins*,[5] *Clifford*,[6] and *Miranda*[7] conjure up not only esoteric legal images and nuances, but also practices and policies with significant real-world implications.

Land use law has its central opinion as well, rendered in a case known by a geographical name, *Euclid*,[8] that suggests to the layperson the lines, points, and planes of elementary geometry. The importance of Justice George Sutherland's nineteen-page opinion is indisputable: Several articles explain the case and debate its import and worth;[9] several pages, each containing columns of case references, appear in *Shepard's United States Citations;* the case has prominent display in casebooks[10] and is discussed in treatises and hornbooks devoted to areas including land use, local government, and constitutional and property law;[11] the term "Euclidean" is used to describe the system of height, area, and use regulation granted the Supreme Court's imprimatur.

Yet *Euclid's* centrality goes beyond the traditional measures noted in the paragraph above. The 1926 decision, unlike such famous cases as the dispute over Dred Scott's future,[12] is much more than a milestone, more than a reference point cited out of habit or to appeal to the audience's familiarity gained over generations of use. The Ambler Realty Company's challenge is exceedingly relevant to student and practitioner: The student who truly masters Sutherland's text has a firm grip on the fundamental rules and rationales found in succeeding cases; even today the typical land use dispute pits a disgruntled property owner (or the disgruntled neighbor of a satisfied owner) against the public zoning decision makers who have failed to appreciate the extent of economic harm caused by their acts or failures to act. Moreover, there are historical, philosophical, and political strata of meanings in *Euclid* that have scarcely been mined.[13]

Sixty years after the Court's approval of zoning, *Euclid* endures as substance and symbol, despite waves of demographic, economic, and political change. This chapter first explores the prescience fixed in the *words* of the *Euclid* opinion, words that anticipate key challenges to the Euclidean regime raised over the subsequent six decades (and, from all indications, beyond); it then examines other legacies of the *form* of the *Euclid* litigation, elements that shaped the seminal (and enduring) posture of American land use disputes; finally it considers *Euclid's* current state of disrepute among the ever-growing body of critics of zoning and the public regulation of land use.

THE FOUR SEEDS

One need only review the table of contents of the latest casebook or treatise to appreciate the complexity and variegation of the field of land use law. In addition to confronting pages and pages devoted to so-called traditional topics such as the power to zone, amendments, variances, nonconforming uses, and accordance with the comprehensive plan, today's reader is invited to master developments in environmental, administrative, and constitutional law, and to ponder readings and concepts drawn from sociology, political science, economic theory, and real estate finance.

The tools of the land use lawyer and planner have indeed changed since the 1920s, as professionals have sought to match the socioeconomic intricacy and technological sophistication of urban and suburban life in the 1980s. Given this profound temporal and developmental gap, it is easy to dismiss *Euclid* as relevant only to a Model-T, "Lochnerian" universe. Such a dismissal, however, would ignore one of the opinion's most important aspects: the manner in which the Court's words and phrases anticipate four principal "modern" objections to Euclidean zoning and comprehensive governmental land use regulation. In fact, to study the *Euclid* opinion absent some appreciation of the "four seeds" planted therein—exclusion, anticompetitiveness, parochialism, and aestheticism—seems as shallow an exercise as Byron's "scarcely skill'd" student pondering Greek geometry.

Excluding Uses and People

The serious question in the case arises over the provisions of the ordinance excluding from residential districts, apartment houses, business houses, retail stores and shops, and other like establishments. This question involves the validity of what is really the crux of the more recent zoning legislation, namely, the creation and maintenance of residential districts, from which business and trade of every sort, including hotels and apartment houses, are excluded.[14]

Exclusion is the essence of Euclidean zoning. Structures and lots are classified according to the height, area, and use deemed appropriate for the specific location. For example, according to the village of Euclid's 1922 "comprehensive zoning plan," the U–1 classification excluded the highest number of potential uses, for only the following were allowed: "single family dwellings, public parks, water towers and reservoirs, suburban and interurban electric railway passenger stations and rights of way, and farming, noncommercial greenhouse nurseries and truck gardening."[15]

The Court had no trouble with the village's segregation of residential and industrial uses, a course of separation in accordance with and abetted by the then-current state of nuisance law.[16] Exclusion of apartment houses and hotels posed the "serious question" left unresolved in "numerous and conflicting" state court decisions. In the name of health, safety, morals, and general welfare—the legitimate goals of the police power—and with the blessings of "commissions and experts"[17] like Alfred Bettman,[18] Sutherland and his brethren refused to find that setting apart single-family housing, in theory, necessarily violated Fourteenth Amendment due process strictures.[19]

The insulation of single-family residences that was approved in *Euclid* was an attempt to use the power of the state (or city) to regulate land uses more rigidly and effectively than had been the case with private devices, particularly covenants and defeasible fees, that ran the risk of unreasonably restricting the essential right of alienation.[20] No longer, it was hoped, would the character of a neighborhood depend on the whims of developers or the insistence of neighbors. Officials of local government—planners, commissioners, inspectors—would devise and enforce a properly legislated zoning plan.

The solution—governmental regulation—was so simple that one wonders why it took until the second decade of the twentieth century for comprehensive land use planning to appear. There are two basic explanations. First, America had only recently turned the corner of urbanization:

> From 1860 to 1910, towns and cities sprouted up with miraculous rapidity all over the United States. Large cities grew into great metropolises, small towns grew into large cities, and new towns sprang into existence on vacant land. While the rural population almost doubled during this half century, the urban population multiplied almost seven times. Places with more than 50,000 inhabitants increased in number from 16 to 109. The larger cities of the Middle West grew wildly. Chicago more than doubled its population in the single decade from 1880 to 1890, while the Twin Cities trebled theirs, and others like Detroit, Milwaukee, Columbus, and Cleveland increased from sixty to eighty percent.[21]

Second, it must be remembered that, although state encouragement of private enterprise is as old as the Republic,[22] it was not until the Progressive era of American history that widespread tampering with the market was broadly accepted, even encouraged by politicians and judges.[23] Even the more conservative members of the Supreme Court, during the initial two decades of the twentieth century, allowed some experimentation under the rubric of the police power, despite some negative impact on cherished constitutional liberties.[24]

By the early 1920s, however, when Sutherland and Pierce Butler joined James C. McReynolds and Willis Van Devanter to form the conservative bloc we know as the "Four Horsemen," the period of judicially approved experimentation swiftly drew to a close. Representative of the new regime was the Court's decision in *Adkins* v. *Children's Hospital,*[25] a 1923 case holding invalid an act of Congress "providing for the fixing of minimum wages for women and children in the District of Columbia."[26] For a five-member majority, Sutherland wrote: "There is, of course, no such thing as absolute freedom of contract. It is subject to a great variety of restraints. But freedom of contract is, nevertheless, the general rule and restraint the exception; and the exercise of legislative authority to abridge it can be justified only by the existence of exceptional circumstances."[27] Those circumstances were absent in the *Adkins* case, as they were in nearly every contract or property rights case to come before the Court until old age (not FDR's Court-packing attempt) took its toll on the elderly Court.[28] *Euclid* v. *Ambler,* a case that split Sutherland from the remaining three (dissenting) "horsemen," was a glaring exception to the pervasive pattern of judicial activism.

In many ways, Euclidean zoning is a quintessential Progressive concept. Many of the key components are present: the reliance on experts to craft and enforce a regulatory scheme;[29] the belief that a pleasant environment would foster healthy, responsible citizens;[30] and the trust in decentralized control, a belief in what Frederic Howe called *The City: The Hope of Democracy.*[31] But there was another sentiment shared by many active in the Progressive movement that was underlying zoning and that contributed to its approval and popularity in the conservative climate of the 1920s: a decidedly negative view of the immigrants, particularly Southern and Eastern Europeans, who from the 1880s to the mid-1920s

poured into America's cities in "alarming" numbers.[32]

The very shape and political structure of many American metropolitan areas were influenced in large part by the influx of "undesirable" newcomers. As Sam Bass Warner, Jr., detailed in relation to Boston and environs,[33] and as recently expanded upon by Kenneth T. Jackson in *Crabgrass Frontier,*[34] the annexation movement lost momentum in the final years of the nineteenth century, allowing for the growth of suburbs that ringed America's burgeoning cities. The new Americans were the catalyst, if not the cause of suburbanization:

> In the face of the continually expanding size of the metropolis, by contrast to the continual waves of poor immigrants that flooded the central city and destroyed its old residential neighborhoods, the new suburbs offered ever new areas of homogeneous middle class settlement. Here, most immigrants spoke English, most were Americanized, and here the evenness of income lessened the scope of political conflict.[35]

With the vast increase in immigration in the late nineteenth century, the core city increasingly became the home of penniless immigrants from Southern and Eastern Europe. And of course, in the early years of the twentieth century, increasing numbers of Southern blacks forsook their miserable tenant farms for a place where, they hoped, "a man was a man." In the view of most middle-class, white suburbanites, these newcomers were associated with and were often regarded as the cause of intemperance, vice, urban bossism, crime, and radicalism of all kinds. And as the central city increasingly became the home of the disadvantaged, the number of white commuters rose markedly.[36]

Unlike New Dealers and post-World War II

liberals who drew political support from inner-city denizens, many Progressives viewed the immigrant, in alliance with the manipulative urban machine, as a barrier to effective political and social reform.[37] The homogeneous suburb, populated by middle-class home owners, offered the hope of good government and local control.

The link between land use regulation and anti-immigrant feelings had been acknowledged by the Supreme Court 40 years before the *Euclid* decision, in *Yick Wo* v. *Hopkins* (1886).[38] The Court, having granted writs of *habeas corpus,* ordered the release from custody of two Chinese immigrants who had been imprisoned for violating an 1880 San Francisco ordinance that read, in part:

> Sec. 1. It shall be unlawful, from and after the passage of this order, for any person or persons to establish, maintain, or carry on a laundry within the corporate limits of the city and county of San Francisco without having first obtained the consent of the board of supervisors, except the same to be located in a building constructed either of brick or stone.[39]

While such regulatory restraint on the use of one's property might appear to be quite a legitimate exercise of the police power (particularly in a city that, with hindsight, we know was a holocaust waiting to happen), the officials' race-based, selective enforcement of the ordinance amounted to a constitutional violation:

> It appears that both petitioners have complied with every requisite, deemed by the law or the public officers charged with its administration, necessary for the protection of neighboring property from fire, or as a precaution against injury to the public health. . . . And while this consent of the supervisors is withheld from them and from two hundred others who have

also petitioned, all of whom happen to be Chinese subjects, eighty others, not Chinese subjects, are permitted to carry on the same business under similar conditions. The fact of this discrimination is admitted. No reason for it is shown, and the conclusion cannot be resisted, that no reason for it exists except hostility to the race and nationality to which the petitioners belong, and which in the eye of the law is not justified. The discrimination is, therefore, illegal, and the public administration which enforces it is a denial of the equal protection of the laws and a violation of the Fourteenth Amendment of the Constitution.[40]

That the crucial issue before the Court in *Yick Wo* was the method of enforcement and not the discriminatory effect is made clear in the opinion, and in a comparison with the Court's holding in a case from the previous year, *Soon Hing* v. *Crowley*.[41] Prosecuted under a different San Francisco ordinance, prohibiting the operation of public laundries and washhouses between the hours of 10 p.m. and 6 a.m., Soon Hing's *habeas* plea fell on deaf ears:

> The principal objection . . . of the petitioner to the ordinance in question is founded upon the supposed hostile motives of the supervisors in passing it. The petition alleges that it was adopted owing to a feeling of antipathy and hatred prevailing in the city and county of San Francisco against the subjects of the Emperor of China resident therein, and for the purpose of compelling those engaged in the laundry business to abandon their lawful vocation, and residence there, and not for any sanitary, police, or other legitimate purpose. There is nothing, however, in the language of the ordinance, or in the record of its enactment, which in any respect tends to sustain this allegation. . . . And . . . even if the motive of the supervisors were as alleged, the ordinance would not be thereby changed from a legitimate police regulation,

unless in its enforcement it is made to operate only against the class mentioned; and of this there is no pretence.[42]

This constitutional challenge came up short. Yet, the link between police power regulation of the use of private property and ethnic discrimination was fixed in the memory of the High Court.

While the Court might not be convinced fully as to the invalidity of regulations that only indirectly discriminated against racial and ethnic minorities, the justices held otherwise when faced with explicit racial zoning by a city ordinance. In *Buchanan* v. *Warley*,[43] a 1917 decision invalidating Louisville's ordinance forbidding blacks to move into a predominantly white neighborhood and whites to move into a predominantly black neighborhood, the Court set aside the regulation designed "to promote the public peace by preventing racial conflicts."[44] The justices found the ordinance an affront to free alienation and a "direct violation of the fundamental law enacted in the Fourteenth Amendment of the Constitution preventing state interference with property rights except by due process of law."[45] Thus, by the time zoning challenges became popular in state and lower federal courts, American jurists were quite aware of the actual or potential use of governmental property restrictions to discriminate against immigrants, or for that matter, any other group out of favor with those in control.

The less than holy alliance between zoning as a particular land use planning tool and anti-immigration sentiment dates back to the birthplace of American height, area, and use zoning—New York City. As has been ably demonstrated by Seymour Toll in his insightful *Zoned American*,[46] one of the driving forces behind passage of New York's 1916 ordinance was a coalition of Fifth Avenue retailers. The garment industry that had worked its way up the avenue over the past few decades, with its mass of Eastern European workers, posed a serious threat to the future of high-class retailing: "What was coming up the avenue in hot pursuit was the garment industry. It sought the same thing as the carriage trade merchant—gain—but its route was lower Fifth Avenue, its great weapon was the tall loft building, its generals were real estate speculators, and its troops were lower East Side immigrants."[47]

The metaphor employed by one key spokesman of the Fifth Avenue Association was far from flattering:

"Gentlemen, you are like cattle in a pasture, and the needle trade workers are the flies that follow you from one pasture to another, nagging you into abandoning one great centre after another and leaving a trail of ruin, devastation, and bankruptcy up and down the length of the city. The rich pasture of your predecessors was in Grand Street. The flies drove the trade to Fourteenth Street, where most of you took up the burden of trying to do business against these odds of a city that had no law and no plan to save itself from the spoilation of its choicest selections. Then you were driven to Twenty-third Street, and again, within a few years, to Thirty-fourth and Forty-second Streets, and here, once more, the flies are threatening to swarm worse than ever."[48]

Compare Henry James's impressions from a visit to New York City less than two decades before:

[I]t was the sense, after all, of a great swarming, a swarming that had begun to thicken, infinitely, as soon as we had crossed to the East side and long before we had got to Rutgers Street. There is no swarming like that of Israel when once Israel has got a start, and the scene here bristled, at every step, with the signs and sounds, immitigable, unmistakable, of a Jewry that had burst all bounds.[49]

Echoes of this type of imagery reverberate in Sutherland's opinion as well. The justice, for example, converted Alfred Bettman's *amicus* reference to a furnace in the living room[50] into *Euclid's* most memorable chestnut: "A nuisance may be merely a right thing in the wrong place,—like a pig in the parlor instead of the barnyard."[51] And how far from the metaphor of swarming flies is Sutherland's characterization of an apartment house as "a mere parasite, constructed in order to take advantage of . . . open spaces and attractive surroundings"?[52] Probably close enough to warrant speculation that the tides (only recently receded) of "new" immigrants, many of whom were current or potential residents of hotels and apartments, in part inspired the justice's rationalization of the legality of land use regulation: "Until recent years, urban life was comparatively simple, but with the great increase and concentration of population, problems have developed, and constantly are developing, which require, and will continue to require, additional restrictions in respect of the use and occupation of private lands in urban communities."[53]

That his contribution in the *Euclid* case was not vintage Sutherland should be apparent when one compares his deference to studies and commissions ("The matter of zoning has received much attention at the hands of commissions and experts, and the results of their investigations have been set forth in comprehensive reports."[54]) to an earlier reference to a business community "beset and bedeviled with vexatious statutes, prying commissions, and government intermeddling of all sorts."[55] Or compare his organic view of a Constitution

that adapts to new circumstances to the following excerpts from his stinging dissent from the majority's support of debtor relief in the 1934 *Blaisdell*[56] decision:

> The words of Judge Campbell . . . are peculiarly apposite. ". . . Constitutions can not be changed by events alone. . . . It is not competent for any department of the Government to change a constitution, or declare it changed, simply because it appears ill adapted to a new state of things. . . ."
>
> . . . .
>
> . . . Constitutional grants of power and restrictions upon the exercise of power are not flexible as the doctrines of the common law are flexible. These doctrines, upon the principles of the common law itself, modify or abrogate themselves whenever they are or whenever they become plainly unsuited to different or changed conditions. . . .
>
> . . . .
>
> The whole aim of construction, as applied to a provision of the Constitution, is to discover the meaning, to ascertain and give effect to the intent, of its framers and the people who adopted it.[57]

It would take nothing short of an emergency (real or only perceived) to move Sutherland away from such dedication to the private property rights protected by the Fifth and Fourteenth Amendments. Or, perhaps, the lone horseman could rationalize his position as protective of the property values (and rights) of established residential users.

That the justices who participated in the *Euclid* case, at least those who read the lower court opinion, were aware of the socioeconomic ramifications of their holding is undeniable. As the members of the Court reviewed Judge Westenhaver's opinion in *Ambler Realty Co.* v. *Village of Euclid,*[58] they should have pondered this direct allusion to the exclusionary purpose and potential of land use controls:

> The purpose to be accomplished [by Euclid's zoning ordinance] is really to regulate the mode of living of persons who may hereafter inhabit [the village]. In the last analysis, the result to be accomplished is to classify the population and segregate them according to their income or situation in life. The true reason why some persons live in a mansion and others in a shack, why some live in a single-family dwelling and others in a double-family dwelling, why some live in a two-family dwelling and others in an apartment, or why some live in a well-kept apartment and others in a tenement, is primarily economic.[59]

Indeed, Westenhaver's prediction of what would have happened had *Buchanan* v. *Warley* gone the other way provided the reader with an important clue as to zoning's exclusionary potential: "[I]t is equally apparent that the next step in the exercise of this police power would be to apply similar restrictions for the purpose of segregating in like manner various groups of newly arrived immigrants. The blighting of property values and the congesting of population, whenever the colored or certain foreign races invade a residential section, are so well known as to be within the judicial cognizance."[60] In 1926, despite this warning, the Supreme Court allowed the bold experiment in urban and suburban planning to continue.

Nearly five decades later, the New Jersey Supreme Court dropped a bombshell on the law and planning community. In their 1975 opinion in *Southern Burlington County N.A.A.C.P.* v. *Township of Mount Laurel*,[61] the justices recognized and attacked the link between land use restrictions and socioeconomic segregation, a tie that was particularly distasteful because of the state's "crisis—a desperate need for housing, especially of decent living accommodations economically suitable for low and moderate income families."[62] To a body of commentators who had perceived this connection two decades before, *Mount Laurel* was an appropriate, if somewhat delayed, judicial response.[63] To a number of critics, particularly local and state legislators and skeptical jurists from other jurisdictions, those who sat on New Jersey's high court were mistaken arbiters at best, socialist usurpers at worst.[64]

During the subsequent decade, the legacy of *Mount Laurel* has been impressive: some corrective legislation,[65] replication in a handful of state courts,[66] oceans of ink in planning and law journals,[67] and stubborn resistance leading to a second (more restrictive and demanding) supreme court decision in New Jersey.[68] Even if one opposed the court's activism and social tampering, it was now evident that zoning and socioeconomic exclusion were intertwined.

The careful student of the Court's opinion in *Euclid* should not be surprised at these recent developments, for the potential use of governmental property restrictions, like private restrictions before *Shelley* v. *Kraemer*,[69] to exclude those "not like us," is one of the seeds of *Euclid*. Buried between the constitutional catchwords and sociological shibboleths are the loaded words and phrases, and a tradition, of segregation.

Controlling the Market

> The bill alleges that the tract of land in question is vacant and has been held for years for the purpose of selling and developing it for industrial uses, for which it is especially adapted, being immediately in the path of progressive industrial development; that for such uses it has a market value of about $10,000 per acre, but if the use be limited to residential purposes

the market value is not in excess of $2,500 per acre. . . .

It is specifically averred . . . that prospective buyers of land for industrial, commercial and residential uses in the metropolitan district of Cleveland are deterred from buying any part of this land . . .; that the ordinance . . . has the effect of diverting the normal industrial, commercial and residential development thereof to other and less favorable locations.[70]

The relatively unrestrained market in industrial and commercial sites in metropolitan Cleveland was one of the first victims of Euclid's comprehensive zoning ordinance, at least according to the Ambler Realty Company. Not only was Ambler's piece of real estate, nestled between Euclid Avenue and the Nickel Plate Railroad, severely devalued, but also certain unnamed parties would have virtual monopolies on the most intensive (and potentially lucrative) uses permitted on selected, choice lots in the newly planned suburb, at least for the foreseeable future.

This second seed planted in *Euclid*—the use of regulatory power to control or eliminate competition—has blossomed into two sets of challenges to Euclidean zoning. First, in the decades following the Court's approval of zoning in theory, many jurisdictions wrestled with a practical problem left unresolved in early ordinances—the nonconforming use.[71] The preexisting gas station, repair shop, or laundry surrounded by block after block of residential and recreational buildings could monopolize business within its captive market. The government officials who, in their wisdom, isolated the nonconforming use with a fervent prayer that it would just disappear, actually freed the owner from the burdens of competition it would have experienced in a zone set aside for similar pursuits. Thus, the judiciary's often tortured attempts to validate

plans for amortizing, purchasing, or severely restricting modifications of nonconforming uses were valid attempts to rid zoning of its inherent anticompetitive nature.[72]

The second set of challenges was inspired largely by two controversial Supreme Court antitrust cases, *City of Lafayette* v. *Louisiana Power & Light* (1978),[73] and *Community Communications* v. *City of Boulder* (1982).[74] In attempting to define the limits of the *Parker* v. *Brown* [75] umbrella that shields states from the devastating torrent of Sherman and Clayton Act antitrust challenges, the Court's rulings on alleged utilities and franchise abuses suggested the possibility of litigation involving a conspiracy to restrain trade between a municipality's zoning authorities and a favored property owner. Justice Potter Stewart, in his dissent in *Lafayette Power*, voiced the fears of many local legislators: "Each time a city grants an exclusive franchise, or chooses to provide a service itself on a monopoly basis, or refuses to grant a zoning variance to a business . . . state legislative action will be necessary to ensure that a federal court will not subsequently decide that the activity was not 'contemplated' by the legislature."[76] When an Illinois federal district court entered a $38 million judgment against local governments that conspired to deprive a developer of a hookup to a public sewer system,[77] chills went up the spines of county and municipal officials throughout the nation.[78] A number of state legislatures reacted to this perceived challenge to the financial health of local governments by extending the state's *Parker* exemption,[79] while Congress enacted the Local Government Antitrust Act to remove the threat of treble damages in future cases.[80] Yet, with injunctive relief and attorneys fees still available, the antitrust count remains an effective component of the litigation package for the late-1980s land use attorney representing disgruntled private interests.[81]

It might seem ironic, given the rich trust-busting image of late nineteenth and early twentieth century reformers, that a program with Progressive roots has such a strong anti-competitive flavor. What is often forgotten in our haste to generalize is that before the First World War public monopolies were often considered the solution to many private sector abuses. So, for example, Frederic Howe proffered municipal ownership of lucrative utilities to avoid the corruption that plagued the awarding of franchises by urban machines:

> In city and state it is the greed for franchise grants and special privileges that explains the worst of the conditions. This is the universal cause of municipal shame. By privilege, democracy has been drugged. . . .
>
> . . . .
>
> . . .That municipal ownership would greatly diminish, if not wholly correct, most of the abuses of municipal administration I am firmly convinced. . . .
>
> . . . .
>
> . . . There seems . . . to be a well-defined line of demarcation between the functions which should be performed by the city and those which should be left to private control. *That line is fixed by monopoly. Whatever is of necessity a monopoly should be a public monopoly,* especially where it offers a service of universal use. . . . Either monopoly will control or seek to control the city, or the city must own the monopoly.[82]

It helps to understand zoning as a variation on this municipal ownership theme, for local governments, particularly in the new suburbs not yet swallowed by annexation, in effect retained control of land development rights through comprehensive land use planning and the restriction of uses. That neither public ownership nor zoning was able to overcome the graft and corruption that infested franchise awards and the unfettered real estate market is yet another example of an ultimately unsatisfying public/private distinction.

The anticompetitive component of zoning also suggests that the reformers who advanced urban planning theory were not solely responsible for the popularity of height, area, and use zoning. One does not have to be an unstinting adherent to Gabriel Kolko's capture thesis[83] to acknowledge that vested real estate interests, such as the Fifth Avenue merchants in New York City, played an important role in the alliance that ensured a future for American zoning.[84] In other words, the attraction and enhanced value of an area set aside as the only available industrial or commercial property were probably hard to overcome in the minds of many influential conservative property owners (or judges) otherwise predisposed to oppose government regulation of land ownership.

Ensuring Local Control

> It is said that the Village of Euclid is a mere suburb of the City of Cleveland. . . . But the village, though physically a suburb of Cleveland, is politically a separate municipality, with powers of its own and authority to govern itself as it sees fit within the limits of the organic law of its creation and the State and Federal Constitutions.[85]

One could easily substitute "City of Petaluma"[86] or "Town of Ramapo"[87]—two municipalities in the vicinity of large central cities (San Francisco and New York City) notorious for their attempts to resist the pressures of growth—for the reference to the "Village of Euclid" in the paragraph above. In many ways, the 1926 decision cleared the way for similarly sited communities to limit population and ward off the evils of urbanization, despite the fact that the municipality in question stood in the way of residential development for central city residents hoping to escape the physical confinement and the social, economic, and political problems of inner-city life.

As noted previously, the use of public and private land use controls was closely connected to the growth of politically distinct suburbs. In the words of one suburban Chicago critic of annexation: "Under local government we can absolutely control every objectionable thing that may try to enter our limits—but once annexed we are at the mercy of city hall."[88] Boston's experience was not atypical:

> It was already apparent in the 1880's that to join Boston was to assume all the burdens and conflicts of a modern industrial metropolis. To remain apart was to escape, at least for a time, some of these problems. In the face of this choice the metropolitan middle class abandoned their central city. . . .
>
> . . . Beyond Boston the special suburban form of popularly managed local government continued to flourish. In suburbs of substantial income and limited class structure, high standards of education and public service were often achieved. Each town, however, now managed its affairs as best it could surrounded by forces largely beyond its control.[89]

Zoning out, or segregating, the city's most distasteful uses could help ensure that the escape to the suburbs would not mean facing again the problems left behind.

Euclid itself, 16 square miles of predominantly agricultural land when it was incorporated in 1903, was a relatively new governmental unit when its officials began studying zoning in 1922.[90] Through the village ran Euclid Avenue, the continuation of a street in Cleveland that boasted one of the nation's grandest, mansion-lined streets.[91] The Cleveland Tractor Company plant was located near the Nickel Plate Railroad.[92] But zoning, even in the village immortalized in the term Euclidean, could not keep metropolitan Cleveland away for long; Euclid today boasts a population of 60,000 (many of whom are of eastern European descent)[93] and a General Motors plant on Ambler Realty's former site.[94]

Because of zoning's contribution to the continued isolation of middle-class communities, courts and legislatures in some states have mandated regional responsibility for suburban areas, while in other areas planning and zoning controls have been recaptured by state officials.[95] Moreover, litigants continue to ask where the obligations of the municipality end—at the town limits, within certain radii extending out from the town's central attraction such as a large employer, a shopping center, or an affluent neighborhood. A broad appreciation of "comprehensiveness" has enabled some jurists to consider the activities and needs of landowners and occupiers in neighboring towns.[96]

These shifts in the nature and operation of zoning law are not timely reactions to late-twentieth century socioeconomic and governance realities. They should be appreciated as inevitable, if sorely delayed, responses to the suburbanization movement that was given credence and support by the Court (and its adherents) in *Euclid.*

Considering Aesthetic Value

> [T]he coming of one apartment house is followed by others, interfering by their height and bulk with the free circulation of air and monopolizing the rays of the sun which otherwise would fall upon the smaller homes, and bringing, as their necessary accompaniments, the disturbing noises incident to increased traffic and business, and the occupation, by means of moving and parked automobiles, of larger portions of the streets, thus detracting from

their safety and depriving children of the privilege of quiet and open spaces for play, enjoyed by those in more favored localities,—until, finally, the residential character of the neighborhood and its desirability as a place of detached residences are utterly destroyed.[97]

One of the most striking departures from "established principles" that land use law has taken of late is the patent acknowledgment of aesthetics as a legitimate goal of the state's police power, either independently or as part of the amorphous concept labeled "general welfare."[98] Some earlier federal and state court decisions had allowed aesthetic regulation in through the back door—for example, by acknowledging the traffic hazards of disturbing signs[99] or the economic benefit of preserving natural beauty.[100] More recent jurists have taken Justice William Douglas's language in *Berman* v. *Parker*[101] as authority for justifying regulations solely on the basis of such subjective qualities as beauty and historical worth: "It is within the power of the legislature to determine that the community should be beautiful as well as healthy, spacious as well as clean. . . ."[102] In the spirit of *Berman,* New York City's landmark preservation program was approved in *Penn Central*[103] and Detroit's anticombat zone ordinance passed constitutional muster in *Young* v. *American Mini-Theatres.*[104]

Precedent for such an expansive understanding of the breadth of the police power can be located in the lines from *Euclid* that introduce this section. Sutherland's language is sprinkled with the buzzwords of 1980s litigation and legislation. The preservation of open space mandated in San Diego[105] and Tiburon, California,[106] and the judicial acceptance of subdivision exactions in the form of parks and other recreational facilities[107] are not too far removed from "the privilege of quiet and open spaces to play" recognized in *Euclid.* The enhanced appreciation of sunlight as an important energy source in the Wisconsin suburb in *Prah* v. *Maretti,*[108] and as a precious urban amenity in the nation's crowded downtowns (with planners seeking to avoid the dark canyons of Manhattan),[109] are 1980s efforts to combat "monopolizing the rays of the sun."

Some official denials to the contrary, aesthetic sensibility originally was an important component of height, area, and use zoning. For every planner who attempted to promote the profession by noting the "The Sheer Cost of Ugliness" (the title of an address to the Sixteenth National Conference on City Planning in 1924),[110] there was the simple assertion that beauty was good in and of itself:

> The object of the City Planning Conference [of 1926], as I understand it, is not only to promote cities and towns which shall be more convenient for business and for traffic, but also to promote cities and towns which shall be more beautiful places in which to live. . . . We must consider for children not only plenty of air and plenty of light and playgrounds, but we must consider also beautiful surroundings in which they shall grow up.[111]

The speaker was Mrs. W.L. Lawton of Glens Falls, New York, in 1926 the chair of the National Committee for Restriction of Outdoor Advertising.[112]

Ambler counsel Baker summarized the point in an argument designed to contrast such unsupportable subjectivity with the mighty demands made by the due process clause, as expansively interpreted by the Four Horsemen: "Even if the world could agree by unanimous consent upon what is beautiful and desirable, it could not, under our constitutional theory, enforce its decision by prohibiting a land owner, who refuses to accept the world's view of beauty, from making otherwise safe and innocent uses of his land."[113] This carefully crafted appeal—though complete with references to Judge Cooley (one of the important influences on Sutherland's jurisprudence)[114]—missed the mark. However, never again would the justice from Utah stray so far from the call of substantive due process.

OTHER LEGACIES OF *EUCLID*

The words and phrases of Sutherland's opinion thus served as a predictive text for legal issues and battles yet to be fought. Equally important, *Euclid* as litigation offered a postural paradigm for the forms of disputation to this day.

Reduced to a sentence, the typical land use case in the 1980s departs little from the Ambler-Euclid fight: A dissatisfied property owner (sometimes one who wishes to develop, sometimes that owner's neighbor) seeks redress from the court for the unreasonable and arbitrary acts or omissions of a public decision maker, with allegations of dire social or economic consequences should the court refuse to act. The typical response of judges—deferring to the wisdom of coequal local or state legislators—emulates the majority of the *Euclid* Court. The warning shot fired in *Nectow* v. *City of Cambridge,*[115] a Sutherland opinion more in line with his writings before and after *Euclid,* was followed by a long period of judicial abstinence in the area of land use regulation.[116] It was left to lower federal courts and especially state jurists to draw useful lines between the valid exercise of the police power and confiscatory or arbitrary regulations that amount to due process violations, if not compensable takings.

We still view nearly every zoning and land use case through this regulation/taking perspective, offering yet further evidence of the centrality of *Euclid.* Apparently we have Alfred Bettman to thank (or to blame) for providing the jurisprudential rationale for shifting development rights from private landowners to the public at large.[117] Bettman's was a mediating position between the alarmism of Baker[118] and the jingoism of Metzenbaum.[119] In the section entitled "Zoning Not a Taking of Property—Question of Compensation Not Involved," Bettman carefully distinguished Ambler's situation from that of the Pennsylvania Coal Company a few years before:[120]

> The case at bar is in no way analogous to that case [*Pennsylvania Coal*] nor remotely similar. No property or contract right created by deed or other instrument is here in any respect abolished, suppressed, destroyed, or even regulated. The property rights asserted are simply those which inhere generally in all owners of land; and it is axiomatic that all property is held subject to the general right of the public to regulate its use for the promotion of public health, safety, convenience, welfare. Zoning regulations are quite free from and outside of the scope of the Pennsylvania Coal Company case, in which specified property interests created by contract were destroyed by the statute. It is quite evident that the court did not consider that case as having any relevancy to regulations of the nature of zoning regulations; for not only did it not overrule, it did not even mention the cases in which it had sustained regulations similar to zoning regulations. . . .[121]

These concepts, and the recognition that reasonable land use regulations are the price we pay for holding land in America, are unshaken. Even Oliver Wendell Holmes, the author of the *Pennsylvania Coal* opinion, could perceive a difference, if not in the logic of the two cases, then in the circumstances resulting from a holding adverse to the village of Euclid.

Today's advocate, student, or scholar, puzzling over the Burger Court's failed efforts to articulate meaningful and useful distinctions between valid regulations and confiscatory takings,[122] can admire the relative resoluteness of the Taft Court and yet regret the failure of Sutherland and his brethren to formulate a simple mathematical formula for deciding future disputes. It is doubtful that the tenuous alliance that led to the village's victory would have survived such a demanding prescriptive effort.

That curious alignment of conservatives and liberals is yet another Euclidean legacy. Comprehensive land use planning made strange bedfellows politically and judicially. The following groups and individuals, drawn from many points on the philosophical and political spectra, are responsible for the promulgation and popularization of comprehensive height, area, and use zoning in this country: the carriage trade merchants on New York's Fifth Avenue;[123] Progressive reformers such as Bettman and Howe;[124] sophisticated attorneys such as Lawson Purdy and Edward Bassett;[125] the Republican Secretary of Commerce Herbert Hoover;[126] the financier and real estate magnate Henry Morgenthau;[127] and Robert Whitten, who played a major role in designing plans for New York City, Cleveland's suburbs, and Atlanta (featuring a heavily racially segregated component).[128]

Judges, too, formed unusual alliances when deciding land use cases. For example, just six years before Sutherland made his temporary break from the other three Horsemen, Justice Brandeis had written a stinging dissent from Holmes's finding of a due process violation in the *Pennsylvania Coal* case.[129] Holmes wrote to Harold Laski concerning the majority opinion, "I fear that I am out of accord for the moment with my public-minded friends."[130] His vote in *Euclid,* endorsing the Brandeisian elevation of the public welfare, ensured that Holmes

was no longer "out of accord," at least in this regulatory arena.

Today we see similar political and juridical mismatches. Litigation often pits traditionally liberal groups (environmentalists, planners, and others) against minority groups eager to share in the American dream of suburban home ownership.[131] Conservatives also are divided, as large-scale developer/capitalists and true believers in the sanctity of private property square off against middle-class suburban whites who are anxious about high-density intrusions, in cases such as *James* v. *Valtierra,*[132] *Arlington Heights,*[133] *Mt. Laurel,*[134] and *City of Eastlake.*[135]

The police power/eminent domain struggle splits old right from new. For example, Richard Epstein, in a body of work that warrants the label "Fifth Horseman," would have us return to a period of strict substantive review of infringements on economic rights, particularly private property rights granted special protection by an almost ubiquitous takings clause.[136] Less activist conservative jurists and commentators, ever on guard to avoid the excesses of the Warren Court, would take, and have taken, issue with Epstein's ruminations.[137]

Observers of the modern Supreme Court can note more than a few aberrant voting blocs in cases in which the justices have been called on to determine the validity of regulations affecting the use and development of property. Justice Douglas's *bête noire* to those on the left was his refusal to recognize associational rights on the part of six unrelated college students in *Village of Belle Terre* v. *Boraas.*[138] Thurgood Marshall used his dissent to point out the inconsistency in his colleague's facility, then apparent inability, to perceive a violation of a fundamental right:

> It is no answer to say, as does the majority, that associational interests are not infringed because Belle Terre residents may entertain

whomever they choose. Only last term Mr. Justice Douglas indicated in concurrence that he saw the right of association protected by the first amendment as involving far more than the right to entertain visitors. . . . As Mr. Justice Douglas there said, freedom of association encompasses the "right to invite the stranger into one's home" not only for "entertainment" but to join the household as well. I am still persuaded that the choice of those who will form one's household implicates constitutionally protected rights.[139]

Seven years later, in *San Diego Gas,*[140] Justice William Rehnquist (who during that 1980 term had voted with Justice William Brennan merely 41 percent of the time)[141] stated that he "would have little difficulty in agreeing with much of what is said" in Brennan's controversial dissent that endorsed awarding compensation for temporary regulatory takings.[142] While justices and other judges have often strayed from familiar positions on a number of legal issues—taking care to resist the hobgoblins of foolish consistency—the philosophical puzzle posed by comprehensive regulation of private property in the name of health, safety, morals, and the general welfare has produced decisional mismatches unlike that found in other areas of constitutional jurisprudence.[143]

One last legacy of *Euclid* was bequeathed in Sutherland's closing paragraph: "[The Supreme Court] has preferred to follow the method of a gradual approach to the general by a systematically guarded application and extension of constitutional principles to particular cases as they arise, rather than by out of hand attempts to establish general rules to which future cases must be fitted."[144] This endorsement of gradual decision making—the refusal to articulate specific constitutional demands and limitations—coupled with the

Court's refusal "to sit as a zoning board of appeals,"[145] has inspired a great deal of governmental experimentation with land use sticks and carrots and has legitimated the land use planner's and counsel's version of what contract lawyers call " 'draft[ing] . . . to the edge of the possible.' "[146]

Indeed, metropolitan Cleveland, the inspiration for the Court's lax review standard, can take pride in (or blame for) fostering something of a land use laboratory. Only a few of the more prominent cases need be recited here, each of which is featured in one or more national casebooks or hornbooks on property or zoning law. The 1963 decision of the Ohio Supreme Court in *Reid* v. *Architectural Board of Review of Shaker Heights*[147] stands for the proposition that reasonable aesthetic regulation will not violate a home owner's freedom of expression. In 1983, a congregation of Jehovah's Witnesses fell victim to the tastes of other suburbanites in *Lakewood, Ohio, Congregation of Jehovah's Witnesses, Inc.* v. *City of Lakewood*[148] as the Sixth Circuit Court of Appeals upheld an ordinance that prohibited churches in residential districts.

Two United States Supreme Court opinions have their origins in regulations restricting the property rights of Cleveland-area residents. In 1977's *Moore* v. *City of East Cleveland,*[149] the city's nuclear family zoning regulation failed to survive the majority's heightened scrutiny, despite the precedent of *Belle Terre.*[150] Only the year before, the Court upheld "a city charter provision requiring proposed land use changes to be ratified by 55% of the votes cast."[151]

Reviewing just these few cases, it is easy to perceive a pattern: the employment of property restrictions to inhibit the activities of, or even to exclude outright, those who do not believe, act, or look like the rest of us. This negative aspect of the Cleveland litigation record is perhaps most apparent in the account of a

Fair Housing Act action brought against the city of Parma, whose officials, according to a federal district court, "had engaged in a number of acts which had the purpose and effect of maintaining Parma as a segregated community in violation of the Act."[152]

The demographic evidence was quite disturbing. In 1970, the suburb could claim a black population of 50 out of a total of 100,216 residents, while in the Cleveland metropolitan area blacks made up 16 percent of the population.[153] This segregation was not a result of happenstance: "The District Court . . . considered the evidence which the government had introduced to prove that Parma had followed racially exclusionary policies and practices. This evidence included testimony that Parma had a reputation and image of being the Cleveland suburb most hostile to blacks and statements of elected officials of Parma which were either overtly racist or found to have racist meanings."[154] In contrast to the Supreme Court's hesitant posture in exclusionary zoning cases like *Warth* v. *Seldin*[155] and *Arlington Heights*,[156] the Sixth Circuit reviewed and for the most part approved District Judge Frank J. Battisti's broad remedial order.[157] Ironically, the residents and officials of the city—many of whom are of Polish descent[158]—were members of the same ethnic groups that were excluded from several of Cleveland's suburbs that featured the Progressive tool of height, area, and use zoning.

Given this duplication and reduplication of some of the more unsatisfying features of the Euclidean model—the stubborn persistence of some of the case's weaker substantive and procedural elements—perhaps zoning is sorely out of place in a society more than half a century removed from 1926 in terms of demographics, technology, politics, and social development. Indeed, many of Euclidean zoning's more prominent critics continue to employ the traditional zoning scheme found in the village of Euclid as either a straw man or a foil that magnifies the economic, social, or practical advantages of alternative systems.

THE HARD QUESTION: WHAT SHOULD REMAIN OF *EUCLID?*

In light of the somewhat "sordid" origins of Euclidean zoning and the reality that the seeds implanted in Sutherland's opinion have often borne poisonous fruit, it is not surprising that a growing body of critics has called for the abandonment of comprehensive governmental regulation of land use, particularly at the local level. The cries for change, much like the voices in support of zoning, cannot be traced to any one ideological or political source. It is possible, however, to delineate three major strategies of attack: deregulation, reregulation, and metaregulation.

The champion of nonzoning is Bernard Siegan, an influential conservative law professor whose imprint easily is discerned in the findings and recommendations of President Reagan's Housing Commission.[159] A devotee of Houston's system of private land use controls, Professor Siegan does not mince words:

> I submit that zoning is not entitled to constitutional protection. It is not necessary; it is not desirable; it is detrimental. It has no relationship to public health, safety, and welfare, except, on the whole, an adverse one. It is regulation almost solely for the sake of regulation.[160]

Siegan has inspired a generation of critics who would have the Supreme Court seriously reconsider the Taft Court's reliance on the expertise of local planners and legislators. These deregulators invite the justices to return us to a pre-Euclidean regime in which the property holder is limited by the vagaries of the market, the constraints of common law nuisance, and the requirements listed in enforceable agreements between neighbors.[161]

The second group of critics, close in spirit and agenda to the deregulators, substitutes an alternative system of controlling or redistributing development rights. For example, Robert Ellickson, though a supporter of revitalized covenant and nuisance doctrines, is no enemy of local governmental regulation:

> First, the state would enact the nuisance rules. . . . The state would then establish metropolitan Nuisance Boards and grant them primary jurisdiction over nuisance cases and exclusive rule making power over land use problems in their metropolitan area. Each Nuisance Board would then use this power principally (a) to publish regulations stating with considerable specificity which land uses are considered unneighborly by that metropolitan population at that time, (b) to identify hypersensitive uses with similar specificity, (c) to establish threshold levels of "substantial harm," and (d) to promulgate schedules of bonus payments for losses of common nonfungible consumer surplus. By thus clarifying entitlements, the Board would assist the private settlement of disputes and thus lower administrative costs.[162]

As for the determination of the amount of compensation paid to the public by an owner of undeveloped land for the right to develop over "normal" levels, Ellickson would turn to a court or again to a special administrative body.[163] Troubled by the inefficiency and inequity of current zoning practices, Ellickson would thus combine "mandatory public regulations" with an improved system of consensual covenants and a modified approach to nuisance law, along with other means of land use control.[164]

The next plan of attack—metaregulation—is reflected in and has been inspired by *The Quiet Revolution in Land Use Control,*[165] Fred Bosselman and David Callies's 1971 review of state and regional initiatives:

> The tools of the revolution are new laws taking a wide variety of forms but each sharing a common theme—the need to provide some degree of state or regional participation in the major decisions that affect the use of our increasingly limited supply of land. . . .
>
> . . .
>
> . . . It has become increasingly apparent that the local zoning ordinance, virtually the sole means of land use control in the United States for over half a century, has proved woefully inadequate to combat a host of problems of statewide significance, social problems as well as problems involving environmental pollution and destruction of vital ecological systems, which threaten our very existence.[166]

The most familiar examples of the metaregulation challenge to local control are statewide legislative efforts (such as those enacted in Maine, Oregon, Vermont, Hawaii, and Florida),[167] the unsuccessful efforts in the early 1970s to adopt a national land use policy act in Congress,[168] and the creative federalism approach implemented through the Coastal Zone Management Act of 1972 and subsequent amendments.[169] To advocates of these and other programs, the solution to the arbitrariness and irregularities of local land use regulation lies in the superimposition of checks or even detailed specifications from above and beyond the immediate political unit. In this manner, yet another essential element of the Euclidean scheme—devolution to municipal decision makers—has been seriously questioned.

It would be foolishly obstinate for contemporary supporters of zoning to ignore the complaints and suggestions of these and other critical observers and to close their eyes to the social and political realities that gave rise to comprehensive height, bulk, and use regulations. We are thus left with a difficult question: What should remain of *Euclid?* Zoning's checkered origins and the body of evidence indicating the arbitrariness and inequities in many cases of local land use planning would seem to warrant a fundamental rethinking, if not a total reversal, of *Euclid.* Indeed, President Reagan's Commission on Housing "recommend[ed] that the Attorney General seek an appropriate case in which to request review of the *Euclid* doctrine in the context of modern land use issues and the due process protections afforded other property rights in the 50 years since *Euclid* was decided."[170]

Such a drastic step is not called for, however, as this and similar proposals are based on a literal reading of the relevant "text"—the 1926 opinion by Justice Sutherland. It is helpful here to analogize to the field of constitutional jurisprudence. Some students of the Constitution view the text of the document as relatively fixed and, when ambiguous, subject to interpretation confined to discerning the intent of the framers.[171] This limited perspective poses real problems. The Constitution was drafted by a group of men celebrated for their political genius, though subject to the racial, sexual, and socioeconomic prejudices of political leaders of late-eighteenth century America.[172] Moreover, it practically is impossible to pinpoint the appropriate individuals or groups whose views are most relevant (framers, those who attended constitutional conventions, voters, etc.).[173]

Because of these and other shortcomings of interpretavism, other scholars, the noninterpretavists, instead consider the Constitution as amended as forming an organic text: words and phrases with meanings and significance that evolve or shift over time, as affected by (and in turn affecting) legal and nonlegal developments.[174] Consequently, there is no need to revise continually the constitutional text, as long as the essential attributes of the document are preserved.

A comparable appreciation of the *Euclid* "text" reveals three such intrinsic elements that have withstood the challenges of time, theory, and practice. First, the Court prescribed a flexible approach in the legislative implementation and judicial review of public land use planning devices. Second, the Court endorsed careful, expert-based planning, eschewing the haphazard vagaries of the market. Third, the Court approved the transfer, from individual to collective ownership, of development rights above a level often labeled "reasonable return." These three elements have remained inviolate, despite years of experimentation and variation.

The judicial, legislative (at all strata), and administrative refinements—experimentation in the best Brandeisian tradition—in many cases have made contemporary zoning much more responsive, creative, and complex than its Progressive precursor. It is easy to dismiss *Euclid* and Euclidean zoning as the misguided or malignant products of a distant past. It is easy, but not fruitful. Many of the negative characteristics of the "four seeds," for example, have been countered by judges and lawmakers working within confines of the three intrinsic elements noted above. Courts in Pennsylvania and New Jersey have spearheaded judicial campaigns against exclusionary zoning,[175] complemented (and on occasion curtailed) by snob zoning acts,[176] inclusionary zoning provisions,[177] and other legislative contributions.[178] Application of the Sherman and Clayton Acts to instances of alleged public/private conspiracies to limit competition, though limited severely by congressional retrenchment, still can have a chilling effect on local government regulation that unreasonably restricts a landowner's right to compete in the property development marketplace.[179]

Unbridled parochialism and aestheticism also have been restrained somewhat by recent judicial and legislative gloss on the *Euclid* text. Courts and legislatures throughout the United States have mandated the regional obligations of communities as part of the "ever-louder revolution" of the past two decades.[180] Similarly, the fears of many of zoning's original opponents—that standardless, purely subjective taste was at the heart of public land use controls—may have been responsible for many of the due process mechanisms employed to ensure that denials of permission are based on ascertainable criteria such as historical and architectural value.[181]

From the 1930s on, the structural framework of Euclidean zoning—the categorization and segregation of height, bulk, and use—has been subject to more than a moderate amount of tampering. Preexisting nonconformities that could not be wished away have been subjected to careful scrutiny and amortization.[182] Municipalities have implemented noncumulative zoning, seeking to segregate intense uses from potential residential neighbors who are more apt to cry "nuisance" and less able to generate revenue.[183] Other approaches may result in the granting of permission to develop above and beyond established limits (transferable development rights,[184] conditional zoning[185]), the provision of public amenities (incentive or bonus zoning),[186] the elimination of harmful spillovers and unimaginative rigidity (performance standards),[187] and the integration of traditionally segregated uses (mixed use[188] and planned unit development[189]).

These are just the more prominent among post-Euclidean techniques for regulating diverse land uses, modifications that have helped zoning adapt to a late twentieth century urban environment featuring suburban nodes, historic preservation districts, and gentrification of inner-city neighborhoods. Municipalities that employ these techniques have learned how to make zoning a more positive tool for encouraging specific forms of development, not just the means for outlawing broad categories of disdained activities.

Jurists have played an important role in amplifying and modernizing the *Euclid* text. For example, the Oregon Supreme Court's elevation of scrutiny in the *Fasano* case[190] can be seen as a logical extension of Charles Haar's influential call for zoning "in accordance with a comprehensive plan."[191] *Fasano* has engendered a great deal of expert commentary, along with judicial and legislative reception, modification, and even well-considered rejection.[192] It is no longer a given that each city council rezoning will be subject to only the most innocuous judicial inquiry.

The constitutional count has proved successful for litigants as well. While the right to develop one's property has not yet attained fundamentality, public regulations that infringe on such interests as free speech,[193] the free exercise of religion,[194] and privacy,[195] have been subjected to elevated scrutiny or careful balancing, in order to ensure that local and state officials do not run roughshod over protected rights. Although one would have liked to hear a clear judicial voice in such cases as *Metromedia,*[196] *Schad,*[197] and *Taxpayers for Vincent,*[198] even these uneven attempts should demonstrate to zoning's critics and supporters alike that judicial abstinence is a thing of the past. Moreover, the decisional void created by the Burger Court's inability or refusal to resolve the regulatory takings puzzle (in *Agins, San Diego Gas, Hamilton Bank,* and *Yolo County*)[199] was filled by the decisions of a number of state and lower federal courts that have rallied around or begged to differ with Justice Brennan's call for compensation for temporary regulatory takings.[200]

Nor have the suggestions offered by free-market critics of zoning fallen on deaf ears. Contract and conditional zoning,[201] and the bargaining over subdivision exactions,[202] are the first steps toward institutionalizing the exchange of development rights and public amenities. In addition, at least one court has given its blessing, despite the disapproval of the local legislature, to a neighborhood's sale of its right to object to a zoning change.[203]

IN CLOSING

For its predictive, postural, and symbolic value, *Village of Euclid* v. *Ambler Realty Co.* legitimately can be offered as one of the great cases of American law. To understand Sutherland's opinion is not just to comprehend the structure and operation of cumulative height, bulk, and use zoning, but also to appreciate the Court's significant and surprising recognition of the public's right to regulate cherished private property rights, even in the absence of a widely perceived general emergency. It is to consider the benefits of comprehensive planning of land use and many other human pursuits. It is to weigh the advantages of flexibility and deference over rigidity and command.

The greatness of *Euclid* is not necessarily equated with worth, particularly given six decades of sharp criticism and profound change. Planners, lawyers, judges, and legislators, in whose hands the future of zoning lies, should consider carefully the justified objections of zoning's critics as well as the concerted efforts to redress inequities, inefficiencies, and arbitrariness. They should strive to resist the temptation to take extreme measures. They should question seriously returning to a purer past or moving to a total regulatory model, for following one path would sacrifice expertise

and predictability while the other road leads to bland uniformity and inefficiency.

A 60-year anniversary is an appropriate time to take an accounting of *Euclid* and its legacy. What one sees, despite some original imperfections and repeated abuses, is a process of synthesis and experimentation that deserves a hard look, a bit of respect, and perhaps some celebration despite the wolves and pallbearers at the door.

AUTHOR'S NOTE

The author thanks Charles Haar for his guidance and constant support, the Lincoln Institute for the opportunity to submit my ideas to the helpful criticisms of others, and Stuart Strasner and Daniel Morgan of Oklahoma City University School of Law for their flexibility and for their appreciation of the importance of scholarly contributions to the constructive development of the law.

NOTES

1. *Palsgraf* v. *Long Island R.R. Co.,* 248 N.Y. 339, 162 N.E. 99 (1928).

2. 5 U.S. (1 Cranch) 137 (1803).

3. *Erie R.R. Co.* v. *Tompkins,* 304 U.S. 64 (1938).

4. *Board of Trade* v. *United States,* 246 U.S. 231 (1918).

5. *Javins* v. *First National Realty Corp.,* 428 F.2d 1071 (D.C. Cir. 1970).

6. *Helvering* v. *Clifford,* 309 U.S. 331 (1940).

7. *Miranda* v. *Arizona,* 348 U.S. 436 (1966).

8. *Village of Euclid* v. *Ambler Realty Co.,* 272 U.S. 365 (1926).

9. The legal periodicals index for 1926–1928 lists the first six reviews of the controversial case, appearing in journals from Cincinnati, Harvard, Minnesota, St. Louis, Virginia, and Yale. *Index of Legal Periodicals* 1 (1928): 694.

10. *See, e.g.,* "Zoning: Classic to Contemporary," in D. Callies and R. Freilich, *Cases and Materials on Land Use* (1986), pp. 34–42; R. Ellickson and D. Tarlock, "Zoning and the Rights of Landowners," in *Land-Use Controls: Cases and Materials* (1981), pp. 43–49; C. Haar, *Land-Use Planning: A Casebook on the Use, Misuse, and Re-use of Urban Land,* 3d ed. (1977), pp. 194–203; D. Hagman, *Public Planning and Control of Urban and Land Development: Cases and Materials,* 2nd

ed. (1980), pp. 468–473; D. Mandelker and R. Cunning-ham, *Planning and Control of Land Development,* 2d ed. (1985), pp. 62–70; R. Wright and M. Gitelman, in "The Zoning Classics," in *Cases and Materials on Land Use,* 3d ed. (1982), pp. 649–657. While preparing the first edition of his casebook, Professor Hagman surveyed a number of case-book and treatise writers concerning "the all-time zoning greats." *Euclid* v. *Ambler* was at the top of the list. D. Hag-man, *Public Planning and Control of Urban and Land Develop-ment,* pp. 465–466.

11. *See, e.g.,* 1 R. Anderson, *American Law of Zoning 3d* § 3.09, at 101–104 (1986); R. Cunningham, W. Stoebuck & D. Whitman, *The Law of Property* § 9.3, at 529–531 (1984); D. Mandelker, *Land Use Law* § 2.18, at 27 (1982); 8 E. McQuillin, *The Law of Municipal Corporations* 3rd ed. § 25.05, at 12 (1983); J. Nowak, R. Rotunda and J. Young, *Constitutional Law,* 3d ed., § 11.12(b), at 404 (1986); 6 R. Powell, *The Law of Real Property* paras. 867[1][a], 79C-10 to 79C-11 (1986); 1 P. Rohan, *Zoning and Land Use Controls,* § 1.02[2][d][i], at 1–11 to 1–13 (1986); 3 C. Sands and M. Libonati, *Local Government Law,* § 16.04, at 16–9 (1982); 1 E. Yokley, *Zoning Law and Practice,* 4th ed., § 3–7, at 43–46 (1978).

12. *Dred Scott* v. *Sandford,* 60 U.S. (19 How.) 393 (1857).

13. William Randle's ambitious contribution to this book does a fine job of exploring uncharted territory, but much more remains to be done until we come closer to a full appreciation of the case—its context and its import.

14. *Euclid* v. *Ambler,* 272 U.S. at p. 390.

15. *Id.* at p. 380.

16. *Id.* at p. 388.

17. *Id.* at p. 394.

18. *See* A. Bettman, *City and Regional Planning Papers* (1946).

19. "[T]he reasons [proffered by the village to justify zoning] are sufficiently cogent to preclude us from say-ing, as it must be said before the ordinance can be de-clared unconstitutional, that such provisions are clearly arbitrary and unreasonable, having no substantial rela-tion to the public health, safety, morals, or general wel-fare." *Euclid* v. *Ambler,* 272 U.S. at 395 (citations omitted).

20. *See, e.g.,* Bruce, "Racial Zoning by Private Contract in the Light of the Constitution and the Rule Against Re-straints on Alienation," *Ill. L. Rev.* 21 (1927): 704.

21. R. Hofstadter, *The Age of Reform* (1955), p. 174 (foot-notes omitted).

22. *See* O. Handlin and M. Handlin, *Commonwealth: A Study of the Role of Government in the American Economy: Massa-chusetts, 1774–1861,* rev. ed., (1969).

23. *See, e.g.,* R. Hofstadter, *The Age of Reform,* pp.

227–256; G. Kolko, *The Triumph of Conservatism: A Reinterpre-tation of American History, 1900–1916* (1963), pp. 2–3.

24. *See, e.g.,* Warren, *The Progressiveness of the United States Supreme Court, Colum. L. Rev.* 13 (1913): 294.

25. 261 U.S. 525 (1923).

26. *Id.* at p. 539 (citation omitted).

27. *Id.* at p. 546.

28. *See, e.g.,* P. Murphy, *The Constitution in Crisis Times: 1918–1969* (1972), pp. 63–67.

29. R. Hofstadter, *The Age of Reform,* at p. 155: "Reform brought with it the brain trust. In Wisconsin even before the turn of the century there was an intimate union be-tween the La Follette regime and the state university at Madison that foreshadowed all later brain trusts. Na-tional recognition of the importance of the academic scholar came in 1918 under Woodrow Wilson, himself an ex-professor, when the President took with him as counselors to Paris that grand conclave of expert advisers from several fields of knowledge which was known to contemporaries as The Inquiry."

30. A. Eckirch, *Progressivism in America* (1974), pp. 77–78: "With [Jacob] Riis, his main prop and comfort, as a guide, Theodore Roosevelt in his capacity as Police Com-missioner of New York from 1895–1897 toured the city streets to observe firsthand the crowded tenements with their inevitable results in poverty, crime, disease, and filth. The social consequences of such conditions contra-dicted Roosevelt's finer instincts and notions of Ameri-can progress. He could agree therefore with those reformers who argued that better housing was a key to the improved health, well-being, and social stability of the hundreds of thousands of new city dwellers in the United States."

31. F. Howe, *The City: The Hope of Democracy* (1905); *see also* R. Hofstadter, *The Age of Reform,* p. 175 (footnote omit-ted): "Even with the best traditions of public administra-tion, the complex and constantly changing problems created by city growth would have been enormously dif-ficult. Cities throughout the industrial world grew rapid-ly, almost as rapidly as those in the United States. But a great many of the European cities had histories stretch-ing back hundreds of years before the founding of the first white village in North America, and therefore had traditions of government and administration that pre-dated the age of unrestricted private enterprise. While they too were disfigured and brutalized by industrialism, they often managed to set examples of local administra-tion and municipal planning that American students of municipal life envied and hoped to copy."

32. *See, e.g.,* G. Mowry, *The Era of Theodore Roosevelt and the Birth of Modern America, 1900–1912* (1958), pp. 91–94;

B. Solomon, *Ancestors and Immigrants: A Changing New England Tradition* (1956). Of course, there were many reformers who were dedicated to "Americanizing" the nation's newcomers, and others who, as cited in J. Higham, *Strangers in the Land: Patterns of American Nativism 1860–1925*, 2d ed. (1977), p.118: "[l]ike the rest of their generation . . . felt little enmity toward the immigrants but little identification with them either."

33. S. Warner, *Streetcar Suburbs: The Process of Growth in Boston (1870–1900)*, 2d ed. (1978).

34. K. Jackson, *Crabgrass Frontier: The Suburbanization of the United States* (1985).

35. S. Warner, *Streetcar Suburbs*, p. 164.

36. K. Jackson, *Crabgrass Frontier*, p. 150.

37. *See, e.g.,* R. Hofstadter, *Age of Reform*, pp. 183–186. *See also* O. Handlin, *The Uprooted*, (1951), p. 217: "It was not surprising that the boss should see in the stirring of reform interests a threat to his own position. But it was significant that the mass of immigrants should regard the efforts of the various progressives with marked disfavor. In part this disapproval was based on the peasant's inherited distrust of radicalism; but it was strengthened by a lack of understanding among the radicals that deprived them of all influence among the newcomers."

38. 118 U.S. 356 (1896).

39. *Id.,* p. 357 (syllabus).

40. *Id.,* p. 374.

41. 113 U.S. 703 (1885).

42. *Id.,* pp. 710–711.

43. 254 U.S. 60 (1917).

44. *Id.,* p. 73.

45. *Id.,* p. 82.

46. S. Toll, *Zoned American* (1969).

47. *Id.,* p. 110.

48. *Id.,* pp. 176–177 (footnote omitted) (quoting address of J. Howes Burton to Fifth Avenue merchants, as reported in the October 22, 1916, *New York Times.*).

49. H. James, *The American Scene* (1968), p. 131.

50. A. Bettman, *Village of Euclid et al.* v. *Ambler Realty Company.* Brief, *amici curiae.* In *City and Regional Planning Papers*, pp. 157, 172 [hereinafter Bettman Brief]: "When we put the furnace in the cellar rather than in the living room, we are not actuated so much by dictates of good taste or aesthetic standards, as by the conviction that the living room will be a healthier place in which to live and the house a more generally healthful place. . . ."

51. *Euclid v. Ambler,* 272 U.S. at 388.

52. *Id.,* p. 394.

53. *Id.,* p. 386–387.

54. *Id.,* p. 394.

55. Sutherland, *"Private Rights and Government Control,"*

A.B.A. Rep. 42 (1917): 197, 198 (presidential address at annual meeting of American Bar Association).

56. *Home Bldg. & Loan Ass'n* v. *Blaisdell,* 290 U.S. 398 (1934).

57. *Id.,* pp. 451–453 (citations omitted).

58. 297 F. 307 (N.D. Ohio 1924).

59. *Id.,* p. 316.

60. *Id.,* p. 313.

61. 67 N.J. 151, 336 A.2d 713 (1975).

62. *Id.,* p. 158, 336 A.2d at 716.

63. *See, e.g.,* Williams, "Planning Law and Democratic Living," *Law & Contemp. Probs.* 20 (1955): 316; Williams and Doughty, "Studies in Legal Realism: Mount Laurel, Belle Terre and Berman," *Rutgers L. Rev.,* 29 (1975): 73.

64. *See, e.g.,* Rose, "The Mount Laurel Decision: Is It Based on Wishful Thinking?" *Real Est. L.J.* 4 (1975): 61.

65. *See, e.g., Cal. Gov't Code* § 65580 (West, 1983).

66. *See, e.g., Surrick* v. *Zoning Hearing Board of Upper Providence Township,* 476 Pa. 182, 383 A.2d 105 (1977); *Berenson* v. *Town of New Castle,* 38 N.Y.2d 102, 341 N.E.2d 236 (1975).

67. *See, e.g., Oakwood at Madison, Inc.* v. *Madison Township,* 72 N.J. 481, 371 A.2d 1192, 1198–1199 n.3 (1977) (citing reactions to *Mount Laurel I*).

68. *Southern Burlington County N.A.A.C.P.* v. *Mount Laurel,* 92 N.J. 158, 456 A.2d 390 (1983) (*Mount Laurel II*). *But cf. Hills Dev. Co.* v. *Township of Barnards,* 103 N.J. 1, 510 A.2d 621 (1986) (*Mount Laurel III*) (upholding state Fair Housing Act that limited breadth of court's holding in *Mount Laurel II*).

69. 334 U.S. 1 (1948).

70. *Euclid v. Ambler,* 272 U.S. at 384–85.

71. *See, e.g., Jones* v. *City of Los Angeles,* 211 Cal. 304, 295 P. 14 (1930).

72. *See, e.g., City of Los Angeles* v. *Gage,* 127 Cal. App. 2d 442, 274 P.2d 34 (Dist. Ct. App. 1954).

73. 435 U.S. 389 (1978).

74. 455 U.S. 40 (1982).

75. 317 U.S. 341 (1943).

76. 435 U.S. at 438 (Stewart, J., dissenting) (footnote omitted).

77. *Unity Ventures* v. *County of Lake,* No. 81 C 2745 (N.D. Ill. Jan. 12, 1984), *j.n.o.v. granted,* 631 F. Supp. 181 (N.D. Ill. 1986). *See* "Developer's Suit Against Localities Nets $28.5 Million Treble Damage Award," 46 *Antitrust & Trade Reg. Rep.* (BNA) 595 (No. 1157, March 22, 1984).

78. *See, e.g., Hearing Before the Comm. on the Judiciary, U.S. Sen., on S. 1578, A Bill to Clarify the Application of the Federal Antitrust Laws to Local Governments,* 98th Cong., 2d Sess. 68–69 (1984) (statement of William J. Althaus, mayor of York, Pennsylvania, on behalf of U.S. Conference of

Mayors): "Local governments throughout the United States are trembling in fear and uncertainty over this issue. The *Unity Ventures, Grayslake* case has served to move local officials up a notch or two on the Richter Scale."

79. *See, e.g., N.D. Cent. Code* § 40–01–22 (1983).

80. Pub. L. No. 98–544, 98 Stat. 2750 (codified at 15 U.S.C. §§ 34–36 (Supp. 1986)).

81. 15 U.S.C. §§ 35–36 (Supp. 1986).

82. F. Howe, *The City: The Hope of Democracy,* pp. 5, 119, 129.

83. *See, e.g.,* G. Kolko, *The Triumph of Conservatism,* p. 3: "It is business control over politics (and by 'business' I mean the major economic interests) rather than political regulation of the economy that is the significant phenomenon of the Progressive Era."

84. *See, e.g.,* S. Toll, *Zoned American,* pp. 174–177.

85. *Euclid* v. *Ambler,* 272 U.S. at 389.

86. *Construction Indus. Ass'n of Sonoma Co.* v. *Petaluma,* 375 F. Supp. 574 (N.D. Cal. 1974), *rev'd,* 522 F.2d 897 (9th Cir. 1975), *cert. denied,* 424 U.S. 934 (1976). ("Petaluma Plan," featuring five-year cap on number of dwelling units, survived challenge.)

87. *Golden* v. *Planning Bd. of Town of Ramapo,* 30 N.Y.2d 359, 334 N.Y.S.2d 138, 285 N.E.2d 291, *appeal dismissed,* 409 U.S. 1003 (1972) (town's plan for timed residential development upheld).

88. K. Jackson, *Crabgrass Frontier,* p. 151 (quoting March 9, 1907, editorial from the Morgan Park *Post*) (footnote omitted).

89. S. Warner, *Streetcar Suburbs,* pp. 164–165.

90. S. Toll, *Zoned American,* pp. 214, 216.

91. *Id.,* p. 214.

92. *Id.,* p. 215.

93. According to the 1980 Census, 3,608 of Euclid's 59,999 residents identified themselves as of Hungarian, Polish, Russian, or Ukranian "single ancestry." Another 2,576 were placed in the "Polish and other groups" "multiple ancestry" category. Bureau of the Census, U.S. Dep't of Commerce, *1980 Census of the Population, Characteristics of the Population, General Social and Economic Characteristics, Ohio* 37–75 to 37–76 (1983) (Table 60, Selected Ancestry Groups: 1980) [hereinafter *Ancestry Groups*].

94. *See* C. Haar, *Land-Use Planning,* p. 204.

95. *See, e.g.,* "Local Government Comprehensive Planning and Land Development Regulation Act," *Fla. Stat. Ann.* §§ 163.3161–.3215 (West Supp. 1988); Pelham, Hyde & Banks, "Managing Florida's Growth: Toward an Integrated State, Regional, and Local Comprehensive Planning Process," *Fla. St. U.L. Rev.* 13 (1985): 515.

96. *See, e.g., Borough of Cresskill* v. *Borough of Dumont,* 15 N.J. 238, 104 A.2d 441 (1954).

97. *Euclid* v. *Ambler,* 272 U.S. at 394.

98. *See, e.g., Metromedia, Inc.* v. *City of San Diego,* 453 U.S. 490, 507–08, 510–11 (1981) (White, J., plurality opinion) (recognizing "appearance of the city" as "substantial governmental goal[]"); *State* v. *Jones,* 305 N.C. 520, 526–27, 290 S.E. 2d 675, 679 (1982) (North Carolina court joined growing number of jurisdictions that authorize "regulation based on aesthetics alone").

99. *See, e.g., Railway Express Agency* v. *New York,* 336 U.S. 106 (1949) (state regulation of advertising vehicles survived equal protection challenge).

100. *See, e.g., City of Miami Beach* v. *Ocean & Inland Co.,* 147 Fla. 549, 3 So. 2d 364 (1941) (resort city's restrictive zoning ordinance upheld).

101. 348 U.S. 26 (1954).

102. *Id.,* p. 33. *See also Metromedia,* 453 U.S. at 570 (Rehnquist, J., dissenting): "In my view, the aesthetic justification alone is sufficient to sustain a total prohibition of billboards within a community. . . ." (citation to *Berman* omitted).

103. *Penn Central Transp. Co.* v. *New York City,* 438 U.S. 104 (1978).

104. 427 U.S. 50 (1976).

105. *See San Diego Gas & Elec. Co.* v. *City of San Diego,* 450 U.S. 621 (1981).

106. *See Agins* v. *City of Tiburon,* 447 U.S. 255 (1980).

107. *See, e.g., Associated Home Builders of the Greater East Bay, Inc.* v. *City of Walnut Creek,* 4 Cal. 3d 655, 484 P. 2d 606, 94 Cal. Rptr. 630 (1971).

108. 108 Wis. 2d 223, 321 N.W.2d 182 (1982) (court recognized property owner's right to receive access to sunlight for solar heating).

109. *See, e.g.,* Vettel, "San Francisco's Downtown Plan: Environmental and Urban Design Values in Central Business District Regulation," *Ecology L.Q.* 12 (1985): 511.

110. Crawford, "The Sheer Cost of Ugliness," in *Proceedings of the Sixteenth National Conference on City Planning* (1924), p. 141.

111. Lawton, "Regulation of Outdoor Advertising," in *Planning Problems of Town, City and Region: Papers and Discussions at the Eighteenth National Conference on City Planning* (1926), p. 86.

112. *Id.*

113. Brief and Argument for Appellee at 48, *Euclid* v. *Ambler,* 272 U.S. 365 (1926) (No. 31).

114. *See* J. Paschal, *Mr. Justice Sutherland: A Man Against the State* (1951), pp. 16–20.

115. *Nectow* v. *City of Cambridge,* 277 U.S. 183 (1928).

116. The Burger Court's willingness to decide some

zoning and other land use disputes, despite its inability to resolve the takings/regulation puzzle, stands in marked contrast to the sparse record of decisions during the four decades following *Nectow*.

117. *See* S. Toll, *Zoned American,* pp. 237–238.

118. *See, e.g., Euclid* v. *Ambler,* 272 U.S. at 379 (argument for appellee): "That our cities should be made beautiful and orderly is, of course, in the highest degree desirable, but it is even more important that our people should remain free."

119. *See* S. Toll, *Zoned American,* pp. 230–231.

120. *Pennsylvania Coal Co.* v. *Mahon,* 260 U.S. 393 (1922).

121. Bettman Brief, p. 165.

122. The litany of frustration began with *Agins,* 447 U.S. at 260 (1980) ("there is as yet no concrete controversy"), and continued through *San Diego Gas,* 450 U.S. at 633 (no final judgment), *Williamson County Regional Planning Comm'n* v. *Hamilton Bank,* 473 U.S. 172, 200 (1985) (premature claim), and *MacDonald, Sommer & Frates* v. *Yolo County,* 477 U.S. 340, 352 (1986) ("the holdings of both courts below leave open the possibility that some development will be permitted"). *See* Wolf, "Three Strikes But Not Out: Hamilton Bank and the Takings Question," *Fla. B.J.,* May 1986, p. 67 (footnote omitted): "The refusal, or inability, of the Court to end this stalemate has resulted in more than the inevitable disagreements between federal and state courts, even within the same state. On occasion, deliberate Supreme Court abstinence can lead to beneficial local innovation. Yet if experimentation is what the Court has in mind in the takings area, the Justices are sending the wrong message by continuing to take regulatory takings cases."

At the end of his first term as Chief Justice, William Rehnquist delivered the majority opinion that broke the stalemate (with a holding in favor of compensation). *First English Evangelical Lutheran Church* v. *County of Los Angeles,* 107 S.Ct. 2378 (1987).

123. *See* S. Toll, *Zoned American,* pp. 110, 158–162.

124. *See id.,* pp. 136, 236–39.

125. *See id.,* pp. 144–145, 149–150.

126. *See id.,* pp. 201–203.

127. *See id.,* pp. 124–126.

128. *See id.,* pp. 220–21.

129. *Pennsylvania Coal Co.* v. *Mahon,* 260 U.S. 393, 416–422 (Brandeis, J., dissenting).

130. M. Howe, ed., *Holmes-Laski Letters* 1 (1963), (letter of Jan. 13, 1923).

131. For example, the local chapter of the NAACP was the lead plaintiff in the litigation challenging Mount Laurel's protective planning and zoning scheme, while environmentalists supporting open space ordinances

faced home builders (and their hopeful clients) in the *Agins* and *San Diego Gas* cases.

132. *James* v. *Valtierra,* 402 U.S. 137 (1971).

133. *Village of Arlington Heights* v. *Metropolitan Housing Dev. Corp.,* 429 U.S. 252 (1977).

134. *See supra* text accompanying notes 61 to 68.

135. *City of Eastlake* v. *Forest City Enterprises,* 426 U.S. 668 (1976).

136. *See* R. Epstein, *Takings: Private Property and the Power of Eminent Domain* (1985); Epstein, "Judicial Review: Reckoning on Two Kinds of Error" *Cato J.* 4 (1985): 711, 717–718: "One only has to read the opinions of the Supreme Court on economic liberties and property rights to realize that these opinions are intellectually incoherent and that some movement in the direction of judicial activism is clearly indicated."

137. *See, e.g.,* Scalia, "Economic Affairs as Human Affairs," *Cato J.* (1985): 703, 705–706: "The Supreme Court decisions rejecting substantive due process in the economic field are clear, unequivocal and current, and as an appellate judge I try to do what I'm told. But I will go beyond that disclaimer and say that in my view the position the Supreme Court has arrived at is good—or at least that the suggestion that it change its position is even worse." One wonders, however, whether now-Justice Scalia's "activist" opinion in *Nollan* v. *California Coastal Comm'n,* 107 S.Ct. 3141 (1987), signals a modest shift in Epstein's direction.

138. *Village of Belle Terre* v. *Boraas,* 416 U.S. 1 (1974).

139. 416 U.S. at 17–18 (Marshall, J., dissenting).

140. 450 U.S. at 636–61 (Brennan, J., dissenting).

141. *"The Supreme Court, 1980 Term,"* Harv. L. Rev. 95 (1981): 93, 340 (Table I(B), Voting Alignments).

142. 450 U.S. at 633–634 (Rehnquist, J., concurring). Indeed, when the *First Church* decision was handed down in late 1987, the five justices joining the new chief included William Brennan (who was aligned with Rehnquist only 40.8 percent of the time during the term) and Thurgood Marshall (who teamed with Rehnquist only 39.5 percent of the time, the low for the term). *See* "The Supreme Court, 1986 Term—Leading Cases," *Harv. L. Rev.* 101 (1987): 119, 363 (Table I(B), Voting Alignments).

143. By no means is such "strange bedfellowing" confined to the land use area. *See, e.g., Metropolitan Life Ins.* v. *Ward,* 470 U.S. 869, 883 (O'Connor, J., dissenting, joined by Justices Brennan, Marshall, and Rehnquist).

144. *Euclid* v. *Ambler,* 272 U.S. at 397.

145. *Belle Terre,* 416 U.S. at 13 (Marshall, J., dissenting).

146. Herbert, "Contracts of Accretion: A Modest Proposal for U.C.C. Section 2-207, *Mem. St. U.L. Rev.* 14 (1984): 441, 473 (quoting Karl Llewellyn's testimony be-

fore the New York State Law Revision Commission for 1954).

147. 119 Ohio App. 67, 192 N.E.2d 74 (1963).

148. 699 F.2d 303 (6th Cir. 1983).

149. 431 U.S. 494 (1977).

150. *See supra* text accompanying note 138.

151. *Eastlake,* 426 U.S. at 670.

152. *United States* v. *Parma,* 661 F.2d 562, 564 (6th Cir. 1981), *aff'g in part & rev'g in part,* 494 F.Supp. 1049 (N.D. Ohio 1980).

153. 661 F.2d at 566.

154. *Id.*

155. 402 U.S. 490 (1975) (restrictive view of federal standing).

156. 429 U.S. at 268–71 (requiring demonstration of discriminatory intent).

157. 661 F.2d at 576–79.

158. Of 92,548 residents of Parma, 9,554 listed themselves as of Polish ancestry, and 7,415 were placed in the "Polish and other groups" category. *Ancestry Groups,* at Ohio 37–79 to 37–80.

159. *See, e.g., Report of the President's Commission on Housing* (1982), p.201 [hereinafter *Commission Report*].

160. B. Siegan, *Land Use Without Zoning* (1972), p. 221.

161. *See, e.g.,* Delogu, "Local Land Use Controls: An Idea Whose Time Has Passed," *Me L. Rev.* 36 (1984): 261; Kmiec, "Deregulating Land Use: An Alternative Free Enterprise Development System," *U. Pa. L. Rev.* 130 (1981): 28; Krasnowiecki, "Abolish Zoning," *Syracuse L. Rev.* 31 (1980): 719.

162. Ellickson, "Alternatives to Zoning: Covenants, Nuisance Rules, and Fines as Land Use Controls," *U. Chi. L. Rev.* 40 (1973): 681, 762–63 (footnotes omitted).

163. *Id.,* p. 763.

164. Professor Ellickson has recently reconsidered the Coasean foundation for his earlier speculation. *See* "Of Coase and Cattle: Dispute Resolution Among Neighbors in Shasta County," *Stan. L. Rev.* 38 (1986): 623.

165. F. Bosselman & D. Callies, *The Quiet Revolution in Land Use Control* (1971).

166. *Id.,* pp. 1, 3.

167. *See, e.g.,* DeGrove & Stroud, "State Land Planning and Regulation: Innovative Roles in the 1980s and Beyond," *Land Use L. & Zoning Dig.* 39 (March 1987): 3.

168. *See* C. Haar, *Land-Use Planning,* pp. 98–102.

169. 16 U.S.C. §§ 1451–1464 (1982). *See* Wolf, "Accommodating Tensions in the Coastal Zone: An Introduction and Overview," *Nat. Resources J.* 25 (1985): 7.

170. *Commission Report,* at 202.

171. *See* J. Ely, *Democracy and Distrust: A Theory of Judicial Review* 1 (1980) (interpretavism "indicate[s] that judges

deciding constitutional issues should confine themselves to enforcing norms that are clearly stated or implicit in the written Constitution").

172. For a fine compilation of exchanges concerning the background and prejudices of the framers, see L. Levy, *Essays on the Making of the Constitution,* 2d ed. (1987).

173. *See* J. Ely, *Democracy and Distrust,* p. 17.

174. *See id.,* p. 1 (noninterpretavists hold "view that courts should go beyond that set of [interpretavist] references and enforce norms that cannot be discovered within the four corners of the document").

175. *See supra* text accompanying notes 61 to 68; *National Land and Investment Co.* v. *Easttown Township Board of Adjustment,* 419 Pa. 504, 215 A.2d 597 (1965); *Appeal of Kit-Mar Builders,* 439 Pa. 466, 268 A.2d 765 (1970).

176. Mass. Ann. Laws, ch. 40B, §§ 20–23 (Law. Co-op. 1983).

177. *See, e.g., In the Matter of Egg Harbor Associates,* 94 N.J. 358, 464 A.2d 1115 (1983).

178. *See, e.g.,* Fair Housing Act, N.J. Stat. Ann. §§ 52: 27D–301 to 27D–329 (West, 1986).

179. *See* Hovenkamp and Mackerron, "Municipal Regulation and Federal Antitrust Policy," *UCLA L. Rev.* 32 (1985): 719.

180. *See, e.g.,* Cal. Gov't Code § 65584 (West Supp., 1988).

181. *See* D. Hagman and J. Juergensmeyer, *Urban Planning and Land Development Control Law* §§ 14.5–14.9, at 458–472 (2d ed., 1986).

182. *See, e.g., Model Land Dev. Code,* art. 4 commentary, pp. 147–148 (1976) (table listing cases in which courts approved amortization).

183. *See, e.g., Kozesnik* v. *Montgomery Township,* 24 N.J. 154, 131 A.2d 1 (1957).

184. *See, e.g., Penn Central Transportation Co.* v. *New York City,* 438 U.S. 104 (1978); Costonis, "Development Rights Transfer," 83 *Yale L.J.* 75 (1973).

185. *See, e.g., Collard* v. *Incorporated Village of Flower Hill,* 52 N.Y.2d 594, 439 N.Y.S.2d 326, 421 N.E.2d 818 (1981).

186. *See, e.g.,* C. Haar, *Land-Use Planning,* pp. 254–267.

187. *See, e.g.,* L. Kendig, *Performance Zoning* (1980).

188. *See, e.g.,* R. Witherspoon, J. Abbett and R. Gladstone, *Mixed-Use Developments: New Ways of Land Use* (1976).

189. *See, e.g.,* D. Hagman and J. Juergensmeyer, *Urban Planning and Land Development Control Law,* at §§ 7.15–.19, pp. 220–233.

190. *Fasano* v. *Board of Commissioners of Washington County,* 264 Or. 574, 507 P.2d 23 (1973).

191. Haar, "In Accordance with a Comprehensive Plan," *Harv. L. Rev.* 68 (1955): 1154.

192. *See* Rose, "Planning and Dealing: Piecemeal Land

Controls as a Problem of Local Legitimacy," *Cal. L. Rev.* 71 (1983): 837, 844–846.

193. *See, e.g.,* Mandelker, "The Free Speech Revolution in Land Use Control," *Chi. Kent L. Rev.* 60 (1984): 51.

194. *See, e.g.,* Reynolds, "Zoning the Church: The Police Power Versus the First Amendment," *B.U.L. Rev.* 64 (1985): 767.

195. *See, e.g., West Side Women's Services, Inc.* v. *City of Cleveland,* 573 F.Supp. 504 (N.D. Ohio 1983).

196. *Metromedia, Inc.* v. *City of San Diego,* 453 U.S. 490 (1981).

197. *Schad* v. *Borough of Mount Ephraim,* 452 U.S. 61 (1981).

198. *Members of the City Council of Los Angeles* v. *Taxpayers for Vincent,* 466 U.S. 789 (1984).

199. *See supra* note 122.

200. *See, e.g., Corrigan* v. *City of Scottsdale,* 149 Ariz. 538, 720 P.2d 513 (1986).

201. *See* Wegner, "Moving Toward the Bargaining Table: Contract Zoning, Development Agreements, and the Theoretical Foundations of Government Land Use Deals," *N.C.L. Rev.* 65 (1987): 957.

202. *See, e.g.,* Bauman and Ethier, "Development Exactions and Impact Fees: A Survey of American Practices," *Law & Contemp. Probs.* 50 (1987): 51.

203. *DeKalb County* v. *Albritton Properties,* 256 Ga. 103, 344 S.E.2d 653 (1986).

10

Euclid's Lochnerian Legacy

Robert A. Williams, Jr.

The right to purchase land in anticipation that development and profits would follow the path determined by the speculator's insight into "natural economic laws" was central to the conception of property in America through the early twentieth century. Professor Morton Horwitz, in his well-known article, "The Transformation in the Conception of Property in American Law, 1780–1860,"[1] has traced the descent and several of the legal by-products of this uniquely American conception of landed property as a dynamic market commodity. The common law's static, agrarian conceptions of property, well-suited to England's long-settled land market, were quickly jettisoned by American judges once it was recognized that doctrines such as prescription, "natural use," and "ancient lights" held profound antidevelopmental consequences if applied too rigidly in the New World. Such doctrines, in the words of a New York court in 1838, would work "the most mischievous consequences" in the "growing cities and villages of this country."[2] In America, as nineteenth century judges came to realize, land was held for the purposes of speculation and development. The role of the court was to adapt common law rules to the changing circumstances of a rapidly expanding nation; the paramount, and oftentimes explicitly stated,

goal was the economic development of land to further "the usages and wants of the community."[3]

The land speculator, the individual who had risked capital and purchased vacant land in anticipation of the natural path of this economic development, was a principal beneficiary of this conception of property. While he was never fully adopted as the favored or ward of the court, he frequently was given more than adequate protection in his expectation of profit. His shrewd calculations that he would enjoy the fruits of his labors and perspicacity were given a special status in American property law through the early twentieth century. The circumstances in which his expectations might be impaired unexpectedly by government allegedly acting in the public interest were limited and clearly defined by the law, most notably by the common law doctrine of nuisance.[4]

It should come as no surprise, therefore, that in the 1926 case of *Village of Euclid* v. *Ambler Realty Co.,*[5] the first case in which the United States Supreme Court considered the validity of governmental control of land uses through the creation of zoning districts, the principal point of debate focused on whether zoning could be analogized to regulation of a nuisance under the police power. Ambler Realty Company's

278

attorneys challenged the attempt by the village of Euclid, Ohio, to defend itself against neighboring Cleveland's sprawling manufacturing growth by arguing that Ambler's contemplated industrial use of its Euclid property did not constitute a nuisance under the common law. Therefore, Ambler's attorneys argued, the village's zoning code placing the realty company's parcel in a residential district was an invalid exercise of the police power.[6]

Nuisance doctrine had long served as the workhorse of American private land use law and its heavy baggage of assumptions about the government's limited role in regulating the landed economy through the police power. According to the brief filed by Newton Baker,[7] Ambler's attorney in *Euclid* v. *Ambler Realty:*

> If I buy a piece of land I have no means of knowing whether or not it will be needed for public use, and if any need develops, I must be compensated when the public takes it. But I always know when I buy land, that I may not devote it to uses which endanger the safety, health, or morals of others or make its use a common nuisance to the prejudice of the public welfare. Because of its nature, the exercise of the police power has always been restrained to those uses of property which invade the rights of others, and courts consistently decline to permit an extension of the police power to uses of property involving mere questions of taste or preference or financial advantage to others.[8]

If Mr. Baker's cramped and constraining vision of the limits of the police power seems alien and anachronistic to "modern" land use practicing and academic lawyers, it is only because we regard the intellectual foundations of his argument that restraints on government are derivable from common law categories such as nuisance a distant relic of a bygone

legal era. But Mr. Baker's archaic discourse on the police power and the public welfare is worth recalling for a number of reasons, not the least of which is that by it we are reminded that *Euclid* v. *Ambler Realty,*[9] the case that established the constitutional validity of comprehensive land use planning by government interference with the natural workings of the market, was decided at the height of what has been derisively labelled the *"Lochner* era."[10] Named after an infamous 1905 Supreme Court decision striking down New York state's minimum hours legislation for bakery employees, the *Lochner* era of American constitutional history conjures images of late nineteenth and early twentieth century judges, particularly the judges who sat on the United States Supreme Court, imperiously striking down social and economic legislation out of harmony with their substantive notions of liberty and due process under the Fourteenth Amendment. While the *Lochner* era Supreme Court did invalidate nearly 200 governmental regulations between 1899 and 1937, an even larger number of regulations did, in fact, survive the *Lochner* Court's aggressive brand of substantive due process scrutiny.[11] Nonetheless, the legacy of *Lochner* has imprinted itself on contemporary legal discourse by means of a pejorative epithet. In modern jurisprudential parlance, a judge accused of Lochnerizing usurps a function most wisely regarded as vested in the legislative branch of government. Why, then, did the Lochnerizing justices who sat on the United States Supreme Court in 1926 feel moved to sustain zoning as a valid exercise of the police power in *Euclid,* while those same justices freely struck down minimum wage and hours legislation, state laws prohibiting "yellow-dog" contracts, and regulations affecting prices and entry into business? The latter exercises of the police power were no more or less perniciously perceived by defenders of the

Constitution during the *Lochner* era than was zoning, a fact demonstrated by Counsellor Baker's able brief in *Euclid* and its defense of Western civilization's most cherished institution, the right to property free from unreasonable government regulation. Why did zoning survive the Supreme Court's skeptical Lochnerizing gaze, while other, progressive initiatives did not?

Perhaps an even more important question arises in considering the distinct connection between the landmark decision in *Euclid* and the *Lochner* era. That is, to what degree did the *Lochner* era shape the Court's opinion in *Euclid* and other early zoning cases, and thereby how and to what degree, if at all, does "modern" zoning law reflect the legacy of *Lochner* and a judicial age that was less ashamed to launch upon inquisitory substantive due process review of governmental choices in the economic and social fields? In this chapter, I investigate *Lochner's* legacy in the Supreme Court's land use planning jurisprudence and attempt to suggest the continuing relevance and centrality of *Lochner* in explaining the Court's most recent land use decisions.

THE BIRTH OF ZONING IN THE *LOCHNER* ERA

Lawyers and specialists trained in the field are familiar with the story of the birth of zoning. The typical nineteenth century American city rivaled the squalor described in any of Dickens's novels. Filth, stagnant water, backyard privies, and poor ventilation all contributed to the frequent urban plagues of yellow fever, cholera, and typhoid arising from unsanitary living conditions. Then, following the Civil War, the sanitary sewer system movement, followed by the City Beautiful movement (an offshoot of the 1893 Chicago World's Fair), contributed to heightened awareness of the economic and social costs attributable to the

unplanned urban environment. It was from this set of circumstances that the zoning movement emerged upon the national scene in the early 1900s, climaxed by the federally sponsored drafting of the Standard State Zoning Enabling Act (SZEA) in 1924, and the Supreme Court's 1926 validation of SZEA-styled zoning in *Euclid* v. *Ambler Realty*.[12]

The "movement" for comprehensive planning of the urban environment through zoning was by no means a unified national crusade supported at all levels of society. The notion of a private property owner's virtually unfettered entrepreneurial right to develop his parcel as he saw fit according to his conceptions of the market's needs was engrained deeply in the popular as well as legal consciousness of the age. The timid approach of many cities in attempting to regulate land uses was excused by one early twentieth century advocate of more aggressive city planning as follows:

> In America, it is the fear of restricting or injuring free and open competition that has made it so difficult for cities to exercise proper and efficient control over their development. The tendency therefore has been to promote those forms of civic improvement which can be carried out without interfering with vested interests.[13]

The fear of "interfering with vested interests" was a fear imposed from above, by a judiciary with definite conceptions regarding the limited extent to which legislatures might interfere with constitutionally protected rights and liberties. We see the fear evidenced concretely. In 1916, New York City became one of the first major urban areas to enact a zoning ordinance. Yet fear of interfering with vested interests is reflected in the gross amount of overzoning in that ordinance; the city set aside enough land in business and industrial zones to accommodate an eventual population of approximately 340 million persons. Several other cities were so nervous about too aggressive an exercise of the zoning power that they turned to eminent domain and payment of compensation as means to regulate land use.[14]

The fears of judicial invalidation of zoning were well founded. While more than half the states had adopted zoning enabling acts, state supreme court decisions in a number of influential jurisdictions continued to strike down zoning ordinances into the early 1920s. The Texas Supreme Court, for example, in 1921 declared that it was "idle" to speak of "the lawful business of an ordinary retail store threatening the public health or endangering the public safety," and thus, capable of being zoned out of a land use district.[15] Maryland's high court, as late as 1925 (*Euclid* would be decided the following year), recognized the pervasiveness of zoning ordinances nationally in its opinion in *Goldman* v. *Crowther*.[16] But the court nonetheless felt compelled to hold that the police power could not be stretched so far as to permit districting a city and declaring which land could be put to which uses, unless such uses were related clearly to a health and safety concern.

The lower federal court decision in the *Euclid* litigation itself,[17] issued by Judge Dale Courtney Westenhaver, the former law partner of the Ambler Realty Company's attorney, Newton Baker, expressed the crystalized judicial wisdom of the age respecting the prevailing conceptions of the right to property and the police power. In striking down the village's zoning ordinance as an unconstitutional taking of Ambler Realty's rightful expectation of profit, Judge Westenhaver admonished Euclid as follows:

> The argument supporting this ordinance proceeds, it seems to me, both on a mistaken view of what is property and of what is police

power. Property generally speaking . . . is protected against a taking without compensation, by the guarantees of the Ohio and United States Constitutions. But [defendant municipality's] view seems to be that so long as the owner remains clothed in the legal title thereto and is not ousted from the physical possession thereof, his property is not taken, no matter what extent his right to use it is invaded or destroyed or its present or prospective value is depreciated. This is an erroneous view. The right to property, as used in the Constitution, has no such limited meaning.[18]

Judge Westenhaver's self-confidence in knowing "what is property" under the Constitution is declaimed in a legal discourse alien to our own, less absolutist "modern" idioms of usage regarding what property is. It is the legal discourse of the *Lochner* era and of an imperious unelected judiciary intent on imposing its own notions of the correct social and economic calculus regarding the general welfare through substantive due process review.

As Professor Laurence Tribe has noted, "The notion that governmental authority has implied limits which preserve private autonomy predates the establishment of the American republic."[19] What distinguished the *Lochner* era, whose boundaries are generally agreed as extending from approximately 1897 to 1937, was the belief that the implied limits on government could be derived from common law categories.[20]

The seeds for the Lochnerian genus of substantive due process review were germinating as early as 1887, in *Mugler* v. *Kansas*.[21] While upholding a Kansas prohibition statute, the United States Supreme Court nonetheless warned that it would freely scrutinize the substantive reasonableness of state legislation under the due process clause of the Fourteenth Amendment. Any law enacted pursuant to the police power would be struck down if it bore, in the Court's opinion, "no real or substantial relation" to the public health, morals, or safety, and was "a palpable invasion of rights secured by the fundamental law."[22]

The tendency of *Lochner* era judges to scrutinize police power initiatives to determine if such actions transcended the implied limits on government derived from the common law posed the constitutional issue in bare relief for zoning advocates in the early twentieth century. Under the common law, government could exercise its police power to control or abate a nuisance, for under the common law, each owner of private property was enjoined by the maxim *sic utere tuo ut alienum,* that is, "use your own [property] so as not to harm another's." The judiciary during the *Lochner* era was particularly careful in assuring that the legislature's declaration of a public nuisance could be defended on rational grounds; i.e., that indeed the thing proscribed posed a significant danger to the health and safety of the public, such that its abatement or regulation was justified under the Constitution. To the Lochnerian judicial mind of the early twentieth century, the implied limits on the exercise of the zoning power would thus invariably have to derive from the implied limits on the legislature to declare a nuisance. Only under common law nuisance theory could the police power be exercised constitutionally to limit the rights of an individual to use his property as he saw fit.

Thus in Lochnerian terms, if zoning legislation rested on the same foundation as common law nuisance doctrine, then the legislature could justify this particular exercise of its police power. But if zoning land uses by district, height, and density could not be adequately analogized to the legislative regulation of nuisances, then it would fail judicial scrutiny, for then all that zoning accomplished, in the famous words of Justice Chase in *Calder* v. *Bull,*[23]

was to take property from A and give it to B. The legislature's attempt at redistribution violated natural rights of property and contract derived from the common law. And these rights, as every Lochnerian knew, were protected from majoritarian whim by the Constitution.

Upon this set of assumptions, the Supreme Court and other lower courts following its ideological banner freely struck down minimum wage and price controls, labor-management statutes, and legislative initiatives. While the legislatures always declared such measures to be in the public interest, the judiciary wisely was vested with the final determination on whether such laws interfered unreasonably with common-law-derived rights of freedom of contract and property. These Lochnerian themes and assumptions focused the arguments of opposing counsel when Euclid's land use ordinance was challenged before the Supreme Court in 1926 as violative of the implied limitations on government and the natural law rights of property holders protected under the Constitution of the United States.

EUCLID V. *AMBLER REALTY*

The Ambler Brief

The Supreme Court brief for appellee Ambler Realty[24] bears all the telltale traces of American law's Lochnerian age and its dominant substantive due process constitutional discourse. Marked by a firm conviction of the state's limited role in restructuring the "natural" workings of the market economy, Ambler's brief assigned to the judiciary an aggressive role in policing the boundaries of the state's police power. The brief's animating vision is based on the belief that the legitimate market expectations of private property owners merit judicial protection from state interference. By placing the company's 68-acre parcel in a residentially zoned district, Euclid's ordinance was in open conflict with "natural economic laws":

> The recent industrial development of the City of Cleveland, following the railroad lines, has already reached the Village. . . . In its obvious course, this industrial expansion will soon absorb the area in the Village for industrial enterprises. It is in restraint of this prospect that the ordinance seeks to operate. In effect, it erects a dam to hold back the flood of industrial development and thus to preserve a rural character in portions of the Village, which, under the operation of natural economic laws, would be devoted most profitably to industrial undertakings. This . . . destroys value without compensation to the owners of lands who . . . are holding them for industrial uses.[25]

The land speculator's right in the uninterrupted operation of "natural economic laws" derives from his expectation of profit in accurately predicting market forces, according to the Ambler brief. For the state to alter the market's operation thus deprives the speculator of his expectation of profit, transferring it to another party, solely on the basis of majoritarian whim:

> Since the industrial development of a great city will go on, the effect of this attempted action necessarily is to divert industry to other less suited sites, with a consequent rise in value thereof; so that the loss sustained by the proprietors of land who cannot so use their land is gained by proprietors of land elsewhere . . . imposing an uncompensated loss on the one hand and a gain which is arbitrary and unnatural on the other hand, since it results not from the operation of economic laws, but from arbitrary considerations of taste enacted into hard and fast legislation.[26]

The village's zoning ordinance, based on matters of pure taste, thus could not be in pursuance of any rational government plan dictated by considerations of public safety, health, and welfare, upon which the police power rests. "On the contrary," Ambler's attorneys argued, Euclid's zoning plan "is an arbitrary attempt to prevent the natural and proper development of the land in the village prejudicial to the public welfare."[27]

The argument of the Ambler brief boils down to the basic propositions that the public interest is in the "natural" operation of the market, and the Court's role is to protect those market actors who by their perspicacity have anticipated the market's laws. According to this vision, land speculators are the vanguard of the public interest, and the Constitution wisely undertakes to protect them in this role from the arbitrary caprice or whim of the majority:

> If the Village may lawfully prefer to remain rural and restrict the normal industrial and business development of its land . . . the areas available for the expanding industrial needs of the metropolitan city will be restricted . . . and industry driven to less advantageous sites. All this would be done at the expense of those land owners whose lands, being most advantageously located from an industrial point of view, have as a part of their right of property, which the constitutions of the Nation and the States undertake to protect, the expectation of value due to their superior availability for industrial development.[28]

Euclid can only limit Ambler's right of expectation of profit in its property if that right's exercise somehow constitutes a nuisance. If Ambler is not committing a nuisance, then the police power cannot be said to be exercised in the public interest:

Unless the theory of our expanding civilization is wrong, the public welfare is advanced by the devotion of the most available sites to business and industry, as the need for them develops.[29]

In other words, the public's interest is in the natural workings of the market; not in what its elected representatives declare to be in the public interest. Ambler's planned industrial use of its land cannot be a nuisance, because such a use harmonizes with the market, and therefore the public interest.

Justice Sutherland's Majority Opinion in *Euclid*

While the Ambler brief's reasoning may appear circular, the energizing force behind this Lochnerian style of legal discourse is a dynamic conception of the judiciary's role in willingly substituting its judgment of what is best for the public in place of the legislature's decision. It is this form of legal reasoning calling for aggressive scrutiny of the police power which in fact animates Justice George Sutherland's majority opinion for the United States Supreme Court in *Euclid* v. *Ambler,* upholding the validity of regulating land use through zoning. With its firm grounding in Lochnerian discourse, *Euclid* represents an odd testament to the *Lochner* era birth of modern comprehensive zoning law.

Justice Sutherland has been called the "intellectual spokesman" for the *Lochner* Court's conservative voting block, less than affectionately referred to as the "four horsemen" in the legal history books.[30] Sutherland's majority opinion for the Court in *Euclid* leaves no doubt of its intellectual grounding. The Court's role as articulated in Sutherland's Lochnerian-inspired *Euclid* text is to closely superintend exercises of the police power by looking to the common law for guidance as to limits on the scope of that power:

The ordinance now under review . . . must find . . . [its] justification in some aspect of the police power, asserted for the public welfare. The line which in this field separates the legitimate from the illegitimate assumption of power is not capable of precise delimitation. . . . In solving doubts, the maxim *sic utere tuo ut alienum non laedas,* which lies at the foundation of so much of the common law of nuisances, ordinarily will furnish a fairly helpful clew. And the law of nuisances, likewise may be consulted, not for the purpose of controlling, but for the helpful aid of its analogies in the process of ascertaining the scope of the power.[31]

This simply stated Lochnerian theme introducing the *Euclid* text is further elaborated in Sutherland's close scrutiny of the legislative ends served by zoning. Under the common law, the exercise of property rights could be limited if the exercise resulted in a nuisance. Sutherland's scrutiny of the ordinance was thus dictated by a strategy grounded in the "helpful . . . analogies" of "the law of nuisances." If zoning could be analogized to declaring a nuisance under the police power, then the limits placed by government on individual property through zoning were within the traditional, legitimate scope of that power.[32] And, in response to the argument that zoning reaches much further than nuisance law in limiting individual rights respecting property, Sutherland could provide the paradigmatic common law judge's answer to the perceived anachronism of a legal system based on the principle of *stare decisis:* "[W]hile the meaning of constitutional guarantees varies, the scope of their application must expand or contract to meet the new and different conditions which are constantly coming within the field of their operation."[33] The majesty of the common law, its signal achievement that rendered it such a useful and elastic tool for

Lochnerian judges interpreting the Fourteenth Amendment's due process clause, was its universally recognized ability to grow and meet "the new and different conditions" of the day. And it was the judiciary that determined the pace of that growth, acting upon clear conceptions of the core values protected by the common law.

Besides the heightened scrutiny of legislative goals to determine their orthodoxy with limitations on government derived from common law categories, Lochnerian jurisprudence also closely examined legislative means in achieving goals. Sutherland's famous analysis of the validity of a total exclusion of apartment houses from single-family residential districts provides just one example of *Euclid's* clear grounding in the Lochnerian discursive mode:

> With particular reference to apartment houses, it is pointed out that the development of detached houses is greatly retarded by the coming of apartment houses . . . very often the apartment house is a mere parasite constructed in order to take advantage of the open spaces and attractive surroundings created by the residential character of the district. . . . Under these circumstances apartment houses, which in a different environment would be not only entirely objectionable but highly desirable, come very near to being nuisances.[34]

Unlike minimum wage or hours laws, price controls or pro-labor legislation, all of which clearly confronted and contradicted common-law-derived principles of contract and property, zoning was easily analogized by the *Lochner* era Supreme Court to a traditional common law maxim: Use your land so as not to cause injury to another. The difference between use zoning by districts and public regulation of nuisances was only one of degree, and impor-

tantly, a degree necessitated by the complex conditions of an urbanized society. Thus, Sutherland's relativizing remark: "A regulatory zoning ordinance, which would be clearly valid as applied to the great cities, might be clearly invalid as applied to rural communities."[35] A modern land use lawyer might wonder by what standard Sutherland could possibly determine validity in one context as opposed to another. For Sutherland, as with any Lochnerian, the answer was as simple as it was reflexive—by the standards set out in the common law to determine a nuisance.

POST-EUCLIDEAN, LOCHNERIAN ZONING LAW

The modern land use lawyer's distance from the common law origins of *Euclid* and zoning indicates just how far we are from the legal discourse of substantive due process review of social and economic legislation that dominated Sutherland's era. The passage of time has obscured origins. The *Lochner* era is a vital part of *Euclid* and the birth of land use planning law, a proposition clearly demonstrated by the handful of post-*Euclid* zoning opinions decided by the Supreme Court through the end of the *Lochner* era.

In *Zahn* v. *Board of Public Works,*[36] decided in 1927 shortly after *Euclid,* and *Gorieb* v. *Fox,*[37] also decided in 1927, Sutherland, writing both unanimous opinions for the Court, upheld exercises of the zoning power challenged in those cases, but only after closely scrutinizing the legislative classification of the affected properties. *Zahn* is a short opinion, but most of it is taken up with a precise and approving reiteration of the reasons presented by the city for placing plaintiff's property in a residential zone.[38] In no sense can the opinion be read as granting mere deference to the legislative classification. Final discretion and discriminations are entrusted to the courts. Sutherland's checklist type of review of the legislative rationales in *Zahn* is wholly substantive in nature and Lochnerian in tone.

In *Gorieb*,[39] Sutherland again engaged in intense scrutiny of the legislatively declared goals behind a zoning setback ordinance. He concluded that the government's reasons justifying the ordinance were "obvious," but only after going through those reasons one by one to prove their obviousness.[40]

The Court's two final zoning decisions of the *Lochner* era actually struck down regulations that the Court felt did not further its own concept of the public interest. Both opinions are grounded solidly on Lochnerian foundations. In the 1928 case of *Nectow* v. *City of Cambridge*,[41] Justice Sutherland, once more writing for the Court in what would be his last zoning opinion, engaged in a full inquiry of the rationality of a residential use zoning classification as applied to plaintiff's parcel of land. Backed by a special master's report, Sutherland freely substituted judicial for legislative judgment and held that the zoning ordinance as applied did not further the general welfare. Then, in the same year, in *Washington ex rel. Seattle Title Trust Company* v. *Roberge*,[42] Justice Butler, writing for a unanimous Court, reminded the land use planning profession that zoning was still subject to *Lochner's* implied limits on government derived from common law nuisance. In that case, a trustee of a home for the elderly was denied a permit to replace the existing structure under a zoning ordinance that required the consent of owners of two-thirds of the property within 400 feet of the proposed building. The permit was denied on the sole ground that such consent had not been obtained. The Supreme Court held that the delegation of the police power to affected property owners was repugnant to the Constitution and therefore void. Significantly, the Court went on to hold that the city could in no way prohibit construction of the new home for there was no evidence suggesting that the structure "would be a nuisance . . . liable to work any injury, inconvenience or annoyance to the community, the district or any person."[43]

Washington was the last of the five zoning cases decided by the *Lochner* era Supreme Court. Consistent with its overall substantive due process review record for the *Lochner* era, the Court struck down two of the five exercises of the zoning police power it reviewed before 1937. The legal discourse of substantive limitations derived from the common law on governments' police power assured that zoning would only interfere with "vested interests" when determined by a conservative judiciary's interpretation of the public welfare. Had *Lochner's* reign of terror continued unabated, zoning would not likely have erupted in the post-World War II era as a powerful tool in the hands of government regulating land uses by comprehensive and purposeful intervention in the natural workings of the market.

LOCHNER'S DEMISE AND *BERMAN* V. *PARKER*

Nectow and *Washington*, both invalidating a zoning ordinance as applied on the basis of the Court's conception of the general public welfare in *Lochner*, should have signaled to those harmed by the zoning process that appeals to the Supreme Court would be welcomed and regarded with earnestness. The Court had indicated a willingness to question the very substance of legislative zoning decisions, both as to ends and means, by assessing whether a proscribed use under a zoning code was analogizable to a common law nuisance.

In fact, however, the promise of continuing heightened Supreme Court scrutiny of the zoning process never materialized. The advocates of zoning were among the many victors who benefitted from the demise of Lochnerian-styled constitutional jurisprudence in the wake of the Depression in the 1930s. Professor Tribe has analyzed the victory of the proponents of an interventionist state during the New Deal era as follows:

> It was the economic realities of the Depression that graphically undermined *Lochner's* premises. No longer could it be argued with great conviction that the invisible hand of economics was functioning simultaneously to protect individual rights and produce a social optimum . . . . Positive government intervention came to be more widely accepted as essential to economic survival, and legal doctrines would henceforth have to operate from that premise.[44]

The progressive undermining of *Lochner's* premises was signaled by a dramatic retreat on the Court's part from the field of social and economic legislation. In 1937, the Supreme Court reversed an earlier ruling and upheld minimum wage legislation in the watershed case of *West Coast Hotel* v. *Parrish.*[45] The following year, in *United States* v. *Carolene Products Co.,*[46] the Court, in an opinion written by Justice Stone, stated that social and economic legislation would be sustained if any state of facts either known or reasonably inferable afforded support for the legislative judgment.[47] In other words, Stone's *Carolene Products* text declared to the world that the Court had virtually no legitimate role to play in assessing the wisdom of legislative judgments in the social and economic fields.[48]

With respect to land use planning and zoning law, *Lochner's* demise and the New Deal era's discrediting of judicial review was reflected in a long silence. After *Nectow* and *Washington,* the Court did not issue a land use planning opinion for a quarter century. The Court's return to land use law, its 1954 opinion in *Berman* v. *Parker,*[49] indicated the reason for the long silence. The *Berman* Court obviously felt that the unelected judiciary had nothing to add to the legislature's declaration and execution of the public interest.

Berman involved a due process challenge to the District of Columbia's Redevelopment Act of 1945. As applied, the act authorized the condemnation of the appellant landowner's building under the power of eminent domain as part of a slum clearance effort. Congress in the case was held to exercise all the legislative police powers over the district that a state might exercise over its affairs. In ruling on whether private property might be condemned under Congress's police power and then redeveloped for private and not public use, Justice Douglas's unanimous opinion declared that the Court was not the proper institution to question the legislative determination of the public interest.[50] Douglas offered[51] a forceful recitation of the judiciary's self-imposed lessons following *Lochner's* demise:

> Subject to specific constitutional limitations, when the legislature has spoken, the public interest has been declared in terms well-nigh conclusive. In such cases the legislature, not the judiciary, is the main guardian of the public needs to be served by social legislation. . . . The role of the judiciary in determining whether that power is being exercised for a public purpose is an extremely narrow one. . . . The concept of the public welfare is broad and inclusive. The values it represents are spiritual as well as physical, aesthetic as well as monetary. It is within the power of the legislature to determine that the community should be beautiful as well as healthy, spacious as well as clean, well-balanced as well as carefully patrolled.[52]

Berman v. *Parker*[53] demonstrated first that the Court had effectively interred *Euclid's* Lochnerian-derived nuisance background.[54] There was no indication in the record that the appellant's building was unsafe or constituted a threat to the public safety, health, or welfare. It was not a nuisance. It simply was in the way of a redevelopment project and therefore had to be sacrificed. This was precisely the type of majoritarian invasion of vested property rights that Lochnerism had sought to protect against.[55] In addition to the Court's clear indication that it no longer felt the judiciary was competent to question legislative ends, Douglas's opinion in *Berman* just as clearly indicated that *Lochner's* close scrutiny of legislative means was no longer regarded as a legitimate judicial function. "Once the object is within the authority of Congress, the means . . . of executing the project are for Congress and Congress alone to determine."[56]

In effect, *Berman* v. *Parker*[57] insulated the local land use process from United States Supreme Court review. Lochnerism, which had provided the original discursive context for zoning as an exercise of the police power, had been suppressed and declared illegitimate by *Berman's* discourse of judicial deference to local land use regulation. The *Lochner* era's concerns with the scope of the police power and the legitimacy of imposing majoritarian preferences on the single individual landowner were safely interred in the post-Lochnerian legal discourse declaimed by Justice Douglas. *Berman's* constrained interpretation of the judicial role in the long, awesome wake of *Lochner's* demise demanded the Supreme Court's near-total deference to the legislature in the social and economic fields. Significantly, having waited a quarter century between land use planning opinions before issuing *Berman,* the Court once again abandoned the field to state court supervision. Fifteen years would pass before the

Court would dare disturb the ghost of *Lochner* by reviewing a local land use decision.

LOCHNER'S GHOST REVIVED: THE BURGER COURT'S EARLY ZONING CASES

The Court's return to land use law is chronicled in a series of decisions issued in the 1970s. *James* v. *Valtierra* (1971),[58] *Village of Belle Terre* v. *Boraas* (1974),[59] *Warth* v. *Seldin* (1975),[60] *Arlington Heights* v. *Metropolitan Housing Corp.* (1976),[61] and *City of Eastlake* v. *Forest City Enterprises* (1976).[62] The texts of these decisions can be fairly interpreted as by-products of two contending discursive forces: the Warren Court's disinterring of *Lochner's* Ghost brought about by the revival of substantive due process analysis in its civil rights constitutional jurisprudence, and the Burger Court's subsequent institutional concern to constrain the interventionist reach of that earlier discourse.

The exclusionary zoning cases, *James* v. *Valtierra,*[63] *Warth* v. *Seldin,*[64] *Arlington Heights,*[65] and *City of Eastlake*[66] all raised, directly or indirectly, the basic question of whether zoning could be used as a tool to exclude low-income and minority persons from a community. Thus, these cases confronted the Court with potentially compelling instances of allegedly abusive zoning processes trammeling important due process, equal protection, and associational interests.

It is worth recalling at this point that zoning had managed to survive *Lochner* era constitutional scrutiny by its ability to regulate and exclude the "nuisance" of high population density. This regulation of a type of land use, usually associated with lower income housing,[67] was, according to *Berman's* post-New Deal discourse, presumptively in the public interest.[68] Thus, the Burger Court's response to the invitation to scrutinize exclusionary zoning practices was not unexpected. The holdings in *James, Belle Terre, Warth,* and *Arlington Heights,* while not resting on analogies showing lower income housing as a nuisance, were nonetheless grounded firmly in the post-Lochnerian conception of the Court's extremely limited reviewing role for economic and social legislation.

In *James,*[69] the Court upheld California's procedure for mandatory referendums for approving low-rent housing projects. The Court declared zoning by referendum to be a valid "procedure for democratic decision making" which ensured "that all the people of a community will have a voice in a decision which may lead to large expenditures of local governmental funds for increased public services."[70]

In *Warth* v. *Seldin,*[71] the Court dismissed a complaint on standing grounds filed by residents of Rochester, New York, against the town of Penfield, a suburb of Rochester. Like many of New York's local governments, Penfield was accused of using its zoning ordinance to exclude persons of low and moderate income from living in the town. Federal court standing and therefore review of the claims of those individuals most affected by a local government's seeming exclusionary zoning practices, that is, those effectively zoned out of a community, were thus denied by *Warth's* holding.

The Court's deferential attitude toward local zoning officials was again demonstrated in the *Arlington Heights*[72] case. There the Court required a proof of racially discriminatory intent or purpose to support a challenge to a virtually all-white suburb's refusal to rezone for racially integrated low- and moderate-income housing. And in *City of Eastlake,*[73] the Burger Court upheld a referendum requirement that gave local voters power to approve any changes (such as changes that might result in the construction of lower income housing in

the community) to a local zoning ordinance. In all these cases, the Court assumed an extremely narrow, limited reviewing responsibility over the local zoning process, consistent with the post-Lochnerian presumption of virtually unquestioned deference to local decision makers and local autonomy.

The majority opinions in *James, Warth, Arlington Heights,* and *Eastlake* successfully suppressed *Lochner's* Ghost by reliance on familiar techniques of judicial avoidance. Reference to "democratic" processes, standing requirements and burdens of proof allowed the Court to avoid any discomforting discussion of the substantive merits of potentially abusive local zoning practices. *Village of Belle Terre* v. *Boraas,*[74] decided in 1974 and written by the author of the *Berman* opinion,[75] Justice William Douglas, thus represents a watershed case in the Supreme Court's modern land use planning law. It was the Court's first decision on the substantive merits of a zoning practice since the *Lochner* era, and the last time that the modern Court would marshall a clear consensus on its reviewing role for land use regulations affecting fundamentally regarded interests.

Belle Terre involved the constitutionally protected right to association versus a city's exercise of its zoning police power to act to exclude undesirable land uses. In *Belle Terre,* the undesired use sought to be excluded was a household of unrelated college students. Relying heavily on the themes of his prior 1954 opinion in *Berman* v. *Parker,*[76] Justice Douglas's 1974 majority opinion in *Belle Terre*[77] declared in plain terms that the Court still saw its role as extremely limited in reviewing the substantive determinations and motivations behind a local zoning ordinance. Douglas, in fact, expanded on *Berman's* benign imagery of the interventionist state in his *Belle Terre* opinion.[78] Assuring local governments that exclusionary and parochial zoning were legislative activities regarded by the Supreme Court as undoubtedly in the public interest, Douglas proclaimed:

> A quiet place where yards are wide, people few, and motor vehicles restricted are legitimate guidelines in a land-use project addressed to family needs. This goal is a permissible one within *Berman v. Parker.* . . . The police power is not confined to elimination of filth, stench, and unhealthy places. It is ample to lay out zones where family values, youth values, and the blessings of quiet seclusion and clean air make the area a sanctuary for people.[79]

Belle Terre,[80] like the other early Burger Court land use cases, indicated clearly that the local zoning process was for all intents and purposes insulated from meaningful federal judicial review. But *Belle Terre* was accompanied by a vigorous and passionate dissent written by Justice Thurgood Marshall, demonstrating that the Warren Court's earlier revival of substantive due process discourse in the 1960s could be extended to the Burger Court's land use planning jurisprudence in the 1970s.[81] Arguing that the students' constitutionally protected right of privacy and association had been violated, Marshall's dissent in *Belle Terre* revived *Lochner's* Ghost and called for substantive due process review and strict scrutiny of zoning laws affecting fundamental interests. While stating that he agreed with *Euclid* and *Berman* v. *Parker's* principle that deference should be given to governmental judgments concerning proper land use allocation, Marshall went on to argue:

> But deference does not mean abdication. This court has an obligation to ensure that zoning ordinances, even when adopted in furtherance of such legitimate aims, do not infringe upon fundamental constitutional rights.[82]

It was as if Marshall had gone back and read

Euclid, Washington v. *Roberge,* and *Nectow* for inspiration, for it was the *Lochner* era Court's recognition that zoning could indeed infringe upon importantly perceived values assertedly protected by the Constitution that led it to closely supervise the zoning process.[83]

THE DISINTERMENT OF *LOCHNER'S* GHOST

The modern Supreme Court has found itself more frequently engaged in reviewing the substance of local zoning decision making. Since *Belle Terre,* the Court has decided nearly 20 land use planning cases, compared to only a dozen such cases between 1926 and 1974. The Court also has found itself more frequently divided as to the issue of its legitimate role in reviewing local zoning decisions affecting fundamental interests and substantive rights. Plurality opinions in land use cases have become the rule rather than the exception in the modern Court's land use planning jurisprudence.

Moore v. *City of East Cleveland,*[84] decided in 1977, represented the first instance since the *Lochner* era in which the Court struck down a local zoning ordinance on substantive due process grounds. East Cleveland had convicted a grandmother of a criminal violation of an ordinance that had limited occupancy of a dwelling unit to members of a single family. The ordinance defined the term "family" essentially as a couple and their dependent children. The grandmother lived in her East Cleveland home with her son and two grandsons (who were first cousins). This type of extended family did not fit the definition of a "family" under the city's ordinance. Grandmother Moore was thus criminally prosecuted by East Cleveland. Justice Powell's plurality opinion in *Moore,* joined by Justices Brennan, Marshall, and Blackmun, held that "when a city undertakes such intrusive regulation of the family, neither *Belle Terre* nor *Euclid* governs, [and] the usual judicial deference to the legislature is inappropriate."[85] The plurality reviewed East Cleveland's legislative definition of "family" on substantive due process grounds, as the ordinance affected "freedom of personal choice in matters of marriage and family life" protected by the due process clause of the Fourteenth Amendment.[86] East Cleveland's ordinance did not survive this heightened level of judicial scrutiny. The city's goals of preventing overcrowding and congestion, though legitimate, were only "marginally" served by the invasive regulation, and therefore, the regulation was required to yield to the protections implied by the Constitution to family rights.[87]

The plurality was aware that its opinion threatened to revive the ghost of *Lochner*, and all that such a revival implied:

> Substantive due process has at times been a treacherous field for this Court. There *are* risks when the judicial branch gives enhanced protection to certain substantive liberties without the guidance of the more specific provisions of the Bill of Rights. As the history of the *Lochner* era demonstrates, there is reason for concern lest the only limits to such judicial intervention become the predilections of those who happen to be members of this Court.[88]

The spectre of *Lochner's* Ghost conjured in the plurality's invalidation of a local zoning ordinance on substantive due process grounds provoked a number of divergent responses from the Court's members. Justice Stevens, concurring in the judgment,[89] argued in anachronistic fashion for analyzing the case within *Euclid's* original Lochnerian framework: as an example of a regulation that could not be justified because it could not clearly be shown to be in furtherance of the public safe-

ty, health, or welfare.[90] While Stevens reminded his brethren of zoning's express origins in common law nuisance, his concurrence was not joined by anyone else on the Court. The three dissents, one by Chief Justice Burger,[91] one by Stewart joined by Rehnquist,[92] and the final dissent authored by White,[93] all invoked in one degree or another fear of *Lochner's* Ghost as a basis for upholding the ordinance.

Besides the lack of consensus evidenced in *Moore* respecting the state's authority to regulate the family, the modern Court has found itself intensely divided over the question of the appropriate level of judicial deference when local zoning and ordinances impinge upon other types of asserted First Amendment interests. In *Young* v. *American Mini Theaters* (1976),[94] Justice Stevens's plurality opinion upheld a zoning ordinance that sought to disperse adult motion picture theaters throughout the city. Planning experts had advised the city of Detroit that location of sexually oriented businesses in the same neighborhood tended to depress property values and create other undesirable side effects. The city's legitimate interest, pursued through its zoning code, of maintaining neighborhood character was held substantial enough to outweigh the limited First Amendment protections afforded erotic materials.

Justice Powell's concurrence in *Young*,[95] perhaps sensing the widening breach on the Court on the issue of the level of scrutiny afforded the local zoning process, sought to remind the Justices of the special status afforded zoning in the post-*Lochner* era:

> While I agree . . . that no aspect of the police power enjoys immunity from searching constitutional scrutiny, it also is undeniable that zoning, when used to preserve the character of specific areas of a city, is perhaps "the most essential function performed by local govern-

ment, for it is one of the primary means by which we protect that sometimes difficult to define concept of quality of life."[96]

A dissent by Justice Stewart in *Young*, joined by Justices Brennan, Marshall, and Blackmun, argued that the case did not "involve a simple zoning ordinance."[97] Stewart took pains to remind his colleagues that important substantive rights guaranteed by the Constitution were implicated by the case, and that by "refusing to invalidate Detroit's ordinance the Court rides roughshod over cardinal principles of First Amendment law."[98]

In a separate dissent joined by Brennan, Marshall, and Stewart, Justice Blackmun also argued that the Court "should not be swayed in this case by the characterization of the challenged ordinance as merely a 'zoning regulation.'"[99] The implications of both dissents were clear. The majority had given indications that zoning regulations—perhaps "the most essential function performed by local government,"[100] according to Justice Powell's concurrence—were entitled to less than searching constitutional scrutiny, no matter what the right or interest implicated.

The Court has decided several major land use/First Amendment cases since *Young* that raise similar issues and evidence the same coalitions. *Metromedia Inc.* v. *City of San Diego*[101] in 1981 and *Members of the City Council of Los Angeles* v. *Taxpayers for Vincent*[102] in 1984 both involved challenges to local ordinances regulating billboards or signs. *Schad* v. *Borough of Mt. Ephraim*[103] in 1981 and *City of Renton* v. *Playtime Theatres*[104] in 1986 raised challenges to local ordinances attempting to regulate sex-related businesses. All four cases brought forth multiple opinions. The proper judicial role and appropriate degree of scrutiny in assessing the validity of local land use ordinances affecting important substantive interests were major

themes of those majority, plurality, concurring, and dissenting opinions. Justice Rehnquist in fact apologized in dissent[105] in one of those cases for contributing to the "virtual Tower of Babel, from which no definitive principles can be clearly drawn" respecting the appropriate standard of judicial scrutiny of "legislative or administrative determinations."[106]

LOCHNER AND THE COURT'S MOST RECENT LAND USE DECISIONS

The divisions in the Court over the basic question of the appropriateness of heightened judicial scrutiny of the local zoning process is not confined merely to these First Amendment-related cases. The Court's recent, highly publicized decisions in *First English Evangelical Lutheran Church* v. *County of Los Angeles*[107] and *Nollan* v. *California Coastal Commission*,[108] both decided in 1987, revealed strong evidence of an intense, near-acrimonious debate on the Court over the question of the appropriate degree of deference due to local zoning decision makers.

Having avoided deciding the issue four times in the 1980s,[109] the Court in *First English* declared that the Fifth Amendment's taking clause requires a remedy of damages when an individual's property rights have been wrongfully invaded, even if only temporarily, by government land use regulations. Chief Justice Rehnquist's majority opinion for the Court declared that "where the government's activities have already worked a taking of all use of property, no subsequent action by the government can relieve it of the duty to provide compensation for the period during which the taking was effective."[110]

Justice Stevens, in a sharply worded dissent (joined in part by Justices Blackmun and O'Connor),[111] called the Court's decision "dangerous,"[112] with "obvious and I fear far-reaching policy implications."[113] Stevens charged that *First English's* mandated damages remedy for invalid regulatory takings would have a chilling effect on local planning initiatives. "Much important regulation will never be enacted, even perhaps in the health and safety area."[114] Calling the majority's decision a "loose cannon," Stevens's dissent concluded with a charge that the Court effectively had overturned "a long line of precedents" in the land use planning area.[115] Stevens did not have to remind his colleagues that these precedents had emerged out of the long wake of *Lochner's* demise and the post-New Deal insulation of the local land use planning process from Supreme Court review.

In *Nollan* v. *California Coastal Commission*,[116] issued shortly after the novel remedy created in *First English,* Justice Scalia's majority opinion illustrated the significance of this new constitutionally mandated damages remedy for invalid regulatory takings. The *Nollan* majority interpreted the Fifth Amendment's takings clause as requiring aggressive judicial scrutiny of police power regulations affecting fundamentally regarded rights in private property. A condition imposed by a government regulatory agency on a land use permit must, according to *Nollan,* "substantially advance" legitimate state interests. The deferential discourse of *Berman-Belle Terre* requiring that a land use ordinance must be merely rationally related to a public purpose in order to avoid a constitutional challenge was directly confronted and overcome by Justice Scalia's full-scale revival of Lochnerian substantive due process analysis.[117]

Nollan did cite previous Supreme Court land use decisions as precedent for the heightened level of Supreme Court scrutiny now to be applied to takings challenges in the Court's land use planning jurisprudence. A vigorous dissent by Justice Brennan, joined by Justice Marshall, charged, however, that the majority had adopted a standard of review for police power regulations affecting land that "has long since been discredited as a judicial arrogation of legislative authority."[118] In effect, Justice Brennan's dissent accused the majority of outright Lochnerizing in *Nollan.* Requiring a demonstration that a government land use regulation substantially advance a valid public purpose was, in Brennan's view, a return to a discredited form of constitutional discourse.

Perhaps even more significant than the charge of judicial interventionism hurled by Brennan's dissent is the fact that *Nollan's* contending discourses respecting the appropriate standard of review for land use regulations contrast opposing judicial visions of property rights in a manner wholly unfamiliar to post-Lochnerian land use jurisprudence. *Nollan's* significance is that for the first time in nearly 60 years, a Supreme Court land use decision has trumpeted property as a fundamental right. According to *Nollan's* holding, regulations impinging on this right are to be subject to an aggressive brand of judicial scrutiny totally unfamiliar to contemporary land use planning law. When combined with *First English's* creation of a damages remedy for invalid regulatory takings, under the Fifth Amendment, the Supreme Court's land use planning jurisprudence possesses an enforcement tool that not even the *Lochner* era judges considered necessary in protecting the fundamental rights of private property under the Constitution.

CONCLUSION

As the debates in *First English* and *Nollan* on the question of the appropriate standard of judicial review in land use planning cases clearly reveal, the ghost of *Lochner* continues to haunt modern land use planning law. *Lochner's* continuing relevance and centrality in these recent land use decisions suggest that the terms of debate on the individual's rights in property in a complex, modern society have remained remarkably static in the 60 years since *Euclid v. Ambler Realty.* The argument that property is a "fundamental" right and therefore requires heightened judicial protection from unjustified and frequently assumed attempts at majoritarian invasion has been ominously revived by the *First English* and *Nollan* decisions. The post-Lochnerian theme, itself more than half a century old, that an unelected judiciary must defer to the legislative definition of the public interest except in the most egregious cases of interference with narrowly defined, vested private rights, continues to be recited in near-dogmatic fashion by those on the Court fearful of the implications of aggressive judicial review of local land use decisions. While this debate remains vigorous on the Supreme Court, its familiarity, and therefore its ultimate utility, must be assessed in light of the fact that since the Court's 1926 decision in *Euclid,* little else in the field of land use planning has remained so obsessively static and unresponsive to "the new and different conditions" of our society. *Lochner's* Ghost, which has haunted the Supreme Court's land use planning law since its inaugural decision in *Euclid,* continues to distract the modern Court from developing a jurisprudence that addresses the needs and wants of a modern society.

NOTES

1. Horwitz, *The Transformation in the Conception of Property in American Law, 1780–1860,* Univ. of Chicago L. Rev. vol. 40 (1973), p. 248.

2. *Parker* v. *Foote,* 19 Wend. 309, 318 (N.Y. Sup. Ct. 1838).

3. *Cary* v. *Daniels,* 49 Mass. (8 Met.) 466, 476–77 (1844). Quoted in Horwitz, *supra* note 1, at p. 260.

4. *See generally* Note, "Land Use Regulation and the Concept of Takings in Nineteenth Century America," Univ. of Chicago L. Rev. vol. 40 (1973), p. 854.

5. 272 U.S. 365 (1926).

6. *Id.* at 376–77.

7. *Id.* at 371–79.

8. *Id.* at 375–76.

9. 272 U.S. 365 (1926).

10. On the "*Lochner* era," see generally G. Gunther, *Cases and Materials on Constitutional Law,* 10th ed., (1980), p. 453 and following; L. Tribe, *American Constitutional Law* (1978), pp. 434–436.

11. *See* sources cited in note 10.

12. *See generally,* D. Hagman and J. Juergensmeyer, *Urban Planning and Land Development Control Law,* 2nd ed., (1986), pp. 13–21.

13. *Id.* at 17–18, quoting J. Nolen, *New Ideas in the Planning of Cities, Towns and Villages* (1919), pp. 133–34.

14. *Id.,* at 21, 40.

15. *Spann* v. *City of Dallas,* 111 Tex. 350, 357, 235 S.W. 513, 516 (1921).

16. 147 Md. 282, 128 A.50 (1925).

17. 297 F. 307 (N.D. Ohio 1924).

18. *Id.* at 313.

19. L. Tribe, *American Constitutional Law,* p. 432.

20. *Id.* at 432.

21. 123 U.S. 623 (1887).

22. *Id.* at 661.

23. 3 U.S. (3 Dall.) 386 (1798). Chase's formulation in *Calder* that a law that "takes property from A and gives it to B" exceeded the proper authority of government exercised a profound influence on later Lochnerian legal discourse. *See* L. Tribe, *American Constitutional Law,* pp. 428–29.

24. 272 U.S. 365, 379 (1926).

25. *Id.* at 371.

26. *Id.*

27. *Id.* at 373.

28. *Id.* at 374.

29. *Id.* at 376.

30. *See generally,* Burner, "George Sutherland," in *The Justices of the Supreme Court, 1787–1969,* Friedman and Israel, eds. (1984), p. 2133.

31. 272 U.S. 365, 387–88 (1926).

32. *See id.*

33. *Id.* at 387.

34. *Id.* at 394.

35. *Id.* at 387.

36. 274 U.S. 325 (1927).

37. 274 U.S. 603 (1927).

38. 274 U.S. 325, 327–28 (1927).

39. 274 U.S. 603 (1927).

40. *Id.* at 609.

41. 277 U.S. 183 (1928).

42. 278 U.S. 116 (1928).

43. *Id.* at 122.

44. L. Tribe, *American Constitutional Law,* pp. 446–47.

45. 300 U.S. 379 (1937).

46. 304 U.S. 144 (1938).

47. *Id.* at 152–53. *See generally* L. Tribe, *American Constitutional Law*, p. 451.

48. "[T]he existence of facts supporting the legislative judgment is to be presumed, for regulatory legislation affecting ordinary commercial transactions is not to be pronounced unconstitutional unless in light of the facts known or generally assumed it is of such a character as to preclude the assumption that it rests upon some rational bases within the knowledge and experience of the legislators." *United States* v. *Carolene Products Co.,* 304 U.S. 144, 152–53 (1938).

49. 348 U.S. 26 (1954).

50. *Id.* at 32.

51. 348 U.S. 26 (1954).

52. *Id.* at 33.

53. 348 U.S. 26 (1954).

54. *See* section III, *supra.*

55. *See* section II, *supra.*

56. 348 U.S. 26, 33 (1954).

57. 348 U.S. 26 (1954).

58. 402 U.S. 137 (1971).

59. 416 U.S. 1 (1974).

60. 422 U.S. 490 (1975).

61. 429 U.S. 252 (1977).

62. 426 U.S. 668 (1976).

63. 402 U.S. 137 (1971).

64. 442 U.S. 490 (1975).

65. 429 U.S. 252 (1977).

66. 426 U.S. 668 (1976).

67. *See* section III, *supra.*

68. 348 U.S. 26 (1954).

69. 402 U.S. 137 (1971).

70. *Id.* at 143.

71. 422 U.S. 490 (1975).

72. 429 U.S. 252 (1977).

73. 426 U.S. 668 (1976).

74. 416 U.S. 1 (1974).

75. 348 U.S. 26 (1954).

76. *Id.*

77. 416 U.S. 1 (1974).

78. *Id.*

79. *Id.* at 9.

80. 416 U.S. 1 (1974).

81. *Id.* at 12–20.

82. *Id.* at 14.

83. *See* section III C.

84. 431 U.S. 494 (1977).

85. *Id.* at 499.

86. *Id.*

87. *Id.* at 500.

88. *Id.* at 502.

89. *Id.* at 515–21.

90. *Id.* at 514.

91. *Id.* at 521.

92. *Id.* at 531–41.

93. *Id.* at 541–52.

94. 427 U.S. 50 (1976).

95. *Id.* at 73.

96. *Id.* at 80.

97. *Id.* at 84.

98. *Id.* at 85–86.

99. *Id.* at 96.

100. *Id.* at 80.

101. 453 U.S. 490 (1981).

102. 466 U.S. 789 (1984).

103. 452 U.S. 61 (1981).

104. 106 S.Ct. 925 (1986).

105. *See Metromedia, Inc.* v. *City of San Diego,* 453 U.S. 490 (1981).

106. *Id.* at 569.

107. 107 S.Ct. 2378 (1987).

108. 107 S.Ct. 3141 (1987).

109. *See MacDonald, Sommer, & Frates* v. *Yolo County,* 106 S.Ct. 2561 (1986); *Williamson County Regional Planning Commission* v. *Hamilton Bank,* 473 U.S. 172 (1985); *San Diego Gas & Electric Co.* v. *City of San Diego,* 450 U.S. 621 (1981); *Agins* v. *City of Tiburon,* 447 U.S. 255 (1980).

110. 107 S.Ct. 2378, 2389 (1987).

111. *Id.* at 2389–2400.

112. *Id.* at 2390.

113. *Id.* at 2397.

114. *Id.* at 2399–2400.

115. *Id.* at 2400.

116. 107 S.Ct. 3141 (1987).

117. *Id.* at 3146.

118. *Id.* at 3153.

IV

Zoning and Economics: Are They Compatible?

It is hardly surprising that economists are among the severest critics of zoning. Through its basic operation, zoning interferes with the workings of the marketplace of land. It intervenes in private development decisions by controlling land use and density. For economists whose disciplinary orientation depends on the utility of the marketplace to measure and fulfill the needs of people, zoning is problematic because of its substitution of government judgment for that of the market. Indeed, to the extent that zoning is seen as the implementation of planning, it is understandable that those economists critical of planned economies would find little positive to say about zoning.

Over the past several years, scholars and practitioners have especially turned to economic analysis to determine the value and efficacy of certain laws. Among other public policies, zoning has been scrutinized and frequently attacked. If the real unzoned Houston cannot be hailed as the paragon of city development, it is the Houston of the mind that captivates some of these observers. That is both the strength and weakness of the economic approach—even as it offers interesting conceptual insights, one misses an empiric testing of the economist's proposals.

It is possible to harmonize traditional planning justifications and the economist's framework of efficiency in discussing zoning. Indeed, the economic concept of negative ex-

ternality serves as corollary to Justice Sutherland's "pig in a parlor" and nuisance analogies. Negative externalities occur when one landowner pursues his or her own self-interest in a way that negatively affects neighbors and that landowner is not forced to pay for such negative effect. For example, a landowner may decide to build a factory that pollutes the air near a residential area. The pollution adversely affects the neighborhood, reducing property values, but the polluting landowner has no reason to consider costs imposed on others and thus has no incentive to reduce or eliminate pollution. Economists would say that the price system fails to reflect the true social cost to the landowner.

Of course, this begs the initial question: What rights should people have in their ownership of land? Is one entitled to a pollution-free environment as part of one's property right? If so, then must the polluter compensate affected landowners for the pollution? And how should this be accomplished? These are the interesting questions posed by economists in the following two chapters. They both recommend the introduction of market mechanisms to make zoning more efficient.

In Chapter 11, "Zoning Myth and Practice—From *Euclid* into the Future," Robert Nelson canvasses the scholars who have turned the economic oculus to zoning. Candidly acknowledging the failure of their proposals to gain popular acceptance, he stalwartly proceeds with his own economics-based prescription. Seeing zoning itself as already establishing a collective private property right to *existing* neighborhood environments, he proposes abolishing zoning and substituting a form of neighborhood fiefdom. Neighborhoods would control decisions about new development, and operate under a system of market incentives. If, for example, neighborhood decisions would be based on market incentives, a developer offering enough of a financial package to the neighborhood could gain neighborhood approval. For undeveloped land under development pressure, Nelson would ensure that the municipality could not impose the will of the majority to stop development on such land, unless it demonstrated a willingness to "pay the cost" for such will.

In Chapter 12, "Zoning and Land Use Planning: An Economic Perspective," William Wheaton exhibits similar concerns. Applying the principle of "Pareto Optimality"—where changes in allocation of resources would make all better off—he criticizes zoning for its failure to impose cost considerations on those making decisions. For example, he describes the common conflict between existing home owners, who want to preserve vacant land for open space, and the landowner who wants to develop the land. Wheaton argues that, because the majority can simply use zoning to preserve open space, they face a zero price for their decision, and thus the trade-offs necessary for achieving Pareto Optimality cannot occur. He urges development of a two-tier system of metropolitan and local planning in which social and private costs may be compared and transacted.

11

Zoning Myth and Practice—From *Euclid* into the Future

Robert H. Nelson

In 1881, Oliver Wendell Holmes published *The Common Law,* since designated as "one of the landmarks" in late nineteenth century American thought.[1] Led also by John Dewey, Thorstein Veblen, and Charles Beard, a "revolt against formalism" occurred in a variety of intellectual disciplines.[2] This revolt generally attacked the idea that social learning could be derived from logical deduction, abstract principles and a priori reasoning. Instead, much influenced by Charles Darwin, the new "pragmatists" of the Progressive era emphasized the importance of history and the process of evolution. Holmes wrote that the law "embodies the story of a nation's development."[3] The proper study of the law required not only the skills of the lawyer but also the talents of the historian, philosopher, anthropologist, economist, and political scientist. The inquirer into the law should be prepared to probe beneath current arguments and rationalizations to find deeper and more complex explanations in the history of the law's development. As Holmes described a "very common" course of the law:

The customs, beliefs, or needs of a primitive time establish a rule or a formula. In the course of centuries the custom, belief, or necessity disappears, but the rule remains. The reason which gave rise to the rule has been forgotten, and ingenious minds set themselves to inquire how it is to be accounted for. Some ground of policy is thought of, which seems to explain it and to reconcile it with the present state of things; and then the rule adapts itself to the new reasons which have been found for it, and enters on a new career. The old form receives a new content, and in time even the form modifies itself to fit the meaning which it has received.[4]

A contemporary of Holmes, Frederick Pollock, demonstrated the insights that could be gained from such an approach in his classic study, *The Land Laws,* first published in 1883.[5] Pollock reviewed the evolution of English land law over many centuries, finding it to be a history filled with legal myths and fictions. The actual result often differed greatly from the expressed intent of the legislature. The accumulation of interpretations and rulings by many individual judges was often the decisive factor. The land law of England was:

An unparalleled accumulation of layer upon layer of diverse materials. Tenure and convention, custom and competition, legislation and usage, the rude common life of the free Teutonic warrior tribes, an aristocratic military system sprung from sheer necessities of mutual defence, and disguised in the terms and reasons of a Romanised law, the subtle deductions of a legal profession trained in scholastic disputes, the attempts of an impatient Parliament to make their crooked things straight, the not less subtle and more flexible inventions of modern lawyers, the partial clearances and half-hearted amendments of modern law reformers: all these have gone to the making of the vast and inextricable mass, and all must be considered in their turn by the seeker who is bold enough to search out the history and the meaning of the land laws of England.[6]

This chapter examines American zoning law in the spirit of Holmes and Pollock. The evolution of American zoning thus is not seen primarily as a matter of legal principles and issues. Instead, it is a reflection of the social and economic forces, as well as political ideologies, social philosophies, and other intellectual influences of its time. It is with an attitude of considerable skepticism toward surface appearances and official explanations that zoning is approached. One begins with the question, what basic social and economic needs did the instrument of zoning serve? A corollary question then is the manner in which the legal system gave legitimacy to and justified such an instrument.

THE *EUCLID* DECISION

It is not a coincidence that the development of American zoning occurs almost simultaneously with the growing importance of the automobile in American life. Automobile sales rose from 4,000 in 1900 to 181,000 in 1910 and then to 1,906,000 in 1920. By the 1920s, residential living patterns were beginning to reflect the new freedom of movement provided by the automobile. Newer cities such as Los Angeles were developing into what eventually would be one vast suburban network. The hallmarks of this pattern of urban development were, of course, low housing densities and a comprehensive system of local roads linked by high-speed freeways. Older cities began taking on a dual character: the older, high-density segments that were shaped by the trolley and subway, and the new, low-density sections that were shaped by the automobile.

Zoning became an integral part of this automotive age. The lower densities of development had a number of consequences that exposed the new neighborhoods of the automobile era to new risks. Because the automobile greatly expanded the amount of land that was convenient to city jobs, the price of land within an acceptable commuting time was substantially reduced. Indeed, it was precisely because land was so much cheaper that it became economical for middle-class families to acquire their own single-family homes on individual lots. However, the low prices also made it much easier for lower income groups to purchase land in higher income neighborhoods. They could do this by sacrificing on their own density in order to live amidst the high environmental amenities of a richer neighborhood. With older, pre-automobile patterns of development, the density of wealthier neighborhoods already was high enough to limit lower income entry. Even today, it is not the well-to-do of Park Avenue in Manhattan but their affluent counterparts in Westchester County who are the primary beneficiaries of zoning exclusions.

The living patterns of an automotive age also emphasized the surrounding out-of-doors environment. The single-family home became the American dream; people enjoyed the barbecues, lawns, swimming pools, and other amenities of low densities. The environmental quality of the suburban neighborhood was more susceptible to intrusion of stores, gasoline stations, restaurants, and other commercial facilities. An apartment house a block away made much more difference in a neighborhood of single-family homes on half-acre lots than it did in the older city. It was in the automobile age that the fear grew, in the words of a more recent commentator, "that less expensive homes than those erected by the first settlers of an area will diminish property values and destroy the atmosphere established by the construction of expensive homes on spacious grounds."[7] As the planner Hugh Pomeroy would explain in 1940, "The important thing is to provide protection for the character of the neighborhood. . . . Low-density neighborhoods occupied by higher income families should not be faced with a danger of intrusion or encroachment by small lot developers which would destroy their character. The danger is always that the less intensive occupancy will be impaired by encroachment by more intensive occupancy."[8]

Given the demand for environmental protection of low-density neighborhoods, there still were other ways this protection might have been provided. Rather than government action, neighborhood environments could have been protected by private convenants or other private mechanisms. For example, the more recent development of condominium forms of collective ownership might have occurred in an earlier era. Private protection works well—in fact, it has long been used—for a large area under single ownership. However, when the homes have numerous individual owners, a voluntary agreement of all owners to a common private system of regula-

tion would be extremely difficult to orchestrate. Instead, it was more practical to have government impose environmental controls on the neighborhood. Because of its unique powers of coercion, government could override any holdouts, implementing the will of the neighborhood majority. Zoning thus became the chosen instrument for the protection of the low-density neighborhood in a new automotive age. It was the regulatory device of an earlier "environmental movement."

Stripped of the many rationalizations offered for it, zoning in truth was a coercive redistribution of property rights within the neighborhood, one which, however, most neighbors favored. The rights to undertake actions significantly affecting the environmental quality of the neighborhood were taken from the individual owners and transferred to the local government. Since the local government would in the great majority of cases follow neighborhood wishes, the practical effect was to substitute collective neighborhood rights for what had been individual rights. Government, in effect, served as the agent for the enforcement of these new neighborhood property rights. The new collective property rights also were, in effect, the "compensation" provided to the individual neighborhood residents for the "taking" of their individual rights that had occurred.

Given the great popularity of zoning, there can be little doubt that this new institution was responding to a widespread public demand. The legal system, however, faced its own problem: There was no principle or sanction in American law for the type of coercive property rights redistribution that zoning in practice accomplished. As a result, zoning purposes could not be explained explicitly and zoning had to be established in the name of some other purpose. New legal myths and fictions had to be invented. The specific form that neighborhood protection took was conditioned by the necessity of winning legal acceptance. In particular, the fixing of districts in advance—the "zones" that were the trademark of "zoning"—were a product of legal necessity, not of economic or other social requirements.

The more direct way of accomplishing neighborhood protection would have been to create a new "special district" for each neighborhood so desiring and to allow the neighborhood residents to vote on a property rights redistribution within the neighborhood. If approved, a private neighborhood body would have taken over the responsibility for maintaining and protecting neighborhood quality. The neighborhood voters could have chosen to vest greater or lesser authority in the new neighborhood body, and defined its specific protective powers, according to their preferences in these matters. Very likely, the regulatory authority approved by neighborhoods would have been discretionary, allowing neighborhoods to accept or reject new uses case by case and on the basis of the best collective judgment of the residents. But for all this, there would have been no justification in American legal traditions.

However, by stretching and straining the existing doctrines of nuisance law, it might be possible to justify a districting form of protection. The creation of fixed zones in advance could be said to provide greater certainty and security in the application of nuisance law, providing protection against arbitrary rulings by individual judges, judges who often were required to make after the fact determinations of nuisances. By some further stretching, it might also be possible to say that a high-density housing facility constituted a nuisance in a low-density neighborhood. This was, of course, the route followed by the legal architects of zoning and eventually given the bless-ing of the Supreme Court. In perhaps the single most famous statement ever made with respect to zoning law, the Court indicated that "under these circumstances, apartment houses, which in a different environment would be not only entirely unobjectionable but highly desirable, come very near to being nuisances."[9]

If fixed zones were to be created in advance, an obvious and troubling question remained for resolution: By what method were these zones to be determined? Here the legal architects of zoning—no doubt acting in good faith—fell back on what now seems an intellectual fad but at the time was one of the great accepted faiths of the day. The veneration of "science" as the basis for social decisions and the belief in "planning" as the means of applying science to practical affairs became a virtual gospel among forward-looking intellectuals of the Progressive era. These attitudes were carried into the 1920s and assumed even greater practical importance as government expanded its role in the New Deal years of the 1930s. A leading political scientist of the post-World War II era, Dwight Waldo, has marveled at the exalted status of planning and planners in administrative thinking of those years:

Planning is the means by which the discipline of Science applied to human affairs will enable man to incarnate his purposes. It is the inevitable link between means and ends. Moreover, it is in itself an inspiring ideal. For once it is realized that there is no natural harmony of nature, no Divine or other purpose hidden beneath the flux and chaos of present planlessness, it becomes immoral to let poverty, ignorance, pestilence, and war continue if they can be obliterated by a plan. Although there is some disagreement as to the nature and desirable limits of planning, students of administration are all "planners."[10]

The Supreme Court in the 1920s was still in the sway of laissez-faire views and was not receptive in most cases to the visions of social engineering offered by planning proponents. Yet, given the opportunity to uphold an essentially conservative institution, which was needed in a new automobile age to ensure the maintenance of high-amenity neighborhoods and economically segregated residential patterns, the Supreme Court was willing to let its doubts be relieved. The problem of the obvious potential of zoning to distort the socially efficient use of metropolitan land, to say nothing of the potential for corruption and other abuse of the wide-ranging powers given to local governments, would be resolved by planning. The science of land use planning, it was argued, would be put to work in the creation of municipal plans. These plans would then serve as a benchmark for both ordinary citizens and the courts in monitoring the municipal exercise of zoning powers. As a scientific activity, land use planning would properly be divorced from politics and would lay the basis for objective, disinterested decisions that would promote economically efficient and environmentally attractive use of urban land.

These arguments all were made persuasively in the famous brief of Alfred Bettman, submitted to the Supreme Court when it surprisingly agreed to rehear the *Euclid* case.[11] That the Court gave some heed to these arguments is seen in the statement of Justice Sutherland that "the matter of zoning has received much attention at the hands of commissions and experts, and the results of their investigations have been set forth in comprehensive reports. These reports, which bear every evidence of painstaking consideration, concur in the view that the segregation of residential, business, and industrial buildings will make it easier to provide fire apparatus suitable for the character and intensity of the development in

each section; that it will increase the safety and security of home life; greatly tend to prevent street accidents, especially to children, by reducing the traffic and resulting confusion in residential sections; decrease noise and other conditions which produce or intensify nervous disorders; and preserve a more favorable environment in which to rear children, etc."[12] As Dan Tarlock has noted, "Bettman's faith in the power of expertise to shape the city was obviously greater than the conservative Justice Sutherland's. Still, at the end of the opinion, Justice Sutherland found the wisdom of zoning 'sufficiently cogent to preclude us from saying . . . that such provisions are clearly arbitrary and unreasonable.' "[13]

In summary, zoning was a new property right institution that responded to the new economic and environmental circumstances of the automotive age. Its specific form, however, was dictated by legal necessity. The creation of fixed zones in advance could be justified as an evolutionary step forward in nuisance law. At the same time, the laying out of fixed zones in advance also corresponded to popular ideas concerning the scientific practice of land use planning, allowing zoning to be justified as one more instrument of the forward march of scientific progress in human affairs. That these justifications would subsequently turn out to be largely myth and fiction would have surprised neither Holmes nor Pollock.

THE PRIVATIZING OF ZONING

As the newly created instrument of zoning was put to use, the practical effect was to treat the neighborhood environment as a private good. Zoning itself was, in effect, a collective private property right to the neighborhood environment. As a result, the well-to-do would be able to employ their financial resources to live in higher quality neighborhood environments, just as they were able to buy higher quality travel, automobiles, food, and other private goods. In a nation where challenges to private property meet with little success, this consequence of zoning has been widely applauded. The National Commission on Urban Problems said in 1968 that "regulations still do their best job when they deal with the type of situation for which many of them were first intended; when the objective is to protect established character and when that established character is uniformly residential. It is in the 'nice' neighborhoods, where the regulatory job is easiest, that regulations do their best job."[14] In 1974, Justice William Douglas delivered an even more enthusiastic Supreme Court endorsement in the *Belle Terre* case.[15]

In early days, zoning was not primarily intended or widely used as a means of controlling the use of undeveloped land. However, once the instrument of zoning was placed in municipal hands, local governments saw that they could use it for this purpose and to their great advantage. Indeed, zoning of undeveloped areas would become just as important as zoning of existing neighborhoods, proving to be much more controversial. It was one thing to redistribute property rights within an existing neighborhood; while legally a radical step, zoning in developed neighborhoods effectively reasserted American property right traditions in a new collective context. However, it was another thing altogether to turn farmland and other undeveloped land into the collective property of people living somewhere else in the municipality—as was often the practical effect of municipal zoning of undeveloped land. Such an action came close to, if not literally constituting, an expropriation of the landowner's development rights. Unlike the existing neighborhood, there was not any *de facto* compensation provided for the loss of individual private rights.

As zoning of undeveloped land became a more common practice, legal supporters argued that any losses in land value experienced by the landowner were justified by the critical importance to the wider community of planning for future land use. However, contrary to received zoning theory, planners and other professional experts typically proved to be weak and ineffectual in their actual influence on the administration of zoning. Instead, as in many other areas of government, administration of zoning reflected the political power and interests of the groups most significantly affected by zoning decisions—in this case groups within each zoning jurisdiction. The planning theory of zoning thus came to be a legal fiction widely offered to justify the exclusion of all but the highest quality development from the municipality. It served the private interests of the already-developed neighborhoods in the municipality that contained most of the voters, if not most of the land. They often preferred to keep the remaining neighborhoods entirely undeveloped in order to maintain their pastoral environment.

Zoning administration in undeveloped areas also gradually evolved to resemble closely the exercise of an ordinary private property right. The most important step was the undermining of the fixed districts of early zoning and the substitution of discretionary zoning changes by the municipality. Municipal residents did not want to commit in advance, but preferred the same freedom of choice and latitude to consider options found in the exercise of ordinary property rights. In some cases, municipal residents literally voted on zoning changes, much as the members of a condominium might hold a vote on the exercise of their property rights. By demanding parks and other developer concessions, municipalities also treated zoning as a transferable right, effectively engaging in the collective sale of development rights.

Municipal governments were not the only ones to benefit from zoning changes and the sale of development rights. Sometimes the gains were much more private. Although the worst abuses seem today to have been cleaned up, contemporary observers in the 1950s and 1960s found zoning corruption and other extralegal activities to be commonplace. These practices undermined the integrity of the regulatory system prescribed by zoning architects, but the unhappy truth is that they were probably socially necessary. Much as there are today many "planned economies" around the world that depend on black markets to meet essential economic needs, metropolitan areas depended on similar underground forces. As a result, the actual social damage done by zoning was considerably less than would have resulted from rigid adherence to proper zoning practice. This was another form of "privatizing" of zoning, one for which, however, little can be said with respect to the distributional consequences and social equity.

Leading writers on zoning in the 1950s and 1960s documented these trends and the resulting demise of Euclidean zoning. They showed how, as a result of widespread zoning practices, zoning was promoting economically inefficient and environmentally unattractive patterns of metropolitan land use. Most important, it was significantly raising housing prices and inducing wasteful leapfrog development. The National Commission on Urban Problems confirmed what commentators such as John Delafons and Richard Babcock had already revealed, that land use planning was playing a minor, often insignificant role in municipal zoning decisions.[16] Much as Holmes and Pollock had described in earlier eras, these writers documented the latest chapter in the continuing saga of the myths and fictions of the land laws.

In 1964 Charles Reich published an article, "The New Property," in which he developed an argument of broad social significance.[17] Reich contended that the beneficiaries of many government programs should receive their benefits, not as matters of "privilege," but as of "right." Their benefits should be regarded as a new type of property, subject to many of the same legal protections afforded traditional property holdings. In a 1966 article, Reich stated that "among the resources dispensed by government which it would seem desirable to treat as property are social security pensions, veterans' benefits, professional and occupational licenses, public assistance, unemployment compensation, public housing, benefits under the Economic Opportunity Act, medicare, educational benefits, and farm subsidies. Planning with respect to such rights can be done on a general basis; the rights themselves should be distributed to all who qualify for a certain status."[18]

As Reich himself recognized, the creation of "the new property" undermined progressive theories of government. Progressives had prescribed a role for expert planners in which they were to design and administer public programs for broad public interests, not to create private rights. However, Reich argued that progressive political theories in practice had already been abandoned in many areas and were discredited. The ability of private interest groups to influence government decisions already had turned many government programs into instruments of private interest. Reich saw his proposal as an egalitarian measure; welfare and other recipients who were less well off should have the same rights to the benefits of their government programs as business had to its own forms of government largess. In short, the transformation of zoning from an instrument of scientific planning into a new private right was not an isolated incident. Rather, it was part of a much broader trend that was attracting attention and commentary over wide areas of American government.

THE PROPERTY RIGHT THEORISTS OF ZONING

The theory of "the new property" was far from the only intellectual response to the loss of faith in the Progressive gospel of scientific planning, disinterested public decisions, and government run by experts rather than politicians. The deregulation movement also argued that the administration of most government regulations had become captive to the business interests that were most affected by the regulations. In a sense, deregulation proponents were saying that the regulatory apparatus had become the "property" of these business interests, property that was paid for by campaign contributions and in other appropriate "currency" of the political system. However, the deregulation movement proposed to solve the problem, not by following Reich in further recognizing and legitimizing the new property, but by abolishing it. Writers on airline, railroad, trucking, communications, securities, banking, and other types of regulation all proposed to cut back on or to abolish altogether existing regulatory systems.

Another important contribution to the tide against regulation was the famous article by Ronald Coase, "The Problem of Social Cost."[19] Coase argued that there was no necessity for government to become involved in regulation of activities such as smokestacks and gravel pits, even though they could have significant adverse effects on their neighbors. If all the parties involved were left free to bargain among themselves, and if property rights were well defined, Coase asserted that market bargaining would produce a satisfactory and economically efficient agreement. In this same spirit, J. H. Dales argued in an influential 1968

book that government command-and-control regulation of air and water pollution was unnecessary; market forces could solve the problem with less administrative burden and greater economic efficiency.[20] An air shed, for example, should be looked on as a scarce resource with a limited capacity to absorb pollution. This was no different, in principle, from the allocation of scarce iron, copper, or other natural resources. The government need only intervene to set a limit on the total pollution emissions for the air shed, and then define pollution rights up to this limit. After that, the mechanism of the private market—perhaps beginning with a government auction of rights—could be counted on to allocate the pollution rights to the users that would make the most efficient use of them.

These same intellectual trends, not surprisingly, spilled over into the land use area, resulting in a variety of proposals for the deregulation of land use, involving radical surgery or even abolition of zoning. The regulation of nuisances, for instance, could be transformed—following the Coase argument—from a direct government responsibility to a problem of appropriately structuring property rights and providing for market financial transactions. Applying the Dales argument, the problem of allocating the development rights to vacant land was almost identical in form to the problem of allocating a fixed total permissible amount of air or water pollution rights. Indeed, Marion Clawson in 1966 already had proposed municipal sale of zoning changes as a superior means of allocating development rights.

In 1972, Dan Tarlock presented a brief sketch of a plan that combined these elements.[21] Given that zoning of existing neighborhoods effectively was serving the functions of a private property right, Tarlock suggested—much in the spirit of the "new property"—that a private covenant scheme be formally substituted for zoning in protecting neighborhood quality. Following Coase, the neighborhood also would be able to negotiate in a market for the sale of these private rights to new neighborhood entrants. If the financial terms offered by the aspiring entrants were attractive enough, the neighborhood would happily take the money and bear with any adverse environmental impacts of the new use. Following Dales and Clawson, Tarlock also suggested that municipalities should be able to market the rights to build on undeveloped land within the municipality.

In two more widely noted articles in leading law journals, Robert Ellickson developed in much greater detail a plan for the application of Coasian principles.[22] In 1973, he proposed that financial compensation be made an integral part of nuisance law. If a new use wanted to enter an existing neighborhood, it could do so by paying monetary compensation to the surrounding neighborhood home owners for any adverse impacts. In 1977, Ellickson extended this proposed approach to the context of suburban undeveloped land, advocating that municipalities be required to purchase new land use restrictions that limited development to densities below a "normal" standard for that municipality.

The writings in the 1970s of Bernard Siegan took the view that zoning of undeveloped land was a property right redistribution that had no legitimate social justification.[23] It amounted to a "taking" or confiscation by the municipality of the development rights, yet served no valid social purpose. Indeed, given the private purposes actually served by zoning, zoning of undeveloped land effectively transferred the development rights from one private party, the land owner, to another private party, the set of higher density property owners that were politically dominant in the municipality.

Disturbed by this naked exercise of government coercive powers, Siegan proposed to solve the problem by abolishing zoning.

In the past 10 years, the new "property right" approach to zoning has influenced a wide range of law journal and other writings on zoning.[24] The Report of the President's Commission on Housing in 1982 found that "excessive restrictions on housing production have driven up the price of housing generally," creating concern for "the plight of millions of Americans of average and lesser income who cannot now afford homes or apartments."[25] The Commission offered recommendations for a "program of land use deregulation." Other researchers found that the regulatory restrictions on development were proliferating in many areas, rather than contracting. One student of land use in the San Francisco Bay area estimated that these regulations had added between 18 and 34 percent to the cost of new housing.[26] Another study found that, nationwide, new home buyers had to pay about 20 percent of their income in 1968 for their homes. But in the early 1980s new home buyers had to spend about 35 percent of their income. Even with declines in financing costs, they still had to spend about 32 percent in 1984.[27] Much of the increase in housing costs reflected a growing scarcity of metropolitan land available for new housing construction.

Although there is little agreement among expert opinions on the solutions, there is close to a consensus on the most important problem of zoning. Zoning is a system that may be acceptable in a static environment such as an existing neighborhood seeking to keep out most new uses. However, zoning fails almost entirely in a dynamic context—either in an existing neighborhood that is facing a transition to new uses or in the development of vacant land. Because of the obstacles zoning and other similar growth controls pose to new development, zoning contributes significantly to higher housing costs and generally to major economic inefficiencies and environmental unattractiveness. Moreover, the distributional consequences of zoning are perverse—the protection of the environmental quality of the richer members of society, while denying housing opportunities to the poorer members.

This assessment of zoning has been common since the 1950s and 1960s. However, the leading zoning critics of those days proposed to solve zoning problems by reviving and reasserting the original ideals of zoning. They sought to institute truly effective land use planning and greater centralization of authority in order to ensure implementation of plans. Thus, the Model Land Development Code of the American Law Institute was built around a much greater state role in land use regulation.[28]

By contrast, the new property right theorists of the 1970s and 1980s, despite many differences in details, all are skeptical of land use planning and centralized authority. They point to the almost universal failure of such approaches over the years. They look instead to decentralized decision making through greater reliance on financial incentives and market forces. The greatest merits of the market mechanism are found in resolving resource allocation problems in a fluid and dynamic environment—precisely the circumstance in which zoning fails.

The following compares some of the specific proposals made and comments briefly on their feasibility.

PROPERTY RIGHT PROPOSALS FOR UNDEVELOPED LAND

A number of proposals have been made to replace the existing zoning system in undeveloped areas with new mechanisms for transfer of development rights. All have in common that they offer some form of financial payment as an inducement for the transfer of the rights, not leaving the transfer simply as a matter of compliance with a government administrative ruling. However, in many other respects the proposals differ. To illustrate some of the issues raised and for purposes of comparison, the key differences among the proposals of Siegan, Ellickson, Fischel, and Kmiec will be briefly examined.[29] (The Fischel proposal examined here is that contained in his 1979 article. His 1985 book on zoning offers a proposal much closer to the Ellickson concept.)

One area in which significant differences arise is the division of development rights between the landowner and the municipality. At present, zoning assigns some of these rights to the existing landowner—the level of development currently allowed without any further zoning change—and the remainder of the development rights are in the possession of the municipality. The simplest and most radical proposal in this regard is the Siegan proposal to return to the prezoning world in which the landowner holds virtually all the development rights. Fischel's proposal, by comparison, would maintain the status quo, allowing the municipality to keep just that level of development rights that zoning now grants it. In a more complicated proposal, Ellickson would define a "normal" level of development that roughly would correspond to current market economics and what economic efficiency would dictate at a particular site. The landowner at that site would be assigned the rights to develop up to this normal level of development intensity. The municipality would in effect be allowed to hold the remaining development rights beyond this level. The Kmiec proposal is the most generous to the municipality. Somewhat in the spirit of Henry

George, Kmiec would assign the right to agricultural use to the landowner, and the remaining development rights would effectively be held by the municipality.

A second key area of difference among the proposals is in the specific mechanism for transferring and setting the payment terms for any transfer of development rights. In the Siegan proposal, the sale of development rights simply would be left to the landowner, who would now possess all of those rights. Under the Fischel proposal, a developer would have to make two separate purchases, first of the land itself from the landowner and, second, a purchase from the municipality of any further development rights needed beyond the status quo of existing zoning. Indeed, the heart of Fischel's proposal is the granting of the new authority to the municipality directly to sell all future zoning changes. No restrictions are placed by Fischel either on the maximum level of development rights that the municipality can sell off, or on the price that it can charge in this transaction. These matters are to be determined by mutual bargaining between the municipality and the developer. Kmiec has also proposed municipal sale of zoning but he would closely control the municipal price. Under Kmiec's proposal, the price for which the municipality could sell development rights would be established by an appraiser's determination of the market value of those development rights. The municipality could not refuse a builder's offer to buy development rights at this appraised price. Thus, Kmiec would make all land immediately available for development, although the municipality would receive the receipts of the development right sales.

Ellickson's proposal in this respect as in others is the most complicated. Ellickson would allow a municipality to restrict development significantly. However, the municipality would then have to buy all those development rights it wanted beyond the current "normal" level of development in the municipality. The municipality also would have to compensate consumers outside its jurisdiction for inflation in metropolitan housing prices that resulted from municipal actions (perhaps accomplished through a consumer class action suit). Ellickson is less precise about the ability of a developer to build at densities higher than the normal development intensity in the community. However, the spirit of his proposal suggests that builders would have such a right, as long as they paid compensation to the municipality for any adverse municipal impacts caused by the unusually high intensity of development. Like Kmiec, Ellickson does not rely on bargaining in the marketplace to determine the prices paid for development right transfers. Instead, the required transfer prices under the various scenarios in Ellickson's proposal would have to be fixed by the courts or by some special administrative tribunal—presumably with the aid of appraisers and other appropriate experts. Ellickson is concerned that development right transfers not only meet efficiency but also equity and social justice criteria that demand government setting of the transfer price. Such a government role might also reduce the transactions costs that would be associated with setting the price through direct bargaining.

In a frictionless world without any transactions and administrative costs and with perfect information, each of these proposals would solve the problem of creating financial incentives for socially efficient transfers of development rights. Only Fischel and Siegan would rely directly on a market mechanism, but Ellickson and Kmiec still would pay the municipality for development right transfers that it currently is asked to grant for free. It is precisely this lack of any financial incentives for the municipality that currently stands in the way of socially desirable transfers of development rights.

In assessing the practicality of these proposals, two further important considerations are administrative complexity and political acceptability. Ranked by administrative complexity, the Siegan proposal would be easiest to administer, followed by the Fischel proposal, then Kmiec, and finally Ellickson. The Siegan and Fischel proposals have the great administrative advantage that they do not require the courts or a government agency to set the financial terms of development right transfers; the proposals rely instead on the market. Proposals such as those of Kmiec and Ellickson that require the public setting of a fair and equitable price are likely to stir a great deal of controversy concerning that price. In not relying on mutually negotiated agreements, the Kmiec and Ellickson proposals both create the prospect of development right transfers coercively imposed against the wishes of one of the two parties. The Kmiec proposal would allow a builder to buy development rights, even when the municipality did not think that the appraised price paid was adequate. Similarly, the Ellickson proposal would allow the municipality to buy development rights, even though the landowner did not think that the price paid to him was adequate.

Politically, the Fischel proposal has the major advantage that it begins from the status quo in the assignment of development rights between the landowner and municipality. By contrast, the Siegan proposal would no doubt incur strong municipal opposition in that it would cancel existing municipal rights and turn them over to the landowner. Similarly, the Kmiec proposal would face strong landowner opposition in that it would eliminate the landowner's rights to the value of the land

beyond its value in agricultural use. The Ellickson proposal is carefully tailored to be equitable to all parties, but the complexity of its administration would threaten to embroil courts and political leadership in contentious disputes. Given the lack of scientific precision achievable in appraisal and other land use fields of expertise, the Ellickson proposal would involve numerous subjective judgments that would be politically difficult to make.

While Fischel's proposal seeks to preserve the status quo in the division of development rights, it might prove objectionable on other social value grounds. It may be argued that the sale of government regulations comes close to, if not literally constituting, bribery, thereby violating basic standards of ethical government conduct. If the regulations create major inefficiencies and otherwise are a failure, so this line of argument would run, the solution is not to put the government regulations on the market but to abolish them. By this standard, the Siegan proposal is superior to the proposals of Fischel, Kmiec, and Ellickson.

In summary, the criteria for assessing the several proposals include at least five elements:

1. The establishment of well-defined entitlements dividing up ownership of development rights among the parties involved;

2. A mechanism for transfer of the development rights with a financial payment to the party giving up rights;

3. A mechanism for determining the size of the transfer payment;

4. An acceptable level of administrative complexity and cost; and

5. An ability to meet prevailing standards of social equity and to win political acceptance.

None of the proposals reviewed here dominates the others on all five grounds, thus requiring some sort of trade-off.

PROPERTY RIGHT PROPOSALS FOR EXISTING NEIGHBORHOODS

As noted previously, zoning has proven more satisfactory in the circumstance for which it was originally intended—the protection of lower density neighborhoods from intrusion of higher density uses. As a result, there has been less writing and commentary on the problems of zoning in existing neighborhoods. Nevertheless, most neighborhoods at some point face the prospect of change; eventually many of them will be superceded by a new type of land use altogether. Zoning has performed just as poorly in this as in other dynamic contexts. Several proposals have been made by Ellickson, Nelson, and Tarlock that seek to establish a system of private property rights to replace zoning in existing neighborhoods.[30] The features to be examined in assessing and comparing these proposals involve basically the same five criteria noted for undeveloped land.

Nelson would abolish zoning in existing neighborhoods and instead transfer the rights to control land uses within the neighborhood to the neighborhood residents themselves. They would have to form a private neighborhood government for the purpose of exercising those rights. The Tarlock proposal is only sketched briefly, but involves a similar direction. As in the case of undeveloped land, Ellickson would base his proposal on the concept of a normal level of development within the neighborhood. The neighborhood would receive the rights to control only uses that were of higher density or otherwise more intensive than normal.

Tarlock and Nelson conceive payments made to neighborhoods as a market price set by bargaining. An aspiring entrant into a neighborhood would have to offer a price and other conditions sufficient to win neighborhood approval. Ellickson, by contrast, would have the courts or a government agency set the transfer price, based on its best estimate of the damages that would be caused by the new use in the neighborhood.

Nelson and Tarlock also would not create any automatic right of entry for new uses into the neighborhood; neighborhood residents collectively could refuse any and all offers of developers, no matter what the price offered. In the Ellickson proposal, however, a new entrant into a neighborhood would be entitled to enter, as long as it was willing to pay the price set as an appropriate level of compensation for adverse impacts. However, Ellickson does offer a means by which the neighborhood residents would still be able to refuse this price and to exclude a proposed new use. Consistent with his basic approach, they could exclude a use by paying the legitimate damages that the use suffered in being excluded from the neighborhood.

Nelson suggests that the creation of a new private neighborhood would be accomplished by a favorable vote of the neighborhood residents—requiring some high percentage but not a unanimous vote. The neighborhood would then form a governing body and establish other necessary rules for collective decision making—a concept based in many ways on the private condominium model. Tarlock does not address the manner of formation of a neighborhood or its governing rules. Ellickson does not envision the permanent formation of new private neighborhoods with their own governing bodies. Rather, collective decision making would occur on an ad hoc basis as a specific use sought to gain entry into an area where surrounding home owners would be adversely affected. At this point, those home owners would band together for the limited purpose of reaching a decision on the new use at issue.

Nelson envisions the possibility of a whole

private neighborhood being sold lock, stock, and barrel to a developer for an entirely new use. Such sales in fact recently have begun to occur through corporate and other collective mechanisms devised by groups of neighborhood home owners themselves on an ad hoc basis. Tarlock and Ellickson do not address this possibility.

All the neighborhood proposals involve significant administrative costs, especially in the start-up phase, when new land use institutions would have to be organized and put in place. Once the new system was operating, the administrative costs might be no greater than the substantial administrative costs currently associated with the zoning system.

Politically, all of these proposals would face the natural resistance to embarking on a radical new departure. The Nelson proposal probably would face opposition from municipal officials who would see new private neighborhoods as a major threat to the current role and authority of the municipality itself. It probably also would be seen as an assertion of "private" over "public" values and as a blow against egalitarian objectives that, even though seldom realized in the land use field, remain an important social ideal. The courts and administrative agencies would probably oppose the Ellickson proposal for fear of the many difficult administrative problems it would create and the fierce controversies likely to result over the setting of fair compensation payments for property right transfers.

Each of these proposals is likely to raise a libertarian objection that individual property owners are coerced to submit to the majority (or supermajority) land use decisions of their fellow neighborhood residents. In establishing a new private neighborhood, some property owners might lose individual rights, even though they had voted against the neighborhood formation. To be sure, zoning many

years ago transferred most of those rights from the individual to collective possession.

Rather than in a comprehensive fashion, these neighborhood proposals might be adopted in a more incremental way. Indeed, the recent block sales of whole neighborhoods represent an important incremental step toward the sale by neighborhood residents collectively of the right to develop within the neighborhood. The spreading use of historic districts also often involves a subterfuge of historic significance. The real purpose is to obtain a new regulatory mechanism for the neighborhood, similar to private mechanisms, that can be exercised by neighborhood residents with much greater discretion than traditional zoning allows.

Although proposals for new property rights in existing neighborhoods have received less scholarly attention, they may have better political prospects than the proposals involving undeveloped land. The aim in existing neighborhoods is to increase and perfect the rights of the neighborhood residents who are presently there. These residents thus represent a concentrated constituency with a strong direct interest in the outcome—a formula for maximum political influence in the American system. There is no similarly concentrated and politically influential group of major beneficiaries to lobby for new property right institutions in undeveloped areas.

THE FUTURE OF ZONING

Most writing on zoning for at least the past 30 years has been critical. Yet, zoning continues to be highly popular with the American public. Richard Babcock and Charles Siemon recently commented that, despite many forecasts of its demise, "zoning is indeed alive and healthy."[31]

The failure thus far of the numerous zoning critics to have a greater influence has several possible explanations. It may simply be that the inertia of political and economic institutions is such that necessary changes are still being blocked, even though they eventually will have their day. American political institutions may face particular problems in asserting larger national and regional interests against parochial but more concentrated political forces—the circumstance faced by zoning reformers.

Another possibility is that the critics of zoning have been too concerned with questions of ideological consistency and have failed to show adequately how the practical consequences of their proposals would benefit the American public. Indeed, a major part of the legal criticism of zoning is directed not so much to practical consequences as to the large discrepancies between the legal theories that justify zoning and the actual practice of zoning. The two discrepancies noted most often have been the absence of professional planning in the actual administration of zoning and the substitution of a discretionary system for a system of zones fixed in advance. More recently, free market critics have objected to zoning as the substitution of a pervasive system of regulation for the forces of the market.

The American public, however, has a high tolerance for ideological inconsistency and does not necessarily find this sufficient grounds for major changes. Moreover, this popular attitude may also exhibit a deeper wisdom. Recalling the writings of Holmes and Pollock, it has been virtually the norm over the centuries that the practice of land law has differed significantly from the accepted theories of the day. Crude fictions and myths often have been required to paper over the ideological inconsistencies. Yet, the light of later history has often revealed that it was the ideology, not the practice, that was most at fault. Ideas often are slower to change than the circum-

stances that the ideas are supposed to explain and legitimize.

It is therefore especially important to try to understand why zoning has proven so popular and why the recommendations of all the scholarly commentators on zoning have so regularly been ignored. It may be useful to observe that the success of zoning is an assertion of local independence and autonomy. Zoning insulates the locality from the forces of the market. Local municipal leaders also have largely fended off any attempts by state or other higher-level governments to assert a greater role in land use regulation. The critics of zoning typically take for granted that localism is a bad thing, since it does in fact promote economic inefficiency and create other problems. However, local independence may foster a sense of community and promote other important social values that are threatened in a mobile, technological age.

Reflecting wider social controversies, debates about zoning often are conducted with the "planners" on one side and the "market advocates" on the other side. However, if the debate is one of localism versus the assertion of wider social interests, the planners and market advocates actually are more allies than opponents. Both are proposing that forces outside the local community should have a greater weight in local land use decisions. The planners seek to exert this outside influence through government planning and an administrative apparatus, while free market proponents would rely on the private forces of the marketplace. The failures of both views in the arena of zoning practice also may reflect a common popular rejection, in principle, of such outside influences in favor of greater local autonomy. This is a fundamental issue that has been little touched in the larger body of zoning writings.

Such issues have been raised in other nonzoning contexts, however. The ideology of government planning and control and the ideology of the free market both are tied closely to the western tradition that calls for individual effort and sacrifice in the name of the overall progress of humanity. The planning and free market traditions might be said to be different "denominations" within a larger modern "religion of progress." Their disagreements—bitter as they have been—have been over means rather than ends.

However, faith in progress has been eroding in recent decades. Many members of the environmental movement today see science as a grave threat and are more concerned with protecting nature from human assault than with the benefits of further "progress." The setting aside of almost 90 million acres in a national wilderness system in part constitutes a symbolic statement in favor of nature and critical of the influence of modern industrial civilization. The author of a recent study of the American conservation movement writes that "to the recurrent question of whether conservationists are against progress, the answer would seem to be yes—at least progress as it has normally been defined in the West."[32]

The attitudes of conservationism and its more recent progeny, environmentalism, have had a significant impact in the zoning arena. The defenders of local zoning and other local controls in many cases defend their actions as necessary protections of the environment. They appeal to a wider public sense that it may often be necessary to sacrifice considerable "progress" (conventionally defined) for new "environmental values." Applied to the zoning context, they ask why local communities should bow to the dictates of modern economic efficiency, when the efficiency of modern productive powers is not put to any good use. The tactics of local defenders of zoning and growth controls are often also borrowed from the methods of resistance pioneered by the environmental movement in opposing dams, coal mines, and many other types of development. In some cases, the defenders of local zoning prerogatives are activists in other environmental causes as well.

Environmentalism in America has been more of a spontaneous, grass roots phenomenon than the product of a well-developed ideology. Indeed, environmentalism has faced strong opposition from all sides of the spectrum of "progressive" ideologies. Yet, its popularity and political impact show that it has tapped an important cord in American life. Coming to terms with the future of zoning may require a more explicit assessment of and coming to terms with the broader localism that the attitudes of environmentalism favor.

The future of zoning will in any case be more a product of broad social forces than of legal theory. In proposing a future of zoning, one is not simply addressing a legal or an economic question but offering a vision of future American society. As Holmes noted, the law is the embodiment of the history of a nation.

COMMENTARY

Balancing the many considerations noted in this chapter, I have my own view of where zoning should be heading. I will conclude the chapter by briefly restating this view, noting the economic assessments and also some value judgments that it implies.

I would bow to localism enough to grant the developed neighborhood independence from outside government control over its land use and to let the neighborhood decide for itself—through some collective mechanism—how to respond to the pressures of outside market forces. The neighborhood response might well be to maintain the existing neighborhood environment just as it is, fending off market pressures. However, I would also allow the neighborhood to profit from market forces to the extent that it wished. This could be done by selling entry rights into the neighborhood for limited new uses or even by selling the whole neighborhood for a new project. It is possible to think of such neighborhood autonomy as a form of neighborhood government, but a more apt characterization would be that it consists of "privatizing" the neighborhood and the neighborhood system of regulatory controls.

However, I would draw the line in granting local autonomy at the boundaries of existing developed neighborhoods. Substantial areas of vacant and undeveloped land should not be insulated from forces for change and maintained in their current state for the purpose of improving the environment of other, more densely settled neighborhoods within the same municipality. The social costs are too high in terms of land that is used at far below its productive potential. It is also an inequitable system in that many members of society in need of housing see their needs frustrated by the high prices and lack of suitable housing within their means.

Fischel's proposal to allow municipalities to sell zoning changes for undeveloped areas largely would take care of the efficiency problem. It would provide the necessary financial incentive to the municipality to open up for building many areas that are now held undeveloped. It would also be an equitable approach in the sense of confirming the current division of development rights between the landowner and the municipality. However, because the original zoning can reasonably be seen as having been a "taking" or "confiscation" of development rights, the Fischel proposal would in effect confirm what was probably an unjust municipal action in the first place. To be sure, since this action typically occurred several or more decades ago, the current landowner in most cases was not the victim, and thus the original inequity today may well be beyond redress.

Another problem with Fischel's proposal is that the current zoning may be less relevant than a realistic expectation of future zoning. The landowner today may be precluded from developing, but have a good chance of winning a court-ordered rezoning five years from today. If this is the case, it would amount to a new "taking" to transfer to the municipality all the additional rights beyond the few allowed by current zoning. The widespread use of "wait-and-see" zoning may mean that the current municipal zoning gives little indication of the true municipal zoning policies. Indeed, partly for these reasons, Fischel himself later shifted away from the proposal of his 1979 article and moved in his 1985 book on zoning toward the Ellickson approach.

However, while Ellickson's design solves equity problems, I wonder about its practicality. In requiring the determination of a "normal" level of municipal development and the making of appraisals of the price of land corresponding to that normal level, Ellickson would impose a major burden of economic calculation, either on the courts or on some other administrative body. Significantly complicating the problem, those development levels and prices will be changing all the time as economic conditions and expectations shift. In a way, Ellickson is offering a new design for land use regulation that will work well only if it is accompanied by the skilled calculations of a new form of central land use agency—in essence, a special type of planning agency. I suspect that the political and informational problems that always have made formal planning difficult in the American system would also act to undermine the intentions of the Ellickson scheme.

As a result, I prefer a more direct reliance on

the market mechanism and on market determination of development levels and land prices. In this regard, the best alternative that I see to the 1979 Fischel proposal would be to turn all the development rights over to the landowner by simply abolishing all zoning in undeveloped areas—the Siegan proposal, and also effectively advocated more recently by Mark Pulliam.[33] Between these two alternatives I can see no compelling case for one or the other. In the past, I have favored the Siegan approach of eliminating zoning in undeveloped areas and giving full development rights to landowners.

As a practical matter, the courts could allow municipal sale of zoning simply by not interfering to prevent municipalities from collecting large cash payments as part of the negotiation for the zoning changes needed to allow new projects. One might imagine an auction at which each developer submitted a proposal for certain physical facilities combined with a direct cash payment to be made to the municipal treasury. The municipality would then pick the offer that was, on balance, most attractive. It might, of course, be necessary to maintain some subterfuge that the payments were related to municipal services, but the courts perhaps could decline to inquire closely into such matters. Washington, D.C., has recently moved in this direction by proposing to allow higher development densities in return for developer cash contributions for low-income housing. These contributions would be made to the city government for use anywhere in Washington.

As a practical matter, courts could implement the proposal to abolish zoning in undeveloped areas through a ruling that would build upon and extend the reasoning of the Supreme Court in the *First English Evangelical Lutheran Church* decision.[34] In this scenario, the courts would acknowledge what they have been denying for many years—that much of the current municipal zoning of undeveloped land represents a taking and that, as such, it requires compensation to the landowner. In other words, the municipality would either have to buy the development rights directly or return them to the landowner.

Whichever approach was adopted, it would be important to allow municipalities to impose full charges on the developer for any new roads, sewers, and other actual costs of new development. Allocative efficiency in the market requires that each private party absorb the burden of the resource costs that it imposes.

As a practical matter, privatization of property rights to existing neighborhoods could take a major incremental step forward with court approval for the arrangements for block sales of whole neighborhoods that are now emerging in some areas around the United States. Courts also might show a lenient attitude toward the creation of historic and other special districts in neighborhoods, going along with the subterfuges involved in many claims to historic significance. Ultimately, however, some government legislative action would be necessary to create a framework for first establishing and then exercising private rights in private neighborhoods.

In conclusion, the courts should look beyond narrow legal theories with their associated zoning myths and fictions. Instead, they should look to the larger social purposes and trends of zoning. In this light, a step forward would be a Supreme Court ruling that at least the most restrictive forms of zoning of undeveloped areas represent a taking. The courts might also permit municipalities to bargain for payments as large as they can get from developers in exchange for zoning changes. Municipalities should be allowed to charge all new development for the full marginal infrastructure costs imposed by the development. The courts also should approve block sales of whole neighborhoods and other actions by neighborhoods in which they assert a private right to profit monetarily and otherwise to deal as they collectively wish with the use of land within their own neighborhood.

NOTES

1. Morton G. White, *Social Thought in America: The Revolt against Formalism* (New York, N.Y.: Viking Press, 1949), p. 59.

2. *Ibid.*

3. Oliver Wendell Holmes, *The Common Law* (Boston, Mass.: Little Brown, 1881), p. 1, cited in White, *Social Thought in America*, p. 16.

4. Holmes, *The Common Law*, p. 5, cited in White, *Social Thought in America*, p. 17.

5. Frederick Pollock, *The Land Laws* (London, England: Macmillan, 1896).

6. *Ibid.*, pp. 11–12.

7. Robert Anderson, *American Law of Zoning* (Rochester, N.Y.: Lawyers Co-operative Publishing Co., 1968), p. 2:48.

8. Hugh Pomeroy, "A Planning Manual for Zoning," unpublished manuscript prepared for American Society of Planning Officials, 1940, p. 57.

9. *Village of Euclid* v. *Ambler Realty Co.*, 272 U. S. 365, 394 (1926).

10. Dwight Waldo, *The Administrative State* 2nd. edition, (New York, N.Y.: Holmes and Meier, 1984), p. 69.

11. *See* Alfred Bettman, *City and Regional Planning Papers* (Cambridge, Mass.: Harvard University Press, 1946).

12. *Village of Euclid* v. *Ambler Realty Co.*, 272 U.S. at 365 (1926).

13. Dan Tarlock, "Euclid Revisited," *Land Use Law and Zoning Digest*, January 1982, p. 8.

14. National Commission on Urban Problems, *Building the American City* (New York, N.Y.: Praeger, 1969), p. 219.

15. *Village of Belle Terre* v. *Boraas*, 416 U.S. 1, 9 (1974).

16. John Delafons, *Land Use Controls in the United States* (Cambridge, Mass.: MIT Press, 1969); Richard Babcock, *The Zoning Game* (Madison, Wis.: Univ. of Wisconsin Press, 1966).

17. Charles A. Reich, "The New Property," *Yale Law Journal*, April 1964.

18. Charles A. Reich, "The Law of the Planned Society," *Yale Law Journal*, July 1966, p. 1,266.

19. Ronald H. Coase, "The Problem of Social Cost," *Journal of Law and Economics*, October 1960.

20. J. H. Dales, *Pollution, Property and Prices* (Toronto, Ontario: Univ. of Toronto Press, 1968).

21. A. Dan Tarlock, "Toward a Revised Theory of Zoning," in *Land Use Controls Annual*, ed. F. S. Bangs (Chicago: American Society of Planning Officials, 1972).

22. Robert C. Ellickson, "Alternatives to Zoning: Covenants, Nuisance Rules and Fines as Land Use Controls," *University of Chicago Law Review*, Summer 1973; and Robert C. Ellickson, "Suburban Growth Controls: An Economic and Legal Analysis," *Yale Law Journal*, January 1977.

23. Bernard H. Siegan, *Land Use Without Zoning* (Lexington, Mass.: Lexington Books, 1972); Bernard H. Siegan, *Other People's Property* (Lexington, Mass.: Lexington Books, 1976).

24. *See* Jan Z. Krasnowiecki, "Abolish Zoning," *Syracuse Law Review* 31 (1980): 719; George Lefcoe, "California's Land Planning Requirements: The Case for Deregulation," *Southern California Law Review*, March 1981; and Orlando Delogu, "Local Land Use Controls: An Idea Whose Time Has Passed," *Maine Law Review* 36 (1984): 261.

25. *The Report of the President's Commission on Housing* (Washington, D.C.: 1982), p. 199.

26. David E. Dowall, *The Suburban Squeeze: Land Conversion and Regulation in the San Francisco Bay Area* (Berkeley, Calif.: Univ. of California Press, 1984).

27. *Home Ownership and Housing Affordability in the United States: 1963–1985*, a report of the Joint Center for Housing Studies of the Massachusetts Institute of Technology and Harvard University, 1986.

28. *A Model Land Development Code* (Philadelphia, Penn.: American Law Institute, 1976).

29. *See* Siegan, *Land Use Without Zoning*; Ellickson, "Alternatives to Zoning"; Ellickson, "Suburban Growth Controls"; William A. Fischel, "Equity and Efficiency Aspects of Zoning Reform," *Public Policy*, Summer 1979; William A. Fischel, *The Economics of Zoning Laws* (Baltimore, Md.: Johns Hopkins University Press, 1985); Douglas W. Kmiec, "Deregulating Land Use: An Alternative Free Enterprise System," *University of Pennsylvania Law Review*, November 1981; and Douglas W. Kmiec, "The Role of the Planner in a Deregulated World," *Land Use Law and Zoning Digest*, June 1982.

30. *See* Ellickson, "Alternatives to Zoning"; Tarlock, "Toward a Revised Theory of Zoning"; Robert H. Nelson, *Zoning and Property Rights* (Cambridge, Mass.: MIT Press, 1977); Robert H. Nelson "A Private Property Right Theory of Zoning," *The Urban Lawyer*, Fall 1979; Robert H. Nelson, "Private Neighborhoods: A New Direction for the Neighborhood Movement," in *Land Reform, American Style*, ed. Charles C. Geisler and Frank J. Popper (Totowa, N.J.: Rowman and Allenheld, 1984); Robert H.

Nelson, "Agricultural Zoning: A Private Alternative," in *The Vanishing Farmland Crisis,* ed. John Baden (Lawrence, Kan.: University Press of Kansas, 1984); and Robert H. Nelson, "Marketable Zoning: A Cure for the Zoning System," *Land Use Law and Zoning Digest,* November 1985.

31. Richard F. Babcock and Charles L. Siemon, *The Zoning Game Revisited* (Boston, Mass.: Oelgeschlager, Gunn and Hain, 1985), p. 263.

32. Stephen Fox, *The American Conservation Movement* (Madison, Wis.: University of Wisconsin Press, 1985), p. 373.

33. Mark S. Pulliam, "Brandeis Brief for Decontrol of Land Use: A Plea for Constitutional Reform," *Southwestern University Law Review* 13 (1983): 435.

34. *First English Evangelical Lutheran Church of Glendale* v. *County of Los Angeles,* 107 S.Ct. 2378 (1987).

12

Zoning and Land Use Planning: An Economic Perspective

William C. Wheaton

The American urban landscape has been shaped by a number of public policies over the past century. Many of these, mostly *implicit* policies, have interplayed smoothly with the operation of the private land market. Government infrastructure, such as highways and water and mass transit, has guided the pattern of land development, while tax policy with respect to energy, capital, and home mortgages has influenced the pattern of consuming both housing and location.

Local zoning ordinances, on the other hand, have emerged over this period as the country's major *explicit* land use policy instrument. By their very nature, zoning powers of the type authorized in the *Village of Euclid* v. *Ambler Realty Co.* decision have a method and intent that runs quite contrary to the operation of the private market. In its current form, zoning has changed private rights into public rights and market decisions into political decisions.

It is argued in this chapter that these changes in rights and decision making have not always operated in the "public interest"— at least as the public interest is perceived by economists. The problems with zoning, as it

currently is implemented, can be described in three ways.

1. Zoning, by being a power of local government, cannot address a range of external "failures" in the operation of the private land market that transcend local boundaries.

2. Those failures of the land market which lie strictly within local jurisdictions are not always regulated in the public interest by current zoning institutions. This results from the political decision making that characterizes zoning decisions in the absence of required compensation.

3. Without the payment of compensation, most zoning decisions focus on the redistribution of wealth and property among different groups, and not on the internalization of externalities that would improve the efficiency of the land market.

To develop these arguments, the chapter is organized into three sections. The first reviews a number of economic theories about the failures of private land markets and the kinds of intervention that have been proposed to correct them. The second section details the structure of present zoning institutions and how the decisions that emerge from them rarely address the failures of the land market identified in the economic literature. The final section offers some suggestions for reorganizing zoning powers to alleviate some of the problems raised throughout the chapter.

EXTERNALITIES AND THE FAILURE OF LAND MARKETS

In traditional economic reasoning, competitive markets produce an allocation of resources that has a very desirable property—usually referred to as "Pareto optimality." The Pareto criterion is quite similar to the legal notion of the "greatest good for the greatest number." In fact, the most straightforward way of explaining the Pareto criteria of economic efficiency is to consider those changes in the allocation of resources that are *capable* of making *all* "better off" (in the utilitarian sense). That is, a change in prices and the assignment of property or goods, in which those who benefit can compensate those who are harmed and still come out with greater utility. An economy or market meets the Pareto criteria when there is *no* change in resources possible that could make all better off. Conversely, a market is inefficient if one or more such reallocations exist.

It is a fundamental theorem in economics that competitive markets will, under certain circumstances, create an allocation of resources that meets the Pareto criteria. A main condition necessary is that there *not* exist any externalities among the agents active in the market. An externality is a service or disservice among agents for which there is no channel of mediation. Traditional scholars have argued that to mediate externalities correctly requires the creation of either a pseudo market, with prices, taxes, and subsidies, or direct government regulation. Other theorists (e.g., the "Chicago school") suggest that externalities exist only because property rights have not

been clearly defined. With a clear definition, the legal system can provide the needed channel of mediation.

It has long been believed that the land market is the one market that abounds with externalities. This becomes especially apparent when one realizes that the traded commodity in the land market is individual parcels of property. Thus, in principle, an externality exists any time the activity or use on one parcel alters the value of other parcels. There is, to be sure, a very active market for parcels of land, but there is no market for the services or disservices that occur among them (Gordon and McRenolds).

While there are literally hundreds of examples of such externalities in the land market, it is useful to review several major ones that illustrate the different scope or types of such effects.

First there are a range of aesthetic external effects in which a building's design, landscaping, or other characteristics bring enjoyment to neighboring property or passersby (Hough and Kratz). The standard argument made is that the owner of each parcel weighs the cost of such features against only his own benefit when installing them, and neglects the impact on others. If the latter is significant, then a private market will underinvest in such characteristics, relative to the level that meets the Pareto criteria. The latter requires that we test to see if the neighbors and passersby might be willing to compensate the builder to invest more in aesthetics. Under these circumstances, all would be better off with more such investment.

A second category of external effects is much broader in its geographic scope and centers around traffic congestion. The best example of this is the recent trend of building large-scale office-industrial complexes in the suburbs. Such developments tend not only to create considerable local congestion, but alter the entire regional flow of traffic as well (White; Tauden and Whitte). In contemplating such a development, the current level of congestion at the site certainly will be a consideration, for it is well known that such congestion is capitalized into land prices or local wages (Eberts). What will not be considered by the private market is the change in congestion resulting from the project. In addition to the private costs of the development, the builder also should compensate all those whose travel will be worsened by the project. If after paying such compensation the project still seems profitable, then it truly has met the Pareto criteria (Solow).

A third example involves the kind of positive linkages that often occur among certain types of retail establishments. If shoppers tend to purchase (for example) clothing and jewelry together, then the proximity of a store selling one benefits the other (Stahl). Consumers will elect to shop at such joint sites in the obvious attempt to accomplish two objectives with one trip. Once a clothing store has located, however, the highest private use for the adjacent site may not be a jeweler (or any other that brings a positive benefit to the clothier). To ensure that the desired adjacency occurs, each establishment must be willing to compensate its neighbor by an amount possibly as great as its consequential gain (Eaton and Lipsey).

This list of examples could go on, but it has by design omitted the most often mentioned negative externalities: nuisances. Zoning, in principle, originally was designed to regulate nuisances. Noise, pollution, and public health or safety are the most frequent justifications for separating uses and requiring minimum lot sizes, setbacks, or building standards. The three examples presented serve to illustrate that in the land market, unregulated external effects may be much more diverse and prevalent than those addressed by current zoning institutions.

From examples such as these, it is possible to construct a descriptive typology of spatial externalities, based on three characteristics: source, scale, and sign.

1. *Source* involves the question of whether the externality exists by the mere proximity or location of two uses (e.g., the jeweler–clothier linkage), or by the nature of each agent's behavior on the site (e.g., design aesthetics). The regulation of the former involves control over the location of uses, while the latter requires more detailed regulations over how uses "operate" at given sites. A noxious use, for example, may be regulated either by isolation from the affected parties, or by intense environmental control at a more "sensitive" site (Henderson).

2. *Scale* involves the issue of how far the influence or impact of an externality is felt. The examples given illustrate that external effects can range from adjacent, to neighborhood, to town, and even to metropolitan in scale.

3. The *sign* of an externality refers to whether the impact between affected parties is positive or negative. It should be noted that two adjacent uses might each impose an externality on the other of opposite sign.

External effects need not be reciprocal. Whatever the nature of the externality, the economic prescriptions proposed tend to fall into two general categories. The first, the Pigouvian approach, calls for public intervention with either financial incentives and penalities, or for direct regulation of private activity. The second, the Chicago approach, calls for the correct definition and assignment of rights, so that either private or legal bargaining can occur.

The Pigouvian economic remedy for externalities is based on the assumption that some neutral third party (i.e., the public) knows of the externality, its characteristics, and the magnitude of its effect. In this case, the externality can be "priced," by charging a tax (subsidy) for each unit of the disservice (service) that is produced (Baumol). If this incentive reflects the incremental cost or benefit to all affected parties, then the producer will make the "correct" (i.e., Pareto) choice of behavior. It is important to note that under this scheme the subsidy (tax) need only be paid (charged) to the creator of the externality—it does not have to originate from the affected parties.

The critiques of this approach center on its assumption of a fully knowledgeable and neutral governmental public. When there exists no (market) data about an externality, the value to be placed upon its costly or beneficial impacts is difficult to ascertain. Furthermore, the diversity and complexity of land market externalities would necessitate an enormous number of such corrective financial incentives. These same problems would exist if the public attempts to correct externalities through regulation. The information requirements and complexity of determining the appropriate regulations are no less than those necessary for the correct taxes or subsidies (Baumol).

As for the neutrality of the public, it is well known that local governments are primarily agents for the interests of the majority of their residents (Fischel). Thus, in many externality situations, the public is often only a voice for one of the affected parties. As such it will not necessarily seek regulations that meet the Pareto criteria.

A somewhat different approach has emerged out of the "Chicago school" of economic thought. The argument here is that the individual parties affected by an externality will bargain over the impact voluntarily *if* the rights involved have been clearly assigned (Siegan). Consider the first case of aesthetic design, above. According to the Chicago view,

if the neighbors and passersby have a clear right to a certain design quality, then the builder must compensate them or pay damages if he installs an aesthetic quality below that level. Alternatively, if the builder has a right to whatever aesthetic quality he wants, then the neighbors must pay him in exchange for his agreement to improve the site. A crucial assertion in the argument is that *either* assignment of rights will accomplish the same end. In *both* cases the higher aesthetic standard will be installed if its value to neighbors and passersby exceeds its cost to the builder.

It should be noted that the assumption of symmetry concerning the assignment of rights also characterizes the Pigouvian approach to externality control. Thus non-Chicago school economists have also asserted that taxing "bad" design and subsidizing "good" aesthetics are behavioral equivalents. The important difference between the two approaches is that the Chicago solution will require that the funds flowing to (from) the externality creator actually come from (to) the affected parties. There is no public to act as a fiscal repository.

The criticism most often made against the Chicago approach involves the assumption that private bargaining can occur in a costless environment. Many economists believe that markets need some form of institutionalization. They argue that if an externality affects many parties, it is not costless to organize them in a way that permits the necessarily complex process of bargaining over compensation. Alternatively, if the number of parties involved is small, then each may engage in strategic behavior, and this does not always lead to the correct level of compensation.

The second criticism of the Chicago approach is that it has tended to ignore the valuation problems that are inherent in the definition of rights. If bargaining is costly, then rights need only be defined generally, so as to establish who has to compensate whom. Bargaining will determine the amount of such payments and the resultant level of externalities. In the more realistic case of costly bargaining, the affected parties will seek redress in the legal system and more specific rights will have to be determined. How much design aesthetics is the public entitled to? What is the maximum level of congestion that drivers should, by right, endure? It is not clear that the legal system is better or more neutral in determining such quantities than a Pigouvian government.

In some respects, then, the difference between the two approaches is not so great. Both require a third party, with extensive information to establish a set of social norms: in the one case financial incentives, in the other detailed legal entitlements. The differences center mostly on implementation, and on how the taxes, subsidies, damages, or bribes are financed. The Chicago school requires that the affected parties pay or be paid by the producer of the externality. With the Pigouvian approach, the payment to or from the producer involves the general fiscal budget.

It is interesting that in addition to these two approaches there is a third solution, at least to certain externalities that operate in the land market. This is to own collectively those parcels of land between which external effects are significant. A single owner of many parcels will not seek the highest use for each one, but rather the combination of uses that yields the highest collective income. There is a conjecture (not yet a proof) that this meets the Pareto criteria, at least with respect to those externalities between the collectively owned parcels.

The operation of the land market provides a number of illustrations of this third, internalization, approach. For example, large–scale residential developments frequently impose design standards at the initial stage of development. Presumably the developer-owner of the project believes that such control will enhance the overall value of the development. Equally common in such projects is the ongoing use of restrictive covenants to maintain these initial standards (Siegan).

A second example is the emergence over the past few decades of large regional shopping centers. Such developments often contain hundreds of separate retail establishments and attempt to create a shopping environment in which total sales are maximized (Weissbrod). The owners of such centers carefully discriminate between tenants in the rent charged for space, and furthermore exercise considerable control over admittance to the center. Again, there is a conjecture that such a form of property ownership and management tends to create retail clusters within which positive externalities are large, and between which negative effects are contained. These centers, then, seem to move the market more toward meeting the Pareto criteria.

The discussion developed in this section might be best summarized in five points:

1. Externalities in the land market are widespread and very diverse in their source, scale, and sign. Very local externalities may be capable of being privately controlled through joint ownership, and primarily at the time new land is developed. The remaining external effects, however, will require some form of public intervention.

2. If the social costs and benefits associated with an externality are known, then the public can, in theory, correct the externality with incentives to the creator, financed from the public treasury and not necessarily from the parties affected by the externality.

3. In many cases, however, a neutral public or government is not present. The normal operation of the political process usually leads the public to be an agent for either those creat-

ing or affected by the externality. This is especially the case with local government and zoning decisions.

4. If the public is not neutral, then it, like any private party, will not act appropriately without the correct incentives. A public decision to regulate an externality should involve compensation to those regulated for the private cost such regulation imposes. Without such compensation, the benefits of regulation cannot be correctly judged, and the public will not act in a manner that is necessarily consistent with the Pareto criteria.

5. The Chicago approach tries to ensure that all costs and benefits will be considered by requiring that the parties in an externality situation actually exchange compensation. This requires a clear assignment of rights and costless bargaining. In the absence of the latter, a neutral third party is still required to more specifically establish the rights of each party.

Against this theoretical discussion, then, where do current zoning institutions fit? What kinds of externalities do they address, and how do they operate? Does the process of zoning decision making lead to the correct control of external effects? These questions are discussed next.

ZONING IN THEORY AND PRACTICE

Zoning, as it exists today, has evolved as an institutionalized regulatory system that has four distinct features:

1. Zoning is a constitutionally approved power of state government, which in almost all cases is delegated to local governments. At present there are only a few state governments that exercise any of these powers themselves.

2. Zoning authorities generally are allowed to define and locate districts and then to limit the land uses allowed therein. In theory, the regulation of use can be quite pervasive, *if* widespread public interest is demonstrated. In

practice, zoning authorities have been allowed control mainly over general lot characteristics and use and not over buildings or behavior within buildings.

3. Zoning of this type is considered to be a police power of the state. A private landowner thus can be required to obey a public standard without compensation for any loss in value.

4. The decision making of zoning authorities is political by design. All local zoning standards must be approved either by a direct popular vote or by a majority of a local government's elected representatives.

Thus zoning is a local political process in which regulations that are for the social good can be instituted without compensating property owners for the private costs that accompany such restrictions. In this context, there is little reason to expect that enacted regulations will meet Pareto criteria, which require that the public benefit of such restrictions exceed the private costs when the impacts on all parties are considered. In fact, quite the opposite is likely to be true. As currently institutionalized, zoning decisions tend to focus on two issues: how to redistribute "wealth" from other jurisdictions, and how to regulate land within jurisdictions by as much as the majority wishes *at zero cost.*

To illustrate these arguments, three of the most typical zoning decisions are considered below. In each case, the motives of the involved parties will be scrutinized to determine how, under current laws, these can differ significantly from the objectives of the Pareto criteria.

Perhaps the most common zoning decision made daily in this country is the minimum lot size required for remaining vacant land in a suburban town that is already partially developed. The conflict is essentially between existing home owners and land owners. In most cases, the home owners are far more numerous and so the local government normally is their agent. Home owners do receive some legitimate social benefit from keeping land in an open state, or having it developed at lower density (Stull). The landowners, on the other hand, generally seek development at that level that maximizes their value—without regard to any broader consequences.

In this situation, the Pareto criteria require that we evaluate the social benefits of "openness" to the existing home owners, against the loss in private value to the landowners. It is also clear that if the town must purchase the right to openness, with compensation to landowners, it will have to make this exact calculation. On the other hand, without any compensation, this test is never made. The existing home owners face a zero price for their decision, and it is in their private interest to zone land as open as possible.

It is interesting that the courts seem partially to have recognized this problem and have set limits to local zoning standards. The most common criterion relates to the existing density of the town. If a community with an average lot size of half an acre tries to zone vacant land for five-acre lots, most courts would rule that the standard was unreasonable or confiscatory, and quite possibly that a taking had occurred. While the difference between existing density and allowed zoning may well reflect the private loss of value to the landowner, the true social benefits to the town may never be revealed or discussed unless the town has to pay for its rights.

Another common decision made by local zoning boards involves the question of whether to allow land for industrial and commercial uses, or whether generally to exclude such development. The town's collective preferences will likely hinge on whether the tax revenue from such development exceeds its broadly defined environmental cost (e.g., congestion,

changing town character). If it does, then the local government as agent of the people will generally permit the development (Fischel). On the other hand, the businesses that might occupy such land are themselves examining different sites. For a particular town's site to be selected, its relative locational advantage (e.g., workers, highway access) must exceed its comparative tax burden.

Comparing the two decisions' criteria, it is clear that if a town decides to allow industrial uses, and industries in turn choose to locate there, then the locational advantage to the firms must exceed their environmental costs. *This is the Pareto test.* However, even if this test is met in principle, a town might exclude such development if the statutory system of taxation yields industrial tax receipts that are less than local environmental costs. Similarly, if the statutory tax is overly lucrative to the town, excessive land may be zoned for industrial development, but no firms will locate there even though the Pareto or compensation test is met.

In this second example, the failure to achieve the Pareto criteria results not from the absence of compensation payments *by* the town, but rather from the inability of firms to pay the correct compensation *to* the town. If taxes were not institutionally delineated, but rather bargained on a case-by-case basis, then in principle the Pareto criteria could be achieved in each instance. Case-specific taxes would serve as prices or compensation for environmental "costs," and the externalities would be controlled correctly.

This example would be considerably more complicated if the environmental costs imposed by the newly locating firm extended outside of the host town. This is most prevalent in the case of large-scale commercial developments that can effect metropolitanwide traffic flows. Even bargaining, or flexible taxation, would insure only that the externalities of the host town were balanced against its locational advantages. To internalize the broader external effects, for all towns, some higher level authority would have to be created with more extended powers of taxation and regulation.

Another example of a zoning decision that has ramifications outside the town that is setting the standards is the process of exclusionary zoning. Many towns bar multifamily housing in a clear attempt to exclude lower income families from settling there. As in the above cases, there is some perceived social cost to the town from allowing such uses, and there are private benefits to the lower income families from being included (Wheaton). There may also be significant third party effects, however, in that keeping low-income families clustered at inner city locations could significantly exacerbate the collective social problems experienced by that group. The Pareto test, then, involves three quantities: the social cost to the town, the private benefits to the potential low-income settlers, and the social benefits to other low-income residents (and perhaps other towns) from "declustering."

Exclusionary zoning actually requires that *several* compensations be paid, if the Pareto criteria are to be met. It has been argued that the private benefits to potential low-income settlers will be reflected in additional land value once zoned for multifamily development (Yinger). When the town excludes such development—and pays no compensation to landowners—it is ignoring these private benefits. However, it is also ignoring the social benefits to the broader area. In other words, if the town wants the "benefit of exclusivity," it must pay compensation both to the local landowners and to some agent who represents the broader public. Alternatively, some agent for the public, as well as those landowners

seeking multifamily housing, must pay compensation to the town for bearing the "cost of heterogeneity."

These examples illustrate three fundamental problems in how zoning currently regulates land market externalities. First, local governments, which generally are the agents for the affected party in an externality, will not make Pareto decisions about the control of externalities unless compensations are actually paid. Second, the assignment of rights is crucial for the determination of the direction of compensation. If towns have the right to open land and exclusivity, then landowners, and agents representing non-local groups, must compensate the town in order to buy these rights. If complete private property "rights" are declared, then the town must compensate landowners, or other affected parties, if it takes these rights. Third, there is a clear need for some higher authority to represent affected non-local parties in many, if not most, zoning issues.

SOME ALTERNATIVES TO PRESENT ZONING

It seems clear from this discussion that many of the problems with current zoning are structural in nature. They will need institutional reform if they are to be properly addressed. Based on the economic character of these problems, several significant changes in land use regulation suggest themselves.

To begin, it would seem necessary to establish some form of higher zoning authority than the city or town. Since most land market externalities are contained within metropolitan areas, this is the logical level at which to create such an institution. It is also true, particularly at this level, that a formal institutional structure is probably necessary since voluntary action among large numbers of parties simply is impractical. Finally, it would seem important not to encumber such an institution with responsibilities beyond its abilities. Thus a potential metropolitan planning board should be charged only with regulating those externalities that occur between towns.

One way of accomplishing those objectives would be to give such a metropolitan planning board the power to assign quotas of development to each town within its jurisdiction. Towns, in turn, would be responsible for how the quotas were achieved. Quotas would be assigned for a wide range of land uses, such as low- and middle-income housing, office, retail, or industrial space, and so forth. The quotas would evolve from an ongoing regional planning process, utilizing current research to determine the metropolitanwide impacts of broadly different land use patterns. Alternative development locations would be evaluated according to how well they fulfilled various objectives such as minimizing congestion, enhancing public open space, and reducing housing prices. Current economic planning techniques probably are capable of providing this kind of information.

It is important to recognize that any such metropolitan planning board would be an intensely political institution by its very nature. While the exact organizational form of such a board is beyond the scope of this chapter, clearly the interests of towns or groups would have to be formally represented. Unfortunately, the behavior of political organizations is well known to produce resource allocations that do *not* always meet the Pareto criteria (Muller). In a metropolitan area of 50 towns, for example, 26 consistently might vote to place all of the undesirable uses in the other 24, while giving themselves all of the beneficial quotas.

In order to enforce the Pareto criteria upon the decisions of such a board, it might be desirable to have the towns engage in direct bargaining with compensation. Each town could be compensated for accepting a quota unit of some undesirable use and would have to pay for receiving beneficial quota units. With such a scheme, it is possible to imagine a hazardous facility being located where its regional harm was minimized, or a park being placed in the town where its overall beneficial effects were greatest. With actual payments occurring, towns would in principle bargain truthfully, and each individual town could override the greater collective good only if its private preferences were strong enough to pay the price.

Under such an arrangement, an entire second tier of planning would have to occur at the town level. Here, decisions would be made about how land would be configured and where different uses would go. The towns could thus district, much in the manner that they do today, in order to define residential areas, industrial zones, parks, and so forth, and locate them in ways that made sense. The overall effect of these local decisions, however, could not violate the town's assigned quotas.

The procedures by which such local planning is conducted might also be altered, so that compensation becomes part of a town's decision making process as well. If local districting and siting decisions are to be efficient, then compensation must be paid between property owners and the town. With such compensation there would be little reason to limit the powers of local zoning again subject to the assigned quotas. Local governments could be given expanded powers to designate architectural design districts, or establish landscaping regulations, as long as compensation were paid, so that unanimous consent is obtained.

As an example of how this two-tier planning system could work, consider the problem of locating a hazardous facility. At the metropolitan level, each town might determine a holdout value they were willing to pay for *not* having the facility, and a set of offer values *for* having it in each other's town. That town for which the holdout payment was smallest and the offers greatest would be the recipient of both the facility and a payment equal to the holdout it had previously declared. The funds for the payment would come from the other towns' offers.

Within the recipient town, the facility would have to be sited again knowing that the affected parties would have to be compensated. In fact, if the system were working correctly, the value declared by the town, at the metropolitan level, would incorporate the costs of the likely local abutters. Thus at least part of the recipient town's compensation from other towns would flow directly down to the project's neighbors.

For a second example, take the case of a prospective major shopping center. A developer has a site in a particular town and is prepared to finance local infrastructure improvements. This, together with the project's tax payment, has convinced the host town that the endeavor is a net gain. A second stage review is necessary, however, in which a metropolitan planning process calculates the regional congestion impact of the project. At this stage, the proposed host town will have to compensate the drivers in other towns with an impact fee. The aforementioned bargaining determines the magnitude of this fee, which the town in turn charges the developer. The developer then considers other sites, and as the process is repeated, the project ultimately is sited where the developer's profit and local benefits are maximized *net* of the impact fee.

These examples are merely illustrations of how zoning issues ought to be evaluated, and decisions made, if the economic Pareto principle is to serve as a social objective. Such decisions need to be made in a broad, metropolitan context, while at the same time being tailored to local needs and situations. In whatever arena the decisions are made, they should never escape the Pareto criteria: Does the social good outweigh the private cost, or does the private good outweigh the social cost? In the modern political environment, requiring compensation is one way to ensure that all costs and benefits are considered and thoroughly evaluated. Just as private property is always subject to the police power of the state, the latter, in turn, must also be subject to some scrutiny. If the power to regulate land is used only parochially, and without cost, it will not be used appropriately.

REFERENCES

Baumol, William. "On Taxation and the Control of Externalities." *American Economic Review* vol. 62 (1972).

Eaton, John and Edward Lipsey. "Comparison Shopping and Firm Clustering." *Journal Regional Science,* November 1979.

Eberts, Roger. "An Empirical Investigation of Intra-Urban Wage Gradients." *Journal of Urban Economics,* July 1981.

Fischel, William. "Fiscal and Environmental Considerations in the Location of Firms." In *Fiscal Zoning and Land Use Controls,* edited by Mills and Oates. Heath Lexington Press, 1975.

Gordon, Peter and William McRenolds. "Optimal Urban Forms." *Journal of Regional Science* 14 (1974): 2.

Henderson, J. Vernon. "Externalities in a Spatial Context, the Case of Air Pollution." *Journal of Public Economics,* February 1977.

Hough, Gordon and Peter Kratz. "Can 'good' Architecture Meet the Market Test." *Journal of Urban Economics,* July 1983.

Muller, Dennis. "Public Choice: A Survey." *Journal of Economic Literature,* June 1976.

Schmenner, Roger. "The Rent Gradient for Manufacturing." *Journal of Urban Economics,* January 1981.

Siegan, Bernard. *Land Use without Zoning,* Heath Lexington Press, 1972.

Solow, Robert. "Congestion Cost, and the Use of Land for Streets." *Bell Journal,* Autumn 1973.

Stahl, Konrad. "Location and Spatial Pricing with Non-Convex Transportation Schedules." *Bell Journal,* Spring 1984.

Stull, William. "Community Environmental Zoning and the Market Value of Homes." *Journal of Law and Economics* vol. 18 (1975).

Tauden, Helen and A. Whitte. "The Socially Optimal and Equilibrium Distribution of Office Activity." *Journal of Urban Economics,* January 1984.

Weissbrod, Glen, Steven Parcells and Culord Kern. "A Disaggregate Model for Predicting Shopping Area Market Attraction." *Journal of Retailing* 60 (1984): 1.

Wheaton, William. "Consumer Mobility and Community Tax Bases: The Problem of Financing Local Public Goods." *Journal of Public Economics,* September 1975.

White, Michelle. "Firm Suburbanization and Urban Subcenters." *Journal of Urban Economics* 3 (October 1976): 4.

Yinger, John. "Capitalization and the Theory of Local Public Finance." *Journal of Political Economy* 55 (1977): 3.

V

Anticipating the Future

The crystal ball is always an uncertain ally. At best, its message is interpreted differently by professional soothsayers; at worst, its image is so cloudy or opaque as to deny meaningful prognostication. Predicting the future of zoning suggests, indeed demands, an understanding of present and future demographic trends, and their resulting spatial implications. If history is any guide, then zoning will both mirror, and at times define, society's proclivities for organizing itself physically, socially, and economically.

The first 60 years offer grounds for optimism and cause for pessimism. Protection of the "haves" in their single-family suburban communities against the "have nots" locked in central cities is surely zoning's most damning legacy. The damage to an open and free society can be only partially redressed by more recent efforts remaking zoning to encourage, rather than discourage, housing for low- and moderate-income families. Artificial separation of uses, the heart of traditional Euclidean ordinances, has resulted in a self-evident sterility, although recent mixed-use strategies have begun to reinvigorate neighborhoods in large and small cities alike. By way of providing public amenities and improving the quality of urban design, newer techniques such as incentive zoning and transfer of development rights promise much, but frequently deliver less than advertised. The problems of growth experienced in many areas of the country cannot be solved by zoning alone. Intelligent public capital spending must be coordinated with comprehensive planning to secure the quality of life citizens have come to expect, if not demand. Local control, the hallmark of zoning, will come under increased pressure to cede authority to regional and state agencies, but abdication will not come easily, if it comes at all.

Ultimately, the central lesson for the future from the past is that zoning is no better or worse than its practitioners. Like all public policies, it is susceptible to gross misuse by those whose purposes deviate from the public interest. But equally true, it offers to planners, lawyers, city officials, and citizen activists the most powerful regulatory tool for shaping the environment in which they live and work. Charles Haar's "Reflections on *Euclid:* Social Contract and Private Purpose" journeys from past to future in discussing zoning's role in American society. His empirical findings and policy recommendations chart promises and pitfalls while outlining a future agenda for this land-use control device.

331

13

Reflections on *Euclid:* Social Contract and Private Purpose

Charles M. Haar

In 1926, without ramparts being mounted or trumpets blaring, a revolution in land use jurisprudence took place in the United States. *Village of Euclid* v. *Ambler Realty Co.*[1] is a landmark case whose effects 60 years after its launching continue to reverberate across the legal landscape. The case brought into focus fundamental questions about the content of private property in the United States, and about the extent of social control over decisions affecting its use—questions whose urgency has only increased with time. In its decision, the Supreme Court defined for its era the role of local and state governments in handling the economic and physical development of communities. Most importantly, the opinion represents a turning point in the continuous pursuit of that elusive balance between freedom and constraint for a society essentially committed to unfettered land transactions yet not fully content with the results this produces in urban environments defined by heavy concentrations of people and ever-tightening markets.

It is the background of the *Euclid* litigation— the legal strategies, the political alliances, the attitudes of contemporaries—that, as much as the words of Justice Sutherland's opinion, re-veals the age-old tensions and conflicts over the uses of land; their provisional resolutions in 1926 still have much to say about the Chicagos, Orange Counties, and Second New Yorks of today. Earlier efforts of the state courts to stretch old theories to fit new economic and social patterns of metropolitan growth led in the 1920s to a redefinition and expansion of the police power in the United States. Today, as we struggle to understand the deeper implications of new versions, of urban form that we recognize as fundamentally different from earlier permutations, a similar reexamination from a contemporary perspective is imperative. Anniversary dates afford us an opportunity to mine the original meaning once more— and to ponder the implications for today and tomorrow.

In looking back upon the series of events culminating in *Euclid,* what is most impressive are the arduous struggles of the courts to adapt the common law to new conditions. They present a clear picture of the shaping of legal institutions to fit emerging social and economic worlds. Intellectual struggles over the appropriate designation of activities as properly private or public—according to common law

333

tradition—appear throughout the briefs and opinions in these cases. But what commands greater attention is the legal profession's perennial effort to create new theories with which to tame new dynamics, drawing upon while transforming the ancient materials of the common law.[2] In harking back to such roots and searching for the basic reasons underlying the birth and survival of formal doctrines, lawyers and judges, through reinterpretation and altered perspectives, adapt and alter and redeploy them for new ends.

To extend the police power to the type of land use control known as zoning meant the regulation of the activities and the aspirations of private property owners without monetary compensation. Permitting this extension must surely be acknowledged as one of the major judicial innovations of our century as well as the most important redefinition of the nature of private property ever made in United States courts. For what the *Euclid* case and its progeny represent is an extraordinary expansion of government power into what previously had been considered a relatively autonomous area of private decision making. What adds to the fascination of this legal revolution is that it occurred in an era not noted for courageous judicial forays into visionary undertakings. Indeed, the climate in 1926 can be fairly characterized as one of general conservatism; the Supreme Court in particular had shown itself hostile to a wider range of social innovation.[3] In comprehending this paradox, perhaps, lies the key to understanding the past and future of *Euclid.* The most perplexing pertinent question for the intellectual historian is why zoning passed successfully through this jurisprudential mine field and became accepted so readily into the zeitgeist of American urban development. And were a *Euclid* case presented for decision today for the first time,

would and should it pass muster in the society of the 1980s?

THE *EUCLID* LITIGATION

At the center of the *Euclid* litigation rests a fascinating question of legal strategy—a recurring question faced by virtually all those who find themselves on the cutting edge of legal reform in the adversarial common law system. Should a new doctrine be acknowledged frankly as a novel approach designed to cope with changing circumstances, or should it be dressed in the reassuring garb of incrementalism, presented as the inevitable product of the evolution of ancient legal principles? How the parties and their lawyers and experts confronted this question, consciously and otherwise, needs close monitoring. The case was not brought to the Supreme Court on the theory of proving that the harshness of the ordinance in its particular application to the property owned by the Ambler Realty Company rendered it outside constitutional protections. True, the plaintiff may have shown that the property was ripe for industrial development, and thus was decreased by $7,500 an acre in value through the residential development restriction. Instead, the litigation became a frontal attack on the ordinance itself: Regardless of the fairness of application, the plaintiff argued, the very concept of the zoning of private land was unconstitutional. Whatever the demerits of this particular ordinance as applied to the particular tract of land on the outskirts of Cleveland, the lawyers for the property owner chose to attack the fundamental concept of zoning as an abstract idea whose inherent unfairness, unreasonableness, and intrinsic inappropriateness should condemn it constitutionally. This type of attack raises the level of discourse to a philosophical and abstract plane which, in the compressed time of litigation, leaves little room for exploring the details, the contours, and the implications of a ruling.

For this reason, the Court's response in *Euclid* was the obverse of the broad question posed to it: In upholding the general validity of the zoning ordinance, it did not bar attacks on the specific application of the rule—a strategy which, if pursued by the plaintiff, at least in hindsight would have been an easier request for a court to grant. The Court was free to respond minimally to plaintiff's broad-ranging arguments. If it could touch only the outer circumference of inquiry, by deciding whether the districting of land uses was a program that could be espoused by a legislature, that would still be deemed a "reasonable" one, then it would have to draw the conclusion that zoning was indeed a tenable policy when adopted by elected officials.[4]

How often we have seen a constellation of tactics and principle, such as those marshalled by Newton D. Baker and his associates in opposition to zoning in *Euclid,* reappear at the turning points of land use history. In general, the more recent annals of the Supreme Court's land use jurisprudence, the conduct of the Covington lawyers in *Penn Central Trans. Co.* v. *New York City* [5] furnishes a prime example. Confronting New York's historic landmark zoning law, the Penn Central attorneys chose to attack the validity *per se* of landmark designations, rather than make the narrow charge of unfairness in the particular case. In such cases, client and lawyer together become so convinced of the merits of their case and the righteousness of their posture, that instead of arguing the wearisome details, they aspire, like Samson, to bring down the entire temple. Unsurprisingly, the post-*Lochner* era Court has barred these general onslaughts on land use restriction schemes.[6]

The *Euclid* Court easily could have avoided the constitutional question. The case arose before the federal Declaratory Judgment Act had been adopted by Congress. Moreover, the Ambler Realty Company had failed to apply for a permit or to seek a variance or an exception to the ordinance, thereby failing to exhaust its administrative remedies. Thus, the complaint did not represent a ripened or matured cause of action. Nevertheless, apparently also eager to decide the issue once and for all, the Court accepted jurisdiction, noting simply that "The relief sought here is . . . on an injunction against the enforcement of any of the restrictions, limitations or conditions of the ordinance."[7] The Court construed the complaint as attacking the "mere existence" of the ordinance.[8]

The attack mounted by the lawyers representing the property interests in *Euclid* centered on the notion that districting—that is, dividing the land of a municipal corporation into separate districts and restricting different uses, bulks, densities, and heights to such districts within the same corporate unit—should be deemed an invalid exercise of the police power. The plaintiff's lawyer argued that districting (and differential regulation within such districts) violated equal protection by arbitrarily subjecting different property holders to different regulations, and further that zoning was a taking in violation of the protection of property conferred by the due process clause of the Constitution. The Euclid ordinance, argued that Ambler Realty Company, did not pursue any rational plan. "[A] municipality may not, under the guise of the police power, arbitrarily divert property from its appropriate and most economical uses or diminish its value by imposing restrictions which have no other basis than the momentary taste of the public authorities."[9] "The ordinance of the village," it asserted, "is not addressed in general to the proper objects of the police power."[10]

Baker, for the property owner, saw the case as an attempt to eliminate a series of local ordinances across the country that were overly intrusive regulations of private property, in the interest of "entirely fanciful or fantastic social or aesthetic grounds . . . ."[11] "[T]he danger of frittering away the constitutional guaranties by successive encroachment," he warned, "has always been apparent to the courts."[12]

The lawyers on the other side were equally determined to make this *the* test case. Metzenbaum, for example, could not be dissuaded despite substantial criticisms that the drafting of the Euclid ordinance was flawed, that its subsequent map amendments had not been adopted by proper procedures, and that its impacts fell too harshly on the Ambler property.[13] Privately, Bettman himself expressed the view that the Euclid ordinance was "arbitrary" and furnished a poor occasion to establish the constitutionality of zoning.[14] Bettman later would write that the *Euclid* plaintiffs "represented a larger group seeking to destroy the zoning movement."[15] And since the contest was now at last elevated to a federal level, it would (for both sides) bring to a resting point what seemed a ceaseless progression of litigation in the state courts: In a bewildering array of rulings, impossible to reconcile by any Aristotelean logic, state supreme courts had divided on the constitutionality of zoning.[16]

The consequence of the *in terrorem* stance of the complaint, and of the broadsides fired both in support of and against the objectives of zoning, was that the Supreme Court gave its reply on the highest level of generalization.[17] The arguments for zoning, the Court observed, are at least sufficiently cogent to preclude a reviewing court from concluding "that such provisions are clearly arbitrary and unreasonable."[18] In its analysis, the Court emphasized that the constitutional conception of police power (and the proper scope of the due process clause) expands and contracts with the changing conditions of a society. Justice Sutherland went on to argue what can be called "the reasonable margin" theory of constitutionalism—leeway should be given the enactors of a regulatory ordinance so that the substance of a law, if otherwise valid, would not be fatally tainted by incidental incursions into areas protected against the police power.[19] "[T]he bad fades into the good by insensible degrees"; society, acting through its executive and legislative branches, must be given the benefit of the doubt.[20]

Essentially, in upholding the validity of the village enactment, Justice Sutherland's opinion threads the justification through the common law of nuisance. "A nuisance may be merely the right thing in the wrong place," Justice Sutherland pointed out, "like a pig in the parlor instead of the barnyard."[21] The "fairly helpful clew" of the common law of nuisance was employed in examining zoning as a novel application of the police power of the state.[22] The Court seemed to accept fully the thrust of Bettman's argument in his brief that zoning is a form of nuisance cataloging, a legislative declaration and codification, as it were, of the common law rules about the compatibilities and incompatibilities of land uses.[23] The twist was that rather than testing on an ad hoc, sporadic basis, as is the nature of judicial declarations of the existence of nuisance, zoning represents a systematic ordering—in advance—of those land uses that could be positioned together and those that should be separated. Thus, zoning is simply a modern application of the recognized and sanctioned methods of centuries-old nuisance law—old wine in new bottles. Under this argument, since zoning is no more an interruption of private property than is the law of nuisance, a law that can be traced back as far as the twelfth century, it need not trigger payment of compensation. The limitations it imposes are but a formerly undeclared part of every piece of property and a delineation of the reasonable expectations of property owners around which constitutional protections are thrown; when buying land, one always knows that it may not be devoted to uses prejudicial to the public welfare.

This nuisance-based justification of zoning reached its most provocative application in the reasoning advanced by Justice Sutherland for the exclusion of apartment houses from residential areas. The apartment house, he wrote, is "a mere parasite constructed in order to take advantage of . . . open spaces and attractive surroundings."[24] Today—in the era of *Mount Laurel,*[25] *National Land,*[26] and *Girsh,*[27] in which courts have confronted the daunting task of disentangling (permissible) attempts of municipalities and suburbs to maintain their local community character from (impermissible) efforts to exclude undesired income, ethnic, and racial groups—the discussion by Justice Sutherland of the apartment districting of the Euclid ordinance is unsatisfactory. Nonetheless, his "parasite" formulation seems less objectionable when it is recalled that this was the birth of a legal doctrine—a time when people are struggling to put ideas forward, make them explicit, and spell them out, and when their full practical implications and consequences cannot be foreseen. By the same token, the Court could hardly be faulted for failing to anticipate the future reactions of developers and their lawyers, their astuteness in dealing with, manipulating, or avoiding the impacts of regulation upon their chosen courses of conduct.

Here again *Euclid* raises the central problem of legal reform. Should a new and dynamic theory of city planning be advanced as the justification for controls to traditional judges, or should zoning be treated as but a recent and

ordinary phase of the old common law protecting property?

At one extreme were those pressing for the new cause. Metzenbaum, the ardent advocate for the village, even went to the point of shrugging off help, disclaiming that part of Bettman's *amicus* brief stressing the nuisance aspect of the zoning control of land uses. He declined the proffered help—most patronizingly!

> We wish here to advert to the brief filed by the National Conference on City Planning, *Amici Curiae.* With no intention of criticism and with a fitting respect for this brief, the Village nevertheless feels that in defense of its own position it does not wish this brief, like its predecessor in the Trial Court below, to prejudice any of the rights of the Village, for (a) the Village earnestly finds itself unable to subscribe to several of the doctrines urged in this brief just as they were urged in the Trial Court, and (b) in addition thereto the Village—having studiously refrained from resting upon citations of so-called "nuisance" and "semi-nuisance" cases as supporting zoning ordinances—the Village cannot conscientiously subscribe to the citation of such cases in the brief of the *Amici Curiae.*[28]

It is hard to look at the case history without wondering about the reasons for this disavowal—pride of authorship aside. The village's argument for sustaining the validity of the ordinance had been lost after its first hearing before the Supreme Court, with Justice Sutherland assigned to write an opinion that would outlaw zoning. Only after the rehearing, when for the first time Bettman advanced the powerful arguments from the nuisance analogy, did zoning emerge victorious.[29] One may conjecture that, without the intervention by the National Conference on City Planning, zoning would have come tumbling down in 1926, and the whole complicated edifice of land use controls in the United States today—of which zoning forms the chief component—would have taken a totally different form. It is mind-boggling to think what the land use regime would be with a 1926 *Euclid* case holding unconstitutional the use of zoning. Invoking the ancient analogies was the canny argument that won over the conscience of the Court's awkward majority.

But while one may remark on the ingeniousness and the elaborateness of the Bettman argument, one slight murmur should be raised on behalf of the approach taken by Metzenbaum. The nuisance origins of the defense of zoning (which probably would have emerged in any event, since the two rules of law are in many aspects similar) have in fact proven a brake upon expansive notions of the planning powers. Indeed, the Court's next major challenge, that of *Nectow* v. *City of Cambridge*[30] (which invalidated a residential designation near a highway planned for expansion), can be understood as a regulation condemned because it went beyond arbitrating the traditional incompatibilities characteristic of nuisance law. Had it been made clear in *Euclid* to Justice Sutherland (who also authored the *Nectow* decision) that zoning can be an affirmative tool of land use planning, incorporating elements that look not just to present but also to future incompatibilities—*unlike* traditional common law nuisance doctrines, raised in higgledy-piggledy fashion by the occasional litigant, of abatements and eliminating past evils—the outcome in *Nectow* might well have been different; the Cambridge zoning designation might have been upheld, as it had been by the Supreme Judicial Court of Massachusetts.

Metzenbaum's brief to the Supreme Court in *Euclid* pressed the view of zoning as enhanc-

ing "balanced" territories;[31] he asked the Court to view the ordinance as an entirety, taking the zone plan as one consistent whole, with parts carefully adjusted to each other.[32] Throughout its subsequent history, however, zoning has been plagued by a nuisance-inspired focus on the single parcel, rather than on the contextual relationships among different parcels and land uses of the entire metropolitan area and on the need for a comprehensive planning approach. The roots of this frustration go back to Justice Sutherland. While his long, original benediction of zoning presents rationales that presage the concerns of comprehensive and forward-thinking planning—the promotion of efficient community service patterns, of reciprocity of benefit and burden, and of equal treatment of other owners similarly situated—the thrust of the Court's opinion rests on the similarity of zoning to traditional efforts to eliminate nuisance.

THE URBAN SETTING FOR ZONING LAWS: THEN AND NOW

There were many remarkable and colorful participants in the *Euclid* litigation. The key dramatis personae were Alfred Bettman, the epitome of the lawyer *qua* public servant; Newton D. Baker, the Washington luminary returning to Cleveland, scene of earlier triumphs as litigator and mayor; and James Metzenbaum, the embattled village lawyer suddenly turned national advocate. In addition to these front and center actors were forces behind the scene, the unruly cast of real estate developers, city planners, public administrators, and reformers. How was this mass of characters able to unite to produce legislation that went against all expectations? In grounding his case on the traditional doctrine of nuisance, Justice Sutherland found a least common denominator on which to establish the constitutional validity of zoning once and for all, but the principle was far removed from the economic and social realities upon which the zoning movement itself was based.

These realities underpinned the formulation and rapid adoption of zoning in this country. For it is truly astonishing how quickly the zoning juggernaut swept across the nation. A wide variety of interest groups, otherwise radically divided by motivation and ideology, joined in support of zoning. It became the grand idea whose time had come. It fell to Herbert Hoover, then secretary of commerce, to chair the committee that put together the zoning and planning state enabling acts, guiding the uses of private property in urban centers that remain even today the predominant framework for our land use controls. The Standard Zoning Enabling Act, published by the United States Department of Commerce, sold 55,000 copies in the years 1924 to 1926, setting a record for technical publications of that type. Zoning enabling legislation was passed in state after state, zoning ordinances by community after community. Why?

This remarkable socio-legislative phenomenon was the result of a confluence of forces. A curious alliance, each of whose components contained great diversity of outlook, produced this transformation in the conception of private property.

The most forthright defense came from reformers, who urged greater public control over private development. A theory of districting to regulate the height, use, and bulk of buildings, as well as the intensity of congestion, was adapted from German analogies to meet American conditions by a group of civic leaders and idealists; it was grafted onto the American legal system of private property by their lawyers, who were also deeply interested in improving the American standard of living and who saw in land use controls a means of struggling with urban blight and improving the shameful conditions of city life.

Many joined together in this camp advocating social change in the governance of urban land. Prominent were the advocates of the City Beautiful; as the aesthetic and architectural branches of the Progressive movement, they believed in the purposeful intervention of government to achieve urban beautification by way of grand boulevards, spacious parks, elaborate street furniture, civic centers, and monuments. Directing attention to the visual disorder of American cities, they called for collaboration and a collectivist spirit rather than uncontrolled individualism in urban development. Overall, design coordination requires centralized land ownership—or, if the institution of private property must be maintained, then, a centralized scheme of land use controls. Chicago's Columbian Exposition, the symbol of the movement, was characterized by Henry Adams as "the first expression of American thought as a unity." Out of the materials of urban building would come an expression of a nostalgic longing to reestablish community by reordering the centers of urban population.

Second, there was a ragtag grouping of idealists and special interest groups of the most diverse origins, social reformers and social workers, pleading the cause of zoning. They paraded forth a host of rationales to justify the exercise of the police power. They attributed to the evils of city life congestion of population. A more vigorous generation would arise under the plenitudes of fresh air and sunlight accompanying zoning ordinances. The housing and living conditions of the urban poor would be improved and humanized. In their view, appalling living conditions were the central justification for comprehensive zoning: Zoning would prevent street car, vehicular, and sidewalk congestion; reduce juvenile delinquency through the use of districting and regulation; diminish accidents through the insulation of industrial and commercial areas; improve mental health through keeping industry and trade from residential sections; eliminate the ills associated with the distances that workers must travel because of improvidently located factories. The expansion of slums, and the desperate needs of immigrants, were pinpointed by still another constituency as a consequence of a lack of zoning. Justice Sutherland echoed the views of many of these groups that zoning would create "a more favorable environment in which to raise children,"[33] even as he excluded the children of apartment dwellers.

A third group—composed of administrators and engineers and lawyers—was also attracted by the prospect of efficiency of municipal investments and economical operations of public services. This aspiration paralleled, in the public governance sphere, the spread of Frederick Taylor's scientific management in the realm of factory work. Costs of street extensions and widenings and the expenses of firehouses and firefighting equipment were singled out as targets for enhanced productivity. Transportation, utility, and antipollution expenditures became expanded budget items. With a system of geographical districts, in which the permitted uses and population densities are spelled out in detail and therefore made predictable, planning and capital budgeting of municipal infrastructure are rendered much more feasible. Coordination of plans and expenditures would eliminate the irrationalities of divided control. An important component of the Progressive movement's platform, it would argue for the planning and zoning system as an antidote to corrupt local political decision making. And decreasing social costs, together with preventing the unwise expenditure of public works funds, are under-

standable, indeed laudable, justifications for cutting into private development.

This efficiency rationale for zoning was most notably espoused from the lawyer's perspective in the 1920s by Professor Ernst Freund, the acknowledged academic expert on the line between permissible exercises of the police power and eminent domain takings. At the annual conventions of the National Conference on City Planning, he continually advanced the proposition that invoking the police power as a justification for zoning was tautological, a way of restating a desired result; he wanted to justify controls over land use on a theory of joint venture between the property owner and the community, whose contribution took the form of public services and delivery of infrastructure. Relying on contract rather than property principles, this theory conditioned the provision of municipal services on the landowner's acceptance of restrictions of land uses; hence, the overall ordinance could be regarded as a wide-ranging social contract rather than, as in the past, a series of individual municipal expenditures. Through the mechanism of providing sewers, water supplies, and streets where it would be most efficient in terms of a cost/benefit analysis, urban growth could be controlled to the advantage of both property owner and public. This coordination of public expenditures within the municipal budget and collaboration with the private sector's expenditures on land development were seen as zoning's contribution. Improved efficiency of the capital budget would be the fundamental consideration put forward to the judges for upholding zoning.

By and large, the diverse groups that subscribed to the design, idealistic, redistributive, and efficiency points of view were interested in establishing a version of public control and dominion over the basic private land resources of the community. Obviously the business groups of society should not have welcomed this objective. Yet, paradoxically, the driving political and economic force that catapulted zoning forward was the real estate industry. Commerce controlled the outcome. Coming from the other side of the ideological spectrum, its members urged the adoption of zoning. Herbert Hoover could write to the president of the National Conference on City Planning:

> The fact is constantly brought before me as Secretary of Commerce that lack of city planning and zoning constantly hampers commerce and industry in their basic function of serving mankind. This is particularly true in connection with housing and general living conditions, while waste and inefficiency in transportation, and losses through bad location of structures are a constant drag on our resources, and tend to retard increases in living standards.[34]

Not that the business group was not also composed of as many diverse and potentially conflicting splinter groups as the camp of idealists. Local owners of real estate, for example, favored congestion and concentration of uses, while commercial and industrial interests required the dispersion of population and commerce. Divisions between manufacturers on the one hand and retailers and bankers in their competition for central city space on the other corresponded with the interests of the real estate industry. Developers, mortgagees, and brokers engaged in the great building boom of the twenties conceived of the proposed land use controls as a means to stabilize property values and rationalize the urban land market, even though they often differed on applications in particular contexts;[35] English common law doctrines of covenants, equitable servitudes, and deed restrictions had proved inade-

quate to the development of active suburban land markets. Indeed, such devices aided the hold out and bogged down transactions in the technical requirements of privity and running with the land. A substitute for English private property notions was sought. Zoning represented an improvement for the real estate market not possible when private property was unrestricted in use; the theory of laissez-faire was not working to the advantage of its supposed beneficiaries who, realists above all, were ready to abandon it when faced with its practical failures. The National Association of Real Estate Boards, for example, could endorse the proposition that "[i]n principle the advisability of zoning of cities can scarcely be questioned." Furthermore, districting legislation could stem declines in land values and property taxes. The alliance between city and real estate developer was cemented by the city planner's assumption that the value of property is a function of the divisions of the market into relatively homogeneous subdistricts and classifications, a process that could not be achieved by common law nuisance mechanisms alone.

Thus, the appeals to the concepts of a public interest and a public good advanced by the idealists also would prove acceptable, garbed in different clothing, to real estate interests who would benefit from the other social ends the zoning movement could claim to serve. Enacted into law, the City Beautiful would enhance social stability. Preventing urban deterioration would stem discontent. To the extended nuisance concept and the efficiency of municipal services were added the values of stabilization of land values and rationalization of the urban land market. Master planning and zoning, especially under a system that conferred mandatory rights to property owners and reserved little public discretion, proved useful to the land development industry because it provided a framework of knowledge and predictability as to neighboring uses previously determined in a random fashion and bounded only by the indeterminate law of nuisance. To large-scale developers, moreover, any kind of allocation would be preferable to none, so long as it was consistent and definite and not totally confiscatory. Strange as this sounds to the modern observer, to many businessmen, furthermore, zoning would transfer land use determinations from politics to the sanitary world of technical experts. The real estate forces were ready to accept controls implemented by a supposedly impartial body, free of the taint of profits and deals, immune from the pressures of machine politics—one that could deduce and enforce a long-range view on the wisest use of land. For property owners, especially in the entrepreneurial class, the prospect of being able to predict the regulatory future of near-permanent building investments made them favorably disposed to this new land use control. Zoning, firmly in the hands of an enlightened planning commission, supported by a competent research and technical staff, could be the tool to remove critical uncertainties. By using scientific methods of prediction and planning, the administrators could provide a framework of future land use patterns on which the individual builder could rely.

To account for political or ideological stances by resorting to global concepts like class is clearly unsatisfactory for understanding the origins of zoning—where quite different constellations of interest converged into a powerful coalition of support for a revolutionary program.[36] This multiplicity of interests is characteristic within the context of land development, where both the structure of the competitive land market and the unique character of the developers mean participants operate more often as individuals than as members of a class. Real estate developers compete with other members of the same group, while the financiers and lenders—also differing among themselves by virtue of their different risk and profit potentials—will urge far different public policies than do the entrepreneurs. Internal divisions, as well as regional differentiations, and ignorance of long-term benefits make it unlikely that the steering and control of the built city is unidirectionally organized, or oriented toward a particular shaping of the city. Add to this the complexity of other nonlanded upper-income powers, such as manufacturers, retailers, and service industries, and it is hard to see a monolithic alliance of the powerful clustering around city planning issues.

Thus, from its very inception, zoning could mean many things to different interest groups. But conceptual murkiness can lead to practical power. The ability to attract diverse supporters from different backgrounds helped its program of market regulation clear the hurdles of political legitimacy and judicial validation. Chambers of commerce and real estate interests could see in this new technique of control the stability of property values and security of lending; public administrators could regard it as a way of producing schools, libraries, streets, water, and sewers at a lower price; home owners could see it as a way of producing a ready supply of land or of assuring neighborhood stability; mayors could see it as the preservation of tax base or the containment of blight; reformers, designers, and aesthetes could see it as the means whereby the city and the life it presented would be transformed into something loftier, richer, and more comfortable. And so this potpourri of groups, swept up in enthusiasm for their ideal images (none of which had yet been tested by reality), could join the good fight for the passage of zoning into the safe harbor of the

American constitutional system. The abstract, general nature of the constitutional attack in *Euclid* could not cope with this range of shifting, amorphous, changing justifications.

UPSETTING THE ASSUMPTIONS OF ORTHODOX ZONING: MUSTERING COALITIONS

Whether one regards law as a primary determinant, insulated and self-propelling, or as a manifestation of underlying social and economic forces, the revolutionary land use controls that evolved in the 1920s demonstrate the hazards of oversimplification in this legal dialectic. Where does the reformist, the law changer, fit in? Many of the lawyers who formulated the first zoning laws were proclaimed Progressives who sought to eliminate the corruption and deterioration of local communities by means of clean government, scientific administrators, and technical experts. Even Baker, the powerful advocate for zoning's opponents, had shared much of the Progressive philosophy as mayor of Cleveland.[37] Indeed, in examining the form of the city and the organization and substance of the primitive zoning ordinances adopted in the 1920s and formally sanctioned in *Euclid,* one can isolate the following range of beliefs and aspirations, held in common by the supporting interest groups that governed the draftsmen of that time. They assumed:

1. That city land is almost entirely developed on the basis of small single parcels;

2. That similar buildings and similar uses in cities tend to congregate to form homogeneous units readily identifiable by the technical expert;

3. That social mobility is limited, occurring at a slow, predictable pace and, therefore, that urban land values in cities shift on a slow and consistent basis;

4. That past trends can be extrapolated into the future, and that society is better off without sharp shifts and abrupt movements either of land or populations; hence, preserving stability and homogeneity is so important that both the public at large and the private property owner have a similar interest in launching a system of controls over the land market; hence the intervention of government in the private market in order to preserve stability is justified;

5. That "clean" government, staffed by experts in technical analysis and stimulated by an aroused citizenry, could rework the cities free of base and corrupt political dealings; and

6. That limited discretion conferred on experts could provide all the necessary constitutional protection of private property while permitting any needed, but circumspect, flexibility in land use regulation.

This is the intellectual background and the prevailing view of cities that dominated the ethos of the middle-class lawyers and judges at the time of *Euclid.* The whole zoning system—districting of uses, automatic permission to develop if a piece of land could be shown to fit into the three maps governing use, area, and height districts, all overlaid by a flexible discretionary system employing a board of appeals that could grant variances in cases of hardships and unique circumstances, and by a commission that could grant special exceptions—was pieced together in the 1920s and finally received its judicial imprimatur by the *Euclid* Court.

All this occurred decades ago. When it comes to predicting intelligently where current trends are leading, the utility of historical perspective and hindsight of experience may be quite limited. Nevertheless, we can examine the present pattern of metropolitan areas and the current assumptions made about land uses and ask whether they uphold and reaffirm the undertakings of the *Euclid* period or whether they call into question the premises—drawn from that period—of the regulatory framework in which modern cities operate.

Such an examination yields but one answer. To put the proposition bluntly, modern conditions have undermined the assumptions underlying Euclidean zoning:

1. Increased use of the automobile, the airplane, and other modern transportation technologies has changed the nature of land uses; it has fostered the growth of isolated yet interdependent suburban areas that are linked together economically and culturally and receding from the central city.

2. The modern technology of retail selling—especially the emergence of the integrated shopping facility—has brought the disruption of historic forms: central business districts cannot dominate the retail market as they did in the past, for suburban access has made possible large commercial parcels assembled under one ownership.

3. As the United States evolves into the next phase of industrial capitalism, the ascendancy of light industry and research establishments means that parcels formally labeled "industrial" for zoning purposes will be quite different from areas traditionally associated with that noisy and smelly classification. Increasingly, local governments deal with the kind of industry represented by the floating industrial zone district upheld in the *Eves* case,[38] insulated and landscaped so as to be residential in appearance, and nearly so in impact.

4. The real estate industry has shattered the assumption that isolation of uses is desirable. The idea never had fully prevailed in Europe, nor had it found favor with the majority of architects in this country. Mixed uses often complement each other, belying the Euclidean ideal of optimizing different uses by separating them. Today's technological and design possibilities for mixing residential, commercial, and industrial uses in large developments indicate that large parcels are an ideal form for development, capable of absorbing integrative yet disparate patterns of development. Moreover, the studies of the American Law Institute[39] all point to the desirability of large-scale and mixed-use development as a dominant (although not exclusive) form of development.

5. Large-scale development and planning encourage the introduction of sophisticated buffering techniques between incompatible uses. By its nature, traditional zoning by districts involves some chafing at the point where adjoining uses meet. As early as 1930, the planner Arthur Comey noted that the typical "sharp" division of cities into districts resulted in "a certain harsh crudeness . . . that blunts the application of city planning techniques" with detrimental effects to property on the edge of one zoning district "resulting from the actual or prospective development of adjacent property in a less restricted district." With the advent of large-scale planned developments and such innovations as cluster zoning, planned unit developments, mixed-use districts, and performance controls, the notion that those at the edge of a zone inevitably must suffer for the greater good of all, as a sort of human buffer, is less acceptable.

6. The emergence of a new economic class of large-scale entrepreneurs—the REITS, the CEF group, the Trammell Crows and Lincoln Property groups, the interstate shopping center developers—who move from state to state, prepared to exploit new trends of economic growth and activity, has changed the idealized picture of the 1920s city. We have even reached the point, unimaginable at the time of *Euclid,* where capitalist entrepreneurs join forces with the NAACP's Legal Defense Fund in bringing actions to invalidate zoning ordinances that create barriers to development.

7. The remarkable change in capital financing of real estate throws the Euclidean axioms into doubt. A new breed of financial institution has emerged in the land development field. For example, a national real estate mortgage market, undreamed of at the time of *Euclid,* has made possible the transfer of capital funds from the proverbial Boston trustee to the Sun Belt subdivisions. New devices abound, such as the wholesale accumulation of packages of mortgages by mortgage bankers who resell them to investors all over the country and the strategies of investment bankers who seek new ways of packaging debt and equity. Further, the insurance of mortgages through the FHA and VA, the secondary market operations of Fannie Mae (FNMA), Ginnie Mae (GNMA), and Freddie Mac (FHLMC), and the recent flurry—now in the billions of dollars and spurred by the Tax Reform Act of 1986—of collateralized mortgage obligations presumably to be enhanced by REMICs (real estate mortgage investment conduits) has meant a massive flow of capital that no longer permits the slow development of land resources according to local habits and ideas. As crucial as grass roots institutions are and as frequently as local myths are employed by embattled local groups, their planning controls, their subdivision exactions, and their zoning powers now are faced with this new array of parachute capitalists, able to transcend boundary lines and, with their economic force, transcend legal lines.

8. A growing body of social science knowledge has shown that urban patterns of homogeneous land uses were exaggerated initially and, in any event, are breaking down. The image of similarity and stability that permeated the thinking of Sutherland, Bettman, Metzenbaum, Baker, and others associated with the *Euclid* case has been overwhelmed by the movements of industry and of corporate employees—by General Motors opening and closing plants in different parts of the country (even on the Ambler Realty parcel itself)—and by the mobility of populations (census data show that one family in five moves each year). Society is characterized by conflicts in racial, class, and ethnic relations. The United States of the 1980s is a restless continent that can hardly be harnessed by the old-fashioned zoning document so painfully supported or opposed by the lawyers in the *Euclid* litigation. Furthermore, city planning theory has developed to the point where a whole school of thought, perhaps epitomized by the work of Jane Jacobs,[40] decries the boredom and sterility of that very separation of uses that was the hallmark of—and was embodied in—the original Euclid ordinance.

9. The same studies by social scientists, verified by the common sense sophistication of lenders as well as by the growing participation of equity partners and real estate syndicators, reveal that shifts of land values in urban areas are extremely rapid and show every indication of continuing the pattern. This cycle of land values was exacerbated by migrations after World War I and II—first from the south to the central cities and later to the Sun Belt as the Rust Belt and its central cities declined in industrial strength.

10. The number and magnitude of urban projects requiring joint actions by the government and the developer mean that line drawing between "private" and "public" becomes even more blurred in the post-Euclidean world. The necessary cooperation between the two sectors also harbors new constitutional inconsistencies and dangers.

11. Finally, there exists today far less faith in a Spencerian evolution toward an ideal social order marked by higher standards of living, social progress, and a general improvement in human welfare. Realizations have grown that life and land are far more

complex than once had seemed the case and that the allocation of urban resources is more puzzling and prone to more stresses and strains than originally conceived. But the policy implications drawn by political leaders and planning theorists vary substantially: One group of political pundits concludes from these complexities that social controls need to give broader scope to the operation of the private land market and to the drives of individual owners as basic allocators; the theorists, presently somewhat in disfavor but sure to re-emerge when the pendulum of planning reverses its swing, argue that this very same complexity calls for increased use of experts, computer models, city laboratories of social experiments, clearing houses, and evaluations of those experiments, as well as for a deeper injection of that elusive creature—the public interest—in deciding land use controversies. Both these groups, however, are united in scoffing at the rather simplistic divisions articulated by zoning maps, which, it must be remembered, automatically confer rights of development on landowners whose proposals—like off-the-rack clothing—fit onto these maps.

Inevitably, all these changes in the society at large were far beyond the ken of the original advocates of zoning. Shifts in the technology, institutions, and economics shaping American cities and metropolitan areas bring about new forms of settlements, be they the automobile cities, suburban villages, or consumer gentrified central cities. Together, these place undeniable strains on the legal and administrative framework of city planning established to assure some reasonable degree of order and amenity. And, inevitably, zoning—the most accepted and widespread tool of all—thus becomes a matter for increased analysis, concern, and criticism.[41] Performance standards, planned unit developments, floating zones, institutional districts, the exclusion of residences from industrial districts, capital budgeting, growth controls, infrastructure contingencies—all these indicate to community officials and city planners that increased refinement in land controls is necessary. At the same time, the lawyers have mounted an attack from their own professional vantage, arguing that the zoning procedures (which may have been implicit in Justice Sutherland's discussion) need to be spelled out and applied in far more detail and specificity. Too often lacking are recordkeeping, findings of fact, formal conclusions of law, notice, and hearings—the whole administrative paraphernalia needs revision, they say, and the state planning enabling acts should take the demands of procedural legitimacy into account.

Another element in the world view that has changed dramatically since the *Euclid* era is the very form of the metropolitan area in the United States today. Newton D. Baker argued that the externalities of Euclid's ordinance affecting the greater Cleveland metropolitan area justified its invalidation;[42] the district court, in holding the ordinance unconstitutional, agreed that the police power was being used in an excessively parochial manner.[43] Justice Sutherland gave passing treatment to the same metropolitan theme, stating that the question of a general welfare greater than that of a particular locality might have to be taken into account some day in ascertaining the constitutionality of a local land use ordinance.[44] His dictum was indeed prescient. Issues concerning the boundaries of local governments have been magnified greatly in recent decades, with well-publicized exclusionary battles, the pitting of suburban areas against "intruders," and the use of such weapons as large-lot zoning, apartment-free districts, overzoning for industry, caps on growth, and failure to supply infrastructure. Localities have employed the police power as a sword rather than a shield, making of zoning a divisive power of Balkanization—quite a different light than the local federalism accepted at the time of *Euclid.*

THE FUTURE OF EUCLIDEAN ZONING

Despite the vision and enduring philosophical core of Justice Sutherland's opinion as it relates to the constitutional demarcation of the public and private sectors, the actual devices dealt with in *Euclid* seem woefully ill-suited for modern urban society. The growing sophistication of planning methodology twinned with the emergence of new social and spatial forms of the postindustrial society; increased awareness in both public and private sectors of the complexity of urban land use problems joined with wider acceptance of the contribution of a private market system; the decline of savings and loan associations as the source of capital for housing development, along with the ascendancy of a new breed of national developers and innovators in the field of capital formation—together, these hallmarks of the modern city make traditional zoning, universally adopted and accepted after 1926 as the model for regulatory control of the land asset, now subject to question and debate if not to repeal and repudiation.

The clearest manifestation of the new skepticism is the emergence of numerous non-Euclidean devices within the framework of the ordinary zoning ordinance. Their aim, by and large, is to provide greater freedom within an area by introducing a range of heterogeneous uses, or by phasing growth where the private market indicates the time is ripe. Again, aesthetic, urban design, and environmental concerns are extended far beyond the *Euclid* ken in the *Berman,*[45] *Penn Central,*[46] and *Vincent*[47] decisions. The more flexible zoning devices also encourage the developer and his architect, along with the public administrator, to exer-cise greater creativity within a project and to introduce more variety in use, dimension, and structural characteristics than is possible under orthodox regulations designed for small, single parcels. These changes in outlook and purpose demand a revision of the Euclidean ordinance and of the framework established by the Standard Zoning Enabling Act to accommodate the kinds of urban developments that have become technologically, socially, or economically desirable in the eyes of both the real estate world and the city planners.

Thus, the challenge of adapting Euclidean land use controls again falls to the lawyers and, ultimately, to the courts. Clearly, under the new zoning regime, designed to make city planning less rigid and abstract, we need even more careful drafting, precise standards, and sharpened performance requirements than prevailed under the old; above all, there must be emphasis on well-crafted comprehensive plans and other explanatory instruments to permit intelligent judicial review of actions taken. But the crucial and most difficult change may involve transforming the institutional arrangements of zoning programs. We need to develop new levels and methods of review: imaginative schemes will call for review by administrative agencies specializing in land transactions and private property, by state or regional boards supervising local zoning efforts with an eye toward reinjecting considerations of the more general welfare, or by agencies directed toward reducing the cacophony of present procedures.

Undoubtedly formidable perils abound in this new planning age. The hallmark of the devices springing up all over the country is the loosing of discretion—increased flexibility augmenting the power of city administrators—which Justice Sutherland would have balked at because of potential excesses and abuses. Further perils loom in the growing recognition that *negative* controls of private development initiatives are inadequate, from the perspective of government and private property owners alike; affirmative mechanisms are required as well, in order to foster and implement comprehensive plans. The role of government as developer and entrepreneur in its own right, as well as a partner in public-private joint ventures, provokes new judicial inquiries into the Constitution's public use and public purpose requirements for the eminent domain and appropriation powers.

Hence, given the careful articulation and drafting of reasonable land planning policies, together with the creation of reviewable standards and procedural safeguards, one can anticipate that the *Euclid* ordinance, so revised and expanded, may yet remain a framework for controlling new forms of land development. Zoning law is opening up in ways that challenge the Euclidean devices that have persisted so long that we regard (and interpret) them as if the social memory runneth not to the contrary. Doubtless many new institutional arrangements and practices are called for. But before we retire Euclidean zoning with an honorable discharge for yeoman service, before society can feel comfortable with the new types of land use control, we must meet some of the following challenges of learning and understanding.

1. Extensive research is needed. Research into the life cycles of cities, into the mechanism of urban growth, development, and decline, and into the relationships among various types of land use within city boundaries, in a way that anticipates and responds to the needs of the public at large is required. We have begun to learn, through the environmental movement and through the neighborhood participation and model cities programs—forms of democratic input not foreseen by the

lawyers arguing the *Euclid* case—that goals and objectives *can* be agreed on and articulated in a way that clarifies the purposes for the public and for reviewing institutions. As the shortcomings of the modern tradition in land use controls have become more apparent, there is an ongoing search for meaningful criteria on which to base planning and design choices. A coherent planning philosophy is desperately required if administrators and planners are to avoid the too-easily-made charge of personal whim and caprice (the major attack that post-*Lochner* courts will consider). Otherwise, we will hear modern variations of the grim image in Baker's final sentence in his reply brief, "the menace . . . the Council of the Village of Euclid claims the power to destroy the value of land lying in it in the interest of undefined objects and to an extent and for purposes which will change from time to time with the personnel of the village legislature."[48] Priorities and intentions need to be made explicit in order to rebut such claims. The movement from the relatively simple mandatory controls of *Euclid* to sophisticated techniques of providing private developers with incentives to meet public goals raises questions about consistency and stability in definitions of public interest; it highlights the tendency of discretionary action to undermine the certainty so essential to the existence of private property. In essence, the "accordance with a comprehensive plan"[49] requirement can provide a framework within which individual decisions can be judged as they are made.

2. Evaluation and clearing-house testing of planning techniques and performance standards are required. Only through a continuous learning process can techniques and standards for the regulation of industry and traffic-generating facilities, for example, be stated in the ordinance to produce desired results—neither too rigid and confining, nor too indefinite to operate as an appropriate restraint. Similarly, experiments in methods of administrative control and review—whether in the form of state agencies whose function is to mitigate the parochialism of local legislation or a requirement of impact statements in order to minimize the power of money in obtaining approval of large-scale development or the use of auction techniques to help reduce favoritism—need to be thoroughly examined for their potential in reducing corruption.

3. The conditions that make the use of new techniques appropriate should be explicitly formulated in the ordinance itself. This should be done as experience develops with flexible zoning, planned unit developments, floating zones, or the novel use of zoning or eminent domain powers for public-private joint ventures. Only in this way will we wean ourselves of the tendency to think of such techniques as exceptions to the rule or as frantic emergency measures undertaken to stave off an unwanted development. The legal standard can be a statement of a general rule instead of an enumeration of particular instances; by spelling out in advance those situations that present judgment predicts will require special treatment and by specifying the factors that need to be taken into account by the decision maker, a discretionary decision can emerge as the predictable outcome of generally applicable principles—as such, it can satisfy judicial concerns.

4. The dominant orientation of zoning is changing and requires response. The political dominance and economic power of real estate interests become more apparent in the struggle for balance between private property and the public interest, signaling a change in the dominant orientation of zoning: The wise planning of metropolitan areas calls for a corps of competent, responsible, and interdisciplinary personnel—adept in the economic special-

ties of job and industrial development and cognizant of the social needs of individuals and classes within a physical context. Zoning, Bettman's brief argued, represents "the application of foresight and intelligence to the development of the community."[50] Economic and social aspects of city planning have assumed an ascendancy that could hardly be conceived of by those early zoners focusing on engineering and physical impacts of land development. The need for new breeds of planners and lawyers who are able to integrate physical, social, and economic concerns into a three-dimensional plan and who understand the financial motivations and income statements of the private property owner comes to the fore; this need is independent of the extent or scale of government intervention in land use decisions.

EUCLID AND POLITICAL CONSENSUS

The evolving techniques of the post-*Euclid* ordinances, thus, inexorably are finding their way into the mainstream of policy-making for urban development and, with the proposed legal and administrative safeguards, frail as they may be, their incorporation could progress without excessive disruption. But these techniques, too, should not be regarded as immutable. For the lesson of *Euclid* primarily is that there are no final answers to the problem of wise land uses, that Justice Sutherland's view of the Constitution as a living and growing guide to unanticipated needs and priorities is the only adequate legal response to the evolution of new metropolitan forms, and that the relations between a free market and government controls continually shift and evolve with differing views of the public interest. Indeed, the enduring legacy of *Euclid* appears in countless modern examples: the isolation of noxious uses in order to prevent depreciation of sections of a municipality; consolidation of mixed uses to support each other synergistically and to provide zones of transition, a technique which on the surface cuts against the grain of Euclidean separation by districts but which nevertheless can be seen as part of its heritage of striving to create livable cities. *Euclid's* legacy, properly understood, counsels flexibility in order to keep pace with new forms of economic and land development and with new methods of finance and capital accumulation. Above all, it exhorts us to recognize that changing conceptions of societal needs compel a continual adjustment between private property and the public good.

Such pragmatism is no stranger to our legal system; the flexibility of the system itself provides the nourishment necessary for the forging of a new consensus for change. But while this flexibility is necessary, it is not sufficient. Without something approaching political consensus and shared goals for a metropolitan area—comparable to the strange, shifting, and ambiguous alliance of interests that converged to form the standard zoning and planning enabling acts in the 1920s—only minor and localized advances in property controls are possible. Yet beyond slight modifications of the existing structure, no common vision exists today regarding the imposition of non-market controls on urban development. Thus, any deeper agreement as to the appropriate balance between public objectives and private property is highly unlikely. Widely divergent views on the efficacy and fairness of the land market, on the capacities and disinterestedness of planning and zoning machinery, and on the contradictions and inconsistencies of the hybrid forms of public and private joint ventures, preclude such consensus. To cite the Supreme Court in another context,[51] no shared view exists for solving the problems of metropolitanism such that an exercise of police power limiting property rights might be

described as "sanctioned by usage," or "held by the prevailing morality," or felt by "strong and preponderant opinion" to be necessary to the general welfare of the inhabitants of our cities.

Agreement upon a coherent philosophy for organizing the metropolitan environment through control of private property, therefore, is more easily called for than accomplished. Indeed, many of the new forms of urban development, by virtue of their complexity, are less conducive to consensus building—hence posing ever-sharper political difficulties and hindrances to success than those confronting the original districting device judicially scrutinized in the 1920s. *Euclid* funneled the political and developmental pressures into a common policy workable within the conditions of the times. The system's simplicity—its lack of detailed control—helped reconcile the public and the private interests at stake. "[S]ustaining of the American People and American Principles" and the American home was the clarion call of Metzenbaum's brief.[52] While zoning meant something different to each of the diverse interest groups, their coalition was protected because potentially conflicting assumptions could at this early stage remain unstated and certain paradoxes left for future resolution.[53] The novelty of a system that left the dynamics of growth to the private sector while enabling the local community to set overall requirements and goals allowed each interest group to overlay its vision of the gains it would derive.

As yet, there was no evidence of the potential disadvantages, such as differential gains to particular groups or too-often corrupt permit systems. There was even less awareness of zoning's potential as an exclusionary engine, manipulated for racial or economic discrimination. Given such a clean slate, the prozoning alliance proved, ironically, as powerful as it was disparate. "The colleges of the Country," in Metzenbaum's sweeping summation, "the municipal authorities, the medical profession, the engineering bodies, the sanitary experts, the traffic authorities, the street car officials, the police departments, the Commerce Department of the Federal government, the banks, the great money lending institutions, the taxation officials, the street cleaning departments, the fire insurance companies, the civic organizations, the institutions for the protection of children, the accident companies, and the fire departments have added their statements to the effect that the modern conditions require and necessitate this kind of exercise of the Police Power."[54]

Although this is strong support for the idea and practice of zoning, we must remember that two interests were largely unrepresented in the alliance. Immigrants and blacks who occupied the city's poorest regions were not included in strategy sessions designed to implement zoning and guide it through political and judicial approval. Hindsight has shown that in the wrong hands land controls have proved effective exclusionary devices. Further, while Theodore Roosevelt, Gifford Pinchot, and others warned pre-World War I America about the dangers of raping the nation's natural resources, it was not until the last half of the century that environmental concerns were translated into legislative measures. Indeed, the "quiet revolution" that still affects statewide planning decision making has been largely inspired by (and directed toward) environmental protection.

Given these new actors and claims, it is not surprising that the relative unanimity of the *Euclid* era has not survived. In fact, in cases such as *Agins*[55] and *San Diego Gas,*[56] those representing the interests of potential low- and middle-income residents are challenging open-space ordinances and other devices designed to conserve and protect precious land.

If the original and fragile coalition's broadly shared assumptions about the certainty of progress and the perfectability of city life have fallen victim to a less sanguine reality, one binding element in the consensus still persists and could operate today to foster a new coalition: an agreement on the evil of uncontrolled growth and on the axiom that land parcels are extremely interdependent and vulnerable. The principle of profit maximization can, in the land development market more than in other markets, take on a distinctly ugly face—in the "selfish" thrusting of bulk and height on individual parcels depriving neighbors of light and air; in indifference to the externality effect of street congestion and overloading of infrastructure; in disregard of spillovers that destroy the environment; in the drive for individual growth that consumes lakes, trees, and hills; in indifference to architectural and historic treasures that gave form to the social aspirations of their day; and in the pricing of land so high that adequate and decent housing is denied to large sectors of the population. Most actors in this market concur in the broad proposition that adequate protection for the values of a home, a business, or a neighborhood against the impacts of contending and incompatible uses cannot be achieved by individual action alone, no matter how heroic. Self-maximization is simply inadequate to the task, for even the selfish stand to lose if property rights are totally unfettered. Moreover, the notion of a public trust in land resources still has power to stir people's blood against "cashing out" municipally held development rights and could provide a thematic basis for the structure of new zoning.

There is also an emerging consensus on the need for joint ventures in land development. The new urban forms and designs require unprecedented amounts of both hard capital and expansive vision; the public and private sectors each are aware of their own inadequacies in working alone on either score. With this awareness has come a recognition that new flexible zoning techniques and devices will be increasingly vital ingredients in the chemistry of innovative collaboration.

On another strand of *Euclid's* legacy, however, no societal agreement seems in sight. Justice Sutherland's signal about metropolitanism may have been picked up by law reviews and, more significantly, some state supreme courts, but the parochialism of local government stands in the way of visions of a more general welfare. Indeed, recent New Jersey history shows how intense is the home rule sentiment when it comes to land use controls and how unlikely is a change in the 1920s philosophy of the delegating of the state police power to cities, villages, and towns.

Nevertheless, the pressure of litigation and the iteration by the judges of the constitutional and common law traditions that underlie zoning may help bring about some agreement on the limits of the power of local government, much as they have done in the area of the provision of municipal services. And there are other signs that jurists have become increasingly skeptical about the motives and practices of local land use decision makers. The burden shifts of *Fasano,*[57] for example, signal that generous deference is no longer in order. Justice Scalia's intriguing intermediate standard of review in 1987's *Nollan*[58] opinion is further evidence of judicial impatience with arbitrary and confiscatory regulation. The debate over the "vital and pressing governmental interest" standard recommended by President Reagan's Housing Commission also calls into question the parochialism encouraged by Sutherland's indulgence.

Affronts abound to the metropolitan settings in which we live, aspire and die: self-seeking by corporate developers, neglect of community needs, destruction of the aesthetic coherence of the urban landscape, and countless opportunities lost in the process of city building. That they do endure poses a continuing challenge to the planning professional and advocate. It was the testimony of national experts on the intimate relationship of zoning to the advancement of the public health, safety, morals, convenience, prosperity, and welfare that helped carry the day for the village of Euclid. Research reports and commission examinations, which "bear every evidence of painstaking consideration," said Justice Sutherland,[59] were undertaken by the planners, lawyers, engineers, doctors, and social scientists in their supporting Brandeis briefs, and the Justice relied on them to uphold the validity of zoning. The empirical data, and the theoretical formulations that flowed from them, helped forge agreement that some form of government intervention is necessary to correct the abuses of overreliance on the operation of the land market. Today, these earlier insights need to be updated, revised, and imbued with constitutional values if a sounder legal ordering for the development and redevelopment of our cities is to be achieved in a way that commands a political consensus.

In the debates over the future of metropolitan areas, therefore, we are faced with the need to strike a new balance between the same competing and contradictory forces that perplexed the actors in *Euclid.* Today, as then, we are burdened with the painful task of measuring the value of the city not only in terms of real estate and financial returns, but also in terms of human costs and values. Inherent contradictions between rights of citizens and the discretion of government, between planning and political bargaining, between elitism and stalemate will always require fresh accommodation as long as we struggle to adjust the private property land market to the conflicting demands of the profit economy and social concerns.

A full-blown political philosophy striking an acceptable social balance between private capitalism and public welfare, relating the social needs to the market economy in the development of urban lands, is hardly likely in the still-early stages of this finance capitalism phase of American economic history. Contradictions between private rights in land and the social character of that land are a centuries-old artifact of the common law—perhaps the most ancient conflict registered in the early reports as the judges struggled with the law of nuisances.[60] The articulation of a coherent planning philosophy to guide the destiny of cities, a revised institutional method of decision making, and the mustering of a political coalition behind the new land use controls required by contemporary metropolitan areas are the tasks that *Euclid* demands from us today. With genuine and committed leadership, the possibility exists for the political and planning processes to come to agreement on an agenda that will bind together the public and private to do jointly what neither can do alone.

NOTES

1. 272 U.S. 365 (1926).
2. A classic treatment of the effort of nineteenth century lawyers and judges to adapt common law rules to the changing circumstances of an industrializing nation is M. Horwitz, *The Transformation of American Law, 1780–1860* (1978). Also see the author's effort to trace one important common law notion through several centuries of permutation and adaptation: C.M. Haar, D.W. Fessler, *The Wrong Side of the Tracks,* Simon & Schuster (1986).
3. *See, e.g., Weaver* v. *Palmer Bros. Co.,* 270 U.S. 402 (1926) (invalidating a state health regulation that prohibited the use of rags for manufacture of bedding material). *See generally* G.Gunther, *Constitutional Law* 458–462 (11th ed., 1985).

4. *See Euclid,* 272 U.S. at 386–97.
5. *Penn Central Trans. Co.* v. *New York City,* 438 U.S. 104 (1978)
6. *See* Justice Brennan's majority opinion in *Penn Central*—itself barring such an onslaught—for a review of the major cases. 438 U.S. at 123–35.
7. *Euclid,* 272 U.S. at 396.
8. *Id.*
9. Brief and argument for appellee at 42, *Village of Euclid* v. *Ambler Realty Co.,* 272 U.S. 363 (1926) (No. 665).
10. *Id.* at 75.
11. Id.
12. *Id.* at 55.
13. *See* reply brief of appellants at 22–34, *Euclid,* 272 U.S. 363 (1926) (No. 665); brief on behalf of appellants on rehearing at 2–16, *Euclid,* 272 U.S. 363 (1926) (No. 665).
14. Letter of A. Bettman to D.J. Underwood, Sept. 29, 1924, quoted in D. Mandelker and R. Cunningham, *Planning and Control of Land Development: Cases and Materials* (1979), p. 213 n.5.
15. A. Bettman, "The Decision of the Supreme Court of the United States in the Euclid Village Zoning Case," *U. Cinn. L. Rev.* 1 (1927): 192.
16. *See Euclid,* 272 U.S. at 390–391; brief on behalf of the National Conference on City Planning at 15–22, *Euclid,* 272 U.S. 363 (1926) (No. 665) (collecting cases).
17. *See Euclid,* 272 U.S. at 396–97 ("[I]t is enough for us to determine, as we do, that the ordinance in its general scope and dominant features, so far as its provisions are here involved, is a valid exercise of authority, leaving other provisions to be dealt with as cases arise directly involving them."); *see also id.* at pp. 394–395 (citations omitted):

> The matter of zoning has received much attention at the hands of commissions and experts, and the results of their investigations have been set forth in comprehensive reports. . . . If these reasons, thus summarized, do not demonstrate the wisdom or sound policy in all respects of those restrictions which we have indicated as pertinent to the inquiry, at least, the reasons are sufficiently cogent to preclude us from saying, as it must be said before the ordinance can be declared unconstitutional, that such provisions are clearly arbitrary and unreasonable, having no substantial relation to the public health, safety, morals or general welfare.

18. *Id.* at 395.
19. *See id.* at 388 ("The inclusion of a reasonable margin

to insure effective enforcement, will not put upon a law, otherwise valid, the stamp of invalidity.'').

20. *Id.* at 389.

21. *Id.* at 388.

22. *Id.* at 388.

23. *See* brief on behalf of the National Conference on City Planning, pp. 23–28, *Euclid,* 272 U.S. 363 (1926) (No. 665).

24. *Euclid,* 272 U.S. at 394.

25. *Southern Burlington County NAACP* v. *Township of Mount Laurel,* 67 N.J. 151, 336 A.2d 713 (1975).

26. *National Land & Invest. Co.* v. *Kohn,* 419 Pa. 504, 215 A.2d 597 (1965).

27. *In re Girsh,* 437 Pa. 237, 263 A.2d 395 (1970).

28. Brief on behalf of appellants (on rehearing) at 42–43, *Euclid,* 272 U.S. 363 (1926) (No. 665).

29. *See* Arthur V.N. Brooks, ''The Office File Box—Emanations from the Battlefield,'' Chapter 1. Mr. Brooks suggests that Bettman's argument carried the day because ''for the court, it gave reassurance that the application of analogous authority—not any radical departure from precedent—was all that was required.'' *Id.* Likewise, Professor Williams argues that, given the *Lochner* era Court's predilection for confining the government's police power within the limits of common law categories, the Court would uphold zoning only to the extent it could be characterized as deriving from nuisance principles; *see also* Robert A. Williams, Jr., ''*Euclid's* Lochnerian Legacy,'' Chapter 10.

30. 277 U.S. 183 (1928).

31. *See* Brief on behalf of appellants at 67, *Euclid,* 272 U.S. 363 (1926) (No. 665).

32. *See id.* at 45–49.

33. *Euclid,* 272 U.S. at 394.

34. Quoted in brief on behalf of the National Conference on City Planning at 34, *Euclid,* 272 U.S. 365 (1926) (No. 665).

35. Of course, the interests of different elements of the real estate and business community were as diverse as those within the camp of idealists. For different approaches to the whole issue of class as it works out in the field of city planning and, most pertinently, how it dominates local ordinances and their subsequent review by the judiciary, see Peter L. Abeles, ''Planning and Zoning,'' Chapter 5, and Jerold S. Kayden, ''Judges as Planners: Limited or General Partners?'' Chapter 8.

36. On the participants in the *Euclid* case and the diversity of interests and classes they represented, see William M. Randle, ''Professors, Reformers, Bureaucrats, and Cronies: The Players in *Euclid* v. *Ambler,*'' Chapter 2.

37. Id.

38. *Eves* v. *Zoning Bd. of Adjustment,* 401 Pa.211, 164 A. 2d 7 (1960).

39. *See* American Law Institute, *A Model Land Development Code* (1975).

40. *See* J. Jacobs, *Cities and the Wealth of Nations: Principles of Economic Life* (1984).

41. In his contribution to this book, Robert H. Nelson discusses aspects of the current debate over zoning and its alternatives, reviewing the work of the debate's major participants. *See* ''Zoning Myth and Practice—From *Euclid* into the Future,'' Chapter 11 and sources cited therein.

42. *See* brief and argument for appellee at 41–43, *Euclid,* 272 U.S. 365 (1926) (No.665).

43. *See Ambler Realty Co.* v. *Village of Euclid,* 297 F. 307, 319 (N.D. Ohio 1924).

44. *See Village of Euclid* v. *Ambler Realty Co.,* 272 U.S. 365, 390 (1926).

45. *Berman* v. *Parker,* 348 U.S. 26 (1954).

46. *Penn Central Transp. Co.* v. *New York City,* 438 U.S. 104 (1978).

47. *Members of the City Council* v. *Taxpayers for Vincent,* 466 U.S. 789 (1984).

48. Reply brief of appellee at 42, *Euclid,* 272 U.S. 363 (1926) (No. 665).

49. *See generally* Haar, ''In Accordance with a Comprehensive Plan,'' *Harv. L. Rev.* 68 (1955): 1154.

50. *See* brief on behalf of the National Conference on City Planning at 37, *Euclid,* 272 U.S. 363 (1926).

51. *Noble State Bank* v. *Haskell,* 219 U.S. 104 (1911).

52. *See* brief on behalf of appellants at 70, *Euclid,* 272 U.S. 363 (1926) (No. 665).

53. On later conflicts among the interests and ideals that converged at the time of *Euclid,* see Joe R. Feagin, ''Arenas of Conflict: Zoning and Land Use Reform in Critical Political-Economic Perspective,'' Chapter 3.

54. Brief on behalf of appellants at 137–138, *Euclid,* 272 U.S. 363 (1926) (No. 665).

55. *Agins* v. *City of Tiburon,* 447 U.S. 255 (1980).

56. *San Diego Gas & Electric Co.* v. *City of San Diego,* 450 U.S. 621 (1981).

57. *Fasano* v. *Board of County Commissioners,* 264 Ore. 574, 507 P.2d 23 (1973).

58. *Nollan* v. *California Coastal Commission,* 107 S. Ct. 3141 (1987).

59. *Euclid,* 272 U.S. at 394.

60. *See, e.g.,* ''Trespass on the Case in Regard to Certain Mills,'' Y.B. 22 Hen. 6, F. 14 (C.P. 1444), excerpted in C.M. Haar, *Land-Use Planning: A Casebook on the Use, Misuse, and Re-Use of Urban Land,* 3rd ed., (1976), p. 126; *see also* Michael Allan Wolf, ''The Prescience and Centrality of *Eucid* v. *Ambler,*'' Chapter 9.

Appendix

(The first seven pages of the appendix present excerpts
from the briefs of the parties involved in *Village of Euclid* v.
Ambler Realty Co. Justice Sutherland's opinion for the Court
begins on page 362.—*Eds.*)

VILLAGE OF EUCLID *v.* AMBLER REALTY
COMPANY.

APPEAL FROM THE UNITED STATES DISTRICT COURT
FOR THE NORTHERN DISTRICT OF OHIO.

No. 31. Argued January 27, 1926; reargued
October 12, 1926.—Decided November 22,
1926.

1. A suit to enjoin the enforcement of a zoning ordinance with respect to the plaintiff's land, need not be preceded by any application on his part for a building permit, or for relief under the ordinance from the board which administers it, where the gravamen of the bill is that the ordinance of its own force operates unconstitutionally to reduce the value of the land and destroy its marketability, and the attack is not against specific provisions but against the ordinance in its entirety.

2. While the meaning of constitutional guaranties never varies, the scope of their application must expand or contract to meet the new and different conditions which are constantly coming within the field of their operation.

3. The question whether the power exists to forbid the erection of a building of a particular kind or for a particular use, like the question whether a particular thing is a nuisance, is to be determined by considering the building or the thing, not abstractly but in connection with the circumstances and the locality.

4. If the validity of the legislative classification for zoning purposes be fairly debatable, the legislative judgment must be allowed to control.

5. No serious difference of opinion exists in respect of the validity of laws and regulations fixing the height of buildings within reasonable limits, the character of materials and methods of construction, and the adjoining area which must be left open, in order to minimize the danger of fire or collapse, the evils of over-crowding, and the like, and excluding from residential sections offensive trades, industries, and structures likely to create nuisances.

6. The same power may be extended to a general exclusion from residential districts of all industrial establishments, though some may not be dangerous or offensive; for the inclusion of a reasonable margin to insure effective enforcement will not put upon a law, otherwise valid, the stamp of invalidity.

7. The power to relegate industrial establishments to localities separate from residential sections is not to be denied upon the ground that its exercise will divert a flow of industrial development from the course which it would follow and will thereby injure the complaining land-owner.

8. The police power supports also, generally speaking, an ordinance forbidding the erection in designated residential districts, of business houses, retail stores and shops, and other like establishments, also of apartment houses in detached-house sections—since such ordinances, apart from special applications, can not be declared clearly arbitrary and unreasonable, and without substantial relation to the public health, safety, morals, or general welfare.

9. Where an injunction is sought against such an ordinance, upon the broad ground that its mere existence and threatened en-

355

forcement, by materially and adversely affecting values and curtailing the opportunities of the market, constitute a present and irreparable injury, the court, finding the ordinance in its general scope and dominant features valid, will not scrutinize its provisions, sentence by sentence, to ascertain by a process of piecemeal dissection whether there may be, here and there, provisions of a minor character, or relating to matters of administration, or not shown to contribute to the injury complained of, which, if attacked separately, might not withstand the test of constitutionality. 297 Fed. 307, reversed.

APPEAL from a decree of the District Court enjoining the Village and its Building Inspector from enforcing a zoning ordinance. The suit was brought by an owner of unimproved land within the corporate limits of the village, who sought the relief upon the ground that, because of the building restrictions imposed, the ordinance operated to reduce the normal value of his property, and to deprive him of liberty and property without due process of law.

Mr. James Metzenbaum for the appellants.

The police power is very wide, *C. B. & Q. Ry.* v. *Drainage Commrs.,* 200 U. S. 561; *Munn* v. *Illinois,* 94 U. S. 113, and adequate to meet new conditions, *Bacon* v. *Walker,* 204 U. S. 317; *Hadachek* v. *Los Angeles,* 239 U. S. 394; *Sligh* v. *Kirkwood,* 237 U. S. 52; *Barbier* v. *Connolly,* 113 U. S. 27; *Gundling* v. *Chicago,* 177 U. S. 183; *Bank* v. *Haskell,* 219 U. S. 104. Legislation under it is presumptively legal. *Sinking Fund Cases,* 99 U. S. 718; *Powell* v. *Penn,* 127 U. S. 684. Courts will not assume the function of the legislative branch, *Barbier* v. *Connolly, supra.* To be unconstitutional, the legislation must have no relation to health and welfare. *Cusack Co.* v. *Chicago,* 242 U. S. 526; *Salt Lake City* v. *Foundry Co.,* 55 Utah 452; *State* v. *Withnell,* 91 Neb. 513; *Armour & Co.* v. *North Dakota,* 240 U. S. 510. Unconstitu-

tionality must be plainly and palpably clear. *Jacobson* v. *Massachusetts,* 197 U. S. 11; *Cusack Co.* v. *Chicago, supra.* The law must be plainly and manifestly unreasonable, *Cusack Co.* v. *Chicago, supra; Porter* v. *Wilson,* 239 U. S. 170. Illegality must be clearly established, *Sinking Fund Cases, supra; Powell* v. *Pennsylvania,* 127 U. S. 678; *People* v. *Warden,* 216 N. Y. 154; *People* v. *Schweinter Press,* 214 U. S. 395. Financial loss is not the test, *Hadachek* v. *Los Angeles,* 239 U. S. 394; *United States* v. *Noble,* 237 U. S. 78; *Reinman* v. *Little Rock,* 237 U. S. 171; *Erie R. R. Co.* v. *Williams,* 233 U. S. 700; *Mugler* v. *Kansas,* 123 U. S. 623; *Sheehan* v. *Scott,* 145 Cal. 684; *Cochrane* v. *Preston,* 108 Md. 220; *State* v. *Cunningham,* 97 Oh. St. 130; *Biggs* v. *Steinway,* 229 N. Y. 320. Local conditions must be considered, *McLean* v. *Denver,* 203 U. S. 38; *Ohio Co.* v. *Indiana,* 177 U. S. 190; *Affeld* v. *N. Y. Co.,* 198 U. S. 361; *Welch* v. *Swasey,* 214 U. S. 91; *Pleasay* v. *Ferguson,* 163 U. S. 537; *Brown* v. *Walling,* 204 U. S. 320.

Though there is unquestionably a "taking" under the exercise of police power, yet that taking is not such as is inhibited by or as requires compensation under the Constitution. This view is recognized in the case of *Interstate Ry. Co.* v. *Commonwealth,* 207 U. S. 79. See also *Hadachek* v. *Los Angeles,* 239 U. S. 394; *Welch* v. *Swasey,* 214 U. S. 91; *Cochrane* v. *Preston,* 108 Md. 220; *Publicity Co.* v. *Supt. of Building,* 218 N. Y. 540; *Doan Co.* v. *Cleveland,* 97 Oh. St. 130; *Barbier* v. *Connolly,* 113 U. S. 27. Classification is permitted and even necessary. *C. & N. W. Ry.* v. *R. R. Comm.,* 280 Fed. 394; *Welch* v. *Swasey, supra; Hadachek* v. *Los Angeles, supra; Powell* v. *Pennsylvania,* 127 U. S. 678.

The courts will not substitute their judgment for that of the legislature. *Armour & Co.* v. *North Dakota,* 240 U. S. 513; *Jacobson* v. *Massachusetts,* 197 U. S. 11; *Benson* v. *Henkel,* 198 U. S. 1; *Cusack* v. *Chicago,* 242 U. S. 526; *Salt Lake City* v. *Foundry Works,* 55 Utah 447; *C. B. & Q. R. R.* v. *Haggarty,* 67 Ill. 113; *Central R. R.* v. *Pettus,* 113

U. S. 127. The general application and not one single instance must be the guide. *Rochester* v. *West,* 164 N. Y. 510; *Tenement House Dept.* v. *Moeschen,* 179 N. Y. 325; *St. Louis Poster Co.* v. *St. Louis,* 249 U. S. 269; *Pierce Oil Corp.* v. *Hope,* 248 U. S. 500; *Benz* v. *Kremer,* 142 Wis. 1.

On the validity of the provisions of the ordinance concerning the Board of Appeals, see *People* v. *Board of Appeals,* 234 N. Y. 484; *Welch* v. *Swasey,* 214 U. S. 91; *Ayer* v. *Cram,* 242 Mass. 30; *Broadway Co.* v. *Nulle,* 203 App. Div. 468; *Sanders* v. *Walsh,* 108 Misc. 193; *Mutual Film Co.* v. *Industrial Comm.,* 236 U. S. 230; *Presbyterian Church* v. *Edgcomb,* 109 Neb. 18; *Chicago R. R. Co.* v. *R. R. Comm.,* 280 Fed. 387; *Merrick* v. *Halsey & Co.,* 242 U. S. 590.

The constitutionality of comprehensive zoning ordinances was involved in the following cases:

New York, (favorable): *Lincoln Trust Co.* v. *Williams Corp.,* 229 N. Y. 313; *People* v. *Board of Appeals, supra; In re Russell,* 158 N. Y. Supp. 162; *People* v. *Ludwig,* 218 N. Y. 240; *Barker* v. *Switzer,* 209 App. Div. 151; *Wulfsohn* v. *Burden,* 241 N. Y. 288. Massachusetts, (favorable): *Building Inspector* v. *Stoklosa,* 250 Mass. 52; *Spector* v. *Milton,* 250 Mass. 63; *Brett* v. *Building Commissioner,* 250 Mass. 73; *Welch* v. *Swasey,* 193 Mass. 364, affd. 214 U. S. 91; *Parker* v. *Commonwealth,* 178 Mass. 199; *Attorney General* v. *Williams,* 174 Mass. 476; *Ayer* v. *Cram,* 242 Mass. 30. New Jersey decisions at least partially opposed are: *State* v. *Nutley,* 99 N. J. L. 389; *Handy* v. *South Orange,* 118 Atl. 838; *Ignaciumas* v. *Risley,* 98 N. J. L. 712; *Max* v. *Building Inspector,* 127 Atl. 785; *Schaite* v. *Senior,* 97 N. J. L. 390; *Cliffside Park Co.* v. *Cliffside,* 96 N. J. L. 278. Maryland, (opposed): *Goldman* v. *Crowther,* 147 Md. 282. Missouri, (opposed): *St. Louis* v. *Evraiff,* 301 Mo. 231; *State* v. *McKelvey,* 256 S. W. 495. Texas: *Spann* v. *Dallas,* 111 Texas 350, is not properly a zoning case. But see *Dallas* v. *Mitchell,* 245 S. W. 944. California, (favorable): *Miller* v. *Board,* 195 Cal. 477; *Zahn* v.

Board, 195 Cal. 497. Cf. *Hadachek* v. *Los Angeles,* 239 U. S. 394; *Ex parte Quong Wo,* 161 Cal. 220. Kansas, (favorable): *Ware* v. *Wichita,* 113 Kan. 153; *West* v. *Wichita,* 118 Kan. 265. Iowa, (favorable): *Des Moines* v. *Manhattan Oil Co.,* 193 Iowa 1096. Louisiana, (favorable): *Calvo* v. *New Orleans,* 136 La. 480; *State* v. *New Orleans,* 142 La. 73; *Civello* v. *New Orleans,* 154 La. 271. Connecticut, (favorable): *Whitney* v. *Windsor,* 95 Conn. 357. District of Columbia, (favorable): *Schwartz* v. *Brownlow,* 50 App. D. C. 279. Minnesota, (favorable): *Banner Grain Co.* v. *Houghton,* 297 Fed. 317; *Twin City Co.* v. *Houghton,* 144 Minn. 1; *Beery* v. *Houghton,* 164 Minn. 146. Wisconsin, (favorable): *Carter* v. *Harper,* 182 Wis. 148; *Holzbauer* v. *Ritter,* 184 Wis. 35. Ohio, (favorable): *Perrysburg* v. *Ridgway,* 108 Oh. St. 245; *Morris* v. *Osborn,* 22 Oh. N. P. (N. S.) 549; *Youngstown* v. *Kahn Bros.,* 112 Oh. St. 654; *Bolce* v. *Hauser,* 111 Oh. St. 402.

See also: *Stephens* v. *Providence,* (not yet officially reported), 133 Atl. 614; *Wood* v. *Boston,* (not yet officially reported), 152 N. E. 62; *Deynzer* v. *Evanston,* 319 Ill. 226; *Aurora* v. *Burns, Id.* 84; *Fourcade* v. *San Francisco,* 196 Cal. 655; *State* v. *New Orleans,* 159 La. 324; *Bradley* v. *Board of Zoning Appeals,* (not yet officially reported), 150 N. E. 892.

The Ambler Company—without any application for revision, amendment or modification of the ordinance and without desiring to build any kind of structure whatsoever—hastened into court and applied for an injunction against the enforcement of the ordinance or any part of it. The decree struck down the entire ordinance. Under the conditions, the Company neither then had nor has now the right to bring into issue any question other than that the ordinance is fundamentally and *per se* in violation of the federal and state constitutions.

Until the complainant shall at least have applied for a permit to build some kind of structure, and until such permit shall have been denied, the complainant does not have the right to obtain an injunction upon the ground that the ordinance is unreasonable in its effect upon the property in question.

Mr. Newton D. Baker, with whom *Mr. Robert M. Morgan* was on the brief, for the appellee.

The recent industrial development of the City of Cleveland, following the railroad lines, has already reached the Village and to some extent extends over into it. In its obvious course, this industrial expansion will soon absorb the area in the Village for industrial enterprises. It is in restraint of this prospect that the ordinance seeks to operate. In effect it erects a dam to hold back the flood of industrial development and thus to preserve a rural character in portions of the Village which, under the operation of natural economic laws, would be devoted most profitably to industrial undertakings. This, the evidence shows, destroys value without compensation to the owners of lands who have acquired and are holding them for industrial uses.

Since the industrial development of a great city will go on, the effect of this attempted action necessarily is to divert industry to other less suited sites, with a consequent rise in value thereof; so that the loss sustained by the proprietors of land who cannot so use their land is gained by proprietors of land elsewhere. In other words, the property, or value, which is taken away from one set of people, is, by this law, bestowed upon another set of people, imposing an uncompensated loss on the one hand and a gain which is arbitrary and unnatural on the other hand, since it results, not from the operation of economic laws, but from arbitrary considerations of taste enacted into hard and fast legislation. Such legislation also tends to monopolize business and factory sites.

In the argument below it is alleged, that the

Company could have no matured right of action until it had first made application for a permit as to specific proposed uses of its lands, taken appeals from refusals to grant such permit, and filed petition with the council of the Village for such amendments as it might deem necessary. The wrong done to the plaintiff below was done when the ordinance was passed and continues as long as the ordinance is in existence. Prospective purchasers of land for commercial and industrial development will not even consider the plaintiff's land so long as the ordinance is in existence. To require the plaintiff to wait until he can find a purchaser sufficiently brave and sufficiently patient to buy a site in the teeth of this ordinance, bear the cost and delay of preparing plans, applying for a permit and having it rejected, perfecting an appeal and having it denied, and then exhausting the possibilities of petitions for amendment of the ordinance which would permit the proposed use, would, in fact, deprive the plaintiff of any remedy whatever, for no such complaisant purchasers can be found in a competitive real estate market. The plaintiff and others similarly situated with regard to their lands would simply be required to sit still and see the normal industrial and commercial development diverted, as purchasers passed them by and took less desirable land, free from the necessities of protracted litigation, in preference to the lands in the Village of Euclid, each acre of which would require litigation and lobbying before it could be devoted to entirely lawful and normal uses.

Ordinance No. 2812 is penal in character. That a court of equity will enjoin the enforcement of a void statute where the legal remedy is inadequate is no longer open to question, in view of the decisions of this Court. *Kennington* v. *Palmer,* 255 U. S. 100; *United States* v. *Schwartz,* *Id.* 102; *Adams* v. *Tanner,* 244 U. S. 590; *Truax*

v. *Raich,* 239 U. S. 33; *Bloch* v. *Hirsch,* 256 U. S. 135; *Brown Holding Co.* v. *Feldman,* 256 U. S. 170.

Whether Ordinance No. 2812 rests for its authority upon the "power of local self-government" granted by § 3 of Art. XVIII of the Ohio Constitution, or upon the attempted donation of power to municipal corporations by §§ 4366–1 to 4366–12 of the General Code, the same tests must be applied to its validity, and those tests are whether or not that ordinance is a reasonable and real exercise of the police power or an unreasonable and arbitrary exercise of the powers of local self-government and an impairment of the rights of property guaranteed to the plaintiff by the constitutions of the United States and of Ohio.

The ordinance does not, in fact, pursue any rational plan, dictated by considerations of public safety, health and welfare, upon which the police power rests. On the contrary, it is an arbitrary attempt to prevent the natural and proper development of the land in the Village prejudicial to the public welfare. This property in the interest of the public welfare, should be devoted to those industrial uses for which it is needed and most appropriate. Therefore, while it will be necessary for us to discuss "zoning" and point out what we believe to be the point of collision between the so-called zoning power and the Constitution of the United States, the appellee's primary interest is to protect its property against the damage wrought by this particular ordinance.

That municipalities have power to regulate the height of buildings, area of occupation, strengths of building materials, modes of construction, and density of use, in the interest of the public safety, health, morals, and welfare, are propositions long since established; that a rational use of this power may be made by dividing a municipality into districts or zones, and varying the requirements according to the characteristics of the districts, is, of course,

equally well established. We believe it, however, to be the law that these powers must be reasonably exercised, and that a municipality may not, under the guise of the police power, arbitrarily divert property from its appropriate and most economical uses, or diminish its value, by imposing restrictions which have no other basis than the momentary taste of the public authorities. Nor can police regulations be used to effect the arbitrary desire to have a municipality resist the operation of economic laws and remain rural, exclusive and aesthetic, when its land is needed to be otherwise developed by that larger public good and public welfare, which takes into consideration the extent to which the prosperity of the country depends upon the economic development of its business and industrial enterprises.

The municipal limits of the Village of Euclid are, after all, arbitrary and accidental political lines. The metropolitan City of Cleveland is one of the great industrial centers of the United States. If the Village may lawfully prefer to remain rural and restrict the normal industrial and business development of its land, each of the other municipalities, circumadjacent to the City of Cleveland, may pursue a like course. Thus the areas available for the expanding industrial needs of the metropolitan city will be restricted, the value of such land as is left available artificially enhanced, and industry driven to less advantageous sites. All this would be done at the expense of those land owners whose lands, being most advantageously located from an industrial point of view, have as a part of their right of property, which the constitutions of the Nation and the States undertake to protect, the expectation of value due to their superior availability for industrial development. *Kahn* v. *Youngstown,* 113 Oh. St. 17; *Pritz* v. *Messer, Id.* 89.

The distinction between the power of eminent domain and the police power is important. In the first place, there must be a public need, the property proposed to be taken must be taken for a public use, all the forms of law must be observed in the taking, and the private owner ultimately compensated. The courts do not allow the private owner to argue with the legislative authority in the exercise of its discretion as to what is a public need and his opinion is not important in the definitions of a public use, but the books are full of cases in which the exercise of this power has been stayed, even against the legislative determination, where the proposed use was only colorably public and the plain purpose of the appropriation was private advantage, no matter how widely distributed. Even where the owner is to be fully compensated, his right to retain and use his own property is protected unless there is a real, as against a pretended, public need to take it and use it.

Quite different is the police power under which the ordinance in this case purports to be passed. In every ordered society the State must act as umpire to the extent of preventing one man from so using his property or rights as to prevent others from making a correspondingly full and free use of their property and rights. The abstract right of a man to build a fire trap is limited by the rights of other people not to have their houses subjected to the peril created by it. The right of a man to maintain a nuisance on his own property is limited by the rights of others not to be subjected to the danger of its proximity. Accordingly, the so-called police power is an inherent right on the part of the public umpire to prevent misuses of property or rights which impair the health, safety, or morals of others, or affect prejudicially the general public welfare.

The limitations imposed by the police power do not have to be compensated for, for the reason that they are inherent in the ownership. If I buy a piece of land I have no means of knowing whether or not it will be needed for the public use, and if any need develops, I must be compensated when the public takes it. But I always know when I buy land, that I may not devote it to uses which endanger the safety, health, or morals of others or make its use a common nuisance to the prejudice of the public welfare. Because of its nature, the exercise of the police power has always been restrained to those uses of property which invade the rights of others, and courts consistently decline to permit an extension of the police power to uses of property involving mere questions of taste or preference or financial advantage to others. Unless the theory of our expanding civilization is wrong, the public welfare is advanced by the devotion of the most available sites to business and industry, as the need for them develops. Restrictions upon limited areas have always been established, when desired, by mutual contracts, and such restrictions have been upheld so long as they were reasonable, in view of the changing growth and development of the country. It has, however, only recently been suggested that use restrictions, which formerly lay in contract, may be imposed or abrogated by municipal regulation and that the fleeting legislative judgment and will of a municipal council can select which, out of a variety of admittedly innocent uses, it will permit the owners of land to enjoy. *Yates* v. *Milwaukee,* 10 Wall. 497.

Even if the world could agree by unanimous consent upon what is beautiful and desirable, it could not, under our constitutional theory, enforce its decision by prohibiting a land owner, who refuses to accept the world's view of beauty, from making otherwise safe and innocent uses of his land. The case against many of these zoning laws, however, is much stronger than this. The world has not reached a unanimous judgment about beauty, and there are few unlikelier places to look for stable judgments on such subjects than in the changing discretion of legislative bodies, moved this way and that by the conflict of commercial interests on the one hand, and the assorted opinions of individuals, moved by purely private concerns, on the other.

Perhaps the most often quoted definition of the police power is that of Judge Cooley. Constitutional Limitations, 7th ed., p. 245. This limits the power to the establishment of rules to prevent the conflict of rights. See also, *Id.* 768, 839; *Truax* v. *Corrigan,* 257 U. S. 336; *People* v. *Road,* 9 Mich. 285; Tiedeman, State and Federal Control, § 146; Freund, Police Power, § 511. *Munn* v. *Illinois,* 94 U. S. 113, sustained the police power in the regulation of grain elevators, because such property was held to be affected with a public use, but the court sharply declined to regard the rule then established as an invasion of rights purely private. See also *Coppage* v. *Kansas,* 236 U. S. 1; *Wolf Packing Co.* v. *Court of Industrial Relations,* 262 U. S. 522; 267 *Id.* 552; *Penna. Coal Co.* v. *Mahon,* 260 U. S. 393; *Eubank* v. *Richmond,* 226 U. S. 137.

It has not been difficult for this Court to vindicate the great guaranties of the Constitution against direct attack. The trouble comes when these guaranties of individual rights of liberty and property appear to stand in the way of some genuinely benevolent and praiseworthy object which enlists support or enthusiasm, and when only a little infringement of the right of the individual is asked to be indulged. Yet the danger of frittering away the constitutional guaranties by successive encroachments has always been apparent. *Railway Co.* v. *Commissioners,* 1 Oh. St. 77; *Miller* v. *Crawford,* 70 Oh. St. 207; *Williams* v. *Preslo,* 84 Oh. St. 345; *Coppage* v. *Kansas,* 236 U. S. 1; *Boyd* v. *United States,* 116 U. S. 616.

It is impossible to reconcile the rulings of the supreme courts of the States upon the questions here presented. Each case is, of course, decided on its own facts. Many of them presented familiar restrictions, more or less demonstrably involving the public safety, health, or morals. In some of the cases, although the opinions seem to sanction very wide extensions of the traditional police power, the facts involved do not necessitate the width of the rulings; but even this consideration does not make it possible to follow through these cases any thread which leads to an authentic definition and application of the constitutional restraints upon unlimited extensions of the police power. *Spann* v. *Dallas,* 111 Tex. 350; *Fitzhugh* v. *Jackson,* 132 Miss. 585; *State* v. *Thomas,* 96 W. Va. 628; *Tighe* v. *Osborne,* 131 Atl. 801; *Goldman* v. *Crowther,* 147 Md. 282; *Mayor* v. *Turk,* 129 Atl. 512; *State* v. *McKelvey,* 301 Mo. 130; *Ignaciunas* v. *Risley,* 98 N. J. L. 712; *Lachman* v. *Haughton,* 134 Minn. 226; *Roerig* v. *Minneapolis,* 136 Minn. 479; *Blackman* v. *Atlanta,* 151 Ga. 507; *State* v. *Edgcombe,* 108 Neb. 859; *Byrne* v. *Realty Co.,* 129 Md. 202; *Illinois* v. *Friend,* 261 Ill. 16; *Windsor* v. *Whitney,* 95 Conn. 357; *Losick* v. *Binda,* 128 Atl. 619; *Sarg* v. *Hooper,* 128 Atl. 376; *Ingersoll* v. *South Orange,* 128 Atl. 393; *Becker* v. *Dowling,* 128 Atl. 395; *Summit Co.* v. *Board,* 129 Atl. 819; *Reimer* v. *Dallas,* 129 Atl. 390; *Plymouth* v. *Bigelow,* 129 Atl. 203; *Printz* v. *Board of Adjustment,* 129 Atl. 123; *Passaic* v. *Patterson Bill Co.,* 72 N. J. L. 285; *Youngstown* v. *Kahn,* 113 Oh. St. 17; *Pritz* v. *Messer,* 113 Oh. St. 89.

New conditions may arise and new discoveries be made that will cause new conceptions of social needs and bring within the legislative power fields previously not occupied; but we frankly do not believe that there has been any such development of new conditions as necessitates or justifies the communal control of private property attempted by this ordinance, or by many others, some of which have been sustained by state courts. Restraints and restrictions upon alienation and use, even when imposed by covenant, are looked upon with disfavor and construed strictly in the interest of the free transfer and use of property. 7 R. C. L. 1115, citing *Hutchinson* v. *Ulrich,* 145 Ill. 335; *Hitz* v. *Flower,* 104 Oh. St. 47. Yet the theory of zoning, in its ampler definitions, assumes that the municipal councils will be able to do, comprehensively, what private owners, most interested, have found it difficult to do, even on a small scale.

That our cities should be made beautiful and orderly is, of course, in the highest degree desirable, but it is even more important that our people should remain free. Their freedom depends upon the preservation of their constitutional immunities and privileges against the desire of others to control them, no matter how generous the motive or well intended the control which it is sought to impose.

MR. JUSTICE SUTHERLAND delivered the opinion of the Court.

The Village of Euclid is an Ohio municipal corporation. It adjoins and practically is a suburb of the City of Cleveland. Its estimated population is between 5,000 and 10,000, and its area from twelve to fourteen square miles, the greater part of which is farm lands or unimproved acreage. It lies, roughly, in the form of a parallelogram measuring approximately three and one-half miles each way. East and west it is traversed by three principal highways: Euclid Avenue, through the southerly border, St. Clair Avenue, through the central portion, and Lake Shore Boulevard, through the northerly border in close proximity to the shore of Lake Erie. The Nickel Plate railroad lies from 1,500 to 1,800 feet north of Euclid Avenue, and the Lake Shore railroad 1,600 feet farther to the north. The three highways and the two railroads are substantially parallel.

Appellee is the owner of a tract of land containing 68 acres, situated in the westerly end of the village, abutting on Euclid Avenue to the south and the Nickel Plate railroad to the

north. Adjoining this tract, both on the east and on the west, there have been laid out restricted residential plats upon which residences have been erected.

On November 13, 1922, an ordinance was adopted by the Village Council, establishing a comprehensive zoning plan for regulating and restricting the location of trades, industries, apartment houses, two-family houses, single family houses, etc., the lot area to be built upon, the size and height of buildings, etc.

The entire area of the village is divided by the ordinance into six classes of use districts, denominated U-1 to U-6, inclusive; three classes of height districts, denominated H-1 to H-3, inclusive; and four classes of area districts, denominated A-1 to A-4, inclusive. The use districts are classified in respect of the buildings which may be erected within their respective limits, as follows: U-1 is restricted to single family dwellings, public parks, water towers and reservoirs, suburban and interurban electric railway passenger stations and rights of way, and farming, non-commercial greenhouse nurseries and truck gardening; U-2 is extended to include two-family dwellings; U-3 is further extended to include apartment houses, hotels, churches, schools, public libraries, museums, private clubs, community center buildings, hospitals, sanitariums, public playgrounds and recreation buildings, and a city hall and courthouse; U-4 is further extended to include banks, offices, studios, telephone exchanges, fire and police stations, restaurants, theatres and moving picture shows, retail stores and shops, sales offices, sample rooms, wholesale stores for hardware, drugs and groceries, stations for gasoline and oil (not exceeding 1,000 gallons storage) and for ice delivery, skating rinks and dance halls, electric substations, job and newspaper printing, public garages for motor vehicles, stables and wagon sheds (not exceeding five horses, wagons or motor trucks) and distributing stations for central store and commercial enterprises; U-5 is further extended to include billboards and advertising signs (if permitted), warehouses, ice and ice cream manufacturing and cold storage plants, bottling works, milk bottling and central distribution stations, laundries, carpet cleaning, dry cleaning and dyeing establishments, blacksmith, horseshoeing, wagon and motor vehicle repair shops, freight stations, street car barns, stables and wagon sheds (for more than five horses, wagons or motor trucks), and wholesale produce markets and salesrooms; U-6 is further extended to include plants for sewage disposal and for producing gas, garbage and refuse incineration, scrap iron, junk, scrap paper and rag storage, aviation fields, cemeteries, crematories, penal and correctional institutions, insane and feeble minded institutions, storage of oil and gasoline (not to exceed 25,000 gallons), and manufacturing and industrial operations of any kind other than, and any public utility not included in, a class U-1, U-2, U-3, U-4 or U-5 use. There is a seventh class of uses which is prohibited altogether.

Class U-1 is the only district in which buildings are restricted to those enumerated. In the other classes the uses are cumulative; that is to say, uses in class U-2 include those enumerated in the preceding class, U-1; class U-3 includes uses enumerated in the preceding classes, U-2 and U-1; and so on. In addition to the enumerated uses, the ordinance provides for accessory uses, that is, for uses customarily incident to the principal use, such as private garages. Many regulations are provided in respect of such accessory uses.

The height districts are classified as follows: In class H-1, buildings are limited to a height of two and one-half stories or thirty-five feet; in class H-2, to four stories or fifty feet; in

class H-3, to eighty feet. To all of these, certain exceptions are made, as in the case of church spires, water tanks, etc.

The classification of area districts is: In A-1 districts, dwellings or apartment houses to accommodate more than one family must have at least 5,000 square feet for interior lots and at least 4,000 square feet for corner lots; in A-2 districts, the area must be at least 2,500 square feet for interior lots, and 2,000 square feet for corner lots; in A-3 districts, the limits are 1,250 and 1,000 square feet, respectively; in A-4 districts, the limits are 900 and 700 square feet, respectively. The ordinance contains, in great variety and detail, provisions in respect of width of lots, front, side and rear yards, and other matters, including restrictions and regulations as to the use of bill boards, sign boards and advertising signs.

A single family dwelling consists of a basement and not less than three rooms and a bathroom. A two-family dwelling consists of a basement and not less than four living rooms and a bathroom for each family; and is further described as a detached dwelling for the occupation of two families, one having its principal living rooms on the first floor and the other on the second floor.

Appellee's tract of land comes under U-2, U-3 and U-6. The first strip of 620 feet immediately north of Euclid Avenue falls in class U-2, the next 130 feet to the north, in U-3, and the remainder in U-6. The uses of the first 620 feet, therefore, do not include apartment houses, hotels, churches, schools, or other public and semi-public buildings, or other uses enumerated in respect of U-3 to U-6, inclusive. The uses of the next 130 feet include all of these, but exclude industries, theatres, banks, shops, and the various other uses set forth in respect of U-4 to U-6, inclusive. (The court below seemed to think that the frontage of this property on Euclid Avenue to a depth of 150 feet came under U-1 district and was available only for single family dwellings. An examination of the ordinance and subsequent amendments, and a comparison of their terms with the maps, shows very clearly, however, that this view was incorrect. Appellee's brief correctly interpreted the ordinance: "The northerly 500 feet thereof immediately adjacent to the right of way of the New York, Chicago & St. Louis Railroad Company under the original ordinance was classed as U-6 territory and the rest thereof as U-2 territory. By amendments to the ordinance a strip 630 [620] feet wide north of Euclid Avenue is classed as U-2 territory, a strip 130 feet wide next north as U-3 territory and the rest of the parcel to the Nickel Plate right of way as U-6 territory.")

Annexed to the ordinance, and made a part of it, is a zone map, showing the location and limits of the various use, height and area districts, from which it appears that the three classes overlap one another; that is to say, for example, both U-5 and U-6 use districts are in A-4 area districts, but the former is in H-2 and the latter in H-3 height districts. The plan is a complicated one and can be better understood by an inspection of the map, though it does not seem necessary to reproduce it for present purposes.

The lands lying between the two railroads for the entire length of the village area and extending some distance on either side to the north and south, having an average width of about 1,600 feet, are left open, with slight exceptions, for industrial and all other uses. This includes the larger part of appellee's tract. Approximately one-sixth of the area of the entire village is included in U-5 and U-6 use districts. That part of the village lying south of Euclid Avenue is principally in U-1 districts. The lands lying north of Euclid Avenue and bordering on the long strip just described are in-cluded in U-1, U-2, U-3 and U-4 districts, principally in U-2.

The enforcement of the ordinance is entrusted to the inspector of buildings, under rules and regulations of the board of zoning appeals. Meetings of the board are public, and minutes of its proceedings are kept. It is authorized to adopt rules and regulations to carry into effect provisions of the ordinance. Decisions of the inspector of buildings may be appealed to the board by any person claiming to be adversely affected by any such decision. The board is given power in specific cases of practical difficulty or unnecessary hardship to interpret the ordinance in harmony with its general purpose and intent, so that the public health, safety and general welfare may be secure and substantial justice done. Penalties are prescribed for violations, and it is provided that the various provisions are to be regarded as independent and the holding of any provision to be unconstitutional, void or ineffective shall not affect any of the others.

The ordinance is assailed on the grounds that it is in derogation of § 1 of the Fourteenth Amendment to the Federal Constitution in that it deprives appellee of liberty and property without due process of law and denies it the equal protection of the law, and that it offends against certain provisions of the Constitution of the State of Ohio. The prayer of the bill is for an injunction restraining the enforcement of the ordinance and all attempts to impose or maintain as to appellee's property any of the restrictions, limitations or conditions. The court below held the ordinance to be unconstitutional .and void, and enjoined its enforcement. 297 Fed. 307.

Before proceeding to a consideration of the case, it is necessary to determine the scope of the inquiry. The bill alleges that the tract of land in question is vacant and has been held for years for the purpose of selling and developing it for industrial uses, for which it is especially adapted, being immediately in the path of progressive industrial development; that for such uses it has a market value of about $10,000 per acre, but if the use be limited to residential purposes the market value is not in excess of $2,500 per acre; that the first 200 feet of the parcel back from Euclid Avenue, if unrestricted in respect of use, has a value of $150 per front foot, but if limited to residential uses, and ordinary mercantile business be excluded therefrom, its value is not in excess of $50 per front foot.

It is specifically averred that the ordinance attempts to restrict and control the lawful uses of appellee's land so as to confiscate and destroy a great part of its value; that it is being enforced in accordance with its terms; that prospective buyers of land for industrial, commercial and residential uses in the metropolitan district of Cleveland are deterred from buying any part of this land because of the existence of the ordinance and the necessity thereby entailed of conducting burdensome and expensive litigation in order to vindicate the right to use the land for lawful and legitimate purposes; that the ordinance constitutes a cloud upon the land, reduces and destroys its value, and has the effect of diverting the normal industrial, commercial and residential development thereof to other and less favorable locations.

The record goes no farther than to show, as the lower court found, that the normal, and reasonably to be expected, use and development of that part of appellee's land adjoining Euclid Avenue is for general trade and commercial purposes, particularly retail stores and like establishments, and that the normal, and reasonably to be expected, use and development of the residue of the land is for industrial and trade purposes. Whatever injury is inflicted by the mere existence and threatened enforcement of the ordinance is due to restrictions in respect of these and similar uses; to which perhaps should be added—if not included in the foregoing—restrictions in respect of apartment houses. Specifically, there is nothing in the record to suggest that any damage results from the presence in the ordinance of those restrictions relating to churches, schools, libraries and other public and semi-public buildings. It is neither alleged nor proved that there is, or may be, a demand for any part of appellee's land for any of the last named uses; and we cannot assume the existence of facts which would justify an injunction upon this record in respect of this class of restrictions. For present purposes the provisions of the ordinance in respect of these uses may, therefore, be put aside as unnecessary to be considered. It is also unnecessary to consider the effect of the restrictions in respect of U-1 districts, since none of appellee's land falls within that class.

We proceed, then, to a consideration of those provisions of the ordinance to which the case as it is made relates, first disposing of a preliminary matter.

A motion was made in the court below to dismiss the bill on the ground that, because complainant [appellee] had made no effort to obtain a building permit or apply to the zoning board of appeals for relief as it might have done under the terms of the ordinance, the suit was premature. The motion was properly overruled. The effect of the allegations of the bill is that the ordinance of its own force operates greatly to reduce the value of appellee's lands and destroy their marketability for industrial, commercial and residential uses; and the attack is directed, not against any specific provision or provisions, but against the ordinance as an entirety. Assuming the premises, the existence and maintenance of the ordinance, in effect, constitutes a present invasion of appellee's property rights and a threat to continue it. Under these circumstances, the equitable jurisdiction is clear. See *Terrace* v. *Thompson,* 263 U. S. 197, 215; *Pierce* v. *Society of Sisters,* 268 U. S. 510, 535.

It is not necessary to set forth the provisions of the Ohio Constitution which are thought to be infringed. The question is the same under both Constitutions, namely, as stated by appellee: Is the ordinance invalid in that it violates the constitutional protection "to the right of property in the appellee by attempted regulations under the guise of the police power, which are unreasonable and confiscatory?"

Building zone laws are of modern origin. They began in this country about twenty-five years ago. Until recent years, urban life was comparatively simple; but with the great increase and concentration of population, problems have developed, and constantly are developing, which require, and will continue to require, additional restrictions in respect of the use and occupation of private lands in urban communities. Regulations, the wisdom, necessity and validity of which, as applied to existing conditions, are so apparent that they are now uniformly sustained, a century ago, or even half a century ago, probably would have been rejected as arbitrary and oppressive. Such regulations are sustained, under the complex conditions of our day, for reasons analogous to those which justify traffic regulations, which, before the advent of automobiles and rapid transit street railways, would have been condemned as fatally arbitrary and unreasonable. And in this there is no inconsistency, for while the meaning of constitutional guaranties never varies, the scope of their application must expand or contract to meet the new and different conditions which are constantly coming within the field of their operation. In a changing world, it is impossible that

it should be otherwise. But although a degree of elasticity is thus imparted, not to the *meaning,* but to the *application* of constitutional principles, statutes and ordinances, which, after giving due weight to the new conditions, are found clearly not to conform to the Constitution, of course, must fall.

The ordinance now under review, and all similar laws and regulations, must find their justification in some aspect of the police power, asserted for the public welfare. The line which in this field separates the legitimate from the illegitimate assumption of power is not capable of precise delimitation. It varies with circumstances and conditions. A regulatory zoning ordinance, which would be clearly valid as applied to the great cities, might be clearly invalid as applied to rural communities. In solving doubts, the maxim *sic utere tuo ut alienum non laedas,* which lies at the foundation of so much of the common law of nuisances, ordinarily will furnish a fairly helpful clew. And the law of nuisances, likewise, may be consulted, not for the purpose of controlling, but for the helpful aid of its analogies in the process of ascertaining the scope of, the power. Thus the question whether the power exists to forbid the erection of a building of a particular kind or for a particular use, like the question whether a particular thing is a nuisance, is to be determined, not by an abstract consideration of the building or of the thing considered apart, but by considering it in connection with the circumstances and the locality. *Sturgis* v. *Bridgeman,* L. R. 11 Ch. 852, 865. A nuisance may be merely a right thing in the wrong place,—like a pig in the parlor instead of the barnyard. If the validity of the legislative classification for zoning purposes be fairly debatable, the legislative judgment must be allowed to control. *Radice* v. *New York,* 264 U. S. 292, 294.

There is no serious difference of opinion in

respect of the validity of laws and regulations fixing the height of buildings within reasonable limits, the character of materials and methods of construction, and the adjoining area which must be left open, in order to minimize the danger of fire or collapse, the evils of over-crowding, and the like, and excluding from residential sections offensive trades, industries and structures likely to create nuisances. See *Welch* v. *Swasey,* 214 U. S. 91; *Hadacheck* v. *Los Angeles,* 239 U. S. 394; *Reinman* v. *Little Rock,* 237 U. S. 171; *Cusack Co.* v. *City of Chicago,* 242 U. S. 526, 529–530.

Here, however, the exclusion is in general terms of all industrial establishments, and it may thereby happen that not only offensive or dangerous industries will be excluded, but those which are neither offensive nor dangerous will share the same fate. But this is no more than happens in respect of many practice-forbidding laws which this Court has upheld although drawn in general terms so as to include individual cases that may turn out to be innocuous in themselves. *Hebe Co.* v. *Shaw,* 248 U. S. 297, 303; *Pierce Oil Corp.* v. *City of Hope,* 248 U. S. 498, 500. The inclusion of a reasonable margin to insure effective enforcement, will not put upon a law, otherwise valid, the stamp of invalidity. Such laws may also find their justification in the fact that, in some fields, the bad fades into the good by such insensible degrees that the two are not capable of being readily distinguished and separated in terms of legislation. In the light of these considerations, we are not prepared to say that the end in view was not sufficient to justify the general rule of the ordinance, although some industries of an innocent character might fall within the proscribed class. It can not be said that the ordinance in this respect "passes the bounds of reason and assumes the character of a merely arbitrary fiat." *Purity Extract Co.* v. *Lynch,* 226 U. S. 192, 204. Moreover, the restrictive provisions of the ordinance in this particular may be sustained upon the principles applicable to the broader exclusion from residential districts of all business and trade structures, presently to be discussed.

It is said that the Village of Euclid is a mere suburb of the City of Cleveland; that the industrial development of that city has now reached and in some degree extended into the village and, in the obvious course of things, will soon absorb the entire area for industrial enterprises; that the effect of the ordinance is to divert this natural development elsewhere with the consequent loss of increased values to the owners of the lands within the village borders. But the village, though physically a suburb of Cleveland, is politically a separate municipality, with powers of its own and authority to govern itself as it sees fit within the limits of the organic law of its creation and the State and Federal Constitutions. Its governing authorities, presumably representing a majority of its inhabitants and voicing their will, have determined, not that industrial development shall cease at its boundaries, but that the course of such development shall proceed within definitely fixed lines. If it be a proper exercise of the police power to relegate industrial establishments to localities separated from residential sections, it is not easy to find a sufficient reason for denying the power because the effect of its exercise is to divert an industrial flow from the course which it would follow, to the injury of the residential public if left alone, to another course where such injury will be obviated. It is not meant by this, however, to exclude the possibility of cases where the general public interest would so far outweigh the interest of the municipality that the municipality would not be allowed to stand in the way.

We find no difficulty in sustaining restrictions of the kind thus far reviewed. The serious question in the case arises over the provisions of the ordinance excluding from residential districts, apartment houses, business houses, retail stores and shops, and other like establishments. This question involves the validity of what is really the crux of the more recent zoning legislation, namely, the creation and maintenance of residential districts, from which business and trade of every sort, including hotels and apartment houses, are excluded. Upon that question this Court has not thus far spoken. The decisions of the state courts are numerous and conflicting; but those which broadly sustain the power greatly outnumber those which deny altogether or narrowly limit it; and it is very apparent that there is a constantly increasing tendency in the direction of the broader view. We shall not attempt to review these decisions at length, but content ourselves with citing a few as illustrative of all.

As sustaining the broader view, see *Opinion of the Justices,* 234 Mass. 597, 607; *Inspector of Buildings of Lowell* v. *Stoklosa,* 250 Mass. 52; *Spector* v. *Building Inspector of Milton,* 250 Mass. 63; *Brett* v. *Building Commissioner of Brookline,* 250 Mass. 73; *State* v. *City of New Orleans,* 154 La. 271, 282; *Lincoln Trust Co.* v. *Williams Bldg. Corp.,* 229 N. Y. 313; *City of Aurora* v. *Burns,* 319 Ill. 84, 93; *Deynzer* v. *City of Evanston,* 319 Ill. 226; *State ex rel. Beery* v. *Houghton,* 164 Minn. 146; *State ex rel. Carter* v. *Harper,* 182 Wis. 148, 157–161; *Ware* v. *City of Wichita,* 113 Kan. 153; *Miller* v. *Board of Public Works,* 195 Cal. 477, 486–495; *City of Providence* v. *Stephens,* 133 Atl. 614.

For the contrary view, see *Goldman* v. *Crowther,* 147 Md. 282; *Ignaciunas* v. *Risley,* 98 N. J. L. 712; *Spann* v. *City of Dallas,* 111 Tex. 350.

As evidence of the decided trend toward the broader view, it is significant that in some instances the state courts in later decisions have reversed their former decisions holding the other way. For example, compare *State ex rel.*

Beery v. *Houghton, supra,* sustaining the power, with *State ex rel. Lachtman* v. *Houghton,* 134 Minn. 226; *State ex rel. Roerig* v. *City of Minneapolis,* 136 Minn. 479; and *Vorlander* v. *Hokenson,* 145 Minn. 484, denying it, all of which are disapproved in the *Houghton* case (p. 151) last decided.

The decisions enumerated in the first group cited above agree that the exclusion of buildings devoted to business, trade, etc., from residential districts, bears a rational relation to the health and safety of the community. Some of the grounds for this conclusion are—promotion of the health and security from injury of children and others by separating dwelling houses from territory devoted to trade and industry; suppression and prevention of disorder; facilitating the extinguishment of fires, and the enforcement of street traffic regulations and other general welfare ordinances; aiding the health and safety of the community by excluding from residential areas the confusion and danger of fire, contagion and disorder which in greater or less degree attach to the location of stores, shops and factories. Another ground is that the construction and repair of streets may be rendered easier and less expensive by confining the greater part of the heavy traffic to the streets where business is carried on.

The Supreme Court of Illinois, in *City of Aurora* v. *Burns, supra,* pp. 93–95, in sustaining a comprehensive building zone ordinance dividing the city into eight districts, including exclusive residential districts for one and two-family dwellings, churches, educational institutions and schools, said:

"The constantly increasing density of our urban populations, the multiplying forms of industry and the growing complexity of our civilization make it necessary for the State, either directly or through some public agency by its sanction, to limit individual activities to a greater extent than formerly. With the growth and development of the State the police power necessarily develops, within reasonable bounds, to meet the changing conditions. . . .

". . . The harmless may sometimes be brought within the regulation or prohibition in order to abate or destroy the harmful. The segregation of industries commercial pursuits and dwellings to particular districts in a city, when exercised reasonably, may bear a rational relation to the health, morals, safety and general welfare of the community. The establishment of such districts or zones may, among other things, prevent congestion of population, secure quiet residence districts, expedite local transportation, and facilitate the suppression of disorder, the extinguishment of fires and the enforcement of traffic and sanitary regulations. The danger of fire and the risk of contagion are often lessened by the exclusion of stores and factories from areas devoted to residences, and, in consequence, the safety and health of the community may be promoted. . . .

". . . The exclusion of places of business from residential districts is not a declaration that such places are nuisances or that they are to be suppressed as such, but it is a part of the general plan by which the city's territory is allotted to different uses in order to prevent, or at least to reduce, the congestion, disorder and dangers which often inhere in unregulated municipal development."

The Supreme Court of Louisiana, in *State* v. *City of New Orleans, supra,* pp. 282–283, said:

"In the first place, the exclusion of business establishments from residence districts might enable the municipal government to give better police protection. Patrolmen's beats are larger, and therefore fewer, in residence neighborhoods than in business neighborhoods. A place of business in a residence neighborhood furnishes an excuse for any criminal to go into the neighborhood, where, otherwise, a stranger would be under the ban of suspicion. Besides, open shops invite loiterers and idlers to congregate; and the places of such congregations need police protection. In the second place, the zoning of a city into residence districts and commercial districts is a matter of economy in street paving. Heavy trucks, hauling freight to and from places of business in residence districts, require the city to maintain the same costly pavement in such districts that is required for business districts; whereas, in the residence districts, where business establishments are excluded, a cheaper pavement serves the purpose. . . .

"Aside from considerations of economic administration, in the matter of police and fire protection, street paving, etc., any business establishment is likely to be a genuine nuisance in a neighborhood of residences. Places of business are noisy; they are apt to be disturbing at night; some of them are malodorous; some are unsightly; some are apt to breed rats, mice, roaches, flies, ants, etc. . . .

"If the municipal council deemed any of the reasons which have been suggested, or any other substantial reason, a sufficient reason for adopting the ordinance in question, it is not the province of the courts to take issue with the council. We have nothing to do with the question of the wisdom or good policy of municipal ordinances. If they are not satisfying to a majority of the citizens, their recourse is to the ballot—not the courts."

The matter of zoning has received much attention at the hands of commissions and experts, and the results of their investigations have been set forth in comprehensive reports. These reports, which bear every evidence of painstaking consideration, concur in the view that the segregation of residential, business, and industrial buildings will make it easier to provide fire apparatus suitable for the character and intensity of the development in each section; that it will increase the safety and security of home life; greatly tend to prevent street accidents, especially to children, by reducing the traffic and resulting confusion in residential sections; decrease noise and other conditions which produce or intensify nervous disorders; preserve a more favorable environment in which to rear children, etc. With particular reference to apartment houses, it is pointed out that the development of detached house sections is greatly retarded by the coming of apartment houses, which has sometimes resulted in destroying the entire section for private house purposes; that in such sections very often the apartment house is a mere parasite, constructed in order to take advantage of the open spaces and attractive surroundings created by the residential character of the district. Moreover, the coming of one apartment house is followed by others, interfering by their height and bulk with the free circulation of air and monopolizing the rays of the sun which otherwise would fall upon the smaller homes, and bringing, as their necessary accompaniments, the disturbing noises incident to increased traffic and business, and the occupation, by means of moving and parked automobiles, of larger portions of the streets, thus detracting from their safety and depriving children of the privilege of quiet and open spaces for play, enjoyed by those in more favored localities,—until, finally, the residential character of the neighborhood and its desirability as a place of detached residences are utterly destroyed. Under these circumstances, apartment houses, which in a different environment would be not only entirely unobjectionable but highly desirable, come very near to being nuisances.

If these reasons, thus summarized, do not demonstrate the wisdom or sound policy in all respects of those restrictions which we have indicated as pertinent to the inquiry, at least, the reasons are sufficiently cogent to preclude us from saying, as it must be said before the ordinance can be declared unconstitutional, that such provisions are clearly arbitrary and unreasonable, having no substantial relation to the public health, safety, morals, or general welfare. *Cusack Co.* v. *City of Chicago, supra,* pp. 530–531; *Jacobson* v. *Massachusetts,* 197 U. S. 11, 30–31.

It is true that when, if ever, the provisions set forth in the ordinance in tedious and minute detail, come to be concretely applied to particular premises, including those of the appellee, or to particular conditions, or to be considered in connection with specific complaints, some of them, or even many of them, may be found to be clearly arbitrary and unreasonable. But where the equitable remedy of injunction is sought, as it is here, not upon the ground of a present infringement or denial of a specific right, or of a particular injury in process of actual execution, but upon the broad ground that the mere existence and threatened enforcement of the ordinance, by materially and adversely affecting values and curtailing the opportunities of the market, constitute a present and irreparable injury, the court will not scrutinize its provisions, sentence by sentence, to ascertain by a process of piecemeal dissection whether there may be, here and there, provisions of a minor character, or relating to matters of administration, or not shown to contribute to the injury complained of, which, if attacked separately, might not withstand the test of constitutionality. In respect of such provisions, of which specific complaint is not made, it cannot be said that the land owner has suffered or is threatened with an injury which entitles him to challenge their constitutionality. *Turpin* v. *Lemon,* 187 U. S. 51, 60. In *Railroad Commission Cases,* 116 U. S. 307, 335–337, this Court dealt with an analogous situation. There an act of the Mississippi legislature, regulating freight and passenger rates on intrastate railroads and creating a supervisory commission, was attacked as unconstitutional. The suit was brought to enjoin the commission from enforcing against the plaintiff railroad company any of its provisions. In an opinion delivered by Chief Justice Waite, this Court held that the chief purpose of the statute was to fix a maximum of charges and to regulate in some matters of a police nature the use of railroads in the state. After sustaining the constitutionality of the statute "in its general scope" this Court said: "Whether in some of its details the statute may be defective or invalid we do not deem it necessary to inquire, for this suit is brought to prevent the commissioners from giving it any effect whatever as against this company." Quoting with approval from the opinion of the Supreme Court of Mississippi it was further said: "Many questions may arise under it not necessary to be disposed of now, and we leave them for consideration when presented." And finally: "When the commission has acted and proceedings are had to enforce what it has done, questions may arise as to the validity of some of the various provisions which will be worthy of consideration, but we are unable to say that, as a whole, the statute is invalid."

The relief sought here is of the same character, namely, an injunction against the enforcement of any of the restrictions, limitations or conditions of the ordinance. And the gravamen of the complaint is that a portion of the land of the appellee cannot be sold for certain enumerated uses because of the general and broad restraints of the ordinance. What would be the effect of a restraint imposed by one or more of the innumerable provisions of the ordinance, considered apart, upon the value or marketability of the lands is neither disclosed by the bill nor by the evidence, and we are afforded no basis, apart from mere speculation, upon which to rest a conclusion that it or they would have any appreciable effect upon those matters. Under these circumstances, therefore, it is enough for us to determine, as we do, that the ordinance in its general scope and dominant features, so far as its provisions are here involved, is a valid exercise of authority, leaving other provisions to be dealt with as cases arise directly involving them.

And this is in accordance with the traditional policy of this Court. In the realm of constitutional law, especially, this Court has perceived the embarrassment which is likely to result from an attempt to formulate rules or decide questions beyond the necessities of the immediate issue. It has preferred to follow the method of a gradual approach to the general by a systematically guarded application and extension of constitutional principles to particular cases as they arise, rather than by out of hand attempts to establish general rules to which future cases must be fitted. This process applies with peculiar force to the solution of questions arising under the due process clause of the Constitution as applied to the exercise of the flexible powers of police, with which we are here concerned.

Decree reversed.

Mr. Justice Van Devanter, Mr. Justice McReynolds and Mr. Justice Butler, dissent.

Index

Abbott, Edith, 44
Abbott, Grace, 44
Abeles, Peter, 71–72, 122–53
Adams, Henry, 337
Addams, Jane, 44, 51
Adkins v. *Children's Hospital*, 47, 51, 52, 254
Aestheticism, and *Euclid*, 262–64, 270
Aesthetic policy, 212
Aesthetics
  as component of city form, 216–17
  legislating, 187–222
  regulation of, 160–61
  and zoning, 159, 160
Agins v. *City of Tiburon*, 232, 233, 234–37, 238, 351
Agricultural land, preservation of, 151
Agricultural zoning, popularity of, 150–51
Aldrich, Nelson W., 53
Alexander, Christopher, 213
Alexandria, Virginia, expulsive zoning in, 115–16
Allen, Florence, 48
Alvarado v. *Independent School District of El Paso*, 118
Ambler Realty Company, in *Euclid*, 5–6, 281–83. *See also Village of Euclid* v. *Ambler Realty Company*
American Bankers' Association, support of, for American Plan, 44
American Bar Association, 47
American Law Institute, 306
American Law Reports, 160
American Plan, 44

Amici Curiae briefs, in *Euclid*, 7, 19–20, 167
Amsterdam canal house, 193, 194
Ancient lights, doctrine of, 278
Anticompetitiveness, and *Euclid*, 259–61
Ashcraft, Garland, 40
As-of-right zoning, 217–18
Atlanta, Georgia
  planning in, 132
  racial zoning in, 106, 107–8
Atlanta plan, 42–43
AT&T building, 207, 208–9, 211, 216
Automobile
  and suburban growth, 137–38
  and zoning, 300–301
Aylesworth, Merlin, 46–47

Babcock, Richard F., 89, 209, 218, 305, 312
Babson, Roger, 44
Baker, George, 1
Baker, Newton D., 11, 41, 45, 47, 48, 82, 168, 170, 171, 172, 173, 174, 263, 264, 279, 335, 336, 338, 345
  files of, relating to *Euclid*, 3–30
  role of, in *Euclid*, 31–32, 33–35
Baltimore, Maryland
  expulsive zoning in, 117–18
  racial zoning in, 106, 107–8
Bank of America, 91
Barnett, Jonathan, 192–93, 214
Bartholomew, Harland, 33
Bassett, Edward M., 33, 44, 47, 48, 105, 107, 265
  and land use reform, 128
  role of, in *Euclid*, 37–38
Battisti, Frank J., 267

Baumol, William, 322
Bay Area Council of San Francisco, 89
Beale, Truxton, 52
Beard, Charles, 43, 299
Beautification, 159
Bell, Daniel, 77
Bemis, Edward W., 33, 34, 45
  role of, in *Euclid*, 43–47
Bentley, Arthur F., 43–44
Berman v. *Parker*, 262, 286–88, 289, 290, 293, 347
Bernays, Eric, 44
Berry, Brian, 76
Bettman, Alfred, 1, 4, 7, 9–10, 11, 19, 20, 33, 40, 168, 169–70, 171, 172, 173, 174, 254, 258, 264, 303, 336, 345
  role of, in *Euclid*, 32, 47–49
Bickel, Alexander, 53
Bigelow, Herbert S., 35
Birmingham, Alabama, racial zoning in, 106, 107
Black, Morris, 39
Blackmun, Harry A., 290, 292
Bly, Richard T., 33
Bosselman, Fred, 268
Boston, Massachusetts, urban renewal in, 152
Boudin, Louis, 54
Boyle, W. C., 7, 9–10, 11
Brainard, Henry S., 3, 4
Brandeis, Louis, 36, 47, 53, 252, 265
Brandeis brief, 4, 20, 47, 51, 225
Brennan, William J., 232, 233, 234, 239, 242, 266, 270–71, 290, 292
Bretano, Simon, 189–90
Brewer, David J., 47

Bronx, New York, and white flight, 137

Brooks, Arthur V. N., 1, 3–30

Brown, Capability, 161

Buchanan v. *City of Jackson, Tennessee*, 113

Buchanan v. *Warley*, 41–42, 103, 106, 107, 257, 259

Building, at time of *Euclid*, 133–34

Bunting v. *Oregon*, 47, 51

Burbank, California, zoning in, 106

Burger, Warren, 288–89, 291

Burgess, Ernest W., 74–75, 83

Burnham, Daniel, 171, 189

Burton, John, 46

Butler, Nicholas Murray, 52

Butler, Pierce, 253

Cadillac-Fairview Corporation, 77, 88

Calder v. *Bull*, 282

California
  environment in, 158–59, 160
  integration of zoning and environmental impact reports in, 157–58
  zoning in, 123

Callies, David, 268

Camden Legal Services, 150

Campbell, James V., 51

Capital budgeting, 346

Cardozo, Benjamin, 53, 252

Carter, Jimmy, 76

Castells, Manuel, 74

CEF group, 344

Centrality, of *Euclid*, 253

Chafee, Zechariah, 40

Charlotte, North Carolina, expulsive zoning in, 110–11

Chaucer, Geoffrey, 154

Cheney, Charles H., 42

Chicago Board of Trade v. *United States*, 252

Chicago Housing Authority (CHA), and construction of public housing, 84–85

Chicago Plan, 189

Chicago school on externalities, 320, 322–23, 324
  criticism of, 322

Citizen mobilization, and land use regulation, 88

City
  after-effects of suburbanization in, 139–40
  aging industrial base of, 136–37
  as commons, 187–92
  investment expansion and growth of, 80
  loss of shopping and services, 143
  and white flight, 137

City Beautiful movement, 189, 280, 339, 341

City design
  role of zoning in, 187–222
  setting standards for, 203–15

City of Eastlake v. *Forest City Enterprises*, 265, 288

City of Lafayette v. *Louisiana Power and Light*, 260

City of Newark v. *Township of West Milford*, 150

City of Renton v. *Playtime Theatres*, 292

Civil Rights challenge, to exclusionary zoning, 84–86

Civil rights movement, 136
  and white flight, 137

Clarke, John H., 34–35, 47, 54

Clarke School Urban Renewal Project Committee v. *Romney*, 114–15, 119

Class, at time of *Euclid*, 132–33

Clawson, Marion, 307

Clear Lake City, Texas, planned unit developments in, 87

Cleveland Chamber of Commerce, filing of *amici curiae* brief by, in *Euclid*, 7

Coase, Ronald, 306

Coastal Zone Management Act (1972), 87, 268

Comey, Arthur, 344

Commager, Henry Steele, 43, 44

Commerce, U.S. Chamber of
  support of, for American Plan, 44
  support of, for zoning, 6

Commerce, U.S. Department of, support of, for zoning, 6

Committee for Economic Development, 89

Committee on Taxation of the City of New York, 36

Commons, 43
  city as, 187–92
  overexploitation of, 187
  zoning of, 189–92

Communal control, versus property rights, as issue in *Euclid*, 5–6

Communities, contracts between, and corporations, 95–96

Community Communications v. *City of Boulder*, 260

Conditional zones, 210

Conservation Foundation, 91

Conservation politics, at time of *Euclid*, 132–33

Contracts, forging, with developers, 96–98

Cook, Dorothy, 3

Cooley, Charles Horton, 38, 44, 51, 52, 264

Cooley, Thomas, 45, 51, 50, 53

Coolidge, Calvin, 5

Corporate flight, legal restrictions on, 95–96

Corporate liberalism, 93

Corporations, contracts between communities and, 95–96

Corrigan v. *Buckley*, 42

Costonis, John, 211–12, 217

Covenant, doctrine of, 267

Craig Jenkins v. *State of Missouri*, 112

Creel, George, 44

Dade County, Florida, racial zoning in, 106

Dales, J. H., 306

Daley, Richard, 92
Dallas, Texas, racial zoning in, 106
Darwin, Charles, 299
Darwinism, influence of, on
  zoning, 103
Davis, John W., 173, 174
Day-Brite Lighting, Inc. v. *Missouri*,
  232, 233
Daylighting standards, in New
  York City, 206–7
Debs, 31, 40
DeForest, Robert W., 47
Delafons, John, 305
Density, aesthetic implications of,
  215
Density controls, ix
Denver Tramways, 45
Deregulation, and zoning, 267, 306
Detroit, Michigan, expulsive
  zoning in, 118
Developers, forging contracts with,
  96–98
Dewey, John, 38, 44, 299
DeWitt, Benjamin P., 43
Dickens, Charles, 49
Dillon, John, 168
Discretionary zoning, 212
  rise of, in New York City, 207–9
District of Columbia,
  Redevelopment Act in (1945),
  287
Donald, David, 43
Douglas, William O., 262, 265,
  287, 288, 290, 304
Downing, Andrew Jackson, 162
Due process clause, 227
  and *Berman* v. *Parker*, 286
  and *Euclid*, 224, 225, 226, 254,
  281–82
  future interpretation of, 242
  and *Nollan*, 233–34, 235, 236, 237
  post *Euclid*, 227, 228
  versus just compensation clause
  analysis, 235–37

Duluth, Minnesota, zoning in, 106

Eaton, John, 321
Eberts, Roger, 321
Ecology, 155
Economic perspective, of zoning
  and land use planning, 319–29
Economics, compatibility of zoning
  and, 297–98
Eliot, Charles, 52
Ellickson, Robert, 268 307, 308,
  309, 310, 311, 312, 315
Elliot, Charles D., 18, 19
El Paso, Texas, expulsive zoning
  in, 118
Ely, Richard T., 40, 43
  role of, in *Euclid*, 43–47
Eminent domain, 350
  distinction between police power
  and, in *Euclid*, 13–14, 22
Empire State Building, 199, 202
Englewood, New Jersey, expulsive
  zoning in, 145–46
Environment
  choice between police power
  and, in *Euclid*, 172–74
  Euclid and, 154–86
  and land use restrictions, 86–87
  meanings of, 154–59
  natural and built, 161–64
Environmental and aesthetic
  considerations, of zoning, 159–61
Environmental impact reports,
  integration of zoning and,
  157–58
Environmentalists, and land use
  reform, 92
Environmental planning, 155–56,
  161, 163
  metropolitan experience in,
  164–65
  and zoning, 161
Environmental zoning, since *Euclid*,
  174–77
Equal protection clause, 227
Erie Railroad Co. v. *Tompkins*, 252

Euclidean zoning, 164, 195–203
  exclusion as essence of, 254
  future of, 347–49
  height and area districts,
  198–200
  and New York Zoning
  Resolution (1961), 200–203
  as Progressive concept, 254
  setting standards for, 203–15
  structure of, 195, 202–3
  use districting, 195–98
  virtues of, 191, 203
Euclid zoning ordinance. *See also*
  Village of Euclid v. *Ambler Realty*
  Company
  adoption of, 4, 5
  amendment of, 4, 5
  appeal to U.S. Supreme Court,
  11–17
  chronology of, 4–5
  observations on, 22–23
  origins of, 5–7
  in U.S. district court, 8–11
  in U.S. Supreme Court, 17–21
Exclusion, and *Euclid*, 253–59
Exclusionary zoning, 124
  civil rights challenge to, 84–87
  court challenges to, 288–89
  in Mahwah, New Jersey, 146
  and payment of compensation,
  327
  racism and, 84–86
  role of, in shaping residential
  patterns, 41
Expulsive zoning, 101–3, 107–8
  adverse impacts of, 118–20
  in Alexandria, Virginia, 115–16
  in Baltimore, Maryland, 107–8
  in Baltimore County, Maryland,
  117–18
  in Charlotte, North Carolina,
  110–11
  in Detroit, Michigan, 118
  in El Paso, Texas, 118
  in Englewood, New Jersey,
  145–46

in Hamtramck, Michigan, 109–10
in Jackson, Tennessee, 112–13
in Kansas City, Missouri, 112
as legacy of *Euclid*, 101–21
in Madison Township, New
Jersey, 146–47
in Mount Laurel, New Jersey,
116–17
in Mount Laurel Township, New
Jersey, 147–48
in Nashville, Tennessee, 111–12
and progressive movement, 103
and property values, 104–6
in Pulaski, Tennessee, 108–9
and segregation, 106–7
in Selma, Alabama, 114–15
in St. Louis, Missouri, 108
Externalities
and failure of land markets,
320–24
Pigouvian economic remedy for,
321–22, 323
Exxon, 77, 87, 91
Exxon building, 207

Fannie Mae, 345
Fasano v. *Board of Commissioners*, 270,
352
Faulkner, Harold U., 43
Feagin, Joe R., 71, 73–100
Federal Housing Administration
(FHA), 142
Feiss, Paul, 40
Fels, Joseph, 36, 45
Fine, Sidney, 43
First Amendment interests, impact
of zoning on, 291–92
First English Evangelical Lutheran Church
v. *County of Los Angeles*, 237, 242,
243, 291, 292, 293, 314
First National Conference on City
Planning, 36
Fischel, William, 308, 309, 310,
315, 316, 322, 324
Fisher, E. M., 46
Fiske, John, 40

Flagg, Ernest, 189, 192
Flexible zoning, 350
Floating zones, 210, 346, 350
Floor area ratio (FAR), 215–16
introduction of, in New York
City, 201–2
Foran, Martin, 34, 39
490 Park Avenue, 211
Frankfurter, Felix, 47, 48, 50, 51,
54
Freddie Mac, 345
French Beaux Arts planning, 189
Freund, Ernst, 50, 340
Friendswood Development
Corporation, 87
Frostbelt-Sunbelt shift in capital
investment, 76
Furuseth, Andrew, 53

Gale, Zona, 163
Gantt, H. L., 44
Garden apartment, 142–43
Garden City, New York, 131, 162
Garfield, Harry, 31
Garfield, James R., 31, 36, 53
Garrett v. *Hamtramck*, 109, 119
Gary, Elbert, 52
Gautreaux v. *CHA*, 85
Gaynor, Mayor, 36
Geddes, Patrick, 162, 175
George, Henry, 33, 34, 35, 43, 54,
93–94, 95, 308–9
Georgian row house, 193
Gerald Hines Interests, 88
G. I. Bill, 142
Ginnie Mae, 345
In re Girsh, 337
Gladden, Washington, 47
Goldblatt v. *Town of Hempstead*, 232,
234, 236, 242
Goldman v. *Crowther*, 281
Goldmark, Josephine, 47
Goldmark sisters, 44, 48, 51
Gompers, Samuel, 44, 53
Goodnow, Frank, 36
Gordon, Peter, 320

Gorieb v. *Fox*, 159, 160, 174, 227,
285–86
Gottdiener, Mark, 77
Government financing, of housing,
142
Grant, Madison, 40
Great Depression
influence of, on zoning, 135
and urban growth, 128
Greater Englewood Housing Corp. v.
DeSimon, 146
Greenbelts, 151–52
Greenville, South Carolina, racial
zoning in, 106
Greenwich Village, 204–5
Gregory, Thomas, 48
Gries, John M., 33
Grosjean v. *American Press Co.*, 53
Growth controls, 346
Gulf Oil, 87

Haar, Charles M., 50, 270, 333–54
Hamilton, Alice, 44
Hamtramck, Michigan, expulsive
zoning in, 109–10
Hanna, Mark, 34
Hardin, Garrett, 187, 191
Harding, Warren, 5, 35, 52, 176
Harvey, David, 74
Hastings, Thomas, 192
Haussmann, Baron, 189
Hawaii Housing Authority v. *Midkiff*,
234
Hays, Samuel P., 43
Height and area districts, 198–200,
206
Height controls, ix
Helvering v. *Clifford*, 252
Henderson, J. Vernon, 321
Herrick, Myron T., 34
Hicks, John D., 43
Highrise office building, 193
Hill, A. J., 18–19
Hill, David Jayne, 52
Hills v. *Gautreaux*, 85
Hofstadter, Richard, 43

Holmes, Oliver Wendell, 10, 50, 173, 239, 264, 299, 300, 313
Home, defense of, in *Euclid*, 6–7
Home Building and Loan Association v. *Blaisdell*, 258
Home use values, and land use controls, 93–94
Hoover, Herbert, 1, 33, 38, 173, 265, 339, 341
Horwitz, Morton, 278
Hostetler, Joseph, 35
Hough, Gordon, 320
Housing Quality Zoning (HQZ), 212–13
  in Neighborhood Impact Program, 214
Howe, Frederic C., 31, 33, 34, 36, 37, 40, 47, 104, 255, 261, 265
  role of, in *Euclid*, 35–37, 38–40
Hughes, Charles Evans, 36, 38
Hunter, Frank, 5–6

IBM building, 208–9, 211, 216
Ihlder, John, 33
Impact zoning, 157
Incentive zoning
  development of, 209
  importance of, in New York City, 209–10
Inclusionary zoning, 244
Indianapolis, Indiana, racial zoning in, 106
Infrastructure contingencies, 346
Institute for Research in Land Economics, 45–46
Institutional districts, 346
Interventionist state, 80–82
Investment expansion, and city growth, 80

Jackson, Henry, 88, 90
Jackson, Kenneth T., 255
Jackson, Tennessee, expulsive zoning in, 112–13
Jacobs, Jane, 345
James, Harlean, 46, 162–63, 166

James, Henry, 257–58
James, William, 51
James v. *Valtierra*, 264, 288
Javins v. *First National Realty Corp.*, 252
Johnson, Tom L., 32, 33, 34, 35, 36, 45
Johnson-Reed Act, 41
Joint ventures, need for, in land development, 351–52
Judges, as planners, 223–51
Judicial standard(s)
  broad versus narrow interpretation, 223, 240–41
  impact of *Nollan* on, 223, 228–39, 242–43
  post *Euclid*, 227–28
  role of planners and judges in, 243–44
  as set in *Euclid*, 223, 224–27
Just compensation clause
  and *Euclid*, 224, 281
  and *First English*, 292
  future interpretation of, 241–42
  and *Nollan*, 228, 229, 230, 232, 235–38, 243, 293
  versus due process-equal protection, 235–37

Kaiser Aluminum, 87
Kansas City, Missouri, expulsive zoning in, 112
Kapp, Karl, 78
Kasarda, John, 76
Kayden, Jerold S., 221, 223–51
Kelley, Florence, 36, 44, 47, 48, 51, 52
Kerner Riot Commission, 89
Kiefer, Daniel, 35
Kmiec, Douglas W., 308, 309, 310
Kolko, Gabriel, 43, 261
Kramer, Samuel, 39–40
Kratz, Peter, 320
Kwartler, Michael, 72, 187–222

LaFollette, Robert M., 36

Lakewood, Ohio, Congregation of Jehovah's Witness Inc. v. *City of Lakewood*, 266
Land, interest in, 74
Land markets, externalities and failure of, 320–24
Land speculation, 278
Land use
  challenges to and conflicts over restrictions in, 84
  environmental restrictions on, 86–87
  historical changes in, in U.S., 122
  impact of *Euclid* on, 122
  values of, and no-growth restrictions, 86
Land use controls, democratizing, 93–94
Land use lawyer, tools of, 253
Land use planning
  economic perspective of, 319–29
  goal of, for environmental purposes, 155
  science of, 303
Land use reform
  classes and class factions in, 91–92
  conflict between zoning and, 73–100
  localized opposition to, 92–93
  regulation versus profit, 89–90
Large-scale development projects, 87–88
Lasker, Bruno, 33, 42–43
Laski, Harold, 50, 265
Lawton, Mrs. W. L., 263
Le Corbusier, 208
Lee, Ivy, 44
Lefebvre, Henri, 74, 77
Levitt, Arthur, 87, 141–42
Liberty League, 174
Lincoln Property groups, 344
Link, Arthur, 43
Linkage, 244
Lippmann, Walter, 44
Lipsey, Edward, 321

Llewellyn Park, New Jersey, 131

Lochner v. *New York*, 47, 50, 221–22, 234, 279, 280, 348
and birth of zoning, 280–82
demise of, and *Berman* v. *Parker*, 286–88
disinterment of ghost of, 290–92

Lochnerian legacy, of *Euclid*, 278–95

Lodge, Henry Cabot, 40, 52

Loft building, 193

Look Building, 216

Los Angeles, California, zoning in, 106

Louisville, Kentucky, racial zoning in, 106

Lubove, Roy, 37

Lynch, Kevin, 193, 202

Lyons, Willie, 51

MacDonald, Sommer & Frates v. *Yolo County*, 270

Madison Township, New Jersey, expulsive zoning in, 146–47

Maeser, Karl, 50, 51, 52

Mahwah, New Jersey, expulsive zoning in, 146

Mainstream ecological analysis, 75–76

Marbury v. *Madison*, 252

Marcus, Norman, 209

Marsh, Benjamin, 35, 36, 103–5

Marshall, Alfred, 78

Marshall, John, 252

Marshall, Thurgood, 265–66, 290, 292

Mason, Alphus, 50

Massachusetts Federation of Town Planning Boards, *amici* briefs of, filed in *Euclid*, 167

Mayo-Smith, Richmond, 45

McAneny, George, 38

McCloskey, Robert G., 54

McHarg, Ian, 155–57, 158, 162, 175

McKenna, Joseph, 5

McMichael, Stanley, 164, 165, 169

McReynolds, James C., 51, 255

McRenolds, William, 320

Members of the City Council v. *Taxpayers for Vincent*, 292, 347

Mercer, New Jersey, 140

Mercer County, New Jersey, preservation of open space in, 150

Metaregulation, and zoning, 268

Metromedia, Inc. v. *City of San Diego*, 270, 292

Metropolitan planning board, and assignment of development quotas, 327

Metzenbaum, James, 1, 4, 6–7, 9, 10, 11–12, 15, 16, 17, 19, 21, 23, 33, 38, 40, 47, 166, 168–69, 174, 264, 337, 345, 350
role of, in *Euclid*, 31–32

Metzger, Walter P., 47

Meyers v. *Nebraska*, 51

Middlesex County, New Jersey, 140
preservation of open space in, 150

Mies van der Rohe, Ludwig, 201

Minimum scrutiny test, 229

Minnesota Rate Cases, 50

Minnesota v. *Clover Leaf Creamery Co.*, 233, 234

Miranda v. *Arizona*, 252

Mitchell, John P., 36

Mitchell, Wesley C., 45

Model Land Development Code, 89, 308

Model Planning Act (1927), 123

Monmouth County, New Jersey, preservation of open space in, 150

Montgomery County, Maryland, preservation of open space in, 150

Moore v. *City of East Cleveland*, 266, 290, 291

Morgan, Lewis H., 44, 51

Morgan, Robert, 4, 11, 18

Morgenthau, Henry, 265

Morris, Clarence, 156–57

Morris, New Jersey, 140

Morris v. *East Cleveland*, 39

Mount Laurel, New Jersey, expulsive zoning in, 72, 98, 116–17, 119, 147–48. *See also* *Southern Burlington N.A.A.C.P.* v. *Township of Mount Laurel*

Mowry, George, 43

Mugler v. *Kansas*, 281

Muller v. *Oregon*, 47, 51

Muller, Dennis, 327

Multifamily housing, 142–43

Mumford, Lewis, 161

Murphy, Earl Finbar, 72, 154–86

Nashville, Tennessee, expulsive zoning in, 111–12

National Association of Manufacturers, support of, for American Plan, 44

National Association of Realtors, 91

National Commission on Urban Problems, 304, 306

National Community Security Act, 94

National Conferences on City Planning, 48
amici briefs of, filed in *Euclid*, 19–20, 167
in 1910, 104
in 1911, 163
in 1912, 104
in 1918, 105
in 1924, 263

National Electric Light Association (NELA) of Cleveland, 46

National Environmental Policy Act, 157

National Grange, support of, for American Plan, 44

National Housing Association, *amici* briefs of, filed in *Euclid*, 167

National Land and Investment Co. v. *Kohn*, 337

National Land Use Policy Act, 90, 91, 92

National Wildlife Federation, 91

Natural environment, 162

Natural use, doctrine of, 278

Nectow v. *City of Cambridge*, 174, 228, 233, 264, 287, 290, 338

Neighborhoods
and land use control, 314–15
property right proposals for existing, 311–12

Nelson, Robert, 299–318

Newark, New Jersey, and white flight, 137

New Jersey, zoning in, 123–24

New Orleans, Louisiana, racial zoning in, 106

New Town movement, 142

New York City
aesthetics in, 216
brownstones in, 193
daylighting standards in, 206–7
density in, 215–16
discretionary review in, 207–9, 216–17
height and area districts in, 198–200, 215–16
housing reform movement in, 36
incentive zoning in, 209–10
landmarks preservation law in, 240
land use changes in, 127
special districts/permits in, 209–15
subdivision patterns of, 125
urban renewal in, 152
use districts in, 190, 195–98, 203–5, 215
wedding cake architecture in, 72, 215, 216
zoning standards in, 203–15

New York City Zoning Ordinance (1916), 1, 37, 81–82, 105, 128, 280–81
creation of standardized building by, 194

use districts in, 190
wedding cake building design produced by, 72, 215, 216
and zoning of commons, 189–192

New York Committee on Congestion of Population, 36

New York Zoning Resolution (1961), 200–203

Noble State Bank v. *Haskell*, 50

No-growth restrictions, zoning for use values, 86

Nolen, John, 33

Nollan v. *California Coastal Commission*, 221, 224, 231–32, 233, 235, 236, 242, 243, 293, 294
application of substantial, 242–43
footnote three, 232–35, 241
impact of, on judicial standards, 223, 228–40
unmasking the real relationship in, 238–40

Norfolk, Virginia, racial zoning in, 106

North Nashville Citizens Coordinating Committee v. *Romney*, 111–12

Nuisance, 267, 302
common law of, as basis for zoning, 336–37
and private land use law, 279
and zoning, 282, 321

Oakwood at Madison, Inc. v. *Township of Madison*, 146–47

O'Brian, John Lord, 48, 173

O'Connor, Sandra Day, 242, 292

Ohio State Conference on City Planning, filing of *amici curiae* brief by, in *Euclid*, 7

Oklahoma City, Oklahoma, racial zoning in, 106

Olmsted, Frederick Law, 161, 195–96

Olympia and York, Ltd., 88

Open shop movement, 44

Open space, preservation of, 150–53

Orgo Farms and Greenhouses, Inc. v. *Township of Colts Neck*, 150–51

Palsgraf v. *Long Island Railroad Co.*, 252

Pareto criteria, 320, 321
enforcement of, 327

Pareto optimality, 320–24
applying principle of, 298

Pareto test, 325

Park, Robert, 74, 83, 177

Parker v. *Brown*, 260

Parks, development of, 161–62

Parma, Ohio, 267

Parochialism, 349
and *Euclid*, 262, 270

Paschal, Joel, 50, 51

Paul, Alice, 52–53

Peccei, Aurelio, 155

Pei, I. M., 211

Penn Central Transportation Co. v. *New York City*, 233, 236, 239, 263, 335, 347

Pennell v. *City of San Jose*, 236, 241

Pennsylvania Coal Co. v. *Mahon*, 10, 50, 237, 264

Perceptual density, 216

Performance standards, 346

Performance zoning, 213, 214

Perlman, Selig, 43

Petaluma, California, 261

Philadelphia, subdivision patterns of, 125

Phipps Houses, 216

Pinchot, Gifford, 351

Pinchot-Ballinger controversy, 53

Pitts, Jon Will, 115

Planned unit developments (PUDs), 87, 209, 346, 349

Planners(s
judges as, 223–51
tools of, 125–26, 253

Planning
major landmarks of, 124

and zoning, 122–53
Plan Voisin, 208
Plotkin, Sidney, 94–95
Police power
   choice between environment
      and, in *Euclid*, 172–74
   definition of, 50
   distinction between eminent
      domain and, in *Euclid*, 13–14,
      22
   and *Euclid*, 16, 38, 41, 48–49,
      281–82
   separation of uses in, 215
   and zoning, 39–40, 334
Polikoff, Alexander, 85
Political consensus, and *Euclid*,
   349–53
Political-economic perspective
   on conflict between zoning and
      land use reform, 73–100
   zoning in, 79–83
Pollock, Frederick, 299, 300, 305,
   313
Pomerene, Attlee, 35
Pomeroy, Hugh, 301
Popper, Frank, 87
Portsmouth, Virginia, racial zoning
   in, 106
Pound, Roscoe, 44, 48
Powell v. *Alabama*, 54
Powell, Lewis F., 290, 291
Power, Garrett, 107
Prah v. *Maretti*, 263
Prescription, doctrine of, 278
Prescriptive zoning, 195
   failure of, in New York City,
      207–9
Preservation, of open space, 150–53
President's Commission for a
   National Agenda for the 80s, 76
President's Commission on
   Housing (1982), 307
Pritz v. *Messer*, 4, 13, 48
Private property
   constitutional rights regarding,
      188

and *Euclid*, 122
Privatizing, of zoning, 303–6
Progressive movement, and zoning,
   103–4
Property right proposals
   for existing neighborhoods,
      311–12
   for undeveloped land, 308–10
Property rights, versus communal
   control, as issue in *Euclid*, 5–6
Proposition 13, 96
Pulaski, Tennessee, expulsive
   zoning in, 108–9
Pulliam, Mark, 316
Purdy, Lawson, 33, 35, 36, 37, 38,
   47, 105, 265

Rabin, Yale, 71, 101–21
Race, at time of *Euclid*, 132–33
Racial zoning, 106–7
   court rejection of, 102, 103
Racism, 42–43
   as aspect of zoning, 40–41
   and exclusionary zoning, 84–86
   as foundation of Southern
      Progressivism, 106
   role of, in *Euclid*, 42–43
Radburn, New Jersey, 131
Ramapo, New York, 261
Rancho, California, planned unit
   developments in, 87
Randle, William M., 1, 31–69
Real estate boards, and
   development of professional
   credentialing system, 46
Regional Plan Association of New
   York, 89
Rehnquist, William, 235, 239, 265,
   292
Reich, Charles, 305
Reid v. *Architectural Board of Review of
   Shaker Heights*, 266
Reiss, Jacob, 129
REITS, 344
REMICs (real estate mortgage
   investment conduits), 345

Rent control, in cities, 139
Reregulation, and zoning, 267
Reston, Virginia, planned unit
   developments in, 87
Richmond, Mary, 44
Richmond, Virginia, racial zoning
   in, 106
Riis, Jacob, 49
Roanoke, Virginia, racial zoning in,
   106
Robinson, Allan, 36
Rockefeller Brothers Fund Task
   Force on Land Use and Urban
   Growth, 90
Rockefeller Center, 199
Rodell, Fred, 54
Roosevelt, Franklin D., 35
Roosevelt, Theodore, 53
Root, Elihu, 52
Ross, Edward Allsworth, in *Euclid*,
   43–47
Rumbold, Charlotte, 11
Rural America, zoning in, 130

Sage, Margaret Olivia, 47
Sage, Russell, Foundation, 47
St. Louis, Missouri
   expulsive zoning in, 108
   racial zoning in, 106
San Diego Gas & Electric Co. v. *City of
   San Diego*, 235, 266, 270, 351
Santa Monica, conflict over the use
   value of land in, 96–98
Scalia, Antonin, 228, 230, 233, 234,
   236, 237, 238, 240, 241, 242, 243,
   293, 352
Schad v. *Borough of Mt. Ephraim*, 270,
   292
Schlesinger, Arthur, 43
Schmidt, Walter, 83
Scientific management, 44
   and zoning, 37, 340
Scott, Sir Walter, 165
Seagram building, 194, 201, 208
Segregation, 262
   Southern Progressives and, 106–7

Seligman, E. R. A., 36–37, 43

Selma, Alabama, expulsive zoning in, 114–15

Services, exodus of, from city, 143

Setback controls, ix

Settlement house movement, 44

Shelley v. *Kraemer*, 259

Shopping, exodus of, from city, 143

Sidlo, Thomas, 35

Siegan, Bernard, 267, 307, 309, 310, 316, 322, 323

Siemon, Charles, 312

Simkhovitch, Mary, 36, 44

Simpson, George T., 17–18, 21

Site plan, as planning tool, 125

Site plan review, 126

Skyscraper, 188

Smith, Adam, 43, 53, 188

Smith, David, 95, 96

Social changes, and zoning, 135–36

Social Darwinism, 52

Social fair share, 135

Social justice, and land use reform, 127–28

Social sciences, new urban paradigm in, 74–79

Soho, 215

Solow, Robert, 321

Soon Hing v. *Crowley*, 256–57

South Bronx, New York, 134

Southern Burlington County N.A.A.C.P. v. *Township of Mount Laurel* (1975), 85–86, 259, 337

Southern Burlington County N.A.A.C.P. v. *Township of Mount Laurel* (1983), 116, 148, 149, 150, 259

Southern progressives, and segregation, 106–7

South Morrisania, New York, 134

Special districts, 209–15

Special permits, 209–15

Spencer, Herbert, 49, 50, 51, 74, 75, 82–83

Stahl, Konrad, 321

Standard State Zoning Enabling Act (SZEA), 48, 89, 280, 339, 347

Standard Zoning and Planning Act (1920), 89

Stare decisis, principle of, 284

State ex rel. Morris v. *East Cleveland*, 34

Stein, Clarence, 216

Stevens, John Paul, 291, 292

Stewart, Potter, 260, 291, 292

Stoddard, Lothrop, 40

Stone, Harlan F., 5, 17, 52, 53, 173

Stull, William, 325

Subdivision
development of, 125–26
as planning tool, 125

Substantial advancing standard, application of, 243

Suburban Action Institute, 150
and Mahwah, New Jersey, 146

Suburban municipalities
growth of, 81
origin of zoning regulations in, 81

Suburbia, 75
after-effects of, in city, 139–40
and automobiles, 137–38
golden age of (1950-present), 136–40
growth of, 131–32
housing in, 140–45
importance of zoning for, 124
independence of, 137
zoning in, 130–35

Sullivan, Louis, 163

Sumner, William Graham, 52

Sumnerology, 52

Sunbelt, and the no-growth movement, 86

Sutherland, George, 1, 5, 20, 21, 32, 35, 47, 50, 52–54, 72, 82, 127, 154, 155, 156, 159, 160, 169, 170, 172–73, 173–74, 190–91, 191, 196, 198, 203, 204, 205, 224, 227, 232, 252, 253, 258, 264, 265, 266, 267, 269, 271, 284, 285, 303, 333, 336, 337, 338, 345, 346, 347–48, 352
role of, in *Euclid*, 49–54

Swann v. *Charlotte-Mecklenberg*, 110

Taft, William Howard, 52, 53

Takings clause *See* Just compensation clause

Tarlock, Dan, 49, 303, 306–7, 311–13

Tauden, Helen, 321

Taxpayers for Vincent, 270

Tax Reform Act (1986), 345

Taylor, Frederick, 44, 340

Taylorism, 44

TDR zoning, 151

Toll, Seymour, 105, 257

Towson, Maryland, expulsive zoning in, 117–18

Trammell Crow, 344

Transfer of development rights (TDRs), 151

Tribe, Laurence, 281, 287

Truman, Harry, 136

Turners Station, Maryland, expulsive zoning in, 117

Udall, Morris, 87, 90

Undeveloped areas
property right proposals for, 308–10
use of zoning for control, 304

United States v. *Carolene Products Co.*, 229, 287

Urban congestion and blight, and planning, 104

Urban construction, replicability and redundancy in, 193–95

Urban design, 192–93

Urban Design Group (UDG), 209

Urban development, alternative strategies for dealing with, 93

Urban Development Action Grants, 125

Urban Development Corporation, 90

Urban ecology, 74–76
Urban growth, and zoning, 126–30
Urban Land Institute (ULI), 88
Urban political economy, 76–79
Urban renewal, invention of, 144–45
Urban setting, zoning laws in, 338–43
Use district, 195–98, 203–5

Van Devanter, Willis, 255
Van Orsdel, Josiah A., 51
Veblen, Thorstein, 44, 299
Veiller, Lawrence, 33, 36, 37, 38
Veterans Administration (VA), 142, 345
Village of Arlington Heights v. *Metropolitan Housing Development Corp.*, 85, 265, 267, 288
Village of Belle Terre v. *Boraas*, 265, 266, 288, 289, 290, 293, 304
Village of Euclid v. *Ambler Realty Company*, ix, 1, 31, 72, 74, 221, 269, 355–71
 and aestheticism, 262–64, 270
 Ambler brief, 282–84
 and anticompetitiveness, 259–61
 building at time of, 133–34
 choice between environment and police power in, 172–74
 and due process clause, 224, 225, 226, 254, 281–82
 and environment, 154–86
 and exclusion, 253–59
 expulsive zoning as legacy of, 101–21
 file contents relating to, 3–30
 future implications of, 267–71
 impact of, 300–303
 judicial standards set in, 223, 224–27
 jurisprudence after, 227–28
 and just compensation clause, 224, 281
 legacies of, 264–67
  Lochnerian, 280–85

 and parochialism, 262
 players in, 31–69
 and police power, 16, 38, 41, 48–49, 281–82
 and political consensus, 349–53
 prescience and centrality of, 256–77
 and private land use, 122
 race, class and conservation politics at time of, 132–33
 social contract and private purpose of, 333–54
 Sutherland's majority opinion in, 284–85
 validation of zoning in, 82–83
 zoning for environment since, 174–77
 and zoning of commons, 190–91

Wait-and-see zoning, 315
Wald, Lillian, 44
Waldo, Dwight, 302
Waldram Diagram, 206
Walker, Francis, 45
Walton, Izaak, League, 91
Ward, Lester, 44, 51–52
Warner, Sam Bass, Jr., 255
Warren, Charles, 40, 48
Warth v. *Seldin*, 267, 288, 289
Washington State, integration of zoning and environmental impact reports in, 157–58
Washington, D.C., subdivision patterns of, 125
Washington ex rel. Seattle Title Trust Company v. *Roberge*, 286, 287, 290
Water Quality act, 125
Weaver, Clifford L., 209, 218
Weber, Max, 74
Weinstein, James, 43
Weissbrod, Glen, 323
West Coast Hotel v. *Parrish*, 287
Westenhaver, Dale C., 4, 10, 11, 33, 34, 35, 49, 167, 197, 205, 258–59, 281
 role of, in *Euclid*, 31, 32, 40–42

Wheaton, William, 298, 319–29
White, Michelle, 291, 321
White flight, and civil rights movement, 137
Whitte, A., 321
Whitten, Robert H., 31, 33, 34, 36, 37, 38, 40, 45, 47, 52, 54, 107, 265
 role of, in *Euclid*, 42–43
Wiebe, R. H., 43
Wilcox, Delos F., 33, 34, 35, 36, 38, 39, 45, 52
William, Frank B., 33, 46
Williams, Norman Jr., 123
Williams, Robert A., Jr., 221–22, 278–95
Williams, Stephen, 213
Williamson v. *Lee Optical of Oklahoma, Inc.*, 232, 233
Williamson County Regional Planning Commission v. *Hamilton Bank*, 270
Willoughby, W. F., 45
Wilson, Woodrow, 33, 34, 36, 43, 52, 54, 173
Winston-Salem, North Carolina, racial zoning in, 106
Wolf, Michael, 221, 252–77
Woodward, C. Vann, 43
World War II, impact of, on zoning, 135–36

Yick Wo v. *Hopkins*, 256
Yinger, John, 326
Young, Arthur, 162
Young v. *American Mini-Theatres*, 263, 291–92

Zahn v. *Board of Public Works*, 227, 285–86
Zoning
 agricultural, 150–51
 alternatives to present, 324–26
 as-of-right, 217–18
 and automobiles, 300–301

birth of, 1, 279–81; *see also* New York City Zoning Ordinance (1916)
broad versus narrow interpretation of, 240–42
in California, 123
in city design, 187–222
compatibility of economics and, 297–98
conflict between land use reform and, 73–100
defense of, in *Euclid*, 6,9,12, 14–15
and deregulation, 267
discretionary, 212
early criticisms of, 83
economic perspective of, 319–29
environmental, 174–77
environmental and aesthetic considerations of, 159–61
Euclidean; *see* Euclidean zoning
evaluation of, ix–xi
exclusionary; *see* Exclusionary zoning
expulsive; *See* Expulsive zoning
flexible, 349
future of, 312–14
goal of, for environmental purposes, 155
historical changes in, 122–23
historical reasons for, 125
impact, 157
incentive, 209–10
inclusionary, 244
influence of Darwinism on, 103
influence of Great Depression on, 135
influence of Progressive movement on, 103
integration of environmental impact reports and, 157–58
judicial literature of, 221–22
legal criticism of, 313
as legal tool, 123,124

linking, with science, 127
major landmarks of, 124
metaregulation and, 268
municipal sale of, 316
myth versus practice in, 299–318
in New Jersey, 123–24
and no-growth restrictions, 86
nuisance doctrine and, 282
performance, 213, 214
planning and, 122–53
as planning tool, 125
in political-economic perspective, 79–83
prescriptive, 195, 207–9
privatizing of, 303–6
problems with, 145–50, 319
property right theorists of, 308–10
racial, 102, 103, 106–7
and reregulation, 268
in rural America, 130
and scientific management, 340
and social changes, 135–36
in suburbia, 124, 130–35
TDR, 151
in theory and practice, 324–26
upsetting the assumptions of orthodox, 343–47
and urban growth, 126–30
for use values, 86
validation of, 82–83
wait-and-see, 315
and World War II, 135–36
Zoning law
post-Euclidean, Lochnerian, 286–88
urban setting for, 338–43
Zoning ordinance, first. *See* New York City Zoning Ordinance (1916)
Zoning out, 262
Zoning regulations
growth of, 81–82
origin of, 81

Contributors

Peter L. Abeles is president of the New York City planning consultant firm of Abeles Phillips Preiss & Shapiro. He is also general partner in Affordable Living Ltd. Partnership and Newlands Limited Partnership and specializes in both affordable housing and zoning.

Arthur V.N. Burns is a partner in the Cleveland law firm of Baker and Hostetler. While serving as a member of the Ohio General Assembly in the 1970s, he was vice-chair of the Ohio Land Use Review Committee, which studied Ohio's state and local land-use laws and practices.

Joe R. Feagin, professor of sociology at the University of Texas, Austin, specializes in urban sociology. He is the author of 18 books and numerous articles dealing with urban issues. His most recent book is *Free Enterprise City: Houston in Political and Economic Perspective,* published in 1988 by Rutgers University Press, New Brunswick, New Jersey.

Charles M. Haar is the Louis D. Brandeis Professor of Law at Harvard University and an expert on property, government finance, land use, and the organizational problems of urban and suburban areas. He served as Assistant Secretary for Metropolitan Development under President Lyndon B. Johnson, has chaired presidential task forces on urban issues, and has served as consultant to the White House and the State Department.

Jerold S. Kayden, a lawyer and city planner, is this year a visiting faculty member at the Lincoln Institute of Land Policy in Cambridge, Massachusetts. During 1986 and 1987, he was the Gerald D. Hines Lecturer in Real Estate at the Harvard Graduate School of Design and has taught courses there on law and design, urban development, and zoning.

Michael Kwartler is a principal in Michael Kwartler Associates, a New York City architecture, planning, and urban design firm. He also is professor of architecture, planning, and historic preservation at Columbia University and directs the university's program in historic preservation.

Earl Finbar Murphy holds a dual appointment at the Ohio State University. He is C. William O'Neill Professor of Law and Judicial Administration in the College of Law and Courtesy Professor of Natural Resources in the College of Architecture.

Robert H. Nelson is an economist with the Office of Policy Analysis, U.S. Department of the Interior. He was a visiting fellow at Woods Hole Oceanographic Institution during 1988.

Yale Rabin is professor of planning and former associate dean for academic affairs in the School of Architecture at the University of Virginia. He is a visiting scholar in the Department of Urban Studies and Planning at the Massachusetts Institute of Technology through the spring of 1989.

William Randle is a lawyer and consultant whose consulting firm, Dr. William Randle and Associates, is located in Cleveland. He is also a visiting scholar at the Annenberg School of Communications, University of Pennsylvania, through the spring of 1989.

William C. Wheaton holds two appointments at the Massachusetts Institute of Technology. He is professor in both the Department of Economics and the Department of Urban Studies and Planning.

Robert A. Williams, Jr., is a professor of law at the University of Arizona.

Michael Allan Wolf is associate professor of law at the University of Richmond. He is an expert on enterprise zones and the coauthor, with Charles Haar, of the fourth edition of *Land-Use Planning,* to be published in 1989 by Little, Brown.